Income Tax 2019/20

Income Tax 2019/20

Sarah Laing CTA

Series General Editor: Mark McLaughlin CTA (Fellow) ATT (Fellow) TEP

Contributing Editor (Scotland): Donald Drysdale CA CTA (Fellow) TEP MBCS CITP

Bloomsbury Professional

LONDON · DUBLIN · EDINBURGH · NEW YORK · NEW DELHI · SYDNEY

Bloomsbury Professional

Bloomsbury Publishing Plc

41–43 Boltro Road, Haywards Heath, RH16 1BJ, UK

**BLOOMSBURY and the Diana logo are trademarks of
Bloomsbury Publishing Plc**

British Library Cataloguing-in-Publication Data

A catalogue record for this book is available from the British Library.

ISBN: 978-1-52650-982-6

Typeset by Evolution Design & Digital Ltd (Kent)
Printed and bound by CPI Group (UK) Ltd, Croydon, CR0 4YY

To find out more about our authors and books visit
www.bloomsburyprofessional.com. Here you will find extracts, author
information, details of forthcoming events and the option to sign up for our
newsletters

Preface

Income Tax 2019/20 is the fourteenth edition of this publication and is part of the Core Tax Annual series published by Bloomsbury Professional. The book is designed to provide a clear, concise reference to all aspects of income tax law and practice, with cross-references to legislation, case law, and other source material.

This edition has been comprehensively reviewed and is up to date to April 2019. Changes implemented by the Finance Act 2019, which received Royal Assent on 12 February 2019, and proposals for future changes, are fully reflected throughout, as are other new developments which have taken place since the last published edition.

The book includes a chapter covering the provisions for the Scottish rate of income tax, which has developed considerably since its introduction in April 2016. This chapter was written by Donald Drysdale, a leading tax expert on this subject, and former author of *Corporation Tax,* one of the Core Tax Annuals published by Bloomsbury Professional. Donald has once again provided a comprehensive update to the chapter for this edition of the book and my grateful thanks go to him again this year for his continued help and expertise on this subject.

Although *Income Tax 2019/20* is part of Bloomsbury Professional's Core Tax Annuals series (see back cover for further details), it is also a useful stand-alone guide to the UK's income tax system. Hopefully readers will find it easy to navigate and more digestible than other reference material. The objective of the book is to provide an easy-to-use, straightforward solution to many common income tax issues, with an emphasis on practical rather than theoretical points.

Bullet points, checklists, summaries, worked examples and tables have been used throughout to aid comprehension.

We have included 'Signposts' at the start of each chapter, which aim to provide a useful summary of the contents of the following chapter. Each chapter also contains a series of 'Focus' points. These are additional points that have been picked out to draw the reader's attention to new developments and proposed changes, planning or practice points, or to provide details of further reference material.

I hope that you find this book useful. We always welcome any comments or suggestions for future editions.

Sarah Laing CTA
May 2019

Contents

Contents

Table of examples

Chapter 7 Self-employment

Chapter 8 Property income

Table of statutes

Table of statutes

Table of statutory instruments and other guidance

[All references are to paragraph numbers]

Table of cases

List of abbreviations

ADR	alternative dispute resolution
AIA	annual investment allowance
ASP	alternatively secured pension
ATED	annual tax on enveloped dwellings
CA	Court of Appeal
CAA 1990/2001	Capital Allowances Act 1990/2001
CDFI	Community Development Finance Institution
CGT	capital gains tax
CIS	Construction Industry Scheme
CPA 2004	Civil Partnership Act 2004
CPI	consumer prices index
CSLM	Collection of Student Loans Manual
CTA 2009/2010	Corporation Tax Act 2009/2010
CTC	child tax credit
CTF	Child Trust Fund
CTT	capital transfer tax
CVS	Corporate Venturing Scheme
DTA	double taxation agreement
DWP	Department for Work and Pensions
EEA	European Economic Area
EIS	Enterprise Investment Scheme
EMI	Enterprise Management Incentive
FA	Finance Act
F(No 2)A 2015	Finance (No 2) Act 2015
FIT	feed-in tariff
FOTRA	free of tax to residents abroad
FYA	first-year allowance
GAAR	general anti-abuse rule
HMRC	Her Majesty's Revenue and Customs
ICTA 1988	Income and Corporation Taxes Act 1988
IHT	inheritance tax
IHTA 1984	Inheritance Tax Act 1984
IHTM	Inheritance Tax Manual
IRC	Inland Revenue Commissioners
ITA 2007	Income Tax Act 2007

List of abbreviations

ITEPA 2003	Income Tax (Earnings and Pensions) Act 2003
ITTOIA 2005	Income Tax (Trading and Other Income) Act 2005
NIC	National Insurance contributions
NICA 2006	National Insurance Contributions Act 2006
NRLS	Non-resident Landlords Scheme
OSPP	ordinary statutory paternity pay
OTS	Office of Tax Simplification
OWR	overseas workday relief
PACE 1984	Police and Criminal Evidence Act 1984
PAYE	Pay As You Earn
PIBS	permanent interest-bearing shares
PILON	payment in lieu of notice
PIP	personal independence payment
POAT	pre-owned asset tax
PSC	personal service company
PTI	Personal Tax International
RBC	remittance basis charge
reg	regulation
RQE	residue of qualifying expenditure
RSTPA 2014	Revenue Scotland and Tax Powers Act 2014
RTI	real time information
s	section
SAP	statutory adoption pay
SAYE	Save As You Earn
Sch	Schedule
SCI	Special Civil Investigations Section
SCO	Special Compliance Office
SDLT	Stamp Duty Land Tax
SED	Seafarers' Earnings Deduction
SERPS	State Earnings Related Pension Scheme
SI	Statutory Instrument
SIP	share incentive plan
SIPP	self-invested personal pension
SITR	Social Investment Tax Relief
SLC	Student Loans Company
SLD	student loan deductions
SMP	statutory maternity pay
SP	HMRC Statement of Practice

SPA	state pension age
SPP	statutory paternity pay
SRT	statutory residence test
SSCBA 1992	Social Security Contributions and Benefits Act 1992
SSP	statutory sick pay
STIU	Special Trades Investigation Unit
TA 1925	Taxes Act 1925
TAD	tax avoidance disclosure
TCEA 2007	Tribunals, Courts and Enforcement Act 2007
TCGA 1992	Taxation of Chargeable Gains Act 1992
TIOPA 2010	Taxation (International and Other Provisions) Act 2010
TMA 1970	Taxes Management Act 1970
TMEs	trustees' management expenses
UITF	Urgent Issues Task Force
VATA 1994	Value Added Tax Act 1994
VCT	venture capital trust
WDA	writing down allowance
WTC	working tax credit

Chapter 1

The UK tax system

SIGNPOSTS

- Scope – Income tax is payable by individuals, trustees and personal representatives (see **1.1**).

- HMRC collect tax through two systems: under the Pay As You Earn (PAYE) system for employed earners and pensioners; and under the self-assessment system for other types of income.

- Income tax is generally payable on the worldwide income of UK residents (see **1.2**).

- Liability to income tax is reportable to HMRC by 5 October following the end of the tax year in which the income arose (see **1.4**).

- Personal allowances may be reduced or lost entirely where adjusted net income exceeds £100,000 (see **1.18**).

- An individual who is not liable to income tax or not liable above the basic rate for a tax year may transfer part of their personal allowance to their spouse or civil partner, provided that the recipient of the transfer is not liable to income tax above the basic rate (see **1.20**).

- From 6 April 2019 most individuals will be entitled to a personal allowance of £12,500 regardless of age (see **1.23**).

- Tax credits (WTC and CTC) are social security benefits, and do not have to be covered by a comparable tax liability. They are not set against an income tax liability, but are paid out directly by HMRC to claimants (see **1.26**).

- Income tax relief may be available for interest payments if a loan relates to a specified category (see **1.37**).

- A cap applies to income tax reliefs that individuals are able to claim (see **1.38**).

- Income tax relief is generally available on most charitable donations, either via the payroll giving or Gift Aid scheme (see **1.42**).

- Employers are required to collect student loan repayments on behalf of HMRC, where instructed to do so (see **1.48**).

- The tax system works on a progressive basis. Tax rates increase as income increases. For 2018/19 and 2019/20 the basic rate is 20%, the higher rate is 40% and the additional rate is 45% (see **1.49**).

- The 10% tax credit attaching to dividends was abolished from 6 April 2016. From that date, the rates applicable to dividend income are the 7.5% ordinary rate up to the basic rate limit, the 32.5% dividend upper rate, and the dividend additional rate of 38.1% on dividends above the higher rate limit (see **1.51**).

- A series of steps must be undertaken to work out an individual's income tax liability for a particular tax year (see **1.54**).

- Double taxation relief may be available where tax has been paid on foreign income (see **1.62**).

- Taxpayers receiving child benefit may be affected by the introduction of the high income child benefit charge (see **1.63**).

INTRODUCTION

Who is liable?

1.1   The following are liable to income tax:

- individuals (including children, although the child's income may be treated as the parent's income, where the capital which gave rise to the income was provided by the parent, if the income exceeds £100 per parent in any tax year (*ITTOIA 2005, s 629(3)*; *R v Newmarket Income Tax Commrs, ex parte Huxley* 7 TC 49);

- trustees; and

- personal representatives of a deceased individual.

Companies pay corporation tax on profits and gains (see *Corporation Tax 2019/20* (Bloomsbury Professional)), but may suffer income tax (eg on investment income) and may be required to account for income tax on certain payments.

What is chargeable?

1.2 Income tax is charged broadly on the worldwide income of UK residents, subject to certain exceptions for individuals who are not domiciled in the UK. A non-resident is generally only liable to income tax on UK income (see **Chapter 10**). Where the same income is liable to both UK and foreign tax, double taxation relief is generally available (HMRC Booklet RDR1: *Residence, domicile and the remittance basis*: https://www.gov.uk/government/publications/residence-domicile-and-remittance-basis-rules-uk-tax-liability).

If a receipt is classified as a capital receipt, it will generally be taxable in accordance with the capital gains tax rules (see *Capital Gains Tax 2019/20* (Bloomsbury Professional)).

The tax year

1.3 The tax year runs from 6 April to 5 April in the following year. The tax year 2019/20 runs from 6 April 2019 to 5 April 2020.

Notification of sources of income

1.4 An individual who is:

- chargeable to income tax (or capital gains tax) for a tax year; and

- has not received a notice from HMRC requiring the completion of a tax return,

must notify HMRC that he is chargeable to tax by 5 October following the end of the relevant tax year in which his income (or gains) arose (*TMA 1970, s 7(1)*).

However, notification is not required where the income comes from certain sources (eg employment income dealt with under PAYE, or investment income taxed at source) and the individual is not a higher or additional rate taxpayer, and where there are no chargeable gains (*TMA 1970, s 7(3)–(7)*).

Focus

An individual must notify HMRC of any new source of chargeable income by 5 October following the end of the tax year in which it first arises.

Focus

Self-employed traders can use form CWF1 to register online for self-assessment and NICs. The form can be found on the gov.uk website at https://www.gov.uk/log-in-file-self-assessment-tax-return/register-if-youre-self-employed.

Legislative framework

1.5   Tax laws are made public mainly through statutes. New tax law is generally drafted in the form of a Bill, which travels through Parliament, being amended during its passage, as appropriate. Once finalised, a Bill will receive Royal Assent and become an Act. Other legislative sources include statutory instruments, made by government departments (eg HMRC) under the authority of 'enabling' Acts of Parliament, and European Community legislation.

The major statutes relevant to income tax are as follows:

- the *Income and Corporation Taxes Act 1988 (ICTA 1988)*, although much of the legislation contained in this Act has now been rewritten into *ITEPA 2003, ITTOIA 2005* and *ITA 2007* for income tax purposes;

- the *Income Tax (Earnings and Pensions) Act 2003 (ITEPA 2003)*;

- the *Income Tax (Trading and Other Income) Act 2005 (ITTOIA 2005)*; and

- the *Income Tax Act 2007 (ITA 2007)*;

The *Taxes Management Act 1970 (TMA 1970)* regulate the institutions involved in the imposing and collecting of the main taxes, and the *Capital Allowances Act 2001 (CAA 2001)* the granting of capital allowances.

The *Commissioners for Revenue and Customs Act 2005* provides the legal basis for the integrated department, Her Majesty's Revenue and Customs (HMRC), and the independent prosecutions office, Revenue and Customs Prosecutions Office.

Income tax is imposed each year by way of a Finance Act (although the legislation authorises the continuity of the operation of the administrative machinery). The Finance Acts also make amendment to the other main statutes and provide additional rules to implement government policy changes or to target avoidance. Social security changes are made by statutes other than the annual Finance Act.

The *Wales Act 2014* contains provisions for devolution of a range of tax and borrowing powers to Wales (see http://www.legislation.gov.uk/ukpga/2014/29/contents). From April 2018 the Welsh Assembly is responsible for the setting and collection of landfill tax (known as landfill disposals tax (LDT) in Wales) and the replacement for stamp duty land tax – Welsh land transaction tax (LTT) – in Wales. The Welsh basic, higher and additional rates of income tax, introduced by the *Wales Act 2014*, are charged on the non-savings and non-dividend income of those defined as 'Welsh taxpayers', with effect from 6 April 2019 (*ITA 2007, s 11B*). The *Government of Wales Act 2006, s 116E* defines who is a Welsh taxpayer for these purposes.

The *Scotland Act 1998* (as amended) gives the Scottish Parliament power to set Scottish income tax rates and thresholds, which apply to Scottish taxpayers and are administered by HMRC as part of the UK-wide income tax regime. The Act also fully devolves the power to raise taxes on land transactions and on waste disposals to landfill (both effective from April 2015), air passenger duty and aggregates levy, allows Scotland to create new taxes, and provides for assignment to the Scottish budget of a proportion of VAT receipts raised in Scotland. Scottish income tax, which applies from April 2017, is covered in detail in **Chapter 3**.

Focus

The *European Union (Withdrawal) Act 2018* received Royal Assent on 26 June 2018. Broadly, the Act repeals the *European Communities Act 1972* on exit day and makes other provision in connection with the withdrawal of the United Kingdom from the EU. The Act came into force on 26 June 2018 in respect of specified provisions and otherwise will come into force on such day as a Minister of the Crown may by regulations appoint.

The House of Commons Library estimates that 13.2% of UK primary and secondary legislation enacted between 1993 and 2004 was EU-related. The review of all EU-related legislation, as well as that which will be transposed by the *European Union (Withdrawal) Act*, makes this potentially one of the largest legislative projects ever undertaken in the UK. The White Paper indicates that the corrections will require between 800 to 1000 statutory instruments.

Non-legislative sources

HMRC often issue statements in which they make known their views on the correct interpretation of statute, or the way in which they propose to apply certain rules. In addition, they may announce a relaxation in their approach to a particular statutory provision, where to adhere strictly to it would cause undue administrative difficulties, or hardship to the taxpayer. Such statements of practice and extra-statutory concessions (ESCs)) lack the force of law and do not affect a taxpayer's rights on appeal. However, concessions can be relied on except where they are being used for tax avoidance purposes.

Interpretations of various points of tax law are often published in HMRC's Briefs publications. Such interpretations are qualified by an important caveat that particular cases may turn on their own facts or context, and that there may be circumstances where the interpretation would not apply. In addition, there may be circumstances in which HMRC would find it necessary to argue for a different interpretation in appeal proceedings. HMRC Briefs also contain articles which give an insight into the thinking of HMRC head office specialists.

In a further step towards greater openness, most HMRC internal guidance manuals are freely available on their website (www.gov.uk/government/collections/hmrc-manuals).

Tax cases

Disputes concerning tax law may be taken for hearing before the tax tribunal (see **2.77**). Appeals from the First-tier Tribunal are invariably heard by the Upper Tribunal. The Upper Tribunal is a superior court of record and has the same status as the High Court itself. Indeed, the Upper Tribunal is often presided over by High Court judges or (in Scotland) judges of the Court of Session.

Introduction of income tax

1.6   Income tax was first introduced as a temporary measure by William Pitt in order to help finance the Napoleonic wars. Unfortunately, a tax on income meant that it became necessary for an individual to declare his income. This was most unpopular and when the then prime minister, Henry Addington, reintroduced income tax in 1803 he chose a method of classifying income by its source and charged each source of income separately under a Schedule. Using this method, a taxpayer's total income could not be ascertained without assessing and computing his income under each source or Schedule.

Income tax was last introduced by Sir Robert Peel in 1842 as a three-year temporary measure, but it has been with us ever since. There have been four consolidations since 1842, in the *Income Tax Acts 1918* and *1952* and in the *Income and Corporation Taxes Acts 1970* and *1988*.

The former Tax Law Rewrite Project was established to rewrite primary tax legislation into a more logical and 'user-friendly' format. The publication of the *Income Tax (Earnings and Pensions) Act 2003 (ITEPA 2003)* covers income from employments, pensions and social security benefits and replaces the former Schedule E. The *Income Tax (Trading and Other Income) Act 2005 (ITTOIA 2005)* covers income from trades, professions and vocations, savings income and investments. It replaced the six cases of former Schedule D and Schedule F. The *Income Tax Act 2007 (ITA 2007)*, which took effect from 6 April 2007, covers basic provisions about the charge to income tax, income tax rates, the calculation of income tax liability and personal reliefs; various specific reliefs (including relief for losses, the enterprise investment scheme, venture capital trusts, community investment tax relief, interest paid, Gift Aid and gifts of assets to charities); specific rules about trusts, deduction of tax at source, manufactured payments and repos, the accrued income scheme and tax avoidance; and general income tax definitions.

Liability to income tax

1.7 Income tax is a tax on income, but also on some capital receipts.

The taxation of employment income is generally charged under the provisions of *ITEPA 2003* from 6 April 2003.

The *Income Tax (Trading and Other Income) Act 2005 (ITTOIA 2005)* took effect from 6 April 2005. The Act covers the taxation of trading, property, savings and investment, and miscellaneous income.

Certain persons are exempt from all taxes on income and gains, while some are specifically exempt from income tax. Certain income is also exempt from income tax.

Focus

Tax avoidance is legal, but tax evasion is not, and it is important to know the distinction between the two. In *IR Commrs v Duke of Westminster* (1936) 19 TC 490 the judge concluded that 'Every man is entitled, if he can, to order his affairs so the tax attaching under the appropriate Act is less than it otherwise would be'.

Provision for charge
1.8

Property income	Formerly Schedule A. Rents (and other receipts) from UK land and buildings; see **Chapter 8**, Property business profits and losses
Trading income	Formerly Schedule D, Case I and II; see **Chapter 7**, Starting a business
Savings and investment income	Formerly Schedule D, Case III, IV and V; see **Chapter 4**, Savings and investments
Miscellaneous income	Formerly Schedule D, Case VI
Employment income	Formerly Schedule E; see **Chapter 6**, Employment, including:
	Earnings of an employee resident in the UK (other than 'foreign emoluments' (ie earnings of non-UK domiciled employees from non-UK resident employers) earned wholly abroad)
	Earnings of an employee not resident in the UK
	'Foreign emoluments' of an employee resident in the UK, which are remitted to the UK
Investment income	Formerly Schedule F. Dividends and distributions of UK resident companies

Basis of charge

1.9   An individual's taxable income is broadly calculated by (*ITA 2007, s 23*):

- adding together the amounts under the various categories of income for that tax year;

- reducing this amount by certain allowable deductions and personal allowances to arrive at total taxable income;

- applying the tax rates in force for the tax year to the total taxable income; and

- reducing the tax calculated by certain other deductions and allowances (if available).

See **1.46** onwards for further details.

Exempt income

1.10   Certain types of income are exempt from income tax, including the following:

- genuine termination payments (generally up to £30,000) (see **Chapter 6**);

- income from certain investments (see **Chapter 4**);

- premium bond prizes;

- casual winnings from competitions and betting;

- maintenance payments;

- genuine statutory redundancy payments (see **Chapter 6**);

- certain social security benefits (eg income support), but various other state benefits (eg jobseeker's allowance) are taxable;

- scholarship income;

- repayment supplement in respect of tax overpayments (including most VAT repayments);

- benefits payable under certain sickness and unemployment insurance policies;

- certain types of pension (eg to war widows, wound and disability pensions to members of the armed forces, and pensions awarded to employees disabled at work);

- damages and compensation for personal injury (including annuities or periodical payments received as damages);

- compensation for certain mis-sold personal pensions;

- housing grants;

- compensation paid by banks on unclaimed accounts opened by Holocaust victims and frozen during World War II; and

- interest on damages for personal injuries.

Basis of charge – example
1.11

Example 1.1—Basis of charge

In 2019/20 a single person aged 35 receives income from employment of £15,000, net rental income of £3,650 (ignoring the property allowance; see Chapter 8), income from writing occasional articles of £650. He also has savings income of £600. His income tax liability for 2019/20 is as follows:

	£	£
Income		
Income from employment (tax deducted under PAYE £500)		15,000
Income from UK land and property		3,650
Other income		650
Total income		19,300
Less personal allowance		12,500
Taxable income		6,800
Income tax due		
£6,800 at 20%		1,360
Less tax deducted at source		
PAYE	500	
		500
Total tax due		860

The savings income of £600 is covered by the personal savings allowance of £1,000 for basic rate taxpayers (see **1.21**).

Taxation of spouses

1.12   A husband and wife, and civil partners, are treated as independent taxpayers. This applies for income tax, CGT and inheritance tax. This independent treatment affects a number of reliefs but principally the 'personal allowances' (see **1.19**) and the capital gains tax annual exemption.

Where income arises from property held in the names of individuals:

(a)   who are married to, or are civil partners of, each other, and

(b)   who live together,

the individuals are treated for income tax purposes as beneficially entitled to the income in equal shares, unless they make a joint declaration (on form 17) to the contrary (*ITA 2007, s 836*). The declaration is ineffective if (*ITA 2007, s 837(3)*):

- notice of it is not given to HMRC (on form 17) within 60 days of its making; or

- the spouses' or civil partners' interests in the property do not correspond to their interests in the income.

Once validly made, the declaration continues in effect, unless and until the spouses' or civil partners' interests in either the income or capital cease to accord with the declaration.

Distributions (usually dividends) from jointly owned shares in close companies are not automatically split 50/50 between husband and wife, or civil partners, but are taxed according to the actual proportions of ownership and entitlement to the income (*ITA 2007, s 837*).

Taxation of minors

1.13   There is a statutory duty on 'every person ¼ who is chargeable' (*TMA 1970, s 7(1)*) to income tax or CGT for a particular tax year, and who has not received a notice to make a return of his total income and gains, to give notice of his chargeability to HMRC not later than six months after the end of that year. 'Every person ¼ chargeable' includes a child under the age of 18: in effect, the obligation to make a return in respect of non-settled property will fall upon the child's parent or guardian. Such a parent, etc may also be held responsible for any tax chargeable on the child (*TMA 1970, s 73*; see also *R v Newmarket Income Tax Commrs, ex parte Huxley* (1916) 7 TC 49).

Same-sex couples

1.14   The *Civil Partnership Act 2004 (CPA 2004)*, which gave legal recognition to same-sex couples, came into force on 5 December 2005. Broadly, the Act allows same-sex couples to make a formal legal commitment to each other by entering into a civil partnership through a registration process. A range of important rights and responsibilities flows from this, including legal rights and protections. For tax purposes, civil partners are now treated the same as husband and wife couples. For example, where one of the partners was born before 6 April 1935, the partners are entitled to an allowance equivalent to the married couple's allowance (*Tax and Civil Partnership Regulations 2005 (SI 2005/3229)*; *Tax and Civil Partnership (No 2) Regulations 2005 (SI 2005/3230)* – see **1.22**).

Focus

Same-sex couples who have entered into a civil partnership are treated as married couples for tax purposes. This means that they are entitled to married couple's allowance, where appropriate.

INCOME OR CAPITAL

Distinction

1.15　　Tax legislation generally makes a distinction between income and capital items when analysing receipts and expenditure.

Revenue receipts must be distinguished from capital receipts, because it is normally only revenue receipts which are chargeable to income tax.

In general, a sum which is derived from the sale of a capital item will not give rise to an income receipt, but it does not follow that what is a capital expense to one party is necessarily a capital receipt to the other party.

What is income and what is capital is a question of law, rather than of fact. However, all of the circumstances surrounding a transaction must be taken into account, and the weight to be given to a particular circumstance depends on common sense, rather than any single legal principle.

The basic principle, in determining whether or not a grant was an income or capital receipt, was set out in *Glenboig Union Fireclay Co Ltd v IR Commrs* (1921) 12 TC 427 by Lord Wrenbury:

> 'was that compensation profit? The answer may be supplied, I think, by the answer to the following question. Is a sum profit which is paid to an owner of property on the terms that he shall not use his property so as to make a profit? The answer must be in the negative. The whole point is that he is not to make a profit and is paid for abstaining from seeking to make a profit ¼ it was the price paid for sterilising the asset from which otherwise profit might have been obtained.'

The test is, therefore, whether the thing in respect of which the taxpayer has received compensation is either:

- a mere restriction of his trading opportunities; or

- the depreciation of one of the capital assets of his business (*Burmah Steam Ship Co Ltd v IR Commrs* (1931) 16 TC 67).

The following two well-known tests are used for distinguishing a revenue receipt from a capital one, although both are of limited value:

(1) The first test is to distinguish receipts which relate to assets which form part of the permanent structure of the business. An example of this would be machinery, the sale of which would give rise to a capital receipt.

(2) The second test is to distinguish between circulating and fixed capital. A fixed capital asset is retained in the business with the object of making profits. An example of this would again be machinery. Circulating capital, on the other hand, is acquired to be used or sold. An example would be the raw materials used in the business (*ITTOIA 2005, ss 105, 207*).

Capital	**Revenue**
Receipts from sale of business assets	Payments *in lieu* of trading receipts, including:
Sale of fixed assets is a capital receipt although a profit on the sale of trading stock constitutes an income receipt	• agreed damages for loss of profits arising from delay in repairs
Receipts for the sale or destruction of the taxpayer's profit-making apparatus	• damages in excess of repair costs to cover lost profits
Receipts in return for restrictive covenants	• compensation for increased revenue expenditure
Payments received in return for the sterilisation of assets are capital receipts, although treatment of lump sums for 'exclusivity agreements' depends on purpose of payment	• damages for negligence of agents resulting in a trading loss
One-off receipts	• rebates against price due for goods supplied
A one-off receipt strongly, but not conclusively, suggests a capital receipt	Recurring receipts are more likely to be revenue receipts

RELIEFS, ALLOWANCES AND DEDUCTIONS

Introduction

1.16 All UK-resident individuals are entitled to personal allowances (*ITA 2007, s 56*). Personal allowances are given by deduction from total income (*ITA 2007, Pt 3*), but all other allowances are given by way of a credit against an individual's tax liability.

Allowances are normally reflected in a PAYE tax coding, but self-employed taxpayers generally claim personal reliefs and allowances through their self-assessment tax returns.

Certain non-residents are also entitled to personal allowances (see **Chapter 10**). An individual who leaves the UK to take up permanent residence abroad is entitled to full personal allowances for the tax year of departure and an individual who comes to the UK permanently is eligible to full personal allowances from the tax year of arrival (*ITA 2007, s 56*).

Income tax allowances

1.17

	2018/19	2019/20
	£	£
Personal allowance for people born after 5 April 1948	11,850	12,500
Marriage allowance	1,190	1,250
Marries couples allowance (born before 6 April 1935 (note (a)) –	8,695	8,915
maximum allowance	3,360	3,450
minimum allowance		
Maximum income before abatement of:	£100,000	£100,000
personal allowance	28,900	29,600
relief for older taxpayers		
Personal allowance abatement income ceiling (note (b)):	123,700	125,000
Blind person's allowance	2,390	2,450
Dividend allowance	2,000	2,000
Personal savings allowance – basic rate taxpayers	1,000	1,000
Personal savings allowance – higher rate taxpayers	500	500

Notes:

(a)   The married couple's allowance is available only where one party is born before 6 April 1935.

(b)   The personal allowance is gradually withdrawn for income over £100,000 at a rate of £1 of allowance lost for every £2 over £100,000 until it is completely removed (*FA 2009, s 4*).

Focus

The personal allowance is set at £12,500 for 2019/20.

The basic rate limit is set at £37,500 for 2019/20. As a result, the higher rate threshold is £50,000 in 2019/20.

Personal allowance

1.18   The personal allowance is currently available to each individual taxpayer, whether single or married, and is deducted from total income for the tax year (*ITA 2007, s 35*).

Since 2016/17 there has been only one rate of personal tax allowance in the UK, regardless of the age of the individual concerned (£11,850 for 2018/19, rising to £12,500 in 2019/20). All age-related personal allowances were abolished from 6 April 2016.

The basic personal allowance is subject to a single income limit of £100,000. Where an individual's 'adjusted net income' is below or equal to the £100,000 limit, they continue to be entitled to the full amount of the basic personal allowance. If 'adjusted net income' exceeds the £100,000 limit, the personal allowance is reduced by £1 for every £2 above the income limit. The personal allowance may be reduced to nil from this income limit (*FA 2009, s 4*). 'Adjusted net income' is the measure of an individual's income that is used for the calculation of the existing income-related reductions to personal allowances (see **1.21**).

As a consequence of the personal allowance abatement, taxpayers with income between £100,000 and approximately £115,000 will suffer marginal tax rates of up to 60% as the personal allowance is withdrawn, where income is above a higher rate threshold of £100,000.

Example 1.2—Personal allowances and marginal rates

Lee, who has no other sources of income, earns £100,000 from his employment. He is paid a bonus of £5,000. His personal allowance in 2019/20 is £12,500, so he loses £2,500 of it (£1 for every £2 earned over £100,000 ((£105,000 − £100,000) /2)), leaving him with an allowance of

£10,000. He will pay tax of £2,000 (£5,000 × 40%) on the bonus, plus an extra £1,000 due to lost allowances (£2,500 × 40%). His total tax attributable to the bonus is therefore £3,000, giving a marginal tax rate of 60%.

Mike earns £125,000 from his employment and is paid a bonus of £5,000. His personal allowance in 2019/20 is £12,500, so he would lose entitlement to all of it because his basic salary exceeds the point at which the allowance is fully withdrawn (£125,000). Receiving the bonus, therefore, results in no further adjustment to his personal allowance. He will simply pay tax of £2,000 (£5,000 × 40%) on the bonus, and his marginal tax rate will be 40%. If Mike's bonus took his income over £150,000, he would be liable to tax at 45% on the bonus.

'Adjusted net income'

1.19   'Adjusted net income' is calculated in a series of steps, as follows:

Step 1

Calculate 'net income' (ie total income subject to income tax). This includes income from employment, profits from self-employment, pensions and income from property, savings and dividends – less specified deductions. The most important of the specified deductions are trading losses and gross pension scheme contributions.

Step 2

Deduct Gift Aid and pension contributions. Net income is then reduced by the grossed-up amount of any:

● Gift Aid contributions; and

● pension contributions where the pension provider has already given basic rate tax relief.

Step 3

Add back any tax relief received for certain payments (eg payments made to trade unions or police organisations which were deducted in arriving at net income in Step 1).

The result is adjusted net income.

Example 1.3—Adjusted net income

Susan has 'adjusted net income' in 2019/20 of £107,000, so her income exceeds the £100,000 limit by £7,000. The personal allowance is therefore reduced by half the amount that exceeds £100,000, ie £3,500. Susan is entitled to a personal allowance of £9,000 for 2019/20 (£12,500 – £3,500).

Focus

Individuals with income slightly exceeding the £100,000 ceiling may avoid losing some or all of their personal allowance by taking steps to reduce 'adjusted net income' to below the abatement threshold: transferring income-producing assets to a lower-earning spouse or partner, increasing pension contributions, or making donations to charity are some areas which may be considered.

Marriage Allowance

1.20 Since April 2015, it has been possible for a spouse or civil partner who is not liable to income tax or not liable above the basic rate for a tax year to transfer part of their personal allowance to their spouse or civil partner, provided that the recipient of the transfer is not liable to income tax above the basic rate. This is known as the 'marriage allowance'. The transferor's personal allowance will be reduced by the same amount. For 2019/20 the amount that can be transferred is £1,250 (rising from £1,190 in 2018/19). The spouse or civil partner receiving the transferred allowance will be entitled to a reduced income tax liability of up to £250 for 2019/20 (£238 for 2018/19). Note, however, that married couples or civil partnerships entitled to claim the married couple's allowance are not entitled to make a transfer (*FA 2014, s 11*, inserting *ITA 2007, Ch 3A*).

Where a couple satisfies the following criteria, it should be possible to claim the allowance:

- The couple must be either married or in a civil partnership – living together is not sufficient for the allowance to be claimed.

- One partner needs to be a non-taxpayer – which generally means they are earning less than the personal allowance (£12,500 for 2019/20).

- The other partner needs to be a basic 20% rate taxpayer, which generally means they are earning less than £50,000 for 2019/20 (£46,350 in 2018/19) (note that rates are different for Scottish taxpayers: see Chapter 3 for details). Higher rate and additional rate taxpayers are not entitled to the allowance.

- Both partners must have been born on or after 6 April 1935.

Individuals who may wish to apply to have part of their allowance transferred in this way to their partner may register with HMRC either online or by phone (HMRC helpline 0300 200 3300). Eligible couples can backdate their claim for the allowance for up to four years; couples will have until 5 April 2020 to backdate their claim to the 2015/16 tax year when the allowance was first introduced.

HMRC will require both partners' national insurance number, and one of a range of different acceptable forms of ID for the non-taxpayer. Note that it is the partner who is the non-taxpayer who must apply for the relevant proportion of their unused personal tax allowance to be transferred to the partner who pays tax at the basic rate.

In most cases, the allowance will be given by adjusting the recipient partner's personal tax code and the allowance will be received via the PAYE system. The partner who transferred their personal allowance will also receive a new, reduced, tax code, which will be operated against their employment income where applicable. If the recipient partner is self-employed, the allowance can be claimed via the self-assessment tax return and the allowance will be given as a reduction against their self-assessment tax liability.

From 29 November 2017, it became possible to make a marriage allowance (MA) claim on behalf of a deceased spouse or civil partner and backdate such a claim by up to four years, where applicable. Previously, the legislation did not allow transfers of personal allowance on behalf of deceased spouses and civil partners, or from a surviving partner to a deceased partner (*FA 2018, s 6*).

Personal savings allowance

1.21   The personal savings allowance (PSA) was introduced with effect from 6 April 2016 for up to £1,000 of a basic rate taxpayer's savings income and up to £500 of a higher rate taxpayer's savings income each year. The PSA is not available for additional rate taxpayers. The allowance will be available in addition to the tax-advantages previously available to investors with individual savings accounts (see **4.25**). A consultation document entitled *Deduction of income tax from savings income: implementation of the personal savings allowance* (July 2015) provided further details.

The PSA applies to 'savings income' as defined in ITA 2007, s 18, and includes interest, income from certain purchased life annuities, profits from deeply discounted securities, accrued income profits, and gains from certain life insurance contracts.

From 6 April 2016 the deduction of tax by banks and building societies from interest they pay on deposits of individuals, partnerships and trusts (known as the Tax Deduction Scheme for Interest (TDSI)) ceased. From that date, such interest is paid without deduction of tax.

The PSA limits remain at £1,000 and £500 respectively for 2017/18 to 2019/20 inclusive.

Example 1.4—Personal savings allowance

In 2019/20, Colin earns £26,000, and has savings income of £600. He will pay income tax at 20% on £13,500 of his earnings (£26,000 less the

---

personal allowance of £12,500). His savings income will be covered by the personal savings allowance and will be tax-free. If his savings income was £1,250 instead of £600, he would have 20% tax to pay on £250. Since tax is no longer collected at source on interest, Colin would have to pay the tax due of £50 to HMRC via self assessment.

Married couple's allowance

1.22   The married couple's allowance (MCA) may only be claimed if at least one of the parties to the marriage or civil partnership was born before 6 April 1935 *(ITA 2007, s 45(2)(c))*. The allowance is £8,915 in 2019/20 (rising from £8,695 in 2018/19).

Where the marriage or civil partnership was entered into on or after 5 December 2005, the claimant is to be the spouse or civil partner with the highest income for the tax year concerned *(ITA 2007, s 46)*. Where the parties to the marriage or civil partnership have the same total income for the year, they are to specify by an election who is to be the claimant for that year *(ITA 2007, s 47)*. The allowance will be restricted if the claimant's income for the year exceeds the specified amount.

The value of the MCA is gradually reduced for taxpayers earning above an income limit, in the same way as the age-related personal allowances were (see below). For 2019/20 this income limit is set at £29,600 (rising from £28,900 in 2018/19). The withdrawal of the MCA from older couples is subject to a minimum allowance set at £3,450 for 2019/20 (rising from £3,360 in 2018/19), restricted to 10%. No couple entitled to the allowance will receive less than this. Where a couple marry during the tax year the allowance is reduced by one-twelfth for each complete tax month pre-marriage. In the first instance the MCA is given to the husband, although if couples elect to do so, the minimum MCA can be transferred to the wife or split equally between spouses. Civil partners may also claim the MCA provided – as with married couples – at least one partner was born before 6 April 1935.

Unlike the personal allowance, the married couple's allowance is not given as a deduction from total income. Instead, relief is allowed at the rate of 10% of the amount of the allowance by means of a reduction in the claimant's income tax liability *(ITA 2007, s 45)*.

Age allowances – income limit

1.23   As it applied up to 2015/16, the age-related personal allowance was restricted to the extent that total income (after allowable deductions but before deducting allowances) exceeded a specified limit (£27,700 for 2015/16 *(ITA 2007, ss 36(2), 37(2))*. The allowances were reduced by half of the excess of income over the limit. The reduction in the age-related personal allowance cannot go beyond that of the amount of the basic personal allowance (£10,600 for 2015/16) (*ITA 2007, ss 45(5), 46(5)*).

It was always the claimant's income that determined the level of abatement (if any). This was so, even if it was the other spouse or civil partner's age that had given entitlement to the higher level of relief. However, the married couple's allowance was only subject to restriction once the claimant's personal allowance had first been reduced to the standard level.

1.24   The abatement process cannot reduce the married couple's allowance (see **1.19**) below the standard amount of that allowance for 1999/2000 and earlier years, or below an equivalent amount for subsequent tax years based on indexation of the 1999/2000 figure of £1,970. For 2019/20, the minimum amount of the allowance is set at £3,450 (rising from £3,360 in 2018/19). Any abatement utilised in reducing the claimant's personal allowance cannot also be used to reduce age-related married couple's allowance.

Blind person's allowance

1.25   An allowance (£2,450 for 2019/20, rising from £2,390 for 2018/19) may be claimed by a blind person, which is given in addition to the personal allowance, and reduces the taxpayer's total income. A married blind person who cannot use all the relief may transfer the unused part to the other spouse (or civil partner), whether the other spouse is blind or not (*ITA 2007, s 39*). A married couple, or civil partners, both of whom qualify for relief, can each claim the allowance.

The allowance can only be claimed by someone who is registered as blind (but not partially sighted). A person may register as blind even if they are not totally without sight. HMRC will, by concession, allow the relief in the previous year if evidence of blindness had already been obtained by the end of it (*ITA 2007, s 38*).

Tax credits

1.26   Working tax credit (WTC) and child tax credit (CTC) are social security benefits, and do not have to be covered by a comparable tax liability. They are not set against an income tax liability, but are paid out directly by HMRC.

Both WTC and CTC are gradually being replaced by Universal Credit (UC), which is administered by the Department for Work and Pensions (DWP) (Department for Communities in Northern Ireland) and will bring together several separate benefits into one benefit with several elements.

The qualification rules and income measures for UC are very different to those for tax credits and its introduction has raised many concerns – it appears that whilst some claimants will be better off under UC, there will be others who will lose out financially.

Focus

- Tax credit claims can be made by contacting the HMRC Tax Credits helpline (0345 300 3900) or online at https://www.gov.uk/browse/benefits/tax-credits.

- There is a three-month residence qualification, with some exceptions, to be satisfied by people who have arrived in the UK before they are able to access Child Benefit or Child Tax Credit awards (*SI 2014/1511*).

- HMRC must be notified of any change in circumstances regarding tax credit claims. Where an overpayment is made, HMRC will seek to recover the money from the claimant.

- Where an employee receives childcare vouchers from an employer, he or she cannot claim for the amount covered by the voucher (even where this is done via a salary sacrifice scheme). As a result, childcare vouchers may affect entitlement to both the childcare element of WTC and also CTC. HMRC have devised a helpful calculator to help ascertain whether a claimant would be better off with tax credits or childcare vouchers. See the gov.uk website at https://www.gov.uk/childcare-vouchers-better-off-calculator.

Working tax credit – basic element

1.27   An individual may be entitled to working tax credit (WTC) if either of the following apply:

- aged between 16 and 24 and have a child or a qualifying disability; or

- aged 25 or over, with or without children.

In addition, the claimant must work a certain number of hours to qualify:

Circumstance	Hours a week worked
Aged 25 to 59	At least 30 hours
Aged 60 or over	At least 16 hours
Disabled	At least 16 hours
Single with one or more children	At least 16 hours
Couple with one or more children	Usually, at least 24 hours between the couple (with one party working at least 16 hours)

A child is someone who is under 16 (or under 20 if they are in approved education or training).

For couples, an individual may be entitled to WTC where they work less than 24 hours a week between them and one of the following applies:

- the claimant works at least 16 hours a week and they are disabled or aged 60 or above; or

- the claimant works at least 16 hours a week and their partner is incapacitated (receiving certain benefits because of disability or ill health), is entitled to Carer's Allowance, or is in hospital or prison.

Working tax credit – other elements

1.28   Provided they are eligible for the basic element of WTC, claimants to WTC may be entitled to various other elements, based on their circumstances:

- *A second adult element.* This is automatic where a joint claim to WTC is made.

- *A lone-parent element.* Where a single claim is made and the claimant is responsible for a child or children.

- *A 30-hour element.* This is designed to encourage those with a disability, or families with children, to move to full-time work. Couples with children will be entitled to it if one of the couple works at least 30 hours a week, or if they jointly work 30 hours a week, provided that one of them works at least 16 hours. Note that, for the purposes of claiming the childcare element of WTC, both partners in a couple must work for at least 16 hours a week.

- *A disability element.* Joint claimants may each claim this if they both qualify.

- *A severe disability element.* Joint claimants may each claim this if they both qualify.

- *Childcare element.* Families are eligible for the childcare element where a lone parent or both partners in a couple work at least 16 hours a week. It is paid directly to the main carer by HMRC, either weekly or four-weekly at the claimant's choice. Up to 70% of qualifying childcare costs may be claimed, although a maximum limit to those costs is set. Childcare costs are calculated on the basis of the average weekly cost, either using the four weeks immediately prior to the claim, or, in the case of monthly payments, multiplying by 12 and dividing by 52.

- A couple where at least one partner is entitled to carer's allowance may also qualify for WTC, including the childcare element, if at least one of the partners works for at least 16 hours a week.

- Any 'relevant' change in childcare costs must be reported to HMRC. A relevant change occurs where there is any change in the childcare provided; or there is an increase or decrease in childcare costs of £10 a week or more for a four-week period.

- When a relevant change occurs, the childcare element of WTC must be recalculated. It is important to note that where childcare costs decrease, and, therefore, less WTC is due, the recalculation will be made from the week following the four-week period of the change. Where costs increase, so that more WTC is due, the recalculation is made from the later of:

    - the first day of the week in which the change occurred; and

    - the first day of the week in which falls the date three months prior to the change being notified to HMRC.

Child tax credit

1.29 Child Tax Credit (CTC) has been replaced by Universal Credit for most people (see **1.26**). New claims are only possible where the applicant receives the severe disability premium, or has received it in the past month and is still eligible for it.

A claimant with a child who is 16 may claim CTC up until 31 August after their 16th birthday.

From 2017/18, the amount of CTC payable depends on how many children the claimant has and whether they are:

- making a new claim for CTC; or

- already claiming CTC.

CTC does not affect payment of Child Benefit. It can only be claimed for children that the claimant is responsible for.

The amount payable depends on when the children were born. If all the children were born before 6 April 2017, the claimant could receive the 'child element' CTC for all of the children. The claimant will also be entitled to the basic amount of CTC (known as the 'family element'). If one or more of the children were born on or after 6 April 2017, the claimant could receive the child element of CTC for up to two children (but they may also be entitled to the child element for more children in certain circumstances: see the gov.uk website at https://www.gov.uk/guidance/child-tax-credit-exceptions-to-the-2-child-limit for details of the exceptions). The claimant will only get the family element if at least one of the children was born before 6 April 2017.

Focus

Individuals must wait three months before claiming Child Tax Credit if they arrived in the UK from the EEA on or after 1 July 2014 and do not work.

Payments are made by HMRC directly to the main carer. Children are eligible up to 1 September following their 16th birthday. The credit remains payable after that date for those in full-time, non-advanced education up to the age of 19. The usual test to be applied is that the child is 'normally living with' the claimant(s). Where there are competing claims, the test is who has the 'main responsibility' for the child. This is subject to a joint election as to who has the main responsibility but, in the absence of such an election, HMRC will decide on the basis of the information available. Child tax credit remains payable for up to eight weeks following the death of a child.

Child tax credit – elements

1.30   From 6 April 2017, CTC is made up of three elements:

- *Family element* – this is the basic element. From 6 April 2017, it is only paid to families who have responsibility for a child or qualifying young person born before 6 April 2017.

- *Child element* – the claimant will receive a child element for all children or young people born before 6 April 2017 for whom they are responsible. Where the claimant is responsible for a child or qualifying young person born on or after 6 April 2017, they will not receive the child element for them unless:

  – there is no more than one child already on the claim; or

  – an exception applies (see below).

- *Disability element* – from 6 April 2017, this is an element in its own right and is no longer part of the child element. The two-child restriction does not apply to the disability element. The disability element is payable at two rates, namely the 'disabled child rate' and the 'severely disabled child rate'. The conditions for each are the same as the previous disabled child rate/severely disabled child rate of the child element.

The exceptions to the two-child limit for children born on or after 6 April 2017 are:

- *Multiple births* – this exception is needed where the claimant already has at least one child on the claim before the multiple birth or there are no children on the claim already but the multiple birth results in triplets (or greater). The first child in a multiple birth will only get the child element if they are the first or second child on that claim; if they are not, then they will not receive the child element.

- *Adoption* – if a child has been placed for adoption with the claimant (or their partner) or adopted by them under certain legislation, this exception may apply. There are some exceptions, for example, if the claimant or their partner were the step-parent of the child immediately before the adoption.

23

- *Non-parental care arrangements* – subject to certain conditions, this exception will apply where the claimant or their partner is a friend or family carer of the child. It may also apply in informal care situations where care has been undertaken where it is likely that the child would otherwise be looked after by the local authority.

- *Child of the claimant has a child of their own* – where the claimant is responsible for a child or young person that they receive a child element for and that child/young person has a child of their own, the CTC rules allow the claimant to claim for both their own child and their child's child.

- *Non-consensual conception* – where the claimant is the child's parent and HMRC determine that the child is likely to have been conceived as a result of sexual intercourse to which they did not agree by choice, or did not have the freedom or capacity to agree by choice, this exception may be applied. There is also a requirement that the claimant is not living at the same address as the other party to that intercourse.

In April 2018, the government announced some changes to the exceptions for non-parental carers and adoptive parents following a legal challenge. If implemented, this will allow the exceptions to be used no matter the order in which the children entered the household.

Working tax credit

1.31

Element	2017/18 £	2018/19 £	2019/20 £
Basic element	1,960	1,960	1,960
Disability element	3,000	3,090	3,165
Severe disability element	1,290	1,330	1,365
30-hour element	810	810	810
Second adult element	2,010	2,010	2,010
Lone-parent element	2,010	2,010	2,010
Childcare element:			
percentage of eligible costs up to weekly maximum of:	70%	70%	70%
(a) for one child	£175	£175	£175
(b) for two or more	£300	£300	£300

Child tax credit
1.32

Element	Circumstance	2017/18 £	2018/19 £	2019/20 £
Family	Family element	545	545	545
Individual	Each child or young person (known as the 'child element')	2,780	2,780	2,780
	Each disabled child or young person	3,175	3,275	3,355
	Each severely disabled child or young person	1,290	1,325	1,360

Income thresholds and withdrawal rates
1.33

	2017/18	2018/19	2019/20
First income threshold	£6,420	£6,420	£6,420
First withdrawal rate	41%	41%	41%
First threshold for those entitled to:			
child tax credit only	£16,105	£16,105	£16,105
Income disregard	£2,500	£2,500	£2,500
Income fall disregard	£2,500	£2,500	£2,500

(The *Tax Credits and Guardian's Allowance Up-rating etc Regulations 2019 (SI 2019/252);* the *Tax Credits (Income Thresholds and Determination of Rates) (Amendment) Regulations 2016, SI 2016/393*)

HMRC guidance on tax credits

1.34 The gov.uk website contains a comprehensive collection of guidance on tax credits. A summary of all guidance can be found at www.gov.uk/topic/benefits-credits/tax-credits.

Qualifying care relief

Relief
1.35 Qualifying care relief allows carers who look after children or young people to receive certain payments (qualifying amounts) tax-free (*ITTOIA 2005, s 803 et seq; F(No 3)A 2010, Sch 1, para 2*).

Previously, there was a statutory tax exemption for foster carers, but shared lives carers were dealt with on an informal concessionary basis. *F(No 3) A 2010, Sch 1* brought the treatment of shared lives carers into line with that of foster carers. The legislation generally applies from April 2010.

The relief applies to individuals who provide care services to local authorities, either directly or indirectly (*ITTOIA 2005, s 804*).

The relief consists of two elements:

- carers whose gross receipts from providing care do not exceed an individual limit (see below) in a year will be exempt from tax on their income from caring; and

- carers whose gross receipts from providing care exceed the individual limit may choose between:

  - computing their business profits using the normal rules; or

  - treating as their profit the amount by which their gross receipts from providing care exceed their individual limit.

Where an individual receives qualifying care receipts for more than three people at any one time, the tax exemption does not apply. Brothers and sisters (including half brothers and sisters) count as one person (*F(No 3)A 2010, Sch 1, para 4*).

The individual limit is made up of two elements (*ITTOIA 2005, s 808*):

- a fixed amount per residence of £10,000 for a full year; and

- an additional amount per child for each week, or part-week, that the individual provides care. The amounts are £200 a week for a child aged under 11, and £250 a week for a child aged 11 or older (see Example 1.6).

For further details, see the HMRC Business Income Manual (BIM52751ff).

Focus

The scope of qualifying care relief has been expanded for 2017/18 onwards, to cover payments made from individuals who self-fund care they receive through a Shared Lives scheme (*SI 2018/317*). Qualifying care relief is an optional tax simplification scheme available to those providing care under Shared Lives schemes which provides a standard relief instead of deductions for their actual expenses, allowing them to keep simpler records. Shared Lives care can be paid for in many ways and one method is self-funded payments. This is where the person receiving Shared Lives care uses their own finances to meet their support costs. This change is designed to ensure that carers who are currently excluded from qualifying care relief because the person they look after happens to self-fund their care, are able to use the simplification scheme, in the same way as carers who look after people whose care is funded by, for example a local authority.

Exemption

1.36 Where an individual's total qualifying care receipts do not exceed his limit, those receipts will be exempt from tax altogether for that year. The mechanism for granting exemption is to treat the profits or losses of the trade as nil. The mechanism for relief is not optional in these circumstances – if the receipts are less than the income limit, it is not possible to claim relief for any loss actually incurred.

The method of calculation varies according to whether or not accounts are drawn up to 5 April. Where the accounting year end is 5 April, or where the profits are calculated simply by reference to the tax year, an individual's qualifying care receipts will be exempt from tax if his total qualifying care receipts do not exceed his limit. His limit for the tax year in question is calculated as his share of the fixed amount, plus each amount per child.

Example 1.7—Qualifying care relief (I)

Anne and Carol live together. Anne has fostered children for many years and Carol now starts to act as a foster parent too. Carol's basis period for the year in question is 270 days.

Anne's share of the fixed amount is £5,000. Carol's share for the first period of her trade is £3,699 ((£10,000/2) × 270/365).

Example 1.8—Qualifying care relief (II)

Angela is a foster carer throughout the tax year. She fosters a ten-year-old boy for 30 weeks and a 14-year-old girl for 40 weeks during the year. Nobody else provides foster care from her home.

Angela's fixed amount is £10,000.

The 'amount per child' for the boy is £6,000 (30 weeks at £200 per week) and for the girl £10,000 (40 weeks at £250 per week).

Angela's limit is therefore calculated as £26,000.

If Angela draws up accounts to 5 April, and her total receipts are under £26,000, the foster income is exempt from tax.

Interest relief

1.37   Income tax relief (at various effective rates, and subject to certain restrictions) is available for an interest payment if it relates to one of the specified categories of loan (see **1.38**) (*ITA 2007, s 383*).

Relief is not granted in the following circumstances (*ITA 2007, s 384*):

- where interest is paid on an overdraft or under credit card arrangements;

- where interest is paid at a rate greater than a reasonable commercial rate (in which case the excess is ineligible for relief);

- where the main benefit of the arrangement is the reduction of tax; or

- where relief is sought by a company within the charge to corporation tax.

Interest paid as a revenue rather than capital item on money borrowed wholly and exclusively for the purposes of a trade, profession or vocation is not subject to the foregoing restrictions.

There are provisions intended to prevent any double deductions for interest.

Where only part of a loan satisfies the conditions for interest relief, only a proportion of the interest will be eligible for relief. That proportion is one which is equal to the proportion of the loan fulfilling those conditions at the time the money is applied.

Full interest relief is generally available on a joint loan to a husband and wife (or civil partner) where only one of them satisfies the qualifying conditions as respects investment in a close company or partnership and that spouse makes the payments or they are made out of a joint account.

Relief generally takes the form of a deduction from or offset against total income in respect of the interest paid. However, as with mortgage interest, if relief is not available at source, relief for interest on a loan to purchase a life annuity is given by way of a reduction in the income tax otherwise payable, though the rate of relief in this case remains the basic rate; an effective order of offset of reliefs is provided. Any necessary apportionment of the interest where a loan is used for the purpose of purchasing such an annuity and for other qualifying purposes is made on a specified basis.

Focus

From 6 April 2013 a cap applies to income tax reliefs that individuals are able to claim. The cap applies only to reliefs that were previously unlimited – eg qualifying interest payments. For anyone seeking to claim more than £50,000 in reliefs, a cap is set at 25% of income or £50,000, whichever is greater (*FA 2013, s 16, Sch 3*).

Categories of qualifying loan

1.38   Interest relief is available on loans applied for the following purposes:

- to purchase machinery and plant (*ITA 2007, s 388*);

- in acquiring an interest in a close company (*ITA 2007, s 392*);

- in acquiring an interest in a co-operative (*ITA 2007, s 401*);

- in acquiring shares in an employee-controlled company (*ITA 2007, s 402*);

- in acquiring an interest in a partnership (*ITA 2007, s 398*); or

- to pay inheritance tax (*ITA 2007, s 403*).

The giving of credit to a purchaser under any sale is treated as the making of a loan to defray money applied by him in making the purchase.

As noted above, from 6 April 2013, the maximum amount of interest relief available is restricted to 25% of income or £50,000, whichever is the greater (*ITA 2007, s 42A* inserted by *FA 2013, s 16, Sch 3*).

Focus

With effect from 6 April 2014, income tax relief for interest paid on loans to invest in certain UK companies has been extended to interest on loans to invest in such companies in the wider EEA.

Legislation is included in *Finance Act 2014* to provide that the relief for investment in close companies is extended to include companies resident in an EEA state other than the UK which would be close if they were UK resident (*FA 2014, s 13*).

The relief for investment in employee-controlled companies has also been extended to include companies resident in an EEA state other than the UK (*FA 2014, s 14*).

Interest on loan to invest in an employee-controlled company – conditions

1.39   Interest may be eligible for income tax relief if it is paid on a loan made to an individual to acquire ordinary shares in an employee-controlled company or to pay off another loan which would have qualified for interest relief. Relief will only be given if the following conditions are satisfied:

(1)   the company must be (from the date on which the shares are acquired to the date on which interest is paid) (*ITA 2007, s 397(2)*):

(a)   an unquoted company that is resident in the UK or another EEA state and is not resident outside the European Economic Area (*FA 2014, s 14*); and

(b)   a trading company or the holding company of a trading company;

(2)   the shares must be acquired before, or not later than 12 months after, the date on which the company first becomes an employee-controlled company;

(3)   during the tax year in which the interest is paid, the company must either (*ITA 2007, s 397(3)*):

(a)   first become an employee-controlled company, or

(b)   be employee-controlled throughout a period of at least nine months;

(4)   the individual must be a full-time employee of the company from the date of buying the shares to the date on which the interest is paid. Relief will continue to be given for interest paid up to 12 months after the taxpayer has ceased to be a full-time employee (*ITA 2007, s 397(4)*);

(5)   the taxpayer must not have recovered any capital from the company unless that amount is treated as a repayment of the loan in whole or in part (*ITA 2007, s 406*).

The maximum amount of interest relief available is restricted to 25% of income or £50,000, whichever is the greater (*ITA 2007, s 42A* inserted by *FA 2013, s 16, Sch 3* with effect from 6 April 2013).

Payments to a trade union, police organisations or friendly society for death benefits

1.40   Relief is available of 50% of that part of a payment of a member's contribution to a trade union or police organisation allocated to superannuation, funeral expenses or life assurance benefits (*ITA 2007, ss 457* and *458*). The maximum amount of relief to which an individual is entitled for a tax year is £100.

Maintenance payments

1.41   Tax relief for maintenance payments was generally withdrawn from 6 April 2000. However, relief is still available if one or both of the parties to the marriage was aged 65 or over at 5 April 2000. Where the relief still applies, the payer is entitled to tax relief in 2018/19 at 10% for qualifying maintenance payments up to the first £3,360. The maximum tax reduction in 2018/19 is therefore £336. All maintenance received after 5 April 2000 is non-taxable income (*ITA 2007, s 453*).

Charitable donations

Payroll giving

1.42   Payroll giving schemes enable full tax relief to be given on donations to charity by employees who authorise their participating employers to deduct the payments from their pay before tax. There is no upper limit for tax relief on donations; employees may give as much as they like under the scheme. Payments by the employer towards the scheme agent's expenses are an allowable deduction for the employer (*ITEPA 2003, ss 713–715; ITTOIA 2005, s 72; FA 2000, s 38; SI 2000/2074*).

The agreed deductions the employer makes from the employee's pay are done before tax is deducted, which means that the employee obtains tax relief included in the donation at his or her top rate of tax. This is illustrated as follows:

Employee's pledge to charity (gross)	Actual cost to employee @ 20% tax	Actual cost to employee @ 40% tax
£5.00	£4.00	£3.00
£10.00	£8.00	£6.00

For example, if an employee pays tax at the basic rate, it will only cost £4.00 to donate £5.00 to the charity of choice, as shown in the table above.

From 2018/19, in the case of Scottish taxpayers, the upper limit for the Scottish basic rate and any Scottish rates above the basic rate will be increased by the grossed-up amount of the gift (see **3.29** for further details).

The main benefit of payroll giving is to create a regular flow of funds for the benefit of the charity or charities supported by the employee.

An individual will be eligible to make donations under a payroll giving scheme provided that they are an employee or pensioner and the employer deducts PAYE tax from their pay or pension.

Most payroll giving agencies make a small charge which they deduct from employee donations before distributing them to charity. The charge is normally no more than 4% of the donation, or 25p per donation, whichever is the greater. Some employers pay the agency's charges so that the full amount of employee donations can go to charity.

'Gift Aid' payments made by individuals

1.43   Individuals can make one-off or regular gifts to charity under the Gift Aid scheme. There is no lower or upper limit on donations upon which tax relief may be claimed. The payment is treated as paid 'net' (ie as if basic rate income tax had been deducted at source). The basic rate tax deemed to have been deducted by the donor is clawed back by HMRC if the donor's income tax and capital gains tax liability for the year is insufficient to match the tax retained. A higher rate taxpayer may claim additional relief against income tax or capital gains tax, as appropriate. Donors may join the Gift Aid scheme by telephone or online, and can complete a single declaration to cover a series of donations (*ITA 2007, Pt 8, Ch 2*).

Focus

Higher rate taxpayers benefit from additional tax relief under the Gift Aid scheme, as they can claim back the difference between the higher rate of tax at 40% and the basic rate of tax at 20% on the total value of their donations. This means that an additional 20% tax relief (40% – 20%) may be claimed. So, if a higher rate taxpayer makes a donation of £100, the gross donation to the charity will be £125 and the donor can claim tax relief of £25 (20% of £125).

Individual donors making Gift Aid donations can elect for the donation to be treated as paid in the previous tax year. The election must be made to HMRC by the date on which the donor's tax return was submitted for the previous tax year and, in any event, no later than 31 January following that tax year. An election can only be made if the gift could be paid out of taxed income or gains of the previous tax year (*ITA 2007, s 426*).

See also **Chapter 4** regarding donations to charities.

Covenants

1.44   A charitable deed of covenant is a legally binding agreement to transfer income to a charity, which is capable of exceeding three years. Covenants were previously a separate form of charitable gift, but tax relief for donations by deed of covenant is given under the Gift Aid rules from 6 April 2000. However, deeds of covenant set up before that date continue to operate. Covenants are treated as Gift Aid donations.

Other charitable donations

1.45   Income tax relief is available for gifts of stock by businesses, and for gifts of quoted shares and securities. Relief is also available for gifts of land and buildings to charity from 6 April 2002, if certain conditions are satisfied. The relief for donations of shares and securities or land and buildings is given by deduction from total income, rather than by extending the basic rate band (*ITTOIA 2005, ss 107–110*).

Example 1.7—Charitable donation using Gift Aid

Olivia makes a Gift Aid payment of £1,000 in 2019/20. Her tax position if she is (a) a basic rate taxpayer, and (b) a higher rate taxpayer, is as follows:

	(a) liable at 20%	(b) liable at 40%
	£	£
Payment made to charity	1,000	1,000
20% treated as deducted by taxpayer (paid to the charity by HMRC)	250	250
Total received by charity	1,250	1,250
Tax relief @ 20%/40%	250	500
Net cost to Olivia	1,000	750

If Olivia is a higher rate taxpayer and she wishes to pass on the benefit of the higher rate relief to the charity, she should make a payment of £1,334. In that case:

- the total received by the charity would be £1,667 (1,334 × 100/80 (ie 100 – 20));

- Olivia would receive tax relief of £667 (1,667 × 40%);

- leaving a net cost to Olivia of £1,000.

If Olivia is an employee and pays all her tax through the PAYE system, the higher rate relief could be given by a coding adjustment.

Otherwise, she would need to claim relief through the self-assessment return. The gross amount (amount paid plus the basic rate tax credit, ie £1,250 in the above example) is added to the basic rate limit, so that income of £1,250, which would otherwise be taxable at the higher rate, is taxed only at the basic rate. The effect of this (assuming all income is earned income) is to reduce the tax liability by £250, giving total relief on the donation of £250 + £250 = £500 (ie 40% of £1,250).

HOW INCOME TAX IS CALCULATED

Introduction

1.46   Tax returns made on paper have to be filed by 31 October. So, a 2018/19 paper return, for example, will have to be filed by 31 October 2019. The date will be the same for taxpayers who want HMRC to calculate their tax liability. The filing date for returns filed online is 31 January following the end of the tax year in question. This means that a 2018/19 electronic return, for example, will have to be filed by 31 January 2020 (see **Chapter 2** for further details).

Calculating the tax payable

1.47   Broadly, the tax liability is calculated by:

• working out 'total income' by adding together all the income under the various categories of income, allowing in each case, for any eligible deductions and expenses as well as any taxable benefits and gains;

• deducting from that amount any reliefs (including any Gift Aid donations) to arrive at total income (for the purpose of the age allowance restriction);

• deducting the personal allowance (and blind person's allowance where applicable) to arrive at 'taxable income';

• applying the relevant tax rates to the taxable income to arrive at the tax due;

• deducting from that amount any relief or allowance given as a tax reduction such as Enterprise Investment Scheme relief to arrive at the total tax liability; and

• adding to that amount any notional tax deducted from payments made by the taxpayer, such as on Gift Aid payments, and deducting tax already paid through PAYE, tax deducted at source and foreign taxes paid where applicable.

Student loans

1.48   Repayment of student loans is a shared responsibility between the Student Loans Company (SLC) and HMRC. Employers have an obligation to deduct student loan repayments in certain circumstances and to account for such payments 'in like manner as income tax payable under the *Taxes Acts*' (*Education (Student Loans) (Repayment) Regulations 2000, SI 2000/944, reg 14*). There are currently two types of student loans: plan 1 and plan 2. With effect from April 2019, the thresholds for making student loan repayments are as follows:

• plan 1 with a 2019/20 threshold of £18,935 (£1,578.00 a month or £364.14 per week); and

• plan 2 with a 2019/20 threshold of £25,725 (£2,143.75 a month or £494.71 per week).

Plan 1 loans are pre-September 2012 income contingent student loans. Loans taken out post-September 2012 in England and Wales have the higher threshold. Previously these have been repaid outside of the payroll directly to the SLC. From April 2016, they will be calculated and repaid via deduction from the payroll, which means that employers and, their payroll software where applicable, need to be able to cope with both types of plans.

Broadly, employers are responsible for:

- checking if a new employee needs to make student loan repayments;

- deducting student loan repayments and passing the payment to HMRC; and

- recording student loan repayments on employee payroll records, pay slips, Full Payment Submissions (FPS) and on a form P45 when an employee leaves.

Employers are not responsible for deciding that employees have to make student loan repayments or handling employees' student loan queries.

Student loan deductions are made from gross pay, alongside tax and NIC. Deductions are rounded down to the nearest pound. Deductions are non-cumulative, and so employers can ignore the question of amounts already deducted. HMRC provide tables, and the employer CD-ROM can be used to calculate the deduction which (because of rounding) may not be exactly 1/52 of the annual amount.

If an employee has two jobs, the employer does not need to be concerned with the employee's other income, but should calculate the deduction based only on amounts paid by him. However, if the employee has two employments with the same employer, these should be aggregated for student loan purposes if they are aggregated for NIC purposes.

Focus

The Department for Education has launched a new student loan product known as postgraduate loans (PGLs). From April 2019, individuals may start loan repayments of this type through PAYE, so employers need to be aware of their new obligations.

Broadly, if an individual has a PGL:

- HMRC will send their employer a new postgraduate start notice (PGL1) to ask them to start taking PGL deductions.

- HMRC will send their employer a new postgraduate stop notice (PGL2) to ask them to stop taking PGL deductions.

- Employers will collect payments through the normal PAYE process.

- Individuals may also be liable to repay a student loan plan type 1 or 2 concurrently with PGL. HMRC will let their employer know this by

---

continuing to send the normal student loan start (SL1) and student loan stop (SL2) notices as well as PGL1s and PGL2s.

HMRC are currently working with software developers to finalise the technical specifications for PGL repayment and hope to publish further guidance in due course.

The earliest individuals can start repayment of PGL via self-assessment is April 2020.

Employees

Employers are required to collect student loan repayments through the PAYE system by making deductions of 9% from an employee's pay to the extent that earnings exceed the relevant threshold each year (see above).

Each pay day is looked at separately, and so repayments may vary according to how much the employee has been paid in that week or month. If income falls below the starting limit for that week/month, the employer should not make a deduction.

Example 1.8—Student loans

Charles leaves university in June 2018, and starts a new job in August 2018 earning £2,500 a month (£30,000 a year).

His student loan repayments will commence in April 2019 and will be calculated as follows:

Income in April 2019: £2,500 – £2,143 (starting limit) = £357

£357 × 9% = £32.13 repaid in April 2019.

Taxpayers who make repayments through PAYE can swap to repaying by direct debit in the last 23 months of their loan if they so wish. SLC will normally contact individuals shortly before this time to offer this option. This payment method enables account holders to choose a suitable monthly repayment date and ensures that they do not repay too much.

Self-employed

For those who are self-employed, the repayments are collected via the self-assessment system. Broadly, repayments will equal 9% of total income (excluding unearned income, if it is £2,000 or less) in excess of the annual threshold for plan 1 or plan 2 loans. They will be collected on the normal self-assessment payment dates (ie 31 January and 31 July each year).

Rates of tax

1.49 The tax system is a progressive one (ie the tax rate increases as income increases), with a basic rate of 20%, a higher rate of 40% and an additional rate of 45% (2019/20) (*FA 2014, s 1; ITA 2007, s 6; FA 2009, s 6*). (Note that, prior to 2008/09, a starting rate of 10% applied to all income. For 2008/09 to 2014/15, the 10% starting rate only applied to savings income below the starting rate threshold (£2,880 in 2014/15; £2,790 in 2013/14) and, if savings income exceeded this limit, the rate band did not apply.)

From 6 April 2015, the starting rate for savings income was reduced to zero per cent, and the maximum amount of an individual's income that can qualify for this starting rate rose to £5,000 (*FA 2014, s 3* amending *ITA 2007, s 7*). The rate of £5,000 remains unchanged for 2016/17 onwards. It remains unchanged for 2019/20.

ITA 2007 sets out different types of income and the order in which they are taxed. The first slice is non-savings income, which is not separately defined in *ITA 2007*, but broadly covers earnings, pensions, taxable social security benefits, trading profits and income from property. The next slice is savings income (broadly, bank and building society interest). Dividend income is the top slice.

Income tax rates

1.50

	2017/18	2018/19	2019/20
Starting rate for savings: 0%	£5,000	£5,000	£5,000
Basic rate: 20%	£0–£33,500	£0–£34,500	£0–£37,500
Higher rate: 40%	£33,501–£150,000	£34,501–£150,000	£37,501–£150,000
Additional rate: 45%	Over £150,000	Over £150,000	Over £150,000

Focus

The basic rate is £37,500 for 2019/20 (rising from £34,500 in 2018/19). This means that the higher rate threshold (taking into account a personal tax allowance of £12,500 in 2019/20) is £50,000 in 2019/20 (rising from £46,350 in 2018/19).

Dividend rates

1.51   Between 2010/11 and 2015/16, there were three rates of tax for dividends as follows (*FA 2009, s 6*):

- dividends otherwise taxable at the 20% basic rate continue to be taxable at the 10% dividend ordinary rate;

- dividends otherwise taxable at the 40% higher rate continue to be taxable at the 32.5% dividend upper rate; and

- for 2013/14 onwards, dividends otherwise taxable at the 45% additional rate (see **1.50**) are taxable at the 37.5% dividend additional rate.

The system for taxing dividends was simplified with effect from April 2016. The dividend tax credit (formerly 10%) was abolished from that date and replaced with a new dividend tax allowance. The allowance was £5,000 a year for 2016/17 and 2017/18, but was reduced to £2,000 from 6 April 2018. It remains at this level for 2019/20.

The rates of tax on dividend income above the allowance are 7.5% for basic rate taxpayers, 32.5% for higher rate taxpayers and 38.1% for additional rate taxpayers.

Focus

The dividend allowance is reduced from £5,000 to £2,000 from April 2018 (*Finance (No 2) Act 2017, s 8*).

Order of allocation of income to tax bands

1.52   Sources of income are treated as the top slice of income in the following order (*ITA 2007, Pt 2, Ch 3*):

(1)   capital gains;

(2)   life insurance policy gains;

(3)   lump sum termination payments from employment;

(4)   dividend income;

(5)   other savings income; and

(6)   all other income and profits.

Repayment claims

1.53   Claims can be made for repayment of tax paid through deduction at source (mainly savings interest prior to 2016/17) where an individual's income does not exceed personal allowances or where reliefs and allowance can be set against income on which tax has been paid (*ITA 2007, s 17*). However, the tax credit on dividends, prior to its abolition from 6 April 2016, was not repayable in any case.

HMRC will deal with repayment claims by issuing a repayment claim form outside the self-assessment system. Where payments on account exceed the final tax liability, a claim for repayment can be made through the tax return or earlier where the taxpayer believes tax has been overpaid. But, if the repayment subsequently proves to be excessive, interest is chargeable on the shortfall.

Income tax computation

1.54   In order to compute an individual taxpayer's liability to income tax, it is first necessary to ascertain his 'total income' for that year of assessment. This is Step 1 in the tax calculation below, as set out in *ITA 2007, s 23*.

Step 1

Identify the amounts of income on which the taxpayer is charged to income tax for the tax year.

The sum of those amounts is 'total income'.

Each of those amounts is a 'component' of total income.

Step 2

Deduct from the components the amount of any relief (under a provision listed at **1.55** below) to which the taxpayer is entitled for the tax year.

The sum of the amounts of the components left after this step is 'net income'.

Step 3

Deduct from the amounts of the components left after Step 2 any allowances to which the taxpayer is entitled for the tax year (under *ITA 2007, Pt 3, Ch 2* (individuals: personal allowance and blind person's allowance)).

At Steps 2 and 3, the reliefs and allowances are deducted in the way which will result in the greatest reduction in the taxpayer's liability to income tax (*ITA 2007, s 25(2)*).

Step 4

Calculate tax at each applicable rate on the amounts of the components left after Step 3 (see **1.49** for rates).

Step 5

Add together the amounts of tax calculated at Step 4.

Step 6

Deduct from the amount of tax calculated at Step 5 any tax reductions to which the taxpayer is entitled for the tax year (under a provision listed in **1.56** below).

Step 7

Add to the amount of tax left after Step 6 any amounts of tax for which the taxpayer is liable for the tax year under any provision listed in **1.57** below).

The result is the taxpayer's liability to income tax for the tax year.

Reliefs

1.55   If the taxpayer is an individual, the provisions referred to at Step 2 in **1.54** above are broadly as follows (*ITA 2007, ss 24* and *25*):

(a)   early trade losses relief (*ITA 2007, s 72*);

(b)   share loss relief (*ITA 2007, Pt 4, Ch 6*);

(c)   gifts of shares, securities and real property to charities, etc (*ITA 2007, Pt 8, Ch 3*);

(d)   payments to trade unions or police organisations (*ITA 2007, ss 457* and *458*);

(e)   pension schemes: relief under net pay arrangement: excess relief (*FA 2004, s 193(4)*);

(f)   pension schemes: relief on making the claim (*FA 2004, s 194(1)*);

(g)   trade loss reliefs: against general income (*ITA 2007, s 64*); carry-forward loss relief (*ITA 2007, s 83*); terminal loss relief (*ITA 2007, s 89*); and post-cessation relief (*ITA 2007, s 96*);

(h)   property reliefs: carry-forward (*ITA 2007, s 118*); against general income (*ITA 2007, s 120*); and post-cessation (*ITA 2007, s 125*);

(i)   employment loss relief against general income (*ITA 2007, s 128*);

(j)   loss relief against miscellaneous income (*ITA 2007, s 152*);

(k)   interest payments (*ITA 2007, Pt 8, Ch 1*); irrecoverable peer-to-peer loans (*ITA 2007, Pt 8, Ch 1A*); and annual payments (*ITA 2007, Pt 8, Ch 4*);

(l)   manufactured dividends on UK shares: payments by non-companies (*ITA 2007, s 574*); manufactured interest on UK securities: payments not otherwise deductible (*ITA 2007, s 579*);

(m)   plant and machinery allowances in a case where the allowance is to be given effect under *CAA 2001, s 258* (special leasing of plant and machinery) (*CAA 2001, Pt 2*);

(n)   patent allowances in a case where the allowance is to be given effect under *CAA 2001, s 479* (persons having qualifying non-trade expenditure) (*CAA 2001, Pt 8*);

(o)   deduction for liabilities related to former employment (*ITEPA 2003, s 555*);

(p)   strips of government securities: relief for losses (*ITTOIA 2005, s 446*);

(q)   listed securities held since 26 March 2003: relief for losses: persons other than trustees (*ITTOIA 2005, s 454(4)*); and

(r)   relief for patent expenses (*ITTOIA 2005, s 600*).

Tax reductions

1.56   If the taxpayer is an individual, the provisions referred to at Step 6 in **1.54** above are broadly as follows (*ITA 2007, s 26*):

(a)   tax reductions for married couples and civil partners (*ITA 2007, Pt 3 Ch 3*);

(b)   transferable tax allowance for married couples and civil partners (*ITA 2007, Pt 3, Ch 3A*);

(c)   EIS relief (*ITA 2007, Pt 5, Ch 1*);

(d)   SEIS relief (*ITA 2007, Pt 5A, Ch1*);

(e)   relief for social investments (*ITA 2007, Pt 5B, Ch1*);

(f)   VCT relief (*ITA 2007, Pt 6, Ch 2*);

(g)   community investment tax relief (*ITA 2007, Pt 7, Ch 1*);

(h)   relief for non-deductible interest on loan to invest in partnership with residential property business (*ITA 2007, s 399B*);

(i)   qualifying maintenance payments (*ITA 2007, s 453*);

(j)   spreading of patent royalty receipts (*ITA 2007, s 461*);

(k)   relief for interest on loan to buy life annuity (*ICTA 1988, s 353(1A)*);

(l)   relief at source: additional relief (*FA 2004, s 192A*);

(m)   property business: relief for non-deductible costs of a dwelling-related loan (*ITTOIA 2005, s 274A*);

(n)   top slicing relief (*ITTOIA 2005, s 535*);

(o)   relief for deficiencies (*ITTOIA 2005, s 539*);

(p)   distribution repaying shares or security issued in earlier distribution (*ITTOIA 2005, s 401*);

(q)   relief where foreign estates have borne UK income tax (*ITTOIA 2005, ss 677 and 678*);

(r)   double taxation relief: relief by agreement (*TIOPA 2010, ss 2 and 6*); and

(s)   relief for foreign tax where no double taxation arrangements (*TIOPA 2010, ss 18(1)(b) and (2)*).

Tax reductions are deducted in the order that will result in the greatest reduction in the taxpayer's liability to income tax for the tax year (*ITA 2007, s 27(2)*).

1.57   If the taxpayer is an individual, the provisions referred to at Step 7 in **1.54** above are broadly as follows (*ITA 2007, s 30*):

(a)   Gift Aid: charge to tax (*ITA 2007, s 424*);

(b)   tainted gift aid donations: charge to tax (*ITA 2007, s 809ZN*);

(c)   tainted charity donations by trustees: charge to tax (*ITA 2007, s 809ZO*);

(d)   high income child benefit charge (*ITEPA 2003, Pt 10, Ch 8*);

(e)   relief at source: excessive relief given (*FA 2004, s 192B*);

(f)   pension schemes: the short service refund lump sum charge (*FA 2004, s 205*);

(g)   pension schemes: the special lump sum death benefits charge (*FA 2004, s 206*);

(h)   pension schemes: the unauthorised payments charge (*FA 2004, s 208(2)(a)*);

(i)   pension schemes: the unauthorised payments surcharge (*FA 2004, s 209(3)(a)*);

(j)   pension schemes: the lifetime allowance charge (*FA 2004, s 214*);

(k)   pension schemes: the annual allowance charge (*FA 2004, s 227*); and

(l)   social security pension lump sum (*F(No 2)A 2005, s 7*).

Allocation of income to tax bands

1.58   To ensure that certain classes of income do not escape charge to tax at the higher and additional rates for higher and additional rate taxpayers, the rules provide for these classes of income to be treated as the 'top slice' of income as follows (*ITA 2007, s 16*):

•   savings income is treated as the top slice of taxable income; and

•   dividend income is treated as the top slice of savings income.

If a person has savings income but no dividend income, the savings income is treated as the highest part of the person's total income (*ITA 2007, s 16(3)*). If a person has dividend income but no savings income, the dividend income is treated as the highest part of the person's total income (*ITA 2007, s 16(4)*). If a person has both savings income and dividend income:

(a)   the savings income and dividend income are together treated as the highest part of total income, and

(b)   the dividend income is treated as the higher part of that part of total income (*ITA 2007, s 16(5)(a) and (b)*).

This is subject to two exceptions. Where a taxpayer receives certain gains from a life insurance policy (*ITTOIA 2005, ss 535–537*) or a taxable lump sum on termination of employment, the income from these sources are generally treated as the highest part of taxable income, with life insurance gains at the top (*ITA 2007, s 16(2)*).

However, capital gains in excess of the exemption limit are treated as the very highest part of taxable income and gains.

Tax at higher marginal rates

1.59   The current tax system has given rise to a series of anomalies in tax rates. In some situations, where a taxpayer has savings or dividend income, the effective tax rate can exceed 40% (or 45% where the taxpayer is liable at the additional rate of tax). It is important to recognise where this might occur and where planning opportunities can be maximised. The total amount of the tax relief should always be considered before undertaking tax planning to ensure that the benefits outweigh the cost and administrative inconvenience.

Marginal tax rate problems may arise in the following situations:

•   Taxpayers with the same amount of income but from different sources can end up paying different amounts of tax (see below).

•   Those claiming Child and Working Tax Credit and whose income is around the thresholds.

•   Taxpayers with 'adjusted net income' of £100,000 and over will have their personal allowance reduced or eliminated. They may suffer marginal tax rates of up to 60%.

•   Those who receive dividends and whose total income is just into the higher rate tax bracket.

•   Those who receive bank or building society interest and whose total income is just into the higher rate tax bracket.

Savings income

1.60   High marginal tax rates can also occur for low earners with savings income, some of which is bank or building society interest. The starting rate for savings applies where the taxpayer's taxable non-savings income is less than the starting rate for savings income threshold (£5,000 for 2017/18 to 2019/20). In such cases, the first portion of taxable savings income up to the savings income threshold is taxed at 0%. Where a taxpayer's taxable non-savings income exceeds (even by £1) the starting rate for savings income threshold, all their savings income is taxed at the basic rate, up to the higher rate threshold.

Focus

- Review non-savings income to keep it below the threshold for the starting rate for savings where possible, for example where a salary is being paid from a family business.

- Bear in mind the 0% starting rate for savings when deciding whether to take a salary or dividend from a family company.

- Where non-savings income is below the starting rate for savings threshold, keep savings income within the 0% band by investing in NISAs/Junior NISAs or exempt National Savings products (see **Chapter 4**).

Deductions and reliefs

1.61   Since the rate at which income (and gains) is taxed depends on the tax band in which it falls, the way in which deductions and reliefs are given is important. Reliefs deductible from total taxable income allow for tax savings at the top rate (*ITA 2007, s 16*).

Focus

The taxpayer can set deductions against different classes of income in the order resulting in the greatest reduction in the tax liability (eg against earned income taxed at 20% before dividend income taxed at 10%) (*ITA 2007, ss 25, 27*).

The personal and blind person's allowances are deducted from income after all other deductions have been made and 'total income' for the purpose of the personal and married couple's age allowance restriction is the income before those deductions. These allowances can be offset against income in the most beneficial way to produce the lowest tax liability.

Double tax relief

1.62   A UK resident taxpayer is normally subject to UK tax on foreign income and a non-resident individual is generally subject to UK tax on income from a UK source. In both cases, the income is liable to tax in the UK and overseas. To prevent a UK resident individual being taxed twice on the same income, relief from double taxation on foreign income is normally available.

If the income arises in a country with which the UK has a double taxation agreement, there may be complete exemption from UK tax on that income. Where there is no double taxation agreement, relief may be claimed against the UK tax liability for the lower of the UK tax or the foreign tax. Otherwise, the income net of any foreign tax paid would be charged to UK tax, but this is not usually beneficial (*ITA 2007, s 28(4)*). See **Chapter 10** for more on double tax relief.

High-income child benefit charge

1.63   The changes to child benefit took effect from 7 January 2013. Broadly, a tax charge will apply where the 'adjusted net income' of a taxpayer or their partner is more than £50,000 in a tax year, and they or their partner receive child benefit. For those with 'adjusted net income' of more than £60,000, the tax charge is 100% of the amount of child benefit. If the 'adjusted net income' is between £50,000 and £60,000, the charge is gradually increased to 100% of the child benefit.

The calculation of 'adjusted net income' is an existing method of determining an individual's income, and is currently used to work out entitlement to personal allowances where an individual has income over £100,000 (see **1.18**).

Where each parent or partner has an income over £50,000, the charge will only apply to the person with the higher income.

For taxpayers with income between £50,000 and £60,000, the amount of the charge will be a proportion of the child benefit received. For taxpayers with income above £60,000, the amount of the charge will equal the amount of child benefit received. The amount of child benefit payable is unaffected by the tax charge.

The charge is 1% of the amount of child benefit for every £100 of income that exceeds £50,000. So, for example, based on a full tax year, child benefit for families with two children is currently £1,752. For a taxpayer whose income is £54,000, the charge will be £700.80, ie £17.52 for every £100 earned above £50,000. For a taxpayer whose income is £60,000 or more, the charge will be £1,752.

Taxpayers affected by the charge were required to report child benefit for the first time on their 2012/13 self-assessment return, which was due for submission to HMRC by 31 January 2014, at which time the tax also had to be paid for the last three months of the 2012/13 tax year. Employees subject to PAYE can choose to pay the tax through their tax code from 6 April 2013 (*Income Tax (Pay As You Earn) (Amendment) Regulations 2013 (SI 2013/521)*). However, it will still be necessary to complete a self-assessment return at the end of the year.

Focus

The case of *Gill* [2018] TC 06566, recently demonstrated how the procedures relating to the high income child benefit charge are difficult for people unfamiliar with the complexity of the tax system to understand. In this case, the First-tier Tribunal (FTT) found that the taxpayer had a reasonable excuse and was not liable to the penalties in respect of the charge.

Chapter 2

Income tax compliance

SIGNPOSTS

- Generally, self-assessment tax returns must be submitted by 31 October following the end of a tax year, if filed on paper, and by 31 January following the end of a tax year if filed electronically (see **2.1**).

- HMRC are currently implementing the 'Making Tax Digital' project (see **2.4**).

- HMRC have powers which enable them to make income tax or capital gains tax assessments without the taxpayer first being required to complete a self-assessment tax return (see **2.8**).

- Sole traders and partners carrying on a business (including letting property) are required to keep all records relevant to a tax return for a period of five years and ten months from the end of each tax year. In other cases, records must be retained for 22 months from the end of the tax year (see **2.25**).

- Most taxpayers pay their tax without the need for direct contact with HMRC, as tax is collected either through the PAYE system (see **2.34**).

- Self-employed taxpayers are generally required to make two equal payments of their income tax liabilities (including any Class 2 and Class 4 NIC liability) on account, by 31 January in the tax year and by 31 July following the tax year. The tax due will usually be based on the total income tax payable directly in the previous tax year (see **2.35**).

- A severe interest and penalties regime exists in relation to tax and national insurance contributions paid late, and to overdue tax returns (see **2.40** onwards).

- If a return is not submitted, HMRC may make a 'determination' of the amount of tax considered to be due, within three years after the normal filing date for the return (see **2.60**).

- Appeals against HMRC decisions may be made to the Tax Tribunal (see **2.77**).

- The alternative dispute resolution (ADR) service provides taxpayers with an alternative way of resolving tax disputes by using an independent facilitator (see **2.96**).

- From 6 April 2017, the Serial Tax Avoidance Regime (STAR) of warnings and escalating sanctions took effect for taxpayers who persistently engage in tax avoidance schemes defeated by HMRC (see **2.115**).

INCOME TAX SELF-ASSESSMENT

Introduction

2.1   Under the system of self-assessment, tax returns are generally required to be filed by 31 January after the end of the tax year to which the return relates (*TMA 1970, s 8, 8A or 12AA*).

Tax returns made on paper must be filed by 31 October (*FA 2007, s 88*). This means that a 2018/19 paper return, for example, will have to be filed by 31 October 2019. The date is the same for taxpayers who want HMRC to calculate their tax liability. Returns filed online must be submitted by 31 January.

Where a notice to file a return has been issued, but no return is filed by the prescribed date, HMRC may serve a determination, to the best of their information and belief, of the amount of the tax due. This then serves as a self-assessment in prescribing how much tax is due, and when, but can be superseded by a self-assessment by HMRC or the taxpayer.

Neither determinations nor superseding self-assessments can be made more than four years from the prescribed filing date or, in the case of a superseding self-assessment, more than 12 months after the determination (*FA 2008, Sch 39, para 48; SI 2009/403, art 2*).

Focus

The time allowed for making a self-assessment was clarified in *Finance Act 2016 (FA 2016, s 168*, inserting *TMA 1970, s 34A*). The time limit is four years from the end of the tax year to which the self-assessment relates. This is the same time limit as for assessments by HMRC. This measure took effect on and after 5 April 2017, although there are transitional arrangements for years previous to this, as follows:

- for tax years prior to 2012/13, taxpayers had until 5 April 2017 to submit a self- assessment;

- for 2013/14, the deadline is 5 April 2018;

- for 2014/15, the deadline is 5 April 2019; and
- for 2015/16, the deadline is 5 April 2020.

Electronic filing

2.2   HMRC's internet service allows taxpayers to send their tax returns over the Internet. This service also allows agents to send tax returns on behalf of their clients. Taxpayers may register to use the internet filing service online via the HMRC website. A user identity is displayed on the screen when the taxpayer has chosen a password and successfully registered online. Confirmation of the user identity is sent by post within seven working days of registering. Before sending the tax return over the Internet, the sender will be asked for a user identity and password. Upon receipt, HMRC immediately forward either an online acknowledgement or a notice of rejection.

Under the self-assessment system HMRC immediately process the return and make basic checks to ensure the accuracy of the calculations. Unless the taxpayer hears otherwise from HMRC, he or she pays any outstanding liability based on the figures shown in the return – HMRC refer to this system as 'process now, check later'. There are two separate filing dates for tax returns. For paper returns, the date is 31 October (for tax year 2018/19, that is 31 October 2019). For returns filed online, the date is 31 January (31 January 2020 for the 2018/19 tax year). A calculation of tax liability is automatically provided when a return is filed online.

It is possible for taxpayers and their agents to file self-assessment returns online for earlier tax years.

Filing the return – relevant dates

2.3   The tax return (form SA100) is usually issued by HMRC during April, shortly after the end of the tax year.

Taxpayers who have previously filed online are no longer issued with a paper return in April, but are sent a letter requiring them to file a return.

Key Dates	What happens/Why is this date important?
6 April 2019	The new tax year starts. A 2018/19 tax return or Notice to Complete a Tax Return (SA316) will be sent out to all people who receive a tax return each year.
31 July 2019	Taxpayers will be charged a second automatic penalty of £100 if their 2017/18 tax return was due back by 31 January 2019 but it has not been sent in.

Key Dates	What happens/Why is this date important?
31 August 2019	For 2018/19 income tax self-assessment returns or notices issued after this date, the normal deadline of 31 October 2019 for HMRC to calculate any tax due is extended to two months from the date on which the return was issued.
5 October 2019	HMRC must be notified of any 2018/19 income tax or CGT liabilities by this date, in respect of those who have not already received a self-assessment return (or a notice to file a return) for the tax year.
31 October 2019	If the taxpayer is completing a paper tax return for 2018/19, he must send it back by this date if he wants HMRC to: ● calculate the tax due; ● tell the taxpayer what to pay by 31 January 2020; and ● collect tax through the taxpayer's tax code.
30 December 2019	If the taxpayer submits returns electronically, it must be sent by this date if he wishes HMRC to collect tax through his tax code.
31 January 2020	If the taxpayer was sent a tax return by 31 October 2019, this is the deadline for sending back the completed 2018/19 tax return.
6 April 2020	The new tax year starts (see above).

'Making Tax Digital' project

2.4   As part of a £1.3bn investment to transform HMRC into one of the most digitally advanced tax administrations in the world, HMRC are implementing new procedures for interacting with HMRC and paying tax under the 'Making Tax Digital' banner.

Most individuals and small businesses now have access to their own secure digital tax account that enables them to interact with HMRC digitally. It is intended that by 2020, businesses and individual taxpayers will be able to register, file, pay and update their information at any time of the day or night, and at any point in the year, to suit them. For the vast majority, there will be no need to fill in an annual tax return.

The Government is also consulting on the issue of payment – on options to simplify the payment of taxes, align payment arrangements and bring payment dates closer to the time of the activity or transactions generating the tax liability.

The 'Making Tax Digital' project has also presented the opportunity to align payment arrangements across different taxes and to provide a more joined-up service for taxpayers. The Government has already brought the collection of Class 2 National Insurance Contributions (NICs) for the self-employed into the arrangements for self-assessment, which means that Class 2 NICs are collected alongside Class 4 NICs for most.

Further information on the 'Making Tax Digital' project can be found at www. gov.uk/government/publications/making-tax-digital.

Focus

Under HMRC's Making Tax Digital (MTD) project, mandatory digital record keeping for VAT for businesses over the VAT threshold (with turnover over £85,000) applies from 1 April 2019. This is an important first step in this modernisation of the tax system to which the government remains committed. The government will operate a light touch approach to penalties in the first year of implementation, so that where businesses are doing their best to comply no filing or record-keeping penalties will be issued. The focus will be on supporting businesses to transition.

At the Spring Statement on 13 March 2019, the Chancellor confirmed that the government will not be mandating MTD for any new taxes or businesses in 2020. However, MTD will be available on a voluntary basis for all businesses before then, so that those who want to engage digitally sooner rather than later, will be able to do so.

HMRC have extended the original MTD income tax pilot to accept quarterly updates from individual landlords with simple tax affairs. Agents can also sign up clients to the MTD for income tax pilot.

The latest extension means that certain taxpayers will be able to opt out of the current self-assessment regime and use software to report their income tax if at least one of the following applies:

- the taxpayer is a sole trader with income from one business; or

- they rent out only UK property but not as furnished holiday lettings.

Those who do not qualify must continue to report their income to HMRC via a self-assessment return in the usual way.

Focus

The Government's consultation entitled *Making Tax Digital: interest harmonisation and sanctions for late payment* ran until 2 March 2018. The consultation proposes to introduce harmonised interest rates and rules and a standardised approach to late payment penalties across taxes. This includes aligning the high level rules for interest on VAT debt, bringing them into line with income tax self-assessment and corporation tax; the consultation also explores how late payment penalties could work and interact with interest. A new hybrid model has been put forward that takes in comments from previous consultations on late payment penalties, and combines a 'penalty charge element' together with an 'interest' type calculation.

The consultation document can be found online at https://tinyurl.com/y8rzcmhv.

Personal tax accounts

2.5   Personal Tax Accounts (PTAs) is an HMRC online service, which enables UK taxpayers to manage their tax affairs online. According to current figures, some eight million people are already using their PTA to complete a variety of tasks, from updating an address to filing their self-assessment return. Tasks which can be completed using the service include:

- checking and changing addresses;

- reviewing tax codes and tax calculations;

- checking state pension entitlement and National Insurance records;

- receiving texts and emails from HMRC rather than letters;

- managing tax credits and Child Benefit payments;

- allowing a family member or friend to manage a taxpayer's affairs; and

- tracking progress of any forms submitted to HMRC.

HMRC state that they will continue to add new services to the PTA.

Further information can be found on the gov.uk website at https://tinyurl.com/yb8y7afj.

Information notices

2.6   HMRC may require certain information from persons generally or from taxpayers in particular (*FA 2008, Sch 36, paras 1* and *2*; *ITA 2007, s 748*).

An officer of HMRC may, by notice in writing, require a taxpayer to provide information or to produce a document if the information or document is reasonably required for the purpose of checking the taxpayer's tax position (*FA 2008, Sch 36, para 1*).

HMRC also have the power to obtain information and documents from third parties if they are reasonably required to check a taxpayer's tax position (*FA 2008, Sch 36, para 2*). However, HMRC may not issue a third party notice without the agreement of the taxpayer or the approval of the tribunal (*FA 2008, Sch 36, para 3*). There is also a requirement that HMRC must provide the taxpayer concerned with a copy of the third party notice, unless the tribunal has disapplied this requirement (*FA 2008, Sch 36, para 4*). HMRC are empowered to obtain, from a third party, information about a taxpayer whose identity is not known (*FA 2008, Sch 36, para 5*). Such notices require First-tier Tribunal approval.

The information requested in an 'information notice' may be specified or 'described' by HMRC, which means that HMRC are not restricted to asking for documents that they can specifically identify (*FA 2008, Sch 36, para 6*). If a tribunal has approved the giving of an information notice, the notice must say so, as there are different rules for the penalties for failure to comply with the notice depending on whether it was issued by HMRC or by the tribunal. For further information on HMRC powers, see the HMRC Compliance Handbook (https://www.gov.uk/hmrc-internal-manuals/compliance-handbook).

2.7   In *R (on the application of Cooke) v HMRC* [2007] EWHC 167 (Admin), the court examined whether a notice given under former *TMA 1970, s 20(3)* to the taxpayer's solicitor (and, therefore, given by a senior officer on behalf of the Commissioners, by virtue of *s 20B(3)*) was subject to the various procedural safeguards to which other notices given under *s 20(3)* (to persons other than lawyers) are subject.

HMRC generally use orders in place of search warrants. HMRC officers, or officers of other government departments who carry out duties under the *National Minimum Wage Act 1998*, can use the information obtained for the assessment and collection of tax and the payment of tax credits.

It is a criminal offence intentionally to falsify or destroy documents called for by HMRC.

TAX RETURNS

Tax returns

2.8   The basic tax return (SA100) currently consists of six pages. There are, in addition, supplementary pages to cover employment, share schemes, self-employment, partnerships, land and property, foreign income, trusts and estates, capital gains and non-residence. The return comes with a tax return guide with notes on how to complete the return.

Additional tax return supplementary pages and helpsheets can be obtained from HMRC using their Orderline: 0300 200 3610 (+44 161 930 8331 if calling from abroad). A tax calculation guide is available to those who wish to calculate their own tax. Taxpayers can obtain advice from their local tax offices, and HMRC operate a Helpline (open during evenings and weekends) on 0300 200 3310 for general advice (+44 161 931 9070 if calling from abroad).

Those with straightforward tax affairs, whose tax liability can be met through PAYE deductions, will not normally be required to complete tax returns, although it is the taxpayer's responsibility to notify HMRC if a return is needed, generally within six months following the end of the tax year. A short tax return is available for those with relatively simple tax affairs (eg employees with a modest amount of property income), consisting of four pages plus accompanying guidance. There are no supplementary pages, except for capital gains. There is no need to calculate the tax on the return, although there is a two-page indicative calculation for those who wish to do so.

Focus

In November 2018, HMRC launched an online tool to check whether a self-assessment tax return needs to be submitted for 2017/18 (https://www. gov.uk/check-if-you-need-tax-return/y).

Taxpayers using certain tax avoidance schemes and arrangements are required to make a disclosure to that effect on their self-assessment returns. HMRC maintain a register of known schemes, each of which has a reference number. Taxpayers are required to enter the reference number on their self-assessment return if appropriate (*TMA 1970, ss 7–9, Sch 3A; FA 2004, ss 306–319*; SP 1/97). See **2.111** for further commentary on disclosure of tax avoidance schemes.

HMRC now have a statutory power enabling them to withdraw notices to file in such circumstances (*FA 2013, s 233, Sch 51*). Previously, HMRC used discretionary powers to withdraw such notices.

Focus

Finance Act 2016 extended HMRC powers to enable them to make income tax or capital gains tax assessments without the taxpayer first being required to complete a self-assessment tax return. Broadly, the provisions, referred to as 'simple assessment' allow HMRC to assess a person's tax liability on the basis of information held by them. For example, they will be used where it is not possible to collect the whole of a person's annual income tax liability through PAYE, and HMRC have sufficient information about the individual to make the assessment. This change applies for 2016/17 onwards (*FA 2016, s 167* and *Sch 23*).

Tax returns and guides

Individuals

2.9   Tax return – SA100

Tax return guide – SA150

Short tax return – SA200

Your guide to the short tax return – SA210

Helpsheets

2.10   HS237: Community Investment Tax Relief

HS320: Gains on UK life insurance policies

HS325: Other taxable income

HS340: Interest and alternative finance payments eligible for relief on qualifying loans and alternative finance arrangements

HS341: Enterprise Investment Scheme – Income Tax Relief

HS342: Charitable giving

Employment

2.11   Employment Pages – SA101

Notes on Employment – SA101 (Notes)

Helpsheets

2.12   HS201: Vouchers, credit cards and tokens

HS202: Living accommodation

HS203: Car benefits and car fuel benefits

HS205: Seafarers' Earnings Deduction

HS207: Non-taxable payments or benefits for employees

HS208: Payslips and coding notices

HS210: Assets provided for private use

HS211: Employment – residence and domicile issues

HS212: Tax equalisation

HS213: Payments in kind

Self-employment

2.13   Self-employment Pages – SA103

Notes on Self-employment – SA103 (Notes)

Helpsheets

2.14   HS220: More than one business

HS222: How to calculate your taxable profits

HS224: Farmers and market gardeners

HS227: Losses

HS229: Information from your accounts

HS231: Doctors' expenses

HS232: Farm stock valuation

HS234: Averaging for creators of literary or artistic works

HS236: Foster carers & adult placement carers

HS238: Revenue recognition in service contracts – UITF 40

HS252: Capital allowances and balancing charges

Partnership

2.15   Partnership Pages (Short Version) – SA104

Notes on Partnership (Short) – SA104 (Notes)

Partnership Pages (Full Version) – SA104F

Notes on Partnership (Full) – SA104F (Notes)

UK property

2.16   UK Property Pages – SA105

Notes on UK Property – SA105 (Notes)

Helpsheets

2.17   HS251: Agricultural land

Trusts

2.18   Trusts etc Pages – SA107

Notes on Trusts etc – SA107 (Notes)

Helpsheets

2.19   HS270: Trusts and settlements – income treated as the settlor's

HS390: Trusts and estates of deceased persons: foreign tax credit relief for capital gains

HS392: Trust management expenses (TMEs)

Corrections and amendments – relevant dates

2.20   In normal circumstances, amendments to a tax return may be made up to one year after the 31 January filing date. So, in relation to a tax return for the year ended 5 April 2018, the amendment deadline date is 31 January 2020.

Time limits for HMRC assessment or determination

2.21   The time limit for the making of assessments by HMRC is four years from the end of the year of assessment (*TMA 1970, s 34(1); FA 2008, Sch 39, para 7; SI 2009/403, art 2*).

The time allowed for making a self-assessment was clarified in *Finance Act 2016* with effect from 5 April 2017, subject to transitional rules – see **2.1** (*FA 2016, s 168*, inserting *TMA 1970, s 34A*). The time limit is four years from the end of the tax year to which the self-assessment relates. This is the same time limit as for assessments by HMRC.

In the case of fraudulent or negligent conduct, prior to 1 April 2010, the time limit was 20 years from 31 January following the end of the year of assessment for income tax and CGT (*TMA 1970, s 36(1)*). However, *FA 2008* amended *TMA 1970, s 36(1)* from 1 April 2010, so that an assessment on a person in a case involving a loss of income tax or capital gains tax brought about carelessly or deliberately by the person can now be made at any time not more than six years after the end of the year of assessment to which it relates (subject to *subsection (1A)* and any other provision of the *Taxes Acts* allowing a longer period) (*FA 2008, Sch 39, para 9; SI 2009/403, arts 3–10*).

For a former Special Commissioners' case relating to the validity of an assessment made by HMRC within the prescribed time limits, see *Mashood v Whitehead* [2002] STC (SCD) 166.

2.22   In the case of assessments on personal representatives, prior to 1 April 2010, the time limit was three years from 31 January following the end of the year of assessment in which the deceased died (*TMA 1970, s 40(1)*). However, *FA 2008* introduced provisions to reduce the time limit, with effect from 1 April 2010, for making assessments to four years from the end of the year of assessment (*FA 2008, Sch 39, para 11; SI 2009/403, art 2(2)*).

Prior to 1 April 2010, where there has been fraud or neglect on the part of the deceased, the six years of assessment before the deceased's death could be reopened, again within three years after 31 January following the end of the year of assessment in which he died (*TMA 1970, s 40(2)*). However, the wording in *s 40(2)* was changed with effect from 1 April 2010 so that it relates to careless or deliberate behaviour by the person who has died (*FA 2008, Sch 30, para 11(3)(a); SI 2009/403, arts 3–10*). The time limit for making the assessment has also been reduced so that, from 1 April 2010, it is not more than four years after the end of the year of assessment (*FA 2008, Sch 30, para 11(3)(a)*).

2.23   From 1 April 2010, where no tax return has been delivered, so that HMRC are empowered to make a determination of the tax liability, there is a time limit of three years from the filing date (*SI 2009/403, arts 3–10*). Prior to 1 April 2010, the time limit was five years from the filing date. Moreover, no self-assessment can supersede such a determination unless made within 12 months of it (*TMA 1970, s 28C(5)*).

Partnership and trustee returns

2.24   *Partnership returns.* In addition to the tax returns for individuals, a separate partnership return (form SA800) must be filed for partnerships, including a 'partnership statement', containing the names, addresses and tax references of each partner, together with their share of profits, losses, charges on income, tax deducted at source, etc.

Trustee returns. A separate trust and estate tax return (form SA900) must be filed by trustees to establish the tax liabilities on any income and gains chargeable on them and on certain settlors and beneficiaries.

Record keeping

2.25   Individuals, trustees and partners are required to keep all records relevant to a tax return, normally until the end of the following periods (*TMA 1970, s 12B, Sch 1A, para 2A*):

- sole traders and partners carrying on a business (including letting property) – five years and ten months from the end of the tax year;

- in any other case – 22 months from the end of the tax year.

However, if HMRC make an enquiry into a return, the records must be kept until that enquiry is completed, if later than those dates.

In addition, where a claim is made other than in a return, supporting records must be kept until any HMRC enquiry into a return is complete, or until HMRC are no longer able to start an enquiry.

Penalties may be charged for a failure to comply (see **2.45**) although, in practice, penalties are usually imposed only in more serious cases of record-keeping failure. Details of HMRC's approach to penalties for failure to preserve records can be found in their Enquiry Manual from EM4645 onwards (www. hmrc.gov.uk/manuals/emmanual/EM4645.htm).

Primary legislation requires records to be kept which enable a taxpayer to make an accurate return. Further detail of the required records is then set out in secondary and tertiary legislation (*TMA 1970, s 12B*, as amended by *FA 2008, s 115* and *Sch 37*; *SI 2009/402, art 2*).

Records to be kept

Taxpayers in business

2.26   *TMA 1970, s 12B* requires a taxpayer to 'keep all such records as may be requisite for the purposes of enabling him to make and deliver a correct and complete return for the year or period'.

The information to be retained includes records of:

- all receipts and expenditure;
- all goods bought and sold; and
- all supporting documents relating to business transactions, including accounts, books, deeds, contracts, vouchers and receipts.

Examples include bank statements, stock and work-in-progress records, details of money introduced into the business, and records of goods or money taken from the business for personal use. Where a car or other asset is used for both business and private purposes, the records should enable an apportionment to be made.

> **Focus**
>
> Employers are required to preserve certain PAYE records for three years following the tax year to which they relate (*SI 2003/2682, reg 97*).

All taxpayers

2.27   The following should be kept by all taxpayers (if applicable):

- employment details supplied by the employer about pay, tax deducted, benefits and expenses payments (eg forms P60, P45, P11D and former P9D);
- records of tips, benefits or other receipts connected with an employment but not provided by the employer;
- a record of state pension and other taxable social security benefits;
- bank and building society records of interest received;
- dividend vouchers; and
- details of purchases, sales and gifts of assets giving rise to chargeable gains.

> **Focus**
>
> Original documents may generally be retained as copies, and computerised records may be kept if they can be reproduced in legible form, but certain tax certificates, statements and vouchers must be retained in their original form.

Some useful HMRC guides

2.28 Note: HMRC are gradually phasing out print versions of some of their leaflets. Where information is now only available electronically, the relevant web address is shown.

General

2.29 Self-assessment tax returns (www.gov.uk/self-assessment-tax-returns).

Savings and investments

2.30 Rent a room in your home (www.gov.uk/rent-room-in-your-home/rent-bills-and-tax)

Tax on savings interest (www.gov.uk/apply-tax-free-interest-on-savings)

Enterprise Investment Scheme (www.gov.uk/government/publications/the-enterprise-investment-scheme-introduction)

Property Income Manual (www.hmrc.gov.uk/manuals/pimmanual/index.htm)

Business

2.31 Booklet 480: Expenses and benefits: a tax guide (www.gov.uk/government/publications/480-expenses-and-benefits-a-tax-guide)

Booklet 490: Employee travel: a tax and NICs guide for employers (www.gov.uk/government/publications/490-employee-travel-a-tax-and-nics-guide)

CIS340: Construction Industry Scheme (https://www.gov.uk/government/publications/construction-industry-scheme-cis-340/construction-industry-scheme-a-guide-for-contractors-and-subcontractors-cis-340)

Employment

2.32 Company cars (https://www.gov.uk/tax-company-benefits/tax-on-company-cars)

Booklet 480: Expenses and benefits: a tax guide (www.gov.uk/government/publications/480-expenses-and-benefits-a-tax-guide)

Booklet 490: Employee travel: a tax and NICs guide for employers (www.gov.uk/government/publications/490-employee-travel-a-tax-and-nics-guide)

CWG2: Employer Further Guide to PAYE and NICs (www.gov.uk/government/publications/cwg2-further-guide-to-paye-and-national-insurance-contributions)

Overseas issues

2.33   RDR1: Residence, domicile and the remittance basis (which replaced former booklet HMRC6) (www.gov.uk/government/publications/residence-domicile-and-remittance-basis-rules-uk-tax-liability)

Tax on your UK income if you live abroad (www.gov.uk/tax-uk-income-live-abroad/rent)

Compliance checks – higher penalties for income tax and capital gains tax involving offshore matters (CC/FS17) (www.gov.uk/government/publications/compliance-checks-penalties-for-income-tax-and-capital-gains-tax-for-offshore-matters-ccfs17)

TAX PAYMENTS

How tax is collected

2.34   Most taxpayers pay their tax without need for direct contact with HMRC as tax is either collected through the PAYE system or, until 6 April 2016, by deduction of tax at source from savings income. Some taxpayers who receive income gross of tax, or who have to pay tax at the higher rate on investment income, or who have capital gains above the annual exempt limit, and all self-employed people, have to pay some or all their income tax directly to HMRC.

Focus

HMRC issue annual tax summaries detailing individual taxpayers' income tax and NICs for the previous tax year, and including a table and chart to show how this contributes to different areas of public expenditure, such as health, education and defence.

Individuals who are registered for SA online can view their tax summary soon after their tax return has been filed. It will be updated if the return is amended.

HMRC have the power to secure payment of tax debts of over £1,000 directly from debtors' bank and building society accounts (including funds held in cash in individual savings accounts that have a minimum aggregate credit of £5,000) (*Finance (No 2) Act 2015, s 47* and *Sch 8*).

HMRC estimate that direct recovery of debts will apply to around 11,000 cases (covering both individuals, including self-employed taxpayers, and businesses) per year. Deposit-takers will be required to provide information to HMRC and hold and transfer sums from customers' accounts to HMRC.

Tax paid directly to HMRC

2.35 Taxpayers are generally required to make two equal payments of their income tax liabilities (including any Class 2 and Class 4 NIC liability) on account:

- by 31 January in the tax year; and

- by 31 July following the tax year,

based on the total income tax payable directly in the previous tax year.

The balance, together with any capital gains tax, is normally payable (or repayable) by 31 January after the tax year. If an HMRC notice requiring a tax return was received after 31 October following the tax year, the balancing payment is due three months from the date of the notice (*TMA 1970, ss 59A, 59B, 86; Income Tax (Payments on Account) Regulations 1996 (SI 1996/1654)*).

Payments on account are not required where (*SI 1996/1654*):

- more than 80% of the previous year's tax liability was covered by tax deducted at source and dividend tax credits; or

- the previous year's net tax and Class 4 NIC liability was less than £1,000.

In addition to this test, there is a power for an officer of the Board to direct that interim payments are not required for a tax year, and make any consequent adjustment. The time limit for making this direction is 31 January following the tax year (*TMA 1970, s 59A(9)*).

HMRC will accept payment of tax by credit card (see www.gov.uk/pay-self-assessment-tax-bill/by-debit-or-credit-card-online for further details).

Example 2.1—Payment on account

Paula's tax liability under self-assessment for 2018/19 is £3,000. She has made two payments on account of £900 each, so has already paid £1,800 in total.

The total amount due by midnight on 31 January 2020 is £2,700, which includes:

- a balancing payment of £1,200 for the 2018/19 tax year (£3,000 minus £1,800); and

- the first payment on account of £1,500 (half her 2018/19 tax bill) towards her 2019/20 tax bill.

Paula must pay her second payment on account of £1,500 by midnight on 31 July 2020.

If her tax bill for the 2019/20 tax year is more than £3,000 (the total of her two payments on account), Paula will need to make a balancing payment by 31 January 2021.

Reducing payments on account

2.36 A taxpayer may claim to reduce the payments on account for any tax year, if he believes that the liability for that year will be less than his liability for the preceding year. The claim may be made at any time before 31 January following the end of the tax year. The reasons for the claim must be given (*TMA 1970, s 59A(3)*).

The claim may be in a standard format (on form SA303), or can be made as part of the tax return, although a letter to HMRC will suffice. Interest is charged where payments on account prove to be inadequate following the claim. In addition, a penalty may be imposed if the claim is made fraudulently or negligently.

Collecting additional tax due through the PAYE code

2.37 For the years up to and including 2014/15, employees and pensioners who submitted their tax returns by 31 October following the tax year could have tax underpayments of less than £3,000 collected through their PAYE tax codes in a later tax year, if preferred. Tax due for say, 2012/13 would normally be collected through the PAYE code in 2014/15 (*SI 2011/1585*; *SI 2003/2682, reg 186*). From 2015/16 the £3,000 limit increased to £17,000 (*SI 2014/2438*). HMRC may use PAYE coding to recover all or part of certain debts owed to them (*SI 2011/1583*; *SI 2011/1584*, amending *SI 2003/2682*). A new graduated scale applies and debtors will be notified in advance of the amounts which will be deducted from their income (see **6.12**).

There is an overriding limit which prevents employers from deducting more than 50% of an employee's pay (*SI 2014/2689*). There is no change in the amount which can be coded out either from debtors whose income is £30,000 or less, or for self-assessment balancing payments and PAYE underpayments.

Business Payment Support Service

2.38 The HMRC Business Payment Support Service (BPSS) provides a fast-track service that offers support to businesses needing more time to pay their tax bills. The taxes covered include corporation tax, VAT, PAYE, income tax and national insurance contributions, and applicants can quickly agree terms they can afford with HMRC over the phone. The majority of businesses applying under the scheme have agreed repayment timetables spread across three to six months. Construction firms account for a quarter of those benefiting from these new arrangements, with many retailers and manufacturers also agreeing payment schedules they can afford.

Focus

The BPSS can be contacted on 0300 200 3835 from 8am to 8pm Monday to Friday, and from 8am to 4pm at weekends. Further information on

---

difficulties with payment of tax is available at www.gov.uk/difficulties-paying-hmrc.

Important dates for income tax

2.39

April 2019	Return issued for 2018/19
31 July 2019	2nd payment on account due for 2018/19
31 October 2019	All paper returns for 2018/19 to be filed: HMRC to calculate tax, or direct tax liability of up to £17,000 (see **2.37**) to be collected through PAYE
31 January 2020	Online returns to be filed for 2018/19; paper returns to be filed for 2018/19 for certain taxpayers (including registered pension schemes set up under trust) for whom no online facilities exist. Balancing payment or repayment due for 2018/19; 1st payment on account due for 2019/20
April 2020	Return issued for 2019/20
31 July 2020	2nd payment on account due for 2019/20
31 October 2020	All paper returns for 2019/20 to be filed: HMRC to calculate tax, or direct tax liability of up to £17,000 (see **2.37**) to be collected through PAYE
31 January 2021	Return to be filed for 2019/20; balancing payment or repayment due for 2019/20; 1st payment on account due for 2020/21

INTEREST AND PENALTIES

Interest

Interest on unpaid tax

2.40   Interest is normally charged on late payments on account and balancing payments (*TMA 1970, s 86*):

- from the due date of payment,

- to the date the tax (and Class 4 NICs) is actually paid.

Interest charges also apply to late payment of penalties and surcharges, and in respect of tax return amendments and discovery assessments.

Focus

Interest is payable gross and is not deductible for tax purposes.

Interest on overpaid tax

2.41 Interest paid by HMRC on tax overpaid is known as a repayment supplement. The supplement normally runs (*ICTA 1988, s 824*):

- from the date of payment (or, in the case of income tax deducted at source, from 31 January following the relevant tax year);

- to the date the repayment order is issued.

Tax deducted at source includes PAYE, but excludes amounts relating to previous years. If a penalty or surcharge is repaid, a repayment supplement is also added to that repayment.

The repayment supplement is tax free (*ITTOIA 2005, s 749*).

Rates of interest on unpaid tax

2.42 The following table shows the rates of interest charged on overdue tax in recent years (*FA 2009, s 101; SI 2011/2446*)

From	To	% Rate
27.1.09	23.3.09	3.5
24.3.09	28.9.09	2.5
29.9.09	22.8.16	3.0
23.8.16	20.11.17	2.75
21.11.17	20.08.18	3.0
21.08.18		3.25

Rates of interest on overpaid tax: repayment supplement

2.43 The following table shows the rates of interest paid on tax repayments qualifying for repayment supplement (*FA 2009, s 102; SI 2011/2446*)

From	To	% Rate
27.1.09	28.9.09	0
29.9.09		0.5

Relevant dates for unpaid tax

2.44   The relevant dates from which interest on unpaid amounts runs are as follows:

Income tax, Class 4 NIC	– payments on account (*TMA 1970, s 59A*)	due date for payment (31 January and 31 July)
	– any other case (and CGT)	31 January after year of assessment or (where taxpayer gave notice of chargeability before 5 October following the tax year and the return was not issued until after 31 October) three months after notice to deliver the return, if later.
		Where a return is submitted by 31 October for calculation by HMRC of the tax due, interest runs from 30 days after the notification of the liability if after 30 December.
PAYE and Class 1 NIC		14 days after end of relevant tax year
Class 1A NIC		19 July after end of tax year in which contributions were payable
Class 1B NIC		19 October after end of relevant tax year
PAYE settlement agreement		19 October after end of relevant tax year

Penalties

Structure of penalties

2.45   HMRC may impose penalties on taxpayers in the following circumstances:

- late payment of tax or duty;
- late filing of returns;
- failure to notify chargeability to tax;
- errors on returns and documents;
- failure to keep or retain records;

- VAT and excise wrong-doing; and

- failure to submit returns online.

The structure of tax penalties is now generally the same across all the taxes administered by HMRC.

The government has taken the first steps to review how automatic HMRC penalties could be made more effective to differentiate between deliberate failure to comply and genuine errors. In addition penalties may be imposed for non-compliance with the GAAR.

UK matters

2.46   The amount of penalty that can be imposed is determined according to the following grid, which relates the behaviour of the taxpayer to the degree of disclosure the taxpayer has made to HMRC, and whether that disclosure was prompted or unprompted (the quality of the disclosure).

	Unprompted disclosure		Prompted disclosure	
Behaviour of taxpayer:	max penalty	min penalty	max penalty	min penalty
Reasonable care taken	0%	0%	0%	0%
Careless	30%	0%	30%	15%
Deliberate but not concealed	70%	20%	70%	35%
Deliberate and concealed	100%	30%	100%	50%

Notes

(1)   This grid applies to penalties imposed for the following:

- errors in returns and documents (*FA 2007, s 97, Sch 24*);

- failures to notify (*FA 2008, s 123, Sch 41*);

- late submission (*FA 2009, s 106; Sch 55*); and

- under-assessment by HMRC (*FA 2007, Sch 24, paras 2, 4C*).

(2)   The penalty provisions generally apply to assessments for tax periods commencing from 1 April 2008, where the filing date is on or after 1 April 2009 (*SI 2008/568, art 2(b)*).

(3)   The percentage of penalty, as determined from the grid above and by negotiation with HMRC, is applied to the amount of 'potential lost revenue' (PLR) (*FA 2007, Sch 24, paras 5–8*). Similar rules apply to failure to notify (*FA 2008, Sch 41, para 7*).

(4) If HMRC become aware of the failure to notify less than 12 months after the tax first becomes unpaid due to the failure, the penalty for careless behaviour ranges from 0% to 30% for unprompted disclosure, and from 10% to 30% for prompted disclosure. Otherwise, the penalty ranges stated above apply *(FA 2008, Sch 41, para 13(3))*.

(5) Error by another person – a penalty can also apply to an error in a taxpayer's document which is attributable to another person *(FA 2007, Sch 24, para 1A)*.

(6) The penalty regime for late returns applies both fixed and tax-geared penalties. A taxpayer may become liable to more than one category of penalty in respect of the same return, etc *(FA 2009, Sch 55, para 1(3))*. However, where more than one tax-geared penalty arises, the aggregate must not exceed a statutory maximum *(FA 2009, Sch 55, para 17(3))*.

(7) No penalty arises if there is a 'reasonable excuse' throughout the period of default for a failure to notify *(FA 2008, Sch 41, para 20)*. Similar rules apply to late returns *(FA 2009, Sch 55, para 23)*.

(8) A penalty can be charged on a person if an HMRC assessment understates the tax payable, and the person fails to take reasonable steps to notify HMRC of the under-assessment within 30 days from the date of the assessment *(FA 2007, Sch 24, para 2)*.

(9) Special reductions – HMRC may reduce a penalty for errors because of 'special circumstances' *(FA 2007, Sch 24, para 11)*. Similar rules apply to a failure to notify *(FA 2008, Sch 41, para 14)* and late returns *(FA 2009, Sch 55, para 16)*.

(10) Further information – see HMRC's compliance factsheets: tinyurl.com/ HMCCFS.

Offshore matters

2.47   Classification of territories

Territories are classified in accordance with the penalty regime for errors *(FA 2007, Sch 24, para 21A; FA 2015, Sch 20)*.

There are different levels of penalty for failure to notify which apply only for income tax and CGT (see tables below). If HMRC become aware of the failure to notify less than 12 months after the tax first becomes unpaid due to the failure, the minimum penalty for a non-deliberate action is reduced for an unprompted disclosure.

Category 1 Territory

Behaviour leading to error:	Unprompted disclosure		Prompted disclosure	
	Maximum penalty	**Minimum penalty**	**Maximum penalty**	**Minimum penalty**
Careless	30%	0%	30%	15%
Deliberate, not concealed	70%	20%	70%	35%
Deliberate and concealed	100%	30%	100%	50%

Reason behind the failure to notify or disclose:	Unprompted disclosure		Prompted disclosure	
	Maximum penalty	**Minimum penalty**	**Maximum penalty**	**Minimum penalty**
Non-deliberate failure within 12 months of tax due	30%	0%	30%	10%
Non-deliberate failure over 12 months of tax due	30%	10%	30%	20%
Deliberate but not concealed within 12 months of tax due	70%	20%	70%	35%
Deliberate but not concealed over 12 months of tax due	70%	20%	70%	35%
Deliberate and concealed	100%	30%	100%	50%

Notes

(1) Category 1 information – this is information involving:

    (a)   a UK domestic matter; or

    (b)   an offshore matter, where the territory is in Category 1 or the tax at stake is income tax or CGT (or IHT from April 2017).

(2) Failure to notify – the penalties for failure to notify only relate to matters connected with income tax or CGT from 2016/17, and for IHT for transfers from 1 April 2017.

(3) Which countries – a list of Category 1 and Category 3 territories is available at: tinyurl.com/OSTRCT.

Category 2 Territory

(FA 2007, Sch 24, para 10)

Behaviour behind inaccuracy or error:	Unprompted disclosure		Prompted disclosure	
	Maximum penalty	**Minimum penalty**	**Maximum penalty**	**Minimum penalty**
Careless	45%	0%	45%	22.5%
Deliberate but not concealed	105%	30%	105%	52.5%
Deliberate and concealed	150%	45%	150%	75%

Reason behind the failure to notify or disclose:	Unprompted disclosure		Prompted disclosure	
	Maximum penalty	**Minimum penalty**	**Maximum penalty**	**Minimum penalty**
Non-deliberate failure within 12 months of tax due	45%	0%	45%	15%
Non-deliberate failure over 12 months of tax due	45%	15%	45%	30%
Deliberate but not concealed	105%	30%	105%	52.5%
Deliberate and concealed	150%	45%	150%	75%

Notes

(1) Category 2 information – This is information involving an offshore matter, in a Category 2 territory, which would enable or assist HMRC to assess an income tax or CGT liability.

(2) Which countries – All countries which are not Category 1 or 3 are Category 2.

(3) Failure to notify – The penalties for failure to notify only relate to matters connected with income tax or CGT from 2016/17, and for IHT for transfers from 1 April 2017.

(4) Further information – See HMRC Compliance Handbook CH11660 and HMRC factsheets CC/FS17 and CC/FS17a.

Category 3 Territory

(FA 2007, Sch 24, para 10)

Behaviour behind the inaccuracy or error:	Unprompted disclosure		Prompted disclosure	
	Maximum penalty	Minimum penalty	Maximum penalty	Minimum penalty
Careless	60%	0%	60%	30%
Deliberate but not concealed	140%	40%	140%	70%
Deliberate and concealed	200%	60%	200%	100%

Reason behind the failure to notify or disclose:	Unprompted disclosure		Prompted disclosure	
	Maximum penalty	Minimum penalty	Maximum penalty	Minimum penalty
Non-deliberate failure within 12 months of tax due	60%	0%	60%	20%
Non-deliberate failure over 12 months of tax due	60%	20%	60%	40%
Deliberate but not concealed	140%	40%	140%	70%
Deliberate and concealed	200%	60%	200%	100%

Notes

(1) Category 3 information – this is information involving an offshore matter, in a Category 3 territory, which would enable or assist HMRC to assess an income tax or CGT liability.

(2) Failure to notify – the penalties for failure to notify only relate to matters connected with income tax or CGT from 2016/17, and for IHT for transfers from 1 April 2017.

(3) Further information – see HMRC Compliance Handbook CH116700.

Late filing

2.48   *(FA 2009, s 106, Sch 55)*

Period	Penalty	Notes
Up to 3 months late	£100	Automatic fixed penalty
More than 3 months late	£10 per day	Maximum of 90 days ie £900.
		Payable only if HMRC give notice of the penalty, and the notice specifies the date from which the penalty is payable.
More than 6 months late	Greater of: 5% of tax liability; and £300	'Tax liability' is any tax which would have been shown in the return in question.
More than 12 months late, except where taxpayer withholds information deliberately (see below).	Greater of: 5% of tax liability; and £300	
12 months + late and information withheld deliberately but not concealed	Greater of: Relevant % of tax liability; and £300	See Structure of penalties above
12 months + late and information withheld deliberately and concealed	Greater of: Relevant % of tax liability; and £300	See Structure of penalties above

Notes

- Effective from – for tax returns for 2010/11 and later tax years (*FA 2009, s 106, Sch 55; SI 2011/702*).

- Further information – see HMRC's Compliance Handbook at CH61120. As to the penalty provisions for earlier returns, see: Penalties for 2009/10 and earlier years below.

Late and on account payments

2.49

Length of delay	Penalty
30 days	5% of the unpaid tax
6 months	5% of the unpaid tax (additional)
12 months	5% of the unpaid tax (additional)

Notes

- Applies to – late balancing payments of income tax and late payments of capital gains tax under self-assessment (ie based on tax returns for individuals or trustees etc, and in certain other circumstances) in relation to 2010/11 and later tax years (*SI 2011/702, art 3*).

- Assessments and appeals – HMRC must assess the late payment penalty, and notify the person liable as to the period to which the penalty relates. The penalty is payable within 30 days from the day on which the penalty notice is issued. There is a right of appeal against both the imposition of a penalty, and the amount involved (*FA 2009, Sch 56, paras 11, 13*).

- Penalty reduction and suspension – HMRC may reduce a late payment penalty in 'special circumstances', which does not include inability to pay (*FA 2009, Sch 56, para 9*). In addition, a defence of 'reasonable excuse' may be available (*Sch 56, para 16*).

- Payments on account – the maximum penalty for fraudulent or negligent claims by taxpayers to reduce payments on account is the difference between the correct amount payable on account and the amount of any payment on account made by him (*TMA 1970, s 59A(6)*).

Focus

HMRC may reduce a late payment penalty in 'special circumstances', which does not include inability to pay (*FA 2009, Sch 56, para 9*). In addition, a defence of 'reasonable excuse' may also be available (*Sch 56, para 16*). In *Horne v Revenue & Customs* [2013] UKFTT 177 (TC), the First-tier Tribunal ruled that HMRC properly imposed a first penalty against a taxpayer for late payment of tax. None of the following were reasonable excuses that existed at the due date of the tax: the taxpayer's mistaken belief that the tax should have been collected via PAYE tax code; HMRC's incorrect calculation of the tax due; the taxpayer's confusion as to the amount of tax he owed; or his alleged overpayment of tax for the next tax year. However, the Tribunal decided that the PAYE overpayment was a 'special circumstance' under *FA 2009, Sch 56, para 9* since the taxpayer

---

could not benefit from the *Income Tax (Pay As You Earn) Regulations 2003 (SI 2003/2682), reg 65*, to claim for overpayment, because of his claim for jobseeker's allowance. Thus, to the extent that the relevant PAYE deduction exceeded his tax liability for the next year, that figure should be notionally deducted from the outstanding tax liability for the relevant year, and the penalty on that part should be reduced to nil.

Prospective late payment penalties for income tax self-assessment

2.50   Draft Finance Bill 2018–19 (published on 6 July 2018) contained proposals to introduce a new aligned penalty regime for late payment of income tax self-assessment and corporation tax. However, at Autumn Budget 2018 (29 October 2018), the government announced that the changes will be introduced in a future Finance Bill to allow more time to consider how to communicate the changes. The government will give notice before these measures are implemented. At present therefore, the following proposals remain subject to change.

The proposed regime will comprise two penalty charges.

The first penalty charge will be payable 30 days after the payment due date and will be based on a set percentage of the balance outstanding as follows:

No of days after payment due date	Payment status	Penalty
0–15	Payments made	No penalty payable
	Time to pay arrangement (TTP) agreed	Penalty suspended
16–30	Payments made	Penalty calculated at reduced percentage
	TTP agreed	
		Penalty calculated using reduced percentage and suspended for the amounts subject to TTP
Day 30	N/A	First charge calculated based on payment activity in the month

A second penalty charge will be payable based on amounts outstanding from day 31 after the payment due date until the outstanding sum is paid in full. Any TTP agreed during the period will result in the suspension of future penalties from the date the TTP was agreed.

Penalties must be paid, or appealed, within 30 days of the date of the penalty notice.

The penalty amounts have not yet been announced.

The new late payment penalties will replace the existing penalties for the late payment of income tax self-assessment in *FA 2009, Sch 56* (see **2.49**).

Failure to notify liability to tax by 5 October after tax year

2.51   The law requires a person to tell HMRC when certain events happen. These events include:

- where a person has income tax, capital gains tax or corporation tax to pay but has not been given notice to make a return for the period;

- when a person starts a new taxable activity;

- when the turnover from an existing activity has reached a certain level; or

- when the nature of the activity changes.

The amount of the penalty which may be charged for failing to notify HMRC about such events is a percentage of the tax:

- that is unpaid at a specified date, or

- to which the person is liable for the relevant period.

This tax is known as the 'potential lost revenue'. The percentage is determined by the behaviour that led to the failure to notify – higher penalties are payable if the failure was deliberate (*FA 2008, Sch 41*).

For further information on failure to notify penalties, see the HMRC Compliance Handbook at CH70000 (www.hmrc.gov.uk/manuals/chmanual/CH70000. htm).

> **Focus**
>
> HMRC are reviewing various options to tackle the hidden economy by making access to licences needed to trade conditional on tax compliance. Licences issued in the following sectors are included for consideration in the consultation:
>
> - private security;
>
> - taxi and private hire vehicles;
>
> - waste management;
>
> - houses in multiple occupation and selective licensing in the private rental sector;
>
> - scrap metal; and

- retail and trade.

The consultation document, entitled *Tackling the hidden economy: public sector licensing* is available online at tinyurl.com/ya6oxmx9.

Failure to maintain records

2.52   A penalty of up to £3,000 per tax year may be charged for a failure to keep and preserve appropriate records supporting personal, trustees' or partnership returns (*TMA 1970, s 12B(5)*; *FA 2008, s 115, Sch 37*).

Self-employed individuals: failure to notify liability to pay Class 2 NICs

2.53   Self-employed individuals are required to notify their liability to pay Class 2 national insurance contributions to HMRC in the same way as liability to income tax must be notified. The penalties set out at **2.45** apply equally to NICs as they do for income tax. The penalty may be reduced at HMRC's discretion, or can be avoided if there is a 'reasonable excuse' for the late notification, or if HMRC are satisfied that the individual's profits were below the small earnings exception threshold for national insurance purposes.

From April 2011, payments for Class 2 NICs become due on 31 July and 31 January along with income tax due under self-assessment (see **7.90** for further details).

Focus

HMRC may collect outstanding Class 2 NICs by adjusting the tax codes of customers in PAYE employment or receiving a UK-based private pension.

Payment requests will be issued to customers showing any Class 2 NICs that they owe. Customers will be asked to pay, or to contact HMRC if they believe the payment request is wrong (for example, because the customer has stopped trading). The payment requests also advise that not paying may mean HMRC will collect the debt through their PAYE code or pass it to a private debt collection agency for recovery.

Offence of fraudulent evasion

2.54   Where a person commits an offence of fraudulent evasion of income tax, he or she is liable to a prison term not exceeding six months on summary conviction or not exceeding seven years on conviction on indictment. In either case, a fine may be levied instead of or in addition to the prison term (*TMA 1970, ss 20BB, 93–107*; *FA 2000, s 144*).

Other penalties

2.55

Negligently or fraudulently making or submitting incorrect returns, accounts, claims for allowances, relief or to reduce or cancel payments on account, etc	Up to the difference between the amount payable under the return, etc and the amount which would have been payable if the return, etc had been correct
Other returns, etc – failure to comply with a notice to deliver any return or other document, to furnish any particulars, to produce any document or record, to make anything available for inspection or give any certificate listed in *TMA 1970, s 98*	(a) An initial penalty up to £300 (b) If the failure continues after the above penalty is imposed, a further penalty up to £60 per day
Negligently or fraudulently delivering any return, incorrect information, etc within the above provisions	Up to £3,000
Assisting in the preparation of incorrect returns, accounts and other documents	Up to £3,000
Fraudulently or negligently giving a **certificate of non-liability to income tax** in connection with receiving bank or building society interest gross or failing to comply with an undertaking in the certificate	Up to £3,000
Refusal to allow deduction of income tax at source	£50
Falsification of documents – intentionally falsifying, concealing or destroying documents in connection with back duty investigations	On summary conviction, a penalty not exceeding the statutory maximum (currently £5,000). On conviction on indictment, imprisonment for up to two years or a fine or both
Witnesses before tribunal – neglect or refusal to appear before tribunal or refusal to be sworn in or answer questions	Up to £1,000

Failure to disclose tax avoidance scheme under *FA 2004* provisions by promoter, etc	(a) An initial penalty up to £5,000 (b) If the failure continues after the above penalty is imposed, a further penalty up to £600 per day
Interest on penalties	Penalties carry interest from the date on which they become due and payable.

> **Focus**
>
> From 1 April 2013, HMRC may issue a tax agent with a conduct notice, if it has been determined that the agent has been engaged in dishonest conduct, to obtain working papers from them, and impose penalties. Where an individual incurs a penalty exceeding £5,000 in relation to dishonest conduct, the Commissioners for HMRC may publish certain information about this individual (*FA 2012, Sch 38*; *SI 2013/279*; see also *SI 2013/280*).

Penalties for the general anti-abuse rule

2.56   The general anti-abuse rule (GAAR) was introduced from 17 July 2013 to identify and counteract tax avoidance arrangements considered to be abusive. Following consultation, the *Finance Act 2016* contained provisions for a new penalty which will apply when a taxpayer submits a return, claim or document that includes arrangements which are later found to come within the scope of the GAAR (*FA 2016, s 158*). The provisions took effect from the date of Royal Assent to *Finance Act 2016* (15 September 2016).

Subject to certain limits, the penalty will amount to 60% of the counteracted tax and will become chargeable at the point where there is no appeal against the counteraction or, if there is, the appeal is unsuccessful. Under the GAAR procedure, the taxpayer will be given the opportunity to correct their tax position (and thereby avoid the penalty) up until the point that their arrangements are referred to the GAAR advisory panel.

In a separate change, the GAAR procedure has been amended so that a GAAR advisory panel opinion will enable counteraction of the same arrangements by other users, and to allow a protective assessment of tax to align the GAAR procedure with the overarching enquiry framework (*FA 2016, s 157*).

HMRC ENQUIRIES

Enquiries into returns

2.57   The period during which HMRC can enquire into returns is broadly linked to the date the return is received by HMRC.

Returns

2.58   The enquiry window closes one year after delivery of the return (*TMA 1970, s 9A(2); FA 2007, s 96*). So, where a return is received before the filing deadline, the enquiry window will close earlier than under previous legislation.

A return may be selected at random, although the majority of returns will be selected for a particular reason. HMRC are not required to state whether the enquiry is random or otherwise. They may send a written notice requiring the taxpayer (and third parties) to produce documents, accounts and other information in order to check the accuracy of a tax return or amendment (*FA 2008, Sch 36, Pt 1*).

HMRC will issue a 'closure notice' notifying the taxpayer when the enquiry is complete, and make any amendments required to the return (or claim). The taxpayer has 30 days in which to appeal against HMRC's amendments, conclusions or decisions. This is also the period by which any tax payable (or repayable) as a result of the amendment must be paid (or repaid). Alternatively, the taxpayer may apply to the tax tribunal for HMRC to issue a closure notice in appropriate cases.

HMRC's enquiry powers equally apply to claims made separately from the return. A return or amendment may not be enquired into more than once (*TMA 1970, ss 28A, 28C*).

Discovery assessments

2.59   The return and self-assessment of tax can usually be regarded as final once the enquiry time limit has expired. However, HMRC may make a 'discovery assessment' to make good a loss of tax due to non-disclosure, if:

- the loss of tax is due to the taxpayer's fraudulent or negligent conduct; or

- HMRC could not reasonably be expected to identify the loss of tax from the information made available.

Put simply, the term 'discovers' means 'finds out' but there must be sufficient evidence to support a genuine discovery by HMRC (see, for example, *Scott (t/a Farthings Steak House) v McDonald (HMIT)* [1996] SpC 91, where an inspector was found to have acted unreasonably, and in bad faith, in making discovery assessments during an investigation case).

In *R v Kensington Income Tax Commrs, ex parte Aramayo* (1913) 6 TC 279, Bray J said at p 283:

'... it seems to me to be quite clear that the word "discover" cannot mean ascertain by legal evidence; it means, in my opinion, simply "comes to the conclusion" from the examination he makes, and, if he likes, from any information he receives.'

The risk of a discovery assessment by HMRC is reduced if all relevant information is disclosed on the tax return and in any accompanying documents if their relevance is explained, and if any contentious issues are brought to HMRC's attention in the additional information space on the tax return. The time limit for making an assessment involving fraud or neglect is 20 years after 31 January following the end of the tax year (*TMA 1970, s 29*).

See also *Singh v R & C Commrs* [2011] UKFTT 707 (TC), in which compensation paid to a sub-postmaster for loss of office belonged to him personally rather than the company through which he traded as a newsagent and so should have been included in his self-assessment return. However, since all the relevant information had been fully disclosed and neither the taxpayer nor his accountant had acted negligently, HMRC were not entitled to issue a discovery assessment.

Determination of tax

2.60   If a return is not submitted, HMRC may make a 'determination' of the amount of tax considered to be due, within three years after the normal filing date for the return. This determination is treated as a self-assessment, until it is superseded by an actual self-assessment, which must be submitted within the same time limit (or 12 months after the determination, if later) (*TMA 1970, ss 28C(5), 31, 36, Sch 1A*).

Enquiry procedures

2.61   When HMRC start an enquiry, it does not necessarily mean that they think something is wrong. Further information is sometimes required to ensure that a return is correct. Returns are also selected at random for enquiry, to ensure the system is operating fairly.

The enquiry might be concerned with one or more particular aspects of a tax return or the whole of it. If nothing is wrong, HMRC will not make any amendments to the return. If the enquiry reveals that an innocent mistake has been made, HMRC will:

- tell the taxpayer in writing that they have completed their enquiries; and
- amend the self-assessment to the correct figures.

Where tax credits are claimed and an enquiry shows that an award may have been wrong, they will review that award.

The extent to which a taxpayer co-operates with HMRC and provides information is entirely a personal choice. However, in calculating the amount of any penalty, HMRC take into account the extent to which the taxpayer has been helpful, and freely and fully volunteered any information about income or gains, which were omitted or understated.

The HMRC Charter (entitled *Your Charter*) sets out the standards of service that taxpayers can expect to receive from HMRC, and the roles and responsibilities of both HMRC and taxpayers in general. The Charter, which was last updated in January 2016, can be accessed on the gov.uk website at https://www.gov.uk/government/publications/your-charter.

What happens first?

2.62   When HMRC are ready to close their enquiries, they will normally ask the taxpayer and their professional adviser, if they have one, to attend a meeting.

HMRC will tell the taxpayer:

- what they have found;

- the amount of tax HMRC believe is owed; and

- how far they believe the late payment or underpayment of tax is due to fraudulent or negligent conduct on the taxpayer's part.

HMRC will listen to any explanations the taxpayer wishes to give. HMRC will then advise the maximum amount of penalties they believe could be determined under formal procedures, and the amount of interest and possibly surcharge that the taxpayer could pay.

Finally, HMRC will explain that it is normal to ask someone in the taxpayer's position to offer to pay one sum for tax, interest, and penalties or surcharge. HMRC will then ask if the taxpayer is prepared to make such an offer. If the taxpayer asks, HMRC will suggest an amount.

HMRC calculate an offer by adding together the tax, the interest on that tax, any surcharge and an amount for penalties. Interest is calculated from the date the tax should have been paid up to the date it was actually paid or will be paid.

The penalty figure will be a percentage of the tax underpaid or paid late. In law, it could be 100% of that amount, but in practice it is always less than that in a negotiated settlement.

HMRC start with a penalty figure of 100% and reduce it by an amount which depends on:

- whether the taxpayer disclosed all the details of his tax affairs;

- how well the taxpayer co-operated over the whole period of the enquiry; and

- the seriousness of the offence.

Disclosure – a reduction of up to 20% (30% for full voluntary disclosure where there was no fear of early discovery by HMRC)

2.63   If a full disclosure was made at the time HMRC first opened the enquiry, the taxpayer will receive a considerable reduction in the amount of the penalty.

If the taxpayer denies until the last possible moment that anything is wrong, he will receive little or no reduction for disclosure.

Between these two extremes, a wide variety of circumstances is possible. HMRC will consider how much information the taxpayer gave, how quickly, and how that contributed towards settling the enquiry.

Co-operation – a reduction of up to 40%

2.64   If the taxpayer supplied information quickly, attended interviews, answered questions honestly and accurately, gave all the relevant facts and paid tax on account when it became possible to estimate the amount due, he will then receive the maximum reduction for co-operation.

If the taxpayer put off supplying information, gave misleading answers to questions, did nothing until HMRC took formal action and generally obstructed the progress of the enquiry, he will not receive any reduction at all.

Between these extremes, there is a wide range of possible circumstances, and HMRC will look at how well the taxpayer has co-operated with the enquiry.

Seriousness – a reduction of up to 40%

2.65   The taxpayer's actions may amount to a pre-meditated and well-organised fraud or something much less serious. HMRC will take into account what he did, how he did it, how long it went on and the amounts of money involved. The less serious the offence, the bigger the reduction in the penalty.

Example 2.2—Penalties resulting from an enquiry

If HMRC think that the reduction for disclosure is 15%, for co-operation 30% and for seriousness 20%, the total reduction will be 65%, making the expected penalty 35% (100% – 65%).

The calculation of what HMRC consider to be a suitable offer may be as follows:

Tax underpaid	£10,337
Interest, say	£4,165
Penalty at 35%	£3,618
Total	£18,120

Negotiations

2.66   HMRC will have already agreed the figures for tax, interest and, where appropriate, surcharge, leaving only the penalty to be negotiated.

The taxpayer will have the opportunity to draw HMRC's attention to any matters affecting the penalty figure, which the taxpayer thinks they have not given enough weight to. HMRC will consider the effect of these on the figure they had in mind, and will comment on any figure the taxpayer might suggest. As a result, HMRC might be able to reach an agreement either straightaway or after a few days' consideration.

If the taxpayer agrees to make an offer, he has to sign a formal letter offering to pay the agreed sum within a stated period and give or send that letter to HMRC. If HMRC are happy with it, they will then issue a letter of acceptance.

The exchange of letters amounts to a legal contract between HMRC and the taxpayer, and both parties are bound by its terms. If the taxpayer pays under the terms of the contract, HMRC cannot use formal proceedings to recover the tax, interest, surcharge or penalties. For this reason, they make sure that the terms of the letter are precise.

When HMRC send the acceptance letter, they will include a payslip showing the Accounts Office Network Unit to which payment should be sent. When the taxpayer pays the amount under the terms of the contract, the matter will be at an end. If the taxpayer does not keep to the terms of the contract, HMRC will charge interest for late payment and may take court action to recover the amount due.

HMRC will not take advantage of the fact that a formal closure notice has not been issued. If any additional liabilities, relating to the years covered by the enquiry, come to light at any time after they have accepted an offer, they will not under any circumstances seek to amend the assessment. But they will arrange to recover any such liabilities.

Where a taxpayer agrees a settlement, but cannot pay the full amount straightaway, it may be possible to arrange payment by instalments. HMRC will expect as large a down payment as possible, and agreement to pay the rest, including an amount for extra interest, by instalments over as short a period as possible. HMRC will suggest payment by direct debit.

If the taxpayer does not want to make an offer, or an offer transpires to be unacceptable to HMRC, HMRC will regard this as the end of negotiations (unless the taxpayer seeks to reopen them). HMRC will then proceed as follows.

HMRC will issue a notice of closure for each self-assessment year that has an open enquiry, which will explain:

- that their enquiries have finished;

- what their conclusions are;

- the amendments being made; and

- that for other years involved they will issue assessments.

The tax due will be shown on the taxpayer's next Statement of Account.

Interest

2.67   When the further tax appears on a Statement of Account, interest will automatically be charged and will run from the date that the tax should have been paid until the date it is actually paid.

Careless and deliberate behaviour

Time limits

2.68   Assessments on an individual, involving a loss of income tax or capital gains tax brought about *carelessly* by the person, can generally be made at any time not more than six years after the end of the year of assessment to which it relates (*TMA 1970, s 36(1)*).

Assessments on an individual in a case involving a loss of income tax or capital gains tax:

(a)   brought about *deliberately* by the person,

(b)   attributable to failure to comply with an obligation to notify HMRC of a liability to tax (under *TMA 1970, s 7*); or

(c)   attributable to arrangements in respect of which the person has failed to comply with an obligation under *FA 2004, s 309, 310* or *313* (obligation of parties to tax avoidance schemes to provide information to HMRC),

can be made at any time not more than 20 years after the end of the year of assessment to which it relates (*TMA 1970, s 36(1A)*).

Fraud

2.69   There is no definition of 'fraud' in the Taxes Acts, so resort must be made to relevant decided cases.

In *Barclay's Bank Ltd v Cole* [1967] 2 QB 738, at 743–744, Lord Denning MR said:

> '"Fraud" in ordinary speech means the using of false representations to obtain an unjust advantage: see the definition in the Shorter Oxford English Dictionary. Likewise in law "fraud" is proved when it is shown that a false representation has been made knowingly, or without belief in its truth, or recklessly, careless whether it be true or false: see *Derry v Peek* (1889) 14 App. Cas. 337 *per* Lord Herschell.'

Willis J in *Ex parte Watson* (1888) 21 QBD 301 stated at 309:

> '"Fraud" in my opinion is a term that should be reserved for something which is dishonest and morally wrong and much mischief is, I think, done, as well as much unnecessary pain inflicted, by its use where "illegality" and "illegal" are really appropriate expressions.'

In *Amis v Colls* 39 TC 148 at 163, Cross J remarked:

> 'Mr Karmel argued that, as the conduct alleged (that is, fraud) might have formed the subject of criminal proceedings, the proper standard is not satisfaction on the balance of probabilities, as is the normal test in civil proceedings, but satisfaction beyond reasonable doubt, the test in criminal cases. I should have thought that, as these are civil proceedings, the civil standard was the proper one to adopt.'

Nevertheless, in *Les Croupiers Casino Club v Pattison* 60 TC1196, Nourse J, in the Court of Appeal, commented:

> '... the standard of proof in civil proceedings, while it is always proof on the balance of probabilities, is nevertheless flexible, being higher or lower according to the nature and gravity of that which has to be proved ... Another, and I think preferable, way of stating this principle is to say that the more grave the act or omission to be proved, the more convincing must be the evidence which is required to tip the balance of probabilities.'

In *Hudson v Humbles* 42 TC 380, Pennycuick J said at 386:

> 'There is nothing in the proviso (to ITA 52/S47(1) – now TMA 70/S36) which in any way restricts the nature of the evidence which the Revenue must give in order to establish prima facie a case of fraud or wilful default ... I do not think it is necessary for the Revenue, in order to raise a prima facie case, to show the particular quality or source of the receipts which had not been accounted for.'

In an attempt to clarify the meaning of fraud and negligence, the heading of *TMA 1970, s 36* (previously entitled 'Fraudulent or negligent conduct') was renamed 'Loss of tax brought about carelessly or deliberately etc' from 1 April 2010 (*FA 2008, s 118* and *Sch 39, para 9(6)*).

HMRC have wide-ranging statutory powers to call for documents or to search premises in cases of suspected fraud or negligence. However, unless they are considering a prosecution, they will normally invite the taxpayer to co-operate and negotiate a settlement without recourse to these powers. Furthermore, the fact that a settlement has been negotiated will not preclude a prosecution in all cases.

FA 2007 contained measures to extend the *Police and Criminal Evidence Act 1984 (PACE 1984)* to all HMRC's criminal investigations in England and Wales (*FA 2007, s 82*), and the *Police and Criminal Evidence Act 1984 (Application to Revenue and Customs) Order 2007 (SI 2007/3175)* brought these new powers into play with effect from 1 December 2007. In particular, the regulations give HMRC a wide range of powers to search, seize and retain items during a criminal investigation into a taxpayer's affairs.

Appeals

2.70 The appeals system was completely reformed from 1 April 2009. The way in which appeals against HMRC decisions were handled up to

1 April 2009 was inherited from the two predecessor departments (namely the Inland Revenue and HM Customs and Excise). The system reflected both developments over a period of time and the different approaches of those two former departments. Appeals were made to different tribunals, and different appeal and review processes operated in different areas depending on the particular tax or scheme involved. In conjunction with the merger of the two departments, HMRC looked at possibilities for the alignment and modernisation of the administration of appeals, particularly in the context of the Review of Powers that was looking at taxpayer safeguards and the reform of the tribunal system being developed by the Ministry of Justice. A consultation document entitled *HM Revenue and Customs and the Taxpayer: Tax Appeals against decisions by HMRC* was published in October 2007, and subsequently, a *Summary of Responses and Future Direction* was published in March 2008.

2.71   The *Tribunals, Courts and Enforcement Act 2007 (TCEA 2007)*, which received Royal Assent on 19 July 2007, is the initial legislation governing the current regime and it provides for a two-tier tribunal structure subdivided into chambers (see below). *TCEA 2007* is supported by *FA 2008, s 124*, which gave the Treasury power, by secondary legislation, to make provisions for reviews of HMRC decisions, and changes to appeals administration procedures, and details the matters that such an Order might cover.

2.72   The subsequent *Transfer of Tribunal Functions and Revenue and Customs Appeals Order 2009 (SI 2009/56)* provides for the actual transfer of the functions of former tax tribunals to the new tribunals established under *TCEA 2007* (broadly effective from 1 April 2009). The Order also makes consequential amendments to legislation relating to tax tribunals and the appeals they consider. In addition, the Order makes changes to HMRC appeals and review processes and related administrative changes.

2.73   The tribunal does not just deal with tax cases. It incorporates a wide range of previously independent tribunals, from the Meat Hygiene Appeals Tribunal and the Antarctic Act Tribunal to the Information Tribunal and the Special Educational Needs and Disability Tribunal, through to the Social Security Tribunal, the Social Security Commissioner and the Lands Tribunal.

Right of appeal

2.74   The taxpayer generally has a right of appeal against any formal decision by an officer of HMRC, the majority of appeals made being against assessments.

Time limits

2.75   Appeals must normally be made within 30 days after the date of the issue of the assessment (or the amendment to the self-assessment), although HMRC may accept a late appeal where there is a reasonable excuse for the delay. The appeal must state the grounds on which the appeal is being made (eg that HMRC's amendment is incorrect).

Procedures

2.76   Where an appeal is not settled between a taxpayer and an HMRC officer, it is listed for hearing by the tax tribunal.

TAX TRIBUNAL

2.77   One of the most important changes brought about by the reformed system is the fact that two different tribunals have been introduced into the tax litigation process. These two tribunals are known as:

- the First-tier Tribunal (*TCEA 2007, s 3(1)*); and

- the Upper Tribunal (*TCEA 2007, s 3(2)*).

The persons hearing cases in the tribunals are referred to as judges or other members (collectively, referred to as 'members'), depending on their qualifications.

2.78   The vast majority of cases are first heard by the First-tier Tribunal, which should therefore be considered as the successor to the former General and Special Commissioners.

Under the old system, appeals from the Commissioners or the VAT and Duties Tribunal would (in England and Wales) almost invariably be heard by the Chancery Division of the High Court – some cases occasionally being able to 'leapfrog' this stage to be heard by the Court of Appeal.

Under the reformed system, appeals from the First-tier Tribunal are invariably be heard by the Upper Tribunal. The Upper Tribunal is a superior court of record and, therefore, has the same status as the High Court itself. Indeed, the Upper Tribunal is often presided over by High Court judges or (in Scotland) judges of the Court of Session. Furthermore, the Upper Tribunal may exercise the same authority, powers and privileges and rights as those higher courts in relation to:

- the attendance and examination of witnesses;

- the production and inspection of documents; and

- all other matters incidental to the Upper Tribunal's functions.

Appeals from the Upper Tribunal are heard by the Court of Appeal (in England and Wales and in Northern Ireland) or the Court of Session (in Scotland).

First-tier Tribunal

2.79   Tax matters are handled by a specialist tax chamber of the First-tier Tribunal (the 'Tax Chamber'). However, it should be noted that tax credit appeals are dealt with in the Social Entitlement Chamber.

Upper Tribunal

2.80   In the Upper Tribunal, there are fewer chambers. Appeals from the Social Entitlement Chamber of the First-tier Tribunal are dealt with by the Administrative Appeals Chamber of the Upper Tribunal. Again, tax matters are heard by a specialist finance and tax chamber of the Upper Tribunal.

Note that *SI 2018/509* transferred functions relating to land appeals from the Upper Tribunal Tax and Chancery Chamber to the Lands Chamber with effect from 14 May 2018.

Bringing cases to the tribunal

2.81   One of the changes that has been introduced under the reformed system is that taxpayers are given greater control over the listing of a hearing before a tribunal, particularly in direct tax cases. Historically, the request for a hearing was generally made by the tax office when negotiations reached an impasse. Whilst this definitely simplified matters for taxpayers (as it removed one level of bureaucracy from them), there was often a perceived 'closeness' between the tax authorities and the independent appeal Commissioners. Once a taxpayer appeals against a decision by HMRC (in writing to HMRC), there are now three possible courses of action. Either:

- the taxpayer can make a formal request that HMRC review the matter in question; or

- HMRC may offer a review of the matter to the taxpayer; or

- the taxpayer may notify the appeal directly to the First-tier Tribunal.

Whichever approach is taken, it does not prevent the parties from settling the dispute by mutual agreement.

2.82   If a taxpayer requires HMRC to review the matter, HMRC must set out their initial view of the matter within 30 days of their receipt of the request for the review, or such longer period as is reasonable.

A request may not be made (and HMRC may not be required to conduct a review) if either:

- the taxpayer has already requested a review in relation to the matter; or

- HMRC have already offered a review in relation to the matter; or

- the taxpayer has already notified the First-tier Tribunal of the appeal.

2.83   When HMRC offer a review to the taxpayer, the offer must include HMRC's view of the matter in question. The taxpayer then has 30 days (starting with the date stated on HMRC's offer of a review) to request that HMRC conduct a review. It is imperative that taxpayers note this time limit carefully, because failure to accept the offer of a review means that the dispute will be treated as settled (in accordance with HMRC's views of the matter).

Furthermore, the taxpayer may not withdraw from any agreement under *TMA 1970, s 54(2)* (requests to repudiate or resile from agreement). However, the matter may still be taken to the First-tier Tribunal (see below).

2.84   HMRC may not offer a review (and HMRC may not be required to conduct a review) if either:

- the taxpayer has already requested a review in relation to the matter; or

- HMRC have already offered a review in relation to the matter; or

- the taxpayer has already notified the First-tier Tribunal of the appeal.

HMRC REVIEW

2.85   There are three outcomes of a review: the original HMRC view is either upheld, varied or cancelled. The nature and extent of the review depends on what appears to be appropriate to HMRC in the particular circumstances. However, HMRC must bear in mind the steps taken by HMRC in first deciding the matter and any steps taken by any person seeking to resolve the disagreement.

2.86   The review must also take into account any representations made by the taxpayer, provided that they are made sufficiently early to give HMRC a reasonable opportunity to consider them. To avoid difficulties with this hurdle, it is therefore suggested that the representations be included in the request for a review (or the acceptance of the offer of the review).

Timescale for review

2.87   HMRC must notify the taxpayer of their conclusions of the review and their reasoning within a 45-day period (unless the parties agree a different timescale). That 45-day period runs:

- in a case where the taxpayer requested the review, from the day on which HMRC notified the taxpayer of their initial view of the matter; and

- in a case where the taxpayer accepted HMRC's offer of a review, from the day on which HMRC received the acceptance of the offer.

The conclusions reached by the review are then deemed to stand (as a *TMA 1970, s 54(1)* agreement) and the taxpayer is unable to withdraw from this deemed agreement under *s 54(2)* (requests to repudiate or resile from agreement).

2.88   If HMRC fail to give their conclusions within the 45-day period (or such other period as agreed), then the initial HMRC view is deemed to stand (as a *s 54(1)* agreement) and the taxpayer is unable to withdraw from this deemed agreement under *s 54(2)* (requests to repudiate or resile from agreement). HMRC are required to notify the taxpayer of the conclusion that is deemed to have been reached.

This provision begs the question: what is the point of asking HMRC for a review? Not only are there concerns about the effectiveness of a review, especially if HMRC reviewers are not able to diverge from HMRC policy; however, if HMRC fail to meet their own 45-day time limit, then the parties are deemed to have agreed to the original HMRC position that was subject to the review in the first place. If taxpayers wish to avoid this 'Catch 22' situation, then they should try to agree with HMRC for an extension of the 45-day period so that HMRC cannot argue that they have run out of time. In either case, however, the matter may still be taken on appeal to the First-tier Tribunal.

Notifying an appeal

2.89   Once HMRC have been notified that their decision is to be appealed against, the taxpayer may notify the First-tier Tribunal of the appeal. Once this is done, it is for the tribunal to decide the matter. However, different procedures apply depending on whether HMRC have given their view of the matter:

- following a review under *TMA 1970, s 49B* (where the appellant requires a review by HMRC); or

- when offering a review under *TMA 1970, s 49C* (ie HMRC offer the review).

2.90   Once a review has been concluded (or once the period for the review expires without HMRC notifying the taxpayer of their conclusion), the taxpayer may notify the First-tier Tribunal of the appeal. This should generally be done within a 30-day period.

If the taxpayer is late in notifying the First-tier Tribunal of the appeal, then the appeal may not proceed unless the tribunal gives permission.

2.91   Once the tribunal has been notified of the appeal, the tribunal will decide the matter in question.

The operation of the period for notifying the tribunal depends on the circumstances of the case:

- If HMRC have notified the taxpayer of their conclusions following the review, the period to appeal runs for 30 days starting with the date of the notice on which HMRC state their conclusions of the review.

- If HMRC have failed to conclude the review in time (usually within 45 days), the taxpayer may notify the tribunal of the appeal at any time between:

    - the conclusion of the review period (usually 45 days); and

    - the 30th day following HMRC giving the document under *TMA 1970, s 45E(9)* – the deemed conclusion of the review (being in accordance with the original decision).

Notifying an appeal to the tribunal (after review offered but not accepted)

2.92   Although the review procedures are likely to catch out many taxpayers, the option of not accepting an offer of a review could be even more troublesome for taxpayers. As previously noted, an offer of a review must be accompanied by a statement of HMRC's position (*TMA 1970, s 49C(2)*). Furthermore, a taxpayer's failure to accept the offer of the review within 30 days means that the HMRC view will be deemed to have been accepted by both parties as their settled position from which the taxpayer cannot withdraw.

2.93   The taxpayer will, however, have the opportunity to notify the First-tier Tribunal of the appeal in such circumstances and the tribunal will decide the matter. Nevertheless, the timing will be critical. If the notification to the tribunal is within the 30-day period (ie within the 30 days after the date of the document by which HMRC send the offer of a review), then the matter can be heard by the tribunal without any additional hurdle. However, if the tribunal is notified later (for example, because the taxpayer is unaware of the consequences of not accepting the offer of a review), then the appeal may not proceed to the tribunal unless the tribunal gives permission.

Procedure if no review offered or requested

2.94   In direct tax cases, the taxpayer will usually have the opportunity to request a review at the same time as notifying HMRC of the appeal against the decision. However, the taxpayer may not necessarily do this and there is no obligation on HMRC to offer one. In such circumstances, the parties will be able to continue to discuss matters until such time as the taxpayer either requests a review or applies directly to the tribunal, or HMRC formally offer a review. Then, the procedures discussed above will be triggered.

2.95   HMRC produce comprehensive guidance on appealing against decisions. See *Disagree with a tax decision* on the GOV.UK website at https://www.gov.uk/tax-appeals.

ALTERNATIVE DISPUTE RESOLUTION SERVICE

2.96   HMRC offer an alternative dispute resolution (ADR) service, which aims to provide an alternative way of resolving tax disputes by using an independent facilitator, who mediates discussions between the taxpayer and the HMRC caseworker in an attempt to resolve the dispute.

ADR can be used before and after HMRC has issued a decision that can be appealed against, and at any stage of an enquiry, including:

● during a compliance check when the taxpayer has been unable to reach an agreement with HMRC, or where progress in the enquiry has stalled; and

- at the end of a compliance check, when a decision has been made that can be appealed against.

ADR does not affect the taxpayer's right to appeal, or to ask for a statutory review.

The ADR service may be particularly useful where the facts of a case need to be firmly established, but where communications have broken down between the taxpayer and HMRC (see *Stirling Jewellers (Dudley) Ltd* [2019] TC 06940).

An application to use the service must be made to HMRC using the application form on the Gov.uk website: Use Alternative Dispute Resolution to settle a tax dispute (https://assets.publishing.service.gov.uk/government/uploads/system/uploads/attachment_data/file/655344/HMRC_Resolving_tax_disputes.pdf).

HMRC will advise within 30 days whether the case can be included in the ADR process.

HMRC will then contact the taxpayer, or their representatives, and introduce them to their facilitator who will explain their role in more detail.

Customers and their representatives will also be asked to complete an ADR Process Agreement to confirm participation and commitment to ADR.

The facilitator will be an HMRC member of staff who has undergone training in facilitation and has had no prior involvement with the dispute.

For further information on using the ADR to settle a tax dispute, see the gov.uk website at https://www.gov.uk/guidance/tax-disputes-alternative-dispute-resolution-adr.

HMRC'S LITIGATION AND SETTLEMENT STRATEGY

2.97   Where possible, HMRC will support taxpayers to get their affairs right without the need for a dispute. However, differences of view – or 'disputes' – between a tax authority and taxpayers on the correct amount of tax owed, or the timing of payment, are a normal feature of tax administration across the world. They arise in cases of all sizes – this may be because HMRC disagree with the interpretation of facts and how the law should be applied to them or the law is complex and its application is not straightforward.

Most disputes can be resolved collaboratively and by agreement once the facts have been established and the points at issue discussed, including cases where there is a formal appeal against the view HMRC have taken. Only a very small minority of disputes need to be resolved by legal action, either in a tribunal or a higher court.

HMRC's Litigation and Settlement Strategy (LSS) sets out the framework within which HMRC seek to resolve tax disputes through civil processes and procedures in accordance with the law. It applies irrespective of whether the dispute is resolved by agreement with the customer or through litigation.

For further reading on LSS, see HMRC's publication 'Resolving tax disputes: Commentary on the litigation and settlement strategy' (https://assets. publishing.service.gov.uk/government/uploads/system/uploads/attachment_ data/file/655344/HMRC_Resolving_tax_disputes.pdf).

Following concerns about the procedures for resolving contentious disputes in high-profile cases, HMRC published a Code of Governance (https://www. gov.uk/government/publications/resolving-tax-disputes), explaining their processes in greater detail.

PUBLISHING DETAILS OF DELIBERATE TAX DEFAULTERS

2.98 HMRC may publish a person's name and other information to identify that person as a deliberate tax defaulter. Personal details will be published where the following three conditions are met (*FA 2009, s 94*):

- As a result of an investigation, it is found that the person has incurred one or more relevant penalties. A relevant penalty is a penalty for a deliberate, or a deliberate and concealed,

  - inaccuracy in a return or other document,

  - failure to comply with certain obligations, or

  - VAT or excise duty wrongdoing.

- The potential lost revenue for the relevant penalty or total relevant penalties exceeds £25,000.

- The penalty reduction for quality of disclosure for any of the relevant penalties is less than the maximum.

HMRC are obliged to notify the person that they are going to publish their information and give them time to make representations about why they should not do so. No information may be published until the relevant penalty becomes final. If there is more than one relevant penalty, HMRC may not publish until the last relevant penalty becomes final.

There are two time limits:

- HMRC must publish the details within 12 months of the relevant penalty becoming final. Where there is more than one relevant penalty, the period of 12 months starts on the date when the last of these penalties becomes final.

- HMRC can only continue to publish this information for 12 months.

Focus

For further details on identifying deliberate tax defaulters, see www.gov. uk/government/publications/compliance-checks-publishing-details-of-deliberate-defaulters-ccfs13.

PAYE COMPLIANCE

Introduction

2.99   Income tax and national insurance contributions collected through the PAYE system on salaries and benefits constitute the Exchequer's largest single item of cash flow. HMRC compliance yield raised additional revenue of £30bn during 2017/18, according to HMRC's annual reports and accounts for that period.

A PAYE compliance check, apart from covering income tax and NICs due on payments of salaries and wages, will also cover many other employer-related issues, including other relevant aspects of the NIC legislation, student loan deductions (SLDs), the national minimum wage, statutory sick pay (SSP), statutory maternity pay (SMP), ordinary statutory paternity pay (OSPP) and statutory adoption pay (SAP). Notification of an impending employer compliance visit or investigation should not, therefore, be taken lightly.

The legislation governing PAYE is found in the *Income Tax (Pay As You Earn) Regulations 2003 (SI 2003/2682)*.

HMRC now have the power to require a financial security from employers where amounts of PAYE income tax and NICs are seriously at risk following a history of serious non-compliance in terms of late or non-payment. HMRC will set the amount of the security based on the potential tax liability (*FA 2011, s 85*). The required security will usually be either a cash deposit from the business or director – held by HMRC or paid into a joint HMRC/taxpayer bank account – or a bond from an approved financial institution which is payable on demand. This will not affect the vast majority of employers who pay their tax on time and in full. It will not be used for employers who are having genuine problems. There is a right of appeal against the imposition of the security and the amount. A new criminal offence has also been introduced where a person fails to give a security when required to do so.

Focus

Under real time information (RTI), information about tax and other deductions under the PAYE system is transmitted to HMRC by the employer every time an employee is paid. Employers are not required to provide information to HMRC using forms P35 and P14 after the end of the tax year, or to send form P45 or P46 to HMRC when employees start or leave a job.

Compliance checks

2.100   A new framework for compliance checks took effect from 1 April 2009 which changed the way that HMRC conduct enquiries, visits and inspections (*FA 2008, Schs 36, 37* and *39*). In summary, *Sch 36* gave HMRC one set of new powers covering all the taxes concerned. This includes powers to visit businesses (without the right of appeal) and inspect the premises, assets and records, and to ask taxpayers and third parties for more information and documents. *FA 2008, s 114* provides the powers to access premises and inspect any computer used by the business.

Further rules, contained in *Schs 37* and *39*, are designed to provide greater flexibility in setting record-keeping requirements after 1 April 2009, along with new time limits for assessment and claims which did not come into force fully until April 2010 (although there were some transitional arrangements from 1 April 2009).

2.101 Under the unified regime, there is a statutory requirement for HMRC to give at least seven days' prior notice of a visit, unless either an unannounced visit is necessary, or a shorter period is agreed. There is also a requirement that unannounced visits must be approved beforehand by a specially trained HMRC officer.

2.102 The legislation, Codes of Practice and guidance governing the regime contain certain safeguards for businesses and taxpayers. Broadly, in carrying out compliance checks:

- HMRC's powers must be used reasonably and proportionately;

- taxpayers should be clear about when a compliance check begins and ends;

- HMRC officers do not have the right to enter any parts of premises that are used solely as a dwelling, whether to carry out an inspection or to examine documents produced under an information notice. They can, however, enter if invited; and

- unannounced visits will be made where agreement has been given by an authorised HMRC officer.

2.103 In addition to examining statutory records (such as PAYE deduction working sheets and expenses payments records), HMRC often ask for supplementary information to enable them to ascertain and quantify a tax position. Examples of supplementary information may include appointment diaries, notes of board meetings, correspondence, commercial employment contracts, explanations and schedules. Under the statutory framework, an information notice for supplementary information must be reasonable, proportionate, and reasonably required to check the tax position. There is a right of appeal against an information notice unless the First-tier Tribunal has approved the issue of the notice. Agreement is required from an authorised HMRC officer before asking for tribunal approval.

2.104 There may be occasions where HMRC cannot obtain information and documents from the taxpayer, or wish to check the accuracy of information and documents provided. Where HMRC think it is necessary to gather information by using a third party notice, they must have the approval of the person whose tax position is being checked and the independent First-tier Tribunal before the notice can be issued. Agreement of an authorised officer within HMRC is required before the request is referred to the First-tier Tribunal. Officers cannot inspect or require auditors or tax advisers to produce documents which ask for or give advice to a client about their tax affairs.

Safeguards

2.105   There are certain things that HMRC are not allowed to request. Such items include information relating to the conduct of appeals against HMRC decisions, legally privileged information, information about a person's medical or spiritual welfare, and journalistic material.

There are also some time constraints relating to information that may be requested. This includes information over six years old, which can only be included in a notice issued by or with the approval of an authorised HMRC officer. In addition, HMRC cannot give a notice in respect of the tax position of a dead person more than four years after the person's death.

Powers can be exercised before a return is received in certain circumstances. This could include a situation where there is a reason to believe that a taxpayer did not notify chargeability to tax, did not register for VAT if required, or is operating in the informal economy.

Settlements

2.106   The majority of compliance visits result in some discrepancies being uncovered, and HMRC will usually calculate the 'lost' tax and national insurance over a period of six years plus the current year. This period may be extended if they suspect that deductions have been withheld deliberately. HMRC may also seek penalties (see below), although these will normally depend on the gravity of the discrepancy and the degree of co-operation and disclosure from the employer.

Often, the audit investigator will be looking only for tax and possibly national insurance on the 'income' not taxed, instead of effecting a gross position. Amounts treated as benefits would not be grossed up or included in the assessment of national insurance under-deduction.

Penalties

2.107   HMRC may seek to impose a penalty where a taxpayer:

- fails to comply with an information notice;
- conceals, destroys or otherwise disposes of documents required by an information notice;

- conceals, destroys or otherwise disposes of documents that they have been notified are, or likely to be, required by an information notice; or

- deliberately obstructs an inspection that has been approved by the First-tier Tribunal.

There are three types and amounts of penalty:

- a standard penalty of £300;

- a daily penalty of up to £60 for every day that the failure or obstruction continues after the date the standard penalty is assessed; and

- a tax-related penalty.

Daily or tax-related penalties cannot be considered unless a standard penalty, in respect of the failure or obstruction, has been assessed. Moreover, they can only be assessed by, or applied with, the agreement of an authorised HMRC officer.

A tax-related penalty is in addition to the standard penalty and any daily penalties. The amount of the penalty is decided by the Upper Tribunal, based on the amount of tax at risk.

A person is not liable to a penalty if they have a reasonable excuse for:

- failing to comply with an information notice; or

- obstructing an inspection;

and they remedy that as soon as the excuse ends. The excuse will then be treated as continuing until the correction is made.

Normally, daily penalties will not be assessed after the failure has been remedied.

Special Civil Investigations Section

2.108 The Special Civil Investigations Section (SCI) investigates the highest-risk areas facing HMRC. These include the tax affairs of individuals, partnerships, companies and particular transactions, and also situations where substantial amounts of tax may be at risk (see HMRC Code of Practice 9, available online at www.gov.uk/government/uploads/system/uploads/attachment_data/file/494808/COP9_06_14.pdf). Investigations are sometimes started in local offices and subsequently handed over to SCI, whilst others are handled by SCI from the outset.

The Special Trades Investigations Unit (STIU) is a subsidiary unit of SCI with offices located both in London and Leicester. It deals almost exclusively with the CMT ('cut, make and trim') sector of the clothing industry in Leicester, Birmingham and the east end of London. Whilst this is a small section, it is very active in its particular sphere and has had a significant impact in raising PAYE/national insurance contributions compliance levels in this sector. A significant proportion of businesses in the CMT sector of the clothing industry are run by Asian immigrants, or second generation UK domiciles of Asian origin. STIU receives a great deal of information (often anonymous in origin) concerning the use of illegal immigrants as direct labour or out-workers by bona fide UK businesses. The employment of illegal immigrants significantly increases the risk that PAYE will not be operated on wages paid to the worker. Whilst there appears to be no provision for information to be swapped between the Home Office and HMRC concerning the use of illegal immigrants by employers, nevertheless STIU is likely to be in the forefront of government agencies with an interest in the provisions of the *Asylum and Immigration Act 1996*.

The Agricultural Compliance Unit is also a subsidiary unit of SCI based in Leeds and deals with self-employed gang masters in order to ensure that they operate the PAYE rules on gangs of casual workers utilised by farmers at peak times during harvesting. There has been an increased tendency in recent years for casual workers in the agricultural sector to be recruited from unemployed peasant workers from Eastern Europe. There is a significant risk that these workers may contravene immigration control regulations and that wages will be paid in cash without deduction of tax under the PAYE regulations.

It is important to establish whether the SCI is involved in an investigation at the outset, because these HMRC staff will usually be more experienced and aware of technical aspects. They may also be more rigorous in the way in which they conduct the investigation.

It is generally perceived that the remit of the SCI is to seek quick and effective settlements, which will promote a speedy cash flow to the Exchequer. In practice, SCI inspectors are often more ready to come to ad hoc arrangements than their counterparts in local tax districts.

Dispensations

2.109   Prior to 2016/17, if an employer paid or reimbursed employees for tax-allowable business expenses, they could apply to HMRC for a dispensation to prevent such expenses or benefits being reported annually on forms P11D. Broadly, a dispensation was granted where HMRC were satisfied that no tax was payable on them. Dispensations generally covered 'qualifying travelling expenses' (other than business mileage payments) or amounts incurred wholly, exclusively and necessarily in the performance of the duties of the employment. HMRC normally accepted that expenses payments which were covered by a dispensation did not count as earnings for NIC purposes. Where an employer had a dispensation the items listed would not be treated as a benefit in kind and liable to Class 1A NICs.

Announcements originally made in the Autumn 2014 Statement confirmed that the administration of tax relief for employee expenses, where the employer pays or reimburses them, or provides benefits in kind in respect of them, was to be simplified. The new provisions subsequently took effect from April 2016. Broadly, the measure removed the reporting requirement and the requirement for employers to apply to HMRC for a dispensation in order to pay qualifying expenses and benefits in kind. The changes also endeavour to more closely align the tax rules to the existing NIC treatment of expenses payments.

From 2016/17, therefore, the dispensations regime has been abolished and, instead, if an employee would have been entitled to tax relief in full for a particular benefit or expense, then the employer will not need to deduct tax or national insurance contributions, and they will not need to report it to HMRC. The exemption does not apply to benefits or expenses paid as part of a salary sacrifice arrangement.

For the exemption to apply to an expense, the amount of the expense must be calculated and paid or reimbursed in an 'approved way'. This means the expense has either been calculated in accordance with regulations on flat rate payments, or at a bespoke rate approved by HMRC.

Complaints

2.110 Most PAYE compliance reviews are settled by agreement. However, if an amount cannot be agreed upon, HMRC may make a formal determination for the tax underpaid, student loan deductions, and penalties. A notice of decision will be issued for outstanding NICs and statutory payments.

An employer can appeal to the tribunal against any determination or notice of decision within 30 days of issue.

There is a set procedure for dealing with complaints concerning the way an investigation has been conducted. Full details are set out in the HMRC Factsheet entitled *Putting things right: how to complain* (www.gov.uk/government/publications/putting-things-right-how-to-complain-factsheet-cfs). Broadly, the steps are as follows:

(1)   The HMRC officer dealing with the investigation should be contacted in the first instance, or their line manager or the person in charge of the HMRC office.

(2)   If the matter cannot be settled, contact the Director with overall responsibility for the office dealing with the investigation. The Director will review the complaint objectively.

(3)   Where matters are still not resolved, contact the Adjudicator (www.adjudicatorsoffice.gov.uk). The Adjudicator acts as an unbiased and independent referee. The Adjudicator can be contacted at:

The Adjudicator's Office
8th Floor

Euston Tower
286 Euston Road
London NW1 3US

Telephone: 0300 057 1111 / 020 7667 1832
Fax: 0300 057 1212 / 020 7667 1830

(4)   If at any time a person is not satisfied with the service they are receiving from HMRC or the Adjudicator, they should contact their MP and ask for the case to be referred to the Parliamentary Ombudsman. The Ombudsman accepts referrals from any MP, but the local MP should be contacted in the first instance.

(5)   Allegations of very serious misconduct by HMRC staff, such as assault or corruption, are dealt with by the Independent Police Complaints Commission (IPCC) (www.ipcc.gov.uk/en/Pages/complaints.aspx).

DISCLOSURE OF TAX AVOIDANCE SCHEMES

Background

2.111   *FA 2004, Pt 7* requires promoters and, in some cases, users to provide HMRC with information ('disclosure') about certain direct tax schemes that might be expected to obtain a tax advantage as one of the main benefits.

The disclosure of tax avoidance schemes (DOTAS) regime covers income tax, corporation tax, capital gains tax, stamp duty land tax, inheritance tax, annual tax on enveloped dwellings and national insurance contributions.

Under the rules, a tax arrangement may need to be disclosed even if HMRC are already aware of it or it is not considered to be avoidance. A tax arrangement should be disclosed where:

- it will, or might be expected to, enable any person to obtain a tax advantage;

- that tax advantage is, or might be expected to be, the main benefit or one of the main benefits of the arrangement;

- it is a hallmarked scheme by being a tax arrangement that falls within any description (the 'hallmarks') prescribed in the relevant regulations.

In most situations where disclosure is required it must be made by the scheme 'promoter' within 5 days of one of three trigger events. However, the scheme user may need to make the disclosure where:

- the promoter is based outside the UK;

- the promoter is a lawyer and legal professional privilege prevents him from providing all or part of the prescribed information to HMRC;

- there is no promoter, such as when a person designs and implements their own scheme. (In such cases disclosure must be made within 30 days of the scheme being implemented.)

Focus

Finance Act 2017 contains provisions to ensure that, on or after 8 March 2017, promoters of tax avoidance schemes (POTAS) cannot circumvent the POTAS regime by re-organising their business so that they either share control of a promoting business or put a person or persons between themselves and the promoting business (*FA 2017, s 24*).

Focus

Under measures contained in *Finance Act 2014 (Pt 4)*, HMRC may issue a notice to the user of a tax avoidance scheme advising that they should settle their dispute with HMRC when the claimed tax effect has been defeated in other litigation. If the taxpayer does not settle, they risk a penalty and must make upfront payment of the tax in dispute.

This requirement to pay upfront also applies to the disputed tax associated with any scheme that falls within the disclosure of tax avoidance scheme (DOTAS) rules and with schemes that HMRC counteract under the general anti-abuse rule (GAAR).

For detailed guidance on follower notices and accelerated payments, see the gov.uk website at www.gov.uk/government/publications/follower-notices-and-accelerated-payments.

Focus

Finance Act 2014 contains provisions that gave HMRC additional powers to tackle non-cooperative promoters of tax avoidance schemes (*FA 2014, Pt 5 (ss 234–283)*). These powers include the ability to issue conduct notices, breaches of which will trigger enhanced information powers with penalties of up to £1 million for non-compliance.

Hallmark schemes

2.112   From 1 August 2006, the schemes required to be disclosed are those that fall within certain hallmarks as prescribed by the *Tax Avoidance Schemes (Prescribed Descriptions of Arrangements) Regulations 2006 (SI 2006/1543)* as amended by the *Tax Avoidance Schemes (Prescribed Descriptions of Arrangements) (Amendment) Regulations 2013 (SI 2013/2595)*. The 2013 Regulations took effect, broadly, from 4 November 2013.

The regulations contain hallmarks (ie descriptions of arrangements in line with the system used for value added tax). If a scheme falls within any one hallmark, it will be notifiable.

The hallmarks fall into three groups:

- three generic hallmarks that target new and innovative schemes;
- a hallmark that targets mass marketed tax products; and
- hallmarks that target areas of particular risk.

The three generic hallmarks are derived from the existing 'filters' of confidentiality, premium fee and off-market terms.

Two specific hallmarks concern:

- schemes intended to create tax losses to offset income or capital gains tax; and
- certain leasing schemes.

Comprehensive guidance on DOTAS can be found at: www.gov.uk/ government/uploads/system/uploads/attachment_data/file/492629/DOTAS_ guidance_Nov_15_version_-_for_publishing-3.pdf.

The forms to complete

2.113 There are four different forms available for use in the following circumstances:

- AAG1 – Disclosure of avoidance scheme (Notification by scheme promoter);
- AAG2 – Disclosure of avoidance scheme (Notification by scheme user where offshore promoter does not notify);
- AAG3 – Disclosure of avoidance scheme (Notification by scheme user where no promoter, or promoted by lawyer unable to make full notification); and
- AAG5 – Disclosure of avoidance scheme (Continuation sheet).

The forms can be downloaded from the Gov.uk website at https://www.gov.uk/ disclosure-of-tax-avoidance-schemes-overview.

On receipt of the above forms, the HMRC Anti-Avoidance Group issues a unique scheme reference number for each disclosure of a hallmarked scheme it receives. The number is issued within 30 days of the Anti-Avoidance Group receiving the disclosure.

The reference numbers are eight digits in length and are issued to either scheme promoters or, where they have the liability to make disclosure, the scheme user.

Scheme reference numbers will be issued where the scheme has been designed for use 'in-house'.

Promoters are required to provide the reference numbers allocated by the Anti-Avoidance Group to clients who use their schemes. Promoters may find it more convenient to issue the number to their clients when it is received, although the strict statutory requirement does not require this. Promoters should ensure that they inform their clients of their obligation to include the reference number on their tax return or form AAG4.

HMRC have published consolidated guidance on disclosure of tax avoidance schemes related to income tax, corporation tax, capital gains tax, National Insurance contributions (NICs), stamp duty land tax and inheritance tax. The guidance can be found at https://www.gov.uk/disclosure-of-tax-avoidance-schemes-overview.

Penalties

2.114   Failure by promoters or scheme users to comply with their obligations to notify prescribed information in respect of notifiable proposals and arrangements or failure by promoters to inform clients of the scheme reference number renders them liable to (*TMA 1970, s 98C(1), (2)*):

- an initial penalty of up to £5,000; and

- a further penalty of up to £600 for each day the failure continues after the imposition of the initial penalty.

Scheme users who fail to supply the prescribed information required in their returns are liable to a penalty of (*TMA 1970, s 98C(3), (4)*):

- £100 for the first failure;

- £500 for a second failure; and

- £1,000 for every failure thereafter.

A failure of this nature will not incur the scheme user a further penalty for the submission of an incomplete return (*FA 2004, s 313(4)*).

Penalties will be determined by an officer of the Board of HMRC, but a right of appeal lies to the First-tier Tribunal (*TMA 1970, ss 100, 100C*).

SERIAL TAX AVOIDANCE REGIME

2.115   The Serial Tax Avoidance Regime (STAR) was introduced from 6 April 2017, under which warnings are issued and escalating sanctions imposed, on taxpayers who persistently engage in tax avoidance schemes defeated by HMRC (*FA 2016, Sch 18*). Following the first defeat of such a scheme after 6 April 2017, HMRC will issue a notice placing the taxpayer on warning that the use of any further avoidance scheme in the following five years, if defeated, will result in a penalty based on the amount of the understated tax.

While on warning, a taxpayer will be required to notify HMRC each year that they have not used any further avoidance schemes or, if they have, to give full details of the schemes and the amount of the tax advantage the schemes are asserted to deliver.

Where a taxpayer on warning uses further avoidance schemes which HMRC defeat, they will face a penalty of 20% of the understated tax on the first occasion, rising to a maximum of 60% on defeat of subsequent schemes.

They will also have their names and other details published by HMRC.

Taxpayers who use at least three tax avoidance schemes during the warning period, exploiting reliefs in a way not intended by Parliament and defeated by HMRC, will be issued with a restriction notice forbidding them for a period of three years from making any claim for relief, except for certain reliefs relating to charities, double tax treaties and registered pension schemes.

HMRC guidance on the STAR regime can be found online at www.gov.uk/government/collections/serial-tax-avoidance-regime.

OFFSHORE TAX EVADERS

Civil sanctions for enablers of offshore tax evasion

2.116   New civil penalties are to be introduced for persons (whether individuals or businesses) who deliberately help taxpayers to hide assets or taxable income or gains outside the UK in order to evade their UK income tax, capital gains tax or inheritance tax responsibilities.

A person enables another person to carry out offshore tax evasion when they knowingly encourage, assist or otherwise facilitate that evasion. The penalties will include a new financial penalty of up to 100% of the tax evaded, and (in the most serious cases) a new power to publish information about the enabler.

The government proposes to extend HMRC's information powers in cases where an information notice is issued to a suspected enabler for the purpose of checking whether they have deliberately enabled evasion.

Focus

In February 2018 HMRC launched a consultation seeking views on the design principles for legislation to implement a new minimum tax assessment time limit of 12 years for HMRC to make assessments or notices of determination in cases involving offshore income, gains or chargeable transfers.

HMRC state that they are extending the time limit because it can take much longer to establish the facts about offshore transactions, particularly if they involve complex offshore structures. More time is needed to address

---

situations where the current assessment time limits of four and six years for offshore non-compliance are not long enough to establish the facts, and determine and assess the amount of tax due.

The consultation document entitled *Consultation: Extension of Offshore Time Limits* can be found online at www.gov.uk/government/uploads/system/uploads/attachment_data/file/682110/Extension_of_Offshore_Time_Limits_consultation_document.pdf. The consultation ran until 14 May 2018.

Increased civil sanctions for offshore tax evaders

2.117 Minimum penalties are to be increased for inaccuracies, failure to notify a charge to tax or failure to deliver a return, where the penalty addresses deliberate behaviour in relation to an offshore matter or transfer.

The provisions in *FA 2009, s 94* for naming deliberate tax defaulters are to be changed. Where an inaccuracy in a taxpayer's document or failure to notify relates to offshore matters or offshore transfers, only disclosures which are both full and unprompted will be outside the scope of the naming provisions. Further amendments will allow the naming of certain people who have benefited from the inaccuracy or failure. A new asset-based penalty, calculated by reference to the value of the underlying asset involved in the evasion, will also be introduced. This will apply in only the most serious cases of deliberate offshore evasion.

Criminal offence for offshore tax evaders

2.118 From a date to be appointed, there are to be new criminal offences for those who evade their UK income tax or capital gains tax responsibilities in respect of income or gains outside the UK. The criminal offences do not require the prosecution to prove intent. They will apply where a person has failed to properly declare offshore income or gains in accordance with *TMA 1970, ss 7, 8*, leading to a loss of tax over a threshold amount which will be defined in regulations.

Requirement to correct

2.119 Broadly, the Requirement To Correct (RTC) legislation contained in *Finance (No 2) Act 2017 (F(No2)A 2017, s 67* and *Sch 18)* required those with undeclared offshore tax liabilities (relating to income tax, capital gains tax or inheritance tax for the relevant periods) to disclose those to HMRC by 30 September 2018. This date was chosen as the final date for corrections as this is the date by which more than 100 countries exchanged data on financial accounts under the Common Reporting Standard (CRS). CRS data significantly enhances HMRC's ability to detect offshore non-compliance and it was therefore in taxpayers' interests to correct any non-compliance before that data was received.

Those who failed to correct any non-compliance existing on 5 April 2017 by 30 September 2018 are liable to new penalties. The penalties are much harsher than those previously applicable and may include:

- a tax-geared penalty of between 100% and 200% of the tax not corrected;
- in serious cases, an asset-based penalty of up to 10% of the value of the relevant asset, naming and shaming by HMRC; and
- enhanced penalties where assets or funds have been moved to attempt to avoid the RTC.

In all cases where a penalty applies, there will be a standard penalty equivalent to 200% of the tax liability which should have been disclosed to HMRC under the RTC but was not. This penalty can be reduced to reflect any combination of the following factors:

- level of co-operation with HMRC; and
- the quality of the disclosure to HMRC (including telling HMRC of anyone who helped enable non-compliance).

The reduction will take account of whether the disclosure was made voluntarily, but the reduction cannot reduce the penalty to less than 100% of the tax involved.

Unlike other penalties, these penalties do not take into account the cause of the non-compliance, so they apply equally to those who failed to pay the correct amount of tax because of a careless error and those who deliberately evaded tax.

For further details on the RTC, see the gov.uk website at www.gov.uk/guidance/requirement-to-correct-tax-due-on-offshore-assets.

Chapter 3

Scottish income tax

SIGNPOSTS

- Background to Scottish income tax, including the Scottish variable rate, the Scottish rate of income tax, the Smith Commission, and other devolved taxes (see **3.1–3.4**).

- Introduction to Scottish income tax – including the tax rates and thresholds for 2017/18, 2018/19 and 2019/20, the impact of income tax divergence, and the legislation and consequential implications of Scottish income tax (see **3.5–3.12**).

- The need for UK-wide awareness of Scottish income tax, the procedure for setting the Scottish rates and thresholds, and the interaction of UK and Scottish rates and thresholds (see **3.13–3.15**).

- Definition of a Scottish taxpayer, including examples (see **3.16–3.24**).

- Income subject to Scottish income tax (see **3.25**).

- The transferable tax allowance for couples (see **3.26**).

- Partnership income, non-UK income, gifts to charities, and general reliefs from income tax (see **3.27–3.33**).

- Pension scheme contributions, including net pay arrangements, retirement annuity premiums, relief at source, and annual allowance or lifetime allowance charges (see **3.34–3.37**).

- Income from trusts, including bare trusts, discretionary and accumulation trusts, deceased estates and onshore interest in possession trusts, offshore interest in possession trusts and settlor-interested trusts (see **3.38–3.43**).

- Social security lump sums (see **3.44**).

- Impact on capital gains tax (see **3.45**).

- Payroll issues for employers, and the construction industry scheme (see **3.46–3.51**).

- Administration of Scottish income tax (see **3.52–3.54**).

- Possible behavioural repercussions of greater divergence (see **3.55**).

BACKGROUND TO SCOTTISH INCOME TAX

The Scottish variable rate

3.1   The Scottish variable rate (SVR) was introduced by *Scotland Act 1998 (SA 1998)*, an Act of the Westminster Parliament, and gave the Scottish Parliament tax-raising powers which they chose not to implement. SVR allowed them (had they chosen to do so) to vary the basic rate of income tax on Scottish taxpayers by up to 3 percentage points above or below the UK basic rate.

The Scottish rate of income tax

3.2   *Scotland Act 2012 (SA 2012)*, amending *SA 1998*, introduced provisions for a Scottish rate of income tax (SRIT), to be charged on certain income of Scottish taxpayers (as defined). *Finance Act 2014* rewrote some of the procedural provisions for SRIT and (paradoxically) a number of changes and prospective changes relating to the definition of a Scottish taxpayer were included in *Wales Act 2014 (WA 2014)*.

HMRC published general guidance on *SA 2012* at www.gov.uk/scotland-act-2012. They published a Technical Note on SRIT in May 2012 at tinyurl.com/nqfu2s2 and updated this in a further Technical Note in December 2014 at tinyurl.com/osxmzw2.

A Treasury order made on 8 December 2015 (*Scotland Act 2012, Section 25 (Appointed Years) Order 2015, SI 2015/2000*) appointed 2015/16 as the last year for which SVR applied and 2016/17 as the first year for which SRIT would apply.

By contrast to SVR, SRIT was actually implemented. From 6 April 2016 the basic, higher and additional rates of UK income tax on non-savings non-dividend income of Scottish taxpayers were cut by 10 percentage points. The Scottish Parliament then had power to substitute a new rate (the Scottish rate) for that reduction, allowing them to reduce the effective basic, higher and additional rates by up to 10 percentage points, or increase them by any amount without limit.

Under what was known as the 'lockstep' system, the same Scottish rate had to be applied to each income tax band – they could not be varied independently. Thus, although the Scottish Parliament had power to set only one rate (the Scottish rate), this effectively gave rise to three rates: the Scottish basic rate; the Scottish higher rate; and the Scottish additional rate. Collectively, these three rates were referred to as the Scottish main rates.

Although the power existed, the Scottish Parliament decided not to vary the rates of income tax in 2016/17. To achieve this, maintaining the rates of tax applied to the non-savings non-dividend income of Scottish taxpayers at the same level as those applied to other UK taxpayers, the Scottish Parliament set SRIT at 10% for 2016/17.

SRIT was administered by HMRC as part of the UK income tax system. A Memorandum of Understanding dated 5 March 2013 between the Scottish Government and HMRC set out arrangements for setting up and operating SRIT (see tinyurl.com/kvtzedp). In 2016/17 the Scottish Government's budget bore £6.3 million in costs of administering SRIT.

For more detailed information on SRIT, see *Income Tax 2016/17* (Bloomsbury Professional).

The Smith Commission

3.3   A referendum on Scottish independence took place in September 2014. The majority voted in favour of Scotland remaining part of the UK, but with each of the main UK political parties promising more powers for the Scottish Parliament. Following this, in November 2014 the Smith Commission on further devolution recommended that the Scottish Parliament should have unrestrained power to set the income tax rates and thresholds applicable to the non-savings non-dividend income of Scottish taxpayers. The Smith Commission also recommended devolution of air passenger duty and aggregates levy, and assignment to the Scottish budget of the receipts raised in Scotland from the first 10 percentage points of the standard rate of VAT. It was subsequently agreed that the assignment of VAT would also apply to the first 2.5 percentage points of the reduced rate of VAT.

Another recommendation of the Smith Commission was that the devolution of further powers should be accompanied by an updated fiscal framework for Scotland, consistent with the overall UK fiscal framework. Following protracted negotiations between the UK and Scottish Governments, a revised fiscal framework was agreed and published on 15 March 2016 (see tinyurl.com/j785d7z). This included agreement that the further income tax powers would be devolved with effect from April 2017.

Scotland Act 2016 (SA 2016), legislated by the Westminster Parliament to bring the Smith Commission proposals into effect, received Royal Assent on 23 March 2016.

Other devolved taxes

3.4   *SA 2012* gave the Scottish Parliament power to levy two new, wholly-devolved taxes – on land transactions and on waste disposal to landfill. From 1 April 2015 these replaced stamp duty land tax and landfill tax in Scotland, and the relevant primary legislation is contained in *Land and Buildings Transaction Tax (Scotland) Act 2013* and *Landfill Tax (Scotland) Act 2014*. For further information about these devolved taxes see www.revenue.scot; also *Land and Buildings Transaction Tax* and *The Management of Taxes in Scotland* (both from Bloomsbury Professional).

From 1 April 2018 a new, wholly-devolved air departure tax (ADT) was to have replaced air passenger duty in Scotland, but its introduction is being deferred until issues have been resolved relating to EU state aid approval for the exemption of flights departing from the Highlands and Islands.

Following the recent withdrawal of litigation against the UK Government and the European Commission, aggregates levy is to be reviewed between now and the end of 2019 – the intention being that aggregates levy in Scotland will be replaced by a wholly-devolved levy.

In the tax year 2019/20, transitional arrangements are coming into force for receipts from the first 10p of the standard rate of VAT and the first 2.5p of the reduced rate of VAT in Scotland to be assigned to the Scottish Government. This partial assignment of VAT receipts will become fully effective in 2020/21. The Scottish and UK Governments have agreed that requiring businesses to report their VAT separately for Scotland and the rest of the UK would impose an unwanted administrative burden. A suggested mechanism for determining what are 'Scottish' VAT receipts was published in November 2018.

SCOTTISH INCOME TAX

Focus

From 6 April 2017, Scottish income tax replaced SRIT, giving the Scottish Parliament full control over the rates of UK income tax on the non-savings non-dividend income of Scottish taxpayers and the thresholds at which these rates apply.

Introduction

3.5   *SA 2016*, amending *SA 1998*, introduced provisions for Scottish income tax (SIT), to be charged on certain income of Scottish taxpayers as defined.

Essentially SIT replaced SRIT while retaining most of its principles and procedural provisions. HMRC published a Technical Note on 30 November 2016 at tinyurl.com/j9rq5e3, setting out the manner in which SIT rates and thresholds interact with various aspects of the UK-wide income tax regime.

A Treasury order made on 29 November 2016 (*Scotland Act 2016 (Commencement No 2) Regulations 2016, SI 2016/1161*) appointed 2017/18 as the first year for which SIT would apply. Related legislative amendments were made by the *Scotland Act 2016 (Income Tax Consequential Amendments) Regulations 2017, SI 2017/468.*

Unlike the SRIT regime (see **3.2**) which applied for 2016/17 only, from 6 April 2017 the Scottish Parliament has had full control over the rates of UK income tax on the non-savings non-dividend income of Scottish taxpayers and the thresholds at which these rates apply. Under SIT the entire income tax charge on non-savings non-dividend income of Scottish taxpayers was replaced by tax at Scottish rates and within Scottish rate bands, all determined by the Scottish Parliament.

Scottish income tax rates and thresholds for 2017/18

3.6   For 2017/18 the Scottish Parliament decided to keep the SIT rates in line with those elsewhere in the UK (ie basic rate 20%, higher rate 40% and additional rate 45%), but held the higher rate threshold at £43,000 instead of the more generous threshold of £45,000 which applied in the rest of the UK.

Scottish income tax rates and thresholds for 2018/19

3.7   On 2 November 2017 the minority Scottish National Party administration in Edinburgh published a paper entitled 'The Role of Income Tax in Scotland' (see tinyurl.com/y9tt8amx) for consultation to inform the Scottish Budget for 2018/19. That Budget was passed on 20 February 2018 following changes to secure the necessary political support, which came from the Scottish Green Party.

Focus

6 April 2018 marked a significant increase in the divergence between SIT rates and thresholds and those for income tax in the rest of the UK.

The Scottish Parliament set SIT rates and thresholds for 2018/19 that were significantly different from those elsewhere in the UK. Instead of the basic, higher and additional rate bands applicable in the rest of the UK, Scottish taxpayers became subject to five distinct SIT rates and bands on their non-savings non-dividend income while remaining subject to the three UK rates and thresholds on their savings and dividend income.

The five SIT bands for 2018/19 were as follows:

Band of non-savings non-dividend income	Name of rate/band	SIT rate
Over £11,850*–£13,850	Starter rate	19%
Over £13,850–£24,000	Basic rate	20%
Over £24,000–£43,430	Intermediate rate	21%
Over £43,430–£150,000	Higher rate	41%
Above £150,000	Top rate	46%

- Assumes the Scottish taxpayer has a UK personal allowance of £11,850 (reduced by £1 for every £2 of adjusted net income over £100,000).

For most Scottish taxpayers, the immediate tax impact of the reform of SIT bands and rates from 6 April 2018 was slight. For those with non-savings non-dividend income up to £24,000, the starter rate (which should not be confused with the UK starting rate for savings, see **1.49**) produced a maximum saving of up to £20 in 2018/19 compared with taxpayers elsewhere in the UK.

On incomes over £24,000 the intermediate rate reversed this saving. Scottish taxpayers with non-savings non-dividend income of £26,000 paid the same tax in 2018/19 as those in the rest of the UK. Those with non-savings non-dividend income of £46,350 (the higher rate threshold south of the border) paid income tax of £788 more than those in the rest of the UK, largely because the higher rate threshold for Scottish income tax was held down at £43,430.

At higher levels of non-savings non-dividend income, Scottish taxpayers paid progressively more tax than those elsewhere in the UK. The differences were not massive compared with their incomes, but might be resented by many high earners. For example, at incomes of (say) £60,000 or £90,000, the extra tax in 2018/19 came to approximately £924 or £1,224 respectively.

Given the increasing divergence of income tax rates and bands north and south of the border, it should be noted that national insurance contributions (NICs) are not devolved. For 2018/19 the upper earnings level for NICs was £46,350 throughout the UK. However, the differing income tax thresholds could cause confusion. On a band of non-savings non-dividend income between £43,430 and £46,350, employed Scottish taxpayers paid income tax and NICs at a combined marginal rate of 53% compared with only 32% in the rest of the UK. For self-employed Scottish taxpayers the equivalent marginal rate was 50% compared with only 29% in the rest of the UK.

For taxpayers, the UK and Scottish Governments and HMRC, the agreement on a new five-band SIT regime only weeks before its implementation on 6 April 2018 raised other concerns. The massive change which brought increasing divergence from income tax in the rest of the UK, with widespread repercussions for Scottish taxpayers, had received only limited parliamentary scrutiny at Holyrood. Understandably this resulted in calls for a review of Holyrood's budget process and the introduction of an annual Scottish Finance Bill to maintain all devolved taxes in a more orderly manner. See, for example, the discussion paper *Devolving Taxes across the UK: Learning from the Scottish Experience* (tinyurl.com/y2ytcq8j) published in October 2018 by the Scottish Taxes Policy Forum.

Scottish income tax rates and thresholds for 2019/20

Focus

From 6 April 2019 the SIT rates and thresholds continued to diverge further from those for income tax in the rest of the UK.

3.8   On 12 December 2018 the minority Scottish National Party administration in Edinburgh presented its Scottish Budget for 2019/20 to the Scottish Parliament, proposing greater divergence of SIT from income tax elsewhere in the UK. Following negotiations to secure the necessary political support, which came from the Scottish Green Party, a Scottish rate resolution (see **3.14**) for 2019/20 was passed on 21 February 2019 and the *Budget (Scotland) Act 2019* was passed on 21 February and received Royal Assent on 29 March 2019.

The SIT rates have remained unchanged from 2018/19. The five SIT bands that apply to the non-savings non-dividend income of Scottish taxpayers for 2019/20 are as follows:

Band of non-savings non-dividend income	Name of rate/band	SIT rate
Over £12,500*–£14,549	Starter rate	19%
Over £14,549–£24,944	Basic rate	20%
Over £24,944–£43,430	Intermediate rate	21%
Over £43,430–£150,000	Higher rate	41%
Above £150,000	Top rate	46%

●   Assumes the Scottish taxpayer has a UK personal allowance of £12,500 (reduced by £1 for every £2 of adjusted net income over £100,000).

For most Scottish taxpayers, the immediate tax impact of the changes to the SIT bands from 6 April 2019 was slight. An inflation-based adjustment increased the starter rate band from £2,000 to £2,049 in 2019/20, boosting the maximum annual saving from this band by 49p to £20.49. On incomes over £24,049 the intermediate rate reverses this saving and Scottish taxpayers with non-savings non-dividend income of £26,993 pay the same tax as those in the rest of the UK.

Similarly, an inflation-adjusted rise lifted the Scottish basic rate band from £10,150 to £10,395, providing a maximum annual tax saving of £2.45.

It is for those on middle incomes and above that SIT really bites. Compared with £50,000 for the rest of the UK, the Scottish higher rate threshold for 2019/20 has been frozen at £43,430 – the same level as in 2017/18 and 2018/19. The top rate threshold has also been held at £150,000, in line with the additional rate threshold for the rest of the UK.

With the freezing of the Scottish higher rate threshold, the gap has widened between SIT on non-savings non-dividend income and income tax on similar income elsewhere in the UK. On various sample earnings, the following table shows the excess of SIT over income tax in the rest of the UK in 2017/18, 2018/19 and 2019/20:

3.9 *Scottish income tax*

Earnings per annum	Excess of SIT over income tax in the rest of the UK			Rise/(fall) in excess in 2019/20
	2017/18	*2018/19*	*2019/20*	
£30,000	£0	£40	£30	(£10)
£43,430	£86	£174	£164	(£10)
£60,000	£400	£924	£1,644	£720
£90,000	£400	£1,224	£1,944	£720
£124,000	£400	£1,683	£2,409	£726
£150,000	£400	£1,943	£2,669	£726

Again, it should be noted that National Insurance Contributions (NICs) are not devolved. For 2019/20 the upper earnings level for NICs is £50,000 throughout the UK. However, the differing income tax thresholds may cause confusion. On a band of non-savings non-dividend income between £43,430 and £50,000, employed Scottish taxpayers pay income tax and NICs at a combined marginal rate of 53% compared with only 32% in the rest of the UK. For self-employed Scottish taxpayers the equivalent marginal rate is 50% compared with only 29% in the rest of the UK.

When comparing 2018/19 and 2019/20, further confusion may arise throughout the UK (including Scotland) because the primary threshold (above which NICs become payable) is to be increased by much less than the substantial rise in the upper earnings limit. As a result, the maximum NIC which an employee can pay at the 12% rate is to increase from £4,555 to £4,967. (For the self-employed, the maximum NIC payable at the 9% rate is to increase from £3,413 to £3,723.)

The impact of Brexit

3.9　　The Scottish Budget for 2019/20 was finalised at a time when there were significant uncertainties about whether and (if so) when and how the UK would leave the European Union.

At the time of writing this, the Scottish Government faced even greater uncertainties because the outcome of the UK Government's negotiations on exiting from the EU was still unknown.

In his Budget speech on 29 October 2018, the Chancellor of the Exchequer had made it clear that as a result of Brexit there might be a need for an emergency UK Budget. The Scottish Finance Secretary had warned that he might have to revisit the priorities in his Scottish Budget, but he could find himself backed into a corner.

For example, if the Chancellor decided to increase income tax rates in the rest of the UK while also cutting back on public expenditure in reserved areas, the

Barnett consequentials could squeeze the Scottish block grant. As a result, the Scottish Government might want to increase SIT revenues – the largest slice of Scottish Government funding over which Holyrood has significant fiscal power.

SA 1998, s 80C requires a Scottish rate resolution (see **3.14**) to be passed by 5 April 2019 in order to set the SIT rates and bands for 2019/20. Beyond that date, the Scottish Parliament is unable to adjust the SIT rates or bands for 2019/20. The Finance Secretary might be reluctant to cut public expenditure, but could find that he had few other options.

Funding the Scottish Government's budget

3.10   The introduction of SIT has an effect on public funding. After a transitional period, the estimated amount raised by SIT is accounted for to the Scottish Government; and the Scottish block grant, paid annually by Westminster to Holyrood to fund devolved public services in Scotland, is reduced by a corresponding amount. Some areas of the funding cycle are being agreed between the Scottish and UK Governments over a period of time, including how estimates are reconciled to forecasts, exactly when this happens, and the process for resolving any disputes.

SIT, like SRIT before it, is administered by HMRC as part of the UK income tax system under a Memorandum of Understanding dated 1 December 2016 between the Scottish Government and HMRC (see tinyurl.com/yaq2sr9p). The Scottish Government's budget bears the costs of administering SIT.

Focus

Unlike the wholly-devolved taxes, SIT is part of the UK income tax regime, and only the power to set the Scottish rates and thresholds is devolved to the Scottish Parliament. Thus, it is UK income tax, administered by HMRC, that is levied on non-savings non-dividend by reference to Scottish rates and thresholds or UK rates and thresholds, depending on whether or not the taxpayer is a Scottish taxpayer.

The Scottish income tax legislation

3.11   The Scottish income tax legislation is not for the faint hearted. SA *1998* provided for SVR. Amendments to *SA 1998* were made by *SA 2012* to introduce SRIT, but these did not take effect until 6 April 2016. Separately, the *WA 2014* made a number of amendments to the *SA 1998* definition of a Scottish taxpayer – some of which took effect on Royal Assent, some of which were to be brought into effect by Treasury order, and some of which only took effect from 6 April 2019 when the new Welsh rates of income tax came into effect.

SA 2016 amended *SA 1998*, extending the income tax powers of the Scottish Parliament and thus introducing SIT, which was implemented with effect from 6 April 2017.

In these circumstances it is not an easy task to interpret the successive provisions of *SA 1998* as they apply on particular dates.

Consequential implications of Scottish income tax

3.12   *SA 2016* and the implementation of SIT gave rise to a number of consequential amendments throughout the income tax regime. For example, references in *ITA 2007, s 13,* to income of a Scottish taxpayer that would otherwise be charged at the dividend ordinary, dividend upper or dividend additional rate are to be read as references to income that would be charged at that rate if the taxpayer in question was not a Scottish taxpayer.

HMRC's Technical Note of 30 November 2016 (see tinyurl.com/j9rq5e3) confirmed that the policies set out in earlier Technical Notes of May 2012 and December 2014 regarding SRIT (see **3.2**) remain unchanged for the devolution of the new income tax powers under *SA 2016*. Therefore, virtually all aspects of income tax interact with SIT in the same way as they interacted with the pre-existing SRIT.

From 6 April 2017 there are no UK-wide higher rate or additional rate income tax thresholds. *ITA 2007 ss 11A, 13,* was amended by *SA 2016, s 14,* so that savings and dividend income of a Scottish taxpayer are subject to income tax as though the individual was not a Scottish taxpayer. This ensures that income tax on savings and dividend income is levied on all UK taxpayers on a uniform basis. The tax thresholds which apply in the rest of the UK are used to determine the personal savings allowance (see *ITA 2007, s 12B,* **1.21**).

Likewise, *TCGA 1992, s 4,* was amended so that for capital gains tax purposes a Scottish taxpayer is treated as though chargeable to income tax at the rates and thresholds which would apply to an individual who is not a Scottish taxpayer. This ensures that capital gains tax is unaffected by the SIT rates and thresholds, and that all UK taxpayers are subject to capital gains tax on a uniform basis (see **3.45**).

These deeming provisions mean that in many cases the tax liabilities of a Scottish taxpayer depend on two separate underlying tax calculations each year (see **3.15**). Although these should be prepared automatically by HMRC's online systems, nonetheless it has now become much more difficult for ordinary Scottish taxpayers (especially those without tax advisers) to check to their own satisfaction that they are paying the right amount of tax.

Other complications arise in any tax year in which the SIT rates and/or thresholds differ from those elsewhere in the UK. For example, thresholds for NICs (a matter reserved to the Westminster Government) are generally aligned with thresholds for income tax, but this is no longer the case in Scotland.

The UK Government has recognised that, following implementation of SIT, there may be a need for changes to the operation of:

- Gift Aid (see **3.29**); and

- pension scheme relief at source (see **3.36**).

To allow for these and other changes, *SA 2016* includes powers to make such amendments by secondary legislation.

On 21 March 2018 HMRC published guidance on changes to tax reliefs from 6 April 2018 onwards, following the introduction of the new starter rate and intermediate rate of SIT (see tinyurl.com/y9777lem). This deals with marriage allowance (see **3.26**), Gift Aid (see **3.29**), finance cost relief for residential landlords (**3.32**), pensions relief at source (see **3.36**), and social security pension lump sums (see **3.44**). *The Scottish Rates of Income Tax (Consequential Amendments) Order 2018 (SI 2018/459)* was made on 29 March 2018 to give effect to related changes.

THE NEED FOR AWARENESS OF SCOTTISH INCOME TAX

Focus SIT has potentially far-reaching implications for practitioners anywhere who have clients living wholly or partly in Scotland, and for employers throughout the UK who may employ Scottish taxpayers.

3.13   Practitioners throughout the UK have good reasons to maintain an awareness of SIT. Individuals may be classified by HMRC as Scottish taxpayers or non-Scottish taxpayers, and this may not always be based on accurate data. Individuals who travel extensively, and those with complex affairs and interests both inside and outside Scotland, may be keen to determine in advance whether or not they are likely to be treated as Scottish taxpayers for a particular tax year; they may be looking to their tax agents for advice in determining their status for this purpose.

Employers located anywhere in the UK, employing Scottish taxpayers (sometimes for the first time), must ensure that their payroll arrangements are adequate to allow them to process PAYE correctly for Scottish taxpayers. HMRC have estimated that some 70% of large UK businesses require to do so. In many cases this is addressed by the employers' payroll software suppliers or payroll bureaux and dealt with seamlessly through software, but appropriate preparation may still be required. For example, it might not be immediately obvious to an employer in (say) southern England or Northern Ireland that they must be in a position to process payroll correctly for a Scottish PAYE code.

3.14 *Scottish income tax*

Individuals living wholly or partly in Scotland should also take an interest in SIT. Whether or not an individual is a Scottish taxpayer liable to SIT affects the calculation of the Scottish block grant paid annually by Westminster to Holyrood to fund devolved public services in Scotland. Thus, if any Scottish taxpayer is incorrectly categorised as non-Scottish, the Westminster Government would gain at the expense of the Scottish Government – regardless of the relative income tax rates and thresholds north and south of the border – and the individual might be liable to interest and penalties.

SETTING THE SCOTTISH RATES AND THRESHOLDS

3.14 For SIT purposes, with effect from the tax year 2017/18, the Scottish Parliament may pass a 'Scottish rate resolution' setting a rate designated as the Scottish basic rate and any other rates of income tax to be paid by Scottish taxpayers on their non-savings non-dividend income for a particular tax year. To be effective, such a resolution must be made within 12 months before the start of the tax year to which it applies.

Where a Scottish rate resolution sets more than one rate it must also set thresholds or make other provision to determine which rates apply in relation to a Scottish taxpayer. Scottish rates may be set at a rate from zero to any number of pence or half-pence in the pound, but different rates may not be set for different types of income (*SA 1998, s 80C*).

There are no other restrictions on the income tax rates or thresholds the Scottish Parliament can set, but all other aspects of income tax remain reserved to the UK Parliament, including the imposition of the annual charge to income tax, the level of the personal allowance, the taxation of savings and dividend income, the ability to introduce and amend tax reliefs, and the definition of income.

Although the level of the personal allowance is a reserved matter, the ability of the Scottish Parliament to set a zero-rate band would effectively allow it to increase the personal allowance but not reduce it.

The Scottish rate resolution is debated and passed as part of the parliamentary process leading to the enactment of the annual Scottish Budget and is an important step in determining the funding available to support that Budget. For 2019/20, a Scottish rate resolution was passed on 21 February 2019, setting the rates and thresholds detailed in **3.8**, and the *Budget (Scotland) Act 2019* was passed on 21 February and received Royal Assent on 29 March 2019.

Under the arrangements for SIT the Scottish block grant, paid annually by Westminster to Holyrood to fund devolved services, is reduced by an amount equivalent to income tax on the non-savings non-dividend income of Scottish taxpayers, calculated by reference to the normal UK rates and thresholds. In place of this reduction, an amount equivalent to the revenue actually raised by SIT, at whatever rates and thresholds are set by the Scottish Parliament, flows to the Scottish Government.

In the absence of a competent Scottish rate resolution, there would be no SIT rates or bands for the fiscal year in question and therefore no charge to SIT. The SIT rates and bands for the immediately preceding year would not apply since they are valid for one year only (*SA 1998, s 80C(3)(a)*). Instead, *ITA 2007, s 10*, implies that the non-savings non-dividend income of Scottish taxpayers would be liable to income tax in accordance with the default and savings rates and thresholds which apply in the rest of the UK. Were there any doubt on this point, it is reasonable to assume that the UK Government would intervene and impose such a charge.

INTERACTION OF UK AND SIT RATES AND THRESHOLDS

3.15   Where a Scottish taxpayer has non-savings non-dividend income such as earnings, property income or pensions, income tax on these must be calculated by reference to the SIT rates and thresholds. However, where they have savings income, dividend income and/or capital gains, tax on these must be calculated by reference to the rates and thresholds applicable in the rest of the UK.

Example 3.1—Dual tax computations

In 2019/20 Hamish, a Scottish taxpayer, receives taxable interest of £2,400 and taxable earnings of £49,300.

His income tax liability on earnings must be calculated by reference to SIT rates and thresholds, as follows:

	Non-savings non-dividend income	SIT payable
Earnings	£ 49,300	
Personal allowance	12,500	
	36,800	
Taxed within SIT starter rate band @ 19%	£ 2,049	£ 389.31
Taxed within SIT basic rate band @ 20%	10,395	2,079.00
Taxed within SIT intermediate rate band @ 21%	18,486	3,882.06
Taxed within SIT higher rate band @ 41%	5,870	2,406.70
Total tax on earnings		£ 8,757.07

By contrast, his income tax liability on interest must be calculated by reference to UK rates and thresholds, as follows:

	Savings/dividend income	*UK income tax payable*
Taxable interest	£2,400	
UK basic rate band	£ 37,500	
UK basic rate band already used against earnings (see above)	36,800	
Balance of UK basic rate band	700	
Taxed within UK basic rate band	(500)	£ 0
@ 0% (covered by personal savings allowance)		
Taxed within UK basic rate band @ 20%	200	40.00
Taxed within UK higher rate band @ 40%	1,700	680.00
Total tax on interest		£ 720.00

Note that Hamish's personal savings allowance is only £500 because he has interest received of £2,400 against the balance of his UK basic rate band of only £700.

His total income tax liability for 2019/20 is therefore £8,757.07 + £720.00 = £9,477.07.

This example shows the need for dual computations where a Scottish taxpayer receives non-savings non-dividend income together with savings income. In a similar way, Hamish would have to prepare dual computations if he had non-savings non-dividend income together with dividend income and/or capital gains.

DEFINITION OF A SCOTTISH TAXPAYER

Focus

Only a UK resident individual can be a Scottish taxpayer, and this is determined for each fiscal year ending 5 April, beginning with 2016/17 for SRIT and continuing in 2017/18 and subsequent years for SIT. *Scotland Act 1998* (as amended) contains statutory rules for determining whether or not an individual is a Scottish taxpayer.

3.16　In the majority of cases, a UK resident taxpayer either lives in Scotland and is a Scottish taxpayer, or lives elsewhere in the UK and is not a Scottish taxpayer. However, the situation for some is more complicated.

SA 1998, ss 80D–80F (as amended) set out the steps necessary to determine whether a UK resident individual is a Scottish taxpayer for the purposes of SIT (and, before it, SRIT). HMRC's guidance on determining Scottish taxpayer status is contained in their Scottish Taxpayer Technical Guidance Manual at STTG1000 onwards (see tinyurl.com/ncrpr9u), and their general guidance for taxpayers is at tinyurl.com/oe7twzd.

Whether or not an individual is a Scottish taxpayer is determined for each fiscal year ending 5 April, beginning with 2016/17, and is a matter for self-assessment by the taxpayer. For an individual to be a Scottish taxpayer in a fiscal year, they must be UK resident for tax purposes and the statutory residence test (SRT) applies for this purpose (see **10.2**). Except in the case of certain parliamentarians (see **3.19**), an individual who is not UK tax resident in accordance with the SRT cannot be a Scottish taxpayer (*SA 1998, s 80D(1)(a)*, as amended by *WA 2014, s 11(3)*).

An individual who is UK tax resident for a fiscal year under the SRT may be eligible nonetheless for the 'split year' treatment for limited UK residence purposes during their year of arrival in or departure from the UK (see **10.3**). Where this applies, only the part year for which they are treated as UK resident will be considered in determining whether they are a Scottish taxpayer for that part year.

There is no such split year treatment for determining whether or not a taxpayer who is UK resident throughout a fiscal year is a Scottish taxpayer during part of that year in which they either leave Scotland to live elsewhere in the UK, or arrive from elsewhere in the UK to live in Scotland. Instead, their circumstances for the whole tax year must be considered in determining whether or not they are a Scottish taxpayer for that year.

An individual is a Scottish taxpayer in any tax year in which he or she is UK resident for income tax purposes and meets any of the following conditions (*SA 1998, s 80D(2)–(4)*):

Condition A

He or she has a close connection with Scotland (see **3.17**).

Condition B

He or she:

- does not have a close connection with England, Wales or Northern Ireland (see **3.17**), and

- spends more days of that year in Scotland than in any other part of the UK (see **3.18**).

Condition C

He or she is (see **3.19**):

- a member of Parliament for a constituency in Scotland,
- a member of the European Parliament for Scotland, or
- a member of the Scottish Parliament.

Condition A – the close connection test

3.17   For any tax year, a taxpayer has a close connection with Scotland or another part of the UK if *(SA 1998, ss 80D(2), 80E(2))*:

- in that year, he or she has only one place of residence (see **3.20**) in the UK;
- that place of residence is in that part of the UK; and
- they live at that place for at least part of the year.

For any tax year, a taxpayer has a close connection with a part of the UK if *(SA 1998, s 80E(3)(c)*, as amended by *WA 2014, s 11(7)* subject to commencement of *s 11(7)(a)* with effect from 6 April 2019 by the *Wales Act 2014 (Commencement No 2) Order 2018, SI 2018/892)*:

- in that year, he or she has two or more places of residence in the UK;
- for at least part of the year, their main place of residence (see **3.21**) in the UK is in that part of the UK;
- the times in the year when their main place of residence is in that part of the UK comprise (in aggregate) at least as much of the year as (or, for 2019/20 and subsequent tax years, more of the year than) the times when their main place of residence is in each other part of the UK (considered separately); and
- for at least part of the year, they live at a place of residence in that part of the UK.

Focus

From 6 April 2019, when the new Welsh rates of income tax came into effect, the rules for establishing whether or not an individual is a Scottish taxpayer were subtly changed.

Where a UK resident individual has more than one place of residence and these are in different parts of the UK, it is necessary to determine which of those places of residence is their main place of residence at any particular time. Initially, this would be determined by the taxpayer's self-assessment, but on enquiry it could become a matter of contention between the taxpayer and HMRC. For further details see **3.21**.

The UK comprises England, Scotland, Wales and Northern Ireland, but excludes the Channel Islands and the Isle of Man.

Condition B – the day-counting test

3.18   A taxpayer who is UK resident for the tax year as a result of the number of days they spend in the UK, but has no place of residence (see **3.20**) in the UK, must count the days in the year which they spend in Scotland and those which they spend in any other part of the UK. Equally a taxpayer who has more than one place of residence and cannot otherwise determine which of these is their main place of residence (see **3.21**) must use this day-counting test. Remember that February has 29 days in a leap year, so 2019/20 contains 366 days.

For a fiscal year up to and including 2018/19, if the number of days they spend in Scotland equals or exceeds the number they spend in any other part of the UK (collectively), they are a Scottish taxpayer for the year (*SA 1998, ss 80D(3), 80F(1)*). Note that for this purpose the number of days spent in any other part of the UK is the aggregate of all days spent anywhere in the UK other than in Scotland.

From 6 April 2019 when the new Welsh rates of income tax came into effect, the day-counting test was amended so that days in Scotland are considered against each of the other parts of the UK individually (rather than collectively). If the number of days they spend in Scotland exceeds the number they spend in each of England, Wales and Northern Ireland, they are a Scottish taxpayer for the year (*SA 1998, s 80F(1)*, as amended by *WA 2014, s 11(8)(a)* subject to commencement with effect from 6 April 2019 by *The Wales Act 2014 (Commencement No 2) Order 2018, SI 2018/892*).

A day spent in Scotland or elsewhere counts as such, depending on where the taxpayer is at the end of the day (*SA 1998, s 80F(1)(a)*). Note that the taxpayer is to be treated as not being in the UK at the end of a day if (*SA 1998, s 80F(2)*, as amended by *WA 2014, s 11(8)(b)*):

(a)   on that day, they arrive in the UK as a passenger,

(b)   they depart from the UK on the next day, and

(c)   between arrival and departure, they do not engage in activities which are to a substantial extent unrelated to their passage through the UK.

Note how strictly HMRC interpret 'substantial' for this purpose. In their guidance (see STTG4500) they state that merely taking dinner or breakfast at a hotel, in the normal course of events, would be related to the taxpayer's passage, but enjoying a film at the local cinema, taking part in a work meeting or catching up with friends or work colleagues should be considered substantially unrelated to the individual's passage through the UK.

Condition C – Scottish parliamentarians

3.19   For a fiscal year up to and including 2018/19, an individual is a Scottish taxpayer in any tax year in which they are UK resident for income tax purposes and meet Condition C by being a Scottish parliamentarian, namely (*SA 1998, s 80D(4)*):

- a member of Parliament for a constituency in Scotland (MP),

- a member of the European Parliament for Scotland (MEP), or

- a member of the Scottish Parliament (MSP).

From 6 April 2019 when the new Welsh rates of income tax came into effect, an individual is a Scottish taxpayer in any year in which they are UK resident for income tax purposes and in that tax year (*SA 1998, s 80DA*, as inserted by *WA 2014, s 11(6)* subject to commencement with effect from 6 April 2019 by the *Wales Act 2014 (Commencement No 2) Order 2018, SI 2018/892*):

- the number of days they are a Scottish parliamentarian exceeds the number of days they are a Welsh parliamentarian, or

- the number of days they are a Scottish parliamentarian equals the number of days they are a Welsh parliamentarian and they would be a Scottish taxpayer by virtue of meeting Condition A (**3.17**) or Condition B (**3.18**).

An amendment that was made to *SA 1998, s 80D(1)(b)*, by *WA 2014, s 11(3) (b)*, might be construed as suggesting that an individual cannot be a Scottish taxpayer unless they are UK resident for income tax purposes by reference to the statutory residence test (SRT). However, it is understood that HMRC regard it as extending also to any Scottish constituency MP, even if not resident under the SRT, since they are deemed to be UK resident for income tax and other purposes under *Constitutional Reform and Governance Act 2010 (CRGA 2010), s 41*.

Other MPs and most members of the House of Lords are also deemed to be UK resident under *CRGA 2010, s 41* if not UK resident under the SRT, so it is understood that such an individual, if not UK resident under the SRT, would nonetheless be a Scottish taxpayer if they meet Condition A or Condition B (see **3.17**, **3.18**).

Meaning of 'place of residence'

3.20   The term 'place of residence' is not defined by the legislation so must be given its ordinary meaning. An individual's place of residence is the dwelling in which they habitually live: in other words, their home. HMRC guidance (see STTG3100) states that it should be regarded as having similarities to the concept of 'home' within the statutory residence test. Places of temporary accommodation such as hotels and holiday homes do not count.

Most individuals have only one home. However, even for those with more complicated affairs, identifying as a matter of fact whether a place is their home, where they habitually live, is central to establishing whether it constitutes a place of residence for the purposes of Scottish taxpayer status.

Based on pre-existing case law, when considering whether a location constitutes a place of residence, the following factors should be considered:

• it is possible for an individual to have more than one place of residence;

• the individual must have actually lived in a place for it to constitute a place of residence;

• living in a place only occasionally or for a short period of time does not preclude it from being a place of residence, but a degree of permanence or continuity is required to turn mere occupation into residence;

• ownership by the individual is not required, and rented or work-provided accommodation may be a place of residence; and

• a place of residence need not be a building – a boat, caravan, lorry or any form of transport or mobile home can constitute a place of residence, if that is the individual's home.

The term 'residence' has been considered in many tax cases relating to principal private residence relief for capital gains tax purposes, and in non-tax cases. HMRC's guidance on Scottish taxpayer status (see STTG3100–STTG3300) refers to:

• several tax cases: *Levene v Inland Revenue Commissioners* [1928] AC 217; *Sansom v Peay* (1976) 52 TC 1; *Frost v Feltham* (1981) 55 TC 10; *Moore v Thompson* (1986) 61 TC 15; and *Goodwin v Curtis* (1998) 70 TC 478; and

• a leading non-tax case: *Fox v Stirk, Ricketts v Registration Officer for the City of* Cambridge [1970] 3 All ER 7.

In 2016 the Ministry of Defence issued guidance (reference 2015DIN01-215; see tinyurl.com/ycf7hchj) for service personnel seeking to establish whether or not they are Scottish taxpayers. All types of service-provided accommodation (eg SFA, SLA, SSFA, SSSA) constitute a place of residence. However, for the same purposes, bed spaces occupied onboard Royal Navy vessels whilst at sea and other temporary accommodation occupied during operational deployments will not be viewed by HMRC as a place of residence; for such periods, whether afloat or on operations (including for called-up reservists), the place of residence will continue to be viewed by HMRC as the last 'main place of residence' (see **3.21**) prior to going to sea or being deployed.

For further discussion on the meaning of 'residence' and reference to other relevant case law, see *Capital Gains Tax 2019/20* (Bloomsbury Professional).

Meaning of 'main place of residence'

3.21   Where an individual has two or more places of residence in the UK, it may be necessary to determine which is their main place of residence in order to establish whether or not they are a Scottish taxpayer. This is not necessarily the residence where they spend the majority of their time, although it often will be. A main place of residence is the place of residence with which the individual can be said to have the greatest degree of connection.

Whether a place constitutes a main place of residence is a matter of fact and all of the facts and circumstances of the particular case must be considered to arrive at a conclusion. The following are among the factors that may be taken into account:

- if the individual is married or in a civil partnership or in a long-term relationship, where does the family spend its time;

- if the individual has children, where do they go to school;

- at which residence is the individual registered to vote;

- how is each residence furnished;

- where are the majority of the individual's possessions kept;

- which address is used for correspondence for banks and building societies, credit cards, HMRC and utility bills;

- where is the individual registered with a doctor or dentist;

- at which address is the individual's car registered and insured; and

- which address is the main residence for council tax.

In the case of a couple (whether spouses, civil partners or cohabitants), for income tax purposes they are treated as two separate individuals each of whom (exceptionally) might have a different main residence if the facts support this. This contrasts with the rules for land and buildings transaction tax, where a couple may have only one main residence for the purposes of the 3% additional dwellings supplement that was introduced from 1 April 2016. Note, however, that for the purposes of the corresponding higher rates of stamp duty land tax for additional dwellings, spouses or civil partners may have only one main residence, but cohabitants may each have a different main residence if the evidence supports this.

For the purposes of capital gains tax, spouses or civil partners may have only one main residence, although there is no such restriction for cohabiting couples. There are cases where, on eventual disposal of a property, HMRC need to determine as a question of fact whether the property was the taxpayer's main residence for principal private residence relief. The rules which apply in determining whether a property is a taxpayer's main place of residence for the Scottish rate of income tax appear to be similar. However, the identity of the main residence for the Scottish rate is not influenced in any way by a capital gains tax main residence election made by the taxpayer under *TCGA 1992, s 222(5)(a)* (for further details see *Capital Gains Tax 2019/20* (Bloomsbury Professional)).

Record keeping

3.22   In their guidance (see STTG5000), HMRC state that in determining Scottish taxpayer status they would look for evidence to establish the taxpayer's presence at a particular home and whether or not a home existed, and they suggest that appropriate evidence should be retained. They emphasise that no single piece of evidence will demonstrate the existence of a place or main place of residence, but they will consider the weight and quality of all the evidence because, taken together, a number of factors may be sufficiently strong to establish a place or main place of residence.

They provide the following list of examples of evidence that might be relevant:

- general overheads such as utility bills that may demonstrate that the taxpayer has been present in that home, eg telephone or energy bills which demonstrate usage consistent with living in the property;
- TV/satellite/cable subscriptions;
- local parking permits;
- membership of clubs, eg sports, health or social clubs;
- mobile phone usage and bills pointing to the taxpayer's presence in a country;
- lifestyle purchases pointing to time spent in the property, eg purchases of food, flowers and meals out
- presence of the taxpayer's spouse, partner or children;
- increases in maintenance costs or the frequency of maintenance, eg having the property cleaned more frequently;
- insurance documents relating to the property;
- SORN notification that a vehicle in the UK is 'off road';
- re-directed mail requests or the address to which the taxpayer has personal post sent;
- the address at which the taxpayer's driving licence is registered;
- bank accounts and credit cards linked to the property address, and statements which show payments made to utility companies;
- evidence of local municipal taxes being paid;
- the address used for registration with local medical practitioners; and

- credit card and bank statements which indicate the pattern and place of the taxpayer's day by day expenditure.

Other practical points regarding Scottish taxpayer status

3.23   In most cases, a UK resident taxpayer will be able to determine in advance whether or not they are likely to be a Scottish taxpayer for a particular fiscal year. However, an individual with a peripatetic lifestyle or complex affairs may not be in a position until after the end of the fiscal year to determine whether or not they are UK tax resident and, if so, whether they are a Scottish taxpayer.

In addition to publishing general and technical guidance on Scottish taxpayer status (see **3.16**), HMRC claimed that in or around December 2015 they wrote to all UK taxpayers with a Scottish postcode, giving them an opportunity to say whether or not they were Scottish taxpayers. Subsequently it became apparent that in this initial exercise they had overlooked some 420,000 Scottish-based taxpayers.

The National Audit Office (NAO) later reported that HMRC had rectified initial issues, but has stated that the biggest challenge facing HMRC in relation to SIT is maintaining accurate address records of Scottish taxpayers on an ongoing basis. Around 80,000 people in the UK move into or out of Scotland each year, but neither taxpayers nor employers are legally required to tell HMRC of changes of address. HMRC carried out an online marketing campaign in early 2017, promoting the message that people should inform them if they moved house, but were unable to assess how effective the campaign had been.

HMRC's ability to assure the amount of tax collected for the Scottish Government will be undermined where taxpayers fail to update their address details, and the NAO has urged HMRC to continue to get this key message over to taxpayers.

Whether or not contacted by HMRC, taxpayers (or their agents) should consider the position carefully because HMRC's information or assumptions may be incorrect in some cases. HMRC have also said that they will monitor address changes on an ongoing basis and maintain an up-to-date record of Scottish taxpayers, issuing new PAYE codes where a taxpayer's status appears to have changed from one tax year to another. Where the address of a self-assessment taxpayer has changed, their tax return asks for the date on which they moved to their current address.

Early in 2019 it became apparent that HMRC had erroneously reclassified a number of Scottish taxpayers as non-Scottish taxpayers, and vice versa. The causes of such errors were unknown, and HMRC were inviting tax agents to notify them of any instances that came to their attention.

HMRC changed their procedures because of difficulties in identifying Scottish taxpayers. Until 5 April 2015 they used to update taxpayer addresses from records identified as new starters in the Full Payment Submission (FPS) under real time information (RTI) online filing, but now they update from any addresses shown in the FPS. In spite of this, HMRC regard it as the employee's responsibility to inform them of any change of address affecting their status as a Scottish or non-Scottish taxpayer. Confusion may arise in cases where HMRC overwrite a taxpayer's preferred correspondence address with a different address provided by the employer, and the employee should correct this by phoning HMRC or notifying them online of a change in personal details (see tinyurl.com/oxsbown).

Confusion may also arise where a non-UK resident has some exposure to UK tax and provides HMRC with a Scottish forwarding address. It is thought likely that HMRC would regard such a person as a Scottish taxpayer based on their Scottish address, but this would be incorrect since a non-UK resident cannot be a Scottish taxpayer. Where possible a non-resident should provide HMRC with an overseas address.

Students are liable to income tax on the same basis as any other taxpayer, if they have income in excess of their personal allowance. The legislation contains no special provisions for determining the Scottish residence status of students, and as with any other UK resident taxpayer their main place of residence must be determined in accordance with the facts of each case. Regarding students from overseas, see also **3.28** (non-UK income) and **10.80**.

Only an individual can be a Scottish taxpayer. A personal representative of a deceased Scottish taxpayer is not acting in their capacity as an individual and therefore cannot fall within the definition, so it follows that any income arising during the administration of the estate of a deceased Scottish taxpayer is not subject to SIT but is liable to income tax at the rates which apply in the rest of the UK.

Definition of a Scottish taxpayer: examples

3.24

Example 3.2—Successive main places of residence – the close connection test

Agnes, a UK resident taxpayer, has only one main place of residence in the UK at any time. She has lived for some time at Norham in the north east of England, but then moves house twice during the tax year 2019/20. Her successive places of residence, and the number of days she lives in each as her main place of residence during 2019/20, are as follows:

Main place of residence	Number of days
Norham, England	26
Ladykirk, Scotland (1 mile from Norham)	170
Belfast, Northern Ireland	170

Although Norham and Ladykirk, 1 mile apart, might be described in common parlance as being in the same part of the UK, this is irrelevant for tax purposes. Instead, Agnes has her main places of residence in three different parts of the UK, namely, England, then Scotland and then Northern Ireland.

Agnes is not a Scottish taxpayer in 2019/20 because her main place of residence is not in Scotland for more of the year than it is in any other individual part of the UK, namely, Northern Ireland (*SA 1998, s 80E(3)(c)*, as amended by *WA 2014, s 11(7)(a)* subject to commencement with effect from 6 April 2019 by the *Wales Act 2014 (Commencement No 2) Order 2018, SI 2018/892*). This is based on Condition A (*SA 1998, ss 80D(2), 80E(2)*; see **3.17**). Note that 2020 is a leap year, in which February has 29 days, so 2019/20 contains 366 days.

Different rules applied before 6 April 2019, when the new Welsh rates of income tax came into effect. For example, if the same pattern of main residences as above had applied in 2018/19, Agnes would have been a Scottish taxpayer because her main place of residence was in Scotland for at least as much of the year as it was in any other individual part of the UK, namely, Northern Ireland (*SA 1998, s 80E(3)(c)*, before amendment by *WA 2014*).

Example 3.3-—No place of residence in the UK – the day-counting test

Kenneth is retired and lives outside the UK. He has no place of residence in the UK but, exceptionally, in 2019/20 he spends 183 or more days in the UK. As a result, he meets the first automatic UK test (see **10.2**) under the statutory residence test (SRT), and on that basis he is resident in the UK for tax purposes for the year.

The number of nights which Kenneth spends in each part of the UK during 2019/20 are as follows:

Scotland	100
England	99
Northern Ireland	8
Wales	4

Kenneth is a Scottish taxpayer in 2019/20, because the time he spends in Scotland (100 days) exceeds the time he spends in any other part of the UK, namely, England – looking at each of England, Wales and Northern Ireland (individually) (*SA 1998, s 80F(1)*, as amended by *WA 2014, s 11(8)* subject to commencement of *s 11(8)(a)* with effect from 6 April 2019 by the *Wales Act 2014 (Commencement No 2) Order 2018, SI 2018/892)*. This is based on Condition B *(SA 1998, ss 80D(3), 80F(1)*; see **3.18**).

Different rules applied before 6 April 2019, when the new Welsh rates of income tax came into effect. For example, if the same pattern of UK visits as above had applied in 2018/19, Kenneth would not have been a Scottish taxpayer for 2018/19, because the time he spent in Scotland – ie 100 days – neither equalled nor exceeded the time he spent (collectively) in any other part of the UK – ie 111 days *(SA 1998, ss 80D(3), 80F(1))*.

HMRC's guidance (see STTG3500, STTG3600) contains a number of practical examples illustrating HMRC's views on how the legislation on determining Scottish taxpayer status should be interpreted. However, there is no guarantee that the courts would agree with all the views put forward by HMRC.

INCOME SUBJECT TO SCOTTISH INCOME TAX

Focus

Scottish taxpayers and their advisers need to understand the distinction between savings or dividend income on the one hand and non-savings non-dividend income on the other, and to differentiate between them.

3.25   Savings income and dividend income are defined in *ITA 2007, ss 18, 19*. As a general rule, the Scottish rates and thresholds under SIT (and not the rates and thresholds applying in the rest of the UK) are charged with effect from 6 April 2017 on the following non-savings non-dividend income of Scottish taxpayers:

- state, occupational and personal pensions (including state pension lump sums), and taxable state benefits (**Chapter 5**);

- income from employment (**Chapter 6**);

- income from self-employment (**Chapter 7**);

- rental income (**Chapter 8**);

- certain payments out of bare trusts (**3.39**);

- payments out of discretionary and accumulation trusts (**3.40**);

- income from deceased estates and onshore 'liferent' (interest in possession) trusts (**3.41**);

- income of settlor-interested trusts (**3.43**);

- income from property income distributions (PIDs) from Real Estate Investment Trusts (REITs) and Property Authorised Investment Funds

(PAIFs) and certain types of non-savings annual payments from which UK basic rate tax is deducted at source; and

- other non-savings non-dividend income.

Note that the deduction of basic rate tax made by the REITs, PAIFs and other organisations continue to be made at the UK basic rate (see HMRC Technical Note, 19 December 2014, tinyurl.com/osxmzw2).

SIT does not generally affect the following, to which the UK rates and thresholds continue to apply where applicable:

- dividends and other savings income (**Chapter 4**);
- partnerships at the partnership level (see **7.95**);
- Construction Industry Scheme (CIS) deductions (**7.117–7.134**);
- non-resident landlord scheme deductions (**8.37–8.47**);
- the annual remittance basis charge on non-UK domiciled individuals (**10.57**); and
- payments to foreign entertainers, sportsmen and sportswomen (**10.42**).

SIT does not affect the income tax treatment of the special 'policyholder rate' of corporation tax used by life assurance companies and friendly societies.

In the interests of avoiding additional complexity for taxpayers and/or costs of collection disproportionate to the revenue raised, there may be certain exceptions to the general rule that SIT always applies to the non-savings non-dividend income of a Scottish taxpayer. The Treasury has wide powers to modify *ITA 2007, s 11A* or other provisions to alter the way they apply to Scottish taxpayers (*SA 1998, s 80G(1)–(1A)*).

The fact that SIT applies only to non-savings non-dividend income of Scottish taxpayers arose largely on account of administrative practicalities, because of pre-existing arrangements for tax credits on dividends and the requirement to deduct basic rate income tax at source from certain interest and other annual payments. With a new UK tax regime for dividends having applied since 6 April 2016 and changes to the rules on deduction of income tax at source from savings income, it seems reasonable to expect that in time SIT might be extended to savings and dividend income.

TRANSFERABLE TAX ALLOWANCE FOR COUPLES

3.26   A transferable tax allowance (the 'marriage allowance') was introduced from 2015/16 for certain married couples and civil partnerships.

An individual who meets certain qualifying residence requirements and is not liable to income tax or not liable above a specified rate for a tax year may claim to transfer part of their personal allowance to their spouse or civil partner, provided that the recipient of the transfer is not liable to income tax above that specified rate. The recipient will then receive a tax reduction of the appropriate percentage of the transferable amount (the transferable amount being 10% of the personal allowance; see **1.20**).

In determining for this purpose in 2017/18 whether or not a taxpayer was liable above the specified rate, it was the UK or Scottish basic rate that applied, depending on whether the taxpayer was non-Scottish or Scottish. In 2018/19 and 2019/20 it is the UK basic rate or the Scottish intermediate rate, as applicable (*ITA 2007, ss 55B, 55C*, as amended by the *Scottish Rates of Income Tax (Consequential Amendments) Order 2018 (SI 2018/459), art 6*).

The 'appropriate percentage' is the UK basic rate where the claimant is not a Scottish taxpayer, and the Scottish basic rate where the claimant is a Scottish taxpayer – both these rates being 20% in 2018/19 and 2019/20 (see tinyurl. com/y9777lem). Where the claimant (whether or not UK resident) is not a Scottish taxpayer, the appropriate percentage remains the UK basic rate even where the non-claiming spouse or civil partner is a Scottish taxpayer.

PARTNERSHIP INCOME

3.27   For the purposes of SIT there are no special rules for partnerships, irrespective of whether the partnership is governed by Scots law or the law of any other jurisdiction.

Partners who are individuals are liable to tax on their own shares of partnership trading income, with each partner being deemed to carry on a separate trade for this purpose. Where a partner is a Scottish taxpayer, their share of non-savings non-dividend income from the partnership is subject to SIT in accordance with the general rules for individuals.

NON-UK INCOME

3.28   In many cases, double tax agreements provide relief from UK income tax or from an equivalent foreign tax charge (see **1.62** and **10.70**). For this purpose it should be noted that SIT is not a discrete tax but is part of the UK-wide income tax regime, so income to which the Scottish rates and thresholds are applied is covered by UK double tax agreements. For observations on double tax relief available to students, see **10.80**.

GIFTS TO CHARITIES

Gift Aid

3.29   The income tax benefits of donations to charities under Gift Aid are explained at **1.43**. When a taxpayer donates to charity through Gift Aid, the donation is treated as made net of income tax at the basic rate and the charity is able to claim repayment of that tax from HMRC.

Charities both in Scotland and throughout the rest of the UK would face heavy administrative burdens if they were required to determine whether each individual donor was a Scottish taxpayer or not, in order to decide whether to recover income tax at the Scottish basic rate or the UK basic rate in the event that these rates were to differ. To avoid such complications, charities continue to claim repayments at the UK basic rate regardless of the tax position of the donor.

In 2017/18, donors who were higher or additional rate taxpayers were able to obtain tax relief on their donations through PAYE or claim the tax relief through self-assessment. This relief was the difference between the basic rate of tax and the higher or additional rate of tax on the grossed-up value of their donation to charity, based on the UK rates and thresholds or the SIT rates and thresholds as appropriate, depending on the status of the taxpayer (*ITA 2007, s 414*, as amended by the *Scotland Act 2016 (Income Tax Consequential Amendments) Regulations 2017, SI 2017/468, reg 10*).

In 2018/19 and 2019/20, donors who are non-Scottish higher or additional rate taxpayers, or intermediate, higher or top rate Scottish taxpayers, are still able to obtain tax relief on their donations through PAYE or claim the tax relief through self-assessment. This relief is the difference between the basic rate of tax and the UK higher or additional rate of tax or (where applicable) the Scottish intermediate, higher or top rate of tax, depending on the status of the taxpayer and their respective marginal rate (*ITA 2007, s 414*, as amended by the *Scottish Rates of Income Tax (Consequential Amendments) Order 2018 (SI 2018/459), art 6*; see tinyurl.com/y7777lem).

Example 3.4—Gift Aid – UK higher rate tax relief

A non-Scottish higher rate taxpayer makes a donation of £100 net to a charity in 2019/20, and the charity can claim Gift Aid at the UK basic rate of 20%, making the gross value of the donation £125.

The taxpayer can claim the difference between the UK higher rate of tax at 40% and the basic rate of tax at 20% on the grossed-up value of their donation, so they can claim 20% of £125, ie a total of £25.

If the taxpayer was an additional rate taxpayer, they could claim the difference between the additional rate at 45% and the basic rate at 20% on the grossed-up value of their donation, so they could claim 25% of £125, ie a total of £31.25.

Example 3.5—Gift Aid – Scottish higher rate tax relief

A Scottish higher rate taxpayer makes a donation of £100 net to a charity in 2019/20, and the charity can claim Gift Aid at the UK basic rate of 20%, making the total value of the donation £125 in their hands.

The taxpayer can claim the difference between the Scottish higher rate of tax at 41% and the basic rate at 20% on the grossed-up value of their donation, so they can claim 21% of £125, ie a total of £26.25.

If the Scottish taxpayer was a top rate taxpayer, they could claim the difference between the Scottish top rate at 46% and the basic rate at 20% on the grossed-up value of their donation, so they could claim 26% of £125, ie a total of £32.50.

In 2017/18, where the grossed-up amount of a gift aid donation was deducted in calculating adjusted net income (**1.18**), the grossing up was based on the UK basic rate or Scottish basic rate as appropriate, depending on the status of the taxpayer. By contrast, in 2018/19 and 2019/20 the grossing-up is based on the UK basic rate regardless of the status of the taxpayer.

It remains a fundamental aspect of Gift Aid that the donor must be able to complete a declaration that they have paid sufficient income tax or capital gains tax to enable the charity to recover the tax relief due to it.

Payroll giving scheme

3.30   Tax relief for donations made to charity under the payroll giving scheme is granted at source before an employee's PAYE tax is calculated, and is given at the employee's marginal rate (**1.42**, **6.29**). Where the employee's marginal rate is derived from the UK rates and thresholds, the relief applies at that UK marginal rate. Where the employee's marginal rate is derived from the Scottish rate and thresholds, the relief applies automatically at that Scottish marginal rate.

Gifts of assets to charity

3.31   Individuals who donate certain shares or land to charity are entitled to income tax relief at the basic, higher and additional rates, or at the Scottish basic, intermediate, higher and top rates (as applicable). This relief has to be claimed through self-assessment (see **1.45**), and is based on the appropriate UK or Scottish rates and thresholds depending on the status of the taxpayer.

FINANCE COST RELIEF FOR RESIDENTIAL LANDLORDS

3.32   Restrictions on the deductibility of residential landlords' finance costs are being phased in, and by April 2020 this tax relief will be restricted to 20% for all individuals (see **8.4**). HMRC have confirmed that this 20% rate, based on the UK basic rate of income tax, will apply to landlords across the UK, regardless of whether they are Scottish or non-Scottish taxpayers (see tinyurl. com/y9777lem).

GENERAL RELIEFS FROM INCOME TAX

3.33 Scottish taxpayers, like non-Scottish taxpayers, are able to offset reliefs and deductions from their total income in such a way as to minimise their total tax liability (*ITA 2007, ss 25, 27*), subject to the overall cap on otherwise unlimited income tax reliefs (**7.75, 8.7**). However, as they are subject to differing Scottish and UK rates and thresholds on different components of their income, their ability to minimise their total tax liability may be restricted by the rules requiring non-savings non-dividend income to be taxed first, followed by savings income, then dividend income, and finally chargeable event gains and payments from trustees of settlor-interested settlements (**1.52**).

For a Scottish taxpayer, the provisions for deficiency relief when a life assurance policy, life annuity contract or capital redemption policy comes to an end take account of income charged at the Scottish rates and thresholds in calculating a tax reduction given if a deficiency arises.

PENSION SCHEME CONTRIBUTIONS

> **Focus**
>
> Scottish taxpayers should receive tax relief on their pension contributions by reference to the Scottish rates and thresholds. In some cases, this will not happen automatically and pension providers are having to implement changes to their systems.

Net Pay arrangements

3.34 Where an occupational pension scheme operates a Net Pay arrangement, pension contributions are deductible from pay before the employee's income tax is calculated under PAYE. This means that relief is given automatically, applying the appropriate UK or Scottish rate and thresholds depending on the status of the taxpayer.

Retirement annuity premiums

3.35 When an individual contributes to a retirement annuity contract, they are able to claim tax relief direct from HMRC through the self-assessment process. This means that relief is given automatically, applying the appropriate UK or Scottish rates and thresholds depending on the status of the taxpayer.

Relief at source

3.36 Income tax relief is given at source for pension contributions made by individuals to personal pension schemes and a few employer pension schemes. Before 6 April 2016 the member automatically received tax relief at the UK basic rate of 20%, and the amount paid into the scheme was treated as having had an amount equivalent to basic rate tax deducted. The scheme administrator claimed the basic rate tax back from HMRC and added it to the pension pot, whether or not the member paid tax. If the member was a higher rate taxpayer, they could claim any extra tax relief due through self-assessment or by contacting HMRC. If the member was an additional rate taxpayer, they had to claim the extra relief through self-assessment.

Under SIT, relief at source ought to be given to Scottish taxpayers by reference to the Scottish rates and thresholds. To achieve this, many pension providers need to change their systems to be able to apply and claim the correct rate depending on the Scottish or non-Scottish taxpayer status of each scheme member. In some cases, shortcomings in the quality of pensioner data they hold makes this problematic.

The UK Government agreed to give the pensions industry time to implement necessary changes. Pension providers were expected to be ready by April 2018 to claim relief at source in respect of Scottish taxpayers at the Scottish basic rate, but that was before the Scottish starter rate was announced. Accordingly, in 2018/19 and again in 2019/20, pension scheme administrators may continue claiming relief at source at the UK basic rate for all members, with HMRC identifying Scottish taxpayers and allowing any adjustment necessary through PAYE or self-assessment to ensure that the correct relief is granted at rates above the basic rate.

Where a Scottish taxpayer is liable to SIT at no more than the 19% starter rate, this arrangement will give them tax relief at 20% on their pension contributions. HMRC have confirmed that for 2018/19 and 2019/20 they will not claw this back from the taxpayer or the pension provider.

Where relief has been given at source at the UK basic rate, Scottish taxpayers who pay income tax at a higher Scottish rate than the Scottish basic rate are (on making a claim) entitled to have their Scottish basic rate limit and any other higher Scottish rate limits increased by the amount of the grossed up contribution (*FA 2004, s 192*, as amended by the *Scotland Act 2016 (Income Tax Consequential Amendments) Regulations 2017, SI 2017/468, reg 3* and the *Scottish Rates of Income Tax (Consequential Amendments) Order 2018 (SI 2018/459), art 3*; see tinyurl.com/yan8tvza).

While these arrangements aim to provide appropriate tax relief to Scottish taxpayers at the SIT intermediate, higher and top rates, it is unclear whether (and how) those not within self-assessment will become aware of the need to claim the relief due to them.

Annual allowance or lifetime allowance charges

3.37   In certain circumstances pension scheme members can become liable to pay lifetime allowance charges or annual allowance charges. With the introduction of SIT there was no change to the basis on which Scottish taxpayers are liable to lifetime allowance charges.

The annual allowance charge is levied at current income tax rates. In the case of a Scottish taxpayer, an annual allowance charge is based on the Scottish rates and thresholds (*FA 2004, s 227*, as amended by the *Scotland Act 2016 (Income Tax Consequential Amendments) Regulations 2017, SI 2017/468, art 4*).

In certain circumstances a taxpayer may require a pension scheme administrator to pay an annual allowance charge on their behalf. The maximum amount of the annual charge that can be specified in this way by a Scottish taxpayer must be calculated by reference to Scottish rates and thresholds (*FA 2004, s 237B*, as amended by the *Scotland Act 2016 (Income Tax Consequential Amendments) Regulations 2017, SI 2017/468, art 5*).

INCOME FROM TRUSTS

Introduction

Focus

Trust or estate income arising to or received by an individual beneficiary who is a Scottish taxpayer is potentially chargeable to SIT. However, it is necessary to consider the circumstances in which income is paid out to beneficiaries.

3.38   The introduction of SIT did not trigger any changes in the residence of trusts. Other things being equal, trusts retain their pre-existing (UK or non-UK) residence status, and are taxed at UK rates where appropriate. Trustees and personal representatives are not generally affected by SIT, which applies only to individuals. A body of trustees (on whom liability for tax due on trust income falls) is treated as a 'person' for tax purposes, but it is not an individual so cannot fall within the definition of 'Scottish taxpayer'. Likewise, a personal representative of a deceased individual is not acting in their capacity as an individual so is not treated as a Scottish taxpayer.

Bare trusts

3.39   Income under a bare trust is treated as income of the beneficiary for tax purposes. Where the beneficiary is a Scottish taxpayer, any non-savings non-dividend income of the bare trust is liable to tax based on the Scottish rates and thresholds.

Discretionary and accumulation trusts

3.40   Income from a discretionary or accumulation trust is distributed to beneficiaries at the discretion of the trustees. The trustees of a UK resident trust are charged on their income at the trust tax rate (45% in 2019/20) or dividend trust rate (38.1% in 2019/20). The beneficiary's income from the trust is treated as being received net of tax at the trust tax rate, so they receive a tax credit of 45% regardless of whether they are a Scottish or non-Scottish taxpayer.

Income flowing through such a trust loses its character. Irrespective of whether the income arising to the trust consists of savings or dividend income, or non-savings non-dividend income, all such income paid out to the beneficiary as income is treated in the hands of the beneficiary as non-savings non-dividend income. Income payments from a discretionary or accumulation trust are therefore liable based on the Scottish rates and thresholds when paid to a beneficiary who is a Scottish taxpayer.

The trustees of a non-resident discretionary trust are generally liable to income tax at the trust tax rate on only the UK source income they receive. They are not liable to UK income tax on foreign source income, although they may suffer overseas tax on such income. Discretionary income distributions from a non-UK resident trust are treated as untaxed income of the beneficiary irrespective of whether the trustees have suffered tax on the trust income, and in certain circumstances the beneficiary may claim credit for some of the tax paid by the trustees. Such income should be included by a Scottish taxpayer beneficiary as part of their total income in the normal way, and this is liable to tax based on the Scottish rates and thresholds.

Deceased estates and onshore interest in possession trusts

3.41   Before the trustees of a UK-resident interest in possession (IIP) or 'liferent' trust make a payment to the beneficiary, they must account for income tax at the UK basic rate.

Similarly, a personal representative dealing with the estate of a deceased person and paying income from the residue of the estate to a beneficiary must account for income tax at the UK basic rate.

In either case, the income paid to the beneficiary could include non-savings non-dividend income which has borne tax at the UK basic rate.

Before SRIT was introduced on 6 April 2016, a beneficiary liable only at the basic rate had no need to do anything further – they did not need to submit a tax return merely to report the IIP or residuary estate income, because there was no additional tax to pay (although, exceptionally, some basic rate IIP beneficiaries might have decided to reclaim tax where the trustees had borne expenses out of the income). A beneficiary liable to higher or additional rate tax had further tax to pay under self-assessment.

It was originally proposed that from 6 April 2016 onwards the tax deductions to be made from non-savings non-dividend income by trustees and personal representatives should continue to be made at the UK basic rate (irrespective of whether the beneficiary was a Scottish taxpayer), and that the income should always be taxed at UK rates in the hands of the beneficiary. This was to avoid basic rate taxpayer beneficiaries facing potentially small over- or under-payments of tax if the Scottish basic rate differed from the UK basic rate.

However, when preparing legislation to achieve this, it proved complicated to identify this income separately in the hands of the beneficiary so that a different treatment could be applied to it; in law, such income is grouped with any other income of the same type arising to the beneficiary (eg property income arising to the individual from a trust is not distinct from property income arising to the individual in their own right).

Given the degree of complexity that would have ensued, it was decided instead that the non-savings non-dividend income from IIP trusts and deceased estates should be subject to SRIT at the Scottish rates when arising to Scottish taxpayer beneficiaries (see HMRC Technical Note, 19 December 2014, tinyurl.com/osxmzw2). The same treatment has been adopted under SIT, so such income is liable to tax based on the Scottish rates and thresholds.

ITTOIA 2005, s 669, provides for a reduction in the residuary income of a deceased's estate in certain circumstances. *ITTOIA 2005 2005, s 685A*, provides for a tax credit where a person other than the settlor receives an annual payment from a settlor-interested trust. Both these provisions were amended to take account of SIT (*Scotland Act 2016 (Income Tax Consequential Amendments) Regulations 2017, SI 2017/468, reg 8*).

Offshore interest in possession trusts

3.42   In the case of a non-UK resident interest in possession IIP trust, the trustees are only liable to UK income tax on UK source income and the trust rate does not apply. The trustees are not liable to UK income tax on any foreign income. Note that the beneficiary's right to income under foreign law in respect of IIP trusts can differ from that for UK trusts, so the treatment of the income in the hands of the beneficiary can differ.

Under some foreign jurisdictions, beneficiaries are entitled to their appropriate share of each item of trust income when it arises to the trustees. These are known as 'Baker-type' trusts, after the case of *Archer-Shee v Baker* (11 TC 749; see tinyurl.com/y454g4lb), and the beneficiaries are chargeable on their share of trust income. If the trust income has borne UK tax, it is treated as taxed income of the beneficiaries, and each beneficiary's share is income that has been taxed at whatever rate of tax it has borne. This income is taxed at the beneficiary's appropriate tax rate. If they are a Scottish taxpayer, they are taxed on non-savings non-dividend income from the trust based on the Scottish rates and thresholds.

Under some other foreign law jurisdictions, beneficiaries are entitled only to their appropriate share of the net trust income that remains after the trustees have paid trust expenses. These are known as 'Garland-type' trusts, after the case of *Garland v Archer-Shee* (15 TC 693; see tinyurl.com/y43k2wgk), and the beneficiaries are chargeable on the arising basis by reference to the income receivable by them from the trust, whether or not it was paid out by the trustees. The income is treated as a new source of untaxed foreign non-savings income. If the beneficiary is a Scottish taxpayer, they are taxed on this income based on the Scottish rates and thresholds.

If trustees have already paid UK or foreign tax on the trust income, the beneficiary can claim relief for this tax, subject to certain conditions being met. If the beneficiary is a Scottish taxpayer, such claims can be set against tax charged at the Scottish rates and thresholds.

Settlor-interested trusts

3.43   Settlor-interested trusts are trusts where the settlor or certain of the settlor's family members can benefit from the trust. The trustees are required to pay tax at the rate appropriate for an accumulation or discretionary trust or an IIP trust, depending on the circumstances. The settlor is liable to pay tax at their marginal rate on the trust income, even if it is not all paid out to them, and they will receive a tax credit for the tax paid by the trustees.

Income in the hands of the settlor is charged at their marginal rate – based on the Scottish rates and thresholds if the settlor is a Scottish taxpayer. This also applies if there is an offshore structure and the transferor or beneficiary is assessable to tax under the anti-avoidance provisions on transfers of assets abroad (*ITA 2007, ss 720, 731*).

SOCIAL SECURITY LUMP SUMS

3.44   *FA 2005, s 7*, imposes a charge to income tax where a person becomes entitled to a social security lump sum. In the case of a Scottish taxpayer, the charge is calculated by reference to the Scottish tax rates and thresholds, including the Scottish starter rate where appropriate (*Scotland Act 2016 (Income Tax Consequential Amendments) Regulations 2017, SI 2017/468, reg 9,* and the *Scottish Rates of Income Tax (Consequential Amendments) Order 2018 (SI 2018/459), reg 5*; see tinyurl.com/y9777lem).

IMPACT ON CAPITAL GAINS TAX

3.45   The UK capital gains tax rates still apply to Scottish taxpayers – notwithstanding the introduction of SIT. For 2017/18, 2018/19 and 2019/20, an individual with taxable income and capital gains falling wholly within their UK basic rate income tax band pays capital gains tax at 10% (or 18% on 'carried interest') on the gains included therein, regardless of whether or not they are a Scottish taxpayer. An individual with taxable income and capital gains exceeding their UK basic rate band pays capital gains tax at 20% (or 28% on carried interest) on the gains within that excess, regardless of whether or not they are a Scottish taxpayer (*TCGA 1992, s 4*, as amended by *SA 2016, s 15*). For further details see *Capital Gains Tax 2019/20* (Bloomsbury Professional).

PAYROLL ISSUES FOR EMPLOYERS

Focus

Employers and pension providers throughout the UK are obliged to operate PAYE correctly for any Scottish taxpayers on their payrolls. In most cases, this should happen seamlessly through the correct operation of payroll software.

PAYE

3.46 A Scottish taxpayer employed by any UK employer, or receiving a pension from any UK pension provider, should have the correct amount of income tax deducted under PAYE, taking account of their liability to SIT. The PAYE Regulations (*Income Tax (Pay As You Earn) Regulations 2003, SI 2003/2682*) were amended to take account of changes on the introduction of SIT (*Income Tax (Pay As You Earn) (Amendment) Regulations 2017, SI 2017/414, reg 2*).

In advance of the introduction of SRIT in April 2016, HMRC announced that they would inform all UK employers which of their employees they should treat as Scottish taxpayers. They said that they would do this by issuing employers with a PAYE code with an 'S' prefix for each employee that HMRC considered should be treated as a Scottish taxpayer. Most of these codes should have been issued in February or March 2016 for the fiscal year 2016/17, although the process was much slower than had been expected (see **3.23**).

An 'S' code for 2019/20 determines the rates at which income tax (including SIT) is to be deducted from the income of a Scottish taxpayer under PAYE during the year to 5 April 2020. It does not change the basis on which personal allowances, etc are taken into account in the PAYE coding process.

Where it is considered necessary or expedient to do so, the Treasury may by order provide that, for a temporary period from the beginning of the tax year, a provision made by a Scottish rate resolution or the absence of a particular provision from a Scottish rate resolution does not require any change in the amounts deductible or repayable under PAYE (*SA 1998, s 80G(1B)*).

Every employer and pension provider, regardless of whether they are located in Scotland or elsewhere in the UK, is obliged to operate PAYE correctly for any employee with an 'S' code. In most cases this means ensuring that they have payroll software that can cope with this, or a third-party payroll service that can do so, in order that they comply with the requirements of real time information (RTI) online filing (see **6.17**).

Exceptionally, some employers process payroll manually and are excused from RTI. Exemption is available to practising members of certain religious societies or orders, and those directly employing certain home care workers. Some others are excused in exceptional circumstances – primarily those unable to file online because of disability, age or lack of internet access. Where employers such as these operate manual payrolls, they must still process 'S' codes correctly. HMRC have published tax tables, including Scottish tax tables, so that the correct tax deductions can be made (see tinyurl.com/obvkuoa).

Scottish taxpayers who are paid under PAYE may not have received notice that an 'S' code for them has been issued to their employer. The addition of the 'S' to the code is not a trigger for the issue of a form P2 coding notice to the employee or pensioner. Where no such notices have been issued, HMRC hope that taxpayers will examine their payslips and inform HMRC if an 'S' code has not been used in a case where one should have been used, or if an 'S' code has been applied in error.

Given that many Scottish taxpayers are liable to income tax at rates above those payable by taxpayers south of the border, and that HMRC are hard to contact, it seems likely that few of them will follow this advice where an 'S' code has not been applied. While their failure to correct the position might have limited impact on their income tax liability for 2019/20, it would result in a much more significant loss of funding by the Scottish Government. Furthermore, interest and penalties might be charged.

SIT brings some additional complications for employers. They do not appear to have any responsibility to take action when an employee apparently living in Scotland has no 'S' code, or an employee apparently living elsewhere in the UK has an 'S' code. They may even have employees who are Scottish taxpayers in some tax years but not in others. Employers, including employers outside Scotland, may find that in practice they need to devote resources to explaining 'S' codes to staff or even helping them identify whether or not they are Scottish taxpayers.

There were consultations on how Scottish taxpayers should be made aware of the amount of income tax they have paid at the Scottish rates, and it was agreed between the Scottish Government and HMRC that this would be shown separately in HMRC's online tax calculator, on the annual tax summary provided by HMRC to each taxpayer, and on HMRC's digital personal tax account for each taxpayer.

There is no requirement that the amount of income tax deducted at the Scottish rates should be identified separately on employees' payslips. There had been an expectation that the amount deducted at the Scottish rates should be identified separately on forms P60 (see HMRC Technical Note, 19 December 2014, tinyurl.com/osxmzw2) but, after consultations, a decision was taken by the Scottish Government not to require this. There is also no requirement to identify tax paid at the Scottish rates on forms P45. However, the P60 and P45 must show the employee's tax code, including an 'S' code where applicable.

There is no emergency tax code based on SIT for use when a new employee starts without a form P45. Even if the circumstances suggest that the new employee is a Scottish taxpayer, employers are not permitted to assume that an 'S' code applies. The usual UK emergency tax code must be applied, and employers may have difficulty explaining this to their employees. There have also been no changes to the pre-existing 'week 1' or 'month 1' processes used where a new starter has to be put on the emergency code on a non-cumulative basis.

HMRC publish technical guidance for payroll software developers to use as part of their own testing routines and check their software against HMRC guidance and specifications (see tinyurl.com/y464kdzx).

Childcare vouchers

3.47 Eligibility to tax-free childcare vouchers depends on an employee's income level. Employers have to estimate the employee's relevant earnings for the tax year since the 'exempt amount' of childcare vouchers is based on their relevant earnings.

ITEPA 2003, s 270A provides that, if the estimated relevant earnings amount:

- exceeds the higher rate limit for the tax year, the exempt amount will be £25 for each qualifying week;

- exceeds the basic rate limit but not the higher rate limit, the exempt amount for that tax year will be £28 for each qualifying week; otherwise

- the exempt amount for that tax year will be £55 for each qualifying week.

Eligibility criteria for employer-provided childcare vouchers are not devolved to the Scottish Parliament, and therefore the basic and higher rate limits referred to above are the UK thresholds. Accordingly, the same income limits apply for all employees in the UK who are in receipt of childcare vouchers.

Payroll giving scheme

3.48 Income tax relief for donations made to charity under the payroll giving scheme is granted at source, before an employee's PAYE tax is calculated, and is given at their marginal rate (see **1.42, 6.29**). This means that relief is given automatically, based on the appropriate UK or Scottish rates and thresholds depending on the status of the taxpayer.

PAYE settlement agreements

3.49 A PAYE Settlement Agreement (PSA) is an arrangement between HMRC and an employer to account for income tax and Class 1B NICs liabilities on certain expenses and benefits given to employees in circumstances where it is impracticable to use normal PAYE or benefit reporting mechanisms (see **6.48**).

PAYE settlement agreements must take account of Scottish taxpayers' liabilities to income tax based on the Scottish rates and thresholds, and other taxpayers' liabilities based on the UK rates and thresholds. This may cause administrative inconvenience where a large payroll consists of both Scottish and non-Scottish taxpayers.

Taxed award schemes

3.50 Taxed incentive award schemes involve employers or third-party providers in negotiating with HMRC on the tax to be paid, based on the grossed-up value of the award to recipients (**6.68**). These negotiations must take account of Scottish taxpayers' liabilities to income tax based on the Scottish rates and thresholds, and other taxpayers' liabilities based on the UK rates and thresholds. Again, this may cause significant administrative inconvenience where a large payroll consists of both Scottish and non-Scottish taxpayers.

CONSTRUCTION INDUSTRY SCHEME

3.51 Under the construction industry scheme (CIS), tax is deducted at different rates (currently 30% or 20%) from payments to sub-contractors who have not been granted gross payment status. These deductions (where applicable) are not intended to match the exact amount of tax (and NICs, where applicable) due by a sub-contractor.

Following the introduction of SIT, CIS is still operated in the same way, with uniform deduction rates throughout the UK regardless of whether or not the sub-contractor is a Scottish taxpayer. This avoids imposing extra administrative burdens on contractors, especially where they operate both in Scotland and elsewhere in the UK.

This does not affect the ultimate liability to tax of non-corporate sub-contractors who are Scottish taxpayers. They are subject through self-assessment to income tax based on the Scottish rates and thresholds.

ADMINISTRATION OF SCOTTISH INCOME TAX

HMRC and the Scottish Government

3.52 SIT is administered by HMRC as part of the UK income tax system. A Memorandum of Understanding dated 1 December 2016 between the Scottish Government and HMRC sets out arrangements for setting up and operating SIT (see tinyurl.com/yaq2sr9p).

3.52 *Scottish income tax*

HMRC identify Scottish taxpayers from information on their systems and by interaction with the taxpayers themselves, and use Scottish taxpayer identifiers in their systems. They update these as they become aware of changes of address. Scottish taxpayers within the self-assessment system must declare their Scottish taxpayer status as part of their annual return.

On the introduction of SRIT, HMRC were supposed to have issued Scottish tax codes ('S' codes) for 2016/17 for all Scottish taxpayers within PAYE. HMRC issue revised coding notices as appropriate, either in-year or as part of the annual coding exercise that normally starts around the beginning of each calendar year. Subject to their obligations about taxpayer confidentiality, HMRC may inform appropriate third parties, such as pension providers, whether or not an individual is a Scottish taxpayer.

Before the start of each fiscal year, the Scottish Government tables a Scottish rate motion before the Scottish Parliament in time for the Scottish rate resolution to be passed by 5 April, and such resolutions are a matter of public record. If the Scottish Parliament has not set the Scottish tax rates and thresholds for any particular fiscal year by the end of the previous November, the Scottish Government and HMRC work together to arrive at an assumption to be used as the basis for PAYE coding purposes.

HMRC have stated that they conduct risk analysis, compliance and anti-avoidance activity on Scottish taxpayers in accordance with their normal approach in relation to income tax. Their risk processes may be influenced by changes in the Scottish rates and thresholds, but make no distinction – pound for pound – between UK income tax and SIT. Risk analysis also extends to individuals in relation to their Scottish taxpayer status, and HMRC consider individually the circumstances of all taxpayers with postcodes spanning the Scotland-England border. HMRC also check on employers to ensure that PAYE systems are properly accounting for SIT. HMRC have a 'high net worth unit' in East Kilbride to focus on the affairs of the wealthiest Scottish taxpayers.

In administering SIT, HMRC are allowed to disclose certain information to the Scottish Government in exercise of their function. However, they are prohibited from providing any analysis that identifies individual taxpayers or would allow amounts of tax relating to individual taxpayers to be inferred.

SA 1998, s 80HA (as amended), requires the NAO to report direct to the Scottish Parliament each year on:

- the adequacy of HMRC's rules and procedures for assessing and collecting SIT;

- whether these rules and procedures are being complied with;

- the correctness of the sums accounted for as SIT by HMRC; and

- the accuracy and fairness of amounts reimbursed to HMRC for administering SIT.

The latest such report by the NAO related to 2017/18 and was published on 30 November 2018 (see tinyurl.com/y2a4tms2).

Revenue Scotland and Tax Powers Act 2014 (RSTPA 2014), which was enacted by the Scottish Parliament and received Royal Assent on 24 September 2014, provided for the establishment of Revenue Scotland as a new tax authority responsible for the collection and management of taxes wholly-devolved to the Scottish Parliament. Revenue Scotland was duly established but is not expected to have any role in relation to SIT, which is not a wholly-devolved tax.

Taxpayer compliance

3.53   Since SIT is part of the UK income tax system, all reporting requirements, time limits, penalties, dispute resolution measures and review and appeal procedures that apply for the UK income tax regime apply equally for the purposes of SIT.

Likewise the UK Tax Tribunals continue to sit in Scotland in relation to all UK taxes, which include income tax regardless of whether it relates to SIT rates and thresholds on non-savings non-dividend income or the UK rates applicable to savings and dividend income. By contrast the Scottish Tax Tribunals deal only with the wholly-devolved Scottish taxes; for more information, see *The Management of Taxes in Scotland* (Bloomsbury Professional).

The relevant 'GAAR'

3.54   *RSTPA 2014* introduced a 'general anti-avoidance rule' (GAAR) designed to combat unacceptable avoidance of devolved taxes. This differs in wording from the 'general anti-abuse rule' (GAAR) introduced by *FA 2013* for UK tax purposes. The Scottish Government has claimed that the Scottish GAAR is significantly wider than the corresponding UK GAAR, which is based on a narrower test of 'abuse' rather than 'artificiality', but this has not been tested.

Since SIT is part of the UK income tax system and not a wholly-devolved tax, only the *FA 2013* UK GAAR applies to it. However, it is possible that both GAARs might need to be considered in the case of tax avoidance arrangements involving both UK and devolved taxes – for example, arrangements concerning both SIT and land and buildings transaction tax.

BEHAVIOURAL REPERCUSSIONS OF INCREASING DIVERGENCE

3.55   Minor differences between the income tax rates and thresholds in Scotland and the rest of the UK might have few practical consequences. However, now that Scottish income tax rates and thresholds differ significantly from those elsewhere in the UK, the behavioural consequences ought to be considered – from the perspectives of both individuals and businesses.

If the divergence of rates and thresholds seems likely to continue, particularly for individuals on high incomes who are often relatively mobile, taxpayers might be inclined to move out of Scotland or avoid coming into Scotland in order to avoid the harsher income tax regime which applies there. Others might see the extra tax as an acceptable price for living in Scotland.

Given the historical strength of the financial services sector in London and Edinburgh, there are a significant number of high earners commuting periodically between those two centres. Where such individuals already have a home in each location or decide to arrange their affairs in this way, they may already have scope to move in or out of Scottish taxpayer status at will, depending on the relative rates of tax for each fiscal year.

So long as the SIT rates and thresholds apply only to non-savings non-dividend income, some Scottish taxpayers may be able to reduce their exposure to Scotland's harsher income tax regime by converting earnings to dividend income. Proprietors of owner-managed businesses already have the freedom to switch from paying earnings to distributing profits by way of dividends.

There are other ways in which Scottish taxpayers might seek to reduce their exposure to SIT. Some might simply decide to work fewer hours, to reduce their liabilities at the Scottish higher rate or top rate. Others might choose to increase their pension contributions to achieve a similar outcome.

For 2019/20 the extra tax liabilities on higher earners in Scotland are significant. Arguably they may have been pitched at levels designed not to trigger large scale behavioural avoidance measures such as incorporation or emigration. However, the increases in SIT proposed for 2019/20 and fears of further rises in future may be enough to discourage some individuals from moving to Scotland and may persuade certain businesses to establish or expand their operations outside Scotland.

In some cases, organisations employing Scottish taxpayers and others elsewhere in the UK may face demands from their Scottish employees for tax equalisation payments to compensate them for the higher taxes payable in Scotland. This has already arisen at the Ministry of Defence, which is reportedly compensating service personnel posted to Scotland.

Tax planning to avoid higher tax in Scotland could become more commonplace if SIT rates and thresholds were to diverge increasingly from those elsewhere in the UK. It remains to be seen whether the definition of Scottish taxpayer might be fine-tuned to counteract tax planning by cross-border commuters, and also whether HMRC might seek further powers to challenge the flexibility between earnings and dividends, or whether there would be pressure from Edinburgh to remove such tax planning opportunities by devolving to Holyrood the power to set income tax rates and thresholds on savings and dividend income.

Until now, Scottish taxes have not been well-understood by ordinary Scots, for whom their long-term implications may be far-reaching. Recent changes made to SIT and land and buildings transaction tax are causing increasing numbers of people to perceive Scotland as the most highly-taxed part of the UK. If this had the effect of discouraging employment, productivity or economic growth in Scotland and thereby reducing Scottish Government revenues, it might take a long time to reverse such trends.

Chapter 4

Savings and investments

SIGNPOSTS

- The starting rate for savings income was reduced from 10% to 0% with effect from 6 April 2015. The maximum amount of an individual's income that can qualify for the starting rate is £5,000. If non-savings income exceeds the annual maximum, the starting rate for savings will not apply (see **4.5**).

- The annual maximum subscription limit for Individual Savings Accounts remains at £20,000 for 2019/20 (see **4.25**).

- Help-to-Buy ISAs provide cash incentives for first time buyers saving to buy their first home (see **4.26**).

- For 2019/20, the annual maximum subscription limit for Junior ISAs is £4,368 (see **4.27**).

- It is now possible to transfer a CTF to a Junior ISA. Investments may be made in any combination of qualifying cash or stocks and shares investments (see **4.27**).

- Innovative Finance ISAs were launched on 6 April 2016 (see **4.28**).

- Offshore funds are popular with UK residents not domiciled in the UK because UK tax is usually payable only on income and gains remitted to the UK (see **4.34**).

- The Enterprise Investment Scheme (EIS) offers income tax relief at 30% on the amount invested, up to a maximum of £1 million per year (see **4.39**).

- Venture capital trusts allow individuals to subscribe up to £200,000 in a tax year and obtain tax relief at the rate of 30% on their investment (see **4.54**).

- Under the gifts to the nation scheme, taxpayers may donate pre-eminent objects or collections of objects to the nation and receive a reduction in their UK tax liability based on a percentage of the value of the donated object(s) (see **4.62**).

- A range of tax reliefs has been is to be introduced for qualifying individuals who make qualifying investments in qualifying social enterprises (see **4.63**).

TAXABLE AND EXEMPT INCOME

Introduction

4.1   Certain types of income are exempt from tax, as are certain types of people. This chapter looks at various categories of savings and investments that are either classed as 'tax efficient' or have various tax exemptions attaching to them. Where any tax-efficient investment is being considered, it is always important to weigh up possible future changes to the tax system. In addition, the possibility of investment transactions being treated as trading by HMRC should also be borne in mind, as once a trade has been established, the more beneficial capital gains treatment (eg use of the annual exemption, special reliefs and use of capital losses) does not apply.

This chapter deals mainly with the position of investors resident and domiciled in the UK. It does not consider the position of the British expatriate.

Focus

In May 2018, the Office of Tax Simplification (OTS) published a report to examine the taxation of savings income with the aim of identifying areas that might be simplified. The report, entitled *Savings income: routes to simplification*, looks at income from savings held in cash or in stocks and shares, including:

- interest and dividend income;

- individual savings accounts (ISAs);

- pension withdrawals;

- life insurance bonds; and

- collective investment vehicles such as unit and investment trusts.

The report identifies areas where further work would be beneficial, including:

- a review of the various savings rates and allowances, and the interactions between them, to identify options to streamline the income tax calculation;

- improving guidance on the taxation of savings income and pension withdrawals;

- considering whether trusts and personal representatives should be entitled to the personal savings allowance;

- simplification of ISAs, including a review of the rules on withdrawals from the Lifetime ISA; and

- a review of the rules on partial redemption of life insurance bonds.

The report can be found online at https://www.gov.uk/government/publications/simplifying-the-taxation-of-savings-income.

Income received without deduction of tax – examples

4.2   Until 6 April 2016, most income from investments (typically bank and building society interest) was subject to the tax deduction at source rules and was paid net of tax to the investor (see **4.5**). There were however, several products on the market where interest was either authorised to be paid gross, or they were entirely exempt from income tax (for example, National Savings Bank interest). From April 2016, the tax deduction at source scheme was abolished and all interest is now paid gross. Certain investment income remains tax-free.

Exempt investment income

4.3   Income from certain investments is exempt from tax, including the following:

- income from Individual Savings Accounts (ISAs) and Junior ISAs;

- accumulated interest on National Savings (including index-linked) Certificates;

- interest and terminal bonuses under Save As You Earn (SAYE) schemes;

- interest awarded as part of an award of damages for personal injury or death;

- dividends on ordinary shares in a venture capital trust.

Joint savings and income

4.4   Where savings or investments are held in joint names, each taxpayer is taxable only on their share of the income. Income from savings or investments held jointly by husband and wife, or civil partners, is usually split equally (*ITA 2007, s 836*). Where the savings and investments, and the income from them, are owned in unequal shares, an election can be made for the income to be split on that unequal basis (*ITA 2007, s 837*). The election cannot be backdated. The election does not apply to life insurance policies, life annuities or capital redemption policies. Income consisting of a distribution from a close company is not split equally in this way, but is taxed in accordance with each spouse's, or civil partner's, actual share in the income.

Tax rates

4.5   Special rates of tax apply to dividends and other savings income. Savings income is taxed at the top slice of an individual's income (except for employment termination payments and life policy gains) and dividend income is treated as the top slice of savings income (*ITA 2007, s 1012*).

The starting rate for savings applies to certain savings income. If an individual's non-savings taxable income exceeds the starting rate (£5,000 for 2015/16 onwards), the starting rate band will be unavailable. Until 5 April 2016, banks and building societies automatically deducted tax at a rate of 20% from interest earned. Individuals who were entitled to have any of their savings income taxed at the starting rate for savings rate were able to claim some tax back from HMRC. From 6 April 2016 onwards, interest is paid tax-free. Broadly, the personal savings allowance (PSA) (see **1.21**) means every basic-rate taxpayer can earn £1,000 interest without paying tax on it (for higher rate taxpayers, the PSA is £500). The PSA remains unchanged at £1,000 and £500 respectively for 2018/19 and 2019/20.

From 6 April 2015, the starting rate for savings income was reduced to 0 per cent, and the maximum amount of an individual's income that can qualify for this starting rate increased to £5,000 (*ITA 2007, s 12; FA 2017, s 4*). Prior to 6 April 2015, the starting rate for savings was 10%.

From 2010/11 to 2012/13, there were three rates of tax for dividends (*FA 2009, s 6*):

- dividends otherwise taxable at the 20% basic rate continued to be taxable at the 10% dividend ordinary rate;

- dividends otherwise taxable at the 40% higher rate continued to be taxable at the 32.5% dividend upper rate; and

- dividends otherwise taxable at the 50% additional rate were taxable at a 42.5% dividend additional rate.

For 2013/14, the additional rate of tax was reduced from 50% to 45%. In consequence of this reduction, the dividend rate for 2013/14 was also reduced from 42.5% to 37.5% (*FA 2012, s 1(2)*).

For 2014/15 and 2015/16, the rates were as follows:

- dividend ordinary rate – 10%;

- dividend upper rate – 32.5%; and

- dividend additional rate – 45%.

For 2016/17 onwards, the rates are:

- dividend ordinary rate – for dividends otherwise taxable at the basic rate – 7.5%;

- dividend upper rate – for dividends otherwise taxable at the higher rate – 32.5%; and

- dividend additional rate – for dividends otherwise taxable at the additional rate – 38.1%.

From April 2016 the dividend tax credit has been abolished and replaced with a new £5,000 tax-free dividend allowance (see **1.51**). However, the dividend allowance is reduced to £2,000 from 6 April 2018 (*F(No 2)A 2017, s 8*).

Focus

A new form of simplified taxation of dividends applies from April 2016. The dividend tax credit has been abolished, and replaced with a dividend tax allowance (£5,000 a year for 2015/16 to 2017/18; reduced to £2,000 from 6 April 2018 *(F(No 2)A 2017, s 8)*). The rates of tax on dividend income above the allowance are 7.5% for basic rate taxpayers, 32.5% for higher rate taxpayers and 38.1% for additional rate taxpayers.

While most taxpayers will thereby pay less tax, people with a portfolio valued at around £140,000 and above a year will pay more. This is part of a strategy to reduce the incentive to incorporate businesses and take remuneration in the form of dividends. In effect, this removes the last vestiges of the 'arcane and complex' imputation system from the taxation of dividends.

Interest and other savings income

4.6   Savings income includes interest from banks and building societies, interest distributions from authorised unit trusts, interest on gilts and other securities including corporate bonds, purchased life annuities and discounts *(ITTOIA 2005, ss 369, 422, 547)*.

This income is taxed in the tax year of receipt, with no relief for expenses. Most of the classes of income are charged to income tax under the provisions of *ITTOIA 2005, Pt 4* (Savings and Investment income).

Until 5 April 2016, in most cases, tax at the 20% basic rate was deducted at source from bank and building society interest *(ITA 2007, Pt 15)* and basic rate taxpayers had no further tax to pay. From 6 April 2016, interest is paid tax-free. Broadly, the personal savings allowance (PSA) (see **1.21**) means every basic-rate taxpayer can earn £1,000 interest without paying tax on it (for higher rate taxpayers, the PSA is £500, remaining unchanged in 2019/20), equivalent to the interest on almost £75,000 in some easy-access savings account.

The PSA does not have to be claimed. Individuals who complete a self-assessment return continue to do this as normal. For sole bank account holders, not in self-assessment, HMRC will normally collect tax due via a reduction in the account holder's PAYE tax code. Banks and building societies will give HMRC the information they need to do this. Joint bank account holders, not in self-assessment, will need to contact HMRC to report the saving income of interest, as appropriate (see the HMRC guidance online at https://www.gov.uk/government/publications/personal-savings-allowance-factsheet/personal-savings-allowance#what-you-need-to-do).

Higher and additional rate taxpayers will have additional tax to pay, to the extent that savings income exceeds the basic rate tax limit.

Dividends

4.7   Special rates of income tax apply to dividend income. These rates are known as the dividend ordinary, the dividend upper rate and (since 6 April 2010) the dividend additional rate (*ITA 2007, s 13*).

Dividend income includes (*ITA 2007, s 19*):

- dividends and distributions from UK companies;

- dividends and 'relevant foreign distributions' from non-UK resident companies. A relevant foreign distribution is a distribution (other than a dividend) corresponding to taxable distributions from UK companies;

- stock dividends from UK-resident companies; and

- the release of a loan to a participator in a close company.

Until 5 April 2016, UK dividends (and certain other distributions) paid by companies carried a tax credit of 1/9th of the amount distributed (equal to 10% of the dividend plus the tax credit). An individual shareholder whose income did not exceed the basic rate limit had no further tax to pay on the dividend.

For the years up to and including 2015/16, higher rate 40% taxpayers paid an additional 22.5% (ie 32.5% less the 10% tax credit), equivalent to 25% of the cash amount received.

From 6 April 2010, individuals are liable to income tax at the dividend additional rate on dividend income which would otherwise be chargeable at the additional rate of income tax (*ITA 2007, s 13(2)*). For 2010/11 to 2012/13 inclusive, the dividend additional rate was 42.5% (*ITA 2007, s 8(3)*). From 6 April 2013 to 5 April 2016, the dividend additional rate was 37.5%. The effective rate with the tax credit was, therefore, 30.6%. The tax credit attaching to dividends and distributions from UK companies was set against the tax charged at the dividend additional rate.

The tax credits on dividends cannot be refunded to non-taxpayers.

From 6 April 2016 the dividend ordinary rate (basic rate taxpayers) is 7.5%, the dividend upper rate (higher rate taxpayers) is 32.5%, and the dividend additional rate is 38.1%. From April 2016 the dividend tax credit has been abolished and replaced with a new £5,000 tax-free Dividend Allowance (see **1.51**). The dividend allowance is however reduced to £2,000 from April 2018 (*F(No 2)A 2017, s 8*).

Other savings income

Relevant discounted securities

4.8   These are certain securities where the investor's return consists mainly of a discount or premium payable on redemption rather than interest payable and involves, or may involve, a deep gain. The discount is the difference between issue price and the amount payable on redemption and it is normally taxable at the date of redemption or disposal. The payment has always been made gross without deduction of tax, so the changes from 6 April 2016 regarding the deduction of tax (see **4.6**) are not relevant here. A 'deep gain' arises if the discount or premium is capable of being more than 15% of the redemption price, or if smaller, 0.5% of the redemption price for each year between issue and redemption (eg the discount on a ten-year bond must be at least 5%) (*ITTOIA 2005, ss 427–432*).

In the recent case of *Pike v R & C Commrs* [2014] EWCA Civ 824 the Court of Appeal upheld the decisions of the First-tier Tribunal and Upper Tribunal that a payment of the premium on a redemption of loan stock was interest, and so the loan stock was not a relevant discounted security.

Strips of government securities

4.9   These are relevant discounted securities, but tax is chargeable on the discount each year even if no disposal is made. The discount is the difference between the market value on 5 April at the end of the tax year and the market value on 6 April at the beginning of the tax year.

Losses

4.10   Losses on disposals of relevant discounted securities before 27 March 2003 may be set against taxable income in the same tax year but cannot be carried forward or back. Relief may generally be claimed for losses on strips of government securities from 27 March 2003, including losses on strips of overseas government securities acquired from that date (*ITTOIA 2005, ss 427–460*). From 6 April 2013, a cap applies to certain previously unlimited income tax reliefs that may be deducted from income under *ITA 2007, s 24*. Relief under *ITTOIA 2005, s 446* (strips of government securities: relief for losses) and *s 454(4)* (listed securities held since 26 March 2003: relief for losses: persons other than trustees) are two areas where the new restriction applies. The cap is set at 25% of income or £50,000, whichever is greater (*FA 2013, s 16, Sch 3*).

Accrued income scheme – government stock, loan stock, etc

4.11   Accrued interest securities include interest-bearing marketable securities, such as government loan stock, company loan stock, permanent interest-bearing shares (PIBS) in a building society but not shares in a company, National Savings Certificates or relevant discounted securities (*ITA 2007, Pt 12*).

The scheme does not apply to companies (*ITA 2007, s 618*). Nor does it apply where the nominal value of all accrued income securities held does not exceed £5,000 at any time either in the tax year in which the next interest payment falls or in the previous tax year. For example, if the next interest payment after a purchase or sale falls between 6 April 2017 and 5 April 2018, the relevant years will be 2017/18 and 2016/17. In addition, the scheme does not apply on death.

A charge arises where the securities are purchased without a right to the next payment of interest (ex-dividend) or sold without a right to the next payment of interest (cum-dividend). The amount taxable on an ex-dividend purchase is the interest accrued on a daily basis from the date of purchase to the next interest date, and on a cum-dividend sale, the amount accrued from the last interest date to the date of sale. This is generally the amount by which the purchase price is reduced or the sale price increased.

Similarly, relief is available for cum-dividend purchases for interest accrued from the last interest date to the date of purchase and, for ex-dividend sales, for interest accrued from the date of sale to the next interest date. The relief is deductible from the gross interest receivable.

If the overall result is an amount chargeable to tax, it is taxed as income received at the end of the interest period.

TAX ON INVESTMENTS

Alternative finance arrangements

4.12   Certain alternative finance arrangements have been developed to cater for investors who require access to products that do not involve the receipt or payment of interest (because for example, it is important to them to adhere to *Shari'a* law, which prohibits receipt or payment of interest). For tax purposes, any profit element attributable to the following financial arrangements entered into on or after 6 April 2005 will be taxed as interest on the payer and recipient (although, for financing purposes, the profit element will continue to be treated as a finance return, not interest) (*ITA 2007, Pt 10A*):

(a)   Purchase and resale arrangements – where an asset is bought for onward sale at a profit and all or part of the sale price is deferred. At least one party to the arrangements must be a financial institution; and

(b)   Profit-share return arrangements – where a person deposits money with a financial institution who invests it as they see fit and shares any profit made with the investor.

FA 2007 contained rules governing the taxation of certain types of investment bonds, known as '*sukuk*', which satisfy the *Shari'a* law prohibition on paying or receiving interest. These products replicate the economic effect of debt securities on which interest is payable, and the measure ensures that they are taxed on a par with equivalent conventional securities (*ITA 2007, s 564R*; formerly *FA 2007, s 53*).

Bank and building society accounts

4.13   Income from savings, including interest arising to a UK-resident individual on an account with a UK bank or building society, has historically been paid with tax deducted at the basic rate of tax. Basic rate taxpayers did not have to pay additional tax, but taxpayers liable at the higher (and, from 2010/11, the additional) rate had a further liability arising on the gross interest (*ITA 2007, s 16*). The automatic deduction of 20% income tax by banks and building societies on non-ISA savings ceased from April 2016 in parallel with the introduction of the tax-free personal savings allowance (PSA) (see **1.21**).

For 2008/09 to 2014/15, individuals whose only taxable income was savings income were entitled to have the first slice of income (£2,880 for 2014/15) above the personal allowance taxed at 10%. Any savings income above this annual threshold was taxed at 20%. Since the bank or building society will normally deducted tax at 20% from interest earned, individuals who were entitled to have any of their savings income taxed at the 10% rate could claim a repayment from HMRC.

From 6 April 2015 (ie for 2015/16 onwards), the starting rate for savings income has been reduced to 0%, and the maximum amount of an individual's income that can qualify for this starting rate has been raised to £5,000 (*FA 2014, s 3*).

Interest is taxed on a current-year basis.

A certificate of deposit or time deposit of over £50,000 made for at least seven days will be credited with gross interest. Companies, clubs, etc and foreign residents with UK bank accounts continue to receive interest gross. Deposits with overseas banks, etc and overseas branches of UK banks (including Channel Islands and Isle of Man) continue to have interest paid gross.

Capital gains tax can apply if currency accounts are operated other than for personal expenditure. Every withdrawal is then treated as a disposal for CGT purposes.

Building societies can offer permanent interest-bearing shares (PIBS). PIBS are a kind of hybrid between shares and a deposit. The main characteristics of PIBS are that they are only repayable on the winding up of the society, or with the prior consent of the Building Societies Commission, and that they rank behind the claims of ordinary shareholders and creditors in a winding up. They are treated as interest-bearing securities. Until 5 April 2016, building societies were required to deduct income tax at the basic rate of tax. They fall within the accrued income scheme, and are treated as qualifying corporate bonds and so are exempt from capital gains tax for individuals.

Normally, a bank account in a foreign currency can be opened at a UK bank as well as in a foreign country. The interest is chargeable to UK income tax if received by a UK resident.

If the account is held abroad, interest will be paid according to local rules and taxed on receipt in the UK. If the interest is paid from abroad with a local withholding tax deducted, this can usually be offset against the UK tax liability.

If an exchange gain is made by converting foreign currency to sterling, this is normally chargeable to capital gains tax for individuals resident in the UK. Losses are allowable. CGT does not apply if the currency was acquired to meet personal expenditure outside the UK, or the gain was made by a non-UK domiciled individual on an account held overseas (it is taxed if remitted to the UK, but with no relief for losses). For further commentary on capital gains tax aspects, see the *Capital Gains Tax Annual* (Bloomsbury Professional).

Betting

4.14 Winnings from betting (including pool betting or lotteries or games with prizes) are normally paid free of tax and are not subject either to income tax or capital gains tax. Rights to winnings obtained by participating in any pool betting or lottery or game with prizes are not chargeable assets. For example, a gain or loss realised on the purchase of a share in the winnings of a ticket which has drawn a horse in a sweepstake is outside the scope of the tax.

Where the prize takes the form of an asset, it should be regarded as having been acquired by the 'winner' at its market value at the time of acquisition (*TCGA 1992, s 51(1)*).

Community investment tax relief

4.15 The community investment tax relief provisions (*ITA 2007, ss 333–382*) borrow much from the Enterprise Investment Scheme (EIS) (see **4.16**), with the position of the SME company in that scheme being taken by an accredited Community Development Finance Institution (CDFI). The investment in the CDFI may be in the form of a loan, shares or securities held for a five-year period.

The investor, which may be a company or an individual, can claim tax relief of up to 25% of the amount invested once a tax relief certificate has been issued by the CDFI, but the tax relief must be spread over the five-year term of the investment giving only 5% tax relief per year. The tax relief reduces the investor's tax liability, and is limited by the amount of that liability. If the investor receives any significant value from the CDFI within a six-year period starting one year before the date of the investment, the tax relief is withdrawn.

Tax relief under this scheme must be claimed on an annual basis at the rate of 5% of the 'invested amount' for the tax year (or accounting period for a corporate investor) in which the investment date falls and the four subsequent tax years (or accounting periods). If the investment was by way of a loan, the 'invested amount' will not necessarily be the amount of the loan made available at the beginning of the five-year investment period. The tax relief due under this scheme is a tax reducer rather than an allowance, so it cannot reduce the taxpayer's tax liability below zero.

The investor must receive a tax relief certificate from the CDFI before claiming any tax relief in respect of the investment.

The rules that govern the speed with which CDFIs must lend on the funding they receive were relaxed from April 2013, and investors may now carry forward unused relief.

For shares and securities the invested amount will normally be the amount subscribed for in cash. However, where the investor has received a significant receipt of value (see below) which does not exceed the permitted levels, the invested amount is treated as being reduced by the amount of value received.

Since an investment made as a loan may be drawn down over an 18-month period and repaid in stages (see conditions of investment below), the 'invested amount' for the tax years or accounting periods corresponding to the five-year investment period is determined according to the average balance of the loan in the relevant 12-month investment period as follows:

- nothing repayable in the first two years after investment;
- in the third year, up to 25% of the capital outstanding after two years;
- in the fourth year, up to 50% of the outstanding loan; and
- in the fifth year, up to 75% of the outstanding loan.

Example 4.1—Community investment tax relief

Alfie makes a loan of £100,000 to P Ltd, an accredited CDFI. The loan is repayable at the rate of £10,000 per year commencing at the beginning of Year 3. In Year 5, the loan is increased to £150,000. The tax relief due is calculated as follows:

Year	Average capital balance of loan in the relevant investment period	Tax relief due at 5% of capital balance in the relevant investment period
1	£100,000	£5,000
2	£100,000	£5,000
3	£90,000	£4,500
4	£80,000	£4,000
5	*see below	£5,000

* Relief in Year 5 is the lower of average capital balance for:

- the year that falls in this tax year – £150,000; and
- the six months beginning 18 months after the investment date – £100,000.

Enterprise Investment Scheme (EIS)

4.16   Under the EIS, qualifying individuals can claim tax relief at the 'EIS rate' of tax (30% from 6 April 2011) on new equity capital of up to £1 million from April 2012 per tax year (£500,000 prior to April 2012) (*ITA 2007, s 158; FA 2011, s 42; SI 2011/2459*). EIS shares must be held for a minimum of three years, and are exempt from capital gains tax on profits after the three-year retention period. Capital losses (reduced by EIS relief not withdrawn) can be set against income tax or capital gains tax (*ITA 2007, Pt 5*).

EIS investments can shelter capital gains. Gains on any asset can be deferred by subscribing for qualifying EIS shares and issued in the period within one year before and three years after the disposal. As 20% CGT can be deferred, and 30% income tax relief claimed, a maximum tax relief of 60% may be available. Any deferred gain becomes chargeable on the happening of certain events, eg on disposal of the EIS shares at any time.

The EIS is covered in further detail in **4.39**.

Venture capital trusts

4.17   Various tax reliefs are available to individuals aged 18 or over who invest in shares in venture capital trusts (VCTs). These are quoted companies that invest in qualifying unquoted companies trading wholly or mainly in the UK (*ITA 2007, Pt 6*).

As a tax shelter, the net of tax return from this investment can be excellent. If an investor can sell out merely at par after five years after a tax refund of £30,000 on a £100,000 investment, he has done tolerably well. If, instead, he is selling his shares at a profit rather than at par plus indexation, the net return could be spectacular given that any profit on that disposal is free of CGT. Much is dependent on the investor being able to make his exit easily and at a good price, which makes this a high-risk investment.

VCTs are covered in further detail in **4.54**.

Chattels, collectables, etc

4.18   Investment into antiques, jewellery, stamps, coins, paintings, works of art, etc can create a liability to capital gains tax if there is a gain at the time of sale, which is not covered by the annual CGT personal exemption.

There is, however, a helpful CGT exemption for chattels (currently £6,000) (*TCGA 1992, s 262(2)*), but a corresponding restriction on loss relief.

The obligation and onus of proof of eligibility are on the taxpayer (see, for example, *Neely v Ward (HMIT)* [1993] BTC 110).

If a set is broken down to try to avoid CGT (eg a pair of candlesticks sold individually), HMRC can invoke anti-avoidance rules to treat two or more transactions as one where parties are acting in concert. Tangible moveable property which is a wasting asset (ie one which has a predictable useful life not exceeding 50 years) is outside CGT, provided it is not used for the purposes of a trade.

The above comments cover collecting only if it remains an investment activity. If HMRC successfully maintain that a trade has developed, then profits will be subject to income tax.

Child Trust Fund (CTF)

4.19 All children born between September 2002 and 1 January 2011 will have received government Child Trust Fund (CTF) vouchers worth between £50 and £500 (depending on their date of birth and whether their family met the conditions for being classed as a low-income family) for investment in a CTF account. Government contributions ceased completely from 1 January 2011.

Family and friends may contribute up to £1,200 a year to each CTF account.

For 2019/20, the annual investment subscription limit for child trust funds is £4,368 (*SI 2019/381*) (rising from £3,260 in 2018/19). There will be no tax to pay on the income or gains arising on the monies in the account, provided the person entitled to the fund is a UK resident at the time the fund is paid out.

The Spring Statement 2019 (13 March 2019) announced that the government is to launch a consultation on draft regulations to ensure that maturing CTFs retain their tax-free status.

There are three types of CTF account to choose from:

(1)   savings accounts;

(2)   accounts that invest in shares; and

(3)   stakeholder CTF accounts.

Stakeholder accounts are the Government's preferred way of saving. The following table shows the key differences between the two:

Stakeholder	Non-stakeholder
Must have exposure to shares	Need not be exposed to shares
Some investments are prohibited (see below)	Almost unrestricted investment choice
Maximum provider charge is 1.5% of the account's value per year	No maximum provider charge
Minimum contribution not exceeding £10	Minimum contribution may be more or less than £10
Until 5 April 2017, accounts had to provide a 'lifestyling' facility (see below)	'Lifestyling' is not compulsory

Both types of account have the following features in common:

- only children born on or after 1 September 2002 are eligible;

- all payments are a gift to the child and cannot be reclaimed;

- the money can only be paid out to the child and is locked in until they are 18; and

- tax-efficient growth.

4.20   A stakeholder account must meet certain requirements, in particular:

- the account must include at least some exposure to equities;

- the underlying investments must represent a mixture of assets which is both appropriate and suitable for long-term savings for a child;

- any underlying investments held directly (rather than indirectly – for example, through a collective investment scheme) for the CTF account must not be, or include:

  - investment trust shares or securities;

  - collective investment scheme shares, if these are dual priced;

  - with-profits endowment policies or rights in contracts of insurance whose value is linked to shares in a dual-priced fund;

  - company shares;

  - company securities whose value could fall below 80% of their purchase price;

  - cash in bank or building society deposit or share accounts whose interest rate is more than 1% below the Bank of England base rate; and

  - depositary interests in any of the above;

- historically, it had to be possible, starting no later than the child's 15th birthday, to gradually move the underlying investments into lower risk assets (such as cash and government bonds) to reduce the chance of losses. This is commonly referred to as 'lifestyling'. However, following a period of consultation, from 6 April 2017, the 'lifestyling' requirement has been removed (*SI 2017/185*);

- the minimum payment amount which the CTF account manager will accept must not be more than £10; and

- the total regular charges which can be made by the CTF account manager must not be more than 1.5% a year.

The registered contact, ie the person who opens a CTF account for a child, will be responsible for managing the account for the child. The registered contact, and the child, when he or she has turned 16, can change account or

CTF provider at any time. The account stops being a CTF account on the child's 18th birthday. The young adult then has full access to the money in the account and can use it how he or she thinks best.

Focus

Since April 2015, it has become possible to transfer savings held in CTFs into Junior NISAs (see **4.27**). Prior to this date, Junior NISAs could only be held by minors who do not hold a CTF account.

Whether a child's CTF should be transferred to a Junior ISA greatly depends on whether the child previously paid tax, and whether they will save enough to pay tax on their savings when they are 18. If the child is likely to save more than £20,000 (the current annual ISA limit) in their first 18 years, then it is probably worth considering a Junior ISA, as these convert to full cash ISAs when the child turns 18.

Some financial advisers suggest that if the parent/guardian is not using all of their own annual ISA allowance, then they could set aside some of this to invest for their children. This means that they still benefit from tax-free savings, but the money will still be under parental control. For many there will be plenty of capacity for this, but for those who use all their ISA allowance, plan on investing a sizeable sum for their children, or have a number of children, this may be restrictive.

It is worth noting that just like adults, children are also entitled to an annual personal allowance (£12,500 for 2019/20). Although Junior ISAs (and CTFs) are tax-free, unless the child stands to earn interest of more than £12,500 from other types of investment accounts, he or she should not pay tax on the interest earned in any case. Therefore, for those with modest savings, one of the most important considerations when choosing a savings plan should be the interest rate on offer and potential return on the investment.

Commodities and financial futures

4.21 Transactions in commodities may take the following forms:

- actual purchases and sales of a commodity ('physicals');

- 'futures' contracts, where there is frequently no intention of supplying or taking delivery of the commodity on maturity of the contract; or

- a combination of both.

If an investor buys physicals and makes his own trading decisions, the profit is likely to be taxable as trading income (*TCGA 1992, s 143*). HMRC will consider on the facts in every case whether, in their view, a trade is carried on.

With futures, a contract is made to buy or sell a quantity at a fixed price. Where the contract is to buy, a price rise meanwhile gives a profit as the investor can buy at the fixed price and sell at the higher market price. If the contract is to sell, a price fall also means a profit for the investor. By buying and selling, traders expecting physical delivery of the commodity can hedge against the risk that unsold goods will depreciate due to a fall in the underlying commodity, or that pre-booked forward sales will show a loss if the price rises. Futures also avoid the difficulties of dealing with the commodity itself, such as storage, perishables, insurance, etc. Statement of Practice 3/02 sets out HMRC's views on the tax treatment of transactions in financial futures and options.

4.22 Gains on disposal of unit trusts specialising in commodities are subject to CGT unless the trust is based abroad. This is inevitable as overseas trusts cannot be 'authorised'. Then, unless the trust or fund has 'distributor' status, the profit will be subject to income tax. The unit trust does not pay tax on capital gains.

Gains (or losses) arising in the course of dealing in commodity or financial futures or options, which do not fall to be treated as trading profits or losses, come within CGT. An outstanding obligation under a futures contract is treated as an asset for CGT and the closing out of it constitutes the disposal of it. If money is received it will be fully taxable as gain and if it is paid out it will constitute a loss (ie the actual price of the underlying physicals is ignored and only the 'differences' on the futures contract are taken into account). Exceptionally, if delivery is taken or made, the full price of the physical will be taken into account.

Investors mainly use financial futures and options to hedge potential losses if the markets or currencies move unfavourably, and resulting profits or losses will be of a capital, not a revenue, nature. Similarly, buying and selling options or futures as an incidental and temporary part of a change in investment strategy will probably result in capital gains or losses. Other transactions accepted by HMRC as capital include where a taxpayer sells gilts and futures to protect the value of his gilts holdings; where a currency future is bought before buying an asset denominated in that currency; where index futures are bought (or put options sold) to protect the value of a taxpayer's portfolio from market falls.

However, the tax treatment of transactions in financial futures or options clearly related to an underlying asset will follow the tax treatment of any underlying asset.

A manufacturer's profits or losses through financial futures to hedge the price of his raw materials are treated as part of the profits or losses of the trade.

Enterprise zones

4.23 Businesses investing in plant or machinery in designated enhanced capital allowance (ECA) sites in enterprise zones may be entitled to additional tax relief. Enterprise zones are part of the government's growth agenda designed to encourage economic growth and investment. ECAs in Enterprise Zones were introduced in 2012 for a five-year period to 31 March 2017. This was extended for a further three years to 2020, giving eight years of ECA.

Gilts (British government stock)

4.24   Stocks are issued by the Government as a way of raising funds. For most stock issues, there will be a guaranteed price and date for redemption. Interest is paid during the lifetime of the stock.

'Gilt-edged securities' means the securities specified in *TCGA 1992, Pt 2, Sch 2*.

The interest is subject to income tax and may be linked to inflation.

Gilts are not chargeable assets for capital gains tax – even if sold in the first year of ownership. There is a charge to income tax on holders of certain securities who realise profits on their sale (or gift) or redemption (including conversion into shares or other securities). This replaces tax under the rules for deep discount and deep gain securities and qualifying convertible securities, abolished from 1996/97 when revised tax rules for corporate and government debt were introduced. The securities concerned are, broadly, securities issued at a discount to their redemption value of greater than 0.5% for each year of their projected lives.

The proceeds of transfer or redemption, less acquisition and certain incidental costs, are charged to income tax. Losses may be set against other income (subject to certain restrictions for trusts and tax-exempt bodies). Death is an occasion of charge, as is the transfer of securities from personal representatives to legatees.

Focus

Special rules apply for gilt strips and securities issued at different times under the same prospectus. Shares, unstripped gilts, life assurance and capital redemption policies, and securities linked to the value of assets dealt with under capital gains tax, are specifically excluded from these rules.

Individual savings accounts

4.25   From 6 April 2017, the annual investment limit into an ISA is £20,000 (SI 2017/186) rising from £15,240 in 2016/17. The annual limit remains at £20,000 for 2018/19 and 2019/20.

Until 30 June 2014, up to one-half of the allowance could be saved in cash with one provider. This restriction was removed from 1 July 2014. Transfers are permitted to be made from a stocks and shares account to a cash account (*SI 2014/1450*).

Husbands and wives, and civil partners, each have their own subscription limits. Income and gains are exempt from tax. From April 2015 it is possible to inherit ISAs tax-free.

Focus

Finance Act 2016 provides that the Treasury may provide by regulations that the ISA savings of deceased individuals can continue to benefit from income tax and capital gains tax advantages, where those savings are retained in an ISA (*FA 2016, s 27,* inserting *ITTOIA 2005, s 694A*).

Withdrawals may be made at any time without loss of tax relief; but, once a withdrawal is made, a further deposit cannot be made to make up for it once deposits have already been made up to the allowed limits.

The general conditions for accounts and subscriptions to accounts are laid out in *Individual Savings Account Regulations 1998 (SI 1998/1870), reg 4.*

Example 4.2—Individual savings account

Bill (aged 35) invests £6,000 in an ISA on 1 September 2019. In January 2020, he withdraws £500. In March 2020, he wishes to make a further investment. The maximum further investment he can make is £14,000 (£20,000 – £6,000). The amount withdrawn is not taken into account.

Help-to-buy ISAs

4.26   Help-to-buy ISAs, designed to help first time buyers save a deposit to purchase their first home, were launched on 1 December 2015. Broadly, this type of ISA enables most potential first-time buyers to save up to £200 a month towards their new home and the government will boost their savings by 25%.

Key features of the help-to-buy ISA are as follows:

- new accounts will be available for four years, but once an account is open there is no limit on how long the investor can hold it;
- initial deposits of £1,000 can be made when the account is opened in addition to normal monthly savings;
- there is no minimum monthly deposit, but up to £200 may be saved each month;
- accounts are limited to one per person rather than one per home, so those buying together can both receive a bonus;

- the scheme is only available to individuals who are 16 and over;

- the bonus is available to first time buyers purchasing UK properties;

- the minimum bonus payable is £400 per person, and the maximum is £3,000 per person;

- the bonus will be available on home purchases of up to £450,000 in London and up to £250,000 outside London;

- the bonus will be paid when the investor buys their first home.

The maximum that can be saved in a help-to-buy ISA is £12,000. The government bonus is added to this amount, so total savings towards the property purchase can be up to £15,000. Since accounts are limited to one per person rather than one per home, a couple buying together will be able to save up to £30,000 towards the purchase of their first home. It will take around four and a half years to achieve this level of savings under the scheme.

The bonus can be claimed once savings have reached the minimum amount of £1,600. There are however, certain restrictions under the new scheme, including:

- help-to-buy ISAs cannot be used if the property is to be rented out;

- purchases of overseas property do not qualify under the scheme;

- only one help-to-buy ISA may be held by an individual; and

- investors cannot open a help-to-buy ISA and a normal cash ISA in the same tax year. Anyone planning to open a help-to-buy ISA later this year should not open a new cash ISA in this tax year. It is not permissible to hold both.

Junior ISAs

4.27 Junior ISAs have been available from providers since 1 November 2011 for UK-resident children (under-18s) who do not have a Child Trust Fund (CTF) account (*SI 2011/1780*). Junior ISAs are tax-relieved and have many features in common with existing ISA products. They are available as a cash or 'stocks and shares' product.

Focus

Key features of Junior ISAs can be summarised as follows:

- until April 2015, only children living in the UK, who did not have a CTF account, were eligible for Junior ISAs. From April 2015 it is possible to transfer from a CTF to a Junior ISA;

- other people (such as parents or grandparents) can make contributions into the child's cash account or 'stocks and shares' account on behalf of the child;

- each child can have one cash and one 'stocks and shares' Junior ISA at any one time;

- there is a total annual limit of £4,368 from 6 April 2019 (rising from £4,260 in 2018/19) (*SI 2019/382*);

- Junior ISA accounts will become 'adult' ISAs when the child is 18; and

- Junior ISAs became Junior NISAs with effect from 1 July 2014.

As with CTFs, the following rules apply to Junior ISAs:

- although the account belongs to the child, the child is not able to withdraw money from it until they are 18;

- the child can become responsible for the account when they are 16;

- interest earned on the money held in the account is paid tax-free; and

- a range of banks, building societies, credit unions, friendly societies and stock brokers offer Junior ISA accounts.

Focus

Junior ISAs operate in much the same way as ordinary 'adult' ISAs. The maximum investment limit for 2019/20 is £4,368, so there is a real opportunity for parents and grandparents to make tax-free savings investments on behalf of their children/grandchildren. Until April 2015 it was only possible for children who did not hold CTFs (see **4.19**) to invest in Junior ISAs, which has meant that many young savers were trapped in accounts yielding poor interest rates.

Since April 2015 all children (under-18s) who are UK resident should be able to hold a Junior ISA and transfers from CTF accounts to Junior ISAs are allowed. This change is important as it will allow parents to look for a better return on their investment, pay lower charges and have more choice of products.

Innovative Finance ISAs

4.28   The Innovative Finance ISA was launched in April 2016. This ISA can hold peer-to-peer (P2P) loans, which often pay significantly higher returns than cash accounts. Broadly, P2P lenders act as middlemen by matching people who wish to invest cash with those who want to borrow money. From 6 April 2016, interest and gains from P2P loans will qualify for tax advantages where these loans are made through an Innovative Finance ISA.

Until April 2016 there were two types of ISA – cash ISA and stocks and shares ISA (see **4.25**). The ISA Regulations specified which investments qualified for each of these accounts and P2P loans were not eligible for either type of ISA, other than where they were included within an investment trust or similar product that was eligible to be held within a stocks and shares ISA. The ISA Regulations also set out which financial institutions can offer ISAs, and specify the information that ISA providers must supply to HMRC. These regulations also specify other rules and features of ISA, including those concerning the ownership, transfer and withdrawal of ISA investments. The ISA Regulations have now been amended by secondary legislation to establish a third ISA type – the Innovative Finance ISA. From 6 April 2016 accounts are available to investors aged 18 or over. Along with loan repayments, interest and gains from peer to peer loans will be eligible to be held within this new type of ISA, without being subject to tax.

P2P lending platforms with full regulatory permissions from the Financial Conduct Authority (FCA) will be eligible to offer the Innovative Finance ISA in accordance with the ISA Regulations. Like other ISA providers, these platforms will be required to supply HMRC with certain information about the accounts they provide. Various account requirements set out in the ISA Regulations will be updated or modified to accommodate the Innovative Finance ISA.

As a result of these changes, an ISA investor is now entitled to subscribe new money each year to a maximum of one Innovative Finance ISA, one cash ISA and one stocks and shares ISA. The amount of new money paid into all of the ISAs held by an investor must not exceed the overall ISA subscription limit for the year.

Investment trusts

4.29 The investor buys shares in public companies, usually via a stockbroker. The portfolio of shares is referred to as an investment trust.

Approved (as opposed to unapproved) investment trusts are now exempt from corporation tax on chargeable gains, but the gains must not be distributed to shareholders as dividends.

Unapproved trusts are not exempt from tax on gains and, on a liquidation, a double charge can arise – one in the hands of the trust and another in the hands of shareholders. The trust must pay corporation tax on any unfranked income received.

When the shares are sold, any gain is subject to CGT. There is a scheme to ease the calculation of indexation allowance for those making monthly contributions to these trusts (SP 2/97).

National Savings

4.30 The forms of National Savings are varied. Current products include:

- *National Savings Income Bonds* – The minimum investment is £500 and the maximum is £1 million per person. There is no fixed investment term.

Interest rates are variable, with tiered rates. They give investors a regular monthly income at a competitive (variable) interest rate. The interest is paid gross but is taxable, subject to the personal savings allowance (PSA) tax-free limit from 6 April 2016 (see **1.21**).

- *National Savings Investment Account* – This is a deposit account run through the post office. Minimum investment is £20, maximum £1 million plus accumulated interest. Notice of one month is needed for withdrawals. Interest is variable. The interest is paid gross but is subject to income tax, subject to the personal savings allowance (PSA) tax-free limit from 6 April 2016 (see **1.21**).

- *National Savings Direct Saver Account* – The minimum opening deposit is £1 and the maximum investment is £2 million per person. Interest is paid gross but is taxable, subject to the personal savings allowance (PSA) tax-free limit from 6 April 2016 (see **1.21**).

- *National Savings Premium Bonds* – Premium Bonds cannot really be called an investment. They are a gamble that the interest forgone on the capital will result in a substantial win in a prize draw. The minimum investment is £100 (or £50 if bought monthly on standing order) and the maximum holding is £50,000. From March 2019, the minimum investment limit has been reduced to £25. Winnings are tax-free. The odds against a £1 bond winning in a particular month are currently approximately 24,500:1. There are two top monthly prizes of £1 million each. The size of each month's prize fund is set by allocating the equivalent of one month's interest on the total value of eligible Bonds. The annual rate is currently 1.40% (April 2019). For current rates, see the National Savings and Investments website at www.nsandi.com/savings-premium-bonds.

- *National Savings Children's Bonus Bonds* – Individuals can invest on behalf of children under 16 a minimum of £25, up to a maximum of £3,000 per child per Issue. A bonus is added on the fifth anniversary of purchase, and all returns are totally exempt from UK income tax, even if funded by a parent.

Focus

The 2018 Autumn Budget announced changes to Premium Bonds (PBs), which should help make them more accessible for all. Formerly, the minimum amount of PBs that could be purchased was £100 (or £50 by standing order). This limit has been cut to £25 from March 2019. This applies to both one-off purchases and regular savings.

The 2018 Autumn Budget also announced that the rules on who can purchase PBs will be changed. Currently, only parents and grandparents can buy PBs for children under 16. Although the timescale is yet to be confirmed, it has been announced that in future, it will be permissible for other adults to buy PBs on behalf of children. The person purchasing the bonds for children will have to be over 16, and must nominate one of the child's parents or guardians to look after the bonds until the child turns 16.

The maximum Premium Bond holding will remain at £50,000.

NS&I has also confirmed that it will be launching a new PB app in the new year, which is designed 'to make saving easier'.

Although Premium Bonds are not strictly an 'investment', they can be encashed at any time with the full amount of invested capital being returned – and in the meantime, any returns by way of 'winnings' will be tax-free.

For full details of National Savings schemes, including current interest rates, see the National Savings and Investments website at www.nsandi.com.

Racehorses

4.31   Profits arising from this type of investment will arise from prize money and from the sale of the horse during or after its racing career.

Under current regulations, not more than 12 people may share in a syndicated ownership with each shareholder contributing to the purchase, training, maintenance and running costs.

Shares can be sold to other shareholders (first offer) or to outsiders.

Investment may also be made into syndicated stallions – the income comes from stud fees – but the rules are not as strict as for racehorse syndication. Frequently, there are up to 40 shareholders, and the syndicate is run by a committee.

Stud fees have been held by a court to be receipt of annual income chargeable under former Schedule D, Case VI, but not trading receipts under former Case I (*Benson v Counsell* (1942) 24 TC 178; *Lord Glanely v Wightman* (1933) 17 TC 634).

Stallions acquired for stud purposes are ineligible for capital allowances. In *Earl of Derby v Aylmer* (1915) 6 TC 665 the taxpayer owned two stallions at stud and was assessed in respect of profits derived from stud fees. He contended that he was entitled to a deduction under the then legislation to take account of the diminished value of the stallions year by year. Both the Special Commissioners and Rowlatt J rejected the taxpayer's claim.

No charge to capital gains tax will arise on the sale of a horse because of the exemption which covers tangible moveable property and a wasting asset (with a predictable life not exceeding 50 years). This is so provided it has not been used for business purposes – so it may be unwise to seek a deduction for costs of purchasing and keeping horses (eg for advertising and promotional purposes) if they are likely to make a fortune either racing or at stud.

Shares

4.32   Successful investors on the stock market will benefit from the capital growth of the share, dividends paid (usually half-yearly by quoted companies) and perhaps 'perks' (eg a discount on company goods).

Due to the risk of investment in unquoted companies, various tax reliefs are available (eg Enterprise Investment Scheme, venture capital trusts: see **4.54**).

Investors receive cash dividends to which a tax credit has formerly attached. From 6 April 2016, the tax credit attaching to dividends was abolished (see **4.7**). From April 2016, the dividend allowance applies, which means that individuals will not have to pay tax on dividend income they receive up to a pre-set annual threshold. The annual threshold was £5,000 for 2016/17 and 2017/18, but has been reduced to £2,000 for 2018/19 onwards.

Capital gains tax is chargeable on the capital growth of the shares on disposal. For 2016/17 onwards, a higher rate of capital gains tax of 20% applies to gains (or part of gains) exceeding the basic rate of income tax. Gains within the basic rate tax band are charged at the lower rate of 10%. Capital losses on a disposal can be set off against gains realised in the same year – if there is an excess of losses, this can be carried forward for use in future years against future gains. For further commentary on capital gains tax aspects, see *Capital Gains Tax* (Bloomsbury Professional).

Unit trusts

4.33   Under this type of investment, the investor (the unit holder) purchases units in a unit trust. The trust would normally consist of a portfolio of shares specialising in certain markets (eg Japan, world technology, American smaller companies, etc). This can spread the risk for the investor, but reduces the opportunity for speculative gain. Some trusts offer a regular income, others capital growth, and some a mixture of both. The units are easily marketable in normal conditions and prices for buying and selling (the spread) are quoted daily. Several unit trust groups also offer savings plans.

Authorised unit trusts are exempt from capital gains tax on gains made within the trust.

Depending on the type of income some unit trusts may prefer to be unauthorised and taxed as trusts (authorised trusts are severely restricted in their types of investment and cannot currently invest, for example, in commodity futures or property).

Until 5 April 2016, dividends paid to unit holders carried a tax credit. Any gain made by the investor on disposal of the units is subject to capital gains tax at the appropriate rate. For further commentary on capital gains tax aspects, see *Capital Gains Tax Annual* (Bloomsbury Professional).

FOREIGN SAVINGS AND INVESTMENTS

Offshore funds

4.34　　Offshore funds are popular with UK residents not domiciled in the UK because UK tax is usually payable only on income and gains remitted to the UK (*ITTOIA 2005, s 832*).

Investors in funds resident overseas have the opportunity to benefit from the advantages of the tax havens where most of them are based. Such funds take the form of open-ended investment companies, or unit trusts. The return can be high, but dangers may lurk in exchange rates when funds are converted into sterling and in the fact that the traditional City safeguards for investors may not apply. On the other hand, currency movement may well be in the investor's favour.

A fund can apply to HMRC for 'distributor' status, the main test being that it distributes 85% of its income which would have been subject to corporation tax if resident in the UK. If the status is awarded, investors will still be subject to capital gains tax on the profit on disposal of the shares or units, but without indexation relief if the fund is 90% or more invested in CGT-exempt assets.

Gains made by investors in non-distributor funds (sometimes called roll-up funds because the income is rolled up into the settlement) are subject to income tax. However, if the interest was acquired before 1984, the part of any gain accruing before 1984 attracts CGT.

Dividends from the funds are paid gross to investors, with income tax payable at basic, higher and, from 6 April 2010, additional rates if applicable.

The funds with non-distributor status may still have strong appeal for some taxpayers.

The advantages are:

- The effective rate of return is much higher because no tax liability arises until the investor sells shares or units in the fund. The tax charge can be reduced to a minimum by selling the shares in a low tax year (perhaps after retirement) or may be eliminated completely by selling during a year of non-residence when the investor is outside the UK tax net altogether.

- Another attractive way to use the funds would be for parents to invest money for their minor children. Income arising during their minority would normally be charged as that of the parent(s). If the money were invested in a sterling fund there would be no taxable income until the shares were sold – and this could be done once the children reached 18, when the income would be treated as their own and not the parents.

- The method of actually taxing an offshore fund also has substantial advantages. The computation of the gain chargeable as income broadly follows the capital gains tax rules which allow a proportionate part of the original purchase price to be deducted as acquisition cost (which may be an advantage over the 5% per annum tax-free 'withdrawal' facility for an insurance bond). One tax disadvantage is that there is a charge to income tax on death.

Foreign securities

4.35 If equities are bought in foreign countries, it will be important to establish the residence of the company, which will decide if the dividends received are franked or unfranked for the UK corporate investor.

It is usual for shares on an overseas company register to be in the name of a nominee – 'marking name' – and this is arranged by a bank or broker. UK stamp duty is not charged when foreign shares are purchased, but other costs (including an equivalent duty in the foreign country) can more than equal this saving.

Dividends and interest may also be received subject to a withholding tax. This cannot be reclaimed from HMRC by non-taxpayers.

Unless the income is assessed on a remittance arising basis, foreign dividends should be regarded as arising when the dividend is payable by the foreign company and not the date of receipt in the UK (*ITTOIA 2005, s 832*). These dates can sometimes straddle the end of a tax year and may need careful attention from the point of view of cash flow.

The UK capital gains tax rules apply to disposals and other capital transactions in overseas shares. The UK gain is calculated by converting both the acquisition costs and disposal proceeds to sterling – not by converting the gain in foreign currency to sterling.

LIFE ASSURANCE GAINS

Gains deemed as income

4.36 Gains may arise on the following policies:

- UK life assurance policies;
- life annuities; or
- capital redemption policies.

Not all policies give rise to chargeable event gains.

Under the provisions of *ITTOIA 2005, s 461*, chargeable event gains are deemed to be income for tax purposes.

Taxable person

4.37   Any such gains of a bare or simple trust are treated as income of the beneficiary.

If the rights of a policy are held in trust, any gain resulting from a chargeable event is usually chargeable on the settlor. If it is the death of the settlor that gives rise to the gain, it is attributable to him. However, the gain is chargeable on the trustee if any of the following apply:

- the individual who created the trust is not resident in the UK at the time of the chargeable event;

- the individual who created the trust is dead at the time of the chargeable event;

- a company or other entity created the trust, and is not resident in the UK at the time of the chargeable event;

- a company or other entity created the trust, and has come to an end at the time of the chargeable event.

Gains that are deemed to be trustees' income are always chargeable at the trust rate.

> **Focus**
>
> HMRC helpsheet 'HS320: Gains on UK life insurance policies' contains more information.

TAX-EFFICIENT INVESTMENTS

Introduction

4.38   What qualifies as a tax-efficient investment depends on the circumstances of a particular individual. An exemption from capital gains tax will be of no benefit to an individual who can confidently expect to have the full annual exempt amount available each year. Similarly, tax relief will not be important to non-taxpayers. Obviously, it would be impossible to cover every aspect in a work of this size, but the more popular vehicles offering various tax breaks are covered in the following paragraphs.

Enterprise Investment Scheme

4.39 The Enterprise Investment Scheme (EIS) aims to promote the raising of equity finance for new and small companies.

The EIS offers a series of potential reliefs for the investor:

- Income tax relief at 30% from 6 April 2011 of the amount invested is available up to a maximum of £1 million per year (from April 2012, see **4.40**), as long as the investor has less than 30% of the shares of the company and certain other conditions are satisfied (*ITA 2007, s 158*; *FA 2012, s 39* and *Sch 7, para 3*; *FA 2011, s 42*; *SI 2011/2459*; *SI 2008/3165*). It is not possible to carry forward unused relief, but there is a limited carry-back facility.

- A gain made by the investor prior to investment can be deferred by rolling into the EIS shares for which the investor subscribes. This relief is available even if the investor has more than 30% of the company share capital. It is even possible for the investor to create the company himself.

- Any gain made on the ultimate disposal of EIS shares is exempt from CGT, if income tax relief was given on the subscription for these shares (ie the investor owned less than 30%, subscribed within the current investment level, and other relevant conditions were satisfied).

- Even though a gain is exempt, the loss arising on the ultimate disposal of shares can be relieved against any capital gains and an election can be made when the loss is suffered to relieve the loss against income.

- If EIS shares that did not qualify for income tax relief are sold, the gain triggered can be rolled into a second EIS investment.

An individual is eligible for EIS income tax relief for cash subscribed for new shares issued to him or her. The shares must be issued in order to raise money for a business activity that qualifies under the EIS scheme (most trades qualify). The company must use the money raised for the trading activity and all money raised by the issue of shares must be wholly employed in a qualifying activity within two years of the EIS share issue, or (if later) within two years of the qualifying activity commencing (*ITA 2007, s 175*).

The subscription must be entirely for cash. In *Thompson v Hart* [2000] STC 381, EIS relief was denied as the shares were issued in exchange for the transfer of properties.

4.40 Relief is available to an individual up to a maximum of £1 million in a fiscal year (*ITA 2007, s 158*). The investment limits are applied separately to spouses and civil partners and so, for 2017/18, can provide a reduction of tax for a married couple of up to £600,000 (2 × £1,000,000 × 30%). The investment can be direct into a company, or can be through an investment fund approved for EIS purposes.

Focus

Finance Act 2018 enacts a series of changes, which affect EIS investments from 6 April 2018 (*FA 2018, ss 14–16,* and *Sch 4*). The changes are summarised as follows:

- The annual limit for individuals investing in knowledge-intensive companies under the EIS is increased to £2 million, in relation to shares issued on or after 6 April 2018, provided that anything above £1 million is invested in knowledge-intensive companies.

- The annual EIS and VCT limit on the amount of tax-advantaged investments a knowledge-intensive company may receive rises to £10 million in relation to new qualifying investments made on or after 6 April 2018.

- Greater flexibility is to be provided with respect to the rules for determining whether a knowledge-intensive company meets the permitted maximum age requirement.

Investor connected with the company

4.41 For EIS income tax relief (but not for the CGT deferral relief), the individual must not be connected with the company into which the individual makes the investment at any time during a period that begins two years before the issue of shares and normally ends three years after that issue (*ITA 2007, s 163*). Where the company has raised funds through the subscription to carry on a trade which has not yet commenced, the three-year period during which the investor must not be connected with the company starts with the date of commencement of the company's trade.

An individual is connected with a company, for the purpose of EIS relief, in any of the following circumstances:

- the individual controls the company;

- the individual owns shares that give him or her more than 30% of the votes;

- the individual's shares plus his loan capital exceed 30% of the company's share capital (measured at par value) plus its loan capital;

- the individual trades in partnership with the company;

- the individual is an employee of the company;

- the individual is a director of the company, unless exempted by the rule below; or

- the individual subscribes for shares as part of an arrangement under which another individual subscribes for shares in another company to which the first individual is connected.

4.42   As stated at **4.41**, a director is connected with a company only if he, or an associate, or a partnership of which he or an associate is a member, receives, or is entitled to receive, any payment from the issuing company or a 'related person' during the period beginning two years prior to the share issue and ending (generally) three years after the issue (*ITA 2007, s 168(1)*). A 'related person' is (*ITA 2007, s 168(4), (5)*):

(1)   any company of which the individual, or an associate, is a director; and

(2)   which is:

   (a)   a 51% subsidiary of the issuing company;

   (b)   a partner of the issuing company;

   (c)   a partner of a 51% subsidiary of the issuing company; or

   (d)   a person who is connected with any of the above companies.

Certain payments are, however, ignored when deciding whether a director is connected. Broadly, payments which do not represent a return of value to the investor are ignored. This includes (*ITA 2007, s 168(2), (3)*):

- reimbursement of expenses wholly, exclusively and necessarily incurred in performance of duties of the director;

- a reasonable return by way of interest on funds lent to the company;

- a 'reasonable' dividend on the investment of the company;

- a market rent on property let to the company; and

- 'reasonable' charges for services provided to the company.

These exclusions are applied from the period of subscription onwards. The EIS income tax relief is not available where the individual has served as a director of the company before the share subscription; the individual is then treated as connected with the company. Where the target company has taken over a trade from another company, a directorship in the predecessor company would also deny relief.

The rule prohibiting 'paid' directors from being eligible for EIS income tax relief is relaxed if an individual is connected with a company only because either he, or an associate, is a director and receiving, or entitled to receive, remuneration, benefits or facilities in that capacity. Such investors are often referred to as 'business angels'. In such circumstances relief will be available provided the following additional conditions are satisfied (*ITA 2007, s 169(1)*):

(1)   the director's remuneration, etc is reasonable in respect of the services rendered to the issuing company, or related person (*ITA 2007, s 169(2)*);

(2)   his relevant shares were issued to him at a time when he had never been either connected with the company or involved in the carrying on of any part of the trade, etc carried on by the issuing company or its subsidiaries (*ITA 2007, s 169(3)*); and

(3)   if the relevant shares were not issued at such a time, they were issued before the termination date for the latest issue of shares which did meet that condition (*ITA 2007, s 169(4)*). This allows for relief on subsequent subscriptions within three years of an initial subscription made at a time when the investor was not connected.

Focus

A requirement for the individual to be independent from the company and hold no shares (other than 'risk finance' or certain subscriber shares) in the company at the time the EIS investment is made applies from 18 November 2015 (*ITA 2007, s 164A*).

If the individual does hold any other shares in the issuing company or any company that is a qualifying subsidiary of the issuing company at the date of the share issue, those shares must either be:

●   a risk finance investment; or

●   subscriber shares that were either issued to the individual and have continued to be held by him or were acquired by him at a time when the company had not issued any shares other than subscriber shares and had not begun to carry on or make preparations for carrying on any trade or business.

Shares are a 'risk finance investment' if they are issued to the individual and the company provides a compliance statement under any of the EIS, Seed Enterprise Investment Scheme (SEIS), or Social Investment Tax Relief (SITR) provisions.

Capital gains tax exemption

4.43   Where shares are issued on which income tax relief has been given, any gain made on the ultimate disposal of those shares by the individual investor is exempt from CGT. In order for this CGT exemption to apply, income tax relief must have been given and not withdrawn, otherwise the exemption is lost. Income tax relief can be withdrawn in two alternative scenarios:

(1)   There can be a clawback of relief by a failure of the conditions that are necessary for the three years following the subscription. This could be a result of an action by the company or by the individual becoming connected with the company, such as taking paid employment or directorship.

(2) The individual's liability to income tax for the year's subscription could be reduced to £nil. This could arise through relief given for trading losses under *ITA 2007, s 72*. Hence, any decision as to the way in which trading losses are to be relieved must take account of the possibility of the withdrawal of EIS relief and its effect on a potential exposure to CGT at a later date.

Capital gains tax deferral relief

4.44 Unlike EIS income tax relief, CGT deferral relief, when there is investment in shares that fulfil the EIS requirements, can be claimed by trustees as well as individuals.

Where a capital gain arises to an individual or to trustees, deferral relief can be claimed if the taxpayer subscribes for shares that fulfil the EIS requirements at any time during a period that begins 12 months before the disposal that caused the gain and ends 36 months after the date of disposal. Deferral relief operates so that the gain that would have been charged is frozen and brought into charge when there is ultimately a disposal of the 'EIS shares'. If the conditions for EIS relief are contravened at any time during the three years following the investment, such as by value being received from the company, the deferred gain is treated as arising on the date that the contravention occurs. It should be noted that the mechanism for the operation of deferral relief is not reduction in the base cost of the shares acquired by subscription; instead, the disposal of those shares causes the original gain to be brought into charge, as well as any gain on the shares themselves.

Unlike the provisions for EIS income tax relief, CGT deferral relief is available to individuals who are 'connected with the company'. This means that a company can be set up to carry on a new trade with the entire shareholding spread around members of the family, whilst still allowing a gain that has accrued to be deferred by reference to the investment made in the company. In contrast to the position for income tax, deferral relief for investment into EIS eligible shares requires the investor to be either resident or ordinarily resident in the UK and not to be exempt from CGT by virtue of a double tax agreement. There is no maximum to the size of the gain that can be deferred. Virtually any gain that arises on an individual or on trustees can be deferred (other than a gain imputed by *TCGA 1992, s 86* or *87* on a settlor or a beneficiary of a non-resident settlement or the gain arising under *TCGA 1992, s 161* where a capital asset is appropriated for trading stock).

A taxpayer obtains deferral relief by making a claim. The taxpayer is free to claim part of a gain. This means that a gain equal to the annual exempt amount can be left in charge, without any actual tax cost. If the investor has capital losses available, a larger part of the gain can be left in charge to be put against the losses. The use of deferral relief is, thereby, very flexible and it can be a valuable planning device.

Criteria for the company

4.45   The restrictions on the relationship between the individual investor and the company apply for a period of three years only. This starts on the date of subscription, unless the company is then not carrying on the trade for which the funds are being raised, in which case the period starts on the later date that trade commences.

The company issuing the shares must, throughout the three-year period, be an unquoted company which exists 'wholly for the purpose of carrying on one or more qualifying trades' (subject to a *de minimis* exemption), or is the parent company of a trading group (*ITA 2007, Pt 5, Ch 4*).

Qualifying trades are all trades other than (*ITA 2007, ss 192–199*):

(a)   dealing in land, in commodities or futures or in shares, securities or other financial instruments;

(b)   dealing in goods otherwise than in the ordinary course of wholesale or retail distribution (*s 193*);

(c)   banking, insurance and other financial activities;

(d)   leasing including ships (*s 194*);

(e)   receiving royalties or licence fees (*s 195*);

(f)   providing legal or accountancy services;

(g)   property development (*s 196*);

(h)   farming and market gardening;

(i)   forestry and timber production;

(j)   shipbuilding (*s 196A*);

(k)   coal production (*s 196B*);

(l)   steel production (*s 196C*);

(m)   operating or managing hotels or comparable establishments (*s 197*);

(n)   operating or managing nursing or residential care homes (*s 198*);

(o)   the subsidised generation or export of electricity (*s 198A*);

(p)   the subsidised generation of heat or subsidised production of gas or fuel (*s 198B*);

(q)   (for shares issued on or after 30 November 2015) making reserve electricity generating capacity available (or using it to generate electricity); and

(r)   provision of services or facilities for another business (*s 199*).

Note that for shares issued on or after 6 April 2016, items (o) to (q) above have been amended to exclude (*FA 2016, s 28*):

- generating or exporting electricity or making electricity generating capacity available;

- generating heat;

- generating any form of energy not within the two categories above; and

- producing gas or fuel.

Permanent establishment

4.46 In respect of shares issued on or after 6 April 2011, the issuing company must have a 'permanent establishment' in the UK throughout the period of the share issue (*ITA 2007, s 180A*). A company has a permanent establishment in the UK if (and only if) either (*ITA 2007, s 191A(2)*):

- it carries on business here wholly or partly through a 'fixed place of business'; or

- an agent in the UK has the authority to enter into contracts on behalf of the company and does so on an habitual basis.

A fixed place of business is not exclusively defined, and can include:

- a place of management;

- a branch;

- an office, factory or workshop;

- a mine, quarry, oil or gas well, or any other place where natural resources are extracted; and

- a building site, or construction or installation project.

However, the company will not be treated as having a permanent establishment in the UK if the activities carried on here are merely of a 'preparatory or auxiliary character', having regard to the activities of the company as a whole.

From 6 April 2011, shares in a company are excluded from qualifying for the purposes of the EIS or VCT legislation if it is reasonable to assume that the company would be treated as an 'enterprise in difficulty' for the purposes of the European Commission's Rescue and Restructuring Guidelines, published in the Official Journal at OJ 2004 C244/02, at section 2.1 (*ITA 2007, s 180B*).

4.47 It is, however, possible for a company to qualify as an EIS company when it has a property-managing subsidiary. (This is permitted by *FA 2004*, which also relaxed some of the more technical restrictions where the company is the parent of a group of companies.)

The balance sheet total of the company must not exceed £15 million before the issue of eligible shares, nor £16 million after the issue of eligible shares. Note that these thresholds were raised from £7 million and £8 million respectively from 19 July 2012 (*FA 2012, s 39* and *Sch 7, para 11*, amending *ITA 2007, s 186 (SI 2012/1896)*).

From 19 July 2012, the maximum amount raised must not be more than £5 million in any 12-month period (£2 million prior to 6 April 2012) (*ITA 2007, s 173A*). A company or group of companies must have no more than 250 full-time employees (or their equivalent) at the date on which the relevant shares or securities are issued (this requirement was 50 full-time employees prior to 6 April 2012) (*FA 2012, s 39* and *Sch 7, para 12*).

The taxpayer must subscribe for 'eligible shares'. These are defined as new ordinary shares which, throughout the period of three years beginning with the date on which they are issued, carry no present or future preferential right to dividends or to a company's assets on its winding up and no present or future right to be redeemed. Ordinary shares are defined as 'shares forming part of the ordinary share capital of the company' (*ITA 2007, s 257(1)*). Shares are treated as never having been eligible if the cash raised by the company on the issue of those shares was used for a purpose other than a qualifying business activity.

Eligible shares are treated as ceasing to be eligible if an event occurs after the date of issue which causes the company not to be a qualifying company or, in the case of a group of companies, to cease to be the parent company of a trading group.

Number of employees

4.48   In respect of shares issued on or after 19 July 2007, the issuing company must have less than 50 'full-time equivalent employees' at the date of the issue of the shares. This limit was increased to 250 with effect from 19 July 2012 in respect of shares issued on or after 6 April 2012. Where the issuer is a parent company, the full-time employees of the parent and all its qualifying subsidiaries are included in the calculation (*ITA 2007, s 186A*).

In determining the number of full-time equivalent employees:

- directors are regarded as employees;
- part-time employees are included as a just and reasonable fraction;
- employees on maternity/paternity leave and students on vocational training are ignored.

From 18 November 2015, the number of employees is subject to a 'permitted limit'. The permitted limit is 500, if the issuing company is a 'knowledge intensive company' at the time the shares are issued. For all other companies, the limit remains at 250.

Procedure

4.49   In order to obtain EIS income tax relief, the company must first apply to HMRC on form EIS1 for permission to grant certificates to its investors. HMRC then issue the company with form EIS2, which is authority to send its investors certificates demonstrating that the company fulfils the EIS requirements (form EIS3). A claim for income tax relief is then made by the investor on receipt of his or her certificate. It is usual for HMRC to ask for certificate EIS3 also in claims for deferral relief. As certificate EIS3 can only be issued after following the procedure of application form EIS1 and authority form EIS2, the effect of HMRC's approach is to force a company to carry through the EIS application procedure even where deferral relief only is being claimed.

Relief can be claimed at any time up to five years after the 31 January following the year in which the shares were issued (*ITA 2007, s 202*).

Focus

HMRC's Small Company Enterprise Centre (SCEC) operates an advance assurance scheme, whereby companies can submit their plans to raise money details of their structure and trade, etc before the shares are issued, and the SCEC will advise on whether or not the proposed issue is likely to qualify. Application should be made to:

HMRC
Small Company Enterprise Centre (SCEC)
Ty-Glas
Llanishen
Cardiff CF14 5ZG

This office also provides advance clearance for companies under the venture capital trust (VCT) scheme, and monitors the action of companies that have issued shares under EIS or the VCT scheme.

Clawback of relief

4.50   EIS income tax relief is clawed back and any CGT deferral relief is brought into charge if, at any time during the three-year period from the date of the issue of the shares (or, if later, the date of commencement of the trade financed by the issue), any one of the following events takes place (*ITA 2007, Pt 5, Ch 7*):

- the shares are sold;
- the company ceases to carry on as a qualifying trade;
- value is received by the investor; or
- the individual becomes 'connected with' the company (income tax relief only).

If the qualifying trade ceases before the issue of shares or, more likely, never commences or, alternatively, if value is treated as being received by the investor before the issue of shares, the shares are treated as having never been eligible.

If the failure of the conditions takes place at a later date, the shares are treated as ceasing to be eligible at that time. It should be noted that the shares ceasing to be eligible causes any gain that was deferred to be brought into charge. Hence, if £100,000 of gain has been deferred but, later, during the three-year period, there is £1 of value received by the EIS investor, the whole £100,000 gain is thereby brought into charge.

4.51   An individual is treated as receiving value from the company if the company:

- repays, redeems or repurchases any of its share capital or securities which belong to the individual or makes any payment to the individual for giving up the individual's right to any of the company's share capital;

- repays any debt owed to the individual (subject to some exemptions) or makes a payment for giving up the individual's right to any debt;

- releases or waives any liability of the individual to a third person;

- makes a loan or advance to the individual;

- provides 'a benefit or facility' to or for the individual;

- transfers an asset to the individual at undervalue; or

- makes 'any other payment' to the individual (unless otherwise exempted).

Payments to an individual investor who is a director are exempted when they are within the categories listed above.

A similar list applies for CGT deferral relief.

If there is reorganisation of the company or there is a 'share for share' exchange, whereby a newly created company issues shares in exchange for 'EIS shares' that are held, the shares acquired on the reorganisation are to be treated as if they were the original shares issued. However, it is necessary for an acquiring company to fulfil the EIS provisions in its own right. The takeover of a company by a quoted company will normally cause clawback and crystallisation of any deferred gain (*ITA 2007, ss 247–249*).

Permitted payments from the company

4.52   *FA 2001* (now dealt with by *ITA 2007, ss 213–223*) introduced complex provisions that omit certain types of payment received from the company without causing clawback of EIS relief. If any of these are in point, careful reading of *ITA 2007, ss 213–223* is essential.

In summary, the following are possible, but all are subject to carefully defined restrictions:

- if a company has been unsuccessful, reorganisation of the company so that trade can continue under the ownership of a new company normally can be achieved without clawback of the EIS relief;

- payments can be made to an investor who sells goods or services to the company as long as the amount paid does not exceed the market value of the supply;

- interest can be paid to the investor on any sum linked to the company, as long as the rate of interest represents reasonable commercial return;

- the investor can sell an asset to the company for its market value;

- rent can be paid to the investor for the company's occupation of property, as long as the payment does not exceed a commercial rent for that property;

- the company can pay off a trade debt owed to the investor;

- the investor can sell other shares to the company, as long as no more than market value is paid;

- other payments totalling not more than £1,000 in aggregate can be made to the investor (described in the legislation as 'receipts of insignificant value') (*ITA 2007, s 215*).

Seed Enterprise Investment scheme

4.53 The Seed Enterprise Investment Scheme (SEIS) is designed to help small, early-stage companies raise equity finance by offering tax reliefs to individual investors who purchase new shares in those companies. It is designed to complement the existing Enterprise Investment Scheme (EIS), which offers tax reliefs to investors in higher-risk small companies. SEIS is intended to recognise the particular difficulties which very early stage companies face in attracting investment, by offering tax relief at a higher rate.

SEIS applies for shares issued on or after 6 April 2012. The rules have been designed to mirror those of EIS as it is anticipated that companies will go on to use EIS after an initial investment under SEIS.

Income tax relief is available to individuals who subscribe for qualifying shares in a company which meets the SEIS requirements, and who have UK tax liability against which to set the relief. Investors do not need to be UK resident.

The shares must be held for a period of three years, from date of issue, for relief to be retained. If they are disposed of within that three-year period, or if any of the qualifying conditions cease to be met during that period, relief will be withdrawn or reduced.

Relief is available at 50% of the cost of the shares, on a maximum annual investment of £100,000. The relief is given by way of a reduction of tax liability, providing there is sufficient tax liability against which to set it. A claim to relief can be made up to five years after the 31 January following the tax year in which the investment was made.

There is a 'carry-back' facility which allows all or part of the cost of shares acquired in one tax year to be treated as though the shares had been acquired in the preceding tax year. The SEIS rate for that earlier year is then applied to the shares, and relief given for the earlier year. This is subject to the overriding relief limit for each year. Note that there is no SEIS rate earlier than 2012/13, so there is no scope for carrying relief back before that year.

The company can follow a share issue under SEIS with other shares under EIS, or investment from a Venture Capital Trust (VCT). It must have spent at least 70% of the monies raised by the SEIS share issue before issuing any more.

A company cannot issue shares under the SEIS scheme if it has already had investment from a VCT, or issued shares on an EIS compliance statement (EIS1).

Venture capital trusts

4.54   The venture capital trust scheme started on 6 April 1995. It is designed to encourage individuals to invest indirectly in a range of small, higher-risk trading companies whose shares and securities are not listed on a recognised stock exchange, by investing through venture capital trusts (VCTs).

In respect of shares or securities issued on or after 6 April 2011, there is a requirement that the issuing company has had a 'permanent establishment' in the UK continuously since the issue of those shares (*ITA 2007, s 286A*). For these purposes, a company has a permanent establishment in the UK if (and only if) either (*ITA 2007, s 302A(2)*):

● it carries on business here wholly or partly through a 'fixed place of business'; or

● an agent in the UK has the authority to enter into contracts on behalf of the company and does so on an habitual basis.

A fixed place of business is not exclusively defined, and can include:

● a place of management;

● a branch;

● an office, factory or workshop;

● a mine, quarry, oil or gas well, or any other place where natural resources are extracted; and

● a building site, or construction or installation project.

From 6 April 2011, shares in a company are excluded from qualifying for the purposes of the EIS or VCT legislation if it is reasonable to assume that the company would be treated as an 'enterprise in difficulty' for the purposes of the European Commission's Rescue and Restructuring Guidelines, published in the Official Journal at OJ 2004 C244/02, at section 2.1 (*ITA 2007, s 286B*).

VCTs are similar to investment trusts, and are run by fund managers who are usually members of larger investment groups. Investors can subscribe for, or buy, shares in a VCT, which invests in trading companies, providing them with funds to help them develop and grow. VCTs realise their investments and make new ones from time to time.

VCTs must be approved by HMRC for the purpose of the scheme. HMRC give approval if certain conditions are met. Investors in an approved VCT will be entitled to various income tax and capital gains tax reliefs, and VCTs are exempt from corporation tax on any gains arising on the disposal of their investments (*ITA 2007, Pt 6*).

An individual can subscribe up to £200,000 in a tax year and obtain tax relief (*ITA 2007, s 262*). For shares issued on or after 6 April 2006, the rate of tax relief is 30% (*ITA 2007, s 263*).

For shares issued on or after 6 April 2006, individuals must hold VCT shares for a minimum period of five years to qualify for income tax relief (*ITA 2007, s 266*).

Focus

Finance Act 2018 enacted a series of changes to both EIS and VCTs, which took effect from 6 April 2018 (*FA 2018, ss 14–17, Schs 4 and 5*). The changes affecting VCTs are summarised as follows:

- The annual EIS and VCT limit on the amount of tax-advantaged investments a knowledge-intensive company may receive is increased to £10 million in relation to new qualifying investments made on or after 6 April 2018.

- Greater flexibility is to be provided with respect to the rules for determining whether a knowledge-intensive company meets the permitted maximum age requirement.

Certain other changes are being made to the rules on investments made by VCTs, including:

- inclusion of a final date of 6 April 2018 in relation to the applicability of certain 'grandfathering' provisions;

- doubling the time VCTs have to reinvest gains from investments from 6 to 12 months;

- requirement that 30% of funds raised in an accounting period must be invested in qualifying holdings within 12 months after the end of the accounting period;

- requirement that qualifying loans are to be unsecured and ensure that returns on loan capital above 10% represent no more than a commercial return on the principal; and

---

- an increase in the proportion of VCT funds that must be held in qualifying holdings from 70% to 80%.

The change concerning unsecured loans applies from 15 March 2018 (the date of Royal Assent to *Finance Act 2018*). The 'grandfathering' provisions and 30% investment in qualifying holdings provisions apply from 6 April 2018. The increased period for reinvestment and qualifying holdings threshold provisions takes effect from 6 April 2019.

Example 4.3—Venture capital trust relief

Sylvia subscribes for shares in Dolly Mixture Ltd at a cost of £180,000. Her tax liability for the year is £19,500. VCT investment relief may be claimed as follows:

		£
Income tax due for the year		19,500
Less:		
VCT investment relief		
Lower of: £180,000 @ 30%	£54,000	
and income tax liability	£19,500	(19,500)
Income tax payable		Nil

4.55   A VCT is required to meet the following conditions (*ITA 2007, Pt 6, Ch 4*):

- its income must be derived wholly or mainly from shares or securities;

- its ordinary share capital (and the share capital of each class, if it has more than one) must be quoted on a recognised stock market (but see **4.54**);

- it must not retain, for any accounting period, more than 15% of the income it derives from shares or securities;

- at least 70% of its investments must be represented throughout its accounting period by 'qualifying holdings' of shares or securities (*ITA 2007, s 280*); and

- from 17 July 2012, the company has not made, and will not make, an investment in a company which breaches the 'permitted investment limits' (*ITA 2007, s 280B*).

With effect from 6 April 2007, any money that a VCT holds (or is held on its behalf) is treated as an investment for the purpose of the 70% and 15% tests above (*FA 2006, Sch 14, para 8*).

At least 50% by value of those 'qualifying holdings' must be represented by 'eligible shares', that is, ordinary shares carrying no present or future preferential rights to dividends or to assets on a winding up, and no present or future preferential right to be redeemed.

VCTs are required to ensure that at least 10% of the total investment from the VCT in any one company is in ordinary, non-preferential shares. Guaranteed loans and securities do not count towards this fixed proportion of qualifying investments, which a VCT must hold.

The specification for the 'qualifying holdings' into which a VCT is permitted to invest is complex. The company must not hold shares or securities listed on any stock market, either in the UK or abroad, nor on the unlisted securities market. However, a VCT is permitted to hold shares that are dealt with on the Alternative Investment Market (AIM). There are provisions whereby the VCT can receive quoted shares as a result of its exercise of conversion rights.

To be a 'qualifying holding', the shares must be in a company that has gross assets that do not exceed £15 million (before the subscription by the VCT) or £16 million (after that subscription). Note that, prior to 6 April 2012, these limits were £7 million and £8 million respectively.

The maximum amount raised must not be more than £5 million in any 12-month period (£2 million prior to 6 April 2012) (*FA 2012, s 40* and *Sch 8, para 8*). A company or group of companies must have no more than 250 full-time employees (or their equivalent) (50 prior to 6 April 2012) at the date on which the relevant shares or securities are issued (*FA 2012, s 40* and *Sch 8, para 9*).

The *Finance (No 2) Act 2015* includes legislation placing a time limit on the availability of relief for VCTs. Only shares issued before 6 April 2025 will be eligible for relief (*ITA 2007, s 261(3)(za)*). However, the Treasury retains the power to amend the end date.

Formerly, the VCT scheme required 80% of the money received by the investee companies to be wholly employed for the purposes of the relevant trade within 12 months and the balance within a further 12 months. *FA 2009* replaced these rules with a single requirement that all the money raised must be wholly employed within two years, or, if later, within two years of the commencement of the qualifying activity (*FA 2009, s 27* and *Sch 8, para 5*).

Each company into which the VCT invests must exist for the purpose of carrying on one or more qualifying trades (*ITA 2007, Pt 6, Ch 4*). Prior to 6 April 2011, the qualifying trade had to be carried on, or intended to be carried on, wholly or mainly in the UK.

An investor receives tax relief on an investment in a VCT only if the VCT is approved by HMRC. To be approved, the VCT must meet a number of conditions *(ITA 2007, s 274)*. The approval process is governed by the *Venture Capital Trust Regulations 1995 (SI 1995/1979,* amended by *SI 1999/819)*. The *Venture Capital Trust (Amendment) Regulations 2008 (SI 2008/1893),* which came into force on 1 September 2008, amended the 1995 regulations to introduce greater flexibility to deal with cases where a VCT has breached, or is likely to breach, the conditions for its approval to continue.

Life assurance (qualifying policies)

4.56 A life assurance company is exempt from tax on both the income arising and the capital gains made in the fund it holds for qualifying life assurance policies. Therefore, for the investor the premium paid on such a policy is invested (after management charges) in a fund that is tax free, and the tax exemption will increase the sums that can be paid out to the investor. In practice, investment in a qualifying life policy falls into two categories:

(1) providing a fund to pay at death, typically either to fund inheritance tax or to take advantage of the facility to write the policy in trust and, thereby, pass the fund free of inheritance tax to the next generation; and

(2) building up a fund, typically over ten years, after which the policy matures and pays out.

Qualifying conditions

4.57 The tax-free fund consists of premiums from 'qualifying policies' only. In order to be a 'qualifying policy', it must satisfy the statutory conditions in *ICTA 1988, s 266*. For whole life or endowment assurances, the term must be at least ten years. The premiums must be payable at yearly or shorter intervals for at least ten years or until the event specified, whether death or disability. The total premiums payable under the policy in any period of 12 months must not exceed twice the amount payable in any other 12-month period or one-eighth of the total premiums payable if the policy were to run for the specified term.

The policy must guarantee that the sum payable on death will be at least 75% of the total premiums payable if the policy were to run its term, except that a 2% reduction for every year by which the person exceeds 55 years of age is permitted and, when a new policy is issued for an old one, the part of the premiums that are attributable to the old policy are ignored. Where a policy includes one or more options, the policy must be tested on each option and will only 'qualify' if it meets the conditions on every such test. A policy may make provision for total or partial surrender without ceasing to qualify; but, if an option in a qualifying policy is exercised after 13 March 1984, and either extends the term of the policy or increases the benefits payable under it, the policy ceases to qualify.

A temporary assurance for a period of not more than ten years may be a qualifying policy, but only if the surrender value is not to exceed the total premiums previously paid. A term policy of less than 12 months cannot be a qualifying policy. This provision is likely to make a policy issued for less than ten years unattractive.

Life assurance (single premium bonds)

4.58   Quite apart from life assurance taken out to provide a lump sum on an individual's death, perhaps to pay funeral expenses or an inheritance tax liability, life policies can be used as an investment mechanism. Although usually referred to as either life assurance bonds or investment bonds, these are, technically, single premium whole life insurance policies. Having taken out such a life assurance bond, the investor can withdraw a sum up to 5% of his or her initial purchase consideration in each fiscal year and the withdrawal is treated as a withdrawal of capital, with no income tax consequences. If less than the 5% is taken in one year, the surplus is carried forward to the following year.

A withdrawal greater than the 5% and, indeed, full encashment of the bond, can be made without any charge to tax by a basic rate taxpayer, as long as the 'chargeable event' that arises, when added to the taxpayer's other income, does not exceed the basic rate band.

For a higher rate tax payer, or one for whom the 'chargeable event' takes the taxpayer into higher rates, there is a charge to income tax at higher rate only.

Chargeable event

4.59   For this purpose, a chargeable event is any one of the following (*ITTOIA 2005, s 484*):

- a payment under the policy at death;
- a payment at the maturity of the policy;
- a surrender of the policy rights;
- an assignment of policy rights for money or money's worth; or
- a withdrawal in excess of 5%.

Even if an assignment is taxed as a chargeable event, this does not stop a later assignment giving a second charge to tax by virtue of the second chargeable event. This provision was introduced to cancel the advantages that were enjoyed under the so-called second-hand bond scheme.

On death, maturity or assignment, the gain is the difference between the amount received from the insurance company and the initial premium paid, less any withdrawals that have been made.

If there is a partial, rather than a complete, encashment of the policy, the gain brought into charge is the sum that is paid out of the policy, less 5% of the initial subscription for each year during the life of the policy, insofar as this has not been taken into account in previous gain computations. The 5% is calculated by reference to the policy year, not the tax year. A policy year commences on the day the policy is taken out and on each 365-day anniversary thereafter. Many modern policies allow partial surrenders at frequent intervals and such surrenders gave rise to complex calculations. In an attempt to reduce the work involved, both for life offices and HMRC, a different system of determining both whether there has been a gain and its extent applies.

On assignment, the gain is the excess of the consideration received, except when assignment is between connected persons when market value is substituted, plus the amount or value of any relevant capital payments over the total amount of premiums paid with adjustments for the assignment.

Where the chargeable gain arises on death, the chargeable event is the income of the individual who owns the policy and not of his or her personal representatives.

Top-slicing relief

4.60   The gain is brought into charge after top-slicing relief (*ITA 2007, s 535*). The gain is spread back over a number of years by dividing it by the number of complete years:

- for the first chargeable event – since the start of the policy;

- for any later chargeable event other than final termination – since the previous chargeable event; and

- on final termination – the number of whole years from the start of the policy.

The slice of the gain is then added to the taxpayer's other income to discover the amount of extra tax payable by reason of its addition. If the addition of that sum does not give rise to anything but tax at the basic rate, no tax is payable. If the sum gives a liability at higher rate, the charge is computed as if there were a credit for tax at basic rate.

When there is a chargeable event through death or maturity and there is a loss, an individual may deduct that loss from total income so far as it does not exceed gains taxed in earlier partial surrender or assignments. Thus, the tax on gains made earlier may be recovered. The relief does not apply to losses on assignments.

Example 4.4—Life assurance top-slicing

Gilbert, aged 60, realises a chargeable event gain in December 2015 of £48,000 on the complete surrender of a life policy taken out in August 2010. During 2015/16, he received a termination payment from his employer of £50,000. He also received a salary of £120,000 from that employment during 2015/16. He had no other income.

His taxable income for that year is £157,000 (£120,000 salary plus £48,000 gain, less £11,000 personal allowance), which means he is liable at the additional 45% tax rate on £7,000. This is deemed to be part of the gain, and the balance of £41,000 is deemed to be charged at 40%. The total tax on the gain is £9,950 (£41,000 at 40% plus £7,000 at 45%, less the basic rate credit of £48,000 at 20%).

There are five complete years from August 2010 to December 2015, so the 'annual equivalent' is therefore £9,600 (£48,000 / 5). By replacing the whole of the gain with the annual equivalent in the earlier calculation, Gilbert's taxable income becomes £118,600 (£120,000 salary plus £9,600 annual equivalent, less £11,000 personal allowance). This means that the whole of the annual equivalent falls within the 40% rate band, and the liability (after allowing credit for basic rate tax) is £1,920. This liability is then multiplied by five to produce the relieved liability of £9,600.

The relief to be given in the income tax calculation is therefore £350, being the difference between the two calculations.

Purchased annuities

4.61   A monthly sum paid from a purchased annuity is treated as if it were two separate payments – a capital content which does not attract a charge to income tax (or CGT), and an income payment which attracts a charge to income tax. However, this treatment is only available where the purchase is made by an annuitant (*ITTOIA 2005, ss 717, 725*).

The apportionment between income and capital is made by dividing the purchase cost into the two elements by reference to Government mortality tables. Even where an individual receives special terms from a company as the individual has a lower than average life expectancy, the Government tables are automatically applied for tax purposes. The capital element that is computed by reference to the table remains constant, even if the individual lives to such an age that the payments made that have been deemed to be capital, exceed, in aggregate, the initial purchase price. In this respect, the treatment is in contrast to that which applies to insurance bonds.

A purchased annuity can be structured so that the monthly payments increase each year in line with inflation. This does not affect the calculation of the division between the deemed capital element and the income element. The calculation of the division is made as at the date of the first payment. The consequence of this treatment is that inflationary increases in the annuity paid are automatically treated as income attracting a charge to income tax.

Gifts to the nation

4.62 A scheme, designed to stimulate lifetime giving by encouraging taxpayers to donate pre-eminent objects, or collections of objects, to the nation, was introduced from 6 April 2012 (*FA 2012, s 49* and *Sch 14; SI 2013/587*). The objects may be loaned or given to appropriate institutions including certain charities and accredited museums for safe keeping and to provide public access. In return, donors will receive a reduction in their UK tax liability based on a percentage of the value of the object they are donating.

Under the scheme, a potential donor may offer to give a pre-eminent object (or collection of objects) to the nation with a self-assessed valuation of the object. A panel of experts will consider the offer and, if it considers the object is pre-eminent and should be accepted, the panel will agree the value of the object with the donor. If the donor decides to proceed based on that valuation they will receive a tax reduction as a fixed percentage of the object's agreed value. The fixed percentage will be 30% for individuals (20% for companies). Individuals may spread the tax reduction forward across a period of up to five years starting with the tax year in which the object is offered. The donor will specify in advance how the tax reduction is to be used. Gifts made under the scheme are not chargeable gains for capital gains tax purposes. The item donated will not be regarded as remitted to the UK under *ITA 2007, s 809Y(1)* for the purposes of the remittance basis rules.

Social investment tax relief

4.63 *Finance Act 2014* introduced a range of tax reliefs for qualifying individuals who make qualifying investments in qualifying social enterprises (*FA 2014, s 57, Sch 11* and *Sch 12*). Income tax relief will be available as a percentage of the amount invested, to be deducted from the individual's income tax liability for the year of investment. In addition, capital gains tax (CGT) on chargeable gains may be deferred in certain circumstances where the person liable to tax invests money in a social enterprise. Capital gains on these social enterprise investments will be free from CGT, subject to conditions being met. The income tax relief was originally to apply to qualifying investments made between 6 April 2014 and 5 April 2019, but the cessation date has been extended to 5 April 2021 (*F(No 2)A 2017, Sch 1, para 2*). The CGT reliefs apply to gains which accrue on or after 6 April 2014. Income tax relief is potentially available at the rate of 30% on the amount invested.

The *Tax Relief for Social Investments (Accreditation of Social Impact Contractor) Regulations 2014 (SI 2014/3066)* supplement the primary legislation in *Income Tax Act 2007, Pt 5B*, relating to social investment tax relief by defining the conditions that must be met for a social impact contractor company to receive accreditation in relation to a relevant contract entered into which allows individual investors to be eligible to claim social investment tax relief in respect of their investment. The Regulations came into force on 10 December 2014. Guidance and an application form for the accreditation scheme for social impact bond contractors eligible for social investment tax relief can be found on the gov.uk website at www.gov.uk/government/publications/social-investment-tax-relief-accreditation-for-sib-contractors.

The Regulations can be found online at www.legislation.gov.uk/uksi/2014/3066/pdfs/uksiem_20143066_en.pdf.

Focus

Finance (No 2) Act 2017 contains provisions designed to enlarge the existing SITR scheme, including an increase in the amount of money newer social enterprises may raise, and provisions to better target the scheme on higher risk activities and deter abuse (*F(No 2)A 2017, s 14* and *Sch 1*). The changes, which broadly have effect in relation to investments made on or after 6 April 2017, are summarised as follows:

- increase the amount of investment a social investment may receive over its lifetime to £1.5m for social enterprises that receive their initial risk finance investment no later than seven years after their first commercial sale (the current limit will continue to apply to older social enterprises);

- reduce the limit on full-time equivalent employees to below 250 employees;

- exclude certain activities, including asset leasing and on-lending, to ensure the scheme is well targeted – investment in nursing homes and residential care homes will be excluded initially, but the government intends to introduce an accreditation system to allow such investment to qualify for SITR in the future;

- exclude the use of money raised under the SITR to pay off existing loans;

- clarify that individuals will be eligible to claim relief under the SITR only if they are independent from the social enterprise; and

- introduce a provision to exclude investments where arrangements are put in place with the main purpose of delivering a benefit to an individual or party connected to the social enterprise.

Chapter 5

Pensions and benefits

SIGNPOSTS

- Pensions are generally treated as earned income, and most of them are taxed under the *Income Tax (Earnings and Pensions) Act 2003* on entitlement in the tax year (see **5.1**).

- Tax on pensions under occupational schemes is usually dealt with under the PAYE system (see **5.6**).

- Individuals can obtain tax relief on pension contributions up to an annual maximum amount, which is £40,000 for 2014/15 onwards. From 2016/17, a tapered annual allowance applies to income over £150,000 (including pension contributions) (see **5.9**).

- There is a single lifetime allowance on the amount of pension savings that can benefit from tax relief. The value of the lifetime allowance is £1,055,000 for 2019/20. (see **5.14**).

- Full membership of a UK-registered pension scheme is available to any person, whether they are resident in the UK or not (see **5.29**).

- Certain state benefits are taxable for income tax purposes (see **5.42**).

- A list of current taxable state benefit rates is shown at **5.54**.

- Class 3 National Insurance contributions (NICs) are voluntary contributions, but a person may be entitled to pay them to protect entitlement to widows' benefits and the basic retirement pension (see **5.57**).

UK PENSIONS

Introduction

5.1   Pensions are generally treated as earned income, and most of them are taxed under the *Income Tax (Earnings and Pensions) Act 2003* on entitlement in the tax year. Examples include:

- state retirement pensions;
- voluntary pensions paid by UK employers (or their successors);

- certain foreign pensions for services to the Crown or a government abroad; and

- other pensions (eg occupational pensions), other than tax-exempt pensions and pensions from abroad.

Tax advantages of making pension contributions include:

- contributions or premiums (up to certain limits) attract tax relief at the individual's top rate (but they do not reduce earnings for National Insurance contributions);

- employers can contribute to an employee's occupational or personal pension scheme reducing their taxable business profits and without the contributions being treated as a benefit in kind to the employee;

- a tax-free lump sum (within permitted limits) can be paid on retirement; and

- non-taxpayers can obtain basic rate tax relief on personal pension contributions of up to £3,600 per tax year.

5.2   With regard to state retirement pensions, everyone is likely to be entitled to different amounts depending on how many years they have paid, been treated as having paid, or been credited with National Insurance contributions.

The earliest an individual can receive a state pension is when they reach state pension age. This age is currently different for men and women, although women's state pension age will gradually increase between 2010 and 2020 to become the same as men's. At the moment, state pension age is as follows:

- men – 65 years old;

- women:

    - 60 years old if born on, or before, 5 April 1950;

    - 65 years old if born on, or after, 6 April 1955;

    - for women born on or after 6 April 1950 but on or before 5 April 1955, it is 60 years old plus one month for each month (or part month) that birth date fell on or after 6 April 1950.

Focus

State pension age (SPA) is set to rise to age 66 from April 2020 and to 67 from April 2028. The government is currently legislating for a new SPA framework. This framework will mean that the SPA will be reviewed every Parliament, with the first review occurring early in the next Parliament. Under the new framework, it is likely that an SPA of 68 will be brought forward from the current date of 2046 to the mid-2030s, and that it will increase further to 69 by the late 2040s.

In April 2011, the government published a Green Paper entitled *A state pension for the 21st century*, which consulted on two broad options for reforming the state pension system for future pensioners. The White Paper which followed in January 2013, entitled *The single-tier pension: a simple foundation for saving*, outlined the government's intentions for reforming the state pension. Those proposals formed the basis for the measures in the *Pensions Act 2014*. Broadly, that Act contained the necessary provisions for implementing the single-tier state pension, which replaced the basic state pension and additional state pension with a flat-rate pension that is set above the basic level of means-tested support for people who reach state pension age on or after 6 April 2016.

The *Pensions Act 2008* allows for the establishment of the personal accounts scheme from 2012. This is as a new low-cost saving vehicle aimed at employees who do not have access to a good quality work-based pension scheme – in the main, medium to low earners. There is a contribution limit of £3,600 per year (based on 2005 earnings levels) and a general ban on transfers in and out of the scheme, to focus the scheme on the target market.

It is possible to obtain a state pension statement showing an estimate of how much state pension (which can be either basic state pension or additional state pension, or both) an individual might expect to receive (reflecting today's position and given in today's values). The older the individual (up until retirement), the more accurate this estimate is likely to be. A state pension statement can be obtained from the government website (www.gov.uk/state-pension-statement).

Pensions exempt from tax

5.3   The following pensions are exempt from tax:

- wounds and disability pensions of members of the Armed Forces;

- pensions awarded to employees disabled at work;

- war widow's pension;

- pensions for victims of Nazi persecution; and

- certain pensions paid to non-UK residents (eg colonial and overseas service pensions).

Benefits paid by any of the following Services schemes are exempt from income tax, even where the recipient continues to serve in any capacity (*ITEPA 2003, ss 639, 640A*):

- new armed forces pensions;

- armed forces compensation schemes; and

- early departure payments scheme.

State pensions guidance

5.4   The gov.uk website provides comprehensive guidance on the state pension. An A to Z list of the guidance can be found at www.gov.uk/browse/working/state-pension.

Guides for those planning ahead

5.5

- Additional State Pension
- Carer's Credit
- Check your State Pension
- Check your State Pension age
- Complain to the Independent Case Examiner
- Contact the Future Pension Centre
- Contact the Pension Service
- Contracted out of the State Pension
- Delay (defer) your State Pension
- Early retirement, your pension and benefits
- Find your pension centre
- Get your State Pension
- Home Responsibilities Protection
- International Pension Centre
- Kindertransport and the State Pension
- National Insurance and tax after State Pension age
- National Insurance credits
- Nominate someone to collect State Pension
- Over 80 pension
- Pension Credit
- Pension Credit calculator
- State Pension if you retire abroad
- The basic State Pension
- The new State Pension

- Voluntary National Insurance

- Your benefits, tax and pension after the death of a spouse

- Your partner's National Insurance record and your State Pension

Occupational pensions income

5.6   Tax on pensions under occupational schemes is dealt with under the PAYE system. Certain lump sum payments (within permitted limits) received on retirement are not taxable.

Pension income is charged to tax under *ITEPA 2003, Pt 9*.

The extent of the charge is to all pension income, excluding any exempt income and less any express deductions permitted (ie payroll giving and the 10% deduction for overseas pensions).

'Pension income' includes pensions, annuities and income of 'other types' that are included in the statutory list provided (*ITEPA 2003, s 566(2), (4)*):

- pensions paid by (or on behalf of) any person who is in the UK (*ITEPA 2003, s 569*);

- pensions paid by (or on behalf of) any person who is outside the UK, to a person who is UK resident (*ITEPA 2003, s 573*);

- UK social security pensions (the state pension, graduated retirement pension, industrial death benefit, widowed mother's allowance, widowed parent's allowance and widow's pension) (*ITEPA 2003, s 577*);

- pensions and annuities paid by an approved retirement benefits scheme (including unauthorised payments) (*ITEPA 2003, s 580*);

- annuities paid under formerly approved superannuation schemes (*ITEPA 2003, s 590*);

- annuities from approved personal pension schemes (including income withdrawals) (*ITEPA 2003, s 595*);

- unauthorised personal pension payments (*ITEPA 2003, s 601*);

- annuities under retirement annuity contracts (*ITEPA 2003, s 605*);

- annuities for the benefit of dependants (*ITEPA 2003, s 609*);

- annuities under sponsored superannuation schemes (*ITEPA 2003, s 610*);

- annuities paid in respect of another person's services in any office or employment (*ITEPA 2003, s 611*);

- pensions payable by or on behalf of certain overseas governments to UK-resident persons (and their dependants) who were engaged in service to the overseas government (*ITEPA 2003, s 615*);

- payments made out of the House of Commons Member's Fund (*ITEPA 2003, s 619*);

- payments representing the return of surplus employee additional voluntary contributions (*ITEPA 2003, s 623*);

- pre-1973 pensions paid under the *Overseas Pensions Act 1973* (*ITEPA 2003, s 629*); and

- voluntary annual payments paid to former employees (and their dependants) by or on behalf of a former employer (or their successor) (*ITEPA 2003, s 633*).

The term 'pension' includes a pension that is paid voluntarily or that may be discontinued.

A special or additional pension paid to a person who has retired because he is disabled following an injury at work, or because of a work-related illness, is not taxed (*ITEPA 2003, s 644*).

TAXATION OF PENSIONS

The simplified pensions tax regime

5.7   A single regime for the taxation of pension income applies from 6 April 2006 (A-Day). From that date, a single set of simplified rules came into effect around how pensions are taxed, designed to offer simpler and more flexible retirement arrangements. Under the unified regime, the tax treatment for all types of approved schemes, including occupational schemes, small self-administered schemes (SSASs, personal pensions, self-invested personal pensions (SIPPs)) and retirement annuity contracts, has been amalgamated into the rules for registered pension schemes. In addition, the tax treatment of unapproved schemes has been changed (see **5.22**).

The main points of the unified pensions regime can be summarised as follows:

- The many former sets of rules governing the taxation of pensions were replaced with a single, universal regime.

- It is possible to save in more than one pension scheme at the same time.

- There is no limit on the amount of money that can be invested in pension schemes, although there are limits on the amount of tax relief available.

- Tax relief is generally available on contributions up to 100% of an individual's annual earnings, up to an annual allowance set at £40,000 for 2014/15 onwards, but subject to tapering from 6 April 2016 (see **5.10**).

- Non-taxpayers are entitled to tax relief on pension contributions. Individuals can invest up to £2,880 in any one tax year and receive tax relief of £720; thus, the total pension savings with tax relief will be £3,600 gross per annum.

- From A-Day, flexible retirement was introduced, allowing people in occupational pension schemes to continue working while drawing their pension, where the scheme rules allow it.

- Where scheme rules allow, up to 25% of a pension fund may be taken as a tax-free lump sum.

- If a pension pot is more than the 'lifetime allowance' when the individual comes to take his or her pension, they may be subject to a tax charge at that time. But this will only apply if total pension savings are in excess of £1.25 million (standard lifetime allowance applying for 2014/15 onwards) (*FA 2011, s 67* and *Sch 18*).

- The rules on when a pension may be taken have changed. From 6 April 2010, an individual cannot take a pension before he or she is 55. There are two exceptions to this: individuals will still be able to retire early due to poor health; and, if they have the right to retire before 50 at 6 April 2006, that right may be protected. From 2010/11 onwards, there is no minimum benefit age.

Legislation

5.8   The legislation governing the unified tax regime applying from 6 April 2006 is found in *FA 2004, Pt 4*. This is supplemented by *FA 2005, Pt 5*, *FA 2006, Pt 7, FA 2007* and numerous regulations. *FA 2007* received Royal Assent on 19 July 2007. The pension provisions are contained within *ss 68–70* and *Schs 18–20* and *27 (Pt 3)*.

Annual allowance

5.9   Individuals can obtain tax relief on contributions up to an annual maximum amount, which is £40,000 for 2014/15 onwards. This is however, subject to tapering restrictions from 6 April 2016, which apply where an individual's income, broadly, exceeds £150,000 (see **5.10**).

Where an individual has flexibly accessed their pension savings on or after 6 April 2015, a £10,000 annual allowance will immediately apply to their future money purchase pension savings. However, those individuals will retain an annual allowance for defined benefits pension savings of at least £30,000, depending on the value of new money purchase pension savings. Unused annual allowance brought forward from earlier tax years will not be available to increase the £10,000 annual allowance for their money purchase pension savings (*FA 2004, ss 227ZA–227G*).

Focus

The Spring Budget 2017 announced a change to the money purchase annual allowance (MPAA) rules, which restrict the amount a person can invest into a 'money purchase' type pension scheme, once that individual has 'flexibly accessed' pension benefits, as defined. Broadly, the MPAA has been reduced from £10,000 to £4,000 per tax year from 2017/18 onwards (*F(No 2)A 2017, s 7*). This change is designed to prevent individuals from 'recycling' pension benefits to accrue further tax relief.

The tax charge on excessive contributions for years up to 2010/11 was at the rate of 40% on so much of the 'total pension input amount' as exceeded the annual allowance for that year. This excess is not treated as income for tax purposes (*FA 2004, s 227(4), (5)*), which in turn means that the tax charge cannot be reduced by losses or reliefs.

'Total pension input amount' is the aggregate of the pension input amounts in respect of each arrangement relating to the individual under a registered pension scheme (*FA 2004, s 229(1)*). The pension input amount depends on the nature of the arrangements. However, if, before the end of the tax year, the individual has become entitled to all the benefits under the arrangement or has died, there is no pension input amount (*FA 2004, s 229(3)*).

Tapered allowance

5.10   In July 2015, HMRC published a policy paper announcing details of a change that restricts pensions tax relief by introducing a tapered reduction in the amount of the annual allowance for individuals with income (including the value of any pension contributions) of over £150,000 and who have an income (excluding pension contributions) in excess of £110,000. The annual allowance taper took effect from 6 April 2016.

The taper works by gradually reducing the existing £40,000 annual allowance down to £10,000. For each £2 of income above £150,000, an individual's annual allowance will be reduced by £1 until his or her income reaches £210,000 or over, when their annual allowance will be £10,000 (*FA 2004, ss 228ZA and 228ZB*). In order to facilitate the taper, legislation has also been introduced to align pension input periods with the tax year as well as transitional rules to protect savers who might otherwise be affected by the alignment of their pension input periods. The legislation took effect from 8 July 2015.

Annual allowance charge 2011/12 to 2013/14

5.11   As mentioned at **5.9**, for years up to and including 2010/11, where pension savings for a 'pension input period' ending in a tax year exceeded the annual allowance for that year, the excess was charged to income tax at a flat rate of 40%, regardless of the individual's marginal rate of tax for that year. From 2011/12 onwards, the excess is taxed at the 'appropriate rate', that is the rate or rates which would be charged on the excess if it was to be added to the individual's 'reduced net income' for the tax year concerned. That figure is the sum calculated at Step 3 of the prescribed method of calculating income tax liabilities (see **1.54**). Any increase in the basic rate or higher rate bands due to pension contributions made under deduction of tax or gift aid payments, will also be taken into account for this purpose *(FA 2004, s 227(4A)–(4C))*.

For 2011/12 onwards, where the annual allowance for a tax year exceeds the pension input amount for that year, a limited form of carry forward is available. Where, in a 'current year' there is an excess of pension input amount over the annual allowance, that allowance may be increased by the 'unused' annual allowance of the three immediately preceding years *(FA 2004, s 228A(1)–(3))*.

However, where the 'current year' is 2011/12, 2012/13 or 2013/14, in determining the unused allowance for tax years ending prior to 6 April 2011, the annual allowance for those years is to be taken as £50,000 rather than the actual allowance *(FA 2011, Sch 17, para 30)*.

An amount of annual allowance is 'unused' to the extent that, ignoring the effect of any carry forward, it exceeds the pension input amount for that year *(FA 2004, s 228A(3))*. Unused allowance is set against the current year's pension inputs on a 'first in, first out basis'. No claim is required and the carry forward is mandatory. This means that unused annual allowance will automatically be set off against the next available year's pension input amount.

Contributions

5.12   Contributions are no longer restricted to a fraction of capped earnings. However, an annual allowance charge may arise on contributions or increases in excess of the annual allowance, but only where tax relief has been given on those contributions. The *de minimis* limit of £3,600 under the old system has been retained.

Contributions may be paid by *(FA 2004, ss 188, 196)*:

- the scheme member;

- the member's current or former employer; or

- a third party on behalf of the member.

In addition to cash, contributions may be in the form of shares from a Share Incentive Plan (SIP), or a Save As You Earn (SAYE) scheme *(FA 2004, s 195)*.

An individual's contributions are usually paid net of the basic rate of tax. Employers who previously used the net pay arrangement for occupational schemes may continue to do so under the unified pensions tax regime *(FA 2004, s 192)*.

Focus

For 2017/18 onwards, an income tax exemption covers the first £500 worth of pensions advice provided to an employee in a tax year, subject to certain conditions being satisfied (*F(No 2)A 2017, s 3*) . The exemption covers advice not only on pensions, but also on the general financial and tax issues relating to pensions. It replaced previous provisions, which limited the exemption solely to pensions advice, capped at £150 per employee per tax year.

The definition of authorised payments has also been extended from 6 April 2017, allowing members and beneficiaries of defined contribution pension schemes and hybrid pension arrangements with cash balance benefits or other money purchase benefits to take pensions advice allowance payments of up to £500 from their scheme, to redeem against the cost of retirement financial advice. They will be able to take £500 tax free, no more than once in a tax year, and up to a maximum of three times in total, without incurring an unauthorised payment tax charge.

Lump sums

5.13   An objection to funding for retirement through tax-relievable premiums to a personal pension has always been that the available lump sum at retirement is limited. Currently, it is possible to take up to 25% of a pension pot as a tax-free lump sum. Withdrawals in excess of the 25% limit are charged to tax. With the remainder, there are four options:

- Those aged 60 and over who have overall pension savings of less than £30,000 (£18,000 prior to 27 March 2014) can take them all in one lump sum (this is known as trivial commutation);

- A 'capped drawdown' pension allows investors to take income from their pension, but there is a maximum amount that can be withdrawn each year (150% of an equivalent annuity from 27 March 2014, 120% prior to that date);

- With 'flexible drawdown' there's no limit on the amount that can be drawn from the pot each year, but the investor must have a guaranteed income of more than £12,000 per year (£20,000 prior to 27 March 2014) in retirement;

- Purchasing an annuity where a fixed sum of money is paid each year.

Regardless of total pension wealth, those aged 60 or over can take any pot worth less than £10,000 as a lump sum (£2,000 prior to 27 March 2014), as this classifies as a 'small pot'. From 27 March 2014 the number of personal pension pots that can be taken as a lump sum under the small pot rules has been increased from two to three.

From April 2015, from age 55, whatever the size of a person's defined contribution pension pot, they will be able to take it how they want, subject to their marginal rate of income tax in that year. 25% of the pot will remain tax-free.

There will be more flexibility. People who continue to want the security of an annuity will be able to purchase one and people who want greater control over their finances can drawdown their pension as they see fit. Those who want to keep their pension invested and drawdown from it over time will be able to do so.

Lifetime allowance

5.14   There is a single lifetime allowance on the amount of pension savings that can benefit from tax relief. The value of the lifetime allowance is £1,055,000 for 2019/20 (rising from £1,030,000 in 2018/19) (*SI 2019/29*).

Finance Act 2013 provides for a transitional protection regime (fixed protection 2014) for individuals with UK tax relieved pension rights (or anticipated rights) of more than £1.25m who notified HMRC by 5 April 2014 (*FA 2013, Sch 22*). *Finance Act 2014* introduced a further transitional protection regime, individual protection 2014 ('IP14') which entitled individuals with pension savings on 5 April 2014 of greater than £1.25m and who did not have primary protection to a lifetime allowance equal to the value of those savings, subject to an overall limit of £1.5m (*SI 2014/1842*).

The lifetime allowance applies to everyone, irrespective of the type of scheme to which they belong. Different forms of calculation are needed to establish an individual's entitlement. For a defined benefit scheme, the single valuation factor is 20:1. This means that a final salary pension that pays £75,000 per annum is deemed to be worth £1,500,000.

An individual receiving payment of a pension at A-Day-minus-one is treated as having used part of his lifetime allowance if, following A-Day-minus-one, he begins to receive a new benefit. In this event the factor is 25:1.

There is a lifetime allowance charge of 25% on funds in excess of the lifetime allowance which are used to provide a pension. If funds in excess of the lifetime allowance are taken as a lump sum, there is a lifetime allowance charge (*FA 2004, s 215*). Historically, this charge has been 55%.

Pension age

5.15   The minimum pension age was increased from 50 to 55 with effect from 6 April 2010. Those with certain existing contractual rights to draw a pension earlier may have that right protected. There is special protection for members of those approved schemes in existence before A-Day with low normal retirement ages, such as those for sportsmen and sportswomen.

It is no longer necessary for a member to leave employment in order to access an employer's occupational pension. Members of occupational pension schemes may, where the scheme rules allow it, continue working for the same employer whilst drawing retirement benefits.

Lump sum death benefits

5.16   From April 2015, the former 55% tax charge on lump sums taken in excess of 25% was reduced to the individual's normal marginal tax rates. Also from April 2015, from age 55, whatever the size of a person's defined contribution pension pot, they will be able to take it how they want, subject to their marginal rate of income tax in that year. 25% of the pot will remain tax-free (see **5.13** for further details).

Non-cash benefits

5.17   Employers may make provision for retired former employees, which takes a form other than cash and these non-cash benefits may be provided together with a pension or entirely separately. Prior to 6 April 2006, these benefits were not taxable if only non-cash benefits were provided but were taxable if provided together with taxable cash benefits. This anomaly was rectified from 6 April 2006 by the new pensions legislation which ensure that most non-cash benefits received by former employees are taxable. This brings more closely into line the taxation on non-cash benefits received by pensioners with those received by employees. A *de minimis* limit exists for benefits which do not exceed £100 in the relevant tax year.

Budget 2007 contained a measure to ensure that the exemptions from tax work as intended, the group of 'excluded benefits' on which there is no tax charge has been expanded to include a number of exemptions similar to those received by employees. Broadly, the additional exclusions relate to continued provision of accommodation and related removal expenses, welfare counselling, recreational benefits, annual parties and similar functions, equipment for disabled former employees, which, with necessary differences to reflect the situation of retired people, mirror exemptions conferred on employees. Exclusions also relate to the writing of wills and benefits which were first provided before 6 April 1998.

Trivial pensions

5.18   From 27 March 2014, the following changes took effect relating to small pots and trivial pensions:

- the size of the lump sum small pot was raised to £10,000; and
- the total pension savings that can be taken from age 60 as a taxed lump sum from other small pots was raised to £30,000. The number which can be taken is also increased to three.

(*FA 2014, ss 41–46* and *Schs 5 to 7*).

Transitional arrangements

5.19 Transitional arrangements protected pension rights built up before A-Day, including protection for rights to lump sum payments that existed at A-Day. There were two options for transitional protection from the lifetime allowance charge:

- primary protection which was given to the value of the pre-A-Day pension rights and benefits valued in excess of £1,500,000; or

- enhanced protection which was available to individuals who ceased active membership of approved pension schemes by A-Day.

Provided that they do not resume active membership in any registered scheme, all benefits coming into payment after A-Day-minus-one will normally be exempt from the lifetime allowance charge.

Personal pension term assurance

5.20 In relation to contributions made after 31 July 2007 under occupational registered pension schemes (unless the insurer received the application for the policy before 29 March 2007 and the policy was taken out as part of the pension scheme before 1 August 2007), individuals cannot obtain tax relief for their contributions to fund pension-related personal term assurance. This change does not affect relief for contributions paid by employers.

For contributions under other registered pension schemes, the change outlined above will take effect for all contributions made after 5 April 2007, unless the insurer received the application for the policy before 14 December 2006 and the policy was taken out as part of the pension scheme before 6 April 2007. The relief may be lost if such a policy is varied.

Deduction for employers

5.21 Employers are able to claim a deduction in computing profits chargeable to UK tax for contributions which are paid by them to registered pension schemes (*FA 2004, s 196*). The previous practice of spreading large contributions over two to four years has been brought into legislation (*FA 2004, s 197*).

To be deductible, employer contributions must actually have been paid, not merely provided for in their accounts.

An anti-avoidance rule applies where an employer contributes to a registered scheme, but the related benefits will not be paid (wholly or partly) out of that scheme because some other arrangement has been made (*FA 2004, s 196A*). In this case, tax relief would be limited to the proportion of contributions relating to benefits which could only be paid out of the registered scheme.

Registration

5.22   A simpler process now applies for scheme registration and reporting (*FA 2004, ss 153, 157, 242*). The former limits on what a scheme may invest have been lifted and replaced by a single set of investment rules that applies for all pension schemes.

FA 2004, Sch 36, paras 1–6 contain provisions which treat certain pension schemes, mainly previously approved schemes, which were in existence immediately before A-Day as registered pension schemes under the unified system. Schemes that can become registered pension schemes with effect from A-Day under the unified registered pension schemes tax regime include certain retirement benefit schemes approved under former *ICTA 1988, ss 590–612*, personal pension schemes approved under former *ICTA 1988, ss 630–655*, and a range of other schemes, funds, etc.

Focus

The Autumn Budget 2017 confirmed the government's intention to make HMRC's tax registration regime even more effective at preventing fraudulent pension schemes, by aligning with the Pensions Regulator's new authorisation and supervision regime for Master Trust pension schemes, and restricting the registration of pension schemes with a dormant company as a sponsoring employer. The provisions, which took effect from 6 April 2018, aim to widen the circumstances in which HMRC may refuse to register a pension scheme, to include where the scheme is a Master Trust pension scheme and has not been authorised by the Pensions Regulator, or where a sponsoring employer of an occupational pension scheme is a dormant company (*Finance Act 2018, s 13* and *Sch 3*, amending *FA 2004*). From the same date, changes were also made to the circumstances when HMRC can de-register a pension scheme, similar to those changes being made to the circumstances when HMRC can refuse to register a pension scheme.

Eligibility

5.23   Individuals who satisfy at least one of the following criteria will be eligible to join a registered pension scheme (*FA 2004, s 189*):

- UK resident at some time during the tax year;

- earnings are chargeable to UK tax; or

- resident in the UK at some time in the previous five years and when they became a member of the pension scheme.

Members who are not resident in the UK and are not in receipt of UK earnings, but used to be UK resident at some time in the last five years, can still contribute to a scheme.

Employees seconded overseas can remain members of an occupational scheme, even where the ten-year limit for foreign service is exceeded before 6 April 2006.

Focus

Individuals coming to work in the UK who are existing members of overseas pension schemes will be eligible for tax relief on their contributions paid whilst in the UK, so long as the previous country of residence also gave relief (an intervening short stay in another country where no relief was available is ignored for this purpose) (*FA 2004, Sch 33*).

Non-registered schemes

5.24 Unapproved pension schemes are now known as employer-financed retirement benefits schemes. There is no facility for such schemes to be registered with HMRC and none of the tax advantages for registered schemes apply. Rights that existed before 6 April 2006 are protected. Amounts in non-registered pension schemes are not tested against the lifetime allowance or the lifetime allowance charge.

For a funded scheme, the following applies:

- Employer contributions, and the scheme administration costs, will only be deductible when pension benefits are actually paid and taxed on the employee (*FA 2004, s 245*).

- Employer contributions are not taxable on the employee.

- Scheme income and gains will be taxed at the rate applicable to trusts.

- The lump sum will be fully chargeable to income tax.

- The value of the fund (even a discretionary fund) will form part of an individual's death estate for IHT purposes.

Where an employee has made contributions to a registered pension scheme, but the related benefits are reduced because benefits are paid out of an unregistered scheme instead, tax relief will be denied on any expenses associated with providing the benefits. However, if the employer has already been denied relief on the contributions into the registered scheme, he will still obtain relief on the cost of the benefits (*FA 2004, s 246A*).

Where an employer guarantees benefits in an unfunded scheme, the cost of the guarantee will be assessed on the employee as a benefit in kind (*FA 2004, s 248*).

Investment

5.25 Under the unified pensions regime, there is a greater measure of freedom of investment choice (*FA 2004, Sch 36*). Thus, a pension fund can invest in residential property, as well as commercial property, works of art, etc (*FA 2004, s 186*). However, the borrowing rules for pension schemes changed on A-Day. The previous 75% limit on borrowing by self-invested personal pensions was reduced to 50% of the value of the fund. Care needs to be taken in this area – significant penalties may be imposed on self-directed pension schemes investing in residential property.

Although investment in pensions is promoted on the basis of tax breaks, there can be draconian tax charges which would eliminate these tax breaks. Besides, the types of investments being promoted often offer tax breaks anyway. The loss of control of such assets is also a disadvantage.

Loans to members (and connected persons) are prohibited and will be treated as an unauthorised payment (*FA 2004, Sch 30*) (see **5.28**).

5.26 Much has been written or said about the advantages of a self-invested personal pension (SIPP). Broadly, a SIPP is a type of personal pension where the policyholder has elected to direct the investments of the scheme fund using non-insurance company assets. SIPP investors can build up diversified portfolios through investment in a wide range of allowable asset classes including cash, UK and international equities, gilts, bonds, exchange traded funds, unit trusts, investment trusts, warrants, covered warrants and even contracts for difference. Commercial property is also allowable in some SIPPs.

Careful consideration of all factors should be undertaken before entering into such an arrangement. The possible advantages are:

- income tax relief is available at rates up to 45%;
- no capital gains tax is payable on any increase in value of the investment on an ultimate sale;
- rental profits (less mortgage payments) can accumulate within the SIPP for reinvestment;
- rental profits are not subject to income tax;
- commercial properties acquired for letting can use pension scheme as shelter;
- choice of property is not limited to UK;
- 25% of sale proceeds can be taken as tax-free lump sum;
- the balance of sale proceeds is taxed as earned income; and
- property may not have to be sold on retirement if sufficient other assets built up in pension fund to pay 25% tax-free lump sum and if income generated is sufficient to meet income requirements.

5.27   However, there are some possible disadvantages:

- there may be difficulty in finding suitable tenants: the property may not be a good investment with no income stream;

- will the property be easy to sell at retirement?;

- substantial costs may arise, such as stamp duty land tax, and legal and professional costs on purchase and on sale;

- concentration of pension investment in one or two properties may be unwise (perhaps indirect investment via property funds would be more sensible);

- control of properties is with pension scheme as landlord/freeholder not the person whose pension fund it is in;

- property may have to be sold to take benefits or to meet lifetime limits;

- transfer of own property into pension scheme may give rise to capital gains tax; and

- new limits on borrowing by pension schemes may restrict ability to invest in property via a pension scheme.

Compliance issues

5.28   The legislation governing the unified pensions regime specifically requires that all scheme tax payments need to be made electronically. Online reporting is also now mandatory.

Where unauthorised payments are made (see below), the following tax charges will arise (*FA 2004, s 208*):

- a higher rate tax charge on the payment; and

- an additional surcharge where the unauthorised payment is 25% or more of the pension fund value.

Furthermore, a higher rate tax charge on the fund value will be payable by the scheme administrator where a scheme makes one or more unauthorised payments in a year or is deregistered.

An unauthorised payment may occur in any of the following situations:

- loans made to a member or connected person;

- payment made after death for the benefit of a connected person;

- reduction in pension payments to increase the lump sum;

- assignment of the benefits of the scheme in order to avoid a lifetime allowance charge; and

- surrender of pension rights in order to avoid a lifetime allowance charge.

Scheme administrators will be required to submit an event report to HMRC in the following circumstances (*FA 2004, s 251*):

- at commencement or cessation of the scheme;

- if the scheme fails to observe any registration requirement;

- on the retirement of a member who is entitled to large benefits, or who has claimed enhanced protection;

- where a member receives benefits early;

- where lump sum payments are made for serious ill health;

- where tax-free lump sums are made under the transitional rules; and

- where benefits are taken before the normal retirement age.

Penalties may be imposed for non-compliance (*FA 2004, ss 257–266*).

FOREIGN PENSIONS

Overseas members

5.29   One feature of the simplified pension regime which came into effect on 6 April 2006 (see **5.7**) is that it allows full membership of a UK-registered pension scheme to any person, whether they are resident in the UK or not. There is no special limit on the period during which an overseas employee can be a member of a UK 'registered pension scheme'.

Foreign pensions

5.30   A foreign pension is defined as being (*ITEPA 2003, s 573(1)*):

- paid by or on behalf of a person who is outside the UK to a person who is resident in the UK; but

- not including any pension subject to *ITEPA 2003, Pt 9, Chs 5–14*.

ITEPA 2003, Pt 9, Chs 5–14 effectively cover all other types of pension apart from those paid by or on behalf of a person who is outside the UK to a person who is resident in the UK.

A UK resident is liable to tax on a foreign pension on an arising basis (*ITTOIA 2005, s 7(4)*) unless the person entitled to the pension:

- is able to satisfy HMRC that he is not domiciled in the UK; or

- is a Commonwealth (including a British) citizen or citizen of the Republic of Ireland and is able to satisfy HMRC that he is not ordinarily resident in the UK.

Such an individual continues to remain chargeable in respect of a foreign pension only on a remittance basis. In all other cases a foreign pension is taxable irrespective of whether it is actually remitted to the UK. However, all such pensions (excluding those taxed only on a remittance basis) are eligible for a 10% deduction.

Focus

Finance Act 2017 made several changes affecting the taxation of foreign pensions, which are designed to bring the UK taxation of foreign pension schemes into line with domestic UK schemes. The measures, which took effect from 6 April 2017, include the following (*FA 2017, ss 9 and 10, and Schs 3 and 4*):

- Foreign pensions no longer be able to enjoy a 10% deduction from the taxable amount. Foreign pensions or lump sums paid to a UK resident will be taxable as to 100% of the amount arising.

- These schemes (*ICTA 1988, s 615* schemes) are now closed to further contributions, and no new such schemes may be created. However, funds accrued prior to 6 April 2017 continue to be paid out according to the current rules.

- With regard to relevant non-UK schemes (RNUKS) that have had UK tax relief, individuals will now need to have been resident outside the UK for ten tax years or more, in order to escape a UK tax charge under *FA 2004, Sch 34* (prior to this change, the rules allowed an individual to access their pension funds free of UK tax after just five tax years).

- The criteria for qualifying overseas pension schemes and qualifying registered overseas pension schemes have been updated; for instance, the requirement that at least 70% of UK tax-relieved funds provide the individual with income for life has been withdrawn.

Republic of Ireland

5.31 Pensions arising in the Republic of Ireland are treated as if they arose in the UK. Such a pension still qualifies for the 10% deduction (*ITTOIA 2005, Pt 8*) (see **5.35**).

Unapproved retirement benefit schemes

5.32 A new charge to tax was imposed on benefits received after 26 July 1989 from unapproved retirement benefit schemes. Individuals in receipt of such benefits are chargeable as employment income taxed under *ITEPA 2003, ss 393* and *394*.

The charge extends, strictly, to lump sums paid to UK residents by schemes established abroad. However, *ITTOIA 2005, s 395B* gives full or partial exemption from income tax, depending on the exact level of foreign service, where the employment giving rise to the benefits was largely carried on abroad.

Income tax is not charged on lump sum relevant benefits receivable by an employee (or by his personal representatives or any dependant of his) from an overseas retirement benefits scheme where the employee's overseas service comprises (*ITTOIA 2005, s 395B(3)*):

(a)   not less than 75% of his total service in that employment; or

(b)   the whole of the last 10 years of his service in that employment, where total service exceeds 10 years; or

(c)   not less than 50% of his total service in that employment, including any 10 of the last 20 years, where total service exceeds 20 years.

If the employee's overseas service is less than described above, relief from income tax will be given by reducing the amount of the lump sum which would otherwise be chargeable by the same proportion as the overseas service bears to the employee's total service in that employment.

In addition, income tax is not charged on lump sum relevant benefits receivable by an employee (or by his personal representatives or any dependant of his) from any Superannuation Fund accepted as being within *ICTA 1988, s 615(6)*.

Overseas Pensions Act 1973

5.33   Under the provisions of the *Overseas Pensions Act 1973*, the UK government assumed responsibility for certain overseas pensions. Where, immediately before 6 April 1973, a UK resident was entitled to a foreign pension, that pension continues to be regarded as a foreign pension notwithstanding that it is now paid by the UK government. Statutory increases in the pension paid by the UK government are not subject to this provision and are taxed in full (*ITEPA 2003, s 629(1)*). A 'statutory increase' is a sum paid under any provision of the *Pensions (Increase) Act 1971* (*ITEPA 2003, s 630*).

Certain foreign pensions for this type are totally exempt from income tax (*Overseas Pensions Act 1973, s 1*). The recipient of such a pension will incur no charge to tax in respect of that pension, provided he or she is the existing pensioner or the widow/widower of the existing pensioner, and the double taxation relief arrangement under which the exemption applies continues in operation. Once again, statutory increases fall outside this provision (*ITEPA 2003, ss 629, 630* and *643*). These provisions apply to those pensions which were paid by the governments of the following countries and which were exempt from tax under a double taxation agreement (*ITEPA 2003, s 643*):

•   Malawi (including those for services to the government of the Federation of Rhodesia and Nyasaland);

- Trinidad and Tobago; and

- Zambia (including those for services to the government of Northern Rhodesia or the government of the Federation of Rhodesia and Nyasaland).

5.34   Relief under *ITEPA 2003, s 629* is extended by ESC A49 to widows' pensions paid to widows of Singapore nationality, who are resident in the UK and whose husbands were UK nationals employed in the service of the government of Singapore. The concession reads as follows:

'WIDOW'S PENSION PAID TO WIDOW OF SINGAPORE NATIONALITY, RESIDENT IN THE UNITED KINGDOM, WHOSE HUSBAND WAS A UNITED KINGDOM NATIONAL EMPLOYED AS A PUBLIC OFFICER BY THE GOVERNMENT OF SINGAPORE

Sections 614 and 615, ICTA 1988 exempt from tax certain overseas pensions, including pensions paid by the United Kingdom Government to non-residents in respect of public service with the governments of former colonies. Section 616 ICTA 1988 extends this relief to United Kingdom residents, in receipt of pensions transferred to the care of the United Kingdom Government, by the Governments of Zambia, Malawi and Trinidad and Tobago. This sub-section should be extended to exempt from tax widows' pensions paid to widows of Singapore nationality, who are resident in the United Kingdom and whose husbands were United Kingdom nationals employed in the service of the Government of Singapore.'

Note that the provisions of former *ICTA 1988, ss 614* and *615* have been rewritten into the provision of *ITEPA 2003, s 643*.

Investment of pension funds for overseas employees

5.35   Some superannuation funds are entitled to relief from UK tax on income derived from investments. The relief takes the form of taxing such income to the same extent as it would be taxed if it was the income of a person who is not resident or domiciled in the UK. Such funds are also exempt from capital gains tax.

Armed forces and war pensions

5.36   Benefits paid by any of the following Services schemes are exempt from income tax, even where the recipient continues to serve in any capacity (*ITEPA 2003, ss 639, 640A; FA 2015, s 15(1)*):

- new armed forces pensions;

- armed forces compensation schemes; and

- early departure payments scheme.

Wounds and disability pensions

5.37 Income from the following list of wounds and disability pensions is exempt from income tax and will not be reckoned in computing income for any of the purposes of the *Income Tax Acts*. The qualifying pensions are (*ITEPA 2003, s 641(1)*):

- wounds pensions granted to members of the armed forces of the Crown;
- retired pay of disabled officers granted on account of medical unfitness attributable to or aggravated by armed forces service;
- disablement or disability pensions granted to members, other than commissioned officers, of the naval, military or air forces of the Crown on account of medical unfitness attributable to or aggravated by armed forces service;
- disablement pensions granted to persons who have been employed in the nursing services of any of the naval, military or air forces of the Crown on account of medical unfitness attributable to or aggravated by armed forces service;
- injury and disablement pensions payable under any War Risks Compensation Scheme for the Mercantile marine; and
- a benefit under a scheme established by an order under *Armed Forces (Pensions and Compensation) Act 2004, s 1(2)*, payable to a person by reason of his illness or injury by way of a lump sum, or following the termination of the person's service in the armed forces or reserve forces.

Where only part of the retired pay or pensions is attributable to the qualifying pensions (above), relief will only extend to that part certified by the Secretary of State after consultation with the appropriate government department, to be attributable to disablement or disability (*ITEPA 2003, s 641(2)*).

Victoria Cross and other awards

5.38 No liability to income tax arises on a pension or annuity if it is paid to the holder of an award for bravery in respect of the award. Awards for bravery include (*ITEPA 2003, s 638*):

- the Victoria Cross;
- the George Cross;
- the Albert Medal or the Edward Medal;
- the Military Cross;
- the Distinguished Flying Cross;
- the Distinguished Conduct Medal;
- the Conspicuous Gallantry Medal;

- the Distinguished Service Medal;
- the Military Medal; and
- the Distinguished Flying Medal.

Pensions in respect of death due to war

5.39   The payment of the pensions or allowances set out below is not treated as income for any purposes of the *Income Tax Acts* (*ITEPA 2003, s 639*). The pensions and allowances are:

(1)   any pension or allowance payable by or on behalf of the Ministry of Defence as relates to death due to:

    (a)   service in the armed forces of the Crown or wartime service in the merchant navy, or

    (b)   war injuries;

(2)   any pension or allowance at similar rates and subject to similar conditions which is payable by the Ministry of Defence in respect of death due to peacetime service in the armed forces of the Crown before 3 September 1939; and

(3)   any pension or allowance which is payable under the law of a country other than the UK and which is of a character substantially similar to a pension or allowance falling within para (1) or (2) above.

If one of the above pensions or allowances is withheld or abated by reason of the receipt of a non-qualifying pension or allowance, then an equal amount of the non-qualifying pension or allowance to the qualifying pension or allowance that is withheld or abated will be treated as falling within the exemption.

NON-TAXABLE STATE BENEFITS

Introduction

5.40   The basic rule is that all benefits payable under *Social Security Contributions and Benefits Act 1992, Pts II–IV* and its Northern Ireland counterpart, the *Social Security Contributions and Benefits (Northern Ireland) Act 1992*, are taxable under the charge on general earnings provisions of the *Income Tax (Earnings and Pensions) Act 2003* (*ITEPA 2003, ss 660* (Taxable benefits: UK benefits – Table A) and *677* (UK social security benefits wholly exempt from tax: Table B)).

Non-taxable benefits

5.41   The following benefits are not taxable (*ITEPA 2003, ss 656–677*):

- attendance allowance;

- bereavement payment;
- child benefit (but may be subject to the child benefit high income charge);
- child tax credit;
- council tax benefit;
- disability living allowance;
- guardian's allowance;
- housing benefit;
- industrial injuries benefit;
- job grant;
- pensioner's Christmas bonus;
- payments out of the social fund;
- severe disablement allowance;
- statutory maternity allowance;
- state pension credit;
- winter fuel payment; and
- working tax credit.

TAXABLE STATE BENEFITS

Taxable benefits

5.42   Social security income is, in principle, taxed in the same way as other sources of income, but the majority of state benefits are not in fact taxable.

The following benefits are taxable as social security income under the *Income Tax (Earnings and Pensions) Act 2003*, broadly on entitlement in the tax year:

- bereavement allowance;
- carer's allowance;
- incapacity benefit (excluding certain long-term incapacity benefit, and short-term incapacity benefit not payable at the higher rate);
- income support (if payable to one member of a married or unmarried couple involved in a trade dispute) up to a taxable maximum;
- jobseeker's allowance (excluding child maintenance bonus) up to a taxable maximum;
- statutory adoption pay;
- statutory maternity pay;

- ordinary statutory paternity pay; and

- statutory sick pay.

Additions to the above taxable benefits for child dependency are not taxable.

Sickness, maternity, paternity, adoption and disability payments

5.43 Sickness or disability payments paid to employees, where such payments have been arranged by the employer, are taxed as employment income (regardless of whether they are paid to the employee or to members of their family or household) (*ITEPA 2003, ss 221, 660*).

Statutory maternity pay (SMP), ordinary statutory paternity pay (OSPP), statutory adoption pay (SAP) and statutory sick pay (SSP) paid by the employer are also taxable under these charging provisions.

A lump sum received under a life, accident or sickness insurance policy is not normally regarded as income for tax purposes. From 6 April 1996, continuing benefits from certain policies are also exempt; otherwise, there is a standard 12-month period for exemption of benefits received in respect of a fall in earnings caused by ill-health or disability.

Agency workers

5.44 In the case of *Commissioners for HMRC v Thorn Baker Limited and others* [2007] EWCA Civ 626, the Court of Appeal upheld the decision of the High Court and dismissed HMRC's appeal concerning the payment of statutory sick pay (SSP) to agency workers. The case confirms that SSP is not payable to agency workers whose contract with the agency is for a specified period of three months or less. However, in response to the court's decision, HMRC published a reminder for agencies who should note that their workers can become entitled to SSP if, in a single contract:

- they work longer than the original period specified and the total period actually worked exceeds three months; or

- the contract is extended for more than three months.

Agency workers whose contracts are for three months or less can also become entitled to SSP if two or more such contracts with the same agency are separated by eight weeks or less (56 days) and:

- the total length of the contracts is more than 13 weeks;

- the total period actually worked becomes more than 13 weeks; or

- the contracts are extended so that together they can run for more than 13 weeks.

The Court of Appeal ruling applies to agency workers only. Other short-term contract workers are unaffected and remain entitled to SSP.

Incapacity benefit

5.45   Incapacity benefits are treated as income for tax purposes (*ITEPA 2003, s 660, Table A*), with the following exceptions:

- benefit payable for an 'initial period of incapacity'; and

- any increase in benefit which is in respect of a child (*ITEPA 2003, s 676*).

An 'initial period of incapacity' is the period for which short-term incapacity benefit is payable otherwise than at the higher rate.

Incapacity benefit is not treated as chargeable income where a person's period of incapacity for work started before 13 April 1995 and, for part of the period prior to that date, the person was entitled to invalidity benefit.

Tax is charged on the amount of benefit accruing in the year of assessment (*ITEPA 2003, s 661*).

Focus

Employment and Support Allowance (ESA) was introduced on 27 October 2008 and replaced Incapacity Benefit and Income Support, paid because of an illness or disability, for new claimants only. Individuals already receiving Incapacity Benefit continue to receive it, but recipients are currently being reassessed and moved to the new benefit.

Employment and Support Allowance

5.46   Employment and Support Allowance (ESA) replaced Incapacity Benefit and Income Support from 27 October 2008. ESA is a benefit for people who cannot work because of illness or disability. It involves a new medical assessment called the Work Capability Assessment, which is designed to ascertain what people can do, rather than what they cannot.

ESA consists of two phases:

- the assessment phase rate is paid for the first 13 weeks of a claim while a decision is made on the claimant's capability for work through the Work Capability Assessment; and

- the main phase starts from week 14 of a claim, if the Work Capability Assessment shows that illness or disability does limit the claimant's ability to work.

There are two groups within the main phase:

- Work Related Activity Group – where claimants are expected to take part in work-focused interviews with a personal adviser; and

- Support Group – in which claimants are placed because their illness or disability has a severe effect on their ability to work. Claimants will not be expected to take part in any work but they can do so on a voluntary basis if they wish. Claimants will receive a support component in addition to the basic rate of ESA.

Income Support

5.47 Employment and Support Allowance (ESA) replaced Incapacity Benefit and Income Support, paid because of an illness or disability, for new claimants only from October 2008. Individuals already receiving Income Support continue to receive it, but it is intended that all recipients will gradually be moved to the new benefit.

Income Support is taxable if the claimant's right to the benefit is subject to a condition that he shall be registered for employment, or he is one of a married or unmarried couple and he is disqualified from receiving unemployment benefit because he is involved in a trade dispute (*ITEPA 2003, s 665*). This means that any Income Support which the striker receives in respect of his partner's needs is taxable.

Where Income Support is taxable, any sum paid in excess of the 'taxable maximum' is not taxable. The taxable maximum is:

- the weekly rate of unemployment benefit if the recipient is an individual;

- the weekly rate of unemployment benefit plus the adult dependent supplement where the recipient is one of a married or unmarried couple and the recipient is not involved in a trade dispute; or

- one-half of the amount which would otherwise be payable where the recipient is one of a married or unmarried couple and he is involved in a trade dispute.

The taxable maximum in respect of part of a week is calculated as follows (*ITEPA 2003, s 668(3)*):

$$\frac{N}{7} \times TMW$$

where:

- N is the number of days in the part of the week for which the claimant is actually paid Income Support

- TMW is the taxable maximum for the whole week, as calculated above.

No liability on income tax arises on payments of Income Support which are attributable to child maintenance bonus (*ITEPA 2003, s 666*).

Jobseeker's allowance

5.48   Payments of jobseeker's allowance are generally taxable as social security income (*ITEPA 2003, s 660*). However, where jobseeker's allowance paid in respect of a week or part of a week exceeds the taxable maximum, the excess is not taxable.

The taxable maximum varies according to whether the payment is of income-based or contribution-based jobseeker's allowance, and whether it is paid to one of a married or unmarried couple, or to a single person. The amount in each case is fixed by regulations under *Jobseekers Act 1995, s 4*.

Retirement pensions

5.49   The state retirement pension (categories A to D) is payable under *Social Security Contributions and Benefits Act 1992, ss 43–55* and the equivalent Northern Ireland provisions, and is accordingly taxable under *ITEPA 2003, s 577*.

5.50   An individual may receive additional money if they defer their state pension.

For those who reach state pension age on or after 6 April 2016, the new state pension will increase by 1% for every nine weeks that a claim is deferred. This works out at just under 5.8% for every full year it is deferred. To receive additional state pension, the individual has to defer claiming for at least nine weeks.

Those who reached state pension age before 6 April 2016 can take extra state pension as either higher weekly payments, or a one-off lump sum. An individual has three months after making a claim to decide how they wish to take the extra state pension. To receive additional state pension, the individual has to defer claiming for at least five weeks. Extra state pension is earned at the rate of 1% of the normal weekly state pension rate for every five weeks the claimant defers (this is equivalent to about 10.4% extra for every year deferred).

> **Example 5.1—Deferring state pension: reaching state pension age on or after 6 April 2016 (I)**
>
> An individual is entitled to full new state pension of £164.35 a week, which works out at £8,546.20 a year.
>
> By deferring for one year, the individual will receive an extra £493 a year (just under 5.8% of £8,546.20).
>
> This example assumes there is no annual increase in the State Pension. If there is an annual increase, the amount received could be larger.

Example 5.1A—Deferring state pension: reaching state pension age before 6 April 2016

An individual is entitled to £125.95 a week (the full basic state pension), which works out at £6,549.40 a year.

By deferring for one year, the individual will receive an extra £681 a year (10.4% of £,549.40).

This example assumes there is no annual increase in the State Pension. If there is an annual increase, the amount received could be larger.

5.51   To receive a lump sum payment, the individual has to defer claiming for at least 12 months (which cannot include any period before 6 April 2005). The lump sum is a one-off, taxable payment based on the amount of normal weekly state pension the claimant would have received, plus interest. They also receive their state pension paid at the normal rate from when they start claiming it.

The interest rate will always be 2% above the Bank of England's base rate (so, if the base rate was 4.5%, the rate of interest would be 6.5%). As the Bank of England base rate may change from time to time, the rate of interest used to calculate the lump sum can also change.

Example 5.2—Deferring state pension (II)

Alan decides to defer claiming his weekly state pension of £105 for three years. When he finally claims, if he chooses a lump sum, he will get a lump sum of around £18,000 (before tax) as well as his normal weekly state pension entitlement.

(In this illustrative example, the lump sum is based on £105 state pension and interest of 6.5% for the whole period. In a real example, the amount will take account of changes in both the weekly state pension and the interest rate.)

Focus

The State Pension Top Up (SPTU) scheme was introduced on 12 October 2015 and ran until 5 April 2017. The scheme allowed anyone entitled to a state pension who reached state pension age before 6 April 2016 to obtain extra state pension income for life by making a voluntary lump sum National Insurance Contribution (Class 3A).

Pension credit

5.52   Pension credit is an income-related benefit for people aged 60 or over living in Great Britain that provides, or contributes to, a guaranteed level of income of £167.25 per week from April 2019 for a single person (£255.25 for a couple from April 2019). These amounts may be more for people who have caring responsibilities, are severely disabled or have certain housing costs.

People aged 65 and over can also be rewarded for some of their savings and income they have for their retirement (Savings Credit). Pension credit gives pensioners a cash addition of 60 pence for every £1 of income they have above the level of basic state pension, up to a maximum of £13.72 (from April 2019) a week (£15.35 a week for couples from April 2019).

After this, the maximum reward is reduced by 40 pence for every £1 of income above the income guarantee.

Those reaching state pension age on or after 6 April 2016 may not be eligible for the pension savings credit. Savings Credit may be payable, however, if both of the following apply:

●   the claimant is in a couple and one of them reached state pension age before 6 April 2016; and

●   the claimant was receiving Savings Credit up to 6 April 2016.

Where the claimant ceases to be eligible for Savings Credit for any reason from 6 April 2016, they will not be able to receive it again (see www.gov.uk/pension-credit/eligibility for further details).

Pension credit is a non-taxable state benefit.

Focus

Full details regarding applications for pension credit are available online at www.gov.uk/pension-credit.

Statutory redundancy payments

5.53   Genuine redundancy payments will be exempt from income tax under *ITEPA 2003, s 309*. 'Redundancy payment' has the same meaning as in *Employment Rights Act 1996, Pt XI* or *Contracts of Employment and Redundancy Payments Act (Northern Ireland) 1965, Pt XII*.

Employers that dismiss employees for redundancy must pay those with two years' service an amount based on the employee's weekly pay, length of service and age. The weekly pay is subject to a maximum amount. From 6 April 2019, this is £525, increasing from £508 (*SI 2019/324*). This means that the top award of statutory redundancy pay also increases from April 2019 to £15,750 from £15,240.

The limit of the amount of compensatory award for unfair dismissal is £86,444 from April 2019 (rising from £83,682) (*SI 2019/324*).

The maximum statutory redundancy payment increases every year in line with the retail prices index.

Taxable benefits rates

5.54

	Weekly from 6 April 2019
Bereavement benefits	
Bereavement allowance – standard	119.90
Carer's allowance	
Each qualifying individual	66.15
Incapacity benefit	
Long-term	112.25
Short-term higher rate (weeks 29 to 52):	
– under pension age	100.20
– over pension age	112.25
Severe disablement allowance	
Basic rate	79.50
Age addition higher rate	11.90
Middle rate	6.60
Lower rate	6.60
Jobseeker's allowance	
Under 25	57.90
25 or over	73.10
Non-contributory retirement pension	
Single person (category C or D)	77.45
Age addition (over 80)	0.25
Retirement pensions	
Single person	129.20
Age addition (over 80) – each	0.25
Statutory adoption pay	
Rate	148.68
(Paid for maximum of 39 weeks)	

	Weekly from 6 April 2019
Statutory maternity pay	
For first 6 weeks – 90% of average weekly earnings with no upper limit	
Remaining 33 weeks – Standard rate or a rate equal to 90% of average weekly earnings, whichever is lower	
Standard rate	148.68
Ordinary statutory paternity pay	
Rate	148.68
(Paid for 2 weeks)	
Statutory sick pay	
(Above earnings threshold of £116)	94.25

Non-contributory benefits

5.55 National Insurance contributions (NICs) pay for only certain state benefits. Many benefits are based on need or circumstantial conditions, with no link to past contributions paid. Instead, they are based on some other link to the system, such as residence, and they are often subject to income limits or means testing. These non-contributory benefits are funded from general taxation and include:

- attendance allowance;
- child benefit;
- constant attendance allowance;
- council tax benefit;
- disability living allowance;
- guardian's allowance;
- housing benefit (including council tax rebate);
- income-based jobseeker's allowance;
- income support;
- industrial injuries disablement benefit;
- invalid care allowance;
- reduced earnings allowance;
- category D retirement pension;

- one parent benefit;

- severe and exceptionally severe disablement allowances;

- social fund;

- statutory adoption pay;

- statutory maternity pay;

- statutory sick pay;

- statutory paternity pay;

- war disablement pension;

- war widow's pension; and

- workmen's compensation supplement.

Focus

Statutory sick pay, statutory maternity pay, ordinary and additional statutory paternity pay and statutory adoption pay are linked with NICs, in that entitlement is based on recent receipt of earnings subject to Class 1 NICs.

Contributory benefits

5.56   Eligibility for the remaining social security benefits depends on an individual satisfying certain requirements as to the level of contributions which have been made (ie contributory benefits), though in some cases certain circumstantial conditions also apply. Contributory benefits include:

- incapacity benefit;

- contribution-based jobseeker's allowance;

- maternity allowance;

- retirement pension (category A and B);

- widowed mother's allowance;

- widow's payment; and

- widow's pension.

The category A pension is payable on the basis of a person's own contributions, while the category B pension is payable to a woman by virtue of her husband's contributions or to a man by virtue of his late wife's contributions. The pension may consist only of the basic component or, if appropriate contributions have been paid, of basic and additional earnings-related components.

CLASS 3 NATIONAL INSURANCE CONTRIBUTIONS

Overview

5.57   Class 3 National Insurance contributions (NICs) are voluntary contributions. A person is never liable to pay Class 3 contributions, but he may be entitled to pay them, to protect entitlement to widows' benefits and the basic retirement pension. In certain limited cases involving overseas employment, voluntary Class 2 contributions may be paid as an alternative to Class 3 in order to protect entitlement to incapacity benefit and maternity allowance on the employee's return to the UK.

Voluntary contributions count towards:

- basic state pension;

- widowed parent's allowance;

- bereavement payment;

- bereavement allowance; and

- child's special allowance.

They do not count towards:

- jobseeker's allowance;

- the earnings-related part of state pension;

- the earnings-related part of bereavement benefits;

- maternity allowance;

- incapacity benefit; or

- industrial injuries disablement benefit.

Focus

Further details on Class 3 NICs, including an application form, can be found in leaflet CA5603, available online at https://assets.publishing. service.gov.uk/government/uploads/system/uploads/attachment_data/ file/743370/CA5603.pdf.

Eligibility

5.58   Class 3 contributions may be paid by anyone who is:

- over 16;

- not working;

- not liable to pay Class 1 and/or Class 2 contributions as an employed or self-employed person;

- been excepted from paying Class 2 contributions; or

- resident in the UK, living or working on secondment abroad. An individual may also pay either Class 2 contributions or voluntary contributions once the initial 52 weeks' Class 1 contributions liability period has ended.

Class 3 contributions cannot be paid if the person:

- is a married woman or widow who opted to pay reduced rate contributions during the whole tax year;

- is paying for the tax year in which they reach state pension age;

- is already entitled to a full basic state pension;

- does not have enough contributions to qualify for a minimum basic state pension unless he or she needs to pay voluntary contributions to qualify for the lump sum bereavement payment; and

- is paying for any week that he or she is entitled to National Insurance credits, including automatic credits, unless he or she needs to pay a voluntary contribution to satisfy the first qualifying condition for basic state pension or bereavement allowance.

Focus

In *Garland v Revenue & Customs Commrs* [2012] UKUT 471 (TCC), the Upper Tribunal upheld the First-tier Tribunal decision ([2011] UKFTT 273 (TC)) on the payment of backdated Class 3 NICs, in which it was ruled that Mr Garland was not entitled to pay contributions for the time that he was employed in Kenya.

Time limits

5.59   To count towards basic state pension and bereavement benefits, voluntary contributions must generally be paid before the end of the sixth tax year following the one in respect of which they are paid.

If voluntary contributions are paid after the end of the second tax year in respect of which they are paid, they will normally have to be paid at a higher rate.

Making payment

Paying for earlier tax years

5.60   An individual who wishes to make payment of Class 3 NICs for earlier tax year(s), and is within the time limit for payment, should contact:

HM Revenue & Customs National Insurance Contributions Office Contributor Caseworker Benton Park View Newcastle upon Tyne NE98 1ZZ

If payment is made before the six-year deadline, the voluntary contributions will be due at the original rate.

Deciding to pay

5.61   Before deciding whether an individual needs to or should pay voluntary contributions, he should consider getting a state pension forecast. The forecast will advise in today's money values:

- the amount of basic state pension earned to date;

- the amount of basic state pension that can be expected at state pension age based on what has been earned already and what might be earned before retirement; and

- if a payment of voluntary contributions will boost basic state pension and the amount that can be paid, at today's rates.

Focus

A state pension statement (formerly known as a pension forecast) can be obtained online at the government information website (www.gov.uk), or by filling in form BR19 State Pension forecast application (www.gov.uk/government/uploads/system/uploads/attachment_data/file/526317/br19-interactive.pdf).

5.62   The number of qualifying years needed to receive a full basic state pension has been reduced to 30 for men born on or after 6 April 1945 and for women born on or after 6 April 1950. (Men born before 6 April 1945 usually need 44 qualifying years, and women born before 6 April 1950 usually need 39 qualifying years to receive a full basic state retirement pension.) The government has confirmed that, where individuals have continued to make voluntary contributions since 25 May 2006, but would have chosen not to do so had they been aware of the government's intention to reduce the number of qualifying years required for a full basic state pension to 30, they may be entitled to a refund.

A person may now want to claim a refund of voluntary contributions that they have made since 25 May 2006 if, for example, they retire after 6 April 2010 and would have had at least 30 qualifying years in their contribution histories even if they had never made any voluntary contributions. Such individuals would be entitled to a full basic state pension without the extra qualifying years earned as a result of the voluntary contributions made.

No refunds will be offered for any NICs that were paid prior to 25 May 2006. These contributions were paid properly at the time in accordance with the law and in line with government policy.

In practice, some people may choose not to claim a refund, as it means they will be forgoing the accruals of entitlement to bereavement benefits that those contributions would have provided.

Chapter 6

Employment

SIGNPOSTS

- Employment status is important for tax purposes, as there are many differences between the tax treatment of employed and self-employed individuals (see **6.1**).

- Income from employment is usually subject to tax and National Insurance contributions under the Pay As You Earn (PAYE) system (see **6.9**).

- Substantial penalties may be imposed on employers for late payment of PAYE and the late submission of returns (see **6.27**).

- Employed earners generally pay Class 1 National Insurance contributions (NICs) on their emoluments from their employment (see **6.33**).

- Class 1A NICs are payable by employers on most benefits in kind liable to income tax (see **6.36**).

- Class 1B NICs are payable by employers on benefits in kind which are subject to a PAYE Settlement Agreement (PSA) (see **6.37**).

- Some expenses payments and benefits are treated as taxable remuneration (see **6.49**).

- The provision by an employer of certain types of benefit in kind may be non-taxable (see **6.80**).

- Employees can generally claim relief for expenses incurred 'wholly, exclusively and necessarily' in the performance of their duties and for travel expenses necessarily incurred by employees in performing those duties (see **6.90**).

- Genuine redundancy of up to £30,000 may be exempt from income tax. From 6 April 2018 all payments in lieu of a notice period will be taxable, regardless of contractual entitlement (see **6.93**).

- When directors and employees acquire shares (and securities) in their company, income tax may be chargeable as employment income (see **6.104**).

- The limit on the value of shares over which options may be held by an employee under the Enterprise Management Incentive (EMI) scheme is £250,000 (see **6.107**).

- Anti-avoidance provisions exist to prevent individuals from avoiding tax and NIC by providing services through an intermediary – known as the IR35 legislation (see **6.116**).

EMPLOYMENT

Employed or self-employed?

6.1   Whether an individual is employed or self-employed is an important question for tax purposes, as there are many differences in the way in which they are taxed.

Employees are taxed under the PAYE system, with income tax and Class 1 NICs being deducted from payments made to them. Class 1 NICs are also payable by their employers (see **6.33**). In contrast, the self-employed currently pay income tax, Class 2 and Class 4 NICs direct to HMRC (see **7.90**).

Some important consequences are that:

- the NIC liability of a self-employed individual is generally lower than that for an employee (especially when taking into account the employer's liability) (see *Athenaeum Club v R & C Commrs* [2010] UKFTT 27 (TC));

- the self-employed have a cash-flow advantage in the timing of tax payments under self-assessment, compared with employees taxed under the PAYE system;

- the rules allowing tax relief for expenses are generally more relaxed for the self-employed; and

- except in limited circumstances, an employer who incorrectly treats an employee as self-employed is liable for the income tax and National Insurance that should have been applied under PAYE (subject to a potential right of recovery from the employee). However, as a result of the *Demibourne* case referred to in **6.3**, *SI 2008/782* came into force from 6 April 2008. The regulations extended the limited circumstances where HMRC may make a direction to transfer an employer's PAYE liability to an employee who has received payments from which tax has been under-deducted.

Indicative factors

6.2   There is no legislation to distinguish between employment and self-employment, but numerous cases decided in the courts have provided guidance as to the indicating factors (see **6.3**). HMRC guidance on employment status can be found on the gov.uk website at www.gov.uk/employment-status. HMRC's Employment Status Manual is a further valuable source of information, which can be accessed at https://www.gov.uk/hmrc-internal-manuals/employment-status-manual.

The guidance given by HMRC in booklet CWG2 (*Employer further guide to PAYE and NICs*) states:

'… "employee" means anyone who is gainfully employed in the UK and is:

- engaged under a "contract of service". Where you pay somebody to work for you, that arrangement will normally amount to either a contract of service (employment) or a contract for services (self-employment). Almost everyone who works for an employer will be employed under a contract of service, including full-time, part-time, casual or temporary employment. A contract need not be written, but can be a verbal or implied working agreement, or

- an office holder with earnings chargeable to tax. An office holder is someone appointed to hold a titled office (including an elective office), for example a company director, or

- engaged through an agency or some other third party …

… In addition "employee" includes, for most PAYE purposes, many pensioners and others who get PAYE income (eg ex-employees). Similarly "employer" includes, for most PAYE purposes, agencies, pension-payers and others who make payments of PAYE income.'

The term 'office' is widely defined in the legislation (*ITEPA 2003, ss 5, 564*) as any position which has an existence, independent of the person who holds it, and may be filled by successive holders. The interpretation of office has historically relied on the element of permanence (*Great Western Rly Co v Bater* [1922] 2 AC 1, 8 TC 231), although the position does not need to be particularly long term. Common examples of office-holders include coroners, company secretaries, clergymen and company directors.

Case law

6.3   The following is a list of case law (in alphabetical order) of the main cases relevant to employment status. Also provided is the HMRC Employment Status Manual paragraph number, where applicable, where a summary of each case can be found, and a brief outline of the point of issue in each case:

ESM Para Number	*Case Title*	*Case Reference*
ESM7060	*Airfix Footwear Ltd v Cope*	**[1978] ICR 1210**

Whether Mrs Cope was engaged under a 'contract of employment' and therefore entitled to claim unfair dismissal under the *Trade Union and Labour Relations Act 1974*.

ESM7150	*Andrews v King*	**64 TC 332**

The tax inspector had contended that Mr Andrews was a self-employed gangmaster and assessable under Schedule D and, further, that he was the employer of the gang members and so obliged to operate PAYE. Mr Andrews contended that he and the other gang members were employees.

ESM7170	*Barnett v Brabyn*	**69 TC 133**

There were two issues the court had to consider in this case. The preliminary issue was whether it was open to Mr Brabyn to challenge additional assessments under Case I Schedule D on the ground that he was never an independent contractor, even though the main assessments had been appealed and determined under *TMA 1970, s 54*. It was decided he could challenge the additional assessments. The second and substantive issue was the nature of his employment status.

	Cable & Wireless v Muscat	**[2006] EWCA Civ 220**

An implied contract of employment was found to exist between Cable & Wireless and Mr Muscat, on the basis that Muscat's contract for services with his agency, Abraxas, did not reflect the reality of his relationship with C&W. In previous cases in which contractors have claimed employment rights from end users, they have failed because no contractual nexus existed: that is, the contractor's company had a contractual relationship with the agency, but not with the end user. This case makes it clear that a contractual nexus in the traditional sense is not necessary and an implied employment contract can be considered to exist.

ESM7200	*Carmichael & Another v National Power plc*	**[1999] 1 WLR 2042**

Whether Mrs Carmichael ('Mrs C') was an employee under a 'contract of employment' as defined in the *Employment Protection (Consolidation) Act 1978* and therefore entitled to written terms of the particulars of employment. Under this Act it was necessary to be engaged under a contract of employment for a minimum of 13 weeks to obtain this entitlement.

ESM Para Number	*Case Title*	*Case Reference*

ESM7190   *Clark v Oxfordshire Health*   **[1998] IRLR 125**
                            Authority

The Oxfordshire Health Authority administered a 'nurse bank' and supplied the services of bank nurses to a number of hospitals within its area. Mrs Clark joined the nurse bank as a staff nurse in January 1991. Her employment ended in January 1994 and she then claimed unfair dismissal and race discrimination. For her case to succeed she had to establish that she had been engaged under a contract of service.

ESM7190   *Dacas v Brook Street*   **[2004] EWCA Civ 217**
                            Bureau UK Ltd

The agency (Brook Street Bureau) was not held to be the employer. However, the Court of Appeal gave a very strong indication that the end user in that case (Wandsworth Council) may have been an employer of the agency worker (Mrs Dacas) under an implied contract of employment.

ESM7020   *Davies v Braithwaite*   **18 TC 198**

Miss Braithwaite claimed that various contracts between her and theatrical producers were contracts of service. The Revenue contended that she was exercising her profession as an actress and was therefore correctly assessed under Case II of Schedule D.

ESM7020   *Demibourne Ltd v HMRC*   **SpC 486**

This case concerned the way in which tax paid by an individual in an employment status case was to be treated for the purpose of a PAYE settlement with the employer. The particular concern was the potential difficulty raised by the case in terms of whether or not it was possible to continue with long-standing arrangements that had often been applied whereby HMRC had allowed an offset of tax paid by an individual whilst they were treated as self-employed in arriving at the PAYE settlement due from the employer, and the method to be adopted.

ESM7080   *Edwards v Clinch*   **56 TC 367**

The question for determination was whether fees paid to Mr Clinch were chargeable to tax under Schedule E as emoluments of an 'office' or chargeable under Schedule D.

ESM7210   *Express & Echo*   **[1999] IRLR 367**
                            Publications Ltd v Ernest
                            Tanton

Whether a newspaper delivery driver was engaged under a contract of service or a contract for services.

ESM Para Number	**Case Title**	**Case Reference**
ESM7055	***Fall v Hitchen***	**49 TC 435**

Whether a professional dancer was engaged under a contract of service or whether he was exercising his profession and, therefore, engaged under a contract for services.

ESM7280	***Future Online Ltd v Foulds***	**76 TC 590**

Whether the *Social Security Contributions (Intermediaries) Regulations 2000* and *FA 2000, Sch 12* applied to the provision of services by an IT consultant working through his own service company.

ESM7050	***Global Plant Ltd v Secretary of State for Social Services***	**[1971] 1 QB 139**

Whether drivers of earth-moving equipment were engaged under contracts of service or contracts for services.

ESM7160	***Hall v Lorimer***	**66 TC 349**

Whether a freelance vision mixer was engaged under a series of contracts of service or assessable under Schedule D as a person in business on his own account.

ESM7165	***Lane v The Shire Roofing Company (Oxford) Ltd***	**[1995] TLR 104**

Whether Mr Lane was engaged under a contract of service or a contract for services.

ESM7140	***Lee Ting Sang v Chung Chi-Keung***	**[1990] 2 AC 374**

During the course of his work at a construction site in Hong Kong, Lee Ting Sang was injured and he claimed compensation under the *Employees' Compensation Ordinance*. The courts had to determine as a preliminary issue whether he was working as an employee under a contract of service.

ESM7220	***MacFarlane & Skivington v Glasgow City Council***	**EAT/1277/99**

Mrs MacFarlane ('Mrs F') and Mrs Skivington ('Mrs S') had previously worked as gymnastic instructors for Glasgow City Council (the 'Council') on a casual basis, when in 1992 the Council attempted to regularise the relationship by sending them a document setting out their terms of engagement. Both declined to sign the document. In 1998, Mrs M and Mrs S claimed unfair dismissal. The preliminary matter was whether they had been engaged under contracts of service or contracts for service.

ESM Para Number Case Title   *Case Reference*

ESM7180   *McMeechan v Secretary of* **[1997] IRLR 353**
                    State for Employment

Mr McMeechan was on the books of an employment agency, Noel Employment Ltd, as a temporary catering assistant for about a year. When the agency became insolvent, he sought to recover from the Redundancy Fund, under *Employment Protection (Consolidation) Act 1978, s 122*, the unpaid earnings due to him in respect of his last engagement. This had been with a client, Sutcliffe Catering, and he was claiming the sum of £105. The underlying matter to be decided was whether Mr McMeechan had been an employee of the agency during the course of this particular engagement.

ESM7040   *Market Investigations Ltd v* **[1969] 2 QB 173**
                    Minister of Social Security

Whether an interviewer, who was engaged on a casual basis, was employed under a series of contracts of service or under a series of contracts for services.

ESM7070   *Massey v Crown Life*   **[1978] 1 WLR 676**
                    Insurance Company

This case involved a claim for unfair dismissal under the *Trade Union and Labour Relations Act 1974*. Mr Massey could only have succeeded if it was found that he was employed under a contract of service.

ESM7240   *Montgomery v Johnson*   **[2001] EWCA Civ 318**
                    Underwood Ltd

Whether a person who was engaged by an employment agency to provide her services as a receptionist/telephonist to a third party was engaged by the employment agency under a contract of service or by the third party under a contract of service.

ESM7025   *Morren v Swinton and*   **[1965] 1 WLR 576**
                    Pendlebury Council

Whether an engineer, who worked for a local authority, was engaged under a contract of service or a contract for services for the purposes of the *Local Government Superannuation Act 1937*.

ESM7090   *Narich Pty Limited v The*   **[1984] ICR 286**
                    Commissioner of Payroll Tax

This is an Australian case that was decided by the Judicial Committee of the Privy Council. Judgments of the Judicial Committee in Commonwealth cases have no value to UK law where the points at issue only concern interpretation of statute of the Commonwealth country. However, they are of relevance where general law principles are considered. The point at issue was whether lecturers engaged to conduct weight-watching classes were employees or not.

ESM Para Number	Case Title	Case Reference
ESM7110	*Nethermere (St Neots) Ltd v Gardiner and Taverna*	**[1984] IRLR 240**

The Industrial Tribunal had to consider as a preliminary issue whether the applicants were 'employees' employed under contracts of service or whether they were self-employed under contracts for services.

ESM7100	*O'Kelly and Others v Trusthouse Forte plc*	**[1984] 1 QB 90**

Mr O'Kelly and some other casual catering staff were claiming that Trusthouse Forte had unfairly dismissed them for an inadmissible reason. The preliminary issue in the case was whether they were employees working under contracts of service or independent contractors working under contracts for services.

	Oziegbe v R & C Commrs	**[2014] UKFTT 608 (TC)**

The First-tier Tribunal allowed the taxpayer's appeal against PAYE and NIC assessments and penalty liabilities, finding that security guards provided by the taxpayer on building construction sites were not agency workers as neither the taxpayer nor the clients had control or the right of control over how security guards performed their work.

	Petrol Services Ltd	*(2019) TC 06907*

The First-tier Tribunal reviewed the directors' contracts and, dismissing the appeal, concluded that they should properly be regarded as contracts of service. The evidence indicated that the directors did not have an independent business which constituted the source of the payments, with the result that those payments arose from the directors' offices or employments with the appellant.

ESM7030	*Ready Mixed Concrete (South East) Ltd v Minister of Pensions and National Insurance*	**[1967] 2 QB 497**

Whether an owner-driver of a vehicle used exclusively for the delivery of a company's ready mixed concrete was engaged under a contract of service or a contract for services.

ESM7120	*Sidey v Phillips*	**59 TC 458**

The point at issue was whether Mr Sidey received part-time lecturing fees under contracts of service or contracts for services.

ESM Para Number	*Case Title*	*Case Reference*
ESM7230	*St John's College School, Cambridge v Secretary of State for Social Security*	**[2001] ELR 103**

Whether visiting instrumental teachers ('VITs') were engaged under contracts of service or contracts for services.

ESM7260	*Synaptek Ltd v Young*	**75 TC 51**

Whether the *Social Security Contributions (Intermediaries) Regulations 2000* applied to the provision of services by an IT consultant working through his own service company.

ESM7250	*Todd v Adams*	**[2002] EWCA Civ 509**

The appellants claimed damages under the *Fatal Accidents Act 1976* and the *Law Reform Act (Miscellaneous Provisions) 1934* from the vessel owners, the respondents. There were two preliminary issues under consideration but only the second issue need be considered here. Under *Merchant Shipping Act 1995, s 185*, liability for maritime claims can be limited in certain circumstances but not where the servants of the ship owners are engaged under contracts of service. The relevant point at issue was, therefore, whether members of the crew of a trawler were engaged under contracts of service.

ESM7270	*Usetech Ltd v Young*	**76 TC 811**

Whether the *Social Security Contributions (Intermediaries) Regulations 2000* and *FA 2000, Sch 12* applied to the provision of services by an IT consultant working through his own service company.

ESM7130	*Walls v Sinnett*	**60 TC 150**

Whether a lecturer was engaged under a contract of service or a contract for services.

	Weight Watchers (UK) Ltd v R & C Commrs	**[2011] UKUT 433 (TCC)**

The Upper Tribunal confirmed a decision of the First-tier Tribunal (FTT) ([2010] UKFTT 54 (TC)) that leaders taking Weight Watchers classes were employees of the taxpayer company for the purposes of PAYE and NICs.

Employed or self-employed – establishing the facts

6.4   No single fact will be decisive in determining employment status. The facts set out in the following paragraphs are based on the guidance provided by HMRC. HMRC also provide an online employment status indicator, which may be of assistance in building the wider picture (see the gov.uk website at www.gov.uk/guidance/employment-status-indicator).

- First, establish the terms and conditions of the engagement – normally established from the contract between the worker and client/employer, whether written, oral or implied or a mixture of all three.

- Then consider any surrounding facts that may be relevant – eg whether the worker has other clients and a business organisation.

Focus

In June 2017, in *Tomlinson* [2017] TC 05943, the First-tier Tribunal found that a double-glazing salesman (Mr Malcolm Tomlinson) was self-employed and not an employee as he had claimed.

As with most employment status cases, this case focused on the details of the terms on which Mr Tomlinson was engaged with the company.

Many facts of the case pointed towards a self-employed status, including the fact that there was no written contract in place and Mr Tomlinson was not required to give notice of leaving. He was paid on a commission-only basis and did not receive holiday pay, sick pay or pension contribution payments. He provided his own car, mobile phone and other equipment. However, many other factors emerged which tended towards employed status. These included authority to sign initial customer contracts on behalf of the company; an expectation for working in the company showroom approximately two days a week; an expectation to complete a holiday request form; appearances in company advertisement; and an expectation that Mr Tomlinson would not work for competitors.

The First-tier Tribunal (FTT) worked its way through various factors which have historically been used to determine employment status cases. Such factors include control, equipment, financial risk and payment terms, personal service and exclusivity, mutuality of obligation, benefits provided, integration within the company's business, and intention.

In concluding its review of the overall effect of all such factors, the FTT found that the details of this case did not clearly point towards either employment or self-employment. However, looking at the overall picture, the FTT's view was that Mr Tomlinson was in business on his own account and was not therefore, an employee. The FTT concluded that it was decisive that both Mr Tomlinson and the company intended and believed that Mr Tomlinson was self-employed and had operated on that basis for almost 25 years.

As Mr Tomlinson had not discharged the burden of proof showing on the balance of probabilities that, during the period in question, he was employed under a contract of service, the decision that Mr Tomlinson was self-employed stood good.

Deciding employment status

Factors indicating employment

6.5

- having to carry out the work personally;

- being told what to do, when and how to do the work;

- payment by the hour, week or month and eligibility for overtime pay;

- working set hours, or a given number of hours per week or month;

- working at the other party's premises, or at a location of the other party's choice;

- being part and parcel of the organisation;

- right of dismissal;

- mutuality of obligations (to provide work on the one hand, and to carry out that work on the other);

- receipt of employee benefits such as holiday pay, sick pay or a company car;

- long periods working for one party.

Factors indicating self-employment

6.6

- the ability to exercise control over the work carried out;

- financial risk;

- responsibility for meeting losses as well as taking profits;

- provision of equipment needed to do the job (as opposed to the small tools that many employees provide for themselves);

- freedom to hire other people on the individual's own terms to do the work taken on (and payment out of own funds);

- the requirement to correct unsatisfactory work in the individual's own time and at his own expense;

- the opportunity to profit from sound management.

Overall picture

6.7   None of these factors are decisive in themselves. It is necessary to look at the circumstances as a whole. Where the evidence is evenly balanced, the intention of the parties may then decide the issue.

HMRC provide an online status tool on the gov.uk website at https://www.gov.uk/employment-status-indicator. If used correctly, HMRC will recognise the decision given by the tool.

What is chargeable?

6.8   Employment income (*ITEPA 2003, s 7*) is assessable as earnings of an employment or office, whether as a payment or benefits in kind. Taxable income may include:

- wages and salaries, fees and overtime;

- holiday pay, sick pay, maternity pay and paternity pay;

- bonuses;

- commissions;

- tips and service charges;

- travelling time payments;

- redundancy payments (subject to possible relief of up to £30,000);

- inducement payments and some termination payments;

- reimbursement of expenses; and

- benefits in kind.

Focus

Recent cases involving earnings

In *Mr A* [2015] TC 04381, the First-tier Tribunal examined whether a £600,000 payment received by the appellant from the bank he worked for before he left had to be taxed as earnings within *ITEPA 2003, s 62*, or whether it was compensation in respect of the appellant's threatened race discrimination claim and was therefore not chargeable to tax on earnings from employment as payment for shortfalls in salary and bonus.

The FTT held that it did not have to 'step into the shoes of an employment tribunal' and consider whether it was satisfied there would have been a successful claim at the tribunal. It was however satisfied that the reason the payment was made by the bank (rightly or wrongly on their part) was to settle a discrimination claim and not to pay back money which they thought the appellant was entitled to under contractual agreement. The FTT concluded that the payment did not fall within *s 62* to be taxed as earnings.

In *Macleod and Mitchell Contractors Ltd and Mitchell* [2017] TC 05633, the FTT found that premiums paid by the employer on insurance contracts taken out erroneously in the name of the director rather than the employer were taxable as income of the director and subject to NICs) by the employer. The appeals were dismissed.

PAYE

Basis of charge

6.9 Employment income (plus pension and social security income) is charged to tax under the *Income Tax (Earnings and Pensions) Act 2003*.

'Employment income' includes earnings (eg salary or benefits), amounts treated as earnings (eg under the provisions for personal services provided by intermediaries) and any amounts counting as employment income (eg termination payments) (*ITEPA 2003, ss 9–13, 62*).

Employment earnings are treated as being paid on the earlier of the date on which (*ITEPA 2003, s 15*):

- the payment is actually made; and

- the employee becomes entitled to the payment.

In the case of directors, earnings are treated as being 'received' on the earlier of the above dates, or the date on which:

- sums on account of the director's remuneration are credited in the company's records;

- the period, during which the director's remuneration is determined, ends; or

- the director's remuneration is determined, if that is after the end of the period.

Exceptions

6.10 These rules do not apply to benefits in kind, which are treated as received in the tax year in which they are provided. Pension and social security benefits are taxable on the amount due in the tax year irrespective of the time of payment (*ITEPA 2003, ss 571, 661, 683, 686*).

Employment income – basis of assessment

6.11

Applies to	**Basis of assessment**
Earnings of an employee resident in the UK (but not emoluments of an employee not domiciled in the UK from a non-UK resident employer for duties performed wholly abroad)	Total earnings in the tax year wherever the duties are performed
Earnings of an employee not resident but domiciled in the UK	Earnings on duties performed in the UK
Earnings of an employee who is resident but not domiciled in the UK, from a non-resident employer for duties performed wholly abroad	Liable on an arising basis or on the remittance basis where claimed

PAYE

6.12 'Pay As You Earn' (PAYE) is the system for deducting income tax (and NICs) from PAYE employment income. The total amount deducted each tax month (ending on the 5th) including employer's NIC must be paid to HMRC within 14 days of the end of the tax month (ie by the 19th) unless the payment is made electronically, in which case the remittance is due within 17 days after the end of the tax month (ie by the 22nd). Employers whose average monthly liability is less than £1,500 can choose to pay quarterly rather than monthly by the 19th (or 22nd) of July, October, January and April (*ITEPA 2003, ss 682–702; FA 2002, ss 135–136; SI 2003/2682, regs 69, 97; SI 2003/2495*).

Focus

The *Income Tax (Pay As You Earn) (Amendment No 4) Regulations 2014 (SI 2014/2689)* took effect from 6 April 2015. The regulations amend the main PAYE Regulations (*SI 2203/2682*) to insert a graduated scale, by reference to which HMRC can collect debts via a PAYE code number (see **2.37**).

Previously there was a limit of £3,000 on amounts that could be coded out, regardless of the income of the person. The total amount of relevant debt and tax credit debt that can be coded out has been increased from £3,000 to £17,000 from 6 April 2015 (*SI 2014/2438*). A graduated scale will apply so that the amount to be coded out from any particular debtor will depend on their PAYE income. This change will increase the maximum amount that can be recovered through coding out from those with higher incomes. There is no change to the amount that can be coded out for those with incomes of up to £30,000, which will remain at £3,000.

The regulations also provide a statutory safeguard to all PAYE tax codes that no more than 50% of income can be deducted from payments.

The graduated scale for the amount of debt that may be collected is as follows:

Expected amount of PAYE income of employee in the tax year for which the code is determined	Total amount of debt that may be recovered from employee in that tax year
Less than £30,000	No more than £3,000
£30,000 or more but less than £40,000	No more than £5,000
£40,000 or more but less than £50,000	No more than £7,000
£50,000 or more but less than £60,000	No more than £9,000
£60,000 or more but less than £70,000	No more than £11,000
£70,000 or more but less than £80,000	No more than £13,000
£80,000 or more but less than £90,000	No more than £15,000
£90,000 or more	No more than £17,000.

Who is included?

6.13   In addition to employees and directors, the PAYE system generally applies to the following workers (although special rules apply in some cases): agency workers, part-time and casual workers, domestic workers and nannies, foreign workers, students and youths in training schemes.

Focus

An increasing number of individuals are finding work through online platforms (for example Deliveroo and Uber workers), usually on a self-employed basis, whereas in the past they might have been employees whose relatively simple tax affairs were dealt with under PAYE. The Office for Tax Simplification (OTS) has published a paper entitled 'Platforms, the Platform economy and Tax Simplification', which explores the possibility of recreating for them, in the context of self-employment, an arrangement that looks and feels more similar to that of an employee from an administrative point of view. Such an arrangement might prevent large numbers of individuals having to submit a self-assessment tax return and a computation of their self-employment income.

In outline, the platform would sign up with HMRC as 'agent' for the platform worker, so that they can apply the equivalent of a tax code.

Workers would be able to have their taxable profits computed in real time. The platform would then withhold tax, either on an even basis or 'back-end' loaded for those with more fluctuating income, which it would then pay on account to HMRC.

The platform will then be able to 'correct' the withholding at the end of the year so the platform worker has nothing further to do. The OTS says this mechanism could initially apply only to large platforms but, over time, could be extended to smaller engagers.

In conjunction with private sector developments in making it easier for people to manage their tax affairs, HMRC might also consider opportunities to streamline its engagement with self-employed platform workers, for example by developing a phone application (for example, along the lines of that available in Australia) which operates alongside these new accounting products.

Work will continue on the proposals, with further announcements to be expected in due course.

When is PAYE operated?

6.14   As a general rule, both NICs and PAYE are operated when a payment of earnings is made to an employee.

If the employee is not a director, PAYE should be operated on the earlier of:

● when the payment is actually made; or

● when the employee is entitled to be paid, even if the pay is not drawn until later.

If the employee is a director, PAYE should be operated on the earlier of:

● when the payment is actually made;

● when the director becomes entitled to be paid; or

● when the payment is credited in the company accounts or records, even if:

    – the director cannot draw the money straightaway because there is a block on the right to payment; or

    – the credit is not specifically in an account in the director's name;

● when the remuneration is fixed or determined:

    – if the amount for a particular accounting period is determined before the end of that period, take the date as being when the period ends;

– if the amount is determined after the period ends, take the date as being when the amount is determined.

Employers have a legal obligation to operate PAYE on the payments made to employees if their earnings reach the National Insurance lower earnings limit (LEL). For 2019/20, this is £118 a week, £512 a month or £6,136 a year.

Focus

Most employers are required to operate PAYE using HMRC's real time information (RTI) system. Broadly, under RTI, information about tax and other deductions under the PAYE system are transmitted to HMRC by the employer every time an employee is paid. Employers using RTI are not required to provide information to HMRC using forms P35 and P14 after the end of the tax year, or to send form P45 or a Starter Checklist to HMRC when employees start or leave a job (see **6.20**).

What is included?

6.15   The HMRC guide CWG2: *Employer Further Guide to PAYE and NICs* provides useful guidance and sets out examples of items that are included in gross pay for income tax and NIC purposes (see https://www.gov.uk/government/publications/cwg2-further-guide-to-paye-and-national-insurance-contributions/2019-to-2020-employer-further-guide-to-paye-and-national-insurance-contributions--3).

PAYE codes

6.16   The tax liability of an employee depends not only on his earnings, but also on the amount of personal allowances and reliefs available to set off against those earnings. The PAYE code represents the total allowances and reliefs available. HMRC provide a set of tax tables for use in conjunction with the codes, to enable the employer to calculate the amount of tax to be deducted from each payment of wages or salary (*SI 2003/2682, regs 13–14*). The tables allow, as near as may be, for the correct time proportion of the employee's annual tax liability to be deducted. Dedicated payroll software is often used instead.

Taxpayers who are registered for HMRC online services and enrolled for self-assessment online can view their PAYE coding notices online for past, current and future tax years. For further information, see https://www.gov.uk/self-assessment-tax-returns.

PAYE in real time

6.17   Real time information (RTI) is the system used by employers operating PAYE to transmit information about tax and other deductions to HMRC.

Broadly, information is submitted to HMRC every time an employee is paid, which means that they are not required to provide information to HMRC using forms P35 and P14 after the end of the tax year, or to send form P45 or P46 to HMRC when employees start or leave a job.

The RTI system supports the introduction of Universal Credit, an integrated working-age credit, which will replace income-related benefits and credits. It will give the Department for Work and Pensions (DWP) access to up-to-date information on a claimant's income from employment.

Each time a payment is made to an employee, a full payment submission (FPS) will be made to HMRC. The FPS includes:

- the amount paid to employees;

- income tax, NICs and other deductions, such as student loans; and

- details of new employees and employees who have left.

Details of all employees paid must be included in the FPS, including those who earn below the NIC lower earnings limit.

There are other submissions that employers may also make. These include:

- an employer alignment submission (EAS), to align employee records with HMRC records before other information is submitted;

- a National Insurance number verification request (NVR), to verify or obtain a National Insurance number for new employees;

- an employer payment summary (EPS) to report a reduction in the amount paid to HMRC, or if any employees have not been paid in a pay period; and

- an earlier year update (EYU) to correct, after 19 April, any of the year-to-date totals submitted in the final FPS for the previous tax year. This only applies to RTI years, and the first year an employer could use an EYU was 2012/13.

- RTI only affects the submission of PAYE information – payment arrangements will remain unchanged.

PAYE electronic communications

6.18   Late filing penalties apply to employer returns for 2014/15 onwards. They started from 6 October 2014 for large employers (with 50 or more employees) and from 6 March 2015 for small employers (with no more than 49 employees at 6 October 2014) and new employers (who become employers after 6 October 2014). Where payment information is not received as expected on an FPS, or HMRC have not been notified that no employees have been paid in a tax period by submission of an EPS, late filing penalties will apply. The rules apply to each PAYE scheme, rather than each employer.

Late filing penalties apply on a monthly basis; however, no penalty will apply for the first month in each tax year that returns are filed late. Until 5 April 2019, HMRC operated a three-day easement for PAYE late filing penalties. See the gov.uk website at https://www.gov.uk/guidance/what-happens-if-you-dont-report-payroll-information-on-time for further details.

New employers will not be penalised if their first FPS is received within 30 days of making their first payment to an employee.

Initial penalties: Number of employees	Monthly penalty
1–9	£100
10–49	£200
50–249	£300
250 or more	£400
Additional penalties where return over 3 months late:	
3 months late	5% of the tax/NIC that should have been shown on the return

Late payment penalties

6.19   Late payment penalties are charged in-year on a late payment for the tax year 2015/16 onwards.

Late payment penalty notices will be issued quarterly in July, October, January and April showing the amount of the penalty due for each tax month. The total penalty charged can be made up of:

• a default penalty, for failure to pay monthly/quarterly payments on time and in full; and

• penalties for amounts still unpaid after 6 and 12 months.

Penalties for late monthly or quarterly PAYE payments

No penalty if only one PAYE amount is late in a tax year, unless that payment is over six months late.

Number of defaults in a tax year	Penalty percentage	Amount to which penalty percentages apply
1–3 (the first failure to pay on time does not count as a default)	1%	Total amount that is late in the tax year (ignoring the first late payment in that tax year)

4–6	2%	
7–9	3%	From April 2014: the total amount that is late in the relevant tax month (ignoring the first late payment in the tax year)
10 or more	4%	

Additional penalties	**Amount**
6 months late	5%
12 months late	Further 5%

New employees

6.20   If a new employee does not have a form P45 (either because he had no previous employment, has lost the form, never received one or does not want the new employer to know his previous pay), the new employer must prepare a starter checklist, which can be downloaded from the gov.uk website (www.gov.uk/government/uploads/system/uploads/attachment_data/file/513621/Starter_checklist_v1.0.pdf). This form is used to gather information about the new employee and, in turn, the information will help the employer fill in his first Full Payment Submission (FPS) for this employee. The information recorded on the Starter Checklist record must be kept for the current and previous three tax years. The Starter Checklist is not sent to HMRC.

Depending on which statement or statements are made, the employer will use either an emergency code (either on a cumulative or a Week 1 or Month 1 basis) to deduct tax allowing for a personal allowance, or code BR to deduct tax at the basic rate. This code will be used until HMRC issue the employer with the appropriate tax code.

If the employee subsequently produces form P45, the code indicated on that form should be used instead.

Further information on new employees can be found on the gov.uk website at www.gov.uk/new-employee.

Employees who leave – P45

6.21   Where an employee ceases to work for an employer, the employer must provide him with a certificate on form P45, which shows the code and the cumulative pay and tax up to the date of leaving. The employee can then produce the form P45 to his next employer to enable him to continue the cumulative system of tax deduction. The employee will also retain a copy of the form which may be needed to complete his tax return (*SI 2003/2682, regs 40, 42*).

National minimum wage

6.22   Employers need to be aware of the implications of the National Minimum Wage (NMW). The NMW rate per hour depends on an employee's age and whether they are an apprentice – they must be at least school leaving age to get it. The rates applicable from 1 April 2019 are as follows:

•   the main adult rate (for workers aged 25 and over) is £8.21;

•   the rate for 21- to 24-year-olds is £7.70;

•   the rate for workers aged between 18 and 20 is £6.15;

•   the rate for workers aged between 16 and 17 is £4.35;

•   the rate for apprentices is £3.90. This rate is for apprentices aged 16 to 18 and those aged 19 or over who are in their first year. All other apprentices are entitled to the NMW for their age.

There are a number of people who are not entitled to the NMW, including:

•   self-employed people;

•   volunteers or voluntary workers;

•   company directors; and

•   family members, or people who live in the family home of the employer who undertake household tasks.

All other workers including pieceworkers, home workers, agency workers, commission workers, part-time workers and casual workers must receive at least the NMW.

National living wage

6.23   The national living wage (NLW) was introduced from 1 April 2016. HMRC have responsibility for enforcing the NLW in addition to the national minimum wage (NMW) (see **6.22**) and will take firm action where an employer fails to pay the correct wage.

The NLW is the national rate set for people aged 25 and over. The rate for the NLW is £8.21 per hour (rising from £7.83 per hour from 1 April 2019). The current NMW for those under the age of 25 continues to apply.

As with the NMW, the Low Pay Commission will recommend any future rises to the NLW rate.

Generally all those who are covered by the NMW, and are 25 years old and over, will be covered by the NLW. These include:

•   employees;

•   most workers and agency workers;

- casual labourers;

- agricultural workers; and

- apprentices who are aged 25 and over.

Focus

Following the Spanish case of *Federación de Servicios Privados del sindicato Comisiones Obreras v Tyco Integrated Security SL (Tyco)* (Case C-266/14), there could potentially be NMW claims if, taking into account travelling time, a mobile worker's hourly pay rate falls below the minimum rate.

In this case, the European Court of Justice (ECJ) gave the judgement that mobile workers who have no fixed place of work, and spend time travelling from home to the first and last customer, should have this time considered as working time. The mobile workers successfully challenged this policy as being contrary to the EU Working Time Directive. The Working Time Regulations 1998 (WTR) give effect to the Directive, which means that the decision of the ECJ is binding on UK courts – so that in the future, travel time to and from home will be deemed as working time under the WTR for workers with no fixed place of work. The impact of the decision on wages is, however, a little more uncertain. The *Working Time Directive* does not stipulate what the employer must pay the worker, except in relation to holidays, and it was not specifically covered in the Tyco decision. Where a contract of employment states that a worker will be paid an hourly rate, the decision opens up the possibility that the worker will be able to bring a claim that they are entitled to pay in respect of the time spent travelling. However, this is currently a point of some controversy as the *National Minimum Wage Regulations 2015, SI 2015/601* expressly provide that travel time between the worker's residence and 'a place of work or a place where an assignment is carried out' is not counted as working time for pay purposes. Several UK professional bodies are currently assessing the impact of the ECJ decision on the NMW and further guidance is expected in due course.

PAYE codes

6.24   The PAYE code is used to deduct more or less the right amount of tax from an employee's pay or an ex-employee's occupational pension (*SI 2003/2682, regs 13, 14*). The number is generally the tax-free income allowed with the last digit removed. The letters following the number are explained below.

L	basic personal allowance
M	the employee has received a transfer of 10% of their partner's personal allowance
N	the employee has transferred 10% of their personal allowance to their partner
S	the Scottish rate of income tax applies
T	used where none of the other code letters apply (eg an age-related personal allowance may be reduced because of income exceeding the income limit or the employee does not want the employer to know what tax allowances are received) does not mean a temporary code has been applied
K	(followed by a number) indicates that total allowances are less than total deductions (eg where benefits exceed personal allowances) and that tax must be deducted at more than the normal rate to take into account the tax due on untaxed income (the maximum rate at which tax may be deducted is 50%)
NT	no tax to be deducted
0T	all earnings to be taxed (ie no tax-free amounts available)
BR	tax collected at the basic rate of 20%
D0	(followed by a number) tax to be deducted at the higher rate of 40%
D1	if earnings in one employment exceed £150,000, all earnings from a second employment will be taxed at 45%
SBR	Scottish taxpayer; all income taxed at the basic rate
SD0	Scottish taxpayer; all income taxed at the higher rate
SD1	Scottish taxpayer; all income taxed at the additional rate
W1, M1, X	denotes the tax code is operating on a non-cumulative basis

See **6.33** for details of new PAYE codes for employees aged under 21, which took effect from 6 April 2015.

A Notice of Coding is usually issued in January or February for the following tax year, allowing employers to use this code from 6 April. Further notices may be issued with any amendments made by the taxpayer or the employer (eg through form P46(Car)).

Coding for benefits – P46(Car)

6.25   In order to ensure the correct amount of tax is deducted from the employee's pay, the tax code takes into account any taxable benefits in kind made to the employee. The code will generally be based on benefits received by the employee in the previous tax year except in the case of company cars for which details must be provided by the employer on a quarterly basis (within 28 days of an income tax quarter) on form P46(Car). The income tax quarter ends are 5 January, 5 April, 5 July and 5 October. Since 6 April 2009, employers have not needed to complete a form P46(Car) for an employee when one car is replaced with another.

PAYE threshold for 2019/20

6.26

Weekly	£240.00
Monthly	£1,042.00
Annual	£12,500.00

(SI 2003/2682, reg 9)

In most years, the PAYE threshold for National Insurance contributions (NICs) is aligned with the personal tax allowance. An employer is not required to operate PAYE in respect of an employee whose rate of pay does not exceed the PAYE threshold.

Interest and penalties on PAYE paid late

6.27   From 2014/15 onwards, HMRC charge in-year, rather than annual, interest on all unpaid:

* PAYE tax, Class 1 National Insurance, and student loan deductions including specified charges (estimates that HMRC make in the absence of a PAYE submission);

* Construction Industry Scheme (CIS) charges;

* in-year late filing penalties, which started from October 2014; and

* in-year late payment penalties, which are charged automatically from April 2015.

(SI 2014/992; SI 2014/2395)

HMRC also charge interest on underpayments that arise because of adjustments reported on earlier year updates submitted in respect of tax year 2014/15 onwards.

For annual payments such as Class 1A and Class 1B National Insurance contributions, HMRC will continue to charge interest on any amount which remains unpaid after the due date.

HMRC will charge interest from the date a payment is due and payable to the date it is paid in full.

Current interest rates are set out at https://www.gov.uk/government/publications/rates-and-allowances-hmrc-interest-rates-for-late-and-early-payments/rates-and-allowances-hmrc-interest-rates.

Payments made 'free of tax and NICs'

6.28   If an employer enters into an arrangement with an employee that all of his or her earnings are to be paid 'free of tax', the employer should note that:

- it is his responsibility to make sure that the employee understands and agrees with the terms under which the payment is made free of tax;
- payments made free of tax can increase employer costs; and
- there are extra PAYE duties involved.

For example, the tax due is worked out by reference to the 'true gross pay', not the amount the employee is actually paid.

Where an employer has such an agreement with employees, he must contact his local HMRC office to obtain a package containing the following forms:

- forms P11 (FOT);
- special 'free of tax' (FOT) Tax Tables, Tables G; and
- leaflet FOT1, which will help work out the 'true gross pay' figure.

If an employer enters into an agreement with an employee that only part of his or her earnings are to be paid 'free of tax', the figure to enter on form P11 (working sheet), to calculate the PAYE and NICs due, is the total of:

- the 'true gross pay' of the 'free of tax' element of the earnings; and
- the actual gross pay not within the 'free-of-tax' agreement.

To work out the 'true gross pay' of the 'free-of-tax' element, the following formula is used:

$$\frac{\text{'Free of Tax' element of pay} \times 100}{(100 - \text{employee's tax rate figure})*}$$

* The tax rate figure will be 20, 40 or 45, depending on the employee's rate of tax.

Example 6.1—Payments made 'free of tax and NICs'

In 2019/20, an employer enters into an agreement to pay an employee a wage of £150 and £20 'free of tax' towards travelling expenses. The employee is a Table B employee.

The figure to use to calculate the PAYE and NICs due is the total of the 'true gross pay' of the 'free of tax' element.

$$\frac{£20 \times 100}{(100 - 20)} \qquad\qquad £25.00$$

The actual gross pay not within the 'free-of-tax' agreement	£150.00
Figure to be entered on form P11 (or equivalent) to calculate PAYE and NICs	£175.00

Payroll giving

6.29   Under the payroll deduction scheme, an employee's donation to charity via the payroll attracts tax relief. Relief is available where (*ITEPA 2003, s 713*):

- an employee suffers deduction of tax under PAYE;

- the employer operates an approved scheme for the deduction of charitable donations;

- the employee authorises the employer to make the deductions;

- the employer pays the deducted sums to an approved agent;

- the approved agent pays the deducted sums to a charity or charities; and

- the sums deducted constitute gifts from the employee to the charity and are not paid under a covenant.

There is no maximum limit for payroll giving. The deduction of a donation to charity under the scheme occurs before PAYE is applied, thus giving relief by means of a 'net pay' arrangement (*ITEPA 2003, s 713*).

There are regulations under which payroll deduction schemes are approved (*SI 1986/2211*).

Employers can obtain tax relief for the costs of administering the scheme. Agencies usually recover their costs by making a deduction from the donations they handle but, if the employer chooses to fund any of the agency's costs, or match its employees' donations, he is entitled to relief for that as well.

Focus

Employers offering payroll giving should remember that employees are entitled only to tax relief, and not relief from NICs. When completing form P11 (or equivalent), therefore, the employer needs to deduct the amount of the authorised donation from the employee's gross pay for PAYE purposes.

The amount of the authorised donation is not deducted from the employee's gross pay for NIC purposes.

Farm workers

6.30   Anyone employed to work on a farm must be paid at least the national minimum wage. Workers employed before the rules changed on 1 October 2013 still have the right to the agricultural minimum wage if it says so in their contract. Agricultural workers in Wales must be paid at least the Agricultural Minimum Wage, or the National Minimum Wage if that's higher. The Agricultural Minimum Wage depends on the worker's job grade and category. See https://www.gov.uk/agricultural-workers-rights/pay-and-overtime for further details. Harvest casuals

6.31   Special rules apply to casual employees only who are taken on for harvest work, who are not family members.

Normal PAYE procedures must be followed for any part-time or casual employees that are taken on for non-harvest work who are family members, regardless of the type of work they do. If earnings do not exceed the primary threshold (£166 per week for 2019/20), no NICs are payable. If earnings reach or exceed the lower earnings threshold (£118 per week for 2019/20) but do not exceed the primary threshold, the employee is treated as having paid NICs when claiming benefit. If earnings exceed the primary threshold, Class 1 NICs are payable by the employee and employer.

The following table is an extract from HMRC booklet CWG2 and sets out these rules.

Employees on the government's Seasonal Agricultural Workers Scheme (SAWS) are not eligible for the special PAYE and NIC concessions for harvest casuals (HMRC booklet CWG2, Chapter 4).

Circumstances	Action
For PAYE	
The person is a daily casual and:	Do not deduct tax.
• is taken on for one day or less • paid off at the end of that period • with no contract for further employment.	Keep a record of the employee's full name, date of birth, gender, National Insurance number, address and amounts paid. This information should be reported through RTI on or before the payment is made (or, if that is not possible, no later than seven days after the payment is made) where the employer has any other employees paid above the LEL.

Circumstances	Action
The employee is taken on for no more than two weeks and has not been taken on previously by you since 6 April and paid above the PAYE threshold without PAYE being applied.	Do not deduct tax.
	Keep a record of the employee's full name, date of birth, gender, National Insurance number, address and amounts paid.
	This information should be reported through RTI on or before the payment is made (or, if that is not possible, no later than seven days after the payment is made) where the employer has any other employees paid above the LEL.
The employee is taken on for more than two weeks.	No special procedures apply, and normal procedures must be followed. See the guidance online at https://www.gov.uk/new-employee.

For NICs

The employee is employed as a regular casual, eg taken on for a specified period and paid at regular intervals.	No special NIC rules apply, and normal procedures must be followed. See the guidance online at https://www.gov.uk/new-employee.
The employee is engaged on an irregular basis: • to work outdoors harvesting perishable crops • is paid off at the end of each engagement, eg at the end of the day • has no contract for further employment.	NICs will not be collected where it is impossible for the employer to identify individuals and record their earnings. If the identity details are known, NICs are due when the earnings for each engagement exceed the secondary threshold (ST) for employers and the primary threshold (PT) for employees: • work out the NICs due at the time the earnings are paid • complete the payroll record. See the guidance online at https://www.gov.uk/new-employee.

National Insurance contributions

6.32 Significant changes were made to the NIC regime in April 1999, when the Contributions Agency merged with the Inland Revenue to become the National Insurance Contributions Office (NICO). Employers no longer face separate audits for PAYE and NIC, and the rules for each of these taxes are being increasingly aligned so that most payments and benefits which are subject to income tax are now also subject to NICs.

Class 1 contributions

6.33   Unless specifically exempted, all employees and employers must pay Class 1 contributions on employee earnings. An outline of the current rules is provided in the following paragraphs, but for detailed commentary, see *National Insurance Contributions 2018/19* (Bloomsbury Professional).

'Primary contributions' are payable by employees, and 'secondary contributions' by employers. Primary contributions are currently payable at the rate of 12% between the lower earnings threshold and the upper earnings limit, with earnings above that limit subject to an additional 2% charge.

The employers' secondary contributions rate is currently 13.8% on earnings above the secondary earnings threshold (£166 weekly for 2019/20). There is no upper earnings limit for employers. Secondary contributions are not however, payable by employers for employees under the age of 21, as long as earnings do not exceed the 'upper secondary threshold for under 21s' (UST) (£962 per week for 2019/20). Where earnings exceed the UST, employer contributions will be payable at the standard rate of 13.8% (see below).

For employees paid within a 'zero rate' band below the earnings threshold (known as the 'lower earnings limit'), the rate of NIC is 0%, but entitlement to benefit is maintained, and earnings count for the purposes of calculating statutory sick pay and statutory maternity pay.

Focus

From 6 April 2015, employers may not need to pay Class 1 secondary contributions to employees aged under 21. The rate of employer contributions for employees under the age of 21 is 0% up to the 'upper secondary threshold' (UST) which is currently the same as the upper earnings limit (UEL). Secondary NICs however continue to be payable on all earnings above this threshold.

For employees who are at, or over the age of 16 and under the age of 21 there will be a range of new NI category letters to use when assessing secondary NICs in respect of the earnings paid to these employees. From 6 April 2015, when submitting PAYE information for employees under the age of 21 employers will need to use the new category letter appropriate to the individual. Seven new category letters have been introduced to support this change; however, three of the new letters were removed in April 2016 in line with the ending of 'contracted-out' in relation to salary-related occupational pension schemes:

- M – Not contracted-out standard rate contributions for employees under 21;

- Z – Not contracted-out deferred rate contributions for employees under 21;

- Y – Mariners not contracted-out standard rate contributions for employees under 21;

- P – Mariners not contracted-out deferred rate contributions for employees under 21;

- V – Mariners Contracted-out Salary Related contributions for employees under 21;

- I – Contracted-out Salary Related standard rate contributions for employees under 21; and

- K – Contracted-out Salary Related deferred rate contributions for employees under 21.

Contracting out

6.34   Until April 2016, contributions payable by the employee and employer were reduced by a rebate where the employee was 'contracted out' of the State Second Pension (S2P) (formerly known as the State Earnings Related Pension Scheme (SERPS)). The rebate was based on contributions from the lower earnings limit, so it was given on contributions (even though they are not paid) between the lower earnings limit and the earnings threshold. Contracting-out in relation to salary-related occupational pension schemes ended in April 2016 in conjunction with the introduction of the state pension provisions.

Employment allowance

6.35   The employment allowance (EA) was introduced from April 2014, potentially cutting every employer's NIC payments by allowing businesses and charities to offset up to a pre-set annual threshold (£3,000 from April 2016, previously £2,000) against their employer PAYE NIC liabilities. To keep the process as simple as possible for employers, the EA is delivered through standard payroll software and HMRC's real time information (RTI) system. To claim the allowance, the employer will have to signify his intention to claim by completing the yes/no indicator just once. The employer will then offset the allowance against each monthly Class 1 secondary NICs payment that is due to be made to HMRC until the allowance is fully claimed or the tax year ends. For example, if employer Class 1 NICs are £1,200 each month, in April the EA used will be £1,200, in May it will be £2,400, and in June £800, as the maximum is capped at £3,000. The following tax year, the allowance will be available as an offset against a Class 1 secondary NICs liability as it arises during the tax year.

The EA applies per employer, regardless of how many PAYE schemes that employer chooses to operate, so each employer can only claim for one allowance. It is up to the employer which PAYE scheme to claim it against.

From 6 April 2015 the EA was extended to individuals who employ care and support workers.

The EA was restricted from April 2016, so that a company no longer qualifies where all the payments of earnings it pays in a tax year, in relation to which it is the secondary contributor, are paid to or for the benefit of one employed earner only who is, at the time the payments are made, also a director of the company. This sounds complicated, but in essence, the purpose of the change was to prevent perceived misuse of the allowance by personal service companies and help focus it on businesses creating employment. The government estimated that this change affected around 150,000 limited companies with a single director.

The Autumn Budget 2018 announced details of a further restriction, expected to take effect in 2020/21, which aims to target the allowance on businesses that need it most.

From 6 April 2020, access to the EA will be limited to businesses and charities with an employer National Insurance contributions (NICs) bill below £100,000. Currently some 1.1 million employers claim the EA and the government estimates that around 93% of these will continue to be eligible once the restriction takes effect, with many paying no employer NICs at all.

Class 1A contributions

6.36 Class 1A NICs are payable on most benefits in kind liable to income tax (eg private medical insurance contracted by the employer, and certain beneficial loans). An outline of the current rules is provided in the following paragraphs, but for detailed commentary, see *National Insurance Contributions 2018/19* (Bloomsbury Professional).

The Class 1A NIC charge is levied on the employer only, based on company car and fuel scale charges, and on the cash equivalent of other benefits as identified on the employee's form P11D. Class 1A NIC does not apply to the following:

- benefits exempt from income tax, covered by a dispensation or Extra-Statutory Concession, or included in a PAYE Settlement Agreement (see **6.48**);

- benefits reported on form P9D (ie relating to lower paid employees, ie those earning at a rate of less than £8,500 a year);

- benefits liable to Class 1 NIC instead (eg shopping vouchers);

- benefits provided for business use, but with insignificant private use; and

- benefits specifically exempt from Class 1 NIC (eg mobile phones) or Class 1A NIC (eg employer provided childcare).

The HMRC booklet CWG5 *Class 1A National Insurance Contributions on Benefits in Kind* provides a useful summary of the liability arising in respect of the provision of benefits in kind (see https://www.gov.uk/government/publications/cwg5-class-1a-national-insurance-contributions-on-benefits-in-kind/2019-class-1a-national-insurance-contributions-on-benefits-in-kind).

Example 6.2—Calculation of Class 1A NICs

During the tax year 2019/20, an employer provides healthcare and company cars to 25 of his employees.

The Class 1A NICs percentage rate for the 2019/20 tax year is 13.8%.

The cash equivalent figures reported on each employee's P11D are £150 healthcare and £3,000 car benefit.

To calculate the Class 1A NICs due:

Step 1 – Add the total cash equivalent figures together:

Healthcare	£150 × 25 =	£3,750
Car benefit	£3,000 × 25 =	£75,000
Total benefits provided:		£78,750

Step 2 – Multiply the figure from Step 1 by the Class 1A percentage rate:

£78,750 × 13.8% = £10,867.50

Class 1A NICs due = £10,867.50

Class 1B contributions

6.37 PAYE settlement agreements (PSAs) (see **6.48**) allow employers to account for any tax liability in respect of their employees on payments that are minor or irregular, or that are shared benefits on which it would be impractical to determine individual liability, in one lump sum. From 6 April 1999, the principle was extended to NICs through a new contribution class: Class 1B. Where an employer has a PSA with HMRC, he will be liable to Class 1B contributions on the amount of the emoluments in the agreement that are chargeable to Class 1 or Class 1A contributions, together with the total amount of income tax payable under the agreement (*SSA 1998, s 53*; *Social Security Act 1998 (Commencement No 4) Regulations 1999 (SI 1999/526)*). For detailed commentary on Class 1B NICs, see *National Insurance Contributions 2018/19* (Bloomsbury Professional).

Class 2 and 4 contributions

6.38 Paid by the self-employed (see **7.90** for an outline of the current rules). For detailed commentary on Class 2 NICs, see *National Insurance Contributions 2018/19* (Bloomsbury Professional).

Class 3 voluntary contributions

6.39   Paid by those who otherwise would not pay enough contributions to earn a full pension (see **Chapter 5**). For detailed commentary on Class 3 NICs, see *National Insurance Contributions 2018/19* (Bloomsbury Professional).

Maximum contributions

6.40   Where an employee has more than one employment (or is also self-employed), liability for Class 1 contributions at the main rate cannot exceed the equivalent of 53 primary Class 1 contributions at the maximum standard rate. The additional 2% rate applies above that limit.

Tax deductions

6.41   Employers' NICs are deductible from taxable profits, but income tax is calculated on employees' earnings before deduction of NICs.

National Insurance contributions from 6 April 2019

6.42

Class 1 NICs	2019/20 £ per week
Lower earnings limit	£118
Upper earnings limit – primary	£962
Primary threshold	£166
Secondary threshold	£166
Upper secondary threshold for under 21s	£962
Apprentice upper secondary threshold for under 25s	£962
Employee contribution rate between primary and upper earnings limit	12%
Employee contribution rate above upper earnings limit	2%
Employers' secondary rate above secondary threshold	13.80%
Employment Allowance	£3,000

Notes:

Class 1A and Class 1B contributions: 13.8%.

Class 1A contributions are payable by employers by 19 July following the tax year. The liability is paid separately from the employer's PAYE and NIC liability.

Class 1B contributions are payable by employers by 19 October following the tax year on the value of any items included in a PAYE settlement agreement which would otherwise be earnings for Class 1 or Class 1A, including the amount of tax paid.

Class 2, 3 and 4 contributions are payable as follows (2019/20 rates):

Flat rate	£3.00 a week
Small profits threshold	£6,365 a year
Class 3 voluntary contributions	£15.00 a week
Class 4 contributions	
Percentage rate	9% payable on profits between £8,632 and £50,000 a year
	2% on profits exceeding £50,000
Exempt if pensionable age reached at start of tax year	

Alignment of income tax and NICs

6.43   At summer Budget 2015, the government asked the OTS to look at options for aligning IT and NICs. This followed on from recommendations made by the OTS as far back at 2011, and the latest report builds on earlier work of the OTS, including the reviews of small business taxation and employee expenses and benefits.

Key recommendations made in the report include:

- moving to an annual, cumulative and aggregated assessment period for employees' NICs similar to that for PAYE income tax;

- replacing employers' NICs with a flat rate charge on employer's total remuneration costs. The Employment Allowance would be retained to remove some small businesses from the charge;

- aligning NICs rates and thresholds between the employed and self-employed. This may mean the self-employed paying more NICs in return for better access to welfare benefits;

- aligning the rules for IT and NICs for employees – for example, a common definition of earnings, similar treatment of business expenses, and the extension of Class 1 NICs to benefits in kind;

- running IT and NICs as common, parallel systems. HMRC are encouraged to bring their IT and NICs teams closer together and to improve their guidance; and

- making NICs more transparent. Few of us understand how our NICs are calculated, what they fund and what we are entitled to. Once this is addressed (perhaps as part of HMRC's digital plans) a decision should be taken on the future of the contributory principle.

If enacted, these measures would significantly change the calculation and collection of NICs, bringing NICs more in line with IT and simplifying the UK's tax system as a result. But this would mean major upheaval and create winners and losers – the OTS estimates that moving to an annual, cumulative and aggregated assessment period for employees' NICs would mean 7.1 million workers paying less NICs (an average of £175 pa) and 6.3 million workers paying more (an average of £275 pa).

The OTS acknowledges that it will take time to achieve what would be a major reform of the UK's tax rules, and that a significant amount of additional work will be required to fully understand all of the implications of the proposed changes. The government will now consider the recommendations made by the OTS.

TAXABLE AND TAX-FREE BENEFITS

Benefits and expenses

6.44 Some expenses payments and benefits are treated as taxable remuneration (*ITEPA 2003, s 63*). From 6 April 2016 the benefits code applies to all directors and employees.

Until 5 April 2016, the benefits code applied only to:

(a) directors and certain other persons in controlling positions whatever their remuneration, but not to certain full-time working directors and certain directors of charities and non-profit making concerns;

(b) employees, including the directors excluded under (a) above, who were remunerated at the rate of £8,500 or more a year including all expenses payments and benefits before the deduction of any allowable expenses other than:

- contributions to an approved superannuation fund in respect of which the individual was entitled to tax relief as an expense;

- exempt profit-related pay; and

- contributions under an approved payroll giving scheme.

'Director' includes directors of companies and any person in accordance with whose instructions the directors are accustomed to act (other than a person who is merely a professional adviser). It also includes a member of the committee which manages such an association and any member of a body whose affairs are managed by its members.

'Company' includes an unincorporated association.

The benefits code does not apply to ministers of religion who are paid at a rate of less than £8,500 a year including all expenses payments and benefits before the deduction of any allowable expenses.

Three significant changes took effect from 6 April 2016, namely:

- the abolition of the £8,500 threshold for taxing certain BIKs;
- the introduction of voluntary payrolling; and
- replacement of the dispensations provisions.

Focus

The 2018 Autumn Budget announced that the government will legislate in Finance Bill 2019–20 so that expenses paid or reimbursed to unpaid office-holders will be exempt from income tax when incurred because of their voluntary duties. Broadly, this will place the existing concessionary treatment on to a statutory basis, providing certainty for those organisations engaging unpaid office-holders. Corresponding legislation will also be introduced to mirror the income tax exemption for National Insurance contributions. The change will have effect on and after Royal Assent to Finance Bill 2019–20.

Voluntary payrolling

6.45 Since April 2016, employers have had the option to collect tax on BIKs through the payroll, a process known as payrolling. HMRC's real time information (RTI) system is able to support voluntary payrolling, which provides the opportunity for employers to report total BIKs which have been taxed through the payroll alongside the total taxable pay to date figure in their normal RTI submissions. The idea is that the voluntary payrolling provisions should result in fewer PAYE tax coding notices being issued, as well as fewer under and overpayments of tax.

Regulations published in December 2015 widened the scope of the initial legislation in this area, such that from April 2016 payrolling is available for all BIKs, other than accommodation, beneficial loans, credit tokens and vouchers. Additional reporting requirements for employers payrolling cars took effect from April 2017.

From 6 April 2017 voluntary payrolling of non-cash vouchers and credit tokens is allowed (*FA 2016, s 15*). The payrolling of these benefits is designed to provide an opportunity to reduce employers' reporting obligations to HMRC. The collection of tax in real time will create efficiencies for employers and a simplified system should prove easier for employees to understand. Payrolling will generally reduce the likelihood of an over or underpayment of tax.

Focus

For 2017/18 onwards, 6 July after the end of a tax year is the set date for 'making good' on benefits-in-kind which are not accounted for through PAYE. The taxable value, and the value on which Class 1A National Insurance contributions (NICs) are payable, will be reduced only if the benefit-in-kind is made good by that date.

The 'making good' provisions generally apply where an employee gives something (usually a cash payment) to the person providing a benefit-in-kind in return for it. The payment has the effect of reducing the taxable value of the benefit-in-kind, often to zero, which in turn reduces the amount of the employee's taxable earnings. Employees will still have the discretion to make good after 6 July, but doing so will not reduce the taxable value of the benefit-in-kind.

Trivial benefits

6.46   From 6 April 2016, certain expenses and benefits can be classed as 'trivial' (subject to certain conditions) and may be exempt from income tax and NICs (*ITEPA 2003, ss 323A to 323C*). Where benefits and expenses meet the conditions of the exemption, the employer will not be required to record the payment of the employee's form P11D.

The exemption may apply where the following conditions are met:

- the cost of providing the benefit does not exceed £50 (see below for definition of 'benefit cost');

- the benefit is not cash or a cash voucher;

- the employee is not entitled to the benefit as part of any contractual obligation (including under salary sacrifice arrangements); and

- the benefit is not provided in recognition of particular services performed by the employee as part of their employment duties (or in anticipation of such services).

The cost of the benefit is defined in the legislation as:

- the cost of providing the benefit; or

- if the benefit is provided to more than one person and the nature of the benefit or the scale of its provision means it is impracticable to calculate the cost of providing it to each person to whom it is provided, the average cost per person of providing the benefit.

271

Example 6.3—Trivial benefits

An employer takes six employees to a restaurant to celebrate recent successes of the business. The total cost of the meal and drinks is £276. Although different employees chose different food and drinks, HMRC will accept that the cost per head can be taken as £46 (£276/6). The benefit of the meal is therefore covered by the exemption as the cost per employee does not exceed the £50 trivial benefit limit. The benefit does not need to be recorded on the employees' forms P11D.

Trivial benefits provided to directors or other office holders of close companies (broadly, those with five or fewer participators), or to members of their families or households, will be capped at £300 per tax year.

The government will be monitoring the use of the exemption, and if it believes it is being abused, adjustments to the qualifying conditions and/or the annual cap are likely.

Focus

Where an employee receives a benefit exceeding £50, the whole amount becomes taxable, not just the excess, and it must be accounted for accordingly.

The exemption applies equally to benefits provided to an employee, or to a member of his or her family or household, subject to the £50 limit.

Dispensations

6.47   The former dispensations regime was replaced from 6 April 2016 with an exemption for paid or reimbursed deductible expenses (*FA 2015, ss 1* and *12*). HMRC retain powers to revoke dispensations issued prior to April 2016.

Formerly, where an employer paid or reimbursed deductible expenses (or provided BIKs covered by a matching deductible expense) to employees, they generally had to report these on form P11D and, in turn, those employees had to contact HMRC to claim back any tax relief they were entitled to. To ease the administrative burden of this 'in-and-out' reporting procedure, employers could apply to HMRC for a 'dispensation' – an agreement that specified specific expenses and benefits that could be provided to employees without deducting tax and NICs, and without reporting them to HMRC.

From 6 April 2016, a new exemption means employers no longer have to agree a dispensation with HMRC or report expenses or BIKs on form P11D where the employee is entitled to tax relief for those expenses or BIKs. Those expenses or BIKs will now be exempt from income tax. This means however, that businesses will need to determine the correct tax treatment of the expenses they pay to their employees and whether a matching deduction is due. Records will still need to be kept of what has been paid or reimbursed to employees. The exemption will not apply in conjunction with a salary sacrifice arrangement.

The exemption will also apply if an employer pays approved scale rates to their employees in respect of certain expenses that they incur, rather than reimbursing the actual amount of the expense. Businesses may use HMRC's benchmark scale rates for subsistence, or apply to HMRC for a 'bespoke scale rate' based on evidence of the amounts employees actually incur on the relevant expense. Where employers have recently agreed a bespoke scale rate with HMRC as part of their dispensation, they will be able to apply to continue to use that scale rate without providing further evidence until the fifth anniversary of the rate being agreed.

Focus

Common items that will be covered by the exemption include:

- travel, including subsistence costs associated with business travel;

- business entertainment expenses;

- credit cards used for business; and

- fees and subscriptions.

The exemption does not apply to expenses or benefits that are paid or provided under a salary sacrifice agreement.

PAYE settlement agreements

6.48   A PAYE settlement agreement (PSA) may be made with HMRC, under which the employer agrees to meet the income tax and Class 1B NIC liability (see **6.37**) on certain expenses and benefits given to employees. This means that the benefits or expenses covered do not need to be taxed under PAYE, or included on the employee's form P11D or P9D. The employer's tax liability under the PSA must be paid to HMRC by 19 October following the end of the tax year to which the payment relates (*ITEPA 2003, ss 703–707*; Statement of Practice 5/96; *SI 2003/2682, regs 105–117*).

The agreement generally covers:

- minor items such as taxi fares, personal incidental expenses in excess of the daily limit, presents for an employee in hospital and other small gifts;

- irregular items such as relocation expenses above £8,000 and one-off gifts which are not minor; and

- items where it is impracticable to apply PAYE, such as Christmas parties and similar entertainment not qualifying for relief.

Example 6.4—PAYE settlement agreements

Client Co Ltd provides taxable benefits of £200 each to four higher rate employees during the year. The company agrees to meet the employees' tax liability under a PAYE settlement agreement. The tax due is calculated as follows:

$$\text{Grossed-up value: } \frac{100}{(100-40)} \times 800 = £1{,}333.33$$

For further information on PAYE settlement agreements, see the gov.uk website at www.gov.uk/paye-settlement-agreements.

Taxable benefits

6.49   Subject to the exemption for 'trivial' benefits outlined at **6.46** above, almost all employees and directors are liable to tax on the provision of certain benefits, including:

- living accommodation;

- non-exempt vouchers, eg travel season tickets, gift vouchers;

- loans written off;

- payments made on the employee's behalf and expenses payments other than those wholly for business purposes (eg travel between home and work);

- certain payments made by employer credit card;

- certain relocation expenses;

- assets transferred at below market value by the employer; and

- gifts (if new, at cost or for 'lower paid' employees at second-hand value).

Prior to 6 April 2016, for employees earning less than £8,500 per annum, these benefits had to be reported on form P9D, where the total expenses payments and benefits exceeded £25 in a tax year.

> **Focus**
>
> The HMRC guidance CWG2 *Employer Further Guide to PAYE and NICs,* provides useful advice on whether benefits and/or expenses are reportable for P9D or P11D purposes (see https://www.gov.uk/government/publications/cwg2-further-guide-to-paye-and-national-insurance-contributions/2019-to-2020-employer-further-guide-to-paye-and-national-insurance-contributions--3).

Cash equivalent

6.50   Benefits provided to directors, and to employees by reason of their employment, are taxed on the cash equivalent of that benefit. This applies whether the benefits and expenses payments are provided by the employer or by a third party.

The 'cash equivalent' of a benefit is generally the VAT-inclusive cost to the employer of providing it, less any amounts made good by the employee. However, there are special rules for valuing certain benefits (such as cheap loans, share options, company cars and fuel for private use, etc).

Where 'in-house' benefits (ie goods, services or facilities) are provided to the employee out of surplus capacity, the value for tax purposes is broadly the additional cost to the employer of providing the benefit.

Prior to 6 April 2016, in determining whether an employee earned more than £8,500 per annum, all expenses payments and the cash equivalent of all benefits were included. Allowable expenses were not taken into account for these purposes, although certain deductions (eg employee contributions to the employer's pension scheme) could be taken into account.

Relocation expenses and benefits

6.51   The limit for qualifying expenses is £8,000.

Expenses must be incurred during the period from the date of the job change to the end of the next following tax year, although this period may be extended with the agreement of HMRC.

Qualifying expenses include (*ITEPA 2003, s 271*):

- *Disposal expenses and benefits* – legal and advertising expenses in connection with the disposal of an accommodation, penalty for redeeming a mortgage, auctioneers' and estate agents' fees, disconnection of public utilities, rent, maintenance and insurance costs while the property is unoccupied.

- *Acquisition benefits and expenses* – legal expenses in connection with the acquisition of a new main residence, loan fees and mortgage insurance costs, survey and land registry fees, stamp duty, connection of public utilities (abortive costs in connection with an acquisition that does not proceed are also allowed).

- *Transportation of domestic belongings* – including insurance costs.

- *Travelling and subsistence expenses and benefits* – for temporary visits to new residence before relocation, travel from old residence to new place of work or from new residence to old place of work where date of move and relocation of work do not coincide, travelling and subsistence costs for child under age of 19 relocating before or after parents for educational reasons, benefit of a car or van for use in connection with the relocation where it is not otherwise available for use.

- *Bridging loan expenses and beneficial bridging loans* – relief on any charge to interest at the official rate on a beneficial loan to the extent that the aggregate value of all other qualifying benefits and expenses falls short of £8,000.

- *Duplicate expenses and benefits in respect of the new residence* – replacement of domestic items (does not cover new school uniforms).

Living accommodation

6.52   There is an exemption to charge where (*ITEPA 2003, Pt 3, Ch 5*):

- it is necessary for the employee to reside in the accommodation, eg a caretaker;

- it is customary for the employee to be provided with accommodation; or

- the accommodation is provided by reason of security for the employee.

A director will not generally qualify for exemption unless the accommodation is occupied for security purposes.

The basic charge is:

- the higher of the annual value or the rent paid by the employer;

- less any rent paid by the employee.

An additional charge arises where the cost of providing accommodation exceeds £75,000 (unless the basic charge above is based on the full open market rent). The extra charge is calculated as follows:

- the excess cost (including cost of improvements) over £75,000 multiplied by the official rate of interest (2.50% from 6 April 2017, remaining unchanged (*SI 2017/305*));

- less the amount by which any rent paid by the employee exceeds the annual value.

The charges are proportionately reduced if the property is provided for only part of a year or if part of the property is used exclusively for business purposes.

Focus

Payments made to members of the armed forces to help meet the cost of private accommodation are to be exempt from income tax and from National Insurance Contributions. The exemption will take effect from a date to be specified under *Finance Act 2018, s 8(2))*. The conditions on the types of allowance that will qualify for exemption will be set out in secondary legislation.

Example 6.5—Benefits in kind: accommodation

A senior executive is provided with a house by reason of his employment from his employer which cost the employer £175,000 in June 2000. The gross rating value of the property is £1,000, and the executive is required to pay his employer a rental of £2,000 per annum. Assuming that the executive occupied the property throughout the tax year and that the 'official rate' in force at 6 April (the beginning of the tax year) was 3.00%, the tax charges on the employee for the year will be:

(a)   benefit under *ITEPA 2003, s 105*:

- (No charge arises because the rental of £2,000 payable by the employee is more than the gross rating value of £1,000)   NIL

(b)   the additional yearly rent ie:

• cost of providing accommodation	£175,000	
Less	£75,000	
Excess is	£100,000	
• £100,000 × 3.00%		£3,000

(c)   Excess of rental payable over gross rating value:

• rental payable by employee	£2,000	
Minus		
gross rating value	£1,000	
unused excess rent		(£1,000)
The cash equivalent of the benefit is		£2,000

Homes owned abroad through a company

6.53   The living accommodation charge outlined above generally applies to overseas property as it does for property in the UK. A particular issue arises, however, where property is held through a company for legal reasons connected with the country in which the property is owned. Individuals buying a home abroad through a company, typically for holiday use, will not face a benefit in kind charge in certain specified circumstances (*ITEPA 2003, ss 100A, 100B*). Subject to certain anti-avoidance rules, the exemption will apply if the following conditions are met:

- the living accommodation outside the UK is provided by a company for a director or other officer of the company ('D'), or a member of D's family or household;

- the company is wholly owned by D (alone or together with other individuals, but not as partnership property), and

- the company has been the 'holding company of the property' at all times since the 'relevant time'.

Employees' additional household expenses

6.54   Payments by employers to cover reasonable additional household expenses incurred by employees in carrying out their regular employment duties at home are exempt from income tax (and NICs). Employers can pay up to £4 per week (£208 per year) without the need for supporting evidence of the costs incurred. Above that level, the exemption is still available, but the employer must provide supporting evidence of the relevant additional household expenses incurred (*ITEPA 2003, s 316A*) (see also **6.64**).

Child care and child care vouchers

6.55   A benefit-in-kind tax exemption applies to the provision of qualifying child care contracted by the employer, and on employer-provided child care vouchers from 6 April 2005. An employee can receive vouchers for registered or approved child care worth up to £55 per week/£243 per month, free of tax and NICs, if certain conditions are met (*ITEPA 2003, ss 318 et seq*; *SI 2006/882*). For individuals who join employer-supported childcare schemes on or after 6 April 2011, the level of income tax relief available to higher rate and additional rate taxpayers is restricted, so that it matches the amount available to basic rate taxpayers (*FA 2011, s 35* and *Sch 8*). From April 2011, an exempt limit of £28 per week applies for higher rate taxpayers and £22 per week for additional rate taxpayers (ie those earning over £150,000 a year). From 6 April 2013, the £22 limit for employees earning over £150,000 a year was increased to £25 (*ITEPA 2003, s 270A*; *SI 2013/513*). The £28 limit for higher rate taxpayers remained unchanged. The change ensures that the benefit of childcare vouchers remained unaffected by the reduction in the additional tax rate from 50% to 45%. The NICs disregard is also aligned to these levels.

With regard to employer-supported childcare, legislation included in *FA 2011, s 36* changed the qualifying conditions for employer-supported childcare (ESC) schemes in relation to childcare vouchers and directly contracted childcare. Under the previous rules, the tax and NIC exemption for ESC schemes was only available where a scheme was open generally to all employees. Many employers use salary sacrifice or flexible remuneration arrangements to provide access to schemes. However, such arrangements could not be applied to workers at or near the national minimum wage (NMW) (see **6.22**) because, by law, an employee's earnings cannot drop below the NMW level as a result of a salary sacrifice or flexible remuneration arrangement. Broadly, the revised legislation amended the qualifying conditions so that employers are able to make their schemes unavailable to those employees earning at or near NMW levels, where the schemes are delivered through salary sacrifice or flexible remuneration arrangements. The legislation contained in *FA 2011* applies with retrospective effect from 2005/06 (see also *SI 2011/1798*, which set out the meaning of 'relevant earnings' and 'excluded amounts' under *ITEPA 2003, ss 270B* and *318AA*).

Guidance on employer-supported childcare can be found in HMRC Employer Helpbook E18 (2018) *How you can help your employees with childcare*, which includes guides on the tax and NIC treatment of workplace nurseries, other childcare premises and childcare vouchers. The booklet is available at https://assets.publishing.service.gov.uk/government/uploads/system/uploads/ attachment_data/file/691358/E18_2018_04_18.pdf.

Tax-free child care

6.56   Tax-free childcare is the government's new initiative to help working parents and guardians with childcare costs.

Under the scheme, the parent/guardian opens an online account and decides how much to pay in. Circumstances are re-confirmed online every three months. Anyone can pay into the account, including grandparents, other family members or employers, giving flexibility to pay in more in some months, and less at other times.

By the end of the year, all eligible parents will be able to receive government top-ups of £2 for every £8 that they pay into their tax-free childcare account, up to a maximum of £2,000 per child (or £4,000 for disabled children), up to a maximum of £10,000. The scheme will be open to all working parents across the UK with children under 12, or under 17 if disabled.

Money can be withdrawn at any time but in doing so, the government contribution will be lost.

Broadly, to qualify for the government contribution, account holders will have to be in work, earning at least £120 a week, but not more than £100,000 each per year.

Unlike the current scheme, tax-free childcare does not rely on employers offering it. Any working family can use a tax-free childcare account, provided they meet the eligibility requirements.

Switching to tax-free childcare is not obligatory – existing employer-supported childcare schemes will continue to run and remained open to new entrants until April 2018. Parents already registered by this date can continue using it for as long as their employer offers it.

Focus

In conjunction with the roll-out, the government's new Childcare Choices website (www.childcarechoices.gov.uk) is now operative, allowing parents to find out about various types of support available, and includes details on how to register for the new scheme.

The website includes a childcare calculator for parents to compare all the government's childcare offers and check what works best for their families, including the new 30-hour free childcare offer, tax-free childcare or universal credit. Through the website, it is also possible to pre-register for email alerts that will notify parents and guardians when they can apply, as well as receiving notifications concerning existing government childcare schemes.

---

30 hours free childcare

The second phase of the roll-out of the new 30 hours free childcare commenced in September 2017. Broadly, the 30 hours free childcare offer for working parents doubled the previous 15 hours of free childcare, saving eligible working families up to £5,000 a year. It became available to parents/guardians of three- and four-year-olds in England in September 2017, and was extended to those with children under six from 24 November 2017. From 15 January 2018, the service became available to parents with children between six and nine (*SI 2018/27*) and it is now available to all qualifying parents and guardians.

Eligible parents can apply online via the Childcare Choices website. On registering, they receive a code, which in turn allows them to arrange their childcare place. Parents can take their code to their provider or council, along with their National Insurance Number and child's date of birth. Their provider or council will check the code is authentic and allocate them a free childcare place.

Parents will be able to apply for tax-free childcare and the 30 hours offer in one go through the government's digital childcare service. Eligible parents can benefit from both tax-free childcare and 30 hours free childcare at the same time.

Company cars

6.57   Company car tax is graduated in relation to carbon dioxide (CO_2) emissions and the list price of the car.

The taxable benefit arising on a car is, broadly, calculated using the car's full manufacturer's published UK list price, including the full value of any accessories. This figure is multiplied by the 'appropriate percentage', which can be found by reference to the car's CO2 emissions level using HMRC's ready reckoner at www.gov.uk/government/uploads/system/uploads/attachment_data/file/356654/TC2b.pdf. This will give the taxable value of the car benefit. The value can be pro-rated where the car is only available to the employee for part of the year. The employee pays income tax on the final figure at his appropriate tax rate (eg 20% for basic rate taxpayers or 40% for higher rate taxpayers). In general terms, less tax will be payable on 'greener' cars.

From 6 April 2012, the 'lower threshold' was replaced with the 'relevant threshold'.

The relevant threshold for 2013/14 to 2018/19 is 95g/km. The benefit is calculated as a percentage of the list price of the car appropriate to the level of the car's CO2 emissions. The 'appropriate percentage' depends on whether the car was registered on or after 1 January 1998 and whether it has a CO_2 emissions figure or is a diesel car. Relevant percentages for cars registered on or after 1 January 2008 (with CO_2 emission figures) for the years up to and including 2019/20, are as follows:

CO_2 emissions	2016/17	2017/18[2]	2018/19[2]	2019/20[3]
50g/km or below[1]	7%	9%	13%	16%
51–75g/km	11%	13%	16%	19%
Above 75g/km up to relevant threshold	15%	17%	19%	22%
Equal to relevant threshold[1]	16%	18%	20%	23%
Above relevant threshold:				
Increase per 5g/km[1]	1%	1%	1%	1%
Up to maximum	37%	37%	37%	37%
Diesel supplement[4]	3%	3%	4%(4)	4%(4)

Notes

(1)   Where CO_2 emissions are not a multiple of five, round down to the nearest multiple of five.

(2)   In 2017/18 and 2018/19, the appropriate percentage of list price subject to tax will increase by two percentage points for cars emitting more than

75g/km CO_2, to a maximum of 37%. In 2017/18, there will be a four percentage point differential between the 0–50 and 51–75g/km CO_2 bands and between the 51–75 and 76–94g/km CO_2 bands. In 2018/19, this differential will reduce to three percentage points (FA 2015, ss 7, 8).

(3) In 2019/20, the appropriate percentage of list price subject to tax will increase by three percentage points for cars emitting more than 75g/km CO_2, to a maximum of 37%. There will be a three percentage point differential between the 0–50 and 51–75g/km CO_2 bands. (*FA 2016, s 8*)

(4) From 6 April 2018, diesel cars are subject to a 4% addition (but subject to the absolute cap) (*FA 2018, s 9*).if:

- the car was first registered on or after 1 January 1998 but before 1 September 2017; or

- the car was first registered on or after 1 September 2017 if it does not meet the Euro 6d emissions standard.

A vehicle meets the Euro 6d emissions standard only if it is first registered on the basis of an EC certificate of conformity which indicates that the exhaust emission level is Euro 6d (and it does not meet that standard if it is first registered on the basis of an EC certificate of conformity which indicates that that level is Euro 6d-TEMP).

Prior to 6 April 2018, the standard diesel supplement was 3%.

6.58

Table of taxable percentages 2012/13 to 2019/20

CO_2 emissions (g/km)	2014–15	2015–16	2016–17	2017–18	2018–19	2019–20
0	0	5	7	9	13	16
1–50	5	5	7	9	13	16
51–75	5	9	11	13	16	19
76–94	11	13	15	17	19	22
95–99	12	14	16	18	20	23
100–104	13	15	17	19	21	24
105–109	14	16	18	20	22	25
110–114	15	17	19	21	23	26
115–119	16	18	20	22	24	27
120–124	17	19	21	23	25	28
125–129	18	20	22	24	26	29
130–134	19	21	23	25	27	30

CO$_2$ emissions (g/km)	2014–15	2015–16	2016–17	2017–18	2018–19	2019–20
135–139	20	22	24	26	28	31
140–144	21	23	25	27	29	32
145–149	22	24	26	28	30	33
150–154	23	25	27	29	31	34
155–159	24	26	28	30	32	35
160–164	25	27	29	31	33	36
165–169	26	28	30	32	34	37
170–174	27	29	31	33	35	37
175–179	28	30	32	34	36	37
180–184	29	31	33	35	37	37
185–189	30	32	34	36	37	37
190–194	31	33	35	37	37	37
195–199	32	34	36	37	37	37
200–204	33	35	37	37	37	37
205–209	34	36	37	37	37	37
210–214	35	37	37	37	37	37
215–219	35	37	37	37	37	37
220+	35	37	37	37	37	37

Notes:

(a)   All diesel cars were subject to a 3% addition (but subject to the absolute cap) until 5 April 2018. From 6 April 2018, diesel cars are subject to a 4% addition (but subject to the absolute cap) (*FA 2018, s 9*).if:

- the car was first registered on or after 1 January 1998 but before 1 September 2017; or

- the car was first registered on or after 1 September 2017 if it does not meet the Euro 6d emissions standard.

A vehicle meets the Euro 6d emissions standard only if it is first registered on the basis of an EC certificate of conformity which indicates that the exhaust emission level is Euro 6d (and it does not meet that standard if it is first registered on the basis of an EC certificate of conformity which indicates that that level is Euro 6d-TEMP).

(b)   The 'list price' is the price published by the manufacturer, importer or distributor (including delivery charges and taxes) at the time of registration. It includes any optional extras supplied with the car when first made available to the employee, together with any further accessory costing £100 or more. The list price is reduced by any capital contributions to the initial cost of the car, capped at £5,000.

(c) For all cars registered on or after 1 March 2001, the definitive CO_2 emissions figure is recorded on the vehicle registration document. For cars first registered between 1 January 1998 and 28 February 2001, the Vehicle Certification Agency supply CO_2 and other relevant information on their website at www.vcacarfueldata.org.uk and in their free, twice-yearly edition of the New Car Fuel Consumption and Emissions Figures booklet. For cars registered after 31 December 1997 with no CO_2 emissions figure, the tax charge is 15% of the list price for engines up to 1,400cc, 25% for engines of 1,401cc to 2,000cc, and 35% for engines above 2,000cc.

For cars registered before 1 January 1998, the tax charge is 15% of the list price for engines up to 1,400cc, 22% for engines of 1,401cc to 2,000cc, and 32% for engines above 2,000cc. Older cars with no cylinder capacity are taxed on 32% of the list price (15% for electric cars).

(d) The value of the benefit is reduced proportionately if the car is not available for part of the year.

Security enhancements

Employers calculating the car benefit charge for 2011/12 onwards can exclude the cost of certain security enhancements where they were provided to individuals who can demonstrate that the nature of their employment creates a threat to their personal security (*ITEPA 2003, s 125A*, inserted by *FA 2012, s 14*).

Focus

In *Jones v Revenue & Customs* [2012] UKFTT 265 (TC), the First-tier Tribunal decided that the taxpayer's specially modified vehicle was not a goods vehicle within the definition of *ITEPA 2003, s 115*. Although the vehicle might have become primarily suited for the conveyance of goods or burden, it was as a result of modifications and not because it was constructed for such a purpose. HMRC were correct in treating the vehicle as a car instead of a van for tax purposes.

Zero emission cars

From 6 April 2010 to 5 April 2015, there was a zero tax charge for cars producing no emissions when driven (eg electric cars).

From 6 April 2015, the special percentage for cars producing no emissions when driven (eg electric cars) is 9%.

Company car fuel rates

6.59   The company car fuel charge operates on the same basis as the car benefit charge. The percentage arrived at under those rules is applied to a single set figure for all cars to give the chargeable amount. The figure for 2019/20 is £24,100 (rising from £23,400 in 2018/19 (*ITEPA 2003, s 150; SI 2018/1176*).

Fuel charges are reduced to nil if the employee is required to make good all fuel provided for private use, including journeys between home and the normal workplace. No taxable benefit arises if the employer only provides fuel for business travel (*ITEPA 2003, s 151*).

The charges are reduced pro rata where a car is not available for any part of the tax year (being at least 30 consecutive days). The charge is also reduced proportionately where an employee stops receiving fuel part way through the year (unless he again receives fuel in the same tax year, in which case the full charge will apply) (*ITEPA 2003, s 152*).

Fuel provided in respect of a private car for private motoring of a director or employee is assessed on the cost to the employer, less any contributions from the employee.

Employers pay Class 1A National Insurance contributions on the fuel charge.

Focus

Finance Act 2019 contains provisions which exempt workplace vehicle-battery charging from being taxed as a benefit-in-kind for 2018/19 onwards. This applies to workplace electricity for electric or hybrid cars and vans owned by employees. The exemption will only apply if the facilities are made available generally to the employer's employees at that workplace (*FA 2019, s 8*, inserting *ITEPA 2003, s 237A*).

Company vans

6.60   In principle, a tax charge will arise if a work's van is made available, by reason of the employment, to an employee or to a member of his or her family or household. It must be made available without a transfer of ownership from the employer to the employee. From 2016/17 onwards, the charge applies regardless of the employee's earnings rate. If the van is only available for part of a tax year, the chargeable benefit will be reduced proportionately.

For 2019/20, the taxable benefit is ££3,430 (rising from £3,350 in 2018/19) (*SI 2018/1176*). There is no benefit if private use is restricted to home-to-work travel. The benefit is proportionately reduced if the van is unavailable for part of the tax year (*ITEPA 2003, s 155*).

Where a van is shared between two or more employees, the taxable benefit is calculated as normal and a reduction is then given for any periods during which the van is unavailable. To recognise that the benefit of the van is shared between more than one employee, a further reduction is then made 'on a just and reasonable basis'. Discretion as what constitutes a just and reasonable proportion is generally left to the employer to evaluate, although HMRC may intervene if they suspect any deliberate manipulation of the rules (*ITEPA 2003, s 156*).

The taxable amount is reduced by any payments made by the employee for private use.

Employer-provided fuel for private use of a van is subject to a taxable benefit charge of £655 per annum for 2019/20 (rising from £633 in 2018/19) (*ITEPA 2003, ss 160 et seq; SI 2018/1176*).

Employers pay Class 1A National Insurance contributions on the fuel charge.

Zero-emission vans

From tax year 2015-16, a rate of 20% of the van benefit charge for vans which emit CO2 applies to zero-emission vans (*FA 2015, s 10*). It was intended that this rate would increase each year, commencing in 2016/17, until it reached the equivalent of 100% of the van benefit charge for vans which emit CO_2. However, Budget 2016 announced that the 20% rate will apply for the tax years 2016/17 and 2017/18, thus deferring the planned increase to 40% until 2018/19. This means that the van benefit charge for zero emission vans will be 60% of the van benefit charge for conventionally fuelled vans in 2019/20, 80% in 2020/21 and 90% in 2021/22. From 2022/23, the van benefit charge for zero emission vans is 100% of the van benefit charge for conventionally fuelled vans.

Subsequently, for vans that emit CO_2, the existing van benefit charge continues to apply. The cash equivalent of the van benefit charge remains at nil where the restricted private use condition is met.

Beneficial loans

6.61   The taxable benefit on cheap or interest-free loans is the difference between any interest paid and the interest payable at the 'official rate' (*ITEPA 2003, s 175*).

The official rate from 6 April 2017 (remaining unchanged) is 2.50% (*SI 2017/305*).

There is no charge where:

- the loan has been made on commercial terms by employers who lend to the general public; or

- the total of all beneficial loans does not exceed £10,000 at any time in the tax year.

Tax is charged on the amount written off of any loans, whether or not the recipient of the loan is still employed.

Focus

From 6 April 2014, the current statutory threshold for the cash equivalent of beneficial loans to be treated as earnings of the employment increased from £5,000 to £10,000. As long as the total outstanding balances on all such loans do not exceed the threshold at any time in a tax year, there is no tax charge.

From 22 March 2006, cheap loans provided by employers to their employees which do not involve the payment of interest are taxed in the same way as conventional employee loans, ie on the difference between the interest (or its equivalent) payable by the employee and the amount of interest that would be payable at the official rate (*ITEPA 2003, Pt 7, Ch 3*, as amended by *FA 2006, s 97*). There are two ways of calculating the taxable benefit:

- the averaging method; and

- the alternative method.

The averaging method will apply unless the taxpayer elects for, or HMRC specifically require, the use of the alternative method (*ITEPA 2003, s 183*). The time limit for an election is the first anniversary of the normal self-assessment filing date for the year in question.

Focus

Where the loan is not at the same level throughout the tax year, it may make a significant difference if one or other method is used.

The averaging method

6.62   The averaging method (*ITEPA 2003, s 182*) applies an average interest rate to an average loan balance. To calculate any tax charge using the normal method, the following steps need to be followed.

Step 1

Find the balance of the loan outstanding on 5 April, ie the day before the start of the tax year. If the loan only came into existence during the year, the balance is taken on the day on which the loan was made.

Step 2

Find the balance on 5 April at the end of the tax year. If the loan was fully repaid during the year, it is necessary to look at the balance on the day of repayment.

In both Steps 1 and 2 above, it is necessary to look at the maximum amount of the loan outstanding on each of the relevant days.

Two successive loans are treated as the same loan for the purposes of these first two steps.

Step 3

Calculate the average of the two figures from Steps 1 and 2 above.

Step 4

Calculate the average official rate of interest. (If the official rate of interest was unchanged for the whole year, or for the part of the year during which the loan was outstanding, this step can be ignored.) The legislation instructs that this should be done as follows:

(1)   multiply the official rate of interest in force during each period by the number of days when it was in force;

(2)   add together these products; and

(3)   divide the result by the number of days in the total period.

The result at this stage is a rough and ready average loan for the whole year.

Step 5

It is now necessary to apply to this average loan figure the average 'official rate of interest' in force during the period for which the loan was outstanding during the year. This is done by using the formula:

$$A \times I \times \frac{M}{12}$$

where:

●   A is the average loan, as calculated above

●   I is the average interest rate, as calculated above

●   M is the number of whole months during which the loan was outstanding in the year. For these purposes, a month begins on the sixth day of the calendar month. A loan taken out on 7 June and repaid on 4 September is therefore treated as outstanding for one month only.

Step 6

Any interest paid by the employee in respect of that loan and for that year is deducted.

The result is the cash equivalent, or taxable value, of the loan in question for the tax year.

Example 6.6—Beneficial loan calculation: averaging method

Sophie's employer lends her £7,000 on 8 June for personal use. She repays £2,000 on 1 December. The remaining balance is still outstanding at the end of the tax year. The official rate of interest is 5% until 5 February when it is reduced to 4%.

The maximum outstanding at commencement of the loan was £7,000.

The maximum outstanding on 5 April at the end of the tax year was £5,000.

The average amount is, therefore, £6,000 ((£7,000 + £5,000) / 2).

The number of whole months the loan is outstanding is nine. (Months run from 6th to 5th, so the loan was not outstanding for the whole month 6 June to 5 July).

Period 8 June to 5 February = 243 days.

Period 6 February to 5 April = 59 days.

Total number of days loan outstanding = 302

The average official rate of interest is $((5 \times 243) + (4 \times 59))$ divided by 302, ie 4.805%.

So, interest payable is £6,000 × 4.805% × 9/12 = £216.

If Sophie has paid no interest on the loan, her taxable benefit for the year will be £216.

Any interest that she does pay reduces the taxable benefit on a pound-for-pound basis.

The alternative method

6.63   Whereas the normal method uses a monthly basis, the precise method considers the amount of loan outstanding each day (*ITEPA 2003, s 183*). This is the process to be followed.

Step 1

For each day in the tax year, multiply the maximum outstanding amount of the loan by the official rate of interest in force on that day.

Step 2

Add together those daily amounts.

Step 3

Divide the result by the number of days in the tax year.

Step 4

Any interest paid by the employee in respect of that loan and for that year is deducted.

Example 6.7—Beneficial loan calculation: alternative method

The facts are identical to those in Example 6.6 above.

Period	A No of Days	B Loan balance £	C Interest rate %	Cash equivalent £
8 June to 1 Dec	177	7,000	5	169
2 Dec to 5 Feb	66	5,000	5	45
6 Feb to 5 April	59	5,000	4	32
Cash equivalent				246

Living expenses

6.64   No liability to income tax arises where an employer makes a payment to an employee in respect of reasonable additional household expenses which the employee incurs in carrying out duties of the employment at home under homeworking arrangements (*ITEPA 2003, s 316A*).

'Homeworking arrangements' are defined as arrangements between the employee and the employer under which the employee regularly performs some or all of the duties of the employment at home. There is no requirement for any part of the employee's home to be used exclusively for the purposes of the employment; if any part of the home is so used, part of the capital gains tax exemption on the disposal of the house may be lost.

'Household expenses' are defined as expenses connected with the day-to-day running of the employee's home (eg heating, lighting). Mortgage interest is unlikely to qualify for the exemption, unless and to the extent that it was an 'additional' household expense. In *Baird v Williams (HMIT)* [1997] SpC 122, the taxpayer failed to obtain a deduction for mortgage interest under what is now *ITEPA 2003, s 336*.

To minimise the need for record-keeping, HMRC have confirmed that employers can pay up to £4 per week (£208 per year) without supporting evidence of the costs the employee has incurred. This rate applies from 2012/13. If an employer pays more than that amount, the exemption will still be available but the employer must provide supporting evidence that the payment is wholly in respect of additional household expenses incurred by the employee in carrying out his duties at home (2003 Budget Day press release REV BN 3, paras 5 and 6) (*ITEPA 2003, ss 318 et seq*; *SI 2006/882*).

Focus

In *Tax Bulletin* number 68 (December 2003), HMRC stated that 'homeworking arrangements' do not cover 'employees who work at home informally and not by arrangement with the employer'. So, for example, the exemption will not apply to employees who simply take additional work home in the evenings.

Example 6.8—Household expenses (I)

Sarah is an employee but works at home each Wednesday under the company's homeworking policy. Her employer pays her £4 per week towards the cost of additional household expenditure incurred as a result of working from home. This payment may be made tax free as the limit of £4 per week is not exceeded. There is no need to prove the additional household expenses in this case.

Example 6.9—Household expenses (II)

Simon also works from home on a full-time basis under his company's homeworking policy. He keeps records of additional household expenses incurred, which total £284 for the tax year. His employer reimburses him with this amount. Although the payment exceeds £4 per week, it can be made tax free because the additional expenses can be substantiated.

Expenses not reimbursed

6.65 If the employer does not reimburse household expenses, the employee will only be entitled to a deduction for household expenses if the strict conditions of *ITEPA 2003, Pt 5* are met. If the employee uses his home as his base of operations and has no permanent office at his employer's base, HMRC will usually allow a proportion of the outgoings as expenses. Note, however, that it may be necessary to use a part of the home exclusively for work purposes to obtain the deduction, and that if the home is owned this may jeopardise part of the capital gains tax exemption. HMRC *Tax Bulletin*, issue 79 (October 2005), contains detailed coverage on this subject.

Gifts, awards, prizes and tips

6.66   A gift received from an employer or third party by an employee may be taxable if it is received as a reward for services past, present or future (or simply, if it is provided by reason of the individual's employment by way of voucher or, in the case of an employee earning at a rate of £8,500 a year or more or a director) (*ITEPA 2003, ss 270* and *324*). Some factors of relevance in deciding whether a voluntary payment, benefit or perquisite may escape tax are as follows:

- Whether, from the recipient's standpoint, it accrues to him as a reward for services.

- If his contract of employment entitles him to receive the payment there is a strong ground for holding that it accrues by virtue of the employment and is therefore remuneration.

- The fact that a voluntary payment is of a periodic or recurrent character affords a further, though less cogent, ground for the same conclusion.

- If it is made in circumstances which show it is given by way of a present or testimonial on grounds personal to the recipient (eg a collection made for a vicar of a given parish because he is so poor, or a benefit for a professional cricketer in recognition of his long and successful career), then the proper conclusion is likely to be that it is not a reward for services and is therefore not taxable.

Long-service awards

6.67   Long-service awards are not taxable, provided the employee has had at least 20 years' service and the cost of the award to the employer does not exceed £50 for each year of service. No similar award must have been made in the previous ten years (*ITEPA 2003, s 323*).

Example 6.10—Long-service awards

Arthur receives long-service awards as follows:

> For ten years' service £250
>
> For 20 years' service £500
>
> For 25 years' service £750
>
> For 30 years' service £1,000
>
> For 40 years' service £2,500

The award of £250 for ten years' service is fully taxable, as he has not completed at least 20 years' service.

The 20-year award of £500 may be paid tax free, as all the conditions are met.

The 25-year award is taxed in full, as there has been an award within the previous ten years.

The 30-year award is also taxed in full, as there has been an award within the previous ten years, even though the earlier award was taxed.

£500 of the 40-year award is taxable, being the excess over £2,000 (40 years × £50 per year).

Taxed award schemes and staff suggestion schemes

6.68   Employers who provide non-cash incentive awards and prizes (eg cameras or holidays), and most of those who provide such prizes for employees of third parties, can operate HMRC's 'taxed award scheme'. Such schemes:

- allow the provider of the incentive to pay the tax due on the award, so that the incentive for the recipient is not blunted by having to pay tax on it; and

- provide an economical means of collecting the tax due (in bulk, instead of from individual recipients).

At commencement, the provider enters into a contract with HMRC's Incentive Award Unit to pay the tax on the total value of the awards to be made. The provider can pay tax at different rates: there are separate contracts for different rate schemes.

The amount of the tax payable is worked out on the grossed-up value of the award to the recipient. Providers must give recipients details of the tax paid so that they can complete their tax returns, or claim repayment if appropriate. Providers give HMRC details of recipients so that any higher-rate tax can be collected.

Most awards under taxed award schemes are suitable for inclusion in a PAYE settlement agreement (see **6.48**) instead of a taxed award scheme. However, a third party who provides awards to the employees of another and who wishes to pay the employees' tax bill must use a taxed award scheme (*ITEPA 2003, s 703*).

Awards made under most staff suggestion schemes are tax free (*ITEPA 2003, ss 321* and *322*).

Christmas parties and gifts provided by third parties

6.69   Gifts made by a third party to any employee are not taxable provided the cost does not exceed £250 in any tax year. If the cost is, say, £251, all of the £251 is assessable. The same concession allows employers to provide one or more annual events at a cost of up to £150 per head without the employees incurring tax liability in respect of the benefit (*ITEPA 2003, s 264*).

Tips and service charges

6.70   Tips are generally part of an employee's taxable income in the same way as his other earnings (*ITEPA 2003, s 692; SI 2003/2682, reg 100*). However, not all employees return full details of the tips they receive. Therefore, HMRC may estimate the tips earned on the basis of the facts available to ensure that the correct amount of tax is paid. Before doing this, HMRC establish first who is in a position to receive them. Wherever possible, they negotiate agreed figures with the employees concerned, or with their representative where large numbers are employed at any one establishment.

Certain organised arrangements fall within the scope of the 'tronc' system which requires PAYE to be deducted by the 'tronc master'. If the tronc master fails to do this, the responsibility falls on the principal employer.

The following flow chart (extracted from HMRC booklet CWG2) provides useful assistance in deciding whether the 'tronc master' rules apply.

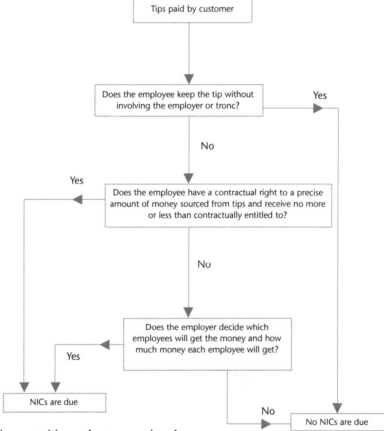

Tips, gratuities, voluntary service charges

Tips and the national minimum wage

6.71 The Court of Appeal ruled in HMRC's favour by upholding current national minimum wage (NMW) legislation relating to tips, gratuities and discretionary service charges in the case of Annabel's restaurant and night club and others. In June 2008, HMRC won an Employment Appeal Tribunal against Annabel's and others. The case involved the calculation of NMW pay where an independent tronc scheme was in operation. Troncs are a system of pooling and distributing service charges, tips and gratuities to staff in the service industries. Under specific circumstances, payments made as tips, gratuities, service charges and cover charges may count towards NMW pay. However, HMRC argued that tips, gratuities and voluntary service charges paid to workers by a tronc master via a tronc did not count towards national minimum wage. Annabel's and others were given leave to appeal against the ruling. The case was heard at the Court of Appeal on 15 January 2009. The court found in HMRC's favour and the judgment was handed down on 7 May 2009. The judgment is legally binding and sets a precedent for other cases.

The judgment confirmed that employers must pay their staff at least the national minimum wage regardless of any tips, gratuities, service charges or cover charges, providing they are not paid by the employer to workers through the employer's payroll.

Use of employer's assets

6.72

- Land is taxable on the annual value.

- Other assets are taxable at 20% when first lent, or rental charge if higher.

Example 6.11—Use of employer's assets

Susan's employer lent her a TV and a home cinema system player for personal use. The assets were first made available in 2010 when they had market values of £400 and £600 respectively. In 2019/20, Susan's employer pays for an annual service contract covering both appliances. The contract costs £100. Susan makes no contribution towards the costs.

Susan's taxable benefit arising in 2019/20 is as follows:

	£	£
TV – higher of:		
• 20% market value when first made available (20% × £400) and		80
• /annual hire/rent		Nil
		80

Cinema system – higher of:	
● 20% market value when first made available (20% × £600) and	120
● annual hire/rent	Nil
	120
	200
Add: associated costs	100
	300
Less: amount made good by employee	(Nil)
Cash equivalent value	300

The charge arises where the asset is available for private use, even if no actual private use takes place.

Vouchers

6.73 Cash vouchers are treated as pay subject to PAYE. Non-cash vouchers are taxable as a benefit in kind, except for vouchers exchangeable for non-taxable benefits such as parking facilities at or near work.

'Non-cash voucher' means (*ITEPA 2003, s 84*):

(a) a voucher, stamp or similar document or token which is capable of being exchanged for money, goods or services;

(ab) a childcare voucher (as defined in *ITEPA 2003, s 84(2A)*);

(b) a 'transport voucher' (as defined in *ITEPA 2003, s 84(3)*) (see below); or

(c) a 'cheque voucher'.

It does not include a cash voucher. A 'cheque voucher' is a cheque:

(a) provided for an employee; and

(b) intended for use by the employee wholly or mainly for payment for:

(i) particular goods or services; or

(ii) goods or services of one or more particular classes (*ITEPA 2003, s 84(4)*).

6.74 *ITEPA 2003, Pt 3, Ch 4* applies to a 'non-cash voucher' which is:

(a) provided for an employee by reason of the employee's employment; and

(b) received by the employee (*ITEPA 2003, s 82*).

If a non-cash voucher is within *ITEPA 2003, Pt 3, Ch 4*, the 'cash equivalent' of the benefit of the voucher is treated as earnings from the employment for the tax year in which the voucher is received (*ITEPA 2003, s 87(1)*). The cash equivalent is the difference between:

(a) the cost of provision; and

(b) any part of that cost made good by the employee to the person incurring it.

The cost of provision means the expense incurred by the employer in, or in connection with, the provision of the voucher and the money, goods or services for which it is capable of being exchanged. Money, goods or services actually obtained by the employee or any other person in exchange for the voucher will be disregarded (*ITEPA 2003, s 95*).

The Treasury may make regulations to remove from a tax charge a voucher or credit token used to provide an otherwise tax-exempt employee benefit (*ITEPA 2003, s 96A*).

Transport vouchers

6.75   The above provisions do not apply in relation to a 'transport voucher' provided for an employee of a 'passenger transport undertaking' under arrangements in operation on 25 March 1982, and intended to enable that employee, or a 'relation' of his, to obtain passenger transport services provided by:

● his employer;

● a subsidiary of his employer;

● a body corporate of which his employer is a subsidiary; or

● another passenger transport undertaking (*ITEPA 2003, s 86*).

For example, there will be no charge on a free train pass of a railway company's employee.

Mileage allowances

Cars and vans

6.76

	Mileage allowance	
	First 10,000	Over 10,000
From 2011/12		
All cars	45p	25p
Each passenger making same business trip	5p	5p

Notes:

(a) There is no charge to tax in respect of mileage allowance payments to employees in connection with business travel in a (non-company) car or van, to the extent that the payments are within the above limits.

(b) Where the employee receives no mileage allowance payments, or the payments are less than the statutory limits, he may claim a deduction from his emoluments equal to the statutory mileage allowance, or, where appropriate, equal to the excess over the payments received.

(c) Where an employee carries one or more other employees on a business journey, there is no charge to tax on passenger payments made to him within the above limit. This applies whether the car or van used is the employee's own or a company car or van. The employee cannot claim a deduction if no passenger payment is made to him.

(d) Employees cannot claim a deduction based on actual expenditure on a car or van. Neither are capital allowances or loan interest relief available.

(*ITEPA 2003, Pt 4, Ch 2*)

Other mileage allowances
6.77

Motorcycle allowance	24p
Cycling allowance	20p

Employers can pay employees up to the mileage allowance tax free for using their own cycles or motorcycles for business travel. Employees can claim tax relief on the mileage allowance if their employer pays no cycle or motorcycle allowance (or on the balance up to the mileage allowance if the employer pays less than this rate).

Advisory fuel rates for business use of company car

6.78   Recent rates are as follows .

From 1 December 2017

Cylinder capacity	Petrol	LPG
Up to 1,400cc	11p	7p
1,401–2,000cc	14p	9p
Over 2,000cc	21p	14p

Cylinder capacity	Diesel
Up to 1,600 cc	9p
1,601–2,000cc	11p
Over 2,000cc	13p

From 1 March 2018

Cylinder capacity	Petrol	LPG
Up to 1,400cc	11p	7p
1,401–2,000cc	14p	8p
Over 2,000cc	22p	13p

Cylinder capacity	Diesel
Up to 1,600 cc	9p
1,601–2,000cc	11p
Over 2,000cc	13p

From 1 June 2018

Cylinder capacity	Petrol	LPG
Up to 1,400cc	11p	7p
1,401–2,000cc	14p	9p
Over 2,000cc	22p	14p

Cylinder capacity	Diesel
Up to 1,600 cc	10p
1,601–2,000cc	11p
Over 2,000cc	13p

From 1 September 2018

Cylinder capacity	Petrol		LPG
Up to 1,400cc	12p		7p
1,401–2,000cc	15p		9p
Over 2,000cc	22p		13p
Cylinder capacity		Diesel	
Up to 1,600 cc		10p	
1,601–2,000cc		12p	
Over 2,000cc		13p	

From 1 December 2018

Cylinder capacity	Petrol		LPG
Up to 1,400cc	12p		8p
1,401–2,000cc	15p		10p
Over 2,000cc	22p		15p
Cylinder capacity		Diesel	
Up to 1,600 cc		10p	
1,601–2,000cc		12p	
Over 2,000cc		14p	

From 1 March 2019

Cylinder capacity	Petrol		LPG
Up to 1,400cc	11p		7p
1,401–2,000cc	14p		8p
Over 2,000cc	21p		13p
Cylinder capacity		Diesel	
Up to 1,600 cc		10p	
1,601–2,000cc		11p	
Over 2,000cc		13p	

Petrol hybrid cars are treated as either petrol or diesel cars for this purpose.

HMRC accept that, where an employer reimburses an employee for the cost of fuel for business mileage in a company car at the above rates, no taxable benefit arises.

Restrictive covenants

6.79   A lump sum payment made in return for an undertaking by an employee to restrict his conduct or activities in some way is fully taxable as employment income. For example, the employee may agree not to set up in competition for a certain length of time or not to behave in any way detrimental to the ex-employer. A termination settlement may include an undertaking by an employee to reaffirm undertakings given as part of the original terms of the employment relating to the individual's conduct or activity after its termination. It may also include an agreement by the employee not to proceed with any legal action. Such undertakings are not considered to be restrictive covenants (*ITEPA 2003, ss 225–226*).

Non-taxable benefits

6.80   Non-taxable payments and benefits include the following:

- free parking facilities;
- work buses with seating capacity of 12 or more (nine or more in the case of minibuses);
- mobile telephones (one per employee);
- free canteen meals (where provided to staff generally);
- child care facilities (where provided by employer);
- contributions by the employer to an approved occupational pension scheme or to an employee's personal pension scheme;
- personal expenses of an employee whilst working away from home of up to £5 a night (£10 if abroad);
- overseas medical insurance and treatment;
- sporting facilities provided in-house;
- bicycles or cycle safety equipment for travel to work;
- gifts not costing more than £250 per year from any one donor;
- qualifying removal expenses and benefits up to £8,000 per move;
- living accommodation provided in the performance of an employee's duties, or due to a threat to the employee's security;
- Christmas and other parties, dinners, etc, provided the total cost to the employer for each person attending is not more than £150 a year;
- long-service awards;
- certain other benefits (eg office supplies or services) provided for the employee's work, where any private use is not significant;
- assistance with home-to-work travel costs for disabled persons;

- retraining expenses and courses to help an employee find another job;

- emergency vehicles for employees required to take the vehicles home in order to respond quickly to emergencies when on call;

- vans provided by the employer for business travel, if any private use is insignificant

- one health screening and one medical check-up per employee, per year (*SI 2007/2090*).

Pensions advice

6.81   For 2017/18 onwards, an income tax exemption covers the first £500 worth of pensions advice provided to an employee in a tax year, subject to certain conditions being satisfied (*F(No 2)A 2017, s 3*). The exemption covers advice not only on pensions, but also on the general financial and tax issues relating to pensions. It replaces previous provisions, which limited the exemption solely to pensions advice, capped at £150 per employee per tax year.

The definition of authorised payments, has also been extended from 6 April 2017, allowing members and beneficiaries of defined contribution pension schemes and hybrid pension arrangements with cash balance benefits or other money purchase benefits to take pensions advice allowance payments of up to £500 from their scheme, to redeem against the cost of retirement financial advice. They will be able to take £500 tax-free, no more than once in a tax year, and up to a maximum of three times in total, without incurring an unauthorised payment tax charge.

Focus

The existing exemption for 'on-call' commuting has been extended for 2017/18 onwards, to allow for ordinary commuting in an emergency vehicle when not on-call (*Finance Act 2019, s 9*, amending *ITEPA 2003, s 248A (1)(b)*).

Broadly, the rules apply to emergency vehicles that are fitted out as such and that are not available for general private use. An emergency vehicle is one which is used to respond to emergencies. It must normally have a fixed lamp that is designed to emit a flashing light for use in emergencies, but this rule may be relaxed if the use of such a lamp could produce a special threat to the personal physical security of those using the vehicle 'by reason of it being apparent that they were employed in an emergency service'. For the exemption to apply, private use must be prohibited except where the person is either on call or 'engaged in on-call commuting'. For these purposes, a person is said to be on-call 'when liable, as part of normal duties, to be called on to use the emergency vehicle to respond to emergencies' (*ITEPA 2003, s 248A(7)*).

Subsidised meals

6.82 The provision by employers of meals in a canteen in which meals are provided for staff generally is exempted from the charge on directors and P11D employees. By concession, tax is not charged on such meals or on the use of any ticket or token to obtain such meals, if the meals are provided on a reasonable scale and either (*ITEPA 2003, ss 266, 317*):

- all employees may obtain free or subsidised meals on a reasonable scale, whether on the employer's premises or elsewhere; or

- the employer provides free or subsidised meal vouchers for staff for whom meals are not provided.

The concession does not apply, in the case of a hotel, catering or similar business, to free or subsidised meals provided for its employees in a restaurant or dining room at a time when meals are being served to the public, unless part of it is designated as being for the use of staff only.

The case of *Ansell v Brown* 73 TC 338, concerning a professional rugby player, confirmed that dietary supplements are not tax deductible, even where the need for extra nutrition arises from the nature of the duties performed.

From 6 April 2002, cyclists' breakfasts were exempted under the minor benefits provisions. No tax charge arose in respect of the first six such breakfasts provided to cyclists in the tax year. If a cyclist was provided with more than six breakfasts, the excess over six was taxed. Further regulations came into force, with effect from 25 June 2003, which removed this limit, and consequently the charge on cyclists' breakfasts was removed with effect from that date. However, due to low take-up of the scheme, the exemption was removed from 6 April 2013 (*SI 2012/1808*).

From 2005/06, the exemption for the tax charge on subsidised meals and recreational benefits is extended to persons other than employees who work on the premises of an employer who provides such benefits for their employees.

See *Income Tax (Exemption of Minor Benefits) Regulations 2002 (SI 2002/205)*, as amended by *SI 2003/1434; SI 2004/3087; SI 2007/2090* and *SI 2012/1808*.

Mobile telephones

6.83 For 1999/2000 and subsequent tax years, an employer-provided mobile telephone (including one mounted in a car, van or heavier commercial vehicle) which is used for private calls is exempted from any income tax charge (but see below). A 'mobile telephone' is one not physically connected to a land line (including a car telephone), but not telepoint telephones or cordless extensions to domestic telephones (*ITEPA 2003, s 319*).

In HMRC *Brief* 02/12, HMRC announced a change of view on the interpretation of *ITEPA 2003, s 319(4)* and now accept that smartphones satisfy the conditions to qualify as 'mobile phones'.

The exemption referred to above was revised from 6 April 2006. There was previously no limit to the number of mobile phones that could be loaned and no financial limit. *FA 2006, s 60* restricts the number of mobile phones that employers can loan to employees for private use tax-free to one per employee, and does not extend to members of the employees' family or household. *ITEPA 2003, s 319* was also amended by *FA 2006* to ensure that, where an employee has been provided with a mobile phone for private use through a salary sacrifice arrangement, no charge arises under the general earnings charge of *ITEPA 2003, s 62(3)*, even if the employee has the right to surrender the phone for additional wages or salary.

Some employers have chosen to use vouchers as the mechanism for making mobile phones available to their employees for private use. In these circumstances, a charge to tax and Class 1 NICs arises on the provision of the voucher. From 6 April 2006, the provision of a voucher is exempt from tax and NICs where it is used to facilitate the loan of a mobile phone to an employee for private use, but only where the benefit in kind arising on the loan of the mobile phone would have been exempt if a voucher had not been used. Effectively, this means that, from 6 April 2006, the method used by employers to loan mobile phones to employees will have no effect on the outcome for tax and NICs purposes.

Computer equipment

6.84   Prior to 6 April 2006, loans of computer equipment, up to the first £500 of benefit including related expenses (providing loans not restricted to directors or senior staff), were non-taxable. However, this exemption was severely restricted by *FA 2006, s 61*. The tax exemption is withdrawn totally from 6 April 2006, unless the computer was first made available to the employee, or a member of his family or household, before 6 April 2006. Transitional rules apply where the employer and employee had agreed in writing the terms on which the computer was made available before 6 April 2006 (*ITEPA 2003, s 320*). There is no benefit in kind where HMRC agree there is no significant use.

Works bus services

6.85   Any benefits attributable to an employee as a result of an employer either directly providing a works bus service or subsidising, in any way, a public transport bus service, are exempt from the general benefit-in-kind charge. Where such a benefit is made available through a ticket or voucher, any charge under the non-cash voucher rules is also exempted.

To qualify for this exemption for a works bus service, the buses used must have a seating capacity of 12 or more (a 'large' bus) and the facility must be available to employees generally. However, to make it easier for smaller employers to offer such a service, from 6 April 2002, the exemption is extended to allow the service to be provided by means of a minibus, which has a seating capacity of at least nine, but not more than 12 seats. To ensure that safety is not compromised by unscrupulous employers squeezing additional seats into vehicles, such as people carriers to bring them within the definition of 'minibus', the exemption will only apply to vehicles originally constructed to carry nine or more seats.

Where a subsidy is provided to a bus service operator, the fares paid by employees must not be lower than non-employee passengers' fares. The exemption only extends to bus services that convey employees on 'qualifying journeys'; these are trips between:

- an employee's home and workplace; or

- one workplace and another.

However, from 6 April 2002, employees may benefit from lower fares without a benefit arising, so long as the service is a local stopping service. From the same date, the definition of a qualifying journey is amended to accommodate the situation where the bus is used for only part of the journey to work (*ITEPA 2003, s 242; FA 1999, s 45*).

Bicycles and cycling safety equipment

6.86   The benefit of bicycles and cycling safety equipment provided by employers to employees for their commuting journey is exempt from the general benefit-in-kind charges.

From 6 April 2005, no tax charge arises where employees buy bicycles from their employer, provided that the bicycle has previously been loaned to them or to another employee, and that they pay market value (*FA 2005, ss 16 and 17; ITEPA 2003, s 244; FA 1999, s 50*).

Eye tests

6.87   From 6 April 2006, no tax or NIC charge arises when employers provide vouchers to employees for eye tests and corrective spectacles for VDU use. Vouchers used to provide equivalent benefits are also exempt (*ITEPA 2003, s 320A; FA 2006, s 62*).

Recommended medical treatment

6.88   From 1 January 2015 a tax- and NIC-free exemption allows employers to meet the cost of recommended medical treatment for employees, up to an annual cap of £500 per employee (*ITEPA 2003, s 320C*). Medical treatment will be 'recommended' where it is provided in accordance with a recommendation from an occupational health service in order to help an employee return to work after a period of absence due to ill-health or injury.

Expenses

6.89   Payments made to directors or employees to cover expenses, or to reimburse them for expenses they incur, are treated as employment earnings. This is irrespective of whether the payments are made by way of a round sum allowance or reimbursed on the submission of an expenses claim (*ITEPA 2003, ss 70–72*).

In *R & C Commrs v Total People Ltd* (decision released 16 August 2011), the Upper Tribunal allowed HMRC's appeal and ruled that payments made by an employer to training advisers travelling in the course of their work were not of relevant motoring expenditure but were emoluments of employment liable for NICs (*ITEPA 2003, s 229(2); SI 2001/1004, reg 22A* (as amended)).

Focus

Finance Act 2019 contains provisions which remove the requirement for employers to check receipts or other forms of documentary evidence of the amounts spent by employees when using the HMRC benchmark scale rates to pay or reimburse their employees' qualifying subsistence expenses. The legislation also makes necessary amendments to allow HMRC to introduce a statutory exemption for overseas scale rates, subject to the same checking requirements as benchmark scale rates (*FA 2019, s 10*).

'Wholly, exclusively and necessarily'

6.90   Employees can generally claim relief for expenses incurred 'wholly, exclusively and necessarily' in the performance of their duties and for travel expenses necessarily incurred by employees in performing those duties.

Until 5 April 2016, the employer could apply to HMRC for a 'dispensation' to avoid having to record these types of expenses on the form P11D so that the employees did not then have to claim the relief (*ITEPA 2003, ss 333–344*). From 6 April 2016, a new exemption means employers no longer have to agree a dispensation with HMRC or report expenses or BIKs on form P11D where the employee is entitled to tax relief for those expenses or BIKs (see **6.47**). Those expenses or BIKs will now be exempt from income tax.

The 'wholly, exclusively and necessarily' test is a very broad one in comparison with expenses allowed as trading income which simply must be incurred 'wholly and exclusively' for business purposes. Numerous cases have decided that relief is not available for such expenses as:

- clothing worn for work which is suitable for use by the employee when not at work (thus failing the 'exclusively' test) (*Hillyer v Leeke* (1976) 51 TC 90);

- costs of cleaning protective clothing (*Higginbottom* [2018] TC 06521);

- newspapers considered necessary reading for journalists (held as not being in the 'performance of their duties' but helping to carry out their duties more efficiently) (*Fitzpatrick v CIR* 66 TC 407);

- travel between home and work (not being in the performance of the employee's duties, if performance does not start until the employee reaches the place of work) (*Kirkwood v Evans* 74 TC 481); and

- rental of a telephone installed in an employee's home (this being a requirement for the particular employee who did not previously have a phone, but not a 'necessary' requirement for the office holder) (*Lucas v Cattell* (1972) 48 TC 353).

Employee expenses not reimbursed

6.91   Employees may also claim tax relief for allowable expenses they incur personally but which are not reimbursed by their employer such as fees and subscriptions to professional bodies, books (required by teachers and lecturers) and allowable training and travel expenditure.

A limited deduction ('flat rate expense allowance') is available for employees in various occupations, towards the upkeep of tools or special clothing necessary for work, although this does not prevent the employee claiming relief for the actual cost incurred, if higher.

Focus

For details of flat rate expenses, the structure of which is currently under review, see the HMRC Employment Income Manual at EIM32730a.

Lump sum payments

On taking up employment

6.92   Payments made to an individual as an incentive to take up an employment, often known as 'golden hellos' or 'golden handcuffs', are generally treated as advance pay for future services of employment and are therefore taxable as employment income. This is not the case where the payment is compensation for the loss or restriction of a right on taking up employment, but this is unusual and often difficult to prove.

In a case involving a football player, a sum paid by his old club when he had already joined his new club was still earnings, even though there was no link between the old club and his future services (*Shilton v Wilmshurst* 64 TC 78).

On termination of employment

6.93   The term 'termination payment' is typically used as a generic summary for a lump sum payment, which is normally (but not always) made to an employee at the time the employment comes to an end. Often referred to as 'golden handshakes', until 6 April 2018, such payments are generally treated as taxable under the normal employment income rules where they are paid for employment services rendered. Where the payments do not fall within those general rules, they are taxable under special rules, subject to an exemption for the first £30,000 (*ITEPA 2003, s 309*).

The rules for the taxation of termination payments are complex. There has been scope for employers to manipulate them by structuring arrangements to include payments that would ordinarily be taxable, in order to minimise the income tax and National Insurance due. The main area of concern has been whether the £30,000 tax-free exemption applies to a payment. Therefore, in an attempt to increase fairness and clarity, the rules governing all termination payments is reformed from 6 April 2018.

HMRC have announced (30 November 2018) that Class 1A employer NICs on termination payments above £30,000 will come into effect on 6 April 2020.

Finance (No 2) Act 2017 contains provisions for a new approach to taxing termination payments (*F(No 2)A 2017, s 5*). The aim of the revised rules is to provide clarity in ascertaining the amount representing basic earnings during the notice period to ensure that it is subject to tax and NICs.

From 6 April 2018, the total amount of any termination payments made will be split into two elements. The first, the pay that is for the post-employment notice period, will be subject to tax and NICs, and the second, which is the remainder, will be taxable subject to the £30,000 exemption. The amount of each part is calculated using a formula (*ITEPA 2003, s 402D*).

The new rules apply to all payments made, and benefits received, on or after 6 April 2018 where employment is terminated on or after 6 April 2018.

The first part of the calculation looks at the 'post-employment notice period'. This is the period from the day after employment ended to the last day of the minimum notice, whether statutory or contractual. It is calculated as:

$$\frac{BP \times D}{P}$$

Where:

- BP is basic pay in the last pay period;

- D is the duration of the post-employment notice period; and

- P is the duration of the last pay period.

The second part of the calculation deducts any taxable termination payment (T), which will include any pay in lieu of notice (PILON) made, whether the PILON is contractual or not. The formula used is as follows:

$$\left(\frac{BP \times D}{P}\right) - T$$

The next step is to deduct post-employment notice period pay (if it is greater than zero) from the total termination package.

'Basic pay' is defined as 'employment income of the employee from the employment' and excludes various items including the following:

- overtime, bonus, commission, gratuity or allowance;
- amounts received in connection with the termination of the employment;
- amounts that would be taxable as benefits or expenses;
- any amount that counts as employment income relating to securities and securities options; and
- any amount that the employee has given up the right to receive but which would have otherwise been earnings.

'Total termination payments' is defined as 'the total of the amounts of any payment or benefit received in connection with the termination that:

- is taxable as earnings;
- is not pay for holiday entitlement taken before the employment ends; and
- is not a bonus payable for termination of the employment;

The trigger date is defined as:

- the last day of the employment if no notice has been given or received; or
- the day the notice is given.

Example 6.12—Termination payment (pre-6 April 2018)

AB ceased employment on 31 January 2016. His termination settlement included £20,000 payable immediately, with a further instalment of £10,000 payable in January 2017. He was also given use of a company car for 24 months. Suppose the cash equivalent of the car use was £2,000 in 2015/16, £8,000 in 2016/17 and £6,000 in 2017/18:

The payments and benefits for AB will be taxed as follows:

2015/16

£20,000 payable on 31 January 2016	
Car benefit £2,000	£22,000 within £30,000 exemption

2016/17	
£10,000 payable in January 2017	
Car benefit £8,000	£10,000 taxable (£18,000 – £8,000 exemption still outstanding)
2017/18	
Car benefit £6,000	£6,000 fully taxable

Tax payable

6.94   The amount of the lump sum received in excess of £30,000 is treated as the top slice of income (whereas, under the normal rules, savings income is treated as the top slice, dividend income being the highest part of that top slice).

Reporting requirements

6.95   If lump sum payments are made to employees before they leave, the excess over £30,000 is subject to deduction of tax under PAYE, as under the normal rules. If the payments are made to employees after they leave, and after they have been given their P45 forms, employers must deduct tax under PAYE at the basic rate. The employee then pays any higher rate tax under the self-assessment system, ie by 31 January after the end of the tax year in which the payment is received. Where a termination payment and benefits package exceeds £30,000, the employer must report details of the package to HMRC by 6 July following the tax year. The details must also be reported to the employee by that date to enable them to complete their tax return.

Payments in lieu of notice (PILON) and compensation for loss of office

6.96   From 6 April 2018, the tax and NIC treatment of payments in lieu of notice (PILONs) is reformed (*F(No 2) A 2017, s 5*, introducing new *ITEPA 2003, ss 402A–402E*). Broadly, from that date, all payments in lieu of notice, not just contractual payments in lieu of notice, are treated as taxable earnings. The result is that all employees will be liable to income tax and Class 1 NICs on the amount of basic pay that they would have received if they had worked their notice in full, even if they are not paid a contractual payment in lieu of notice. The reform is designed to ensure that the tax and NICs consequences will be the same for all employees and will no longer be dependent on how the employment contract is drafted or whether payments are structured in some other form, such as damages.

The existing £30,000 exemption under *ITEPA 2003, s 309* will be retained and employees will continue to benefit from an unlimited employee NICs exemption for payments associated with the termination of employment.

HMRC have announced (30 November 2018) that Class 1A employer NICs on termination payments above £30,000 will come into effect on 6 April 2020.

Pre-2018/19

Prior to the reform from 2018/19, if the contract obliged the employer to make a payment where due notice was not given, the payment arose under the contract and was taxable as an emolument in the normal way. Where the contract provided only for notice to be given, failure to give the notice was regarded as a breach of the contract. The payment was compensation for that breach rather than arising under the contract, and would therefore be taxable under the special rules, provided that it was not the employer's normal practice to make such payments and there was no understanding that the payment would be made (*ITEPA 2003, ss 401–416*).

The phrase 'payment in lieu of notice' (PILON) could be used to describe a range of payments made in a variety of legal situations. In considering the taxation of such payments, it was therefore important to establish the precise circumstances in which they were made.

In particular, it was necessary to distinguish between a PILON and a gardening leave situation (see **6.100**).

In the latter, an employee would typically be given proper notice of termination of employment but told not to attend work during the notice period. As proper notice was given, payment for the period to the termination date could not properly be described as made in lieu of notice. The payment was simply the salary due for the period of notice and so taxable under *ITEPA 2003, s 62*, whether or not it was paid as a lump sum. In this case, the employment continued to the termination date, whether the employee worked or not.

Where a PILON was given instead of notice, how it was taxed depends on whether it was contractual, customary or a payment of damages. In *SCA Packaging Ltd v R & C Commrs* [2007] EWHC 270 (Ch), the High Court upheld a decision of a Special Commissioner that sums paid to certain employees who were made redundant were emoluments from the relevant employees' employments, so that the employer should have deducted and accounted for PAYE and National Insurance contributions (NICs).

Focus

Up to and including the 2017/18 tax year, payments made in lieu of notice could be exempted from tax and NICs up to the £30,000 limit, but not if there was an entitlement to the payment under the contract of employment. From April 2018, PILONs will be taxed as earnings and liable to National Insurance contributions regardless of whether the PILON is contractual or not. For further details, see the *National Insurance Contributions Annual 2018/19* (Bloomsbury Professional).

Contractual payments (pre-6 April 2018)

6.97 From 6 April 2018, the tax and NIC treatment of payments in lieu of notice (PILONs) is reformed (*F(No 2) A 2017, s 5*, introducing new *ITEPA 2003, ss 402A–402E*). Broadly, from that date, all payments in lieu of notice, not just contractual payments in lieu of notice, are treated as taxable earnings. The following paragraphs therefore are applicable only to years up to and including 2017/18.

For years up to and including 2017/18, where an employee received a contractual PILON, it was chargeable under *ITEPA 2003, s 62* as earnings from the employment. A contractual PILON is one that has its source in the contractual arrangements between employer and employee. Such arrangements could take a variety of forms, including:

- the main contract document;

- a side letter to the main contract document;

- a staff handbook;

- a letter of appointment;

- a redundancy agreement; or

- an employer-union agreement.

Sometimes, arrangements gave the employer a choice or discretion of giving notice or making a PILON. In *EMI Group Electronics v Caldicott* 71 TC 455, under the terms of the contract the employer had a reserved right to make a payment in lieu of notice. It was accepted that the right was exercised and the Court of Appeal held that such a payment was chargeable under *ITEPA 2003, s 62*.

An employer in this situation could choose not to give proper notice and also not to make a payment in lieu under the contract. If so, the terms of the contract were breached, and a payment for that breach fell within *ITEPA 2003, s 401*. It was dealt with as a damages payment. HMRC generally examine such cases critically to ensure that there is evidence that the employer did in fact choose to breach the contract. *Richardson v Delaney* 74 TC 167 is an example of a case where the High Court rejected the employer's claim that such a breach had occurred.

Customary payments

6.98 As explained above, prior to 6 April 2018, a payment made without legal obligation could be chargeable under *ITEPA 2003, s 62* if it was customary to make it. This was to be considered when there was no written reference in employment terms to PILONs (see *Corbett v Duff* 23 TC 763 and *Laidler v Perry* 42 TC 351). From 6 April 2018, the tax and NIC treatment of payments in lieu of notice (PILONs) is reformed *(F(No 2) A 2017, s 5,* introducing new *ITEPA 2003, ss 402A–402E).* Broadly, from that date, all payments in lieu of notice, not just contractual or customary payments, are treated as taxable earnings.

Payments of damages

6.99   Where:

- there is no entitlement to or custom of making a PILON (see above); and

- the employer unilaterally dismisses the employee with less notice than the employee is entitled to,

the employer has breached the contract.

In such circumstances, a PILON represents damages for breach of contract and is taxable under *ITEPA 2003, s 401.* The employment terminates with the employer's action.

Focus

It should be remembered that an employer would not normally breach a contract if it can be avoided due to the threat of legal action for damages. The working presumption to adopt is, therefore, that the employee will have been given proper notice. This presumption should be overturned only if there is evidence to support it.

Example 6.13—PILON (I) (pre-6 April 2018)

Gordon earns £60,000 per annum and his employment is to be terminated. His contract specifies a six-month notice period, with a discretionary PILON clause. Gordon works out three months of his notice period. His employer makes a payment of £40,000 at the end of this period. It is likely that the following treatment will apply:

- £20,000 will be taxed as a contractual payment in lieu of the three months' salary which Gordon would have received if he had worked out his notice period; and

- £20,000 will be treated as a termination payment.

Compensation payments for loss of office or a variation of employment are usually treated as valid termination payments, and are therefore not treated as taxable earnings from the employment.

The concept of damages can apply to any contract, including an employment contract. Whenever one party to a contract acts contrary to its terms (ie breaches the contract), and by doing so inflicts a loss on the other party, the latter can sue for damages. So rules that apply to calculating damages generally also apply where an employer breaches an employment contract. Probably the most common breach is where an employer fails to give proper notice of termination. A payment of damages falls within *ITEPA 2003, s 401*.

When an employment tribunal, a court or parties to a termination settlement calculate damages they will often follow the *Gourley* principle. This principle is a rule of non-tax law that derives from *British Transport Commission v Gourley* (1955). The principle is that a person must not be placed in a better or worse position than if the contract had actually been carried out. The following example is slightly adapted from the guidance given in the HMRC Employment Income Manual (EIM13995):

Example 6.14—PILON (II)

An employer fails to give proper notice of termination to an employee, and there is no contractual provision or expectation relating to payments in lieu of notice. The employer has breached the contract and the employee can claim damages.

The damages are first calculated by reference to the pay and benefits that the employee would have received during the notice period if proper notice had been given, for example gross pay of £2,000. Note that this is not, in fact, pay but is merely part of the calculation of the appropriate level of damages.

The payment of £2,000 would place the employee in a better position than if the contract had been carried out. If the employee had received pay during notice, it would have been taxed and liable to NICs, leaving (say) £1,500 in hand. As the damages payment itself is exempt from tax and not liable to NICs the employee would keep the whole £2,000. So, to satisfy the *Gourley* principle, the damages payment is adjusted to £1,500.

It is important to recognise that the £500 adjustment to the sum of damages in the above example is not a deduction of tax and must not be repaid as such. The actual payment made to the employee (£1,500) must be considered under the normal taxation rules for that termination payment.

Gardening leave

6.100   If a payment is made where notice has been given but not worked, the employee continues to be employed until the end of the period and the payment is taxable as an emolument under the normal rules.

Redundancy payments

6.101   Genuine redundancy payments (ie where the job no longer exists) are taxable under the special rules, the first £30,000, including any statutory redundancy, being exempt from tax (*ITEPA 2003, s 309*).

Retirement

6.102   An ex-gratia lump sum payment made on an employee's retirement or death may be treated by HMRC as fully taxable employment income as a payment under an unapproved 'retirement benefit scheme'. This will not apply where the employer obtains tax approval for the payment to be treated as a relevant benefit under an approved scheme (*ITEPA 2003, ss 393–400*).

Exempt payments

6.103   Certain termination payments may be completely exempt (ie not just the first £30,000). These include payments on termination of employment by the death of the employee, or on account of injury or disability. Payments relating to employment which included an element of foreign service may be wholly or partly exempt, depending on the extent of that overseas work.

SHARE SCHEMES

Introduction

6.104   When directors and employees acquire shares (and securities) in their company, income tax may be chargeable as employment income, for example where:

- the market value of the shares exceeds their cost price – the employee is liable to tax on the difference between cost and market value; or

- the employee has a right to acquire shares (an option) – the employee is liable to tax on the difference between the market value of the shares when the option is exercised and the cost of the shares (plus any amount paid for the option).

Legislation exists to counter avoidance schemes using employment-related securities to reward employees. Backdated to 5 December 2004, the legislation contained in *FA 2006, s 92* (amending *ITEPA 2003, s 420*) makes it clear that all options fall within the definition of securities. Options that are a right to acquire securities (call options) are not securities unless the main purpose of acquiring them is to avoid tax and NICs. *FA 2006, s 94* legislates for PAYE to be applied to employment-related options as a result of the retrospective changes introduced by *s 92* via the provisions in *ITEPA 2003, ss 222, 684* and *710* relating to notional payments.

Favourable tax treatment is, however, available to share incentive schemes approved by HMRC as detailed below.

Reportable events

6.105   There is an obligation for the 'responsible person' (normally the employer) to provide details of 'reportable events' to HMRC in respect of employment-related securities and options, eg certain acquisitions of shares by reason of employment, or chargeable events relating to restricted or convertible securities (*ITEPA 2003, s 421J*).

For tax years up to (and including) 2013/14, reportable events had to be notified (using Form 42), to HMRC by 6 July in the tax year following that in which the reportable event took place.

From 2014/15 onwards, reporting has moved onto more of a 'self-assessment' approach. Returns and any supporting information must be submitted electronically, unless HMRC give permission for an alternative method (*ITEPA 2003, ss 421JA–JB*).

Reportable events (*ITEPA 2003, s 421K*) are as follows:

- acquisition of securities or securities option;

- chargeable events affecting restricted securities;

- chargeable events affecting convertible securities;

- events where there is artificial enhancement of the value of securities;

- discharge of notional loan in relation to securities (partly paid securities);

- disposal of securities for more than market value (stop loss);

- receipt of benefit arising from a security;

- assignment or release of securities option; and

- compensation or other benefit on securities option.

6.106   The legislation requires companies to disclose to HMRC details of company shares and unapproved share options issued to their directors and employees if this is by reason of a former, current or prospective employment. This must be done irrespective of whether the employees face an income tax and NIC liability from the transaction. Failure to comply could prove to be very costly. If an individual, who has shares in a company, subsequently becomes a director or employee of that company, the acquisition of shares is reportable to HMRC. A £300 penalty applies to each reportable event.

HMRC have confirmed that a reportable event does not occur in relation to incorporation of a company where the company formation agent is the subscriber shareholder. However, if the subscriber shareholders are the prospective directors, this is likely to be a reportable event and, consequently, a return is required. Where an existing director or employee transfers shares to another director or employee (or prospective director or employee), a reportable event will arise and a return must be submitted.

A reportable event may arise where shares are issued to someone who is not an employee or director at the time of the issue but becomes one at a future date. This will, however, depend on whether the shares are employment-related securities made available by reason of employment or prospective employment. The company will know why it is issuing shares to someone who is not an employee or director, and the likelihood is that it relates to prospective employment and is, therefore, reportable.

Focus

See the HMRC guidance on share schemes at www.gov.uk/tax-employee-share-schemes.

Enterprise Management Incentive scheme

6.107   The Enterprise Management Incentive (EMI) scheme allows certain independent trading companies to offer tax-favoured share options to employees.

The legislation governing EMIs is found at *ITEPA 2003, ss 417–421L, 527– 541* and *Sch 5*.

From 16 June 2012, the company can grant EMI options worth up to £250,000 per employee (*SI 2012/1360*), provided that the total value of unexercised EMI options does not exceed £3 million.

The company must satisfy certain conditions to qualify. For example, it must:

- be an independent company (*FA 2014, Sch 37, para 22; SI 2014/2461*);

- for options granted on or after 16 December 2010, have a permanent establishment in the UK (*F(No 3)A 2010, s 6*); and

- have gross assets worth not more than £30 million.

The scheme is open to the employees of the EMI company or certain subsidiaries. The individual must be committed to working for at least 25 hours a week (or 75% of his working time, if less). Employees with a 'material interest' are excluded (ie where the individual and/or his associates control more than 30% of the company's ordinary share capital (or the assets on a winding up of a close company)).

Where all the conditions are satisfied, there will normally be no income tax for the employee to pay:

- when the option is granted; or

- on any increase in value between the grant and subsequent exercise of the share option (where the option can be exercised within ten years of its grant, and the employee pays not less than the market value of the shares when the option was granted).

The *Finance Act 2013* contains provisions which change the holding period to obtain entrepreneurs' relief on shares acquired by exercising EMI share options, so that it will commence on the date the option is granted (*FA 2013, s 64* and *Sch 24*).

Share incentive plans

6.108 A company participating in a share incentive plan (SIP) may give free shares to employees and employees of group companies without an income tax charge. Employees may also allocate part of their salary to purchasing tax-advantaged shares in their employer company, and receive tax relief for the cost of the shares (*FA 2000, s 47, Sch 8*; *FA 2001, Sch 13*; *ITEPA 2003, ss 488–515, Sch 2*; *FA 2003, Sch 21*).

A plan may offer the following types of shares:

- 'free shares' – from April 2014 a company can give an employee shares worth up to £3,600 per annum free of tax (£3,000 prior to April 2014);

- 'partnership shares' – from April 2014 an employee may buy shares by deductions from salary, up to a maximum of £1,800 per tax year (£1,500 prior to April 2014) (or 10% of salary, if less), these being allowable deductions for income tax and NICs; and

- 'matching shares' – the company may give an employee up to two free shares for each partnership share purchased.

The shares must normally be kept in the plan for three years. Employees who keep their shares in the plan for at least five years pay no income tax or NICs.

6.109 Income tax charges generally arise when free and matching shares are withdrawn from the plan, or when partnership shares are removed as below:

Shares held in plan	Income tax charge
0–2 years	Market value of shares withdrawn
3–4 years	Lower of initial value of shares and market value on withdrawal*
5 years and over	No tax (or NIC) charge

* For partnership shares, the market value of the shares removed, or the salary used to acquire the shares (if lower).

Other conditions and reliefs include:

- employees may reinvest dividends on plan shares up to £1,800 per year to acquire further ('dividend') shares in the company tax free (subject to a minimum holding period of five years beginning with the date of award of the plan shares in respect of which the dividend applied);

- the company may claim tax relief on the costs of setting up and running the plan, and for the market value of any free or matching shares used in the plan;

- the scheme must be open to all individuals on similar terms. However, directors and employees with a 'material interest' are excluded (ie where the individual and/or his associates control more than 25% of the company's ordinary share capital (or the assets on a winding up of a close company)).

Focus

Share incentive plans were formerly known as employee share ownership plans (ESOPs).

6.110 Employees working for a group of companies could be prevented from benefiting from the plan where they have been moved around within the group. Changes in *FA 2001* ensure that an employee will satisfy a qualifying period of employment by having worked for any group company. When a group restructures, employees' participation in an SIP may be affected as prior to 10 July 2003 they could not participate in two SIPs run by connected companies in the same year. This unnecessary restriction was removed from 10 July 2003 for cases where a group restructures and an employee transfers to another company within the group.

The legislation specifies that the purpose of the plan must be to provide employees with shares in the company, which in turn, gives them a continuing stake in that company. The plan must not contain, and the operation of the plan must not involve, features which are neither essential nor reasonably incidental to that purpose. No conditions, apart from those required or authorised by the provisions of *ITEPA 2003, Sch 2, Pt 2* (ie those set out below), may be imposed on an employee's participation in an award of shares under the plan.

Although the scheme rules must require that all qualifying employees participate on the same terms, the rights of those participating in the scheme to obtain and exercise share options may vary according to level of remuneration, length of service, or any similar factors. There must not, however, be any preferential treatment for directors and senior employees.

The arrangements for the plan must not make any provision, or be associated in any way with any provision made, for loans to some or all of the employees of the company, or in the case of a group plan, of any constituent company. The operation of the plan must not be associated in any way with such loans (*ITEPA 2003, Sch 2*).

Approved Save As You Earn (SAYE) share option schemes

6.111   A company may obtain HMRC approval to operate a scheme for its directors and employees, under which options are granted to employees to acquire shares without an income tax charge arising on receipt of the option, or on any growth in value of the shares between the option being granted and exercised (*FA 2003, s 139, Sch 21*; *ITEPA 2003, Schs 3, 4*; *Finance Act 1995 (Contractual Savings Schemes) (Appointed Day) Order 1995 (SI 1995/1778)*).

There are a number of conditions to be fulfilled to obtain approval, including the following:

- the shares must be bought through a certified contractual savings scheme and any loans must not be payable before a date approved by HMRC except where the employee dies or leaves his job before that date;

- the price paid for the shares must not be less than 80% of their market value when purchased;

- all employees or directors must be able to participate in the scheme, except individuals who have held 5% of the share capital of a close company in the last 12 months;

- all those who have worked for a qualifying period must be permitted to participate in the scheme (the qualifying period must not exceed five years); and

- the shares must be fully paid ordinary shares which are non-redeemable and they must be either quoted on a stock exchange or be shares in a subsidiary company.

From 1 September 2018, employees on maternity/parental leave will be allowed to pause contributing to their SAYE share scheme for up to 12 months, instead of the existing six months (HMRC's *Employment-Related Securities Bulletin* No 26 (March 2018)).

6.112   It is possible to subject shares within savings-related share option schemes to restrictions connected with the termination of employment.

On a takeover of a company, scheme participants may exchange their rights of option in shares of the company taken over for equivalent rights in the acquiring company or another company. Scheme rules may be changed so that an exchange of rights is permissible and such a transaction will not give rise to a CGT charge.

The cost of the shares is funded by 'Save As You Earn' (SAYE) contracts taken out by the employee with a bank or building society. Interest and bonuses on scheme savings are exempt from tax.

From April 2014, the employee may save between £5 and £500 per month (£250 per month prior to April 2014), usually as a deduction from pay (although tax relief is not given for SAYE contributions).

Options may be granted to acquire shares at their market value on that date subject to a maximum discount of up to 20%.

The options will normally be capable of being exercised after three, five or seven years, when the SAYE contract ends. The shares are purchased out of the employee's SAYE contract.

The scheme must be open to all directors and employees with at least five years' service, and on similar terms. Individuals with a 'material interest' in a close company are excluded.

Approved company share option plan (CSOP) schemes

6.113 Company share option plans (CSOPs) are HMRC-approved, tax advantageous share option plans. The schemes are discretionary, which means that the company is to select which directors and employees can participate in the scheme *(ITEPA 2003, Schs 3, 4)*.

Under a CSOP, options are granted to the employee/director. No income tax is payable on grant. Normally, there is no income tax payable on the increase in value of the shares between grant and exercise provided that certain conditions have been met. For capital gains tax purposes, the cost of the shares is normally the price paid for them.

The value of shares for which a person may hold options under any approved scheme established by his employer or any associated company is limited to £30,000.

The share price must be specified at the time the option is granted and must not be manifestly less than their market value at that time.

The employee must not exercise his option less than three years or more than ten years after the date on which it was granted. *FA 2003, s 139, Sch 21*, removed the charge to income tax on a second option exercise within three years of a previous exercise.

The procedure for obtaining approval is substantially the same as that for approved savings-related share option schemes.

6.114 It is possible within limits to subject shares within an approved scheme to restrictions where the restriction is either attached to all shares of the same class or requires that the directors and employees sell all the shares upon cessation of employment and that shares be sold when acquired, if the acquisition of the shares occurs after cessation of employment.

Restrictions which are not permissible include those attaching to shares which limit the holder's freedom to dispose of the shares, or their proceeds of sale, or to exercise any right conferred by the shares; they do not include restrictions imposed by the Model Code for Securities Transactions by Directors of Listed Companies (see ESSUM43670), nor to any terms of a loan relating to repayment or security.

Only full-time directors and employees may participate in a scheme approved before 1 May 1995. The 'full-time' requirement is removed in respect of schemes approved on or after that date.

A company may include provisions in a scheme which permit options to be exercised by participators who, by the time of the exercise, may no longer be full-time employees. A provision may also be included allowing options to be exercised by the personal representatives of a deceased participator; in such cases, the exercise must take place within one year of the employee's death, but subject to the ten-year limit.

A person holding a 'material interest' in a close company is ineligible to participate in an approved share scheme involving that company. Broadly, a person has a 'material interest' for this purpose if he, alone or with any 'associate(s)', beneficially owns or is able to control more than 10% of the ordinary share capital of the company. A 'close company' for these purposes is, broadly, one which is controlled by five or fewer 'participators' or over half the assets of which could be distributed on its liquidation between five or fewer participators or director participators.

'Employee shareholder' status

6.115   The *Growth and Infrastructure Act 2013* came into force on 25 April 2013. *Section 31* of that Act contained provisions for a new 'employee shareholder' status, which in turn allowed individuals adopting the status to receive between £2,000 and £50,000 of CGT-exempt shares (see *Capital Gains Tax 2019/20* (Bloomsbury Professional), Chapter 17). As far as income tax is concerned, *Finance Act 2013* introduced provisions which amended *ITEPA 2003* so as to reduce the income tax due when employee shareholders acquired shares under their employee shareholder agreement, by deeming that they had paid £2,000 for these shares (*FA 2013, s 55* and *Sch 23*). Following Royal Assent to the *Finance Act 2013* (17 July 2013), amendments were also made to the *Social Security (Contributions) Regulations 2001*. These ensured that, when an employee shareholder acquired shares, the same amount counted as earnings for Class 1 NIC purposes as counted as employment income for income tax purposes, and that the first £2,000 of the value of the shares also remained NIC-free.

At Autumn Statement 2016, the government announced that the tax advantages linked to shares awarded under the employee shareholder shares regime would be abolished for arrangements entered into on or after 1 December 2016 and that the employment status itself would be closed to new arrangements 'at the next legislative opportunity'. Due to legislative requirements, HMRC subsequently confirmed that the effective date was 2 December 2016 where the relevant independent advice was received on 23 November 2016 before 1.30pm. This change was enacted by *Finance Act 2017* (*FA 2017, ss 12–14*).

PERSONAL SERVICES PROVIDED THROUGH INTERMEDIARIES

6.116   Detailed anti-avoidance rules prevent individuals paying less tax and National Insurance through the use of personal service companies and other intermediaries (*ITEPA 2003, ss 48–61*). The rules broadly apply where, but for the intermediary, the income arising from an engagement would have been treated as employment income of the individual.

The intermediary will be responsible for applying PAYE and NIC to earnings received from any engagements caught by the rules. The income from the worker's relevant engagements in the tax year, less amounts provided as salary and benefits in kind and less allowable expenses, are deemed to be paid as salary on 5 April. Allowable expenses include normal employment income expenses, employers' NICs and pension contributions and 5% of earnings. For the calculation of the deemed payment, see **6.120**. See also the HMRC guidance *IR35: find out if it applies*, which is available online at www.gov.uk/ir35-find-out-if-it-applies.

Legislation

6.117   Anti-avoidance provisions to prevent individuals avoiding tax and NICs by providing services through an intermediary, such as a personal service company, came into effect from 6 April 2000. The legislation is widely referred to as the 'IR35 rules' after the number of the Budget press release in which they were first announced.

The rules were extended from 9 April 2003 so that income received by domestic workers, including nannies and butlers, in respect of services provided after this date via an intermediary, are also caught by the intermediaries legislation. This anti-avoidance measure means that workers who would otherwise be treated as employees, if they were engaged directly, can no longer avoid paying tax and NICs on any payments of salary by using a service company. Additional tax and NICs may have to be paid on the 'deemed payment' (see below).

The IR35 rules provide that (*ITEPA 2003, s 49*):

* where an individual ('the worker') personally performs, or has an obligation personally to perform, services for another person ('the client');

* the performance of those services by the worker is referable to arrangements involving a third party, rather than referable to a contract between the client and the worker; and

* the circumstances are such that, were the services to be performed by the worker under a contract between him and the client, he would be regarded as employed in the employed earner's employment by the client,

the relevant payments and benefits are treated as emoluments paid to the worker in respect of his or her employment. These rules apply irrespective of whether the client is a person with whom the worker holds any office or employment. Under the rules, a deemed salary payment, subject to tax under PAYE, may fall to be made to the worker on 5 April at the end of the tax year. The tax and NICs due on this deemed payment must be accounted for by 19 April.

The IR35 legislation was tightened for 2013/14 onwards, and this has an impact on individuals who hold an office (an executive or non-executive director) on the board of a company and are paid via a personal service company (PSC). Historically, there has been a view that income received by a PSC did not fall within the existing IR35 legislation and was therefore not treated as employment income subject to PAYE. However, from 6 April 2013, any payment to a PSC from a third party for the provision of an individual as an 'office holder' is deemed to be employment income, regardless of whether the PSC or the individual is registered as the office holder of the engager (*ITEPA 2003, s 49(1)(c)*).

HMRC guidance on this change states:

'The change applies when a worker's personal services are supplied via an intermediary to perform the duties of an office, including when:

- A worker is personally appointed to perform the duties of an office.

- An intermediary is appointed as a corporate office-holder, provides the worker to perform the duties of that office and the worker's personal services are required.

- A worker is engaged both as an office-holder and to perform other duties in circumstances when they would be regarded as an employee if they were engaged directly by the client. (For example, a director also engaged as a CEO who has some duties arising from their office but in addition has managerial duties whereby they are mainly responsible for the client company's day to day activities).

- A worker has earnings from an employment that have already been subject to PAYE/NICs by a client but they are also engaged by that client as an office-holder. (For example, the salaried Chief Financial Officer of a charity who is also engaged as a director of the charity).

The change applies for tax purposes when a worker is an office-holder or performs duties arising from an office. The other rules relating to IR35, including when the IR35 NICs rules apply, are unchanged.

For example, a non-executive director who also provides consultancy services to an organisation will always be subject to IR35 for NICs and will be brought under IR35 for tax from 6 April 2013 when performing their duties as holder of the office of non-executive director. However, IR35 will not apply to the consultancy services, unless they are provided in circumstances when the worker would be regarded as an employee if they had been engaged directly by the client.

These new rules do not apply:

- simply because a worker is a director of their own personal service company

- nor just because their job title refers to them as an "officer" but they do not hold an office

- nor when a company engages another firm as auditor and there is no requirement for an individual's personal services.'

The change outlined above means that HMRC can invoke IR35 and seek recovery of tax under PAYE from the PSC when PAYE has not already been applied. This places office holders in the same position as contractors and other workers that currently have to apply IR35.

Focus

From 6 April 2016, certain temporary workers are not able to claim tax relief or a disregard for NICs on the travel and subsistence expenses they incur on an ordinary commute from home to work. The restrictions apply to workers who are employed through an employment intermediary, such as an umbrella company, or a recruitment agency/employment business, and who are supplying personal services (largely supplying their skills or labour) under the supervision, direction or control, of any person, in the manner in which they undertake their role.

Those individuals who supply their services through small limited companies (generally known as personal service companies), may no longer claim tax relief or a NICs disregard for those contracts where they are required to operate the intermediaries legislation (commonly known as IR35), or they would otherwise be operating IR35 if they were not receiving all their remuneration as employment income.

Factors determining employment status

6.118   Given that the issue of employment status has such far-reaching consequences, both for tax purposes and otherwise, it would be helpful to have a system that could determine the issue in any given circumstances. In most cases, it is clear whether a relationship is one of employment or of self-employment. There are however, many cases where it is unclear and there is currently no definitive guide providing absolute certainty. The basics of employment status are discussed at **6.1** onwards. With regard to personal service companies in particular, this is an area where judgement, experience and legal precedents all come into play. The point was highlighted in *Hall v Lorimer* 66 TC 349, as follows:

> 'In order to decide whether a person carries on business on his own account it is necessary to consider many different aspects of that person's work activity. This is not a mechanical exercise of running through items on a check list to see whether they are present in, or absent from, a given situation. The object of the exercise is to paint a picture from the accumulation of detail. The overall effect can only be appreciated by standing back from the detailed picture which has been painted, by viewing it from a distance and by making an informed, considered, qualitative appreciation of the whole. It is a matter of evaluation of the overall effect, which is not necessarily the same as the sum total of the individual details. Not all details are of equal weight or importance in any given situation. The details may also vary in importance from one situation to another. The process involves painting a picture in each individual case.'

In recent years, implied employment contracts have been examined in detail by the courts, with particular reference to personal service companies. In *Brook Street Bureau v Dacas* [2004] EWCA Civ 217, there was relief in the recruitment community that the agency (Brook Street) was not held to be the employer. However, the Court of Appeal gave a very strong indication that the end user in that case (Wandsworth Council) may have been an employer of the agency worker (Mrs Dacas) under an implied contract of employment.

Following on from the *Dacas* case, the Employment Appeal Tribunal (EAT) upheld a decision of an employment tribunal that an agency worker, operating through a personal services company, is the employee of the end user. In *Cable & Wireless v Muscat* [2006] EWCA Civ 220, an implied contract of employment was found to exist between Cable & Wireless and Mr Muscat, on the basis that Muscat's contract for services with his agency, Abraxas, did not reflect the reality of his relationship with C&W. In previous cases in which contractors have claimed employment rights from end users, they have failed because no contractual nexus existed: that is, the contractor's company had a contractual relationship with the agency, but not with the end user. This case makes it clear that a contractual nexus in the traditional sense is not necessary and an implied employment contract can be considered to exist.

More recently, in *Island Consultants Ltd v R & C Commrs* [2007] SpC 618, the Special Commissioners decided that, for the purposes of the IR35 legislation, a worker who had provided his services through a personal service company would have been regarded as an employee if he had contracted direct with the client.

In *Primary Path Ltd v R & C Commrs* [2011] UKFTT 454 (TC), the First-tier Tribunal confirmed that, where the taxpayer company provided the services of its sole director and shareholder to a client through the services of agency companies, the arrangements were such that, had they taken the form of a contract between the worker and the client, the worker would not have been regarded as an employee of the client, so that the IR35 legislation did not apply.

Control and substitution

6.119   In September 2008, the High Court held that the IR35 legislation applied to the services of an IT consultant. The failure of the appeal against an earlier ruling of the Special Commissioners in December 2007 (*Dragonfly Consulting Ltd v R & C Commrs* [2007] SpC 655) represented a huge defeat for both Jon Bessell, the owner of Dragonfly Consulting, and the Professional Contractors Group (PCG) who supported him. In this case the provision of personal services and substitution was the main issue and, ultimately, the one on which Mr Bessell's case collapsed. In *Dragonfly Consulting Lt v HM Revenue & Customs* [2008] EWHC 2113 (Ch), four issues were argued before Mr Justice Henderson, namely: the relevance of the concept of 'worker'; intention; control; and substitution/personal service. HMRC will usually agree that a person who is an expert in their field is unlikely to be controlled as to 'how' he does the work. However, that does not preclude the possibility that the work provider could retain the right to control 'how' the work is done.

In the *Dragonfly* case, the Automobile Association (AA) wished to use Mr Bessell's services because he was an experienced expert who knew what he was doing. However, the contracts included terms that indicated that the AA could exert control and supervision rights. In addition, the team managers said they could monitor his work, could check it if there was a complaint, asking him to undertake certain tasks so they could check the quality of his work. The High Court approved the Special Commissioner's description of this as 'an on-going informal appraisal of the quality of the work'. This, they said, is unlike a self-employed person, where you would not expect to find such regular appraisal and monitoring.

As a separate issue of control, the court also looked at 'what' was done. The AA allocated tasks to Mr Bessell, and his progress was reviewed by a manager. In his assessment of the facts, the Special Commissioner said that 'the engagement simply would not have worked if he did not do what was allocated to him' and he had to 'accept the AA's reasonable directions in relation to what he was doing (rather that how he did it)'.

In *Talentcore Ltd (t/a Team Spirits) v R & C Commrs* [2011] UKUT 423 (TCC), the Upper Tribunal upheld a decision of the First-tier Tribunal ([2010] UKFTT 148 (TC)) that workers supplied by the taxpayer agency to act as consultants in duty free shops at airports were not employees of the taxpayer, since the workers had an unfettered right to substitution, even though they were subject to, or to the right of, supervision, direction or control as to the manner in which the services were provided.

Focus

In March 2019, TV presenter Lorraine Kelly has won an appeal at a First Tier Tribunal (FTT) over a £1.2m demand for unpaid income tax and NICs arising from a challenge to her employment status under IR35. In *Albatel Ltd and the Commissioners for Her Majesty's Revenue and Customs* [2019] UKFTT 195, TC07045, HMRC argued that if there had been a direct contract between Lorraine Kelly and ITV Breakfast Ltd during the relevant period in connection with her work for the programmes 'Daybreak' and 'Lorraine', it would have been a contract of service, meaning the company would need to account for income tax and NICs as she was effectively an employee of ITV. Albatel appealed HMRC's decision on the basis that the nature and range of Kelly's work meant that she should be treated as a self-employed star.

In evidence, it was found that ITV is under no obligation to pay Kelly if she is unable to present the show. Kelly is not provided with office space and explained that she carries out her preparation at home. In the hour that Ms Kelly is contracted to work she stated she had total control; any additional work related to the show is her choice. Any requests to appear as a guest on another ITV show would go via Kelly's agent and be subject to separately negotiated contracts. Kelly also highlighted that she is taken off air if a new story breaks.

The tribunal had to decide whether the contract was a contract of services or a contract for services, considering issues such as mutuality of obligation and control. In looking at the overall picture, the tribunal reached the view that the relationship between Kelly and ITV was a contract for services and not that of employer and employee, and so found in her favour.

Focus

In February 2018, HMRC won a significant appeal concerning the application of the IR35 legislation to BBC television presenters. In *Christa Ackroyd Media Ltd and the Commissioners for Her Majesty's Revenue and Customs*, [2018] UKFTT 0069 TC06334, the First Tier Tribunal (FTT) ruled that the legislation applied to the arrangements under which the BBC contracted one of the presenters of the regional news programme Look North.

Christa Ackroyd, whose 'personal service company' (Christa Ackroyd Media Ltd (CAM)), was engaged under a seven-year contract with the BBC to provide her services on up to 225 days per year. Ackroyd was appealing against demands for some £419,151 from HMRC relating to income tax and National Insurance contributions (NICs) for the tax years 2006/07 to 2012/13.

This appeal is specifically concerned with 'hypothetical contract'. HMRC argued that such a contract between the BBC and Ackroyd would have been a 'contract of service' rather than a 'contract for services', that her status was that of an employee, and that CAM Ltd should therefore account for tax and NICs accordingly. The taxpayer however, contended that she was a self-employed contractor, and there was no further liability on the part of CAM Ltd.

The FTT found that the hypothetical contract would have been a contract of employment. Such factors as:

- mutuality of obligation;
- control of what, when, where and how the taxpayer performed her role;
- right of substitution; and
- whether the taxpayer was in business on her own account,

were all considered in depth.

In his ruling, the judge said that a hypothetical contract of seven years, for at least 225 days per year, and terminable only for a material breach, pointed towards a contract of employment. In particular, the length of the contract was 'pursuant to a highly stable, regular and continuous arrangement'. It involved a high degree of continuity rather than a succession of short term engagements. However, he also went on to say (at para. 171): 'We do not consider that the fact the fees were payable on a monthly basis akin to the way an employee might be paid is significant. Nor is the absence of any provision for holiday, sick pay or pension entitlement.'

In this case, it was the ability of the BBC to 'control' the taxpayer, and the fact that there was a seven year contract for what was effectively a full time job, that were the significant factors in the Tribunal's findings that the taxpayer was an employee under a hypothetical contract.

The FTT said that whilst this appeal is one of a number of other appeals involving television presenters and PSCs, it is not a lead case as such. It is a significant ruling though as, not least, it indicates that the IR35 can be enforced where HMRC see fit to do so.

Focus

In *Jensal Software Ltd v HMRC Commrs* [2017] TC 00667, an IT contractor, Ian Wells, successfully appealed a tax bill relating to a succession of contracts during the 2012/13 tax year. Wells provided his services through his limited company, Jensal Software Ltd, to the Department of Work and Pensions (DWP), via recruitment agency Capita.

Wells worked on a project which formed part of the DWP's universal credit rollout, which involved attending a DWP office and travelling to different sites. He had the use of a secure DWP laptop and the tribunal heard evidence of meetings between Wells and DWP managers on the project.

HMRC contended that there was a direct contract between Wells and the DWP during the period of engagement, and that this represented a contract of services (as opposed to a contract for services).

HMRC relied heavily upon evidence provided by DWP officials, who noted that Wells was required to give feedback on the progress being made throughout the project. They also argued that Wells was expected to come to work each day.

However, Wells' submissions demonstrated that he had full autonomy over the work completed while noting that he would regularly work off-site under his own volition. This was confirmed by a project colleague, who noted that Wells managed his own time and location around the demands of the role.

Three conditions determining employment status were examined in depth by the Tribunal. The first is commonly known as 'mutuality of obligation', the second relates to the degree of control and the third is a negative condition, ie where it is shown that there is 'requisite mutuality of work-placed obligation and the requisite degree of control, then it will prima facie be a contract of employment unless, viewed as a whole, there is something about its terms that places it in a different category.'

Mutuality of obligation

Judge Jennifer Dean stated:

> 'The essence of the relationship was that there was no continuing obligation on the part of the DWP to provide work; if it chose to abandon the project there was no contractual basis upon which Mr Wells could demand further work.

> 'Although there is mutuality of obligation it does not, in my view, extend beyond the irreducible minimum nor does it demonstrate that the relationship was one of a contract of employment. Moreover, the level of control falls far below the sufficient degree required to demonstrate a contract of service.'

The judge also pointed out that each contract lasted a short duration. The break between the penultimate and final contracts of approximately two weeks indicates that there was no contractual obligation for the DWP to provide continuous work.

The judge said:

> 'It was also clear from the evidence of all of the witnesses that Mr Well's engagement did not extend beyond the specific project in respect of which his skills were required.

> 'The position as borne out by the facts is that there was a period during which one contract ended and the DWP was under no obligation to continue to offer a further contract. No further work was offered for a short period. Moreover, Mr Wells was under no obligation to perform the work and in relation to the final contract Mr Wells terminated the final contract when a better offer presented itself.'

Control

On this subject, the judge commented: 'The level of control exercised did not go beyond that which was usual for an independent contractor. In balancing all of the factors I conclude that Mr Wells was not subject to the degree of control which would be necessary to constitute a contract of employment.'

In this case, the judge concluded that the appellant's circumstances were such that they were not caught by the IR35 legislation, and in turn, this outcome now throws further uncertainty into the IR35 framework. On 18 May 2018, the government launched a consultation on proposals to extend the IR35 rules to the private sector (see 'Off-payroll working in the private sector'). This consultation ran until 10 August 2018 and it now seems very likely that changes to the regime will be announcement in due course.

Deemed salary calculation

6.120   To ascertain whether a deemed salary payment falls to be made, and the extent of any such payment, the following procedure is used:

Step 1

The total amount of all payments and other benefits received by the intermediary during the tax year in respect of relevant engagements (*ITEPA 2003, s 55*) is reduced by 5%.

Step 2

Add to the result of Step 1 the amount of any 'payments and benefits' received by the worker (or the worker's family: *ITEPA 2003, s 61(3)(b)*) in respect of 'relevant engagements' during the tax year, from any person other than the intermediary, where such amounts are not chargeable to income tax as employment income and would be so chargeable if the worker were employed by the client.

This rule ensures that any amounts paid directly to the worker as part of an arrangement to avoid the application of these provisions is caught.

Step 3

Deduct from the total of Steps 1 and 2 the amount of any expenses met in the year by the intermediary, or (from 6 April 2002) met by the worker and reimbursed by the intermediary, that would have been deductible from the emoluments of the employment if the client had employed the worker and the expenses had been met by the worker out of those emoluments. For 2002/03 onwards, where the intermediary provides a vehicle for the worker, deduct any mileage allowance that would have been available had the worker been directly employed and provided their own vehicle (*ITEPA 2003, s 54(4)*).

If the result of applying Step 3, or at any later point, is nil or a negative amount, there is no deemed employment payment. Neither, by implication, is there a deductible deemed amount.

Step 4

Deduct the amount of any capital allowances for expenditure incurred by the intermediary that could have been claimed by the worker had he been employed by the client and had incurred the expenditure (*CAA 2001, s 262*).

Step 5

Deduct any contributions made in that year for the benefit of the worker by the intermediary to an approved retirement benefit scheme or personal pension plan that, if made by an employer for the benefit of an employee, would not be chargeable to income tax as income of the employee.

Step 6

Deduct the amount of any employer's NIC (Class 1 or 1A: *ITEPA 2003, s 61(1)*) paid by the intermediary for the year in respect of the worker.

Step 7

Deduct the amount of any payments or other benefits received in the year by the worker from the intermediary that are chargeable to income tax and do not represent items in respect of which a deduction was made at Step 3 above. From 6 April 2002, mileage allowance payments and passenger payments are deemed to be chargeable under the charge on employment income provisions and therefore included in the amount to be deducted.

If the result at this point is nil or a negative amount, there is no deemed charge on employment income.

Step 8

Assume that the result of Step 7 represents an amount together with employer's NICs on it, and deduct what (on that assumption) would be the amount of those contributions. The result of this 'netting down' is the deemed employment payment.

Example 6.15—Deemed salary

James and Matthew are directors of a service company – Techies Ltd – and they each own 50% of the shares. During 2016/17, they each undertake some engagements that are treated as relevant engagements under the IR35 rules. They also undertake some other engagements that are not relevant engagements.

During the year, Techies Ltd received income of £50,000 in respect of relevant engagements undertaken by James and a further £30,000 in respect of relevant engagements undertaken by Matthew. The company also has further income of £40,000, which is not derived from relevant engagements.

James and Matthew each draw a salary of £30,000. NICs of £3,020 are paid in respect of each salary payment ((£30,000 – £8,112) × 13.8%). The company also makes a contribution of £5,000 each to a registered employer's pension scheme.

James incurs travelling expenses of £2,500 in relation to the relevant engagements undertaken by him, and Matthew incurs travelling expenses of £1,000 in relation to the relevant engagements undertaken by him.

At the end of the tax year, the company must calculate whether a deemed payment falls to be made. This is calculated as follows:

	James £	Matthew £
Income from relevant engagements	50,000	30,000
Less: travelling expenses	(2,500)	(1,000)
pension contributions	(5,000)	(5,000)
employer's NICs paid in year	(3,020)	(3,020)
5% deduction for expenses (£50,000/£30,000 × 5%)	(2,500)	(1,500)
	36,980	19,480
Less: salary paid in year	(30,000)	(30,000)
		(10,520)
Deemed payment and employer's NIC	6,980	
Less: employer's NIC $\frac{13.8}{113.8} \times £6,980$	(846)	
Deemed salary payment	6,134	

No deemed salary payment falls to be made to Matthew, as the salary paid to him during the year exceeds the intermediary's income from relevant engagements that he undertook during the year, after taking account of relevant expenses.

However, a deemed salary payment of £6,134 falls to be made to James on 5 April 2017.

Managed service companies

6.121   Legislation contained in *FA 2007, s 25* and *Sch 3* deems income to be employment income where individuals provide their services through managed service companies (MSCs) and their income is not already treated as employment income. This means that, from 6 April 2007, MSCs have to operate and account for PAYE on all payments that individuals receive for services provided through the MSC. If the MSC does not pay the tax and NICs, HMRC can recover them from others, principally the MSC's director and the person who provided the company to the individual.

Broadly, MSCs are multi-person, personal service companies, often referred to as 'managed personal service companies' or 'composites'.

In a composite company scheme, several (typically ten to 20) otherwise unrelated workers are made worker-shareholders of the company. The size of the company is restricted to ensure that profits do not exceed the threshold for the small companies' rate of corporation tax. Each worker usually holds a different class of share in the company. This enables the company to pay different rates of dividend to each worker, and in practice the dividend received will be directly related to the company's income from the end client for work undertaken by that worker.

In a managed personal service company (MPSC) scheme, in contrast to a composite company, there is only one worker per company structure. The MSC scheme provider performs similar functions for MPSCs as for composite companies – it usually provides a director and exercises financial and management control of the company, typically performing this function for many MPSCs.

Broadly, the changes mean that HMRC no longer have to rely on the IR35 legislation to require the operation of PAYE and payment of NICs by the MSC.

Tax relief for travel expenses paid to MSC workers may be restricted.

Partnerships and companies

6.122   Since the introduction of the managed service company (MSC) legislation (*ITEPA 2003, Pt 2, Ch 9*) with effect from April 2007, HMRC have seen a growth in intermediary companies which are marketed to individuals for the provision of their services to clients. The companies claim that they are not MSCs, usually by virtue of the fact that the provider of the intermediary is an officer or partner of the intermediary and that consequently, as there is no separate MSC provider, the MSC legislation does not apply. HMRC have subsequently taken counsel's advice and have confirmed that they consider that companies and partnerships that otherwise fall within the MSC legislation (that is, fulfil the criteria of *ITEPA 2003, Pt 2, Ch 9*), but claim not to be MSCs because the provider is an officer or partner of the intermediary, *are* nevertheless MSCs.

HMRC will challenge and litigate in relevant cases. Where HMRC successfully challenge a company as being within the MSC legislation and that company is unable to pay the resultant PAYE and National Insurance debt, HMRC will invoke the transfer of debt provisions.

Chapter 7

Self-employment

SIGNPOSTS

- There are three main vehicles through which a business may be conducted in the UK: sole trader; in partnership with others; or through a limited company. The tax rules, rates and reliefs vary according to the chosen vehicle (see **7.1**).

- The profits of a trade, profession or vocation are taxed on the basis of the business accounts (see **7.18**).

- The profits in the accounts of the business are not always the same as taxable profits, and it is usually necessary to make adjustments to the accounts to arrive at the taxable profit for the accounting period (see **7.22**).

- Eligible unincorporated businesses are allowed to calculate taxable income figures on a simpler cash basis if this suits the business. There are also simplified arrangements for certain expenses (see **7.23**).

- Apart from business expenses specifically allowed by tax law, expenditure cannot be claimed for tax purposes unless it is 'wholly and exclusively' for the purposes of the business (see **7.27**).

- When a business ceases, some adjustment may be made for overlap profits/relief (see **7.34**).

- Special rules apply where a business changes its accounting date (see **7.39**).

- Businesses can claim capital allowances on expenditure on qualifying plant and machinery (see **7.45**).

- Business losses are generally calculated in the same way and using the same basis periods as business profits. Relief for trading losses may be available (see **7.73**).

- Self-employed earners over the age of 16 and below state retirement age are liable to both Class 2 and Class 4 National Insurance contributions (NICs), unless specifically excepted (see **7.85**).

337

- Annual profits from farming and market gardening may be averaged for income tax purposes (see **7.111**).

- All businesses in the construction industry (individuals, partnerships and companies) are subject to the Construction Industry Scheme (CIS) (see **7.117**).

STARTING A BUSINESS

Introduction

7.1　　Broadly, there are three main vehicles through which a business may be conducted in the UK. These are as a sole trader, by a partnership, or through a company (either private or public).

Sole trader – this means that the trader is an individual who is self-employed. He will pay income tax through the self-assessment system, as well as Class 2 and Class 4 National Insurance contributions (NICs) (see **7.85**), and VAT if the registration threshold is reached (£85,000 from 1 April 2017, remaining unchanged for 2018/19 and 2019/20).

Partnership – if there are two or more people in the business, they might want to consider a formal deed of partnership. Each partner pays income tax, through the self-assessment system, as well as Class 2 and Class 4 NICs (see **7.85**), and the business itself pays VAT once the registration threshold is reached. The concept of a limited liability partnership (LLP) was introduced from 6 April 2001 and broadly provides the organisational flexibility of a partnership, but with limited liability status for its members (see **7.91**). See *Partnership Taxation 2019/20* (Bloomsbury Professional) for further commentary.

Limited company – a company registration agent may be used to buy a company 'off the shelf' or a new one can be created and registered with Companies House. Limited companies should always display their full corporate name outside the business premises, and registration details must also appear on the stationery and on e-mail communications and websites. Company directors have certain obligations. They need to file statutory documents, such as accounts and annual returns. Companies are liable to corporation tax on company profits. Company directors are also employees of the company, so there are different national insurance and PAYE obligations. Even though a company director is an employee, they still need to register for self-assessment. The same applies to each director in a limited company. The taxation of companies is dealt with in *Corporation Tax 2019/20 (Bloomsbury Professional)*.

Focus

For further details on starting up in business, see www.gov.uk/working-for-yourself.

Choice of vehicle

7.2 If the particular trade involves a risk, isolating that risk within a company environment may seem favourable. Otherwise the choice of unincorporated or incorporated business vehicle often depends on whether trading losses are expected in the early years of trade. Most businesses that develop to a considerable size find the inconveniences of a sole trader or partnership structure too constraining. Thus, if growth is anticipated, the choice is effectively between sole trader or partnership status initially, followed by transfer of the business to a company, or trading through a company from the start.

Focus

If losses are anticipated in the early years, and the proprietors have other taxable income, earliest relief (subject to restrictions) for the losses is obtained through an unincorporated business. Company losses are effectively locked into the company. A new company is unlikely to have other income against which to relieve the losses in the short term. Thus, they must be carried forward for relief against trading profits when and if these materialise.

Anti-avoidance

7.3 Certain transactions designed to avoid tax on the sale of land by direct or indirect means are specifically brought into the charge to tax (*ITA 2007, Pt 13, Ch 3*).

Whilst tax avoidance arrangements have diminished over recent years, due to the alignment of income tax and capital gains tax rates, the provisions are nevertheless very wide in scope and apply to all persons (which include companies and unincorporated bodies), whether or not resident in the UK. However, the land in question (or part of it) must be situated in the UK for the provisions to apply.

The anti-avoidance rules apply where (*ITA 2007, s 755*):

- land, or any property deriving its value from land (including shares in a land-owning company), is acquired with the sole or main object of realising a gain from disposing of the land;

- land is held as trading stock; or

- land is developed with the sole or main object of realising a gain from disposing of the land when developed;

and any gain of a capital nature is obtained from the disposal of the land, by the person acquiring, holding or developing the land, or by any 'connected person' or, where any arrangement or scheme is effected in respect of the land which enables a gain to be realised by any indirect method, or by any series of transactions, by any person who is a party to, or concerned in, the arrangement or scheme, and whether any such person obtains the gain for himself or for any other person (*ITA 2007, s 759*).

7.4   There are also supplementary provisions which ensure that the rules apply to many transactions whereby a person indirectly benefits, though where one person is assessed to tax in respect of consideration receivable by another person there is a right of recovery (*ITA 2007, s 761*).

However, the operation of the provisions is restricted where a company holds land as trading stock, or where a company owns 90% or more of the ordinary share capital (directly or indirectly) of another company which holds land as trading stock, and there is a disposal of shares in either the land trading company or the holding company, and all the land so held is disposed of in the normal course of trade by the company which held it, and all the opportunity of profit or gain in respect of the land arises to that company (*ITA 2007, s 766*).

It is worth noting that adjustments have been upheld in respect of:

- the grant by trustees of a lease of land to a developer, with a clause ensuring that the premium payable should be linked with the prices obtained from the sale of the underleases following the redevelopment of the land (*Page (HMIT) v Lowther* [1983] BTC 394); and

- the sale of properties through the medium of Bahamian companies (*Sugarwhite v Budd (HMIT*) [1988] BTC 189).

Trading indicators

7.5   There is no statutory definition which will absolutely define whether someone is trading. Case law provides the main pointers in this area. In statute the definition 'includes every trade, manufacture, adventure or concern in the nature of trade'. The most important aspect of the statutory definition is that it makes clear, by the use of the word 'adventure', that an activity does not need to become an established and successful one before the tax regime begins to take effect.

The indicators, pointers or 'badges of trade' are derived from case law and subject to gradual modification and extension. Whilst each pointer should be examined in isolation, the situation as a whole must also be considered. When applied to the facts of a new situation, some of them may point towards there being a trade and others toward the opposite conclusion. It is their cumulative effect that is decisive.

The badges of trade were reviewed in *Marson v Morton* (1986) 59 TC 381, [1986] STC 463, [1986] 1 WLR 1343. Eight points were made which expanded upon the badges of trade originally put forward by the *Royal Commission on the Taxation of Profits and Income* (1955).

The following introduces the tests developed by the courts.

Profit-seeking motive

7.6   Generally, an intention by the taxpayer to make a profit is an indicator that he is trading, but it is not conclusive. In particular, two factors may lead to the opposite conclusion:

- the trader may be acquiring and realising capital investments rather than trading; and

- an intention to make a profit may be simply wishful thinking, if the facts are such that the individual is most unlikely to ever make a profit.

Equally, the fact that a taxpayer does not intend to make a profit or even positively wishes not to do so does not prevent a taxable profit arising if one is, in fact, made.

Type of asset

7.7   The type of asset, whether normally traded or not, will determine the initial presumption toward or away from trading. But this initial presumption may be overturned in the light of other factors.

Some assets, typically raw materials for manufacturing processes, tend to be acquired only for trading purposes. Their purchase and sale would indicate trading other than in the most exceptional circumstances. Other assets, however, may be acquired for personal pleasure (for instance, antiques), and as capital investments (for instance, shares).

Capital equipment that in most businesses is regarded as a fixed asset (for instance, heavy lorries) can also be traded.

If an asset produces income, such as rent, it is much more likely to be treated as an investment than an asset producing no income. This tendency is reduced, however, where the expenditure on maintaining the asset is such that the owner can make a return only by selling it at a profit.

In *CIR v Fraser*, CS 1942, 24 TC 498, three reasons were put forward for purchasing an article:

- own use or consumption;

- investment, possibly to yield income; and

- resale at profit, ie trading.

Repetition of transactions

7.8   Trades tend to be characterised by systematic buying and selling many transactions of an essentially similar character. Clearly, the more frequent and systematic the pattern of buying and selling, the more likely the activity will be regarded as trading.

An isolated transaction is not prevented from being 'an adventure' in the nature of trade, but other indicators would need to point in that direction. Sometimes a transaction, the first of what turns out to be a series, is not recognised as trading at the time. But the courts have agreed that later transactions may be taken into account in reaching a conclusion about the nature of the first one.

What was treated as a hobby may develop into a trade (*Hawes v Gardiner* (1957) 37 TC 671, [1957] TR 341).

Asset modification

7.9   Doing something to the purchased asset before sale is an indication that the person is engaged in trading. Typically, this may be of two kinds:

(1)   an asset may require development, such as refitting (*IR Commrs v Livingston* (1926) 11 TC 538); or

(2)   the owner may fulfil the role of a wholesaler, buying in bulk and dividing into smaller lots for retail sale – sometimes the owner may both develop the asset and divide it into smaller lots (*Cape Brandy Syndicate v IR Commrs* (1921) 12 TC 358).

See also **7.27**.

Circumstances of asset sale

7.10   Consideration should be given as to whether the sale is conducted in the usual way for dealings in that type of asset. If so, and particularly if that involved the person in establishing a sales office or sales team, there is a strong pointer that the activity amounted to trading. Disposal in an amateurish fashion, or to meet a clearly non-trading need, such as cash to make repayments on personal borrowings, points toward the opposite conclusion.

Time period between purchase and sale

7.11   Looking at the time interval between purchase and resale is one means of attempting to distinguish between a person who is trading and one who periodically changes investments.

Finance

7.12   The source of finance may be a neutral factor. When, however, a person borrows to finance a purchase in circumstances that make it necessary to resell promptly, it tends to indicate a trading intent. This argument was used in the *Wisdom* case where silver bullion was purchased using borrowings (*Wisdom v Chamberlain (HMIT)* (1968) 45 TC 92). The high interest rate indicated that a quick sale would be needed and this was what occurred.

Means of acquisition

7.13   Most assets are purchased rather than acquired by gift or inheritance. When the acquisition is other than by purchase it does present a strong indication that the person had no trading intention. Such a means of acquisition points toward non-trading at the start. That does not mean, however, that whatever the owner does subsequently with the asset, it can never be trading.

Trades and professions

7.14   Profits are charged to tax as trading income under *ITTOIA 2005*. The income tax charge applies to annual business profits, but can apply equally to occasional activities or even single transactions. The issue of what constitutes a trade, or whether a transaction is a trading receipt (or, for example, a capital receipt), may not be clear in every case (*ITTOIA 2005, Pt 5*).

It is important to establish whether an activity constitutes trading (or a profession) as different rules apply to the taxation of the income, the deductibility of expenses and, in particular, to the ways in which losses can be relieved. In the legislation, the word 'trade' is taken to include 'every trade, manufacture, adventure or concern in the nature of trade'. This definition has caused much difficulty in the past but has been adhered to nevertheless. The difficulty has been overcome to a large extent by decided cases.

It is equally important to consider whether income relates to professional or vocational work, or whether it amounts to casual income or profits taxable as miscellaneous income. For example, the royalties received by an established author would be taxable as professional or vocational work, but receipts for the occasional writing of articles would be taxable as miscellaneous income.

Case law has determined that the profits of an illegal trade will still be taxed (*Mann v Nash*, 16 TC 523, [1932] 1 KB 752; *Southern v AB*, 18 TC 59, [1933] 1 KB 713; and *IRC v Aken* [1988] STC 69).

What constitutes a trade?

7.15   The miscellaneous examples below are mainly based on decisions in court cases.

	Trading	**Not trading**
Betting	Professional bookmakers (even if unlawful)	Private betting (even if habitual)
Divers and diving supervisors	Emoluments of person employed in the UK to exploit the sea-bed	

Futures and options	Dealing in the course of a trade (ie by a bank or similar financial institution)	Dealing by pension schemes; relatively infrequent transactions; transactions to hedge specific investments; purely speculative transactions
Horse racing	Racing and selling the progeny of a brood mare; profits from stallion fees	Private horse racing and training
Illegal trading	Profits of a commercial business even if carried on unlawfully, eg bootlegging and prostitution	Crime, eg burglary
Liquidators and personal representatives	Where continuing the company's/deceased's trade	Where merely realising the assets
Miscellaneous	Profits from promoting a series of driving schools	The activities of the British Olympic Association
Property transactions	Established business of property development	Property held as an investment or residence; isolated transactions
Share dealing	Under the *Financial Services Act 1986* and also where transactions amount to trading	Prudent management of an investment portfolio

What is a profession?

7.16

	Trading	**Not trading**
Actors/artists	Normally trading even where based in UK with engagements abroad	Performers engaged for a regular salary, eg permanent members of some orchestras and of an opera, ballet or theatre company (taxable as employment income)
Authors	Regular newspaper articles; sale of authors' notebooks and memorabilia	Occasional writing or articles (taxable as Miscellaneous income under *ITTOIA 2005*)
Dramatist	A successful play after a series of failures	

Informing the authorities of a new business

7.17   In the UK, an individual starting in business on their own account does not generally need permission to do so. Exceptions to this general principle apply when entry to the sector concerned is regulated, either by government (such as the medical profession) or by professional institutes.

Any person starting up as self-employed must register with HMRC (*TMA 1970, s 7*). A self-employed person can use a single form, CWF1, to tell HMRC that they are self-employed for income tax and NICs. They can also notify on the same form that they need to register for VAT.

Focus

Form CWF1 is used to register for self-assessment and NICs. An online version of the form is available and is designed to work in all up-to-date browsers, and on mobile devices such as iPads, smartphones and tablets. The form can be found on the gov.uk website at www.tax.service.gov.uk/shortforms/form/CWF1ST?dept-name=CWF1&sub-dep.

FA 2008, s 123 and *Sch 41* introduced a new penalties regime for failure to notify HMRC of a taxable activity under *TMA 1970, s 7*. The changes took effect from 1 April 2010 (*SI 2009/511, arts 2, 3*). A penalty will only be charged if tax and NICs have been lost because of the failure to notify. When someone tells HMRC they should have registered a new taxable activity within a year of a penalty becoming due, any penalty can be reduced to nil. The penalties which may be charged for failure to notify liability are as follows:

- 30% of tax unpaid for non-deliberate failure to notify;

- 70% of tax unpaid for a deliberate failure to notify; and

- 100% of tax unpaid for a deliberate failure with concealment.

Each penalty will be substantially reduced where the taxpayer makes a disclosure (takes active steps to put right the problem), and more so if this is unprompted.

For further information on starting a business, see www.gov.uk/working-for-yourself.

BASIS OF ASSESSMENT

7.18   The profits of a trade, profession or vocation are taxed on the basis of the business accounts (*ITTOIA 2005, ss 196–225*). A business may choose the date to which accounts will be prepared. In general, income tax is charged on profits arising in the tax year, based on the 12-month accounting period ending in that tax year (ie a 'current year' basis). Capital allowances are treated as a trading expense of the accounting period, and balancing charges as a trading receipt (*CAA 2001, s 2*).

Special rules apply when a business commences or ceases, and where the business accounts are for a period longer or shorter than 12 months.

New businesses

7.19   On the commencement of a new business by an individual, the following rules apply.

First tax year – the new business is taxed on profits from the date of commencement to the end of the tax year (*ITTOIA 2005, s 199*).

Second tax year – the tax charge is based on the profits of the accounting period ended in the second tax year. However (*ITTOIA 2005, ss 200 and 201*):

●   if the first accounts are made up to a date in the second tax year, but for a period of less than 12 months, the charge for the second tax year is based on the profits of the first 12 months;

●   if the accounts are made up to a date in the second tax year, but for a period of more than 12 months, the charge for the second tax year is based on the profits of 12 months to the accounting date;

●   if the first accounts are made up for more than 12 months and no account ends in the second tax year, the charge for that year is based on the profits of the tax year itself.

Third tax year – the tax charge is normally based on the accounts for the 12 months to the accounting date ending in the tax year.

Businesses ceasing

7.20   When a business ceases, it is usually taxed on profits from the end of the basis period for the previous tax year to the date of cessation (but see **7.34** for tax relief on 'overlap profits' upon cessation) (*ITTOIA 2005, s 202*).

Other points

7.21   *Overlap profits* – in the opening years of a new business, profits may be taxed more than once. This can also happen on a change of accounting date. The profit taxed in two successive tax years is called 'overlap profit'. Tax relief for overlap profits may be available on a change of accounting date, and can also be claimed on the cessation of business (see **7.33**) (*ITTOIA 2005, s 204*). Overlap profits are not indexed, so will diminish in value in real terms over several years.

Time-apportionment – in calculating business profits for a tax year, it may be necessary to time-apportion the profits for long accounting periods, or to combine the profits of two short accounting periods. Time-apportionment may be calculated in days, months or fractions of months, providing that the method is used consistently (*ITTOIA 2005, s 203*).

Example 7.1—Basis of assessment: starting a business

Arnold commences trade on 1 September 2016 and prepares accounts to 30 April, starting with an eight-month period of account to 30 April 2017. His profits (as adjusted for tax purposes and after capital allowances) for the first three accounting periods are as follows:

	£
8 months to 30 April 2017	24,000
Year to 30 April 2018	39,000
Year to 30 April 2019	40,000

His taxable profits for the first four tax years are as follows:

	Basic period		£	£
2016/17	1.9.16 to 5.4.17	£24,000 × 7/8		21,000
2017/18	1.9.16 to 31.8.17:			
	1.9.16 to 30.4.17		24,000	
	1.5.17 to 31.8.17	£39,000 × 4/12	13,000	37,000
2018/19	Y/e 30.4.18			39,000
2019/20	Y/e 30.4.19			40,000
Overlap relief accrued:				
1.9.16 to 5.4.17 (7 months)				21,000
1.5.17 to 31.8.17 (4 months)				13,000
Total overlap relief accrued				£34,000

Example 7.2—Basis of assessment: cessation of business

Barbara commenced trading on 1 May 2015, preparing accounts to 30 April. She permanently ceases trading on 30 June 2018, preparing accounts for the two months to that date. Her profits (as adjusted for tax purposes and after capital allowances) are as follows:

	£
Year ended 30 April 2016	24,000
Year ended 30 April 2017	48,000
Year ended 30 April 2018	96,000
Two months ended 30 June 2018	5,000
	£173,000

Her taxable profits for the four tax years of trading are as follows:

	Basic period		£	£
2015/16	1.5.15 to 5.4.16	£24,000 × 11/12		22,000
2016/17	Y/e 30.4.16			24,000
2017/18	Y/e 30.4.17			48,000
2018/19	1.5.17 to 30.6.18:			
	1.5.17 to 30.4.18		96,000	
	1.5.18 to 30.6.18		5,000	
			101,000	
	Deduct overlap relief		22,000	79,000
				173,000

COMPUTING PROFITS

Profit and accounts

7.22   The profits in the accounts of the business are not always the same as taxable profits, and it is usually necessary to make adjustments to the accounts to arrive at the taxable profit for the accounting period. The business profits must generally be computed in accordance with 'generally accepted accounting practice', subject to any adjustment required or allowed by tax legislation or case law (*ITTOIA 2005, s 25*). However, legislation contained in *FA 2013* provides that eligible unincorporated small businesses may choose to use the cash basis when calculating taxable income, and all unincorporated businesses have the option to use certain flat-rate expenses when calculating taxable income. The measures took effect from the tax year 2013/14 (*FA 2013, ss 17, 18, Schs 4, 5*) (see **7.23**).

Focus

Two new income tax allowances of £1,000 each, for trading and property income, are available for 2017/18 onwards (*F(No 2)A 2017, s 17* and *Sch 3*). Individuals with trading income or property income below the level of the allowance no longer need to declare or pay tax on that income. The trading income allowance also applies to certain miscellaneous income from providing assets or services.

Simplified income tax for small businesses

7.23   From 2013/14 onwards, eligible unincorporated small businesses may choose to use the cash basis when calculating taxable income, and all unincorporated businesses have the option to use certain flat-rate expenses when calculating taxable income (*FA 2013, ss 17, 18, Schs 4, 5*).

Cash basis

7.24   Under the cash basis, small businesses are taxed on the basis of the cash that passes through their books, rather than being asked to spend their time doing calculations designed for big businesses.

The cash basis eligibility threshold was raised significantly from 6 April 2017. The increase forms part of the Government's initiative for simplifying tax paid by unincorporated businesses and runs alongside the 'Making Tax Digital' project. Amendment to the legislation (currently contained in *ITTOIA 2005, Pt 2, Ch 3A*) took effect from 6 April 2017 (operative for 2017/18 onwards) and increased the threshold for the cash basis from £83,000 to £150,000 (*SI 2017/293*). The increase is expected to have a significant impact on businesses with an estimated 135,000 additional small businesses becoming eligible to choose the cash basis for their business.

The exit threshold above which the cash basis may not be used is set at double the entry threshold. This means that from 6 April 2017, the exit threshold is £300,000.

Companies and certain other specified businesses (including farmers or authors who have a current averaging claim under *ITTOIA 2005, Ch 16*, farmers etc who have or make herd basis elections, and members of Lloyd's) are not permitted to use the scheme. Many landlords are permitted to use the cash basis for 2017/18 onwards (*F(No 2)A 2017, s 16* and *Sch 2*) although the existing rules remain for certain landlords (including companies, LLPs, corporate firms, and trustees of trusts) (see **Chapter 8** for further commentary).

General partnerships may use the cash basis – as long as the partnership meets the receipts and other entry criteria, the partners are all individuals, and either there is no individual treated as controlling the partnership, or any such individual would be eligible to use the cash basis if they were conducting the business as a sole trader.

Generally, an individual who undertakes (whether as a sole trader or a partner) more than one unincorporated trading or professional business will only be eligible for the cash basis if all those businesses are also eligible for, and use, the cash basis. Additionally, it is envisaged that any subsequent use of the 'ordinary' rules for any of those businesses should have the effect of precluding eligibility for the cash basis for all such businesses. This is because simultaneous use of two different regimes would cut across the simplification benefits of the cash basis.

An exception would be where an individual is a partner in a partnership that they do not control that uses the ordinary rules. So, for example, a partner in a large professional partnership would be eligible to use the cash basis in respect of any separate unincorporated businesses they conduct as a sole trader, as long as those businesses meet the eligibility criteria.

The cash basis is available to foreign resident individuals, to the extent that they carry on a trade, profession or vocation in the UK, provided that the other eligibility criteria are met.

The cash basis operates by reference to the tax year. This means small businesses can calculate their taxable income for the tax year by adding or subtracting:

- receipts in connection with the business received in the tax year;

- payments made in the tax year to cover allowable expenses; and

- amounts allowed for simplified expenses.

There is no requirement to apply generally accepted accounting practice (GAAP) or calculate profits/losses.

The cash basis operates on a VAT-inclusive basis. This means that full amount of receipts and payments will be counted including any VAT element. If a business is registered for VAT, any VAT paid to HMRC will be an allowable expense, and any VAT refund received from HMRC will be taxable as a receipt in connection with the business.

Income

7.25 Receipts in connection with the trade will be counted as income in the tax year in which the income is received. This will include all receipts treated as trading income by virtue of *ITTOIA 2005, Pt 2*. Receipts in the form of 'money's worth' will be included, for example the value of goods or services received from customers. Also, a reasonable amount will need to be added to income reflecting any deficiency arising from a transaction being made other than on a commercial basis. (An example would be if, after expensing the cost of purchasing stock, an item of the stock was taken for personal use without any actual payment being made for it.)

Sale proceeds for capital assets (such as plant or machinery) whose purchase costs have previously been relieved will be taken into account as a receipt.

Where there is a significant reduction in the business use of an asset whose purchase costs have previously been relieved (eg a switch to partial private use), a reasonable amount representing the appropriate proportion of the value of the asset at the time will need to be added to income.

The following items are not treated as income under the cash basis scheme:

- capital introduced by the owner of the business for purposes of financing the business;

- changes in the form of money, eg cash withdrawals from bank accounts;

- loan capital borrowed by the business from third parties for financing purposes;

- proceeds from disposals of durable assets, eg land and property, intellectual property, shares; and

- refunds of income tax, capital gains tax, or tax credits.

With regard to expenses, the 'wholly and exclusively' rules continues to apply under the scheme. Allowable expenses include certain capital expenditure. This removes the need for capital allowance calculations and claims, and so no capital allowances will be available.

Capital expenditure on wasting assets such as plant or machinery are allowable (with the exception of expenditure on cars or motorcycles – see below). Where an asset is used for non-qualifying purposes, for example it is partly used privately, the proportion of the expenditure that represents the qualifying proportion of use will be allowable as a deduction – although the full cost will be deductible where private use was insignificant or immaterial.

A deduction will be allowed for the purchase cost of other motor vehicles (eg vans), unless the business chooses to use the fixed mileage rate allowance for such vehicles. All vehicles of the same type will be treated in the same manner, and the fixed mileage rate can only be used if the business has obtained no relief previously for purchase costs under the cash basis (or through claiming capital allowances or annual investment allowance).

Focus

For the years up to and including 2016/17, individuals (and partnerships comprised only of individuals) that make use of the cash basis for calculating taxable profits were unable to claim tax relief for capital expenditure unless the expenditure would qualify for capital allowances – a level of complexity deemed undesirable by the government. The Spring 2017 Budget announced details of reforms to the cash basis to restrict the scope of the general disallowance for capital expenditure so that relief will be prohibited only in relation to costs incurred in relation to the provision, alteration or disposal of:

- any asset that is not a 'depreciating asset' (to be defined as having a useful life of up to 20 years);

- any asset not acquired or created for use on a continuing basis in the trade;

- a car (but of course business mileage-based relief is available);

- land (as defined);

- a non-qualifying intangible asset, (as per financial reporting standard 105) including education or training; and

- a financial asset.

Costs in relation to the acquisition or disposal of a business, or part of a business, will also be excluded.

This change was legislated for in *Finance (No 2) Act 2017*, and applies from 2017/18 onwards (*F(No 2)A 2017, s 16 and Sch 2*).

Simplified expenses

7.26   The provisions include simplifying arrangements for some business expenses (later referred to as 'simplified expenses') to complement the cash basis (*FA 2013, s 18* and *Sch 5*). The cash basis and simplified expenses will be used to calculate taxable income. In essence, claiming expenses should be a lot less complicated under the new regime.

The following simplified expenses should be an integral part of the cash basis (see *ITTOIA 2005, Pt 2, Ch 5A* for further details):

- standard mileage rate for business use of cars or motorcycles;

- flat rate expenses for business use of home; and

- flat rate adjustment for personal use of business premises.

With regard to business use of a home, a deduction per month will be allowable if certain criteria are satisfied (*ITTOIA 2005, s 94H*). The current rates are as follows:

No of hours worked	Applicable amount
25 or more	£10.00
51 or more	£18.00
101 or more	£26.00

The number of hours worked in a month is the number of hours spent wholly and exclusively on work done by the person, or any employee of the person, in the person's home wholly and exclusively for the purposes of the trade.

Where a person uses premises for both business and private use, he or she may, instead of making the standard deduction outlined above, make a deduction for the non-business use. The allowable deduction will therefore be the amount of the expenses incurred, less the non-business use amount. The non-business use amount is the sum of the applicable amounts (see below) for each month, or part of a month, falling within the period in question (usually the tax year). The applicable amounts are as follows (*ITTOIA 2005, s 94I*):

Number of relevant occupants	Applicable amount
1	£350
2	£500
3 or more	£650

A relevant occupant is someone who occupies the premises as a home, or someone who stays at the premises otherwise than in the course of the trade (*ITTOIA 2005, s 94I*).

No deduction will be allowed for any of the following expenses:

- entertaining, expenditure for private purposes, bribes etc;
- non-cash costs such as amortisation of assets or accounting provisions;
- payments of income tax, capital gains tax or Class 2 and Class 4 NICs;
- changes in the form of money, such as purchase of foreign currency; and
- costs of borrowings, including arrangement fees, capital repayments, and interest.

Allowable trading expenses

7.27 Expenditure is generally allowable in computing profits for tax purposes, provided it is:

- wholly and exclusively for the purposes of the business; and

- not capital expenditure (although such expenditure may be eligible for capital allowances instead; see **7.25** for details of a relaxation in the capital expenditure general disallowance from 2017/18).

Appropriations of profit (eg proprietors' drawings and income tax) are not allowable business deductions, but should not normally appear as expense items in the accounts (*ITTOIA 2005, ss 32–55*).

The main work base needs to be identified to determine a claim for travelling expenses (*Horton v Young* (1971) 47 TC 60 and *Newson v Robertson* (1952) 33 TC 452, [1953] Ch 7, [1952] 2 All ER 728).Note that repair works on a newly acquired asset will not generally be allowed for tax purposes if the repairs must be made to enable the asset to be brought in to business use (*Law Shipping Co Ltd v CIR*, CS 1923, 12 TC 621, but contrast *Odeon Theatres Ltd v Jones* (1971) 48 TC 257, [1973] Ch 288, [1971] 1 WLR 442, [1972] 1 All ER 681).

Focus

The case of *Huntley v R & C Commrs* [2010] UKFTT 551 (TC), [2011] TC 00804 examined the taxpayer's claim for reasonable subsistence costs for time spent working away from home. The taxpayer's appeal was allowed in part.

'Wholly and exclusively'

7.28 Apart from business expenses specifically allowed by tax law, expenditure cannot be claimed for tax purposes unless it is 'wholly and exclusively' for the purposes of the business.

An expense incurred for both business and private purposes cannot be deducted unless the business part of the mixed expense can be separately identified. The business element may then be claimed, provided it was incurred wholly and exclusively for business purposes (*ITTOIA 2005, s 34*).

In *Huhtala v R & C Commrs* [2011] UKUT 419 (TCC), the Upper Tribunal decided that the First-tier Tribunal should reconsider the question whether a journalist was entitled to a deduction for costs incurred while researching a book since, although the tribunal had identified some duality of purpose, it had not gone on to consider whether a deduction might be available for any identifiable part of the expense incurred wholly and exclusively for the purposes of the taxpayer's trade within *ITTOIA 2005, s 34*. The Upper Tribunal (Judge Colin Bishopp) (allowing the appeal and remitting the case for rehearing) said that the taxpayer's claim to HMRC was presented in a confusing and incorrect manner, and it was not altogether surprising that it had been disallowed.

Capital expenditure

7.29 It is important to distinguish between 'revenue' expenditure, which can be deducted from profits, and 'capital' expenditure, which cannot be deducted, although certain capital expenditure may qualify for capital allowances (see **7.25**). Where capital expenditure does not qualify for capital allowances, it will generally form part of the allowable cost for capital gains tax purposes.

There is no definition of capital and revenue expenditure in the tax legislation, although their meaning has been considered in a number of court cases. Expenditure is commonly defined as capital if it brings about an 'enduring benefit of a trade'. In deciding whether an expense is capital or revenue it will generally be necessary to consider such factors as the type of asset on which the expenditure was incurred and the nature of the expenditure (eg repairs expenditure is normally allowable revenue expenditure, whereas improvement expenditure is not).

In *Strick v Regent Oil Co Ltd* (1965) 43 TC 1 at page 29 (see HMRC Business Income Manual at BIM35560), Lord Reid described the difficulties in making sense of the large number of decisions on this topic:

> 'It may be possible to reconcile all the decisions, but it is certainly not possible to reconcile all the reasons given for them. I think that much of the difficulty has arisen from taking too literally general statements made in earlier cases and seeking to apply them to a different kind of case which their authors almost certainly did not have in mind – in seeking to treat expressions of judicial opinion as if they were words in an Act of Parliament.'

Non-trading income

7.30 Any non-trading income and capital profits included in the business accounts are not usually taxed as part of the business profits, but may be liable to tax under separate rules (eg rental income under the property income business regime, or capital profits assessed to capital gains tax).

Pre-trading expenditure

7.31 A deduction may be claimed for expenses incurred within seven years prior to the commencement of trading, where those expenses would have been allowed after trading commenced. The expenditure is treated as incurred on the first day of trading (*ITTOIA 2005, s 57*).

Disallowable expenses

7.32 Disallowable expenses include:

Bad debts (*ITTOIA 2005, s 35*)	general bad debts provision or debts relating to capital items, such as the sale of a fixed asset
Entertaining	entertaining expenses and hospitality except staff entertaining or advertising to the public generally
Gifts	except where carrying prominent advertising costing less than £50 per person per annum (but not food and drink)
Premises and plant*	costs of acquiring premises and fixed assets
Depreciation*	of fixed assets; profit or loss on sale (special rules apply to assets held on finance leases)
Legal and professional costs	relating to tax disputes; or purchasing of fixed assets (treated as part of the cost of the fixed asset)
Employee costs	wages, salary, drawings, benefits, pension payments, except relating to bona fide remuneration for employees
Car hire	for leases entered into from April 2009, there is broadly a fixed 15% restriction for cars with CO_2 emissions above 110g/km (from 1/6 April 2018) but no restriction for cars with lower emissions (*ITTOIA 2005, s 48 et seq; SI 2016/984, art 5*). The 15% disallowance applies to cars that do not fall into any of the following categories:

- a car that is first registered before 1 March 2001;
- a car that has low CO_2 emissions;
- a car that is electrically propelled, or
- a qualifying hire car.

The restriction applies to the actual rent paid plus any element of unrelievable VAT. If, however, the rental agreement separately identifies charges for costs such as maintenance, those costs should not be included when calculating the restriction, and the restriction is only applied to the rental payment

Personal	eg ordinary clothing, even if for business use; fines; fuel expenses for private use of vehicles; travel between home and business; non-business premises expenses
Repairs and renewals	general provisions for future repairs and renewals; alteration, improvements or replacement of fixed assets*

Interest and finance charges	on unpaid tax; otherwise generally allowable but not capital repayments or premiums on mortgage repayment
Annual payments	eg annuities, royalties, paid under deduction of tax at source – treated as 'charges on income'
Sundry	payments to political parties, some payments to charities

* See Capital allowances (**7.45** onwards).

Focus

In the first-tier tribunal case *Healy v HMRC* [2015] UKFTT 233 (TC), the First-tier Tribunal (FTT) found that an actor who had rented a flat in London for nine months close to the theatre in which he was appearing in a musical was not entitled to deduct the rental payments against his business income. The FTT found that when he chose to rent the three-bedroom flat, Mr Healy partly did so to enable friends and family to come and stay. This meant that the expenditure on the flat had a dual purpose and was therefore not incurred wholly and exclusively for the purposes of his business. There was also no 'identifiable part or identifiable proportion of the expense which [was] incurred wholly and exclusively for the purposes of the trade' and therefore not even a proportion of the expense could be allowed.

Allowable trading expenses – example

7.33

Example 7.4—Allowable trading expenses

A UK trader commences trading on 1 October 2016. He is not using the cash basis or simplified expenses regime for computing his taxable profit. His profit and loss account for the year to 30 September 2017 is therefore calculated as follows:

	£	£
Sales		110,000
Deduct purchases	75,000	
Less: Stock and work in progress at 30.9.17	15,000	60,000
Gross profit		50,000

7.33 Self-employment

Deduct:		
Salaries (all paid by 30.6.18)	16,500	
Rent and rates	2,400	
Telephone	500	
Heat and light	650	
Depreciation	1,000	
Motor expenses	2,700	
Entertainment	600	
Hire-purchase interest	250	
Repairs and renewals	1,000	
Accountant's fee	500	
Bad debts	200	
Sundries	700	27,000
Net profit		23,000
Gain on sale of fixed asset		300
Rent received		500
Profit		£23,800

Further information

(i)   Rent and rates. £200 of the rates bill is for the period from 1.6.16 to 30.9.16.

(ii) Telephone. Telephone bills for the trader's private telephone amount to £150. It is estimated that 40% of these calls are for business purposes.

(iii) Motor expenses. All the motor expenses are in respect of the proprietor's car. 40% of the annual mileage relates to private use and home to business use.

(iv) Entertainment. Includes entertainment of staff of £100 and of customers £500.

(v)   Hire-purchase interest. This is in respect of the owner's car.

(vi) Repairs and renewals. There is an improvement element of 20% included.

(vii) Bad debts. This is a specific write-off.

(viii) Sundries. Includes £250 cost of obtaining business loan finance, £200 agent's fees to obtain a patent for trading purposes and a £50 'political donation' (in fact a bribe to a local council official).

(ix) Other. The proprietor obtained goods for his own use from the business costing £400 (retail value £500) without payment.

(x) Capital allowances for the year to 30 September 2016 amount to £1,520.

Trading income computation – Year to 30.9.17

	£	£
Profit per the accounts		23,800
Add:		
Repairs – improvement element	200	
Hire-purchase interest (40% private)	100	
Entertainment note (e)	500	
Motor expenses (40% private)	1,080	
Depreciation	1,000	
Telephone (60% × £150)	90	
Goods for own use	500	
Illegal payment	50	
		3,520
		27,320
Deduct:		
Rent received	500	
Gain on sale of fixed asset	300	
		800
		26,520
Less capital allowances note (b)		1,520
Trading income profit		£25,000

Notes:

(a) Costs of obtaining loan finance are specifically allowable.

(b) Capital allowances are in all cases deductible as a trading expense (see **7.45**).

(c)   The adjusted profit of £25,000 would be subject to the commencement provisions for assessment purposes.

(d)   Pre-trading expenses are treated as incurred on the day on which trade is commenced if they are incurred within seven years of the commencement and would have been allowable if incurred after commencement.

(e)   All entertainment expenses, other than staff entertaining, are non-deductible.

(f)   Expenditure incurred in making a payment which itself constitutes the commission of a criminal offence (or would do if committed in the UK) is specifically disallowed. This includes payments which are contrary to the *Prevention of Corruption Acts*.

Profit adjustments

Overlap relief

7.34   The effect of the rules for taxing business profits using tax years often means that some profits are taxable more than once due to the profits in one accounting period overlapping two tax years. However, the rules for overlap profits ensure that the business is taxed over its life on the actual profits made by providing overlap relief.

Where accounting periods coincide with the tax year throughout the life of the business, overlaps will not occur. The tax year is the year ending 5 April. There are rules to avoid short overlap periods (*ITTOIA 2005, ss 208–210*). For example, if the first accounting date is 31 March, or 1, 2, 3 or 4 April, the accounts are treated as being to 5 April, unless an election is made to the contrary (*ITTOIA 2005, ss 204–207*).

Overlap profit

7.35   An 'overlap profit' is the amount of profit in an accounting period which is taxed in two successive tax years (*ITTOIA 2005, s 204*). Overlap profits can occur:

●   as the result of transitional rules when pre-6 April 1994 businesses changed over from the 'preceding year basis' to the 'current year basis';

●   due to the rules for taxing the profits of the opening years of a new business; or

●   on a change in basis period for taxing the profits following a change of accounting date (*ITTOIA 2005, s 220*).

Overlap profits may arise more than once for different reasons. Where this occurs, those profits are combined to give a single figure.

A record needs to be kept of the amount of any overlap profits and of the overlap period as relief will be provided for these profits as set out below.

Overlap relief

7.36 Overlap relief reduces the profits of the tax year in which it is given. It may convert a profit into a loss, or increase a loss. The relief may be claimed:

• when the business ceases;

• if the business is sold; or

• if the basis period is longer than 12 months due to a change of accounting date.

Overlap losses

7.37 If a loss arises for the overlap period, so as to be included in the computations of two successive tax years, the amount in the second year is excluded from the computation. The loss will be subject to separate loss relief claims and is deemed to be 'nil' for overlap purposes.

Overlap relief – example

7.38

> **Example 7.5—Overlap relief**
>
> Geraldine commences trade on 1 September 2015 and prepares accounts to 30 April, starting with an eight-month period of account to 30 April 2016. She ceases trading on 31 October 2018, preparing accounts for the six months ending on that date. Her profits (as adjusted for tax purposes and after capital allowances) for the four accounting periods to cessation are as follows:
>
> | | £ |
> |---|---|
> | 8 months to 30 April 2016 | 24,000 |
> | Year to 30 April 2017 | 39,000 |
> | Year to 30 April 2018 | 40,000 |
> | 6 months to 31 October 2018 | 22,000 |
> | | 125,000 |

Her taxable profits for the four tax years 2015/16 to 2018/19 are as follows:

	Basis period		£	£
2015/16	1.9.15–5.4.16	£24,000 × 7/8		21,000
2016/17	1.9.15–31.8.16:			
	1.9.15–30.4.16		24,000	
	1.5.16–31.8.16	£39,000 × 4/12	13,000	
				37,000
2017/18	Y/e 30.4.17			39,000
2018/19	Y/e 30.4.18		40,000	
	1.5.18–31.10.18		22,000	
			62,000	
	Less overlap profit		34,000	
				28,000
				125,000

	£
Overlap relief accrued	
1.9.15–5.4.16 (7 months)	21,000
1.5.16–31.8.16 (4 months)	13,000
Total overlap relief accrued	34,000

The business is taxed over its life on its total profits earned of £125,000.

Change of accounting date

7.39   Unless certain conditions are met, HMRC will not recognise a change of accounting date, in which case profits will continue to be taxed for 12-month periods ending on the original accounting date (*ITTOIA 2005, s 198*).

The conditions for a change of accounting date to apply are that:

- the change must be notified to HMRC normally by 31 January following the tax year of change;

- the first accounts to the new accounting date must not exceed 18 months; and

- there has been no change of accounting date in the last five tax years, or HMRC are satisfied that the change is for commercial reasons.

If these conditions are satisfied, or if the change takes place in the second or third tax years of the business, profits are taxed as follows (*ITTOIA 2005, s 200*).

Focus

In *Grint v R & C Commrs* [2019] UKUT 28 (TCC), the Upper Tribunal dismissed an appeal by a taxpayer who claimed that the First-tier Tribunal (FTT) erred in law when deciding that he could not change his annual accounting date in order to give himself a 20-month basis period.

The FTT ([2016] UKFTT 537 (TC)) found that the taxpayer had failed the test in *ITTOIA 2005, s 217* by not having existing accounts with an accounting period of less than 18 months when he notified HMRC of the change.

The taxpayer had an annual accounting date of 31 July. In the tax year 2009/10, he decided on professional advice to change his accounting date to 5 April and so bring into account in that tax year income earned in the 20-month period 1 August 2008 to 5 April 2010 (the 'long accounts').

The reason for creating a 20-month, rather than a 12-month, basis period in 2009/10 was that it enabled the taxpayer to bring forward his liability to tax on eight months' income which otherwise would have been subject to income tax in the tax year 2010/11. This was advantageous to him because in 2010/11 the top rate of income tax increased from 40% to 50%.

The dispute centred on the condition in *ITTOIA 2005, s 217(1)(b)* and whether the taxpayer's accounts satisfied the 18-month test set out in *ITTOIA 2005, s 217(3)*. Under the terms of *ITTOIA 2005, s 217(3)* the test was met 'if the period of account ending – (a) with the new accounting date in the tax year in which the change of accounting date occurs … is not longer than 18 months.' The FTT interpreted *ITTOIA 2005, s 217* as requiring the basis period to be declared when the tax return was submitted in order for the 18-month test to be met. If the 18-month test only needed to be met at any point in the future, and had not actually been met at the filing date, yet the other conditions in *ITTOIA 2005, s 217* were met when the tax return was filed, it could not have been known at the point of filing what the basis period actually was for that tax return and the tax liability could not be determined.

For the change in accounting date to be effective, the taxpayer was obliged to show that his period of account to 5 April 2010 was no longer than 18 months. The parties disagreed over which of four sets of documents produced by the taxpayer were his 'accounts'; there was also a dispute over the period to which he drew up accounts, which the taxpayer considered to be eight months and HMRC to be 20 months.

The FTT decided that the return accounts were not 'accounts', and the new accounts were prepared too late to be relevant. The long accounts were the only accounts that actually reflected the taxpayer's financial performance over the period to which they related. The taxpayer therefore failed the *s 217* test because he did not have accounts with an accounting period of less than 18 months to the accounting date of 5 April 2010 when he notified the change in his accounting date. The appeal was dismissed.

The taxpayer appealed to the UT, claiming that the FTT had made four errors of law, which were: (1) the finding that for the purpose of ascertaining the relevant 'period of account' for the purposes of *s 217(3)* the long accounts were the relevant accounts rather than the 2010 schedule accounts; (2) if, as the FTT found, the test was which were 'the more important' accounts, it should have found the schedule accounts were more important for the taxpayer than the long accounts; (3) the finding that the return accounts were not accounts at all; (4) the new accounts should have been held to be relevant, as *s 217* did not set a deadline by which the accounts that determined the 'relevant period of account must be drawn up.

The UT agreed with the FTT that of the various competing accounts put forward the long accounts best fitted the description in *ITA 2007, s 989* of being 'the accounts of the business.' The 'period of account' was the period covered by the long accounts. The UT also agreed with the FTT that the return accounts did not constitute accounts. Even if the return accounts were accounts, there was no reason why they would constitute the 'accounts of the business' in preference to the long accounts. Finally, the new accounts could not be relied on because they only came into existence after 31 January 2011 when the taxpayer submitted his tax return. The taxpayer's appeal was dismissed.

Where the accounting period changes to an earlier date in the tax year

7.40 The basis period for the tax year is the 12 months ending with the new accounting date. The period to the new accounting date will be less than 12 months, so part of the profits in the previous accounting period will be taxed again in the subsequent tax year. These overlap profits should be recorded for a later relief claim (*ITTOIA 2005, s 216*).

Where the accounting period changes to a later date in the tax year

7.41 The basis period for the tax year will be a period of longer than 12 months ending with the new accounting date (*ITTOIA 2005, s 216*).

The profits chargeable will be subject to deduction of any overlap relief previously accrued. The length of the overlap period determines how much relief may be claimed.

The overlap relief deduction is calculated as follows using the following six-step process:

Step 1

Find total overlap profits for all overlap periods.

Step 2

Deduct any overlap relief previously claimed, to arrive at the remaining overlap profit.

Step 3

Find the total number of available overlap days (ie after any overlap days previously claimed).

Step 4

Divide the remaining overlap profit (Step 2) by the available overlap days (Step 3).

Step 5

Deduct the number of days in the tax year from the number of days in the period to the new accounting date.

Step 6

Multiply the overlap profit in Step 4 by the number of days in Step 5.

Change of accounting date in second year of business

7.42   If the change occurs in the second tax year of a new business, the basis period for the tax year is the 12 months to the new accounting date. If the period from commencement to the new date is less than 12 months, the basis period is the first 12 months of the business (*ITTOIA 2005, ss 214–220*).

Change to an accounting date earlier in the tax year – example

7.43

Example 7.6—Change to an accounting date earlier in the tax year

Harry has been trading for a number of years, preparing accounts to 31 August. In 2018, he changes his accounting date to 31 May, preparing accounts for the nine months to 31 May 2018. His taxable profits are as follows:

	£
Year ended 31 August 2017	21,500
9 months to 31 May 2018	17,000
Year ended 31 May 2019	23,000

Taxable profits for the years 2017/18 to 2019/20 are as follows:

	Basis period		£	£
2017/18	Y/e 31.8.17			21,500
2018/19	1.6.17–31.5.18:			
	1.6.17–31.8.17	£21,500 × 3/12	5,375	
	1.9.17–31.5.18		17,000	22,375
2019/20	Y/e 31.5.19			23,000
Overlap relief accrued 1.6.17–31.8.17 (3 months)				5,375

Change to an accounting date later in the tax year – example 7.44

Example 7.7—Change to an accounting date later in the tax year

Irene has been trading for a number of years, preparing accounts to 30 June. On the change from the preceding-year to the current-year basis, overlap relief was accrued of £13,500 for an overlap period of nine months. In 2017, she changes her accounting date to 31 December, preparing accounts for the six months to 31 December 2017. Her taxable profits are as follows:

	£
Year ended 30 June 2016	21,500
Year ended 30 June 2017	23,000
6 months to 31 December 2017	12,000
Year ended 31 December 2018	27,000

Taxable profits for the years 2016/17 to 2018/19 are as follows:

	Basis period	£	£
2016/17	Y/e 30.6.16		21,500
2017/18	1.7.16–31.12.17:		
	1.7.16–30.6.17	23,000	
	1.7.17–31.12.17	12,000	
		35,000	
	Deduct overlap relief	9,000	26,000
2018/19	Y/e 31.12.18		27,000
Overlap relief carried forward (£13,500 – £9,000)			4,500

Utilisation of overlap relief in 2017/18

$$£13,500 \times \frac{18 - 12}{9} = £9,000$$

CAPITAL ALLOWANCES

General

7.45 Business profits, after any adjustments for tax purposes (eg depreciation of fixed assets), are reduced by capital allowances to arrive at taxable profit (*CAA 2001, ss 2–6*).

Allowances may be claimed on certain capital expenditure, including (*CAA 2001, ss 393A–393W*):

- plant and machinery;

- hotels;

- mineral extraction;

- patent rights and know-how; and

- research and development.

Plant and machinery allowances are normally given by way of:

- the annual investment allowance (see **7.57**);

- first-year allowances (see **7.53**); or

- writing down allowances (see **7.55**).

Basis periods

7.46   Capital allowances are treated as a trading expense of the accounting period. This means that they can increase a loss, or turn a profit into a loss (*CAA 2001, s 2*).

Short and long accounting periods

7.47   If the business accounts are shorter or longer than 12 months, the allowances are generally reduced or increased pro rata on a time basis.

If the accounts are more than 18 months long, they are divided into separate periods, the first being 12 months long and the subsequent period(s) being 12 months or less to cover the remainder of the long accounting period. The total allowances of each period are then added together and deducted as a trading expense of the whole period.

Time expenditure incurred

7.48   Capital expenditure is generally treated as incurred when the obligation to pay becomes unconditional (eg the invoice or delivery date), whether or not the payment is in whole or part or is required at some later date. However, expenditure is treated as incurred on the date when payment is due where (*CAA 2001, s 5*):

- the credit period for that part of the expenditure exceeds four months; and

- an obligation to pay becomes unconditional earlier than usual to bring forward a capital allowances claim.

Where payments for building work are made in stages, ownership may pass at an earlier date (on the issue of an architect's certificate) than the time when the obligation to pay becomes unconditional. In this case, where ownership has passed in one basis period, but the obligation becomes unconditional in the first month of the next period, the expenditure is treated as incurred in the earlier period.

Assets purchased under hire-purchase agreements

7.49   The expenditure is treated as incurred when the asset is brought into use (note that finance charges are not part of the purchase price but are deductible from profits) (*CAA 2001, s 67*).

Time limits, claims and elections

7.50   Claims for capital allowances must be made in the tax return, or amended return and are subject to the same time limits for the return, ie normally by the 31 January filing date following the tax year or, for amendments, normally by 12 months after that filing date (*CAA 2001, s 3*).

Focus

There is no need to make a full claim for capital allowances where it is not tax efficient to do so, ie where better use could be made of other available reliefs and allowances. Where reduced claims are made for first-year or writing down allowances for machinery or plant, the allowances would be deferred to a future period. Note, however, that unclaimed research and development allowances will usually be lost.

Time limits for claims

7.51

Claim	Time limit
Amendment of claim where HMRC enquiries made into the tax return	30 days after settlement of enquiry (provided the original return was submitted by the filing date)
Further claims where assessment made by HMRC under powers of discovery	12 months from end of tax year in which assessment is made
Plant or machinery to be treated as a short-life asset	First anniversary of 31 January next following the tax year in which the chargeable period (in which the expenditure occurs) ends
Transfer of short-life asset to a connected person to be treated as taking place at tax written-down value	Two years from end of chargeable period in which disposal occurs
Relief for excess capital allowances of a property income business to be set against other income of the same or following tax year	First anniversary of 31 January next following the tax year in which the chargeable period (in which the excess arises) ends
Plant or machinery which becomes a fixture subject to an equipment lease or energy services agreement to be treated as belonging to the lessor or energy services provider. Election to be made by both lessor/provider and lessee/client (provided unconnected)	First anniversary of 31 January next following the tax year in which the chargeable period ends

Claim	Time limit
Plant or machinery which becomes a fixture on land which is subsequently let to be treated as belonging to tenant. Election to be made by both lessor and lessee (provided unconnected)	Two years from date on which lease takes effect
Grant of long lease of building to be treated as sale of relevant interest by lessor. Election to be made by both lessor and lessee	Two years from date on which lease takes effect
Succession of trade between connected persons to be ignored in computing capital allowances	Two years from the date of succession
Disposal and acquisition of property between persons, one of which controls the other or both of which are under common control, to be treated as made at the lower of open market value and tax written-down value	Two years from the date of the disposal
Acquisition of relevant interest in capital expenditure on agricultural land and buildings to be treated as a balancing event	First anniversary of 31 January next following the tax year in which the chargeable period ends

Plant and machinery

First-year allowances

7.52   Allowances at the rate of 100% are available for the following types of expenditure incurred by a business of any size. If full FYAs are not claimed, writing down allowance (WDA) is normally available at 18% on a reducing balance basis.

Expenditure	Legislation (*CAA 2001*)
Energy-saving plant or machinery	*ss 45A–45C*
Cars with very low CO_2 emissions	*s 45D*
Zero-emission goods vehicles	*s 45DA*
Plant or machinery for certain refuelling stations	*s 45E*
Plant or machinery for electric vehicle charging points	*s 45EA*
Plant or machinery for use in a ring fence trade	*s 45F*

| Environmentally beneficial plant or machinery | *ss 45H–45J* |
| Certain new investment by companies in new plant or machinery in designated assisted areas in Enterprise Zones | *s 45K* |

Focus

Businesses can claim a 100% first-year allowance (FYA) in relation to qualifying expenditure incurred on the acquisition of new and unused electric charge-points. The allowance was due to end on 31 March 2019 for corporation tax purposes and 5 April 2019 for income tax purposes, but *Finance Act 2019* extended the provisions for four years until 31 March 2023 for corporation tax purposes and 5 April 2023 for income tax purposes (*FA 2019, s 34*).

The measure complements the 100% FYA for cars with low carbon dioxide (CO_2) emissions, and the 100% FYA for cars powered by natural gas, biogas and hydrogen.

Focus

The 100% first year allowance (FYA) for businesses purchasing zero-emission goods vehicles (*CAA 2001, ss 45DA, 45DB*) or gas refuelling equipment (*CAA 2001, s 45E*) has been extended, by statutory instrument for a further three years with effect from 1 April 2018 (*SI 2017/1304*). These allowances were due to end on 31 March/5 April 2018 for corporation tax and income tax respectively, but will now end on 31 March/5 April 2021 accordingly.

Structures and buildings

7.53   A new capital allowance for structures and buildings is introduced from 29 October 2018 (*Finance Act 2019, s 30*), although the detail is subject to consultation. The new structures and buildings allowance (SBA) will be available for eligible construction costs on new non-residential structures incurred on or after 29 October 2018. The allowance will be given at an annual rate of 2% on a straight-line basis. The aim of the relief is to relieve the costs of physically constructing new structures and buildings that are intended for commercial use. The relief will be available both to businesses chargeable to income tax and to those chargeable to corporation tax. A technical note explaining the new relief is available on the gov.uk website: www.gov.uk/government/publications/capital-allowances-for-structures-and-buildings-technical-note.

371

7.54 No first-year allowances are available, for a business of any size (*CAA 2001, s 46(2)*), for:

- expenditure incurred in the final chargeable period;
- cars (other than those with very low CO_2 emissions);
- certain ships and railway assets;
- long-life assets;
- plant or machinery for leasing;
- in certain anti-avoidance cases where the obtaining of a FYA is linked to a change in the nature or conduct of a trade;
- where an asset was initially acquired for purposes other than those of the qualifying activity;
- where an asset was acquired by way of a gift; and
- where plant or machinery that was provided for long funding leasing starts to be used for other purposes.

Writing down allowances

7.55 Recent writing down allowances (WDAs) (*CAA 2001, s 56; FA 2019, s 31*) rates are as follows:

	Standard rate (%)	Special rate (%)
From April 2019	18	6
April 2012 to April 2019	18	8
April 2008 to April 2012	20	10

WDAs may be claimed on a reducing balance basis. The allowance is given on the amount of a 'pool' of unrelieved expenditure (or written-down value) brought forward from earlier periods after adding eligible expenditure during the period and deducting the proceeds on disposals (or original cost if lower) during the period.

Integral features

7.56 The following assets qualify as integral features (*CAA 2001, s 33A*):
- electrical systems (including lighting systems);
- cold water systems;
- space or water heating systems, powered systems of ventilation, air cooling or air purification, and any floor or ceiling comprised in such systems;

- lifts, escalators and moving walkways; and

- external solar shading.

Expenditure on thermal insulation and long-life assets is also allocated to the 'special rate' pool (see **7.62**).

Annual investment allowance

7.57 The annual investment allowance (AIA) for capital allowances purposes is a 100% allowance for qualifying expenditure on machinery and plant. The AIA was set at a temporary level of £500,000 to 31 December 2015, reverting to £25,000 from 1 January 2016. *Finance (No 2) Act 2015* contained provisions to set the AIA at the permanent limit of £200,000 from 1 January 2016 (*F(No 2)A 2015, s 8*). However, Autumn Budget 2018 announced that the AIA is to be increased from £200,000 to £1 million for the two-year period from 1 January 2019 to 31 December 2020. It will revert to the permanent level of £200,000 from 1 January 2021. Where a business has a chargeable period that spans either 1 January 2019 or 1 January 2021, transitional rules will apply under which the AIA will be computed in two parts. Where the period spans 1 January 2019, the allowance will be calculated by reference to an AIA of £200,000 for the period before 1 January 2019 and by reference to an AIA of £1 million for the period after the change. The reverse will apply where the period spans 1 January 2021 (*Finance Act 2019, s 32* and *Sch 13*).

For a period of account more or less than six months, the AIA is proportionately increased or reduced.

The AIA applies to businesses regardless of size and can be applied to expenditure on long-life assets and integral features as well as on general plant and machinery, but not on cars. Expenditure over the AIA limit will be dealt with within the normal capital allowances regime.

The term 'car' was specifically defined, until April 2009, to include a motorcycle, so no AIAs were given for expenditure on motorcycles. However, the definition was amended, broadly from April 2009, to exclude a motorcycle (*CAA 2001, s 268A*). It follows, therefore, that AIAs are available for expenditure on motorcycles from (broadly) 6 April 2009.

Assets classified as plant and machinery

7.58 The terms 'plant' and 'machinery' are not defined in the legislation. 'Machinery' is therefore given its ordinary meaning (but includes such items as cars and ships). The uncertainty as to what constitutes 'plant' has resulted in a large number of court cases over the years. Broadly, it is necessary to distinguish between:

- assets used to carry on a business (which will generally be plant); and

- the setting in which that business is carried on (which usually will not). See *JD Wetherspoon plc v R & C Commrs* [2012] UKUT 42 (TCC), in which the Upper Tribunal substantially upheld a decision of the First-tier Tribunal as to what amounted to alterations to an existing building incidental to the installation of machinery and plant within *CAA 1990, s 66* (now contained in *CAA 2001, s 25*).

Focus

As announced in the Autumn Budget 2018, *Finance Act 2019* contains provisions aimed at clarifying the scope of relief given by *CAA 2001, ss 21–22* for expenditure incurred in altering land (*Finance Act 2019, s 35*). The changes, which apply to claims for capital allowances made on or after 29 October 2018, make it clear that the allowances are only available for expenditure altering land for the installation of qualifying plant and machinery, which itself qualifies for capital allowances, and not for expenditure incurred altering land for the installation of assets which do not qualify for capital allowances.

When the business ceases

7.59 When the business ceases, no first-year or writing down allowances can be claimed in a period in which the business ceases.

Balancing adjustments

7.60

- A 'balancing allowance' is given if the sale proceeds are less than the balance of unrelieved expenditure (although, where assets are 'pooled' together, a balancing allowance only arises when the business ceases).

- A 'balancing charge' arises where disposal proceeds exceed the pool balance, so that capital allowances previously given are clawed back. However, if the proceeds exceed original cost, the excess is generally subject to capital gains tax rules. The charge is treated as an addition to profits (or a reduction in losses).

Asset pools

7.61 All qualifying expenditure on plant and machinery is included in a single 'main' pool, except in certain cases where separate pools must be maintained, including the following (*CAA 2001, ss 53–54*).

From 6 April 2008, businesses can claim a writing down allowance of up to £1,000 for each pool, where the balance of unrelieved expenditure in a general capital allowances pool, or the special rate pool (see below), has fallen below £1,000 (*FA 2008, s 81*, inserting *CAA 2001, s 56A*).

Special rate pool

7.62   Since 6 April 2008, a special rate pool applies to certain plant and machinery. With effect from that date, expenditure on long-life assets, thermal insulation and integral features is allocated to the special rate pool, and the rate of WDA applicable to that pool was 8% per annum between 6 April 2012 and 5 April 2019 on a reducing balance basis (*FA 2008, s 82* and *Sch 26*). The special rate pool has subsequently been reduced from 8% to 6% with effect from 1 April 2019 for corporation tax purposes and from 6 April 2019 for income tax purposes (*Finance Act 2019, s 31*). Where the chargeable period spans 1 April/6 April (as appropriate), a hybrid rate will apply to unrelieved expenditure in the special rate pool based on the proportion of the chargeable period falling before the change date and the corresponding proportion falling after the change date.

Special rate expenditure also includes expenditure on high emission cars (110g/km where the expenditure is incurred on or after 1 April 2018).

Cars

7.63   The tax rules granting relief for business expenditure on cars were changed quite significantly from April 2009. Formerly, the amount of relief claimable was based on the cost of the vehicle. From April 2009, the rate of relief is determined primarily by the level of engine emissions.

There is a revised definition of a car for capital allowance purposes (*CAA 2001, s 268A*). Until April 2009, a car was specifically defined to include a motorcycle, so no AIAs were given for expenditure on motorcycles. However, this definition was amended (broadly from April 2009) to exclude a motorcycle.

7.64   The main features of the rules are as follows:

- The previous concept of 'expensive' cars is abolished, and the rate of tax relief is now based on the level of the vehicle's CO_2 emissions.

- For 2015/16 to 2017/18, cars with emissions of 75g/km or less attract 100% first year allowance (*CAA 2001, s 45D*). The threshold was reduced to 50g/km from April 2018; cars with emissions over 75g/km up to 130g/km were eligible for capital allowances at the main rate (currently 18%). From April 2018 the lower and upper thresholds were reduced to 50g/km and 110g/km respectively. Cars with emissions exceeding 110g/km (from April 2018) go into the 'special rate' pool and attract capital allowances at the rate of 8% (6% from April 2019: see **7.62**).

- Cars with private use are kept in a single asset pool, but the rate at which allowances are given is still determined by reference to emissions.

Cars with very low CO_2 emissions

7.65 Until April 2021, expenditure by any size of company on cars with ultra-low CO_2 emissions, or electric powered, should qualify for first year allowances (FYAs) if the car meets both of the following conditions:

- when the car is first registered, it is so registered on the basis of a qualifying emissions certificate (*CAA 2001, s 104AA(3)*); and

- the applicable CO2 emissions figure in relation to the car does not exceed 110g/km for expenditure incurred on or after 1 April 2018 for corporation tax or 6 April 2018 for income tax (between April 2013 and March 2018, the threshold was 130g/km) (*CAA 2001, s 104AA(4)*; *SI 2016/984*).

The car must be unused and not second-hand; however, it may have been driven a limited number of miles for the purposes of testing, delivery, test driven by a potential purchaser, or used as a demonstration car (HMRC Capital Allowances Manual CA23153).

From 1 April 2013, no FYA is available if the car is leased (*FA 2013, s 68*). Information regarding a car's CO^2 emissions figure can be found on the vehicle registration document (the 'V5') or on the Vehicle Certification Agency's website at www.dft.gov.uk/vca.

Areas designated as enterprise zones

7.66 The current regime provides for 100% enhanced capital allowances (ECAs) for qualifying expenditure in enterprise zones (*FA 2012, s 44, Sch 11*). Originally the expenditure had to be incurred between 1 April 2012 and 31 March 2017, but *Finance Act 2014* extended this period to 31 March 2020 (*FA 2014, s 64*).

Short-life assets (on election by the taxpayer)

7.67 'Short-life assets' are qualifying assets which are expected to be disposed of within five years. Where the asset is disposed of within four years from the end of the accounting period in which it was acquired, a balancing allowance can be obtained (or a balancing charge made). If the asset is still held at the end of that period, the tax written-down value is transferred to the main pool (*CAA 2001, ss 83–89*).

Long-life assets

7.68 'Long-life assets' are plant and machinery with an expected useful life of 25 years when new. Such assets normally only qualify for writing down allowances of 6%, instead of the usual 18% (from April 2019). The long-life asset rules do not generally apply where the total expenditure incurred during the period is less than £100,000. In addition, the provisions do not apply to certain types of asset including motor cars, or to plant and machinery in a dwelling house, retail shop, showroom, hotel or office (*CAA 2001, ss 90–104*).

Private use assets

7.69   There is a restriction in allowances if a sole trader or partner uses an asset partly for private use. Allowances are calculated and deducted from costs as normal, but only the business proportion of the allowances are allowed as a trading expense (*CAA 2001, ss 205–208*).

Assets leased to non-residents

7.70   Certain assets leased to non-residents who do not use them in a UK trade attract writing down allowances of only 10% and are subject to balancing charges and allowances (*CAA 2001, ss 107, 109*).

Connected persons

7.71   Where an asset is sold to a 'connected person' for use other than in a business, the sale proceeds are usually to be taken as the open market value. First-year allowances cannot be claimed on transactions between connected persons. A 'connected person' includes a spouse, certain close relatives, business partners, companies under common control, etc. On the succession of a business by a connected person (eg a business incorporation), an election can be made to substitute open market value with the asset's tax value if appropriate (*CAA 2001, ss 214, 217–218*).

Business premises renovation allowance

7.72   From 11 April 2007, 100% business premises renovation allowances (BPRAs) are available on qualifying expenditure incurred on the renovation of business properties that have been vacant for at least one year, in designated disadvantaged areas of the UK (*CAA 2001, Pt 3A; SI 2007/949*).

Originally, BPRAs were expected to be available for a period of five years from the start date. However, the scheme was extended for a further five-year period and therefore ended on 31 March 2017, for businesses chargeable to corporation tax, and 5 April 2017, for businesses chargeable to income tax (*SI 2012/868*). At Budget 2016 it was announced that there would be no further extension. The following section therefore applies for periods up to the cessation date.

Since the scheme was first announced in *FA 2005* (*FA 2005, s 92* and *Sch 6*), two changes were made (*SI 2007/945*). First, disadvantaged areas are defined as Northern Ireland and the areas specified as development areas by the *Assisted Areas Order 2007*. Secondly, excluded from scheme are any premises that are refurbished by, or used by, businesses engaged in the following trades:

- fisheries and aquaculture;

- shipbuilding;

- the coal industry;

- the steel industry;

- synthetic fibres;

- the primary production of certain agricultural products; and

- the manufacture of products which imitate or substitute for milk or milk products.

There is a clawback of relief if, within seven years of the premises being made available for letting, there is a sale, grant of a long lease or demolition or destruction of the premises. Initially, the relief was to be available only for a period of five years from April 2007. However, in the March 2011 Budget, the government announced that it would be extended for a further five years, to April 2017 (*SI 2012/868*; *SI 2007/945*). Anti-avoidance provisions apply in connection with sales where the control test is met, or the sale has been artificially arranged in order to obtain a tax advantage (*CAA 2001, s 568*), and sales where, as part of a tax avoidance scheme, the proceeds are less than they would be on the open market (*CAA 2001, ss 325, 357, 570A*).

Focus

Legislation was introduced in *FA 2014* to clarify the scope of the expenditure that qualifies for BPRAs (*FA 2014, s 66*). Broadly, the legislation provides that only the actual costs of construction and building work, certain specified activities (eg architectural and surveying services) and additional associated but unspecified activities (eg project management services) qualify for relief, up to a limit of 5% of the actual costs. In addition:

- a rule has been introduced preventing claims to BPRA from being made if another form of state aid has been or will be received;

- the rule preventing expenditure incurred on buildings from qualifying for relief before they have been unused for a year has been clarified;

- where expenditure is paid in advance and tax relief immediately claimed, the works to which that expenditure relates must be completed within 36 months or the relief has been withdrawn; and

- the period in which balancing adjustments must be made, if certain events occur, has been reduced from seven to five years.

The changes have effect for qualifying expenditure incurred on and after 1 April 2014 for businesses within the charge to corporation tax, and 6 April 2014 for businesses within the charge to income tax.

LOSSES

General

7.73   Business losses are generally calculated in the same way and using the same basis periods as business profits. Relief for trading losses may be obtained by (*ITA 2007, Pt 4*):

- set-off against other income in the same or preceding tax year (*s 64*);

- carry-forward against subsequent profits of the same trade (*s 83*);

- carry-back in the early years of a trade (*s 72*);

- set-off against capital gains of the same or preceding tax year (*s 71*); or

- carry-back of a terminal loss (*s 89*).

Restrictions

7.74   From 12 March 2008, loss relief is restricted for individuals who carry on a trade but spend an average of less than ten hours a week on commercial activities. This measure is designed to counteract the use of contrived arrangements that generate trade losses which may be claimed as sideways relief or capital gains relief ('sideways loss relief'), by an individual, other than a partner, carrying on a trade in a non-active capacity.

Where a loss arises to an individual carrying on a trade in a non-active capacity as a result of tax avoidance arrangements made on or after 12 March 2008, no sideways loss relief will be available for that loss. Otherwise, there will be an annual limit of £25,000 on the total amount of sideways loss relief that an individual may claim from trades carried on in a non-active capacity (*FA 2008, s 60* and *Sch 21*).

Transitional rules apply to the computation of losses subject to the annual limit where these arise for an individual's basis period which begins before 12 March 2008 and ends on or after that date.

Cap on income tax reliefs

7.75   From 6 April 2013, a cap applies to certain previously unlimited income tax reliefs that may be deducted from income under *ITA 2007, s 24* (*FA 2013, s 16* and *Sch 3*). The cap is set at £50,000 or 25% of income, whichever is greater. In relation to trading income, the reliefs affected by the cap are as follows:

(a)   *ITA 2007, s 64* (trade loss relief against general income);

(b)   *s 72* (early trade losses relief);

(c)   *s 96* (post-cessation trade relief);

(d)   *s 120* (property loss relief against general income); and

(e)   *s 125* (post-cessation property relief).

'Income' for the purposes of the cap is calculated as 'total income liable to income tax'. This figure is then adjusted to include charitable donations made via payroll giving and to exclude pension contributions – this adjustment is designed to create a level playing field between those whose deductions are made before they pay income tax, and those whose deductions are made after tax. The result, known as 'adjusted total income', will be the measure of income for the purpose of the cap.

The cap applies to the year of the claim and any earlier or later year in which the relief claimed is allocated against total income. The limit does not apply to relief that is offset against profits from the same trade or property business.

Losses set against total income (s 64 relief)

7.76   Providing the trade is carried on with a view to making a profit on a commercial basis, a sole trader or partner may claim relief for the trading loss of a tax year (*ITA 2007, s 64*):

- against his total income of that tax year; and/or

- the preceding tax year,

in any order.

From 6 April 2013, a cap applies to the amount of loss relief that may be claimed under *s 64*. The cap is set at £50,000 or 25% of income, whichever is greater (see **7.75**).

Where a claim is made to relieve profits in one basis period by losses of both the same basis period and a subsequent period, the claim for the loss in the same period takes precedence.

Where basis periods overlap, and a loss would otherwise fall to be included in the computations for two successive tax years (eg in the opening years of a business), it is taken into account only in the first of those years.

Relief is not normally available for farming and market gardening losses, where losses were also incurred in the previous five years (calculated before capital allowances).

Losses set against gains (s 71 relief)

7.77   A claim for loss relief (under *s 64*) against total income of a tax year may be extended to capital gains, for the tax year of the loss and/or the previous year (*ITA 2007, s 71*).

- The trading loss must first be relieved against other income for the year of claim, and is also reduced by any other relief (eg under *s 72* – see below) already claimed in respect of the loss.

- The maximum capital gains available for relief is the amount of net gains (ie after deducting capital losses of the same year and losses brought forward from earlier years).

- The trading loss is treated as an allowable capital loss of the current year, and relief is therefore given against the capital gains available for relief, before capital losses brought forward.

From 2004/05 to 2007/08 (and for 2002/03 and 2003/04 by election), the maximum trading losses available for relief equalled the gains before taper relief and the annual exemption (not after taper relief, as is otherwise the case) (*FA 2002, s 48*).

Losses carried forward (s 83 relief)

7.78   Any trading losses not otherwise relievable may be carried forward without time limit and set off against the first available profits of the same business carried on by the same owner in subsequent years.

Where a business is incorporated (ie transferred to a company), any unrelieved losses of the business may be carried forward and set off against the former sole trader's or partner's first available income derived from the company, first against earned income (director's salary, benefits, etc), then against investment income (dividends or interest from the company). The relief is available where the proceeds for the business consisted mainly of the issue of shares (more than 80% of which are retained), and provided the company continued the trade (*ITA 2007, s 83*; HMRC Business Income Manual at BIM75500).

Losses in early years of trade (s 72 relief)

7.79   A loss incurred in any of the first four tax years of a new business may be carried back against the sole trader's or partner's total income of the three previous tax years, starting with the earliest year (*ITA 2007, s 72*). The relief must be set off to the maximum possible extent against all three tax years. It is not possible to restrict the claim to a particular year.

From 6 April 2013, a cap applies to the amount of loss relief that may be claimed under *s 72*. The cap is set at £50,000 or 25% of income, whichever is greater (see **7.75**).

Relief is not available unless the trade is operated on a commercial basis, in such a way that a profit could be expected in that period within a reasonable time thereafter. In practice, this may be difficult to prove in the case of a new business and a viable business plan may be necessary to support a carry-back claim.

Terminal loss relief (s 89 relief)

7.80 Relief may be claimed for a loss incurred in the final 12 months of trading to be set against the trading income of the tax year in which the business permanently ceases and the three previous years, starting with the latest year. Capital allowances are treated as an expense in computing the loss (*ITA 2007, s 89*).

The terminal loss is calculated in two parts:

- the unrelieved trading loss of the tax year in which the business ceases (ie from 6 April to the date of cessation); and

- the unrelieved trading loss from a date 12 months before cessation, up to the following 5 April.

Profits must be taken into account in calculating the figures for each part but where the amount calculated in either part is a profit it is treated as nil.

The terminal loss may be increased by any unrelieved trade charges, and also by any available overlap relief (without restriction). The deduction for overlap relief is given in calculating the profit or loss in the final tax year (ie 6 April to the date of cessation) and is not relevant to the period prior to 6 April that falls within the 12 months prior to cessation (*ITA 2007, s 90(5)*).

Losses in early years of trade – example

7.81

Example 7.8—Loss in earlier years

Edna commences to trade on 1 December 2014, preparing accounts to 30 November. The first four years of trading produce losses of £12,000, £9,000, £2,000 and £1,000 respectively (after being adjusted for tax purposes and after taking account of capital allowances). For each of the four years of assessment 2011/12 to 2014/15, Edna had other income of £8,000.

The losses for tax purposes are as follows:

	£	£
2014/15 (1.12.14–5.4.15) (£12,000 × 4/12)		4,000
2015/16 (y/e 30.11.15)	12,000	
Less already allocated to 2014/15	4,000	
		8,000
2016/17 (y/e 30.11.16)		9,000
2017/18 (y/e 30.11.17)		2,000
2018/19 (y/e 30.11.18) note (b)		1,000

Loss relief for early losses is available as follows:

	2014/15	2015/16	2016/17	2017/18
	£	£	£	£
Losses available	4,000	8,000	9,000	2,000
Set against total income				
2011/12	4,000			
2012/13		8,000		
2013/14			8,000	
2014/15			1,000	2,000
	4,000	8,000	9,000	2,000

Revised total income is thus £4,000 for 2011/12, nil for 2012/13 and 2013/14, and £5,000 for 2014/15.

Notes:

(a)   Where part of any loss would otherwise fall to be included in the computations for two successive tax years (as is the case for 2014/15 and 2015/16 in this example), that part is excluded from the computation for the second of those years.

(b)   The loss for the year ended 30 November 2018 in this example is not available for relief for early year losses (*s 72* relief) as it does not fall into the first four tax years of the business, even though it is incurred in the first four years of trading. It is, of course, available for the alternative reliefs, ie offset against total income of the same or preceding tax year (*s 64* relief) (depending on other income for 2017/18 and 2018/19) or carry-forward against profits of the same trade.

Terminal losses – example

7.82

Example 7.9—Terminal losses

Frank, a trader with a 30 September year end, ceases to trade on 30 June 2018. Tax-adjusted results for his last two accounting periods are as follows:

	Profit/(loss)
	£
Year ended 30 September 2017	30,000
9 months to 30 June 2018	(9,000)

Frank has overlap reliefs brought forward of £2,000.

The terminal loss available is as follows:

			£	£
2018/19	(6.4.18 to 30.6.18)			
	(£9,000 × 3/9) + £2,000			5,000
2017/18	(1.7.17 to 5.4.18)			
	1.10.17 to 5.4.18	£9,000 × 6/9	6,000	
	1.7.17 to 30.9.18	(£30,000) × 3/12	(7,500)	
			(1,500)	—
Terminal loss				£5,000

In determining the part of a terminal loss arising in a part of the final 12 months (the terminal loss period) that falls into any one year of assessment, a profit made in that period must be netted off against a loss in that period. In this example, no net loss is incurred in that part of the terminal loss period falling in 2017/18. However, the two different years of assessment are looked at separately, so that the 'net profit' of £1,500 falling within 2017/18 does not have to be netted off against the 2018/19 loss and is instead treated as nil.

The £6,000 losses which cannot form part of the terminal loss claim may be claimed under the alternative *s 64* relief for offset against total income of the same or preceding tax year. In practice, where other income is sufficient, the whole of the £9,000 would in many cases be claimed under *s 64* relief in preference to terminal loss relief.

Post-cessation expenses

7.83   Relief for expenses related to a business incurred within seven years after trading has ceased is given against income and capital gains of the year in which the expense is paid (*ITTOIA 2005, s 250*). Any expenses which cannot be relieved in this way can only be set against any post-cessation receipts arising from the business.

The expenses allowed are those amounts spent:

● in remedying, or as damages for, defective work done, goods supplied or services rendered in the course of the former business activity;

● for legal or professional services in connection with any claim that the work, goods or services were defective;

● for insurance against expenses described above;

- recovering debts which have been included in business profits before cessation; and

- debts which have been included in business profits before cessation but which have subsequently (within seven years of cessation) become bad debts or have been released under a formal voluntary arrangement.

Claims must be made through the self-assessment return form within 12 months of the filing date (ie for expenditure in 2017/18, the claim should be made in the 2017/18 return due on 31 January 2019, or notified by way of amendment of the return by 31 January 2020).

A targeted anti-avoidance rule ('TAAR'), which applies to events occurring on or after 12 January 2012 (*FA 2012, s 9*), prevents post-cessation trade relief from being available where a payment, or event for which relief is sought, arises from 'relevant tax avoidance arrangements' (*ITA 2007, s 96*). Similar provisions to those restricting post-cessation property relief apply to trade relief. 'Relevant tax avoidance arrangements' are arrangements (*ITA 2007, s 98A*):

- to which the person is a party; and

- the main purpose or one of the main purposes of which is the obtaining of a reduction in tax liability as a result of the availability of post-cessation trade relief.

Focus

In *Sinclair* [2019] TC 06873, the First-tier Tribunal restricted the amount of post-cessation trade relief claimed, first to the amount of legal fees actually paid in the tax year (where relief had been claimed and second, by denying relief in respect of an invalid declaration of trust.

Time limits for claims

7.84

Claim	Time limit
Set-off against income or gains of the same or preceding tax year (*s 64*)	Anniversary from 31 January after end of tax year in which loss occurs
Set-off losses in early years of trade against three previous tax years (*s 72*)	Anniversary from 31 January after end of tax year in which loss occurs
Carry-forward against future profits of the same trade (*s 83*)	Four years from the end of the tax year in which loss occurs
Carry-back of terminal losses (*s 89*)	Four years from the end of the tax year in which loss occurs

NATIONAL INSURANCE CONTRIBUTIONS FOR THE SELF-EMPLOYED

National Insurance contributions

7.85   Self-employed earners (ie sole traders or partners) over the age of 16 and below state retirement age are liable to both Class 2 and Class 4 National Insurance contributions (NICs) unless specifically excepted (*SSCBA 1992, ss 11, 15; SI 2001/1004, regs 45, 87, 94, 100*).

Class 2 contributions

7.86   Class 2 contributions are payable at a flat weekly rate (see **7.89**). Self-employed individuals with small earnings may apply for a certificate of exemption from paying Class 2 contributions if net earnings for the tax year are below a specified limit or if earnings for the previous tax year were below the limit for that year and there has been no material change in circumstances.

For these purposes, 'net earnings' are the profits of the business, as shown in the profit and loss account. If an individual has more than one self-employment, the profits (and losses) of each business are added together to arrive at earnings.

The newly self-employed must notify their liability to pay Class 2 contributions to HMRC. Penalties may be imposed for failure to notify chargeability (see **7.17**).

From April 2011, payments for Class 2 NICs became due on 31 July and 31 January, along with income tax due under self-assessment. HMRC issue two payment requests (instead of four quarterly bills) in October and April, showing payments due by 31 January and 31 July respectively.

An option to pay by six-monthly direct debits, collected in January and July each year, is available for those who do not wish to spread their payments.

HMRC now consider that sleeping and inactive limited partners (see **7.90**) are (and have in the past been) liable to pay Class 2 NICs as self-employed earners and Class 4 NICs in respect of their taxable profits. 'Inactive limited partners' are limited partners who take no active part in running the business. This view represents a change from that previously held by HMRC and the Department for Work and Pensions (DWP). Sleeping or inactive limited partners who have not paid Class 2 or Class 4 NICs for a past period will not be required by HMRC to pay those contributions. In relation to the payment of Class 2 NICs from 6 April 2013, sleeping and inactive limited partners must check their Class 2 NICs position, and those who are not already paying Class 2 NICs as a result of being self-employed must advise HMRC of their self-employed status and arrange to pay NICs or seek exception/deferment, etc, according to their individual circumstances. Many sleeping and inactive limited partners will qualify under one of these exceptions, but there is a need to ensure that the appropriate action has been taken.

Class 4 contributions

7.87 Class 4 contributions are payable on the profits of a trade, profession or vocation at a main percentage rate between a lower and upper profits limit, and at an additional rate on profits above that upper limit. The income tax and Class 4 contributions of a self-employed individual are collected together under self-assessment.

'Profits' for Class 4 purposes are generally calculated in the same way as for income tax. However, where trading losses have been relieved against other income or gains, they may nevertheless be carried forward and deducted from future profits for the purposes of computing the Class 4 liability.

If the taxpayer has more than one self-employment, the profits of each business are aggregated to calculate the Class 4 liability. Individual business partners are each liable to Class 4 contributions on their profit shares.

Maximum contributions at the main rate

7.88 An individual who is both self-employed and employed is liable to pay Class 1, 2 and 4 contributions. The overall maximum for contributions at the main rate is based on 53 times the maximum weekly Class 1 contributions at the main rate.

The liability for Class 4 contributions at the main rate cannot exceed a maximum based on 53 times the weekly Class 2 contributions plus the maximum Class 4 contributions paid at the main rate.

Class 4 contributions above that limit are payable at the additional rate. A claim for repayment of contributions may be made in appropriate circumstances; and, where contributions are expected to exceed the maximum amount at the main rate, an application to defer payment of contributions can be made.

Rates and exemptions

7.89   Class 2 contributions

	2017/18	2018/19	2019/20
Flat rate	£2.85 a week	£2.95 a week	£3.00 a week
Small profits threshold	£6,025	£6,205	£6,365
Annual maximum payable	£148.20	£153.40	£156.00

Exempt for:

● men and women over state retirement age;

● married women who elected before 12 May 1977 to pay reduced rate Class 1 or no Class 2 NICs (provided election not revoked by divorce or widowhood);

- someone not 'ordinarily self-employed' with small earnings from self-employment who does not therefore need to apply for a certificate of exemption;

- someone who is incapable of work, in legal custody or prison, or is receiving incapacity benefit or maternity allowance for a full week; and

- someone receiving invalid care allowance for any one day in a week.

Class 3 voluntary contributions

	2016/17	2017/18	2018/19	2019/20
Flat rate	£14.10 a week	£14.25 a week	£14.65 a week	£15.00 a week

May be paid by those who would otherwise not have paid sufficient contributions to earn a full state pension.

Class 4 contributions

	2016/17	2017/18	2018/19	2019/20
Percentage rate up to upper annual limit	9%	9%	9%	9%
Percentage rate above upper annual limit	2%	2%	2%	2%
Lower annual limit	£8,060	£8,164	£8,424	£8,632
Upper annual limit	£43,000	£45,000	£46,350	£50,000

Exempt for:

- men and women over state retirement age at the start of the tax year;

- someone who is 16 at the start of the tax year and holds a certificate of exemption for that year;

- someone not 'ordinarily self-employed' with small earnings from self-employment who does not therefore need to apply for a certificate of exemption;

- someone not resident in the UK for income tax purposes;

- 'sleeping partners' who receive a share of profits but take no part in actively running the business;

- trustees and executors chargeable to income tax on income received on behalf of others (eg incapacitated persons); and

- divers and diving supervisors employed in the UK to exploit the sea-bed.

SOLE TRADER OR PARTNERSHIP?

Partnerships

7.90   Although, under the law of England and Wales, a partnership is not a separate legal person, it is treated as a separate entity for tax purposes (*ITTOIA 2005, ss 848–850; TMA 1970, s 42*). Within the partnership, entitlement to shares of profits and losses between the separate legal persons, the partners, is regulated by the partnership agreement. Their relationship with third parties is governed principally by the *Partnership Act 1890*. It makes partners responsible jointly for the debts and losses of the firm. Like sole traders, partners have no protection from creditors; their private assets are available to creditors for the payment of business debts. In Scotland a partnership is a separate legal person but this distinction is not important for tax purposes.

A partnership may be 'limited' (by the *Limited Partnerships Act 1907*). A limited partnership is one that has one or more limited partners. Limited partners are liable for the debts of the firm only up to the amount of the capital they have contributed. Both individuals and companies may be limited partners. Being a limited partner has implications for tax, particularly in restricting the amount of loss relief. Every partnership with limited partners must also contain at least one general partner, liable in full for the debts of the firm. Every limited partnership must register with the Registrar (who is the Registrar of Companies). Without registration a limited partnership becomes a general partnership.

In addition to full or general partners, who have unrestricted liability, and limited partners, there are two other types of partner, as follows:

(1)   sleeping partners – a sleeping partner is one who plays no active role in the business; involvement is limited to an investment and a share of profits; and

(2)   salaried partners – these may be full partners who choose to divide up the firm's profits first by reference to fixed amounts, described as 'salaries'; alternatively they may be individuals who are employees and are described as partners for prestige reasons only.

Limited liability partnerships

7.91   Limited liability partnerships (LLPs) were introduced from 6 April 2001. An LLP broadly provides the organisational flexibility of a partnership, but with limited liability status for its members. For tax purposes, an LLP carrying on a trade, profession or other business with a view to profit is generally treated as a partnership. The transfer of an existing partnership business to an LLP will not normally give rise to income tax or capital gains tax consequences. However, there is a potential restriction in loss relief for

389

members of LLPs that carry on a trade. An LLP is taxed as a company during a liquidation of the business (*ITA 2007, Pt 4, Ch 3*).

Disguised employment via LLPs

7.92   A series of anti-avoidance measures were announced in the 2014 Budget relating to the 'disguised employment' rules as they affect LLPs. By law, the members of an LLP cannot be employees and are therefore treated as self-employed, with lower NICs and, of course, the deferral of income tax payments. HMRC perceived that there was abuse at both ends of the spectrum, so that 'groups of low paid workers who would normally be regarded as employees are being taken on as LLP members as a condition for their obtaining work' and 'individuals who would normally be regarded as employees in high salary professional areas such as the legal and financial services sectors are benefiting from self-employed status for tax purposes'. The rules were accordingly revised from 6 April 2014 to counter these types of situation (*FA 2014, s 74* and *Sch 17*).

The revised rules will only apply to individuals that are members of LLPs; and, to fall within the rules, those individuals have to satisfy conditions A to C as follows:

Condition A is that there are arrangements for the individual to perform services as a member of the LLP, and it is reasonable to expect that the amounts payable for those services will be wholly, or substantially wholly, disguised salary. 'Substantially wholly' will be defined to be at least 80%.

'Disguised salary' is defined as being where the remuneration is varied without reference to the overall partnership profits, or is not affected by the partnership profits. In many cases, this will not lead to any difficulties, as partners in an LLP will be remunerated by reference to the overall profits available. There is concern, however, for the treatment of salaried partners or fixed share partners. HMRC's guidance suggests that it is important to ensure that at least 20% of partner remuneration is by reference to the overall partnership profits, but that this can include various points arrangements or pooling arrangements, so long as the overall 'pot' is based on the overall partnership profits.

Condition B is that the person concerned does not have significant influence over the affairs of the partnership. This is causing concern, particularly amongst the larger professional services and law firms, where only a very small proportion of the partners can be said to have any real influence over the affairs of the partnership. HMRC have stated that they do not consider that many of the partners of, for example, the Big Four accounting firms would have significant influence over the affairs of their firm, so arguably a lot of people will satisfy condition B (or fail it, depending on your perspective).

Condition C is that the person's partnership capital is less than 25% of the amount of reasonable expected disguised salary for the tax year. In other words, the person concerned has to have at stake capital of at least one quarter of their partnership income to avoid satisfying this test. The partnership capital is determined on 6 April 2014, or at the date of appointment of the partner, and then at the beginning of each subsequent tax year or whenever the partnership sharing arrangements change. This condition, again, reflects HMRC's views that partnership includes having a substantial amount of capital at stake. The test will be accepted as satisfied if there is a firm commitment to contribute capital within three months of 6 April 2014, or within two months of becoming a member of an LLP after that date, so long as the capital is actually contributed.

If a person satisfies all three conditions, then that person is taxed as if they were an employee of the partnership, although their wider legal status as a member of the LLP is not changed. In other words, this is purely a tax measure. The legislation also introduces statutory deductions for the salaries and taxes, and the salaried member will not have to be included on the partnership returns.

Partnership tax return

7.93   Each partnership is required to submit a partnership tax return, showing business profits and the allocation of those profits between the partners. Each partnership must nominate a representative partner who is responsible for the submission of the partnership return. It is this partner who receives the notice from HMRC to complete a return and all other correspondence from HMRC concerning the partnership (*TMA 1970, s 12AA(1)–(3)*).

The partnership itself is not liable to tax on the profits allocated to each partner. Each partner is separately responsible for the tax on their own share of partnership income and gains, which is reported and assessed on their own individual self-assessment tax returns. Every partner is responsible for reporting his source of partnership income on his own tax return.

The trading profits, income and gains of the business are dealt with in a partnership tax return, made on behalf of all the partners each tax year. The return includes a partnership statement that may be a short or detailed (full) version. Most partnerships can adequately return details of the partnership profits on the short version, but if the partnership has particularly complex affairs the full version should be used.

A separate return is required for each accounting period ending in the tax year, based on the accounts of the period concerned. However, details of taxed income, trading charges on income and disposals of partnership assets are entered on those returns for the tax year in question. It is not strictly necessary to submit a copy of the partnership accounts and computations with the tax return unless the turnover exceeds £15 million. However, the Chartered Institute of Taxation recommends the submission of all accounts to give maximum protection in the event of an enquiry.

The partnership return must be submitted by 31 January following the end of the tax year to which it relates. However, if the return is not issued until after 31 October following the tax year, the filing date is extended to three months from the date the return is issued. Different filing dates apply to partnerships with corporate partners (*TMA 1970, s 12AA(4), (5)*).

Partnership tax returns are subject to largely the same amendment and HMRC enquiry procedures as for individual returns. An enquiry into a partnership return is automatically extended to include the partners' own tax returns, although this does not cover non-partnership aspects of an individual partner's return (*TMA 1970, ss 12AA–12AE*).

The partnership tax return must include the following details for every partner who was a member of the partnership at some time during the accounting period covered by the return:

- name;
- private address;
- personal tax reference;
- registered office; and
- National Insurance number.

Penalties

7.94 Penalties for late partnership tax returns are not imposed on the partnership itself, but on the partners individually (*TMA 1970, ss 93A and 95A*). No tax-related penalties are imposed for late partnership returns, as the partnership itself has no liability to tax. However, there is no reduction in the fixed penalties where the outstanding tax at the filing date is less than the amount of those penalties, as there is for individual taxpayer's returns.

A tax-related penalty may be imposed on the partners where a partnership return has been made fraudulently or negligently, up to a maximum of the additional liability properly payable by each partner. A penalty of up to £3,000 may be imposed for a failure to keep adequate records in support of a partnership tax return (*TMA 1970, s 12B(5)*). There are also penalties for failing to provide HMRC with records and documents when required (*FA 2008, s 115, Sch 37*; *TMA 1970, Sch 1AA*).

Calculating profits and losses

7.95 The rules for calculating partnership profits and losses are the same as for self-employed individuals (see **7.22**). However, all business expenses incurred by the partners individually must be deducted from partnership profits in arriving at taxable profits on the partnership tax return.

This also applies to capital allowances claimed on business assets provided by individual partners. Partners are not permitted to claim relief for such business expenses on their own individual tax returns.

If any of the partners is a company, the partnership profits are computed using corporation tax rules, but profits are allocated to individuals using income tax rules. Two separate computations are therefore required (*CTA 2009, s 1262*).

Reform of partnership taxation

7.96   The 2017 Autumn Budget announced a series of measures, which followed a consultation on modernising the taxation of partnerships (*FA 2018, s 18* and *Sch 6*). In summary, the measures cover:

- the calculation and allocation of partnership profits for tax purposes;

- the mechanism for resolution of partnership disputes;

- partners who are bare trustees or nominees for other persons;

- partnerships with partnerships as partners;

- investment partnerships; and

- partnerships that are partners in another partnership.

Partnership profits

One of the measures provides that the allocation of partnership profits shown on the partnership return is the allocation that applies for tax purposes for the partners (but see 'partnership disputes' below).

Partnership disputes

As indicated above, the partnership return determines the allocation of profits between partners. Where a dispute arises between partners over how the profits are allocated (rather than the overall quantum of profits), a new process allows disputes over the correctness of the allocation of profits (or losses) for tax purposes to be referred to the tribunal to be resolved. However, disputes over the quantum of partnership profits are not within the scope of the new process.

Partners in nominee or bare trust arrangements

Where a beneficiary of a bare trust is absolutely entitled to any income of that trust consisting of profits of a firm, but is not a partner in the firm, they will be subject to the same rules for calculating profits and reporting, etc as actual partners.

Partnerships with partnerships as partners

For a partnership with partners that are themselves partnerships, there is a requirement to include, for each of the 'participating' partnerships, the share of the partnership's profit or loss calculated on all four possible bases of calculation, unless details for all partners (and indirect partners) are included in the partnership statement.

Investment partnerships

Where a partnership does not carry on a trade, profession or UK property business, it is not necessary to include the tax reference for a partner who is not chargeable to income tax or corporation tax in the UK on the partnership return if the partner's details are instead reported by the partnership to HMRC under the Common Reporting Standard or Foreign Account Tax Compliance Act.

Partnerships that are partners in another partnership

If a partnership (the reporting partnership) is a partner in more than one partnerships carrying on a trade, profession or business, the legislation provides that the profits or losses from each partnership must be shown separately, and separately from any other income or losses, on the reporting partnership's return.

The rules for the allocation of partnership profits and losses have effect for accounting periods and periods of account starting after 15 March 2018 (the date of Royal Assent to the *Finance Act 2018*). The changes to give effect to the new return relaxation in respect of overseas partners in investment partnerships have effect for returns made after 15 March 2018. The other changes outlined above have effect for 2018/19 returns.

For further commentary, see *Partnership Taxation 2019/20 (Bloomsbury Professional)*.

Capital gains

7.97   Partnership capital gains are assessed to capital gains tax on the partners themselves, and not on the partnership (*TCGA 1992, s 59*).

Allocating profits and losses

7.98   The taxable profits are allocated to each partner according to the profit-sharing arrangements for the accounting period. Partners' salaries, commissions and interest on capital accounts are not deducted in arriving at taxable profits; they are treated as a prior share of profits and are allocated to the partners concerned. The balance of profits is then allocated in accordance with the profit-sharing proportions in operation. This allocation cannot create or increase a loss for a partner. Any 'notional' loss calculated in this way must be reallocated to the other partners.

Each partner is treated as if his share of the partnership profit (or loss) had arisen from a separate trade carried on by that individual as a sole trader. The rules for taxing profits in the opening and closing years of a business therefore apply to each partner upon joining and leaving the firm. A change in the members of a partnership is not treated as a cessation of the business for tax purposes if at least one of the old partners continues after the change (*ITTOIA 2005, ss 846–863*).

Partnerships with mixed membership

7.99 Where, for example, one or more individuals form a partnership with a non-individual member, such as a company or a trust, in many cases, the corporate member of the partnership performs few, if any, duties but is allocated a substantial proportion of the profits. HMRC see this as tax avoidance, on the basis that profits parked in the company are only charged to corporation tax at 20%, in contrast to the much higher rates of income tax and National Insurance contributions applicable to the profits allocated to individual partners. From 6 April 2014 (subject to certain anti-avoidance rules, which came into force on 5 December 2013), HMRC have the legislative facility to allocate the profits of a partnership to the individual members, replacing any allocation to non-individual partners. In order for this to apply, there are two conditions (X and Y) that must be satisfied (*FA 2014, s 74* and *Sch 17*).

Condition X is that it is reasonable to suppose that profits are allocated to the corporate member with a view to reducing the profit share of the individuals so that the tax is less than it would have been. HMRC's guidance says that their general approach is that the legislation will not apply unless there is actually evidence of profits being shifted to the corporate member, although it is not entirely clear what they mean by this, and it will be interesting to see what happens in practice.

Condition Y is that the corporate member's profit share exceeds the 'appropriate notional profit', the individual member or members can enjoy those profits, and it is reasonable to suppose that the allocation of profits is attributable to that ability for the individual members to enjoy those profits.

The appropriate notional profit is the aggregate of the 'appropriate notional return' on capital and the 'appropriate notional consideration' for services. The appropriate notional return on capital is the return at a commercial rate of interest, effectively reflecting the time value of money on the contribution made by the corporate member to the partnership capital and the level of risk. The appropriate notional consideration is the arm's length remuneration for services provided.

Both of these look like fairly onerous tests, requiring some form of transfer pricing review. In practice, however, in the majority of cases where the non-individual member is not really carrying out any material activities for the partnership, there will be no appropriate notional profit and these tests will merely allow HMRC to unwind what they see as an unwarranted tax advantage.

The ability of the individual member to enjoy the profit share of the corporate member is defined as applying where the individual is connected with the non-individual member (under *ITA 2007, s 993*). For example, if there were a close company member and the individual member was also a participator in that company, the individual would be deemed to be able to enjoy the company's profit share.

Even without a connection, the 'enjoyment' conditions are satisfied where the profits of the corporate enure to the benefit of the individual, enhance the value of the individual's assets or benefit the individual, or where the individual can control the application of the company's profit share. In all cases, the enjoyment conditions are also satisfied if any of these factors apply in relation to persons connected to the individual.

The consequences of satisfying conditions X and Y above are that the individual's profit share is increased by an appropriate amount and that of the corporate is reduced.

The rules also apply similarly where the partnership does not have any individual members but where the corporate members are in effect owned by those people who would otherwise have been the individual members (eg a firm of three partners where each of the partners is a company and each of those companies is owned by an individual). A more normal structure (at least in HMRC's view) would have been for the three individuals to form a partnership. In these cases, if conditions X and Y are satisfied, the individuals are charged to income tax as if they were directly the partners in the partnership.

Sideways losses

7.100   *FA 2005* brought in measures to restrict loss relief available to partners in certain circumstances (*FA 2005, s 74*). The rules are now contained in *ITA 2007, Pt 13, Ch 5*.

ITA, 2007, ss 64, 71 and *72* allow trading losses arising to an individual to be set against other income and capital gains. The amount of loss relief available may be subject to the new cap, which took effect from 6 April 2013 (see **6.84**). These reliefs may be claimed by individuals who carry on a trade in partnership – generally referred to as 'sideways loss reliefs'.

The amount of trading losses for a tax year for which a non-active partner can claim sideways loss relief is restricted broadly to the amount of capital that the partner has contributed to the partnership (*ITA 2007, Pt 4, Ch 3*), although certain capital contributions are excluded from this amount.

The capital contributions excluded are those paid by non-active partners on or after 2 March 2007 where the main purpose, or one of the main purposes, for contributing the capital to the partnership is for the partner to have access to losses for which sideways loss relief can be claimed.

An annual limit on the amount of trading losses for a tax year for which an individual who is a non-active partner in a partnership can claim sideways loss reliefs applies to trading losses sustained as a non-active partner on or after 2 March 2007. The limit for each tax year, for trading losses from all partnerships in which the individual was a non-active partner for that year, is the lower of:

- £25,000; and

- the amount of trading losses for the tax year for which the individual would otherwise be able to claim sideways loss reliefs.

A non-active partner for these purposes is a limited partner or any other partner who spends an average of less than ten hours a week personally engaged in carrying on the partnership's trading activities.

A trading loss for which sideways loss relief is not available can be carried forward and set against the individual's share of the partnership's trading profits for future tax years.

The limit does not apply to losses from carrying on a profession or a Lloyd's underwriting business.

Limited liability partnerships and members of LLPs are equally affected by these provisions.

Allocation of profits – example

7.101

Example 7.10—Allocation of profits

Andrew, Barry and Clarisa trade in partnership. Their profit and loss sharing ratios are 1:2:3. They are allocated salaries in the year to 31 March 2019 of £100,000, £60,000 and £10,000 respectively. Each is entitled to interest of £1,000 on capital per year. The partnership makes a taxable profit of £233,000 in the year to 31 March 2019. The profit allocation for tax purposes is:

	Total	Andrew	Barry	Clarisa
	£	£	£	£
Salary	170,000	100,000	60,000	10,000
Interest on capital	3,000	1,000	1,000	1,000
Balance of profits (in ratio 1:2:3)	60,000	10,000	20,000	30,000
Chargeable on partners for 2018/19	233,000	111,000	81,000	41,000

Allocation of notional loss – example

7.102

Example 7.11—Allocation of notional loss

The facts are as above, but the partnership made a profit of only £149,000 in the year to 31 March 2019.

	Total	Andrew	Barry	Clarisa
	£	£	£	£
Salary	170,000	100,000	60,000	10,000
Interest on capital	3,000	1,000	1,000	1,000
Balance of profits (in ratio 1:2:3)	(24,000)	(4,000)	(8,000)	(12,000)
	149,000	97,000	53,000	(1,000)
Apportionment of Clarisa's loss		(667)	(333)	1,000
Chargeable on partners for 2018/19	149,000	96,333	52,667	—

Actual loss allocation – example

7.103

Example 7.12—Actual loss allocation

Brad and Leonardo have been in partnership for several years, sharing profits and losses equally. On 1 July 2019, they change the profit/loss-sharing ratio to 60:40. They make a loss in the year to 30 September 2019 of £100,000.

The loss will be divided as follows:

	Total	Brad	Leonardo
	£	£	£
1.10.18–30.6.19 (50:50) £100,000 × 9/12	75,000	37,500	37,500
1.7.19–30.9.19 (60:40) £100,000 × 3/12	25,000	15,000	10,000
	100,000	52,500	47,500

Non-trading income

7.104   The partnership non-trading income is also divided between the partners according to the sharing arrangements for the trade in that accounting period.

Taxed income

7.105   Income taxed at source is included in the partnership tax return as the income of the tax year itself, which will normally differ from the accounting period. This will either require an apportionment of income received in different accounting periods or, alternatively, details of taxed income actually received in the tax year.

Untaxed income

7.106   The partnership tax return should include details of untaxed income received in the partnership's accounting period. A partner's share of untaxed income is treated as arising from a separate business carried on by that individual. This income is therefore subject to similar opening and closing year rules as for trading income, and the rules for overlap relief may apply if untaxed income is taxed more than once in the early years of a business, or on a change in the partnership's accounting date. The 'separate business' rules start when an individual becomes a partner (or when the firm starts trading, if later) and end when he ceases to be a partner (or when the firm ceases trading, if earlier). The opening and closing year rules for untaxed interest are not applicable to changes in individual sources of untaxed income.

Partnership statement

7.107   The partnership statement must contain the following for each period of account ending within the tax year of the return:

- the amounts of income or loss from each source;

- tax deducted or credited;

- partnership charges on income;

- proceeds from disposals of partnership assets; and

- each partner's share of each of the above, for the period covered by the return.

> **Example 7.13—Reporting of partnership income**
>
> Angela is admitted to a partnership on 1 January 2019. She needs to report her share of the partnership income, to be assessed for the period 1 January to 5 April 2019, on her 2018/19 tax return by 31 January 2020. This income will be a proportion of her partnership profits for the accounting period to 31 December 2019, which are unlikely to be finalised by 31 January 2020.
>
> The amount of partnership profits included in Angela's 2018/19 tax return will have to be a provisional figure. The relevant box should be ticked on the tax return so the HMRC computer can flag the return as containing provisional figures that are to be finalised later. Angela is obliged to report the final amount of her partnership profit for the year to HMRC as soon as the figure becomes available.

Use of provisional figures

7.108   HMRC's approach to dealing with provisional figures in tax returns was set out in *Tax Bulletin* number 57 (January 2002). HMRC accept that a taxpayer has made a return where a provisional or estimated figure is used, and will not send back a return as incomplete if it does not have an adequate explanation for the use of the figure, or if no date is given for the supply of the final figure. The use of a provisional or estimated figure may nevertheless make a return incorrect, in which case a penalty will be charged if there is negligence or fraud.

HMRC Helpsheets for the partnership tax return

7.109

Name	Title
SA850	Partnership Tax Return Guide
SA801(notes)	Notes on Partnership UK Property
SA802(notes)	Notes on Partnership Foreign
SA803(notes)	Notes on Partnership Disposal of Chargeable Assets
SA804(notes)	Notes on Partnership Savings, investments and other income
HS380	Partnerships: Foreign Aspects

FARMING AND MARKET GARDENING

Introduction

7.110   Farming or market gardening in the UK is treated for income tax purposes as the carrying on of a trade or part of a trade (whether or not the land is managed on a commercial basis and with a view to the realisation of profits) (*ITTOIA 2005, s 9*).

'Farming' means the occupation of land wholly or mainly for the purposes of husbandry, but does not include market gardening. Husbandry includes hop growing, and the breeding and rearing of horses and the grazing of horses in connection with those activities (*ITTOIA 2005, s 876*). 'Farming' has different meanings in different contexts for tax purposes. For example, for the purposes of restricting certain loss reliefs which would otherwise be available to farmers or market gardeners, 'farming' and 'market gardening' are interpreted as above, but with the difference that activities carried on outside the UK are included.

'Market gardening' means the occupation of land as a garden or nursery for the purpose of growing produce for sale (*ITTOIA 2005, s 876(5)*).

All farming (but not market gardening) carried on by one person (or partnership or body of persons) is treated as one trade.

Since 29 November 1994, 'short rotation coppice' is regarded for tax purposes as farming rather than forestry (*ITTOIA 2005, s 876(3)*). Consequently, the land on which it is undertaken is regarded as farmland or agricultural land and not commercial woodland. 'Short rotation coppice' means a perennial crop of tree species planted at high density, the stems of which are harvested above ground level at intervals of less than ten years.

'Farm land' excludes 'market garden land' (*ITTOIA 2005, s 876*). 'Market garden land' means 'land in the UK occupied as a nursery or garden for the sale of produce (other than land used for the growth of hops) and 'market gardening' is construed accordingly.'

Under strict interpretation of the law, anyone whose house has a garden attached may be a market gardener. However, in order to counter the use of a small garden as a mere device for tax avoidance, the rule which HMRC apply in practice is that only if commercial purposes predominate will the garden be regarded as a market garden. However, this rule is unlikely to be rigidly applied where the taxpayer sells fruit or vegetables as part of a wider business. For example, a farm shop on farm premises which sells farm produce is unlikely to be treated as a separate trade even if, in order to keep the shop worker busy, the taxpayer brings in goods from outside for resale.

Focus

HMRC have produced an online tax guide for farmers. The *Starting your own Business* e-learning tutorial, covers a wide range of issues including an overview of tax, NI contributions and VAT, registering as self-employed and help with completing tax returns. The tutorial can be accessed online at www.hmrc.gov.uk/courses/syob3/a_b/HTML/a_b_menu.html.

Trading

7.111   All farming which is carried on by a sole trader, persons in partnership or body of persons is treated as one trade. Accordingly, profits derived from more than one farm must be aggregated into a single chargeable source of income where the taxpayer operates more than one farm at the same time, whether the farms are in the same or in different parts of the country.

Where the giving up of farming on one farm and the commencement of farming on another is treated as having taken place, the following consequences occur.

Trading losses from the farming operation which has ceased cannot be set off against profits generated from the new farm. The trading losses from the first farming operation could only be brought forward against trading profits from the second farming operation if the two sets of farming operations amounted, for income tax purposes, to a single continuing trade.

If the farmer is treated as having ceased to trade in respect of one farm, then any accumulated income tax losses at the date of such cessation are 'wiped out' and are not available for set-off or carry-forward (*ITA 2007, s 83*).

If a particular activity does not fall within the definition of 'farming' and 'market gardening', it may still be treated as being some other trade or part of some other trade within the ambit of *ITTOIA 2005*.

The taxpayer should take particular care to avoid the activity being regarded as casual or occasional. If the activity is treated as such, profits derived from it will be charged to income tax.

Share farming

7.112   'Share farming' is a method of farming where the owner or tenant of farmland (the landowner) enters into a contract with a working farmer (the share farmer). Typically:

- the landowner provides the farmland and buildings, fixed equipment and machinery, major maintenance of the buildings and his expertise;

- the share farmer provides labour, field and mobile machinery and his expertise;

- other costs such as seed, fertilisers and feed are shared. If there is a livestock enterprise then ownership of the animals is shared on the basis that each party owns a share in each animal;

- each party is rewarded by a share in the produce of the farm which he is free to sell as he likes; and

- each party produces his own accounts and is responsible for his own tax and VAT returns.

HMRC consider that both parties to a genuine share farming agreement are carrying on a 'farming' business for tax purposes.

Relief for fluctuating profits

7.113 Because personal reliefs which are unused in one tax year cannot be carried forward or backward to another tax year, and because of the progressive nature of income tax liability, a person who earns, say, £40,000 in one tax year and £10,000 in the next, pays more income tax than a similarly placed person who earns £25,000 in each of two succeeding tax years. Special relief is accordingly available to individuals and partnerships engaged in a farming or market gardening business to take account of fluctuating profits (*ITTOIA 2005, ss 221–225*).

Focus

Prior to 2016/17 farmers and market gardeners could generally claim to average their profits in any two consecutive tax years, provided that the profits in either year did not exceed 75% of the profits for the other year or the profits of one of the years were nil. From 2016/17 onwards it is possible to make an averaging claim to average farming profits in:

- any two consecutive tax years, provided that the profits in either year do not exceed 75% of the profits for the other year or the profits of one of the years are nil (marginal relief is abolished); and

- any five consecutive tax years, provided that either the average of the first four years' profits are less than 75% of the last year's profits or vice versa or the profits of one or more of the five years are nil.

Farming, for these purposes, includes the intensive rearing of livestock or fish on a commercial basis for the production of food for human consumption.

Prior to 2016/17 a marginal relief was available where profits for one year were more than 70%, but less than 75%, of the profits of the other year.

A year in which a loss is incurred is, for the purposes of the relief, deemed to be a year of nil profit. Loss relief is, nevertheless, still available.

The introduction of self-assessment changed the method of dealing with capital allowances in the computation of profits, and consequently it also changes the measure of profits to be used in an averaging claim. The profits to be taken are the profits before any deduction for losses.

A claim for the relief must be made in writing within two years of the end of the second tax year to which the claim relates. Under self-assessment, the claim is to be related to the later year, with any necessary adjustments in respect of the earlier year being given in the later year.

The average profits for the second year can provide the basis for averaging the profits for years two and three.

> ### Example 7.14—Farming: relief for fluctuating profits (I)
>
> A farmer's profits for recent years are as follows:
>
> Year 1 = £30,000; Year 2 = £10,000.
>
> So, Year 2 profits are less than 75% of Year 1 profits. The farmer claims the relief.
>
> His profits for each of Year 1 and Year 2 will be deemed to be:
>
> $$\frac{£30,000 + £10,000}{2} = £20,000$$
>
> The profits in Year 3 are £10,000. The farmer again claims relief. His profits for Years 2 and 3 will each be adjusted to:
>
> $$\frac{£20,000 + £10,000}{2} = £15,000$$
>
> A claim for relief cannot be made for a year of commencement or discontinuance.

> ### Example 7.15—Farming: relief for fluctuating profits (II)
>
> A farmer's profits were £16,000 in 2014/15 and £30,000 in 2015/16, and an averaging claim was made so that the profits of each year became £23,000. Assume the 2014/15 tax is increased by £1,680 (but the 2015/16 tax is reduced by £2,800, giving a significant reduction overall). The increase in the 2014/15 tax would be given effect by increasing the tax payable for 2015/16.
>
> A claim was then made to average the previously averaged 2015/16 profits of £23,000 with those of 2016/17. The calculation of the effect on the tax position for 2015/16 would not treat the increase of £1,680 relating to 2014/15 as part of the tax payable for 2015/16.

Restriction of loss relief

7.114 In general, any loss incurred in farming or market gardening is unavailable for loss relief by offset against general income if, in each of the prior five years, a loss was incurred (disregarding capital allowances) in carrying on that trade, ie losses can only be relieved against general income for five years. The restriction also applies to capital allowances related to the loss (*ITA 2007, s 67(2)*).

In *Donaghy v R & C Commrs* [2012] UKUT 148 (TCC), the Upper Tribunal decided that the inability of a farmer to carry back losses through averaging of farming profits was neither discriminatory nor in breach of his human rights.

Focus

In *French v HMRC* [2015] UKFTT 173 (TC), the First-tier Tribunal considered the correct interpretation and application of *ITA 2007, s 68(3)* and found that its objective is to preclude a farmer from enjoying the sideways and carry-back offset for farming losses in excess of five years' continuous losses only if the farmer has been slower in anticipating profit than 'the notional competent farmer'.

In the FTT case of *Erridge v HMRC* [2015] UKFTT 89 (TC), the FTT dismissed a taxpayer's appeal against HMRC's decision to disallow sideways loss relief in respect of the taxpayer's share of farming losses. The FTT found that the farming activities did not meet the 'reasonable expectation of profit' test because at the beginning of the prior period of loss a competent person could not have taken into account the banking crisis and alleged mis-selling by the taxpayer's bank because it would have been entirely unforeseeable and they would therefore have reasonably expected the farming activities to have become profitable before the current year; therefore the taxpayer did not meet the test in *ITA 2007, s 68(3)(b)*.

Livestock, tillages and harvested crops

7.115   The treatment and valuation of stock-in-trade is a particular problem for farmers. This applies to livestock, tillages, harvested crops, etc. As a general rule, animals kept for farming are treated as trading stock; however, animals are not so treated where the farmer makes an election for 'the herd basis' (see below).

A number of long-standing practices were called into question by the Revenue, their views being set out in a business economic note (BEN 19) issued in April 1993. The Revenue later commented on their revised practice in ascertaining the cost of harvested crops (from 85% of market value to 75% thereof) and clarified further the areas in which they expected changes to valuation methods: full way-going valuations, dilapidations reserves, certificates under the 1942 NFU arrangement and production animals taken at cull value.

BEN 19 is reproduced in full in the HMRC Business Income Manual at BIM55410.

Herd basis

7.116   Where animals are treated as part of the trading stock, payments and receipts for animals bought and sold are dealt with in the accounts in the usual way. Trading stock will have to be revalued at the end of the period of account.

However, where an election for the herd basis is made, the initial cost of the herd, and of any animal added to the herd which is not a replacement animal, is not deducted in the accounts as an expense and the value of the herd is not brought into account (*ITTOIA 2005, s 111*).

Generally, where an animal is sold, or dies, and is replaced, the proceeds of sale are included as a trading receipt and the cost of the replacement animal is deductible as an expense. It is not always clear whether the acquisition of one animal is necessarily a 'replacement' for another.

HMRC have confirmed that they will accept that replacement treatment is applied where an animal is brought into the herd within 12 months of the corresponding disposal. If the interval is longer than 12 months, replacement treatment may be accepted if the facts of the case support it (BIM55520).

Where at least 20% of the herd is sold within a 12-month period, and is not replaced within five years, any profit or loss is treated as a capital profit or loss. However, no chargeable gain will accrue on disposal as animals are wasting assets which are tangible moveable property.

An election for the herd basis can only be made in relation to 'production herds': ie herds of animals of the same species kept wholly or mainly for the sake of the products which they produce for the farmer to sell, eg dairy herds. An election must be made in writing and must specify the class of herds to which it relates. An election is irrevocable and must normally be made within two years of the end of the first chargeable period for which the farmer is chargeable under *ITTOIA 2005*, or is given relief for trading losses against general income. In commencement cases, the time-limit is extended to two years after the end of the first period of account if that is later.

The herd basis extends to cases where several farmers hold shares in one animal for the purposes of a herd, or in animals forming part of a herd.

Where there is a change in any of the persons carrying on the farming trade, HMRC's view is that the herd basis election made by the old 'farmer' ceases and the new 'farmer' can decide whether to make a fresh election.

Capital allowances cannot be claimed with regards to animals in respect of which the herd basis is used to compute profits.

SUBCONTRACTORS

Construction Industry Scheme

7.117   All businesses in the construction industry (individuals, partnerships and companies) are subject to the Construction Industry Scheme (CIS). This applies not only to construction work but also to work including installation (of most items from heating systems to shop fittings), repairs, decorating and demolition.

7.118 'Contractors' for these purposes include construction firms and any other business involved in construction work, although private householders and businesses spending less than £1 million per annum on construction work are excluded (*FA 2004, s 59*).

A 'subcontractor' is any business which has agreed to carry out construction operations for a contractor – whether by doing the operations itself, or by having them done by its own employees, or in any other way.

Key aspects of CIS

7.119 The legislation governing the CIS is contained in *FA 2004* and regulations (*SI 2005/2045*). Broadly, the rules provide for a verification service run by HMRC, periodic returns and an employment status declaration.

7.120 Key aspects of the CIS are as follows:

- Certificates, CIS cards or vouchers no longer exist.

- Contractors must check or 'verify' new subcontractors with HMRC.

- Subcontractors are paid either net or gross, depending on their own circumstances, but HMRC tell the contractor which treatment to use during verification.

- There is a higher rate tax deduction if a subcontractor cannot be 'matched' on the HMRC system. This rate applies until the subcontractor contacts HMRC and registers or sorts out any matching problem.

- There are no CIS annual returns.

- Contractors must make a return every month to HMRC, showing payments made to all subcontractors. Contractors must declare on their return that none of the workers listed on the return are employees. This is called a Status declaration.

- Nil returns must be made when there are no payments in any month. These can be made over the telephone as well as via the Internet or on paper. There are financial penalties for failure to submit a return.

Focus

In the Autumn 2014 Statement, the Chancellor announced a series of changes designed to improve the operation of the CIS. The changes are as follows:

Measures which apply from 6 April 2015

- the nil return obligation will be amended (SI 2015/429);

- joint ventures where there is already one member with gross status will be allowed easier access to gross payment status (SI 2015/789);

- earlier repayment to liquidators in insolvency proceedings will be allowed (SI 2015/429).

Measures applying from 6 April 2016

- a reduction of the turnover test limit to £100,000 in multiple directorships;

- the initial and annual compliance tests will focus on fewer obligations.

Measure applying from 6 April 2017

- mandation of filing of CIS returns and online verification.

Employment status

7.121   Under the CIS, contractors must check or 'verify' new subcontractors with HMRC. Broadly, this means that HMRC will check that the subcontractor is properly registered for income tax and National Insurance contributions (NICs) purposes.

A worker's employment status, that is whether they are employed or self-employed, is not a matter of choice. Whether someone is employed or self-employed depends upon the terms and conditions of the relevant engagement. The tax and NICs rules do, however, contain some special rules that apply to certain categories of worker in certain circumstances. A worker's employment status will determine the charge to tax on income from that employment or self-employment. It will also determine the class of NICs which are to be paid.

Focus

HMRC provide an 'employment status indicator (ESI) tool' on their website at https://www.gov.uk/employment-status-indicator. Employers and contractors may use the tool to obtain an HMRC 'view' of the employment status of their workers. It should be noted that the tool will provide a general guide only, which would not be binding on HMRC. To obtain a written 'opinion' of employment status in the construction industry, the contractor will need to telephone the CIS Helpline on 0300 200 3210.

Payments to subcontractors

7.122   There are a number of obligations that a contractor must comply with before payments can be made to subcontractors.

Verification

7.123 Verification is the process that HMRC use to make sure that subcontractors have the correct rate of deduction applied to their payments under the CIS. There are three main steps to the process:

- the contractor contacts HMRC with details of the subcontractor;

- HMRC check that the subcontractor is registered with them; and

- HMRC tell the contractor what rate of deduction to apply, if any.

Before a contractor can make a payment for construction work to a subcontractor, they must decide whether they need to verify the subcontractor.

The general rule is that a contractor does not have to verify a subcontractor if they last included that subcontractor on a return in the current or two previous tax years.

If a contractor does not have to verify a subcontractor, they must pay the subcontractor on the same basis as the last payment made to them. This means that, if the subcontractor was last paid under the standard rate of deduction, the current payment must also be made under the standard rate of deduction. If the last payment was made gross, because a deduction was not required, the current payment must also be made gross.

Verification reference number

7.124 Once HMRC have received the above information, they will check their records to see if the subcontractor is registered for tax and then tell the contractor to pay the subcontractor in one of the following ways (*SI 2007/46, reg 2*):

- gross – ie without any deductions taken from the payment;

- net of a deduction at the standard rate (currently 20%); or

- net of a deduction at the higher rate (currently 30%) because:

    - HMRC have no record of that subcontractor's registration, or

    - HMRC are unable to verify the details for any other reason.

When HMRC verify a subcontractor, they will give the contractor a verification reference number. The verification reference number will be the same for each subcontractor that they have verified at the same time. If it is not possible to verify a subcontractor, HMRC will add one or two letters to the end of the number, so that it is unique to that subcontractor.

Payments under deduction

7.125 Deductions must only be made from that part of the payment that does not represent the cost of materials incurred by the subcontractor.

Any travelling expenses (including fuel costs) and subsistence paid to the subcontractor must be included in the gross amount of payment and the amount from which the deduction is made.

There are two steps that contractors must follow:

(1) Calculate the gross amount from which a deduction will be made by excluding:

– VAT charged by the subcontractor if he is registered; and

– any amount equal to the Construction Industry Training Board (CITB) levy.

The contractor will need to keep a record of the gross payment amounts so that they can enter these on their monthly returns under real time information (RTI).

(2) Deduct from the gross payment the amount the subcontractor actually paid for the following items used in the construction operations, including VAT paid if the subcontractor is not registered for VAT:

– materials: the contractor can ask the subcontractor for evidence of the direct cost of materials. If the subcontractor fails to give this information, the contractor must make a fair estimate of the actual cost of materials. The contractor must always check, as far as possible, that the part of the payment for materials supplied is not overstated. If the materials element looks to be excessive, HMRC may ask the contractor to explain why;

– consumable stores;

– fuel (except fuel for travelling);

– plant hire; and

– the cost of manufacture or prefabrication of materials.

The contractor must provide a written statement, to every subcontractor from whom a deduction has been made, within 14 days of the end of each tax month. A tax month runs from the 6th of one month to the 5th of the next month, so the statement must be provided by the 19th of the month.

Monthly returns

7.126 Each month, contractors must send to HMRC a complete return of all payments made to all subcontractors within the CIS in the preceding tax month (*FA 2004, s 70*). This is regardless of whether the subcontractors were paid gross or net of either the standard or higher deduction. Monthly returns must reach HMRC within 14 days of the end of the tax month they are for. Returns may be made electronically or by post (*SI 2005/2045, reg 4*).

Contractors who have not paid any subcontractors in the previous tax month must nevertheless submit 'nil' returns, unless HMRC have been notified that no further payments will be made, in which case HMRC may cease to require monthly returns for up to six months, or until payments to subcontractors recommence (www.hmrc.gov.uk/cis/returns/returns-records.htm#4).

Penalties

Late returns (from October 2011)

7.127 *FA 2009, s 106* and *Sch 55, paras 8–13* introduced a new penalty regime for the submission of late CIS returns, which took effect from October 2011 (*SI 2011/2391*; *SI 2011/2401*). The first return to attract a penalty under *FA 2009, Sch 55* will be the return due for the month ended 5 November 2011. The penalties which may apply are as follows:

Period	Penalty
Up to 2 months late	£100
More than 2 months late	£200
More than 6 months late	Greater of: • 5% of tax liability; and • £300
More than 12 months late	
Other cases (ie not included below)	Greater of:
(Also see below for returns relating only to persons registered for gross payment)	• 5% of tax liability; and • £300
Information [deliberately]* withheld:	
Deliberate but not concealed	Greater of: • 70% of tax liability; and • £1,500
Deliberate and concealed	Greater of: • 100% of tax liability; and • £3,000
More than 12 months late – Information [deliberately]* withheld: Return relating only to persons registered for gross payment	
Deliberate but not concealed	£1,500
Deliberate and concealed	£3,000

* 'Deliberately' inserted by *F(No 3)A 2010, s 26, Sch 10 paras 1, 5, 6*, with effect from 6 October 2011 (*SI 2011/2391*).

The penalty regime for failing to make CIS returns under *FA 2009, Sch 55* took effect from October 2011. The first return to attract a penalty under *Sch 55* is the return due for the month ended 5 November 2011.

For contractors who have not submitted any previous returns and are filing their first returns late, an upper limit of £3,000 applies to the total 'fixed' penalties (ie £100 and £200) arising. The £3,000 upper limit does not replace any 'tax geared' penalties, but the £300 minimum penalty that would otherwise be charged, where the tax geared penalty is less than £300, is removed (*FA 2009, Sch 55, para 13*).

Payments

7.128   Contractors are normally required to make monthly payments to HMRC of deductions from contract payments, within 17 days after the end of the tax period if made electronically, or otherwise within 14 days after the end of the tax period.

A contractor who has reasonable grounds for believing that the 'average monthly amount' will be less than £1,500 can choose to pay tax on a quarterly basis (ie for quarters ending 5 July, 5 October, 5 January and 5 April) (*SI 2005/2045, reg 8*).

FA 2009, s 107, Sch 56, paras 6–8 introduced a new penalty regime, applicable from 6 April 2010 (*SI 2010/466, art 3*), in relation to late payments of PAYE, which apply equally to CIS payments (for details of the penalties which may be imposed, see **6.26**). The potential penalties for a tax year comprise 'default' penalties for unpaid CIS deductions at the penalty date, and two further penalties for CIS deductions which are more than 6 and 12 months late. Penalties apply for the failure to pay all or part of the amounts due. HMRC guidance, and worked examples regarding the late payment regime for CIS purposes, are contained in the Compliance Handbook (at CH153000 onwards).

The imposition and/or amount of penalty are subject to an appeal procedure. HMRC may also reduce a penalty due to 'special circumstances' at its discretion. Penalties are suspended if the contractor has an agreement for deferred payment in place (ie a 'time to pay' arrangement) with HMRC, which is not broken. Liability to a penalty does not arise if there is a 'reasonable excuse' for the failure (*FA 2009, Sch 56, paras 9, 10, 13, 16*).

Registration as a subcontractor

7.129   A subcontractor starting working in the construction industry on a self-employed basis for the first time should register for CIS if they do not want deductions at the higher rate made from their payments.

HMRC will only authorise a contractor to make gross payments to a subcontractor where the following conditions are satisfied.

The business test

7.130 To satisfy this condition, the subcontractor must provide evidence that he is carrying on a business in the UK which:

(a) consists of or includes the carrying out of construction operations or the furnishing or arranging for the furnishing of labour in carrying out construction operations; and

(b) is, to a substantial extent, carried on by means of an account with a bank.

Evidence prescribed to satisfy the business test is as follows (*SI 2005/2045, reg 27*):

- the business address;

- invoices, contracts or purchase orders for construction work carried out by the applicant;

- details of payments for construction work;

- the books and accounts of the business; and

- details of the business bank account, including bank statements.

The turnover test

7.131 The applicant must satisfy HMRC that, in the year following the making of the application:

- as an individual, his net business turnover from construction work (ie after the cost of any materials used to earn that income) is £30,000 a year or more (*SI 2005/2045, reg 28*); or

- as a partnership or company, the net business turnover from construction work (ie after deducting the cost of any materials) is £30,000 a year or more multiplied by the number of partners or directors.

In the case of 'close companies' (broadly, companies controlled by five or fewer individuals), the figure will be multiplied by the number of individuals who are directors and/or shareholders. For a husband and wife team, for instance, it would be £60,000.

An alternative test for partnerships and companies is that the business has an annual net turnover from construction work (after deducting the cost of materials) of £100,000 or more (prior to 6 April 2016 the threshold was £200,000) (*SI 2005/2045, reg 28*).

Following the Spring Budget 2017, the Government issued a consultation document entitled *Fraud on provision of labour in construction sector: consultation on VAT and other policy options*. One of the policy options under review is a change to the turnover test for companies. Future changes may therefore, be expected in this area.

The compliance test

7.132   From 6 April 2016, the compliance test has been somewhat relaxed and now focuses on fewer obligations. From that date, the relevant person(s) must have done the following, in respect of the qualifying period:

- paid by the due dates any deductions due as a contractor in the construction industry;
- completed and filed any required monthly CIS returns;
- paid by the due dates any PAYE and NICs due as an employer; and
- completed and filed any required self-assessment returns or corporation tax returns.

Items that are disregarded for the compliance test include any or all of the following, during the same 12-month period:

- three late submissions of the contractor's monthly return – up to 28 days late;
- late payments of PAYE/NICs/CIS deductions of less than £100;
- three late payments of PAYE/NICs/CIS deductions of at least £100 – up to 14 days late; and
- any self-assessment return made up to 28 days late.

The compliance test does not need to be met where, at the time of the application, one of the members is already registered for gross payment; or where the member possesses (or is entitled to acquire) at least 50% of the share capital or the voting rights or so much of the share capital or the rights as would on a winding up entitle the member to receive at least 50% of the assets or the amounts available for distribution.

Focus

In the recent case of *JP Whitter (Water Well Engineers) Ltd v R & C Commrs* [2018] UKSC 31, the Supreme Court dismissed the appeal by the taxpayer company against removal of gross payment status under the CIS. This case demonstrated the importance of ensuring that the strict conditions applicable to registration for gross payment status in the CIS are adhered to.

7.133

Subcontractor administration

Historically, some smaller subcontractors have often failed to keep the records of payments given to them by contractors. Moreover, contractors sometimes fail to give their subcontractors the required payment and deduction statements. Difficulties can subsequently arise because, when it comes to the completion of their annual tax return, the subcontractor concerned will not have a full record of his earnings and receipts. Subcontractors in this position usually contact HMRC at the end of the year and ask them to give back to them details of their payments and deductions, as reported on the returns of contractors for whom they have worked during the period, or year, in question. HMRC are often able to help out with this information where the subcontractor clearly has a genuine need for it. However, providing details of all payments and deductions reported on contractors' returns can cause problems. HMRC cannot know at all times which contractors a subcontractor may have worked for, nor can they ever be fully aware of what payments and deductions may have been made by any particular contractor. Although contractors are under a legal obligation to report this information to HMRC on a monthly basis, there have been occasions where a contractor's monthly return has not been accurate, complete or even received by HMRC in the first place. Subcontractors that rely on this information as a complete record in order to complete their own tax returns run the serious risk that they are making an incorrect or incomplete return and could be making themselves liable to a penalty for doing so.

HMRC say that this is a growing problem, with many subcontractors and some agents seeking to obtain this information from HMRC rather than keeping their own records. One of the aims of the reformed CIS was to improve subcontractors' compliance with their tax obligations.

In order to stem the ever rising number of time- and resource-intensive, multiple and bulk requests for data that HMRC are receiving, the Department will no longer be able to provide this information on a bulk basis. Requests for missing details from individual subcontractors or their agents will continue to be provided when they can demonstrate that they have been back to the contractor concerned to request a duplicate or missing payment and deduction statement but have failed to obtain one. In cases where it is alleged that a contractor has refused to issue one or more original payment and deduction statements, HMRC will require the subcontractor or their agent to give details of the contractor so that further enquiries may be made.

Once HMRC are satisfied that a subcontractor has tried to obtain details of the missing payment and deduction statement, they will supply the missing information if they possibly can and, of course, where the information is currently held on the HMRC CIS system.

HMRC guidance on CIS

7.134 HMRC produce comprehensive guidance on the Construction Industry Scheme (see www.gov.uk/business-tax/construction-industry-scheme).

Focus

For information regarding employment status, see www.gov.uk/ government/collections/employed-or-self-employed. The HMRC 'employment status indicator (ESI) tool' can be accessed at www.gov.uk/ employment-status-indicator.

Chapter 8

Property income

SIGNPOSTS

- From 2017/18 onwards, most landlords will calculate profits on property business income using the cash basis. An election may be made to continue using the accruals basis (see **8.1**).

- Expenses are generally allowable if they are incurred wholly and exclusively for business purposes, and are revenue as opposed to capital in nature (see **8.2**).

- An allowance of £1,000 to cover income from property is available from 2017/18 onwards (see **8.3**).

- Revised rules govern the treatment of capital expenditure under the cash basis for 217/18 onwards (see **8.9**).

- Premiums in respect of leases of more than 50 years' duration are charged to CGT. Grants, variations, surrenders and other lump sum payments in respect of leases which do not exceed 50 years are charged partly to CGT and partly to income tax (see **8.12**).

- The rent-a-room scheme allows people to receive up to £7,500 a year tax-free from renting out furnished accommodation in their home (see **8.20**).

- The commercial letting of furnished holiday accommodation in the UK is treated as a trade, and landlords may benefit from various income tax reliefs afforded to trading profits (see **8.26**).

- Rent and other receipts from properties outside the UK are taxed separately on an arising basis (see **8.32**).

- The Non-resident Landlords Scheme (NRLS) is a scheme for taxing the UK rental income of non-resident landlords (see **8.37**).

- The annual tax on enveloped dwellings (ATED) may be levied on owners of high-value UK residential property which is held by non-natural persons (see **8.52**).

PROPERTY BUSINESS PROFITS AND LOSSES

General

8.1 Income from property is taxed under *Income Tax (Trading and Other Income) Act 2005 (ITTOIA 2005), ss 260–262, 263–267, 268–275* and *859.*

Receipts, in relation to any land, include:

- any payment for a licence to occupy or otherwise to use any land or in respect of exercising any other right over the land; and

- rental charges, ground annuals and (in Scotland) feu duties, and any other annual payments reserved in respect of, or charged on or issuing out of, the land.

Excluded from the charge are profits:

- relating to farming and market gardening, mines, quarries and similar concerns, rents from mines, etc or rent from electric line wayleaves; and

- from letting tied premises, the rent from which is deemed to be a trading receipt.

Rents for 'caravans' confined to use at a single UK location and for permanently moored houseboats come within the property income charge. 'Caravan', for this purpose, broadly means any structure designed or adapted for human habitation which is capable of being moved. Sums payable, or valuable consideration provided, by a tenant or licensee for the use of furniture also come within the rules, unless they constitute receipts of a trade which consists in, or involves, the making available of furniture for use in premises (including caravans and houseboats) (*ITTOIA 2005, s 20*).

It is the person who is receiving or entitled to the income from the property who is charged to tax. It is important to note that beneficial entitlement may be unnecessary as far as, for example, an estate agent or other agent in receipt of such property is concerned (*ITTOIA 2005, s 271*).

The charge to income tax is computed on the full amount of the profits arising in the tax year.

Subject to any express contrary rules, property income profits are computed as if the trading income deductions rules were, in general, applicable. All businesses and transactions carried on or entered into by a person or partnership are treated as a single business for the purposes of calculating trading profits (*ITTOIA 2005, ss 264, 270*).

Example 8.1—Property income: calculation of taxable profit

John has a property business and makes his accounts up to 31 December each year. In recent years, his profits have been as follows:

31 December 2016	£10,000
31 December 2017	£8,000
31 December 2018	£9,500

The profits will be taxable as follows:

2016/17		£	£
6 April 2016 to 31 December 2016 (270 days)	270/365 × £10,000	7,397	
1 January 2017 to 5 April 2017 (95 days)	95/365 × £8,000		2,082
			9,479
2017/18			
6 April 2017 to 31 December 2017 (270 days)	270/365 × £8,000	5,918	
1 January 2018 to 5 April 2018 (95 days)	95/365 × £9,500		2,473
			8,391

Focus

Partnerships are charged to tax on property income arising in the accounting period ending in the tax year in question, ie on the same basis as for trading income.

Property business profits

8.2   Proposals to allow landlords to use the cash basis for calculating taxable profits were enacted by *Finance (No 2) Act 2017*, applying retrospectively for 2017/18 onwards (*F(No 2)A 2017, s 16* and *Sch 2*).

Up to and including the 2016/17 tax year, profits of a property business must be calculated in accordance with generally accepted accounting practice (GAAP), commonly referred to as the accruals basis.

Although the existing rules remain for certain landlords (including companies, LLPs, corporate firms, and trustees of trusts), the basis on which many landlords are taxed for 2017/18 onwards has changed.

The general rule will be that the cash basis must be used. However, this is subject to some exceptions and there will be scope for the individual to elect to continue using the accruals basis if they so wish. In addition, whilst the new property allowance (see below) will remove some landlords from income tax altogether, for others it will simply provide a deduction from profits of £1,000.

For commentary on capital expenditure under the cash basis, see **8.9**.

Focus

In June 2018, HMRC extended their MTD income tax pilot (see **2.4**) to accept quarterly updates from individual landlords with simple tax affairs. Agents can also sign up clients to the MTD for income tax pilot.

The latest extension means that certain taxpayers will be able to opt out of the current self-assessment regime and use software to report their income tax if at least one of the following applies:

- the taxpayer is a sole trader with income from one business; or

- they rent out only UK property but not as furnished holiday lettings.

Those who do not qualify must continue to report their income to HMRC via a self-assessment return in the usual way.

Property allowance

8.3   At the 2016 Budget, the government announced two new allowances of £1,000 each – one for property income, and the other for trading income. The legislation for these allowances was enacted by *Finance (No 2) Act 2017 (s 17 and Sch 3)* and applies for 2017/18 and subsequent tax years. The allowances are designed to 'provide simplicity and certainty regarding income tax obligations on small amounts of income from providing goods, services, property or other assets'.

In relation to property income, the allowance means that if all of an individual's 'relevant income' (broadly, gross income before expenses) is less than £1,000 for the tax year, then they will no longer have to declare or pay tax on this income. The effect of the relief will be that the income and expenses will not be brought in to account when calculating profits of a property business.

There are, however, two important exceptions worth noting:

- the allowances will not apply to partnership property businesses; and

- the allowances will not apply in addition to relief given under the current rent-a-room relief scheme (but see below).

Those with property income exceeding the £1,000 allowance threshold have the choice, when calculating their taxable profits, of deducting the allowance from their receipts, instead of deducting the actual allowable expenses. This option takes the form of an election which will apply to the calculation of the profits from property businesses for a particular tax year. The effect of the alternative method will be that the income receipts are brought in to account only in calculating the profits for the tax year. Any expenses associated with the income receipts will not be brought in to account. In calculating the profit a deduction will be allowed for the £1,000 property allowance.

It is worth noting that the Treasury has confirmed that although the new tax relief cannot be used on the same income by someone who is taking advantage of the rent-a-room allowance, if they were letting out furnished accommodation in their home but then also renting out their driveway as a parking space, they could benefit from both allowances.

Interest relief

8.4   Until 5 April 2017, individual landlords could deduct their costs – including mortgage interest – from their profits before they pay tax, giving them an advantage over other homebuyers. Wealthier landlords therefore received tax relief at 40% and 45%. Restrictions on this type of tax relief are now being phased in and by April 2020 this tax relief will be restricted to 20% for all individuals (*F(No 2)A 2015, s 24*).

Landlords will be able to obtain relief as follows:

- In 2017/18 the deduction from property income (as is currently allowed) will be restricted to 75% of finance costs, with the remaining 25% being available as a basic rate tax reduction.

- In 2018/19, 50% finance costs deduction and 50% given as a basic rate tax reduction.

- In 2019/20, 25% finance costs deduction and 75% given as a basic rate tax reduction.

- From 2020/21 all financing costs incurred by a landlord will be given as a basic rate tax reduction.

A separate restriction applies from April 2017, for investment loan interest in the case of property partnerships.

Furnished holiday lettings are excluded from this reform.

Legal and professional expenses in a letting business

8.5

Deductible from rental income	Not deductible
Insurance valuations	Purchasing or selling a property
Negotiation of rent reviews	Architect's and surveyor's fees, etc for improving a property
Evicting a tenant in order to re-let the property	Planning applications (unless for permission to carry out repairs on a listed building)
Accountancy fees for preparing the letting business accounts	First letting or subletting of a property for more than one year
Renewing the lease for less than 50 years	
First letting or subletting of a property for one year or less	

Losses

8.6   The losses of a property business are computed in the same way as profits (see **7.78**). Rental business losses are generally carried forward and set off against future property business profits. Alternatively, it may be possible to set off losses against total income of the same year (or the next following year), to the extent that they relate to capital allowances or allowable agricultural expenses.

Example 8.2—Property income: calculation of losses

Graham owns a house in Cyprus, which he only managed to let for seven weeks in 2018/19. As a result, he made a net loss from that property of £1,500. He also owns a flat in London which was let for the whole year and generated a net profit of £4,000 for 2018/19.

The loss from the Cyprus property of £1,500 cannot be set against the profit of £4,000 from the London flat, as it arose on an overseas property and must be kept separate. The Cyprus loss can be carried forward to set against future letting profits from overseas properties.

Cap on loss relief

8.7   From 6 April 2013, a cap applies to certain previously unlimited income tax reliefs that may be deducted from income under *ITA 2007, s 24*

(*FA 2013, s 16* and *Sch 3*). Property loss relief against general income (under *ITA 2007, s 120*) (see **8.6**) and post-cessation property relief (*ITA 2007, s 125*) are two reliefs affected by this cap. The cap is set at £50,000 or 25% of income, whichever is greater.

'Income' for the purposes of the cap will be calculated as 'total income liable to income tax'. This figure will then be adjusted to include charitable donations made via payroll giving and to exclude pension contributions – this adjustment is designed to create a level playing field between those whose deductions are made before they pay income tax, and those whose deductions are made after tax. The result, known as 'adjusted total income', will be the measure of income for the purpose of the cap.

The cap will apply to the year of the claim and any earlier or later year in which the relief claimed is allocated against total income. The limit will not apply to relief that is offset against profits from the same trade or property business.

Capital expenditure

8.8   Expenditure on land and the structure of buildings is treated as part of the cost of the asset for capital gains tax purposes. Until 6 April 2013 (1 April 2013 for corporation tax purposes), 100% capital allowances could be claimed for the cost of renovating or converting certain space above commercial properties into flats for short-term letting. If the 100% allowance was not claimed in full, a writing down allowance of 18% (from 6 April 2012) a year (on cost) (20% prior to April 2012) could be claimed until the expenditure was fully relieved (*CAA 2001, s 35*, former *CAA 2001, ss 393A–393W*; *FA 2001, s 67* and *Sch 19; FA 2012, s 227* and *Sch 39, para 37*).

From 11 April 2007 until 5 April 2017, business premises renovation allowances (BPRAs) may be claimed for the costs of renovating or converting certain unused business property in any of the 2,000 or so areas of the UK that are designated as disadvantaged. The allowances offer 100% up-front tax relief and may be claimed by individuals or companies incurring capital expenditure on bringing qualifying business premises back into business use. The allowances are available both to landlords and to businesses occupying their own properties (*CAA 2001, s 360A*). Initially, the relief was to be available only for a period of five years from April 2007 but was subsequently extended to 5 April 2017.

Plant and machinery allowances are available for expenditure on certain types of equipment used in the rental business. Such expenditure is 'pooled' together for capital allowances purposes.

Capital allowances are not available for expenditure on furniture and furnishings for use in dwelling houses (*CAA 2001, s 15(3)*). However, until 5 April 2016 (1 April 2016 for corporation tax), a deduction for wear and tear could be claimed (known as a 'wear and tear allowance election'), equal to

10% of the 'net rents' from furnished lettings (ie after deducting payments that would normally be borne by the tenant, such as water rates) (see **8.10**) (*ITTOIA 2005, ss 308A–308C*). In addition, a deduction could be claimed for replacing fixtures that are an integral part of a building (eg central heating systems), but excluding additional expenditure on 'improved' versions of those items. Replacing single glazed windows with double glazed units was treated as allowable repairs and not disallowable improvements.

In relation to expenditure incurred on or after 1 April 2016 (for corporation tax) and 6 April 2016 (for income tax), the former wear and tear allowance for fully furnished properties has been replaced with a relief enabling all landlords of residential dwelling houses to deduct the costs they actually incur on replacing furnishings, appliances and kitchenware in the property (see **8.10**).

Capital expenditure and the cash basis

8.9   The cash basis operates by reference to the tax year (see **8.2**). This means that profits are calculated for the tax year by adding or subtracting:

- all income received in connection with the property business in the tax year;

- any income that is not taxable and for expenses which are not allowable.

Prior to 2017/18, the cash basis rules prohibited a deduction for expenditure of a capital nature unless such expenditure would qualify for plant and machinery capital allowances under the ordinary tax rules (see **8.8**). However, the *Finance (No 2) Act 2017* provisions, which apply for 2017/18 onwards, replaced this general disallowance of capital expenditure rule with a more limited disallowance of capital expenditure incurred in relation to assets which are not used up in the business over a limited period. Relief will be prohibited only in relation to costs incurred in relation to the provision, alteration or disposal of:

- any asset that is not a 'depreciating asset' (defined as having a useful life of up to 20 years);

- any asset not acquired or created for use on a continuing basis in the trade;

- a car (but of course business mileage-based relief is available);

- land (as defined);

- a non-qualifying intangible asset, (as per Financial Reporting Standard 105) including education or training; and

- a financial asset.

Costs in relation to the acquisition or disposal of a business, or part of a business, will also be excluded.

Focus

On switching to the cash basis, which many taxpayers will do for 2017/18, it will be necessary to adjust for:

- amounts which, applying the cash basis, would have been brought into account for a period before the change and were not brought into account; and

- amounts which, applying the cash basis, should be brought into account for a period after the change and were brought into account for a period before the change.

Replacement domestic items relief

8.10 The wear and tear allowance has been abolished from 6 April 2016 and replaced with revised provisions for a deduction for expenditure on the replacement of domestic items such as furniture, furnishings, appliances (including white goods) and kitchenware in a let dwelling-house. The deduction applies for expenditure incurred on or after 6 April 2016 for income tax payers and 1 April 2016 for corporation taxpayers on an item that is substantially the same as the item being replaced, plus any costs incurred in disposing of, or less any proceeds received for, the item being replaced.

The availability of the relief is conditional on certain conditions being met:

- the expenditure must relate to the replacement of a domestic item for use solely by the lessee in the let property;

- the old item must no longer be available;

- the expenditure is capital in nature and incurred wholly and exclusively for the purposes of the property business;

- capital allowances are not available in respect of the expenditure; and

- rent-a-room relief has not been claimed.

The new relief given will be for the cost of a like-for-like, or nearest modern equivalent, replacement asset, plus any costs incurred in disposing of, or less any proceeds received for, the asset being replaced.

The amount of the deduction is:

- the cost of the new replacement item, limited to the cost of an equivalent item if it represents an improvement on the old item (beyond the reasonable modern equivalent); plus

- the incidental costs of disposing of the old item or acquiring the replacement; less

- any amounts received on disposal of the old item.

This deduction will not be available for furnished holiday lettings as capital allowances continue to be available for them.

Note also that the renewals allowance for tools (*ITTOIA 2005, s 68*) is no longer available for property businesses from the same date.

Where the replacement is superior to the old item, the deduction is limited to the cost of an equivalent replacement.

Example 8.3 – Replacement domestic items relief

George is the landlord of a furnished property. In 2018/19, he replaced the sofa at a cost of £600 and the washing machine at a cost of £300. He paid £20 to dispose of the old washing machine and he sold the old sofa for £50.

For 2018/19, George can claim a deduction of £870 (the cost of the replacement items (£600 + £300), plus the cost of disposing of the washing machine (£20), less the proceeds from the sale of the old sofa (£50)).

The legislation accommodates part-exchanges and letting arrangements without a formal lease and clarifies that the item being replaced should no longer be available for use in the dwelling-house.

The tax charge

8.11   Unlike normal trading income, property business profits are taxable as investment income. This distinction is important because there are more reliefs available for trading income than non-trading income.

The profits of a property business are normally charged to tax based on the tax year itself (different rules apply to trading partnerships). Income from both furnished and unfurnished lettings is included as profits of the property business. Furnished holiday lettings income is also currently taxed as a property business, although it is effectively treated as trading income for most tax purposes. Income tax on property business profits is usually collected as part of the self-assessment system of payments on account and balancing payments.

Special rules apply to the UK rental income of non-resident landlords (see **8.37**).

Lease premiums

8.12   Premiums in respect of leases of more than 50 years' duration are charged to CGT. Grants, variations, surrenders and other lump sum payments in respect of leases which do not exceed 50 years are charged partly to CGT and partly to income tax under the property income provisions; such 'short leases' are also potentially subject to charges under *ITTOIA 2005* in the case of a sale with a right to reconveyance or leaseback or of a profit on sale. The duration of a lease is determined by reference to certain specific principles.

A 'lease' includes an agreement for a lease as well as any tenancy, but does not include a mortgage. A 'premium' includes:

'any like sum, whether payable to the immediate or a superior landlord or to a person connected [see below] with the immediate or a superior landlord.'

A person is 'connected' with an individual if that person is the individual's spouse or civil partner, or is a relative, or the spouse or civil partner of a relative, of the individual or of the individual's spouse or civil partner. 'Relative' means brother, sister, ancestor or lineal descendant (*ITA 2007, s 993*).

Duration of lease

8.13   There are rules for determining the duration of a 'lease', as follows (*ITTOIA 2005, s 303*):

- **Rule 1** – If–

  (a)   the terms of the lease or any other circumstances make it unlikely that the lease will continue beyond a date before the end of the term for which the lease was granted, and

  (b)   the premium was not substantially greater than it would have been had the term been one ending on that date,

  the lease is treated as ending on that date (or the earliest such date).

  The term 'premium' includes (*ITTOIA 2005, s 303(2A)*):

  –   amounts treated as a premium under *ITTOIA 2005, s 278* (amount treated as lease premium where work required);

  –   sums payable by the tenant under the terms subject to which the lease is granted instead of the whole or a part of the rent for a period;

  –   sums payable by the tenant under the terms subject to which the lease is granted as consideration for the surrender of the lease; and

  –   sums payable by the tenant (otherwise than by way of rent) as consideration for the variation or waiver of a term of the lease.

- **Rule 2** – Where there is provision for the extension of the lease beyond a given date by notice given by the tenant, account may be taken of any circumstances making it likely that the lease will be so extended.

- **Rule 3** – Where the tenant, or a person connected with him, is, or may become, entitled to a further lease or the grant of a further lease (whenever commencing) on the same premises, or on premises including the whole or part of the same premises, the term of the lease may be treated as not expiring before the term of the further lease.

Under this rule, the premium, or an appropriate part of it, payable on or in connection with either of the leases mentioned in the rule, may be treated as having been required under the other lease mentioned (*ITTOIA 2005, s 306(5)*).

The rules above are applied by reference to the facts known or ascertainable at the time of the grant of the lease or, in the case of a variation or waiver of a lease, the facts known or ascertainable at the time of the waiver etc (*ITTOIA 2005, s 304(1)*).

Focus

Where a premium is paid for the grant of a lease of less than 50 years, this is generally treated as being an income payment for tax purposes (as opposed to a capital payment) (see **8.13**). This may also be the case in some situations where the term of the lease is more than 50 years and there are rules designed to prevent leases being artificially extended beyond 50 years by landlords to avoid the tax charge. The legislation also treats work required to be carried out by a tenant as a premium in certain circumstances.

In relation to leases granted on or after 6 April 2013 (1 April 2013 for companies), relief will no longer be available to a trader or intermediate landlord that pays a lease premium on a lease that is only deemed to be short because of the operation of 'Rule 1' in *CTA 2009, s 243* (*FA 2013, s 75* and *Sch 28*).

Example 8.4—Lease premiums (I)

Richard grants a lease of a property known as Sunnyside. The lease is expressed in the deed as being for a 51-year duration. Paul pays a premium of £3,000 in consideration of his being granted the lease. The normal rate that would be expected by way of premium for the grant of a ten-year lease of Sunnyside is £3,000. In addition, the terms of the lease specify that although the rent is £3,000 per year, after ten years the rent required under the lease will rise to £100,000 per year, which is a prohibitive amount for a property such as Sunnyside. This transaction will be caught by Rule 1 above. The lease would be treated as being a ten-year lease, and thus the premium would be regarded as one in respect of a lease of ten years' duration.

Tax treatment

8.14   The tax treatment of lease premiums paid to landlords depends on the length of a lease. If a lease is assigned, or granted for more than 50 years, it is treated as a whole or part disposal for capital gains tax purposes. If the duration of the lease is 50 years or less, part of the lease premium is treated as income in addition to actual rent. The income portion is normally calculated using the following formula:

$$P \times (50 - Y/50)$$

where:

- P = the premium
- Y = the number of complete years of the lease, except the first.

The remainder of the premium is subject to the capital gains tax regime.

The income element of the premium is taxed on the landlord in the year the lease is granted.

The income element of the premium paid by a business tenant may be deducted as a business expense, but is spread evenly over the lease period (*ITTOIA 2005, ss 60–67, 276–307*).

Example 8.6—Tax treatment of lease premium

Bob grants Jean a lease for 21½ years for a premium of £10,000.

	£
Premium	10,000
Less: $(21 - 1) \times 2\% \times £10,000$	(4,000)
Taxable amount	6,000

The part of the premium chargeable is taxable in full in the chargeable period in which the lease is granted.

8.15   In applying the above, it is assumed that all parties concerned act as they would act if they were at arm's length and that, where an unusual benefit is conferred by the lease, the benefit would not have been conferred had the lease been for a period ending on the likely date of determination, rather than on the actual date. The likely date of determination is in most cases the end of the period of the lease. An unusual benefit would be any benefit other than the right to enjoy the beneficial occupation of the premises or the right to receive a reasonable commercial rent in respect of them.

Where provision is made in the lease for the tenant to carry out work instead of paying a premium, the amount by which the landlord's estate has been increased in value by the provision requiring the work to be done is treated as a premium. However, if the work is of a type which, if the landlord and not the tenant were obliged to carry it out, would be deductible from the rent under general rules or as an expense of a property income business, the rule does not apply.

A complex form of relief may also be available (and continues to be available in the case of a property income business), if the premium arises on the grant of a sublease out of a head lease in respect of which a charge under these provisions has previously been made; also if a charge would have been made except for any exemption from tax; similarly, relief may be available if the previous charge arose as a result of the grant of a lease at undervalue.

Where it appears to an HMRC officer that the amount chargeable affects the tax liability of any other person, he may notify those other persons of the amount he proposes to charge. All parties may then object if they so wish and the amount will be determined by the Commissioners as if it were an appeal.

The various payments under the present provisions are taxable in full in the chargeable period in which payment is received.

In general, the whole of a discounted premium is taxable in the relevant chargeable period. However, there is a relief where a premium is payable by instalments: originally, a taxpayer who satisfied HMRC that he would otherwise suffer undue hardship could elect to pay the tax chargeable by such instalments as HMRC might allow over a period not exceeding eight years. As this did not fit with self-assessment, the income or corporation tax payer now has the option to pay tax by instalments over the eight-year period.

Short leases: sale and leaseback income charges

8.16   In addition to the anti-avoidance provisions which deal with the duration of the lease and those which deal with the sale of land with the right to reconveyance, the legislation deals with ascertaining the charge to tax where land is sold and the agreement contains a provision for its lease back to the vendor or a person connected with him (rather than a reconveyance as such) (*ITTOIA 2005, s 285*).

The amount of the premium payable on the grant of the lease, plus the value at the date of sale of the right to purchase the reversion when the lease is granted, is taken to be the reconveyance price. The date of reconveyance is deemed to be the date of the grant of the lease.

> **Example 8.7—Short lease**
>
> A landlord sells the property to the tenant for £30,000 but the agreement gives the landlord the right to take a 999-year lease for £15,000 after ten years.
>
> If the value of the reversion was £500, the landlord would be charged as follows:
>
> £30,000 – (£15,000 + £500) = £14,500 over ten years, discounted in accordance with the provisions treating only a portion of any premium as income.

This type of transaction is frequently used, not as a means of avoidance, but as a bona fide commercial method to finance the development of land; therefore, an express proviso excludes situations where the lease is granted and begins to run within one month after the sale.

The amount deemed to have been received is taken into account in computing profits in the period in which the estate or interest is 'sold'. The estate or interest is treated as 'sold' when any of the following occurs:

- an unconditional contract for its sale is entered into;

- a conditional contract for its sale becomes unconditional; or

- an option or right of pre-emption is exercised requiring the vendor to enter into an unconditional contract for its sale.

Where it appears to HMRC that the amount chargeable affects the tax liability of any other person, they may notify those other persons of the amount that they propose to charge; all parties may then object if they so wish, and the amount will be determined by the Tribunal as if it were an appeal.

Reverse premiums

8.17   Reverse premiums are the sums that landlords pay to induce potential tenants to take a lease.

Reverse premiums received on or after 9 March 1998 are taxable as revenue receipts (*CTA 2009, s 98(1)*). However, the charge to tax does not apply to a premium to which the recipient was entitled immediately before that date, arrangements made on or after that date being ignored for this purpose.

Payments or other benefits made by a landlord to induce potential tenants are treated as taxable income of the tenant, except in certain specific circumstances. Benefits not involving an actual cash outlay by the landlord, such as the grant of rent-free periods of occupation, are not subject to tax (*ITTOIA 2005, ss 99–103*; HMRC Business Income Manual at BIM41050).

Inducements

8.18 The legislation taxes 'a payment or other benefit by way of inducement'. Such an inducement may take the form of a cash payment by the landlords, a period of rent-free occupation, a contribution to the tenant's costs or the assumption by the landlord of the tenant's liabilities. However, not all such inducements are caught by the rules. The following table summarises those inducements that are taxable under the reverse premium provision and those that are not:

Taxable	Non-taxable
Cash payments	The grant of a rent-free period of occupation
Contributions towards specified tenant's costs, eg relocation costs, start-up costs or fitting-out costs	The replacement by agreement of an existing rent with a lower rent because market conditions have made the original rent onerous
Sums paid to third parties to meet obligations of the tenant, eg rent to a landlord due under an old lease or a capital sum to terminate such a lease	A new lease by agreement without an onerous condition present in the former lease
An effective payment of cash by other means, eg the landlord writing off a sum owed by the tenant	

Broadly, inducements are caught if they involve the laying out of money. Benefits representing amounts foregone or deferred are not generally caught as they do not involve an outlay.

Tax treatment of receipts by way of reverse premiums

8.19 For tax purposes, a reverse premium is treated as a revenue receipt taxable under *ITTOIA 2005, s 99*.

The timing of the charge generally follows accepted principles of commercial accounting, the broad effect of which is to spread the reverse premium over the period of the lease, or to the first rent review, whichever is the shorter.

An anti-avoidance provision aims at preventing the exploitation of timing differences by the grant of a lease to a connected person on clearly uncommercial terms (eg a 25-year lease with no rent review clause).

The above provisions do not apply to a payment or benefit:

- if or to the extent that it is taken into account under the capital allowances provision relating to subsidies, contributions etc to reduce the recipient's expenditure qualifying for allowances;

- received in connection with a relevant transaction where the person entering into the transaction is an individual and the transaction relates to premises occupied or to be occupied as his only or main residence; or

- to the extent that it is consideration for the transfer of an estate or interest in land which constitutes the sale in a 'sale and leaseback transaction' as described in *ITA 2007, Pt 12A*.

RENT-A-ROOM RELIEF

Rent-a-room relief

8.20   The rent-a-room scheme is an optional exemption scheme that lets people receive a certain amount of tax-free 'gross' income (receipts before expenses) from renting furnished accommodation in their only or main home. The annual exemption is £7,500 a year for 2016/17 (£3,750 if letting jointly) (*ITTOIA 2005, Pt 7, Ch 1*). For 2015/16 and earlier years, the annual exemption was £4,250 (£2,125 if letting jointly).

Individuals can choose to take advantage of the scheme if they let furnished accommodation in their only or family home to a lodger. A lodger is someone who pays to live in the house, sometimes with meals provided, and who often shares the family rooms.

A lodger can occupy a single room or an entire floor of the house. However, the scheme does not apply if the house is converted into separate flats that are rented out. Nor does the scheme apply to let unfurnished accommodation in the individual's home.

An individual does not need to be a homeowner to take advantage of the scheme. Of course, those who are renting will need to check whether their lease allows them to take in a lodger.

If the lodger is charged for additional services, for example, cleaning and laundry, the individual will need to add the payments they receive to the rent, to work out the total receipts. If income exceeds £7,500 a year in total, a liability to tax will arise, even if the rent is less than that.

> **Focus**
>
> The emergence and growth of peer-to-peer online marketplaces and digital platforms (for example Airbnb) has made it significantly easier to advertise rooms and put those with spare accommodation in touch with a national and global network of potential occupants. HMRC believe that this type of income should not be eligible for rent-a-room relief, but should instead be taxed under the normal property business income rules. Consequently, during 2018, HMRC worked on proposals to introduce a 'shared occupancy' test. The test would provide that the individual, or a member of their household, in receipt of income must have a 'shared occupancy', a physical presence for all or part of the period of the rental, with the individual whose occupation of the furnished accommodation is generating receipts.
>
> Although it was intended that this change would take effect from 6 April 2019, the government announced in the Autumn Budget 2018 that, in order to maintain the simplicity of the system, the legislation would not be included in Finance Bill 2018/19. Therefore, the rules currently remain unchanged, and rent-a-room continues to provide a valuable exemption in many cases.

Rent-a-room scheme and running a business

8.21   The rent-a-room scheme can apply to taxpayers running bed and breakfast businesses or guest houses, or providing catering and cleaning services as part of a letting business. In such cases, the taxpayer must complete the relevant parts of the self-employment pages of their self-assessment tax return.

> **Example 8.8—Rent-a-room: joint residents**
>
> Jo and Sinisha are single persons sharing a house as their main residence. They have for some years taken in lodgers to supplement their income. As Jo pays the greater share of the mortgage interest on the house, she and Sinisha have an agreement to share the rental income in the ratio 2:1, although expenses are shared equally.
>
> Sinisha and Jo have elected for only the excess over the exemption amount to be taxed.
>
> Sinisha has losses of £350 brought forward, which arose from this letting because he elected in one tax year for the exemption not to apply.
>
> For 2015/16, the position is as follows:

	Jo	Sinisha
	£	£
Gross rents (y/e 5.4.16)	4,000	2,000
Allowable expenses	1,250	1,250
Net rents	2,750	750

Sinisha's share of gross rents is below his one-half share of the exempt amount (£2,125), so his election to tax only the excess is deemed to be withdrawn and his share is treated as nil. Jo's election to tax only the excess over the exemption continues to apply, so that her property income assessment will be £1,875 (£4,000 – £2,125).

For 2016/17, the position is as follows:

	Jo	Sinisha
	£	£
Gross rents (y/e 5.4.17)	6,400	3,200
Allowable expenses	2,250	2,250
Net rents	4,150	950

Again, Sinisha's share of gross rents is below his one-half share of the exempt amount (£3,750), so his share is treated as nil and his loss of £350 from the earlier year is once again carried forward. Jo's election to tax only the excess over the exemption continues to apply, so that her property income assessment will be £400 (£4,150 – £3,750).

Interpretation of rent-a-room relief and business use

8.22   Rent-a-room relief is not available to exempt from tax income from the letting of part of a residence as an office or for other business purposes (see the HMRC Property Income Manual at PIM4002). The relief only covers the circumstance where payments are made for the use of living accommodation. However, the relief is not denied where a lodger living in the home is provided with a desk, or the use of a room with a desk, which he or she uses for work or study.

Advantages and disadvantages of the scheme

8.23   There are advantages and disadvantages of the scheme – it is simply a matter of working out what is best for the individual concerned.

The principal point to bear in mind is that those using the rent-a-room scheme cannot claim any expenses relating to the letting (eg wear and tear, insurance, repairs, heating and lighting).

To work out whether it is preferable to join the scheme or declare all of the letting income and claiming expenses via a self-assessment tax return, the following methods of calculation need to be compared:

- *Method A*: paying tax on the profit they make from letting worked out in the normal way for a rental business (ie rents received less expenses).

- *Method B*: paying tax on the gross amount of their receipts (including receipts for any related services they provide) less the £7,500 (or £3,750) exemption limit.

Method A applies automatically unless the taxpayer tells their tax office within the time limit that they want method B – see below.

Once a taxpayer has elected for method B it continues to apply in the future until they tell their tax office they want method A. The taxpayer must tell their tax office within the time limit if they decide they no longer want method B to apply. They may want to do this where the taxable profit is less under method A, or where expenses are more than the rents (so there is a loss).

Example 8.9—Rent-a-room: business use

A taxpayer may have gross receipts of £15,000 but their expenses are £16,000, so they have a loss of £1,000. Unless they opt out of method B, they will still be taxed on the excess of the gross receipts of £15,000 over the exemption limit of £7,500; that is, the taxable profit from letting in their own home will be £7,500.

Example 8.10—Rent-a-room: business use: where method B is better

In 2015/16, Florence lets out a room in her own home for £100 a week. Nobody else lets a room in the house. Her gross receipts for the year are £5,200. She is not exempt from tax because her gross receipts exceed the exemption limit of £4,250. She has expenses of £1,000 so her profit is £4,200. The excess of her receipts over £4,250 is £950 (£5,200 less £4,250).

Using method A, she pays tax on her actual profit of £4,200.

Using method B, she pays tax on a profit of £950.

In Florence's case, method B is better and she elects for it. The profit of £950 is included in Florence's overall business computation if she has other rental business income from lettings outside her home. The profit of £950 will be the only rental business profit if Florence has no other letting income.

Example 8.11—Rent-a-room: business use: where method A is better

In 2015/16, John lets out a room in his own home for a rent of £100 a week plus contributions to the heating and lighting. His total letting receipts for the year from letting the room are £5,200 rent plus £200 for lighting and heating = £5,400. He has expenses of £4,500 so his profit is £900. The excess of his gross receipts over £4,250 is £1,150 (£5,400 less £4,250).

John pays tax on his actual profit of £900 if he uses method A.

John pays tax on a profit of £1,150 if he uses method B.

In John's case, method A is better. Therefore, he either does not elect for method B or, if he has already done so, he tells his tax office that he no longer wants it to apply. The profit of £900 is included in John's overall business computation if he has other rental business income from lettings outside his home. The profit of £900 will be the only rental business profit if John has no other letting income.

Changing from method A to method B, and vice versa

8.24   A taxpayer can change from method A to method B (or vice versa) from year to year. But each time they want to change, they must tell their tax office within the time limit. The assessment is not out of time if it is made on or before the first anniversary of the normal self-assessment filing date for the tax year for which the election was made or notice was given (or treated as given) (*ITTOIA 2005, s 801*).

Method B will automatically cease if the rent drops below the annual exemption limit. The taxpayer will then be automatically exempt from tax unless they ask within the time limit for their actual profit or loss to be taken into account. If, in the following year, their gross receipts go up and they want to use method B again, they must tell their tax office within the time limit. Otherwise, they are automatically taxed on the normal rental business basis (receipts less expenses) (HMRC Property Income Manual at PIM4050).

Alternative method of calculation

8.25   The simplified method of calculation ('method B' above) is contained in *ITTOIA 2005, ss 795–798*, and elections for it are covered in *ITTOIA 2005, s 800*. An individual may elect for the alternative method of calculating profits given in *ss 796–798* to apply if:

(a)   the individual qualifies for rent-a-room relief for a tax year, and

(b)   the individual's total rent-a-room amount for the tax year exceeds the individual's limit for the tax year.

Any balancing charge is not counted in the total for this purpose. Under the alternative method of computation, tax is simply charged on gross receipts less the exemption limit, and no other expenses can be claimed, no capital allowances can be given, but any balancing charge is still taxable.

In practice, balancing charges in a continuing case are likely to be rare. This measure is to prevent exploitation of rent-a-room. It deals, for example, with the case where a taxpayer with a substantial boarding house business might otherwise elect for the alternative basis on a cessation of trading simply to avoid a large balancing charge.

The election must specify the tax year for which it is made, and has effect for that year and subsequent tax years (unless withdrawn by notice given by the individual).

An election or notice of withdrawal must be made or given to an officer of Revenue and Customs on or before the first anniversary of the normal self-assessment filing date for the tax year specified in the election or notice of withdrawal, or such later date as an officer of Revenue and Customs may, in a particular case, allow.

FURNISHED HOLIDAY LETTINGS

Trading income

8.26   The commercial letting of furnished holiday accommodation in the UK has always been treated as a trade, and landlords have been able to benefit from various income tax reliefs afforded to trading profits. Overseas properties were not included in the UK furnished holiday lettings provisions. However, in 2009, it was decided that this might not comply with EU law and the rules had to be amended. Originally, the plan was to end the system altogether but, following representations from various interested groups, it was decided to retain the system, extending it to include both UK and EEA properties but tightening up the rules. *FA 2011* contains the relevant provisions.

The valuable capital gain tax reliefs such as roll-over relief and entrepreneurs' relief, which are usually only allowed for trading companies, were expanded from April 2011 to include both UK and non-UK furnished holiday letting businesses (*FA 2011, s 52* and *Sch 14, paras 14–17*).

Where a person owns and uses plant or machinery at different types of property business (ie both furnished and non-furnished lettings in either the UK or EU), for capital allowance purposes the capital expenditure is to be treated as though the expenditure had been incurred on the date that it was used (or reused) in the second business when it ceased being used in the first business. The amount of qualifying expenditure is treated as the market value of the plant or machinery, or the amount of the original expenditure if lower (*FA 2011, Sch 14, paras 12* and *13*).

> **Focus**
>
> Income from property held jointly by married couples or civil partners living together is treated as arising in equal shares under *ITA 2007, s 836*. The exception to this general rule is for income from furnished holiday lettings in the UK. *FA 2011* confirms this exception for income from EEA furnished holiday lettings.

Commercial letting

8.27   The beneficial tax treatment afforded to furnished holiday lettings applies to the 'commercial letting of furnished holiday accommodation'. 'Commercial letting' requires that the property be let (*ITTOIA 2005, s 323(2)*):

●   on a commercial basis; and

●   with a view to the realisation of 'profits'.

'Profits' here means the 'commercial', not the 'tax adjusted', profit. It should be noted that HMRC take the view that the required income profit motive may be displaced where the taxpayer's motive is the acquisition of a second, or retirement, home, or securing a long-term capital profit on disposing of the property. Claimants may also fail the above requirements where the size of the mortgage used to purchase the property is so large that the projected profitability is jeopardised or the commercial credibility of the scheme as a whole is, consequently, questionable even though individual lettings are on a commercial basis. In such cases, HMRC expect a written business plan to be prepared, with credible figures.

The separation of property income from trading income is a long-established principle in UK tax law. In *Salisbury House Estate Ltd v Fry* (1930) 15 TC 266, Lord Atkin said:

> '… the schedules are mutually exclusive; the specific income must be assessed under the specific schedule.' (page 319)

and Lord MacMillan said:

> 'A landowner may conduct a trade on his premises, but he cannot be represented as carrying on a trade of owning land because he makes an income by letting it.' (page 330)

Lord MacMillan goes on to raise the possibility that a landowner may be providing services which are a separate trade.

The principle of *Salisbury House Estate Ltd v Fry* has often been applied by the courts subsequently.

In practice, it may sometimes be difficult to distinguish between a hotelier and a landlord of property which is let furnished. Generally, the essential distinction is taken to be the extensive degree of exclusive occupation of the accommodation that is granted in the course of a letting as opposed to the much more limited occupation rights of a guest in a hotel or lodging house. In *Griffiths v Jackson* (1982) 56 TC 583, Vinelott J said:

> 'The distinction between a hotelier or a lodging house keeper, on the one hand, and the owner of property who lets furnished rooms and provides services is no doubt in practice a narrow one, more particularly in these days of self-service hotels and motels, but the principle is clear and in the present case there can be no doubt on which side of the line the taxpayers' activities fall. It is quite clear from the terms of the tenancy agreements and the taxpayers' form of letter that they let rooms furnished to tenants, albeit with shared facilities and some services.'

Where the taxpayer seeks relief for losses in the early years of a trade, there is an additional, objective, condition that profits could reasonably be expected to be realised in the year of the loss or within a reasonable time thereafter. HMRC's view is that this test must be considered for each year for which relief is claimed and that it is necessary to look at the year of the loss and whatever, on the facts, is a reasonable time thereafter. And they dissent from a Special Commissioner's view that this relief is available so long as profits may be expected not later than a reasonable time after the end of the statutory four-year period (*Walls v Livesey (HMIT)* [1995] SpC 4).

Holiday lettings – from 6 April 2012

8.28   From April 2012, certain changes apply to the taxation of furnished holiday lettings (*FA 2011, s 52* and *Sch 14*). From that date, the qualifying conditions are as follows (*ITTOIA 2005, s 325*):

(a)   available to let for commercial letting by the public for at least 210 days in a tax year (ie increased from 140 days); and

(b)   actually let for at least 105 days in a tax year (increased from 70 days).

There is an 'averaging election' which can be made for any year where one or more properties fails the 'qualifying period' test. The 'election' treats each of the properties as satisfying the 'day count' test for that year. In the situation where furnished holiday lettings are owned both in the UK and EEA, the averaging election is made separately for each of the two categories of property.

There is a 'period of grace' which will help properties that may meet the 'qualifying period' rules for one year but fail the next. An election needs to be made on or before the 31 January self-assessment filing date for the tax year which will allow the property to be treated as satisfying the 'letting condition' for that coming year. The 'period of grace' can include the following year if required, but must not be made should the 'averaging election' above have already been made. If the election is made for the first year, it need not be made for the second; however, it cannot be made for the second year without also having been made for the first. The 'period of grace' provisions take effect from 6 April 2010 (*ITTOIA 2005, s 326A* inserted by *FA 2011, Sch 14, para 2*).

Losses

8.29   Losses of a property business are calculated in the same way as profits (*ITTOIA 2005, s 272(2)*) (see **8.6**). In relation to furnished holiday lettings, from April 2011 the use of loss relief is restricted, such that losses can only be carried forward against future profits of the same trade. Sideways relief against general income, terminal loss relief and corporation tax relief for the offset of losses against total profits are no longer allowed.

Losses cannot be offset against profits from other non-furnished lettings property income. However, where a business ceases to qualify for one tax year, any losses previously incurred will be available for offset against subsequent profits made from the same property (ie they will not be 'lost').

Example 8.12—Furnished holiday lettings

Mrs Brown owns and lets out furnished holiday cottages. None is ever let to the same person for more than 31 days. Three cottages have been owned for many years, but Rose Cottage was acquired on 1 June 2016 and first let on that day. Rose Cottage was also let for 30 days between 6 April and 31 May 2017.

In 2016/17, days available for letting and days let are as follows:

	Days available	Days let
Honeysuckle Cottage	250	160
Primrose Cottage	200	110
Bluebell Cottage	220	90
Rose Cottage	220	110

Qualification as 'furnished holiday accommodation'

Honeysuckle Cottage qualifies as it meets both the 210-day availability test and the 105-day letting test.

Primrose Cottage does not qualify although it is let for more than 105 days as it fails to satisfy the 210-day test. Averaging (see below) is only possible where it is the 105-day test which is not satisfied.

Bluebell Cottage does not qualify by itself as it fails the 105-day test. However, it may be included in an averaging claim.

Rose Cottage qualifies as furnished holiday accommodation. It was acquired on 1 June 2016, so qualification in 2016/17 is determined by

---

reference to the period of 12 months beginning on the day it was first let, in which it was let for a total of 110 days.

Averaging claim for 2016/17:

	Days let
Honeysuckle Cottage	160
Bluebell Cottage	90
Rose Cottage	110

$$\frac{160 + 90 + 110}{3} = 120 \text{ days}$$

All three cottages included in the averaging claim qualify as furnished holiday lettings, as each is deemed to be let for 120 days in 2016/17.

Reliefs for which furnished holiday lettings are treated as a trade

8.30   Reliefs for which furnished holiday lettings are treated as a trade include:

- retirement annuity relief and personal pensions;

- relief for losses;

- relief for pre-trading expenditure;

- treatment as earned income;

- Landlord's Energy Saving Allowance (LESA);

- rollover relief for capital gains tax;

- relief for gifts of business assets for capital gains tax;

- entrepreneurs' relief; and

- relief in respect of loans to traders for capital gains tax.

Benefits of furnished holiday lettings

8.31   Benefits for the taxpayer of treatment as a trader include the following:

- capital allowances are available for expenditure on plant and machinery acquired for purposes of the letting;

- CGT rollover reliefs are available, where applicable and subject to the usual rules; likewise, relief for gifts of business assets and in respect of loans to traders;

- CGT entrepreneurs' relief may be due on the sale of property; and

- the income attracts retirement annuity or personal pension relief.

It should nevertheless be noted that the 'rent-a room' exemption may prove more advantageous to the taxpayer.

RENT FROM PROPERTY OUTSIDE THE UK

Overview

8.32 Profits of an overseas property business are chargeable to income tax under *ITTOIA 2005 Pt 3, Ch 3* only if the business is carried on by a UK resident.

A person's overseas property business consists of (*ITTOIA 2005, s 265*):

- every business which the person carries on for generating income from land outside the UK; and

- every transaction which the person enters into for that purpose otherwise than in the course of such a business.

The special rules for furnished holiday lettings (see **8.26**) do not apply to overseas properties.

The current fiscal year basis applies to income from properties that were first let on or after 6 April 1994. The basis period is, therefore, the year to 5 April.

Capital allowances are available, but normal capital allowances rules apply.

Computing profit

8.33 The rules for computing the amount of rental profit or loss are the same as those used for UK property income businesses. Every property outside the UK has its profits computed using trading income principles, whatever basis periods are used.

The taxpayer computes the profit or loss for the rental business as a whole and not the result for individual properties. But they will need to make separate computations for tax credit relief purposes. This is to ensure that the overseas tax they pay on income from a property in one foreign country is only set against the UK tax on that property; they cannot set that foreign tax against UK tax due on income from a property in another country.

Travel

8.34 There are special rules for travel connected with overseas trades. These do not apply to rental income. However, deductions may be made for travel costs on the same basis as for UK property income businesses. That is, the taxpayer must be able to show that the travel was incurred wholly and exclusively for business purposes and not (wholly or partly) for some other purpose (such as a holiday).

Losses

8.35 All the overseas properties are treated as a single overseas letting business. Hence, excess expenditure on one overseas property is automatically set against surplus receipts from other overseas properties. Any overall overseas rental business loss can be carried forward and set against future overseas rental business profits; but it cannot be set against UK rental business profits or against any other income.

Foreign tax

8.36 Normally, the tax authorities of the country where the let property is situated will also charge tax on the letting profits. This means that a UK resident landlord will pay tax on the same profits both here and abroad. However, the double charge is relieved by deducting the overseas tax paid on the property income from the UK tax due on the same income. This is done either under the terms of a double taxation treaty with the overseas country or, where no treaty exists, under separate UK rules.

If the overseas income has suffered foreign tax and a claim to tax credit relief is made, it will be necessary, for the purposes of the source by source rules, to identify the amount of UK tax attributable to income from each particular property. Where, therefore, tax credit relief is claimed, separate computations of profits and losses for each property will be required.

For the purposes of calculating tax credit relief, losses should be deducted in the order most favourable to the taxpayer's claim. Normally, this will mean that losses should be allocated first against the source that has suffered the lowest rate of foreign tax.

Example 8.13—Foreign property

A taxpayer has income assessable for 2018/19 from properties in the following countries:

	Country A	Country B	Country C	Total
Income	£6,000	£4,000	£6,000	
Expenses	£1,000	£6,000	£4,000	
Profit (loss)	£5,000	(£2,000)	£2,000	£5,000

The following amounts of foreign tax have been paid:

	Taxable	Rate of foreign tax	Tax deducted
Country A	£5,000	11%	£550
Country B	Nil		
Country C	£2,000	30%	£600
Total foreign tax			£1,150

Assuming that the overseas rental income is wholly chargeable at the basic rate of income tax (and that the basic rate of income tax is 20%), the income tax due will be £5,000 × 20% = £1,000.

Calculation of tax credit relief

Allocate losses to the income that has suffered the lowest rate of foreign tax (income from Country A):

Country A Profit	£5,000
Losses	£2,000
Net	£3,000 @ 20% = £600

All of the foreign tax paid of £550 relating to Country A is available for tax credit relief.

Country C Profit £2,000 @ 20% = £400

Although foreign tax of £600 has been paid, the amount available for tax credit relief is limited to the amount of UK tax charged on the same income (ie £400).

Summary

Income tax due	£600 + £400 =	£1,000
Tax credit relief	£550 + £400 =	(£950)
Net UK tax payable		£50

The balance of Country C's tax of £200 (£600 – £400) cannot be offset against the income tax attributable to the Country A income and cannot be repaid.

Note that, if all or part of the Country B loss of £2,000 had been set against income from Country C, the overall tax bill in the UK would be higher.

NON-RESIDENT LANDLORDS SCHEME

Overview

8.37 The Non-resident Landlords Scheme (NRLS) is a scheme for taxing the UK rental income of non-resident landlords.

The rules governing the scheme are contained in the *Taxation of Income from Land (Non-residents) Regulations 1995 (SI 1995/2902)*.

The HMRC website contains much useful information on the scheme at https://www.gov.uk/tax-uk-income-live-abroad/rent.

The scheme requires UK letting agents, referred to as 'non-resident landlord representatives', to deduct basic rate tax from any rent they collect for non-resident landlords. If non-resident landlords do not have UK letting agents acting for them, and the rent is more than £100 a week, their tenants must deduct the tax. When working out the amount to tax, the letting agent/tenant can take off deductible expenses.

Letting agents and/or tenants do not have to deduct tax if approval is obtained from HMRC. But, even though the rent may be paid with no tax deducted, it remains liable to UK tax. So, non-resident landlords must include it in any tax return that HMRC send to them.

A 'non-resident landlord representative' is defined as (*ITA 2007, s 971(3)*):

'(a) a person by whom any sums are payable to the non-resident which are to be treated as receipts of a UK property business (within the meaning of *Chapter 2 of Part 3 of ITTOIA 2005* or *Chapter 2 of Part 4 of CTA 2009*), carried on by the non-resident, or

(b) a person who acts on behalf of the non-resident in connection with the management or administration of any such business.'

Applications for payments with no tax deducted

8.38 Non-resident landlords who are eligible can apply at any time for approval to receive their UK rental income with no tax deducted. This includes applying before they have left the UK or before the letting has started.

When approval has been given, HMRC send a notice of approval to receive rent with no tax deducted to the non-resident landlord, and a separate notice to the letting agents or tenants named on the application form authorising them to pay rent to the non-resident landlord without deducting tax.

Authority to pay rent to a non-resident landlord with no tax deducted is generally backdated to the beginning of the quarter in which HMRC receive the non-resident landlord's application.

As the tax year for the NRLS starts on 1 April, the quarters are the three-month periods that end on 30 June, 30 September, 31 December and 31 March. So, if a non-resident landlord applies to HMRC on, say, 20 September, the authority they send to his letting agent/tenant will usually take effect from 1 July.

HMRC may refuse approval if they are not satisfied that the information in the application is correct, or the non-resident landlord will comply with their UK tax obligations.

HMRC may withdraw approval if:

- they are no longer satisfied that the information in the application is correct;

- they are no longer satisfied that the non-resident landlord will comply with their UK tax obligations; or

- the non-resident landlord fails to supply information requested by HMRC.

Where HMRC refuse, or withdraw, approval to receive rent with no tax deducted, the non-resident landlord can appeal to them within 90 days.

Where HMRC and the non-resident landlord cannot reach agreement, the appeal will be referred to the tax tribunal.

HMRC will tell an agent/tenant not to deduct tax if the non-resident landlord has successfully applied for approval to receive rents with no tax deducted. But rent paid with no tax deducted remains liable to UK tax. So, non-resident landlords must include it in any tax return that HMRC send to them.

All non-resident landlords who receive rents with no tax deducted will have a tax district.

Some individuals who are not resident in the UK for tax purposes are not sent an annual tax return automatically, even though they have UK rental income. This is because many non-residents will have sufficient UK personal allowances to cover any liability.

Conditions for approval

8.39 Non-resident landlords can apply to receive their rent with no tax deducted, on the basis that either:

- their UK tax affairs are up to date;

- they have not had any UK tax obligations before they applied;

- they do not expect to be liable to UK income tax for the year in which they apply; or

- they are not liable to pay UK tax because they are Sovereign Immunes (these are generally foreign Heads of State, governments or government departments).

'Usual place of abode'

8.40   Although HMRC refer to 'non-resident' landlords, it is usual place of abode and not non-residence that determines whether a landlord is within the scheme or not.

In the case of individuals, HMRC normally regard an absence from the UK of six months or more as meaning that a person has a usual place of abode outside the UK. It is therefore possible for a person to be resident in the UK yet, for the purposes of the scheme, have a usual place of abode outside the UK.

Letting agents

8.41   A letting agent is a person who:

- has a 'usual place of abode' (see **8.40**) in the UK;

- acts for a non-resident landlord in the running of their UK rental business;

- has the power to receive income of the non-resident landlord's rental business, or has control over the direction of that income; and

- is not an 'excluded person'.

An excluded person is someone whose activity on behalf of a non-resident landlord is confined to providing legal advice/services. However, solicitors who draw up a lease and collect the rent for the first period are not excluded persons.

Focus

HMRC produce comprehensive online guidance for the NRLS. *Non-resident Landlords – Guidance Notes for Letting Agents and Tenants* can be found on the gov.uk website at www.gov.uk/government/publications/non-resident-landord-guidance-notes-for-letting-agents-and-tenants-non-resident-landlords-scheme-guidance-notes.

Letting agents' obligations

8.42   Letting agents that have to operate the NRLS must:

- register with HMRC's (see the gov.uk website at www.gov.uk/guidance/paying-tax-on-rent-to-landlords-abroad for further information on registration);

- account quarterly for the tax due under the scheme by 5 July following the year ended 31 March;

- complete an annual information return; and

- where they have deducted tax, give the non-resident landlord a tax deduction certificate NRL6.

Tenants

8.43   Tenants of non-resident landlords have to operate the scheme if:

- the rent that they pay is over £100 a week; and

- either:

    - they pay the rent direct to a non-resident landlord;

    - they pay the rent to a person outside the UK; or

- they pay the rent to a person who is not a letting agent in the UK.

HMRC's PTI may sometimes instruct tenants to operate the scheme even where the rent paid is less than £100 a week.

Tenants' obligations

8.44   Tenants who have to operate the NRLS have to:

- account quarterly for any tax due under the scheme by 5 July following each year ended 31 March;

- give the non-resident landlord a tax deduction certificate NRL6; and

- complete an annual information return.

HM Armed Forces personnel and other Crown Servants

8.45   The NRLS applies to members of HM Armed Forces and other Crown Servants – for example, diplomats – if they have a 'usual place of abode' outside the UK. They are treated no differently from any other non-resident landlords, even though their employment duties overseas are treated as performed in the UK for the purpose of charging their salaries to tax. So if their absence from the UK is for more than six months, they are within the scheme.

Administration of the scheme

8.46   The NRLS is administered by HMRC. Completed NRL applications should be sent to:

Charities, Savings and International 1
HM Revenue and Customs
BX9 1AU

For further information, contact the Non-Resident Landlord Scheme Helpline on 03000 516 644.

Expenses

8.47   Letting agents or tenants must generally tax the rental income they pay to non-resident landlords unless HMRC have told them not to. In calculating the amount to tax, they take into account any 'deductible expenses' they pay in a quarter. These are expenses that they can reasonably be satisfied will be allowable expenses for the non-resident landlords when the profits of their rental businesses are computed.

Allowable expenses of a rental business

8.48   Broadly, in calculating the profits of a rental business, expenses are allowable where:

- they are incurred wholly and exclusively for the purposes of the rental business; and

- they are not of a 'capital' nature.

Expenses paid by letting agents and tenants which will normally be allowable expenses are:

- accountancy expenses for the rental business;

- advertising costs of attracting new tenants;

- cleaning;

- costs of rent collection;

- council tax while the property is vacant but available for letting;

- gardening;

- ground rent;

- insurance on buildings and contents;

- interest paid on loans to buy land or property;

- interest paid on loans to build or improve premises;

- legal and professional fees;

- maintenance charges made by freeholders, or superior leaseholders, of leasehold property;

- maintenance contracts (eg gas servicing);

- provision of services (eg gas, electricity, hot water);

- rates;

- repairs which are not significant improvements to the property, including:

  - mending broken windows, doors, furniture, cookers, lifts, etc,

  - painting and decorating,

  - replacing roof slates, flashing and gutters; and

450

- water rates.

Letting agents and tenants can deduct only those expenses which they pay or which are paid on their direction. This means they cannot deduct:

- expenses which the landlord pays, even if they have details of the expenses;

- expenses which have accrued in a quarter but which have not been paid in the quarter;

- capital allowances; and

- any personal allowances due to the landlord.

Calculating the tax due

8.49   In order to calculate the tax due, the letting agents/tenants should:

- add together the rent they actually receive in the quarter plus:

  - any rent that they had the power to receive, and

  - any rent paid away at their direction to another person,

- less:

  - any deductible expenses that they paid in the quarter; and

  - any deductible expenses that were paid away in the quarter at their direction by another person.

It is the date on which the letting agents/tenants actually receive/pay the rents (or pay the deductible expenses) that determines when they calculate tax. The periods for which the rents (or expenses) are due are not relevant.

Example 8.14—Non-resident landlord (I)

Anytown Lettings Ltd is due to collect rental income of £5,000 a quarter for Mr Anderson, who is a non-resident landlord. In one quarter, it collects only £2,500. It pays out £200 for gardening and cleaning.

The calculation is:

	£
Rental income received	2,500
Less deductible expenses paid	200
	2,300

Basic rate tax (at 20%) on £2,300 = £460

Example 8.15—Non-resident landlord (II)

Anytown Lettings Ltd is due to collect rental income of £3,000 a quarter for Mr Brown, a non-resident landlord. But Anytown Lettings Ltd authorises the tenant to pay £1,000 to a third party in settlement of a loan (this is not a deductible expense).

The calculation is:

	£
Rental income received	2,000
Plus rental income paid away at Anytown Lettings Ltd's direction	1,000
	3,000

Basic rate tax (at 20%) on £3,000 = £600

Example 8.16—Non-resident landlord (III)

If, in Example 8.15, Anytown Lettings Ltd had authorised the tenant to pay £1,000 to a builder to repair a leaking roof, instead of the payment to a third party to repay a loan, the £1,000 would be a deductible expense. The calculation would then be:

	£
Rental income received	2,000
Plus rental income paid away at Anytown Lettings Ltd's direction	1,000
Less deductible expenses	(1,000)
	2,000

Basic rate tax (at 20%) on £2,000 = £400

Tenant-finders

8.50   Some people enter into arrangements with non-resident landlords whereby they find a tenant for the landlord's property. The tenant-finder then collects rent for a period from which he or she recovers the fee. The tenant subsequently pays rental income directly to the landlord. In such circumstances the tenant-finder does not have to operate the NRLS in respect of the landlord, provided:

- the period for which rent is collected is no more than three months; and
- the tax which would be payable would be no more than £100.

Example 8.17—Tenant-finders (I)

Mr Jones finds a tenant for a non-resident landlord in respect of a property rented at £500 per month. Mr Jones collects two months' rent in order to recover his fee of £700. The tenant pays the rent direct to the landlord from the third month.

If Mr Jones were required to operate the scheme, his tax calculation would be:

	£
Rental income received	1,000
Less deductible expenses	700
	300

Basic rate tax on £300 = £60

As the tax is less than £100, Mr Jones does not have to operate the scheme.

Example 8.18—Tenant-finders (II)

Mrs McGregor finds a tenant for a non-resident landlord in respect of a property rented at £2,000 a year. Mrs McGregor collects six months' rent in advance, from which she recovers her fee of £500. She also pays insurance and repairs of £400.

Mrs McGregor's tax calculation is:

	£
Rental income received	1,000
Less deductible expenses	900
	100

Basic rate tax (at 20%) on £100 = £20

The tax is only £20 but, because Mrs McGregor collects more than three months' rent, she must operate the scheme. She should deduct the tax of £20 and pay it with her quarterly return.

Where tenant-finders collect a period's rent and do not have to operate the scheme, the non-resident landlord will receive rental income with no tax deducted for that period. Subsequently, tenants will pay rent direct to the landlord and may have to operate the scheme. In these circumstances, it would be helpful if tenant-finders notify the tenant of his or her obligations under the NRLS.

Record-keeping requirements and penalties

8.51   Letting agents and tenants must keep adequate records to satisfy HMRC auditors that they have complied with their obligations under the scheme. In particular, for each non-resident landlord, letting agents and tenants should keep separately:

- a record of rental income received by the letting agent or paid by the tenant (showing the date and amount of each receipt or payment);

- copies of any correspondence with the landlord regarding their usual place of abode;

- unless the letting agent is authorised to pay rental income with no tax deducted, a record of expenses paid (showing the date and amount of each payment and a brief description of the expense); and

- invoices and receipts (or copies) to provide evidence of expenses paid.

Letting agents and tenants should retain records for six years after the end of the year to 31 March to which they relate.

Penalties may be charged under *TMA 1970, s 98* for failure to make a return or for making an incorrect return.

ANNUAL TAX ON ENVELOPED DWELLINGS

8.52   An enveloped dwelling is an interest in a single residential property located in the UK, owned by a non-natural person, which includes companies, collective investment schemes (unit trusts) and partnerships with corporate members. Such structures have been used in the past to avoid stamp duty land tax (SDLT) and capital gains tax on the transfer of the residential property.

To discourage such tax avoidance the government introduced three measures which apply to enveloped dwellings owned by non-natural persons:

- SDLT on purchase at 15% – effective from 22 March 2012;

- annual tax on enveloped dwellings (ATED) – effective from 6 April 2013; and

- CGT charge at 28% on gains made on disposal where the ATED has applied.

These measures first applied to enveloped dwellings worth over £2m, but that threshold has gradually been reduced to over £500,000 (*FA 2015, Sch 8, paras 3, 4*).

The main points are summarised in the following paragraphs, but, for further commentary, see *Capital Gains Tax 2018/19 (*Chapter 10*)* and *Stamp Taxes 2018/19 (*Chapter 2*)* (both from Bloomsbury Professional).

The ATED is a charge which is levied annually on owners of high-value UK residential property which is held by a non-natural person. The amount of the charge is based on the value of the property, and the band into which the property falls (*FA 2013, s 99*). Current rates are as follows (*SI 2016/401*):

Property value	Annual tax 2017/18	Annual tax 2018/19	Annual tax 2019/20
£500,000 – £1m	£3,500	£3,600	£3,650
£1m – £2m	£7,050	£7,250	£7,400
£2m – £5m	£23,550	£24,250	£24,800
£5m – £10m	£54,950	£56,550	£57,900
£10m – £20m	£110,100	£113,400	£116,100
£20m and over	£220,350	£226,950	£232,350

Properties will need to be revalued every five years. For properties whose values fall within 10% of the thresholds, there is a facility to agree a value with HMRC.

There are a number of anti-avoidance rules designed to prevent the ATED being circumvented. For example, it is not possible to grant a lease to a connected person and then argue that this has reduced the value of the property interest retained by the non-natural person.

There are reliefs available to eliminate the tax, but these need to be claimed in an ATED return. The reliefs from ATED may be available for properties:

- let to an unconnected third party on a commercial basis;
- held for charitable purposes;
- open to the public for at least 28 days per annum;
- that are part of a property trading business;
- for the use of employees of the company, for the company's commercial business and where the employee does not have an interest (directly or indirectly) in the company of more than 5%;
- that are farmhouses, if they are occupied by the farmer who farms the associated farmland full-time and the farmhouse is of an appropriate character; or

- held as part of a commercial property development business, where the property was purchased with the intention to redevelop and sell it on, and the property is not at any time occupied by anyone connected with the owner.

There are also special rules for alternative finance arrangements, and there are exemptions for diplomatic properties and some other publicly owned residential properties.

Chapter 9

Trusts and estates

SIGNPOSTS

- A trust is the relationship which exists where a person or persons hold property for the benefit of others. Where property is set aside on trust for beneficiaries, the property may be referred to as 'settled' or 'comprised in a settlement'. These two terms are often used interchangeably (see **9.1**).

- For 2019/20, the trust rate remains at 45% and the dividend trust rate remains at 38.1% (see **9.6**).

- Trustees' management expenses (TMEs) are paid out of taxed income and cannot, therefore, be relieved against trust income. However, TMEs are deductible in computing the trust rate (with discretionary powers) in full or in part (see **9.8**).

- Special rules apply to the taxation of trustees acting for incapacitated persons (see **9.10**).

- Several types of trust exist, and different taxation rules apply to each (see **9.15–9.24**).

- There are two sets of rules for deciding trustees' residence status: one for income tax, and the other for capital gains. The residence status for income tax purposes can be different from that for capital gains (see **9.25**).

- Penalty provisions apply to late filing of tax returns and late payments of tax (see **9.33**).

- Separate provisions apply for the taxation of estates in administration (see **9.36**).

- An income tax charge may arise on benefits received by the former owners of property, referred to as the 'pre-owned assets' rules (see **9.48**).

TRUSTS AND SETTLEMENTS

Trust or settlement

9.1   A 'settlement' is sometimes referred to as a trust, implying that they share the same meaning. However, a settlement can include any disposition, trust, covenant, agreement, arrangement or transfer of assets.

From 6 April 2006, settled property is redefined as any property held in trust other than property held as nominee, bare trustee for a person absolutely entitled, an infant or disabled person (*Taxation of Chargeable Gains Act 1992 (TCGA 1992), s 60*). References in the legislation to a settlement are construed as references to settled property and the meaning of settlement is determined by case law. This measure effectively aligns what is treated as a settlement for the general purposes of income tax and tax on chargeable gains (*FA 2006, ss 88 and 89, Schs 12 and 13*).

The effect is that income tax will be charged on income arising to the trustees of a 'settlement' with the definition of settlement being derived from existing trust law and case law, and 'settled property' being defined in the tax legislation.

The existing definition of settlement in *Income Tax (Trading and Other Income) Act 2005 (ITTOIA 2005), s 620* still applies for the purposes of the settlements anti-avoidance legislation.

Since 6 April 2006, the trustees of a settlement have been treated as a single person for income tax and capital gains tax purposes.

The settlements legislation can apply if an individual enters into an arrangement to divert income to someone else, resulting in a tax saving. If those arrangements are bounteous, or uncommercial, or not at arm's length, or (for gifts between spouses or civil partners) wholly or substantially a right to income, the settlements rules can apply to cancel the income tax advantage.

Focus

In recent years, the term 'settlement' has been used with increasing frequency in tax legislation. There is no general definition of the term within the legislation, and so its meaning has historically been determined by case law. Settled property is, however, defined as any property held in trust other than property held as nominee, bare trustee for a person 'absolutely entitled', an infant or disabled person (*ITA 2007, s 466(2), (3)*). This measure effectively aligns what is treated as a settlement for the general purposes of income tax and capital gains tax.

Note that a 'settlement' can be wider than a trust for tax purposes; for example, a joint bank account which is funded by a gift will be a settlement in certain circumstances.

The law was examined in *Wagstaff v Revenue and Customs Commissioners* [2014] UKFTT 43 (TC). The three certainties to establish a trust – certainty of intention, subject matter and objects – were referred to by the Tribunal and need to be present to establish a valid trust.

Trust documentation

9.2 Under self-assessment, HMRC generally rely on information shown by trustees, settlors and beneficiaries in their annual tax returns or repayment claims. They do not usually request a copy of a new family trust document (HMRC Trusts, Settlements and Estates Manual at TSEM1705). When a new trust is created, trustees are sent a form which asks them to give some basic factual information about the identities of the trustees and settlor and whether the trustees can accumulate income or distribute it at their discretion.

Trust income

9.3 A trust broadly arises when assets are transferred to trustees, who hold them on behalf of one or more beneficiaries. A trust is usually created by a written document, possibly during an individual's lifetime or perhaps by a will upon death.

For the purpose of determining liability for income tax, the liability of trustees to tax on income of a trust fund must not be confused with the liability of a beneficiary to tax on distributions from a trust fund.

The rate of tax borne by trustees depends largely on whether the trust is a discretionary trust, or whether a beneficiary is absolutely entitled to the trust income.

Trust income is treated as the highest part of a settlor's total income (*ITTOIA 2005, s 619A*).

Trust income may be treated as the settlor's for income tax purposes where (*ITTOIA 2005, ss 619–648*):

- the settlor (or spouse or civil partner) retains an interest in the settled property (for example, as trust beneficiaries);

- an unmarried child of the settlor who is under the age of 18 receives settlement income (to the extent that the income exceeds £100 for a particular child); or

- capital sums (eg loans) are paid by the trustees to the settlor (or spouse/ civil partner). Such amounts may be treated as the settlor's income for the year, within certain limits.

Focus

HMRC belatedly recognised that the combined effect of the 2016/17 introduction of the revised dividend rates with its removal of the notional dividend tax credit and the cessation of tax withholding at source for most interest receipts would have caused a substantial increase in the number of trusts that should register under self-assessment. Following representations from the various professional bodies, HMRC announced as an interim measure for 2016/17 that trustees would not need to register under self-assessment to report savings interest income alone if the income tax liability concerned was under £100 in total provided that the trust has no other income. HMRC confirmed that this relaxation in reporting requirements also applies for 2017/18 and in the HMRC Trusts and Estates Newsletter dated December 2017, this has been further extended to 2018/19.

The modified reporting relaxation does not apply to discretionary or accumulation trusts with savings income in excess of the standard rate band.

Settlor

9.4   *Income Tax Act 2007 (ITA 2007), s 467* defines a settlor for income tax purposes. This is based on the wider definition in the settlements anti-avoidance legislation. The measure took effect from 6 April 2006 and affects settlements whenever created.

A person is a settlor in relation to a settlement if it was made (or treated as made) by that person directly or indirectly, or if it arose on his or her death. A settlor of property means that which is settled or derived from settled property and a person is treated as having made a settlement if he or she has provided (or undertaken to do so) property directly or indirectly for the settlement. If A enters into a settlement where there are reciprocal arrangements with B, B is treated as the settlor for these purposes.

With effect from 6 April 2006 in relation to settlements whenever created, *ITA 2007, s 470* identifies the settlor where there is a transfer of property between settlements made for no consideration or less than full consideration. Where property is disposed of from settlement 1 and acquired by settlement 2 (even if in a different form), the settlor(s) of settlement 1 will be treated as the settlor(s) of settlement 2, unless the transfer occurs because of a will variation.

9.5   *ITA 2007, s 472* identifies the settlor in relation to will and intestacy variations occurring on or after 6 April 2006 regardless of the deceased's date of death. The measure applies where there is a variation in accordance with *TCGA 1992, s 62(6)* and property which was not settled property under the will becomes settled. In this case, a person mentioned in the group below is treated as having made the settlement and providing the property for it (*ITA 2007, s 472(3)*):

- a person who immediately before the variation was entitled to the property, or to property from which it derives, absolutely as legatee (as defined);

- a person who would have become entitled to the property, or to property from which it derives, absolutely as legatee but for the variation;

- a person who immediately before the variation would have been entitled to the property, or to property from which it derives, absolutely as legatee but for being an infant or other person under a disability; and

- a person who would, but for the variation, have become entitled to the property, or to property from which it derives, absolutely as legatee if he had not been an infant or other person under a disability.

If property would have been comprised in a settlement as a result of the deceased's will but the effect of the variation is that it becomes comprised in another settlement, the deceased will be treated as the settlor. He or she will also be the settlor if an existing settlement of which the deceased was settlor becomes comprised in another settlement. In both cases, the deceased is treated as having made the settlement immediately before his or her death unless the settlement arose on the person's death.

Trustees' income tax position

9.6   Trustees are liable to tax on trust income (whether by deduction or direct assessment) at the basic rate. From 6 April 2004, the special rate of tax applicable to trusts (now referred to as the trust rate) was increased from 34% to 40%, ie the same as the higher rate of income tax. The trust rate is currently 45% (2013/14 to 2019/20; it was 50% in 2012/13). The special trust rate does not apply to the first £1,000 of 'trust rate income', where the normal income tax rates apply, as appropriate (*ITA 2007, s 491(1)–(3)*). Anti-avoidance measures prevent multiple standard rate bands from being obtained where a settlor has made more than one settlement (*ITA 2007, s 492*). This restricts the band to the lesser of £200, or £1,000 divided by the number of settlements made by the same settlor.

Any one or more of several trustees is assessable and chargeable in respect of the trust income. However, trustees are regarded as representing the beneficiaries and are not treated as individuals for tax purposes, ie their personal circumstances are disregarded. Thus, trustees cannot set their own entitlement to personal reliefs against trust income. Further, resident trustees are not liable to tax on foreign income paid directly to a non-UK domiciled beneficiary, though a UK-resident beneficiary may be liable to tax on income arising to non-resident trustees under certain anti-avoidance provisions (see **9.25**).

The trustees of a settlement are treated as a single person for both income tax and capital gains tax purposes.

Trust income is assessed under the provisions appropriate to its source: eg income from a trade is assessed under *ITTOIA 2005* and the trustees are entitled to claim any relief applying to that source of income (eg loss relief).

Employee share schemes

9.7   Trustees of employee share schemes are exempt from income tax in respect of interest received from such individuals to the extent that it is matched by interest paid to the company (*ITTOIA 2005, s 752(1), (2)*).

Trustees' management expenses

9.8   Trustees' management expenses (TMEs) are paid out of taxed income and cannot, therefore, be relieved against trust income for the purposes of basic or lower rate tax (prior to 6 April 2008) (*ITA 2007, Pt 9, Ch 8*). However, TMEs are deductible in computing the trust rate (with discretionary powers) in full or in part.

To be an allowable TME, an item must at least be an expense. Not all payments out of the trust can be categorised as expenses. Some are distributions.

A distribution is a payment out of the trust that is either itself a gift made directly to the beneficiary, or is payment to a third party that procures a benefit for a beneficiary (as distinct from a benefit to the trust funds). Examples of distributions are:

- payment of cash or a grant to a beneficiary;

- the costs of procuring a benefit in kind for a beneficiary, such as the payment of a beneficiary's utility bills; and

- the cost of providing gifts, medical treatment, support or entertainment to beneficiaries.

Distributions are not expenses, and so are never allowable TMEs.

TMEs are not like any other expenses for tax purposes.

There is a common misconception that they are on a par with tax deductions for trading. Where a trust carries on a trade, the normal trading income rules apply to the computation of the profit/loss of that trade. In contrast, TMEs are expenses incurred in the capacity of trustee, not in any other capacity such as a trader. They are not related to the expenses or deductions of a trade or rental business. Even if a large trust is run like a business, for TMEs' purposes the rules for allowable trading deductions are not in point. A separate set of principles, legislation and case law apply.

TMEs are the expenses of managing the trust, not the expenses taken into account in computing the profit/loss of a trade. The more common tax notions of 'capital' and 'income', eg construction of a new building versus repairs, do not apply. What is relevant is 'capital' and 'income' in trust law.

The allowance of TMEs for tax purposes is based, to a large extent, on trust law (see eg *Carver v Duncan* [1985] AC 1082).

9.9   In managing a trust, the trustees may incur expenses in the course of exercising their duties and powers. These are to be distinguished from payments made to beneficiaries (distributions).

Expenses may be referred to as 'capital' or 'income' expenses, depending on which fund they are to be paid out of. For an expense to be properly chargeable to income in trust law the trustees must have authority to put the final burden of that expense on the income fund.

The administrative powers of trustees derive from four sources, any one or more of which might apply:

(1)   an order of the court in a specific case;

(2)   the provisions of the trust deed;

(3)   trust statute; and

(4)   general law in the field of trusts and equity (including principles to be discerned from case law).

In order to decide whether expenses are to be paid out of capital or income, trust law looks at the four sources in the above order. So, for example, for trust law purposes, a court order has priority over the provisions of the trust deed, and the provisions of the trust deed have priority over general trust law.

The main case on trust management expenses is *Carver v Duncan* [1985] AC 1082. The more recent case of *Trustees of the Peter Clay Discretionary Trust v Revenue and Customs Comrs* [2007] SpC 595 offers some further guidance in this area. In that case, the trustees claimed certain expenses (ie trustees' fees, investment management fees, bank charges, custodian fees and professional fees for accountancy services), some of which contained elements of both income and capital. The Special Commissioners held that, in principle, a proportion of all the expenses, apart from the investment management fees, was attributable to income and properly chargeable to income for the purposes of *Income and Corporation Taxes Act 1988 (ICTA 1988), s 686(2AA)* (now *ITA 2007, s 484*). In addition, the Commissioners held that the accruals basis was a proper way of allocating trust management expenses to particular tax years, as opposed to when such expenses were incurred and paid.

Whilst the decision will clearly be welcomed by most trustees and professional advisers, in appropriate cases they will be required to apply their judgment in apportioning trust management expenses between income and capital. This could be the 'trigger' for enquiries by HMRC and possible disagreements over the correct proportions to be used. Full disclosure of the expenses apportioned and the basis of apportionment will be necessary in such cases, to reduce the possibility of a subsequent 'discovery' by HMRC outside the normal enquiry window.

Trustees acting for incapacitated persons

9.10   The trustee, guardian, tutor, etc of any incapacitated person is chargeable to income tax to the extent that the incapacitated person would be charged and assessed. This is so where the trustee, etc has the direction, control or management of the property of the incapacitated person, whether or not that person resides in the UK.

A new tax regime for certain trusts with vulnerable beneficiaries took effect from 6 April 2004 (*FA 2005, s 23*). Certain trusts and beneficiaries can elect into the regime and, where a claim for special tax treatment is made for a tax year, no more tax will be payable in respect of the relevant income and gains of the trust for that year than would be paid had the income and gains accrued directly to the beneficiary.

A 'vulnerable beneficiary' is defined as (*FA 2005, ss 38–39*):

- a disabled person, including cases where a person is receiving kidney treatment or is living in certain prescribed accommodation; or

- a child under the age of 18 when at least one of his parents have died (subsequent remarriage by the surviving parent is disregarded).

Income and gains arising from the property held on qualifying trusts for the benefit of a vulnerable person will be eligible for the special tax treatment. This treatment does not apply in cases where the settlor is regarded as having an interest in the property from which the qualifying trusts income arose (*FA 2005, s 24*).

Broadly, the amount of income tax relief due is the difference between two amounts. The first of those amounts is what (were it not for the rules in *FA 2005*) the income tax liability of the trustees would be in respect of the qualifying trusts income for the tax year. The second amount is the amount of extra tax to which the vulnerable person would be liable if the qualifying trusts income were that person's own income (see **9.24** for further details) (*FA 2005, ss 26–29*).

The tax legislation relating to vulnerable beneficiary trusts was amended by *Finance Act 2013* (*FA 2013, s 216* and *Sch 44*), to ensure that the tax benefits for these trusts are appropriately targeted following the introduction of the *Welfare Reform Act 2012*. The definition of a 'qualifying person' has been amended to include those in receipt of the personal independence payment (PIP) by virtue of entitlement to the daily living component at either the standard or enhanced rate.

In addition, the capital and income rules have been harmonised, so that the capital or income is applied for the benefit of the vulnerable beneficiary. However, trustees will be able to apply small amounts of income and capital without having to prove that it is for the benefit of the vulnerable beneficiary. This amount is the lower of £3,000 or 3% of the trust fund each year (*FA 2005, s 35(4B)*, as amended). There will be no roll-over of unused amounts. The measure took effect from 8 April 2013. Transitional arrangements apply where a trust ceases to be a qualifying vulnerable beneficiary trust by reason only of the revised income and capital conditions.

Finance Act 2014 contains further measures which expand the range of trusts qualifying for the special income (and CGT/IHT) treatment and enable the CGT uplift to apply on the death of the vulnerable beneficiary (*FA 2014, s 291*).

Example 9.1—Discretionary trust with vulnerable beneficiary

Charles qualifies as a vulnerable beneficiary of a discretionary trust. The trustees make an election and claim in relation to rental income of £10,000 received by the trust in 2018/19. Charles's gross income in 2018/19 is £12,000 bank interest.

The trustee's income tax liability for the year is as follows:

	Gross	Tax
	£	£
Bank interest	12,000	–
Rental income	10,000	
	22,000	–
Less:		
Personal allowance	(11,850)	
Savings allowance	(1,000)	
Taxable income	9,150	
Tax due:		
£9,150 × 20%		1,830

If a claim had not been made, the trustees' income tax liability would have been as follows:

	Gross	Tax
	£	£
Rental income	10,000	

Tax due:

Basic rate band £1,000 × 20%	200
(10,000 – 1,000) × 45%	4,050
	4,250

Note: The *Finance (No 2) Act 2017* introduction of £1,000 property allowance is not available to trusts (bare trust excepted).

Focus

An election for the special tax treatment to apply must be made jointly by the trustees and the beneficiary and specify the commencement date. It must be made by 31 January following the tax year in which the commencement date falls (*FA 2005, s 37*). The election will be effective until the trust terminates, the trust ceases to be a qualifying trust, or the beneficiary ceases to be a vulnerable beneficiary.

Beneficiaries' income

9.11   To determine whether trust income is treated as the income of the beneficiary as it arises, or only on distribution to him, depends on whether the beneficiary has a vested or contingent interest in the income of the trust fund. If a beneficiary would have an interest in possession had a trust had effect under English law, he is so treated if it has effect under Scots law and the trustees are UK-resident (*ITA 2007, s 464*).

The following possibilities may arise.

(i) Adult beneficiary with a vested interest in income

The income is regarded as the beneficiary's income as it arises, even though it may not be paid over to him.

Example 9.2—Adult beneficiary

The settlor of a trust directs the trustees to accumulate the income of the trust fund and to hold it along with the income for James upon his attaining 18 years of age. James becomes 18 but directs the trustees to receive the income from the trust fund and to continue to invest and accumulate it. Until James reaches his 18th birthday, he cannot demand the income be paid to him. Once he is 18, both the capital and income become his and the trustees continue to accumulate only at James' sufferance.

(ii) Infant beneficiary with a vested interest in income

If the beneficiary has an indefeasible vested interest, the income is treated as the beneficiary's as it arises. If there is a power of accumulation (eg the statutory power of maintenance and accumulation in *Trustee Act 1925, s 31*), the beneficiary is treated as having a contingent interest.

> **Example 9.3—Minor beneficiary**
>
> Matthew, currently a minor, becomes entitled to a vested interest in certain estates. The trustees accumulate income, in accordance with *Trustee Act 1925, s 31*, until Matthew is 18. During his minority, Matthew is in the same position as if his interest was a contingent one and the income does not become his until he reaches 18.

(iii) Beneficiary with a contingent interest

Trust income is not regarded as the beneficiary's unless it is paid to him, eg under a discretionary power. A beneficiary with a contingent interest in the capital of a trust fund is, nevertheless, entitled to the income of the trust fund arising after he attains 18 years of age if *Trustee Act 1925, s 31* (above) applies.

Income applied for beneficiary's benefit

9.12   Income used at the discretion of trustees for the maintenance, education or benefit of a beneficiary is treated as the beneficiary's income in the year of receipt. The beneficiary is treated as having received the grossed-up amount. However, in some cases the income is treated as that of the settlor and not of the beneficiary, for example, where the beneficiary is an infant child of the settlor.

Payments out of capital

9.13   Whether or not a payment is treated as having been made out of trust income or capital is usually of significance only if the beneficiary is entitled absolutely to both income and capital of the trust fund. In such cases, payments to the beneficiary out of income retain their income character whilst payments to the beneficiary out of capital retain their character as capital. In other cases, it is the character of the payments in the hands of the beneficiary which is important.

> **Example 9.4—Payment out of capital**
>
> Trevor, the testator, directs trustees to pay his widow £6,000 out of income of the trust fund and, where the income is not sufficient to meet this

obligation, the trustees are to raise and pay the balance out of capital. The payments out of capital are annual payments chargeable to income tax as part of the widow's total income.

Treatment of trust beneficiary's income

9.14 A beneficiary's share (as grossed-up) of the income of a trust fund forms part of his total income in the tax year in which it arises. The income is from the trust and not from the underlying property; hence, except in relation to discretionary trusts, the grossing-up process is at the basic rate by virtue of the deduction at source being under the normal rules for payments out of profits chargeable to income tax, etc in the hands of the trustees.

Example 9.5—Treatment of beneficiaries

In 2018/19, David has £10,000 of trading income, and trust income of £2,500 (received under deduction of basic rate income tax). His total income is thus £13,125 (ie £10,000 + (£2,500 × 100/80)) and his tax liability should be £255 (ie 20% × (£13,125 − £11,850)). As David has already suffered £625 by deduction (£3,125 × 20%), he can reclaim the balance of £370 from HMRC.

TYPES OF TRUST

Bare trusts

9.15 A bare trustee holds the trust property as its legal owner, but the beneficiary is absolutely entitled to the trust property, including any income or gains arising. The beneficiary is, therefore, taxable on the trust income, notwithstanding that the trustees may retain that income (eg in the case of a bare trust for a minor, until the age of 18).

However, where a parent creates a bare trust for an unmarried minor child, the trust income is treated as the parent's, subject to the £100 limit mentioned above. This applies to settlements made, or property added to existing settlements, after 8 March 1999 (otherwise, if the income is accumulated within the settlement while the child is unmarried and under 18, the normal bare trust treatment applies).

In addition, where settlement income has previously been accumulated (and treated as income of the settlor's child), if it is subsequently paid whilst the child is still unmarried and under 18, the income is treated as the settlor's for tax purposes, subject to the normal threshold of £100 (per parent, if appropriate).

Types of trust – examples

9.16 The following examples, taken from the HMRC Trusts, Settlements and Estates Manual, illustrate whether or not a trust is a bare trust.

Example 9.6—Types of trust (I)

Mrs A left the residue of her estate to such of her grandchildren as were alive at the date of her death.

She directed that the funds should not be paid to the grandchildren until they respectively attain age 21 years.

All of the grandchildren who were alive when Mrs A died are entitled to an equal share in the residue of the estate. There are no other conditions that they must fulfil before they become entitled. The direction about payment does not affect this basic position.

The beneficiaries have a vested interest and the trust is a bare trust.

Example 9.7—Types of trust (II)

Mr B left the residue of his estate to 'such of my grandchildren as survive me and attain age 21 years'. If any grandchild dies before age 21, his/her prospective share goes to the other grandchildren who do attain that age.

Here there are two conditions to be met before the grandchildren become entitled to their shares in the estate:

(1)   they must survive Mr B; and

(2)   they must attain age 21 years.

Here the grandchildren did not take immediate vested interests at the death of the testator.

This is not a bare trust and the trustees must make a tax return.

Example 9.8—Types of trust (III)

The trustees of a pension scheme decide under their discretionary powers to grant the sum of £20,000 to the child of a deceased member of the pension scheme. Because the child is only nine years old, they decide to appoint trustees to administer the fund and protect the child's interests until she attains age 18 years. The terms of the appointment from the pension scheme were in favour of the child absolutely.

This is a bare trust. The income ought to be returned as the child's own income and not that of the trustees.

Interest in possession settlements

9.17   An 'interest in possession' settlement exists when a beneficiary has an immediate right to the trust income. The trustees are liable to income tax in a representative capacity where a beneficiary is entitled to the trust income, generally in accordance with the nature of that income.

The trustees receive no tax relief for expenses of managing the trust. The expenses are generally treated as being paid first out of the trust's dividend income, then savings income and finally other income. The net income of the trust (ie after expenses, etc) is paid to beneficiaries including a tax credit at rates applicable to the income source.

Focus

Discretionary powers and powers of accumulation generally prevent an interest in possession. The most common example of an interest in possession is that of a life tenant.

Following *FA 2006*, most interest in possession trusts created on or after 22 March 2006 will, for IHT purposes, be treated in the same way as discretionary trusts (being 'non-estate' interests in possessions). Exceptions to this principle are 'transitional serial interests', trusts for a disabled person and 'immediate post-death interests' (IPDI) arising under a will.

To qualify as an IPDI following *IHTA 1984, s 49A*, certain conditions must be satisfied:

●   the IPDI must be effected by will or on intestacy;

●   the life tenant must have become beneficially entitled to the interest in possession on the death of the testator or intestate; and

●   it is not a bereaved minor trust or disabled trust.

Rates of income tax for interest in possession trusts

9.18   Income from property and savings is charged to tax at the basic rate of 20%. UK dividends are charged at ordinary dividend rate.

Finance (No 2) Act 2017 introduced a fresh £1,000 trading and property tax allowance; effective from 6 April 2017, but it will not be extended to trusts (bare trust excepted).

Order of set-off of trust expenses against income

9.19

Trust expenses are offset against income in the following order:

(1)   dividend income;

(2)   savings income; and

(3)   other income.

Income from an interest in possession trust – example 9.20

Example 9.9—Income from an interest in possession trust

In 2015/16, the Attree Trust has income and expenses of:

	£	£
Property income		500
Taxed savings income (tax deducted at source: £300)		1,500
Dividends	900	
Add tax credits	100	
		1,000
		3,000
Expenses chargeable to revenue		400

The tax assessable on the trustees will be £100 (£500 at 20%). The expenses are not deductible in arriving at the tax payable by the trustees.

Arthur is sole life tenant of the Attree Trust and, as such, is absolutely entitled to receive the whole trust income. His income for 2015/16 will include the following:

	£	£	£
Trust dividend income (gross)	1,000		
Trust interest income		1,500	
Other trust income			500
Deduct investment income ordinary rate tax (10%)	(100)		
Basic rate tax (20%)		(300)	(100)
	900	1,200	400
Deduct expenses (note (b))	(400)		
Net income entitlement	500	1,200	400

Grossed-up amounts:

£500 × 100/90	556	
£1,200 × 100/80		1,500
£400 × 100/80			500

Notes:

(a) This income falls to be included in Arthur's return even if it is not actually paid to him, as he is absolutely entitled to it. He will receive a tax certificate (form R185E) from the trust agents, showing three figures for gross income:

Trust income	Gross income	Tax deducted	Net income
	£	£	£
Income taxed at investment income ordinary rate	556	56	500
Income taxed at basic rate	1,500	300	1,200
Income liable at basic rate	500	100	400

(b) The trust expenses are deducted from savings income falling in priority to other income, first against dividend and similar income and then against other savings income.

(c) That part of Arthur's trust income which is represented by dividend and other savings income (£500 and £1,200 net) is treated as if it were received directly by Arthur. It is chargeable at the investment income ordinary rate and basic rate only, the liability being satisfied by the 10% and 20% tax credit respectively, except to the extent, if any, that it exceeds his basic rate limit.

Discretionary trusts

9.21 The trustees have discretionary powers to pay income at their discretion, or to accumulate it.

For years prior to 6 April 2016, a dividend from a UK company carried a 10% notional tax non-repayable credit, available for offset against the trust's liability to tax (*ITTOIA 2005, s 397*). The same principle applied to 'other qualifying distributions' from UK companies, which were not dividends and qualifying foreign dividends (with effect from 2008/09). Similarly, with dividend distributions from UK-authorised unit trusts and open-ended investment companies, shown separately on page 4 of the tax return.

9.22 Post-5 April 2016, UK dividend income paid is treated as gross income which no longer carries the notional 10% credit. Such income received by the discretionary or accumulation trustees attracts tax at 7.5% to the extent the dividend income is sheltered within the standard rate band and 38.1% on any excess. Such income received by the interest in possession trustees attracts tax at 7.5%.

A basic rate band of £1,000 is available, so that the above rates do not apply to the first £1,000 of trust income, which is instead taxed at the basic, lower or dividend ordinary rate, depending on the type of income (*ITA 2007, s 491*).

The trustees may claim tax relief on certain expenses. The order of set-off for trust expenses is the same as for interest in possession trusts. Income paid to the beneficiaries is grossed up for income tax at the current rate of 45% (for 2013/14 onwards). The beneficiary will receive a tax certificate from the trustees, and the gross trust income forms part of the beneficiary's total income for the tax year of payment. The tax credit is set off against the beneficiary's income tax liability (*ITA 2007, Pt 9, Ch 7*).

Example 9.10—Distribution of dividend income by discretionary trust (2016/17)

In 2016/17, the trustees receive dividends from UK companies totalling £4,500 and dividends totalling £1,000 from UK Unit trusts.

The amounts are entered as follows:

Box

9.10	£4,500
9.11	£1,000

Bereaved minor trusts and 'age 18 to 25' trusts

9.23 Bereaved minor trusts ('BMTs') and 'age 18 to 25' trusts were introduced by *FA 2006* to replace accumulation and maintenance (A&M) settlements; however, both these types of trusts are far more restrictive in their application than A&M settlements. The provisions governing the trusts can be found in *IHTA 1984, ss 71A–71D*.

Following *IHTA 1984, s 71A*, BMTs can only arise on the death of a parent. They can be established following the terms of the will of a deceased parent, following the Criminal Injuries Compensation Scheme, or held on statutory trusts following intestacy. A bereaved minor must become entitled to the trust property at age 18.

For income tax and capital gains tax, BMTs are taxed like discretionary trusts. *IHTA 1984, s 71B* provides that BMTs are not subject to exit charges or a ten-year anniversary for IHT, provided that the conditions of *s 71A* are complied with.

Similar to BMTs, an 'age 18 to 25' trust can only arise on the death of a parent or legal guardian (see *IHTA 1984, s 71D*). An 'age 18 to 25' trust can only be created either under the will of a deceased parent or under the Criminal Injuries Compensation Scheme. In addition, such trust must satisfy the following conditions:

- a beneficiary must become absolutely entitled to the trust property, its income and any accumulated income at the age of 25; and

- for as long as the beneficiary is under the age of 25, the settled property must be applied for his benefit; and

- he must be entitled to all the income arising on the settled property, or no such income may be applied for the benefit of another person.

For income tax and capital gains tax, 'age 18 to 25' trusts are taxed like discretionary trusts. *IHTA 1984, s 71F* provides that 'age 18 to 25' trusts are subject to the IHT relevant property regime, except that the time for calculating exit charges only runs from the beneficiary's 18th birthday. This has the effect that there will not be any ten-year anniversary charges, and the maximum rate of an exit charge will be 4.2% when a beneficiary becomes absolutely entitled to trust property at the age of 25.

Finance Act 2013 introduced provisions to allow the use of income and capital by some other person without the trust losing its favoured status. Regulations made by the Treasury will determine the amounts.

Example 9.11—'Age 18 to 25 trust'

An accumulation and maintenance settlement set up by Walter for his grandchildren in 1983 now comprises quoted investments and an industrial property. The property is let to an engineering company. Charges for rates, electricity, etc are paid by the trust and recharged yearly in arrears to the tenant. As a result of the delay in recovering the service costs, the settlement incurs overdraft interest.

The relevant figures for the year ended 5 April 2016 are as follows:

	£
Property rents	40,000
UK dividends (including tax credits of £500)	5,000
Taxed interest (tax deducted at source: £700)	3,500
Total tax borne	48,500

	£
Trust administration expenses – proportion chargeable to revenue	1,350
Overdraft interest	1,050
	2,400

The tax liability of the trust for 2015/16 is as follows:

	£	£
Property income £40,000 at 50%		20,000
Gross interest £3,500 at 30% (ie 50 – 20)		1,050
Net dividends	4,500	
Deduct expenses	(2,400)	
	2,100	
£2,100 grossed at 100/90 = £2,333 @ 32.5% (ie 42.5 – 10)		758

	£
Tax payable by self-assessment	21,808
Add: Tax deducted at source	700
Tax credits	500
Total tax borne	20,608

Notes:

(a) Expenses (including, in this example, the overdraft interest) are set first against the investment income and then against the other savings income, before other income. The effect is that the expenses, grossed up at 10%, save tax at 32.5% (the difference between the 10% rate applicable to dividend income and the investment income trust rate of 42.5%).

(b) The net revenue available for distribution to the beneficiaries, will be:

	£
Gross trust income	48,500
Less tax borne	(20,608)
Less trust expenses	(2,400)
Available for distribution	25,492

475

(c)   Of the tax borne, only £21,108 goes into the tax pool. Tax credits on dividends cannot enter the pool, unless there is sufficient balance brought forward from earlier years. The effect is that if the whole of the distributable income is in fact distributed, there will be insufficient tax in the pool to frank the distribution, and the trustees will have a further liability which they may not have the funds to settle.

Trusts for the vulnerable

9.24   A separate tax regime applies for certain trusts with 'vulnerable' beneficiaries (ie disabled persons or relevant minors, as defined), from 6 April 2004 (see **9.10** for details regarding the special tax treatment available to such trusts). If a claim for special tax treatment is made, tax on trust income (and gains) is restricted to the tax that would be paid had the income and gains accrued directly to the beneficiary. The claim must be made by the first anniversary of 31 January following the end of the tax year in which it is to have effect, or longer if HMRC allow (*FA 2005, ss 23–29, 34–39, Sch 1*).

RESIDENT AND NON-RESIDENT SETTLEMENTS

Residence rules for trustees

9.25   There are two sets of rules for deciding trustees' residence status: one for income tax, and the other for capital gains. The residence status for income tax purposes can be different from that for capital gains. The rules for capital gains are covered in *Capital Gains Tax (2019/20)* (Bloomsbury Professional).

9.26   The rules for determining the residence of trusts were simplified from 6 April 2007. Trustees are treated as if they were a single person, and the deemed person is treated as resident in the UK when: all of the trustees are resident; or at least one trustee is resident and at least one is not and the settlor is resident or domiciled in the UK when the settlement was created (*ITA 2007, ss 474–476*).

Trustees may be resident in the UK and another country at the same time (dual residence). The HMRC Centre for Non-Residents checks in detail any claim for dual residence. If there is a double taxation agreement with another country, it may have a 'tie-breaker' provision. A 'tie-breaker' makes the trustees a resident of one of the countries, but this is only for the purposes of applying the provisions of the double taxation agreement (*TCGA 1992, s 69*).

Information needed for trusts

9.27   In January 2017 HMRC announced the intention to introduce an online system to administer their trusts register and to replace the former form

41G (Trusts) process. Broadly, the service is designed to provide a single point of access to register and update records online. HMRC have indicated that the registration process will be mandatory and will apply to existing as well as new trusts, but, whilst the date of its introduction has not yet been announced, it is assumed the likely date will be 6 April 2018 at the earliest. To validate compliance, it is proposed to include a tick box on the self-assessment to confirm the trust register has been checked and updated and a similar box will potentially be included on the IHT100. The registration service can be accessed at https://www.gov.uk/government/publications/trusts-and-estates-trust-details-41g-trust.

Broadly, trustees of non-resident trusts do not pay UK tax on foreign income that they receive. For most discretionary or accumulation trusts, trustees pay tax at:

- the nil rate on the first £1,000 of taxable income;

- 38.1% (2019/20) on dividend income from stocks and shares;

- 45% on UK interest (including 'free of tax to residents abroad' securities) if a beneficiary (or someone who might become one) is resident in the UK; and

- 45% on all other non-dividend income arising in the UK.

For interest in possession trusts, the trustees pay tax at:

- the dividend ordinary rate on trust dividend income; and

- the basic rate on all other types of income.

Non-resident trustees should use form SA900 Trust and Estate Tax Return to declare any UK source income due from a non-resident trust. This can be downloaded from https://www.gov.uk/government/publications/self-assessment-trust-and-estate-tax-return-sa900. Where appropriate, form SA906 (the Trust and Estate Non-Residence supplementary pages) may also be required (www.gov.uk/government/publications/self-assessment-trust-and-estate-non-residence-sa906).

Bare trusts

9.28   A bare trust, also known as a simple trust, is one in which each beneficiary has an immediate and absolute right to both capital and income. The beneficiaries of a bare trust have the right to take actual possession of trust property (see **9.15** for further details).

The property is held in the name of a trustee, but the trustee has no discretion over what income to pay the beneficiary. In effect, the trustee is a nominee in whose name the property is held and has no active duties to perform.

Bare trustees are not obliged to complete trust returns, but they can choose to make a return of trust income. They would then account for the UK income tax due.

The beneficiary gets credit for UK income tax that the bare trustee has paid.

The beneficiary of a bare trust returns the income on his personal self-assessment tax return.

The beneficiary enters it on the page for the particular income in question. There are instructions in SA107(Notes) under the heading 'Income from trusts and settlements'. The notes can be downloaded from https://www.gov.uk/government/publications/self-assessment-trusts-etc-sa107.

Income tax liability of non-resident trustees

Discretionary and 'age 18 to 25' trusts

9.29 First, it is necessary to decide if the settlement is within *ITA 2007, s 479*. This will be so if:

- the trustees have the power to accumulate income or make discretionary payments; and

- the trust income is not treated as that of the settlor.

Generally, discretionary and accumulation and maintenance settlements will fall into this category.

Tax is charged at the trust rate. For 1999/2000 onwards, dividend-type income is charged at the dividend trust rate.

Foreign income is not chargeable to UK tax.

Interest from FOTRA (free of tax to residents abroad) securities remains chargeable to UK tax unless:

- the Centre for Non-Residents confirms that it is exempt; or

- the provisions of *ITA 2007, s 811* (limit on liability to income tax of non-UK residents) apply. Briefly, if no beneficiaries are resident in the UK, the trustees do not pay tax on interest they receive gross.

With regard to other income received gross, if no beneficiaries are resident in the UK, the trustees do not pay tax on interest they receive gross (*ITA 2007, s 811*). If *ITA 2007, s 811* does not apply, the trustees are chargeable to tax.

Subject to the possible effects of *ITA 2007, s 811*, other UK income remains chargeable to UK tax.

Interest in possession settlements

9.30 A non-resident trust, which is not within *ITA 2007, s 479*, is called an 'interest in possession settlement' (see **9.17**).

Foreign income is not chargeable to UK tax.

ITA 2007, s 811 applies to interest from FOTRA securities. Briefly, if no beneficiaries are ordinarily resident in the UK, the trustees do not pay tax on interest they receive gross.

Subject to the possible effects of *ITA 2007, s 811*, other UK income remains chargeable to UK tax.

ADMINISTRATION OF TRUSTS

Self-assessment

9.31   Trustees and personal representatives are required to complete tax returns (form SA900), and are generally subject to the same self-assessment regime as individuals in terms of filing deadlines, payments on account of tax, interest and penalties, etc *(TMA 1970, s 8A)*.

The extent to which trustees are liable to tax depends upon their residence status and the type of trust (see **9.25** for further details concerning residence).

Notices are given, by an officer of the Board of HMRC, for the purposes of establishing the amounts in which the following persons are chargeable to income tax and CGT, and the amount payable by them by way of income tax:

- the 'relevant trustees' (see below);

- the settlor or settlors; and

- the beneficiary or beneficiaries.

Notices may be given to any relevant trustee, or separate notices given to each relevant trustee, or to such of the relevant trustees as the officer thinks fit.

'Relevant trustees' are:

- for the purpose of trust income, any person who was a trustee at or after the time when the income arose;

- for the purpose of trust gains, any person who was a trustee during or after the tax year in which the gain accrued.

The relevant trustees are liable for any tax which falls due as a result of the self-assessment included in the return.

In the absence of a return, an officer of the Board may determine the amount of the relevant trustees' liability. Similarly, an assessment may be made on the relevant trustees where a loss of tax is discovered.

Bare trusts under self-assessment

9.32   Trustees of bare trusts (see **9.15**) are not expected to account for tax at the appropriate rate on income paid over to beneficiaries. Any income which is received gross by the trustees will be paid gross by them. In addition, trustees of bare trusts will not be required to complete self-assessment returns or make payments on account. (However, they are entitled, if they so wish, to make a self-assessment return of income (not capital gains) and to account for tax on it at the appropriate rate.) Beneficiaries must include income and gains from these trusts in their returns.

Penalties

9.33   *FA 2009, s 106* and *Sch 55* introduced a reformed penalties regime for filing late returns, which applies equally to trustee returns as it does to personal tax returns under self-assessment. The provisions apply with effect from 6 April 2011 in respect of returns for 2010/11 and later years (*SI 2011/727*). Full details of the penalty provisions are set out at **2.48**.

9.34   A revised penalty regime also applies to late payments of tax from 2010/11 onwards (*FA 2009, s 107* and *Sch 56*). The penalties are as follows:

Payment made	Penalty
30 days late	5% of the unpaid tax
6 months late	Further 5% of the unpaid tax
12 months late	Further 5% of the unpaid tax

The above penalties apply to late balancing payments of income tax and late payments of capital gains tax under self-assessment (ie based on tax returns for individuals or trustees etc, and in certain other circumstances) with effect from 6 April 2011, in relation to 2010/11 and later tax years (*SI 2011/702, art 3*).

HMRC must assess the late payment penalty, and notify the person liable. The penalty notice must state the period to which the penalty relates. The penalty is payable within 30 days from the day on which the penalty notice is issued. There is a right of appeal against both the imposition of a penalty and the amount involved (*FA 2009, Sch 56, paras 11, 13*).

HMRC may reduce a late payment penalty in 'special circumstances', which does not include inability to pay (*FA 2009, Sch 56, para 9*). In addition, a defence of 'reasonable excuse' may also be available (*Sch 56, para 16*).

HMRC Helpsheets for the Trusts and Estates tax return
9.35

Number	Title
HS390	Trusts and estates of deceased persons: foreign tax credit relief for capital gains
SA901(Notes)	Notes on Trust and Estate Trade pages
SA901L(Notes)	Notes on Trusts and Estate Lloyd's Underwriters pages
SA902(Notes)	Notes on Trust and Estate Partnership pages
SA903(Notes)	Notes on Trust and Estate UK Property pages
SA904(Notes)	Notes on Trust and Estate Foreign pages
SA905(Notes)	Notes on Trust and Estate Capital Gains pages
SA906(Notes)	Notes on Trust and Estate Non-residence pages
SA907(Notes)	Notes on Trust and Estate Charities pages
SA950	Trust and Estate tax return guide

TAXATION OF ESTATES

Death

9.36   On death, the property of a person passes to their personal representatives.

Personal representatives can be either executors of a will of a deceased person or administrators of the estate if there is no will. The roles of trustees and executors are quite different. The executors have a duty to gather in the assets, pay the liabilities and then to distribute the surplus according to the will. If any surplus is to be held on trust, the trustees then take over in respect of that part of the estate. The date at which this is deemed to happen is important for some tax purposes, but in general the trustees are deemed to inherit at the end of administration by the personal representatives (*TMA 1970, s 74*).

The personal representatives of a deceased individual are responsible for discharging the liabilities and obligations of the deceased, as part of the administration of an estate. This includes unpaid tax liabilities for periods up to the deceased's death, and also tax on income of the estate during administration (*TMA 1970, s 40*).

A personal representative is defined for income tax purposes as someone who is responsible for administering the death estate, whether in the UK or elsewhere (*ITA 2007, s 989*).

Focus

HMRC have four years after the end of the tax year in which the deceased died to assess the liability on the executors or administrators of a deceased person in respect of the income, or chargeable gains, which arose or accrued to him before his death (*TMA 1970, s 40*). In cases involving a loss of tax brought about carelessly or deliberately by a person who has died (or another person acting on that person's behalf before that person's death), an assessment on his personal representatives to tax for any year of assessment ending not earlier than six years before his death may be made at any time not more than four years after the end of the year of assessment in which he died (*TMA 1970, s 40(2)*).

Income during the administration period

9.37   Income arising from the deceased's estate from the date of death to the completion of the administration of the estate is taxable on the personal representatives. When the income is distributed to the estate beneficiaries, it then forms part of their taxable income.

Personal representatives must pay income tax on the estate income during the period of administration. They are not entitled to personal reliefs and allowances, although the income they receive is taxed only at the dividend ordinary rate or basic rate.

Example 9.12—Income during the administration period

Graham dies unmarried on 25 July 2019. His executors are entitled to set off his full personal allowance of £12,500 for 2019/20 against his income tax liability for that year.

Expenses of administering the estate are not allowable deductions for income tax purposes, although relief for interest on a loan taken out to pay IHT is available for up to one year from the making of the loan (*ITA 2007, s 403*).

Estate income is paid to beneficiaries according to whether they are entitled to the estate assets (ie an 'absolute interest'), or whether they are entitled to income from an estate asset only (ie a 'limited interest').

Broadly, a beneficiary entitled to an income-producing asset is generally taxable on income arising from the asset since the date of death. Any sums payable by the personal representatives to a residuary beneficiary during the administration of the estate are treated as the beneficiary's income for the tax year of payment. The payments are treated as net income, after deduction of tax at rates applicable to the types of income out of which they are paid.

The beneficiary is taxable on the gross equivalent of the estate income. Estate distributions are treated as paid first out of basic rate taxed income, followed by savings income and then dividend income (*ITTOIA 2005, ss 649–682*).

End of the administration period

9.38   Upon completion of the administration period, the overall amount of income due to each beneficiary is compared with the payments already made. Where an amount remains payable to a beneficiary, the gross equivalent is treated as income of the tax year in which the administration period ends (or the tax year in which a beneficiary's interest ends, if earlier), regardless of when it was actually paid over to the beneficiary.

UK and foreign estates

9.39   A 'UK estate' is defined as an estate, the income of which comprises only income which either (*ITTOIA 2005, s 651*):

● 　 has borne UK income tax by deduction; or

● 　 is directly assessable to UK income tax on the personal representatives.

To be a UK estate, the personal representatives must not be entitled to claim exemption from UK income tax (in respect of any part of the income of the estate) by reason of their residence outside the UK.

Focus

Finance (No 2) Act 2017 includes provisions designed to bring all UK residential property held indirectly through an offshore structure or trust within the UK IHT net. The changes apply from 6 April 2017 (*F(No 2)A 2017, s 33 and Sch 10*). See *Inheritance Tax Annual (2019/20)* (Bloomsbury Professional) (at 9.33) for further details.

If all the trustees are resident in the UK during the whole tax year, they are liable to income tax on UK and overseas trust income. If the trustees were only resident for part of the tax year, they will generally only be liable to income tax on overseas income for that part of the tax year in which they were UK resident (*FA 2013, Sch 45*).

In the case of mixed (ie resident and non-resident) trustees, their income tax liability depends upon the domicile and residence status of the settlor. The trustees are jointly treated as UK resident if the settlor was UK resident or domiciled when funds were provided to the settlement (or at the time of the settlor's death). Alternatively, the trustees are jointly regarded as non-UK resident if the settlor was not resident or domiciled in the UK at those times.

Income of person with limited interest in residue

9.40   Special provisions apply to persons with limited interests in the residue of the whole or part of an estate during the administration period (or part of it) (*ITTOIA 2005, s 678*).

A person is deemed to have a limited interest if he does not have an absolute interest and the income of the residue (or part of it) would be properly payable to him, or directly or indirectly paid for his benefit, if the residue had been ascertained at the commencement of the administration period. A life interest is a limited interest.

Any sum paid during the administration period in respect of a limited interest is, subject to adjustment on the completion of administration (or its Scottish equivalent), deemed to have been paid as income in the tax year in which the sum was paid. Where the sum is paid in respect of a limited interest which has ceased during the administration, the sum paid after the interest has ceased is deemed to have been paid in the last tax year in which the interest subsisted. Personal representatives may be treated as residuary beneficiaries in such a way that the deemed income forms part of the estate of a second deceased person. The legislation also caters for discretionary payments.

In the case of a 'UK estate' (see **9.39**) the personal representatives will have paid tax of 10% and any sum paid to a beneficiary is treated as a net amount after the application of the 10% rate. Payments are made first out of payments bearing tax at the 10% rate and there are provisions for effecting a reasonable apportionment of amounts between persons with different interests.

In the case of a 'foreign estate' (ie an estate that is not a 'UK estate'), the sum paid is treated as gross income chargeable under *ITTOIA 2005, Pt 5, Ch 6* with a possible proportionate reduction on proof of tax deduction in respect of the aggregate income of the estate.

Between April 2008 and April 2016, provided certain conditions were met, dividends from non-UK companies were given the same notional tax credit that was afforded to dividends paid by UK companies.

9.41   In respect of discretionary payments out of income, beneficiaries are treated as receiving income on which tax has been paid at the basic rate or, in the case of payments routed through trustees, at the rate applicable to trusts.

A residuary beneficiary who is not resident in the UK may claim to have his income from an estate in the course of administration treated as if it had arisen directly to him, so that he will not be liable to tax on, for example, foreign source income of the estate.

On the completion, after 5 April 1995, of the administration of an estate, where an amount remains payable in respect of a limited interest, the amount is deemed to have been paid as income of the tax year in which the administration period ends; if the sum is deemed to be paid in respect of an interest which ceased before the end of the administration period, then it is deemed to have been paid in respect of the last tax year in which that interest subsisted.

In many cases, therefore, adjustments will have to be made to assessments already made on the beneficiary during the administration period. The adjustments may be made within three years of 31 January following the end of the tax year in which administration of that estate was completed. This treatment is given in HMRC Extra-statutory Concession (ESC) A14, the full text of which is as follows:

'Extra Statutory Concession A14

Deceased person's estate: residuary income received during the administration period

A beneficiary who for a year of assessment is not resident or not ordinarily resident in the United Kingdom, and is deemed under *ss 657, 658(2) and 830(1), (2), Income Tax (Trading and Other Income) Act 2005 ('ITTOIA')* to have received income from a UK estate in that year, may claim to have their tax liability on that income from the estate adjusted to what it would be if such income had arisen to them directly and as a result they:

● could claim relief under *section 278, ICTA 1988* (claim to personal reliefs by certain non residents); or

● could claim entitlement to exemption in respect of FOTRA Securities issued in accordance with *section 714, ITTOIA*; or

● could claim relief under the terms of a double taxation agreement; or

● would not have been chargeable to income tax.

Relief or exemption, as appropriate, will be granted to the beneficiary only if the personal representatives of the estate:

● have made estate returns for each and every year for which they are required, and

● have paid all tax due and any interest, surcharges and penalties arising, and

● keep available for inspection any relevant tax certificates, together with copies of the estate accounts for all years of the period of administration showing details of all sources of estate income and payments made to beneficiaries.

Relief or exemption, as appropriate, will be granted to the beneficiary on a claim made within five years and ten months of the end of the year of assessment in which the beneficiary is deemed to have received the income.

No tax will be repayable to the beneficiary in respect of income they are deemed to have received where the basic amount of estate income, if

485

received by a UK resident beneficiary of an estate, is paid sums within *sections 657(3), (4)* and *680(3), (4), ITTOIA*.'

Income of person with absolute interest in residue

9.42   Special provisions apply to persons who, during the administration period (or part of it), have an absolute interest in the whole or part of the residue of the estate of the deceased. A person is deemed to have an absolute interest if and so long as the capital of the residue (or of the relevant part) would, if the residue had been ascertained, be properly payable to him or, directly or indirectly, payable for his benefit (*ITTOIA 2005, ss 660* and *665*).

A person entitled to an absolute interest may receive payments during the administration period made out of either income or capital and these have to be distinguished. This is done by first calculating the residuary income during such part of the administration period in which the beneficiary had an absolute interest.

The 'residuary income' is ascertained by deducting from the income of the estate for that year (*ITTOIA 2005, s 666*):

- annual interest, annuities or other annual payments for that year which are a charge on residue (see below), except for any interest, etc which is allowable in computing the income of the estate;

- management expenses (unless allowable in computing the aggregate income of the estate) which, in the absence of any express provision in a will, are properly chargeable to income; and

- the income of the estate to which any person is specifically entitled as a devisee or legatee.

There is also a reduction in residuary income by way of relief for higher rate tax purposes ('excess liability'), where accrued income has also been included in the value of the estate for IHT purposes; the reduction is the grossed-up value of IHT attributable to the accrued income net of accrued liabilities.

9.43   The importance of calculating the residuary income lies in the fact that any sum paid during the administration period in respect of the absolute interest is deemed to have been paid as income to the extent that it does not exceed the residuary income for that year (less basic rate tax for that year in the case of a UK estate). Personal representatives may be treated as residuary beneficiaries in such a way that the deemed income forms part of the estate of a second deceased person. The legislation caters for successive absolute interests and discretionary payments.

Where any deductions exceed the amount of residuary income, the excess may be carried forward and treated as an amount to be deducted from the aggregate income of the estate for the following year. This replaces an earlier concession which stated that where the allowable deductions exceeded the gross income, the residuary income was nil and the excess could be carried backwards or forwards to other years for higher rate tax purposes.

In the case of a 'UK estate' (see **9.39**), the sum deemed to have been paid as income includes the amount by which the aggregated income entitlement of the person for the tax year exceeds the aggregate of all the sums which have been paid (as income) to that person in respect of that absolute interest. It is, therefore, grossed-up at the basic rate in force for the year of payment; payments are made first out of payments bearing tax at basic rate and there are provisions for effecting a reasonable apportioning of amounts between persons with different interests. In the case of a 'foreign estate', the amount paid is treated as gross income with a possible proportionate reduction on proof of tax deduction in respect of the aggregate income of the estate.

A residuary beneficiary who is not resident in the UK may claim to have his income from an estate in the course of administration treated as if it had arisen directly to him, so that he will not be liable to tax on, for example, foreign source income of the estate.

On the completion of administration certain adjustments may be necessary, giving rise to additional assessments or a claim for relief. Any further or adjusted assessment or claim for relief may be made within four years from the end of the tax year in which the deceased died.

Charges on residue

9.44   'Charges' on residue means the following liabilities (to the extent that the liabilities fall ultimately on residue) properly payable out of the estate and interest payable in respect of those liabilities:

- funeral, testamentary and administration expenses and debts;
- general legacies, demonstrative legacies, annuities and any sum payable out of residue under an intestacy;
- any other liabilities of the personal representatives; and
- (relating to Scotland only) any sums required to meet claims in respect of legal rights by the surviving spouse or children.

Thus, for example, interest payable in respect of a general legacy is a charge on residue and is not taken into account in calculating residuary income. In Scotland, sums required to meet certain claims by a surviving spouse or child are also charges on residue (*ITTOIA 2005, Pt 5, Ch 6*).

Income of legatees and annuitants

9.45   In the case of a specific legacy, the legatee is entitled to the income (subject to a contrary provision in the will) from the relevant property from the date of the testator's death. The income from the property, therefore, forms part of the legatee's total income as it arises, notwithstanding the general charge on the personal representatives.

In the case of a general legacy, the legatee is entitled to interest at 5%. If the legacy is an immediate one, the interest is generally payable (subject to a contrary provision in the will) only after the end of the executor's year. Such interest is charged to tax under *ITTOIA 2005* as part of the legatee's total income. However, a legatee may refuse to accept payment of the interest and in such instances the interest is only treated as his income if there is identifiable income which he can claim, eg from a fund set aside to meet the legacy.

In general, an annuitant is not entitled to the capital value of his annuity, though he is entitled to have a fund set aside to secure the annuity. The first instalment of the annuity is payable only at the end of the executor's year, but (subject to a contrary intention) the annuity runs from the testator's death and forms part of the annuitant's total income from that date.

In some cases, and in particular where the estate is insufficient to provide an annuity fund and also to pay the pecuniary legacies in full, the annuitant is entitled to the actuarial value of his annuity (duly abated, if necessary). This is regarded as a capital payment and is not included in the annuitant's total income. Thus, payments made in respect of an annuity are regarded as capital payments where the payments are made before it is discovered that the income of the estate is insufficient to pay the annuity in full.

References in a will or codicil to payments by reference to the former 'surtax' and 'standard rate' are treated as if they were to higher rate(s) and basic rate.

Estate in administration – example

9.46

Example 9.13—Estate in administration

Sam died in March 2015. Ann is the residual beneficiary of his estate and she has an absolute interest. In the year to 5 April 2016, the personal representatives received the following income:

UK dividends (net)	10,000
Interest on deposit monies	4,000
Rental income	6,000

In January 2016, shares in M&S Plc valued at £5,000 were transferred to Ann, and in March 2016 she was paid £4,000 in cash. Expenses charged to income are £500.

The transfer of shares and the cash payment create the following taxable income of £9,000 net for Ann in 2015/16, which is calculated as follows:

	Gross £	Tax £	Net £
Property income less income tax at 20%	6,000	1,200	4,800
Interest	4,000	800	3,200
Dividends	1,111	111	1,000
	11,111	2,111	9,000

The balance of the UK dividends is calculated as:

	£
Gross dividends	10,000
Expenses	500
Distributed in 2015/16	1,000
Balance held	8,580

This amount will be carried forward to be treated as income of the beneficiary when it is paid in succeeding years, or on completion of the administration of the estate.

Early settlement of a deceased taxpayer's tax affairs

9.47 HMRC will, if requested, issue a tax return for a deceased person before the end of the tax year in which the individual dies. This will allow the personal representatives to deal with the deceased's tax affairs without delay.

HMRC will also give early written confirmation if they do not intend to enquire into that return. This will enable the deceased's personal representatives to finalise the estate.

PRE-OWNED ASSETS

Introduction

9.48 *FA 2004, s 84* and *Sch 15* introduced an income tax charge on benefits received by the former owners of property, referred to as pre-owned assets. Broadly, it applies to individuals (the chargeable person) who continue to receive benefits from certain types of property they once owned after 17 March 1986, but have since disposed of. The rules have effect for 2005/06 onwards.

The property within the scope of the charge can be grouped into three headings:

(1)   land;

(2)   chattels; and

(3)   intangible property.

If the chargeable person has either disposed of any property within these headings by way of gift or, in some circumstances, sale, or contributed towards the purchase of the property in question and they continue to receive some benefit from the property, they are potentially liable to the charge. The benefit may be occupation of the land, use of the chattel or the ability to receive income or capital from a settlement holding intangible property.

There are several types of transactions relating to land and chattels that are excluded from the scope of the charge (see **9.53**). There are also provisions exempting the relevant property from the charge where the property is subject to a charge to IHT or where specific protection from IHT is given by legislation.

If the income tax charge applies, *FA 2004, Sch 15* contains provisions enabling the taxable benefit to be calculated. In the case of the occupation or use of land and chattels, the calculation of the taxable benefit will be determined to a large extent by the proportion which the value of the chargeable person's original interest in, or contribution to the purchase, bears to the current value of the property.

The conditions required for the charge to apply are virtually identical where the property in question is land or chattels, but they differ slightly in respect of intangible property.

Land and chattels

9.49   The charge applies where the chargeable person occupies any land or uses or possesses any chattels, either alone or with other persons, and either the 'disposal condition' or the 'contribution condition' is met.

Disposal condition

9.50   The disposal condition will apply if the chargeable person, at any time after 17 March 1986, owned relevant land or chattels, or other property whose disposal proceeds were directly or indirectly applied by another person towards the acquisition of the relevant land or chattels, and then disposed of all or part of their interest in the relevant land or chattels (or other property). If the disposal was an excluded transaction (see **9.53**), the disposal condition will not apply.

Note that the disposal condition will apply to the chargeable person's occupation or use of property even if that property was never actually owned by them. If they gave away other property (apart from cash) to another person who sold such property and used these proceeds to purchase the relevant land or chattel, the disposal condition is satisfied, unless it qualifies as an excluded transaction.

A disposition that creates a new interest in land or in a chattel out of an existing interest is taken to be a disposal of part of the existing interest.

Contribution condition

9.51   The contribution condition will apply if the chargeable person, at any time after 17 March 1986, provided any of the consideration given by another person for the acquisition of an interest in the relevant land or chattel, or for the acquisition of any other property the proceeds of the disposal of which were directly or indirectly applied by another person towards an acquisition of an interest in the relevant land or chattel. As with the disposal condition, if the provision of the consideration qualifies as an excluded transaction, this condition will not apply.

It can be seen that the contribution condition can apply not only where the contribution provided by the chargeable person is directly used to purchase the relevant land or chattel but where the contribution is indirect, too. If they provided all or part of the consideration (eg a cash gift) for the purchase of property by another person, who then sold the property and used the proceeds to purchase the land occupied, or the chattel used, by the chargeable person, the contribution condition is satisfied, unless it qualifies as an excluded transaction.

Focus

HMRC do not regard the contribution condition set out in *FA 2004, Sch 15, para 3(3)* as being met where a lender resides in property purchased by another with money loaned to him by the lender. Their view is that, since the outstanding debt will form part of his estate for IHT purposes, it would not be reasonable to consider that the loan falls within the contribution condition (and, therefore, not reasonably attributable to the consideration (*Sch 15, para 4(2)(c)*)), even where the loan was interest free. It follows that the 'lender', in such an arrangement, would not be caught by a charge under *Sch 15*.

Intangible property

9.52   The charge applies where the chargeable person settles intangible property or adds intangible property to a settlement after 17 March 1986 on terms that any income arising from the settled property would be treated under *ITTOIA 2005, s 624* (income arising under a settlement where the settlor retains an interest) as income of the chargeable person as settlor and any such income would be so treated even if *sub-section (2)* of that section did not include any reference to the spouse of the settlor. The settlor in this case is, of course, the chargeable person.

In this context, 'settlement' has the same meaning as it does for IHT purposes (*Inheritance Tax Act 1984 (IHTA 1984), s 43(2)*).

Intangible property means assets such as stocks and securities, insurance policies and bank and building society accounts. The provisions of this paragraph do not apply to land and chattels included in a settlement.

Excluded transactions

9.53   There are a number of situations where a charge to tax will not arise. Certain transactions are excluded from the charge, and there are also exemptions from the charge where certain conditions are met (*FA 2004, Sch 15, para 10*).

The concept of excluded transactions has no application to intangible property. They only serve to exclude from the income tax charge certain transactions relating to land and chattels.

Excluded transactions – disposal condition

9.54   For the purposes of the disposal conditions relating to land and chattels, the disposal of any property is an excluded transaction in relation to the chargeable person in any of the following situations (*FA 2004, Sch 15, para 10*):

- It was a disposal of their whole interest in the property, except for any right expressly reserved by them over the property, either:

  – by a transaction made at arm's length with a person not connected with them; or

  – by a transaction such as might be expected to be made at arm's length between persons not connected with each other.

- The exclusion clearly only applies to sales of the entire interest in the property at full market value, although the words 'except for any right expressly reserved' would envisage the sale of a freehold reversion subject to a lease, but only if it was on arm's-length terms.

- Concern was expressed that sales of a part share of property to commercial providers of equity release schemes would not qualify as an excluded transaction and an individual would be subject to the charge if he remained in occupation of the land. This concern was recognised in the rules governing the charge which specifically exempted from the charge disposals of part of an interest in any property by a transaction made at arm's length with a person not connected with the chargeable person. Furthermore, the exemption is extended to disposals of a part share to anyone, provided that they were made on arm's-length terms and either took place before 7 March 2005, or took place on or after that date for a consideration not in the form of money or assets readily convertible into money.

- The property was transferred to their spouse or civil partner, or former spouse or civil partner where the transfer has been ordered by a court.

- The disposal was by way of gift (or in accordance with a court order for the benefit of a former spouse or civil partner) by virtue of which the property became settled property in which his spouse or civil partner or former spouse or civil partner is beneficially entitled to an interest in possession. The spouse or civil partner must take an interest in possession from the outset. It is not an excluded transaction, however, if the interest in possession of the spouse or civil partner or former spouse or civil partner has come to an end other than on their death unless the spouse or civil partner or former spouse or civil partner has become absolutely entitled to the property, in which case HMRC would accept that the benefit of the exclusion is not lost.

- The disposal was a disposition falling within *IHTA 1984, s 11* (disposition for maintenance of family).

- The disposal is an outright gift to an individual and is wholly exempted from IHT by either of the following sections of *IHTA 1984*:

  – *s 19* (£3,000 annual exemption); or

  – *s 20* (£250 small gifts exemption).

Excluded transactions – contribution condition

9.55   For the purposes of the contribution conditions relating to land and chattels, the provision by the chargeable person of consideration for another's acquisition of any property is an excluded transaction in relation to the chargeable person in any of the following situations:

- The other person was their spouse or civil partner, or former spouse or civil partner where the transfer has been ordered by a court.

- On its acquisition, the property became settled property in which their spouse or civil partner or former spouse or civil partner is beneficially entitled to an interest in possession. The spouse or civil partner must take an interest in possession from the outset. It is not an excluded transaction, however, if the interest in possession of the spouse or civil partner, or former spouse or civil partner, has come to an end otherwise than on their death, unless the spouse or civil partner or former spouse or civil partner has become absolutely entitled to the property.

- The provision of the consideration constituted an outright gift of cash by the chargeable person to the other person and was made at least seven years before the earliest date on which the chargeable person occupied the land or had possession or use of the chattel.

- The provision of the consideration is a disposition falling within *IHTA 1984, s 11* (maintenance of family).

- The provision of the consideration is an outright gift to an individual and is, for the purposes of *IHTA 1984*, a transfer of value that is wholly exempt by virtue of *s 19* (£3,000 annual exemption) or *s 20* (£250 small gifts exemption).

Property in the estate

9.56   The charging provisions relating to land, chattels and intangible property do not apply to a person at a time when their estate for the purposes of *IHTA 1984* includes the relevant property, or other property which (*FA 2004, Sch 15, para 11(1)*):

- derives its value from the relevant property; and

- whose value so far as attributable to the relevant property, is not substantially less than the value of the relevant property.

Where their estate includes property which derives its value from the relevant property and whose value, so far as attributable to the relevant property, is substantially less than the value of the relevant property:

- the appropriate rental value of the relevant land;

- the appropriate amount in respect of the chattel; or

- the chargeable amount in relation to the relevant intangible property;

must be reduced by such proportion as is reasonable to take account of the inclusion of the property in their estate.

> **Example 9.14—Value of estate property**
>
> If Mr Big transfers his house to a company wholly owned by him, then, provided there are no loans to the company, one can say that the value attributable to the company is not less than the value of the house. But, if Mr Big gave the house to a company which was owned 25% by his wife, the value of the 75% shares that he holds would be substantially less than the value of the house. If he has lent money to the company and the company holds the house, we take the view that the company's value is less than the house unless (possibly) the loan is charged on the house.

Gifts with reservation

9.57   The charging provisions also do not apply to a person at a time when, for IHT purposes, the relevant property or property deriving its value from relevant property falls within the 'gifts with reservation' provisions set out in *FA 1986 (FA 2004, Sch 15, para 11(3))*.

In addition, the legislation does not apply if the property:

- would fall to be treated as subject to a reservation but for any of *FA 1986, s 102(5)(d)–(i)* (certain cases where disposal by way of gift is an exempt transfer for purposes of IHT). But, where *s 102(5)(h)* is in point, *Sch 15* is disapplied only when the property remains subject to trusts complying with the requirements of *IHTA 1984, Sch 4, para 3(1)* (maintenance funds);

- would fall to be treated as subject to a reservation but for *FA 1986, s 102B(4)* (gifts with reservation: share of interest in land), or would have fallen to be so treated if the disposal by way of gift of an undivided share of an interest in land had been made on or after 9 March 1999. This refers to situations where the chargeable person transfers a share (usually 50%) of their property to the donee, and both the donee and the chargeable person continue to occupy the property, paying their share of household expenses; or

- would fall to be treated as subject to a reservation but for *FA 1986, s 102C(3)* and *Sch 20, para 6* (exclusion of benefit). This refers to situations where the chargeable person continues to use or occupy the property but pays full consideration in money or money's worth, or where they leave the property but have to move back at a later date due to an unforeseen change in their circumstances and are unable to look after themselves because of age or infirmity.

Where the contribution condition relating to land or chattels applies, *Sch 20, para 2(2)(b)* (which excludes gifts of money from the provisions that apply where property is substituted for the original gift) should be disregarded. For example, if A gives cash to his son and they buy a home jointly and live together, then, while they live together, the pre-owned assets tax charge will not apply.

Schedule 15 also contains provisions for the chargeable person to elect that the relevant property that would otherwise be subject to the charge be treated as property subject to a reservation for the purposes of *IHTA 1984*. If the election is made, no charge under the Schedule will apply.

Excluded liability

9.58   Where, at any time, the value of a person's estate for the purposes of *IHTA 1984* is reduced by an 'excluded liability' affecting any property, only the excess of the value of the property over the amount of the excluded liability will be treated as comprised in their estate.

A liability is an excluded liability if:

- the creation of the liability; and

- any transaction by virtue of which the person's estate came to include the relevant property or property which derives its value from the relevant property or by virtue of which the value of the property in their estate came to be derived from the relevant property,

were 'associated operations', as defined in *IHTA 1984, s 268*.

The 'amount' of the excluded liability will be the face value of the debt, including any rolled-up interest or accrued indexation where this has been allowed for under the terms of the agreement. For the purposes of computing the charge, it will be sufficient for the debt to be revalued taking into account outstanding interest, or accrued indexation, at the five-yearly valuation dates. Any reduction of the debt resulting from a repayment can be taken into account as it occurred, and may be reflected in a revised computation of the tax in the relevant year and subsequently.

Residence or domicile outside the UK

9.59   There is no charge to tax where an individual is not resident in the UK during the year of assessment in question.

If the individual is resident, but not domiciled, in the UK in any year of assessment, the legislation only applies to land, chattels or intangible property situated in the UK.

In applying the rules to a person who was at any time domiciled outside the UK, no regard should be had to any property which is excluded for IHT purposes under *IHTA 1984, s 48(3)(a)*.

Focus

An individual will be treated as domiciled in the UK at any time if they would be treated as such for inheritance tax purposes. This means that the 'deemed domicile' rules for inheritance tax will apply for the purposes of this income tax charge.

De minimis exemption

9.60   An exemption from charge applies where, in relation to any person in a year of assessment, the aggregate of the amounts specified below in respect of that year do not exceed £5,000 (*FA 2004, Sch 15, para 13*).

Calculating the tax

9.61   The approach to valuing property for the purpose of the pre-owned assets rules is generally the same as for IHT purposes (*IHTA 1984, s 160*). In other words, it is the price that the property might reasonably be expected to fetch if sold in the open market at that time, without any scope for a reduction on the ground that the whole property is to be placed on the market at one and the same time.

The valuation date for property subject to the charge is 6 April in the relevant year of assessment or, if later, the first day of the taxable period.

When valuing relevant land or a chattel, it is not necessary to make an annual revaluation of the property. The property should rather be valued on a five-year cycle. Before the first five-year anniversary, the valuation of the property will be that set at the first valuation date. Thereafter, the valuation at the latest five-year anniversary will apply.

> **Example 9.15—Valuation**
>
> Andrew is first chargeable on 6 April 2014. A valuation is obtained on that date. He becomes non-UK resident for three years from 6 April 2015 to 6 April 2018. The charge does not apply during this period. He returns to the UK on 7 April 2018. A new valuation is made on that date, which is the start of the next five-year anniversary.

Land

9.62   The chargeable amount in relation to the relevant land is the appropriate rental value, less the amount of any payments which the chargeable person is legally obliged to make during the period to the owner of the relevant land in respect of their occupation.

The appropriate rental value is:

$$\frac{R \times DV}{V}$$

where:

- R is the rental value of the relevant land for the taxable period

- DV is:

    – where the chargeable person owned an interest in the relevant land, the value as at the valuation date of the interest in the relevant land that was disposed of by the chargeable person or, where the disposal was a non-exempt sale, the 'appropriate portion' of that value;

- – where the chargeable person owned an interest in other property, the proceeds of which were used to acquire an interest in relevant land, such part of the value of the relevant land at the valuation date as can reasonably be attributed to the property originally disposed of by the chargeable person or, where the original disposal was a non-exempt sale, to the appropriate portion of that property; or

- – if the contribution condition applies, such part of the value of the relevant land at the valuation date as can reasonably be attributed to the consideration provided by the chargeable person

- V is the value of the relevant land at the valuation date.

The 'rental value' of the land for the taxable period is the rent which would have been payable for the period if the property had been let to the chargeable person at an annual rent equal to the annual value. The annual value is the rent that might reasonably be expected to be obtained on a letting from year to year if:

- the tenant undertook to pay all taxes, rates and charges usually paid by a tenant; and

- the landlord undertook to bear the costs of the repairs and insurance and the other expenses, if any, necessary for maintaining the property in a state to command that rent.

9.63 The rent is calculated on the basis that the only amounts that may be deducted in respect of the services provided by the landlord are amounts in respect of the cost to the landlord of providing any relevant services. 'Relevant service' means a service other than the repair, insurance or maintenance of the premises. In other words, if the landlord provides other relevant services that are reflected in the rent, for example the maintenance of the common parts in a block of flats, then the cost of providing those services may be deducted from the rent.

The regulations do not specify the sources from which the required valuations should be obtained. However, HMRC would expect the chargeable person to take all reasonable steps to ascertain the valuations, as they would do if, for example, they were looking to let a property on the open market.

FA 2004, Sch 15, para 4(4) introduced the concept of a 'non-exempt sale' for a disposal which is a sale of the chargeable person's whole interest in the property for cash, but which is not an excluded transaction as defined in *para 10*. The 'appropriate proportion', which is relevant for ascertaining the appropriate rental value, is calculated as follows:

$$\frac{MV - P}{MV}$$

where:

- P is the amount paid
- MV is the value of the interest in land at the time of the sale.

Example 9.16—Pre-owned asset tax

Andrew sells his house to his daughter for £100,000. It is worth £300,000. He lives in the house. In these circumstances we would say that only two-thirds of the value of the house is potentially within the charge to pre-owned asset tax (POAT). However, since he made a gift of that two-thirds, HMRC would accept that he is protected under *FA 2004, Sch 15, para 11(5)* from a charge on that two-thirds. Note that, if he sold part of his house to his daughter at an undervalue, the non-exempt sale provisions would not apply. So, in Example 9.15, if he sold half his house to his daughter for £100,000 and that half share was in fact worth £300,000, although he would have reserved a benefit in two-thirds of that half share, the £100,000 cash would be subject to POAT.

Chattels

9.64   The chargeable amount in relation to any chattel is the appropriate amount, less the amount of any payments that the chargeable person is legally obliged to make during the period to the owner of the chattel for the possession or use of the chattel by the chargeable person (*FA 2004, Sch 15, para 7(2)*).

The appropriate amount is:

$$\frac{N \times DV}{V}$$

where:

- N is the amount of the interest that would be payable for the taxable period if interest were payable at the prescribed rate on an amount equal to the value of the chattel at the valuation date (the prescribed rate is the official rate of interest at the valuation date)

- DV is the value at the valuation date of the interest in the relevant chattel that was disposed of by the chargeable person or, where the proposal was a non-exempt sale, the appropriate proportion of that asset

- V is the value of the chattel at the valuation date.

Example 9.17—Chattels

In 2017/18, Andrew was caught by *Sch 15* in respect of an earlier disposal of chattels. The chattels were worth £1 million at the relevant valuation date on 6 April 2017. He will be treated as receiving a taxable benefit of 2.50% (official rate of interest in 2017/18) × £1 million = £25,000.

Note that the charge is computed differently from land and, while any rental payments made to the owner will reduce the amount on which he is chargeable, the fact that he pays a market rent for their use does not prevent an income tax charge arising. Hence, if he pays £10,000 rent, he will still be taxable on a £15,000 benefit. Tax is due on 31 January 2019 unless Andrew elects.

Intangible property

9.65 The chargeable amount in relation to the relevant property is N minus T.

N is the amount of the interest that would be payable for the taxable period if interest were payable at the prescribed rate on an amount equal to the value of the relevant property at the valuation date. The prescribed rate is the official rate of interest at the valuation date.

T is the amount of any income tax or CGT payable by the chargeable person in respect of the taxable period by virtue of any of the following provisions:

- *ITTOIA 2005, s 461 or 624*;

- *ITA 2007, ss 720–730*; or

- *TCGA 1992, s 86*;

so far as the tax is attributable to the relevant property.

Example 9.18—Intangible property

Mr A is the UK-resident and domiciled settlor of a non-resident settlor-interested settlement. (You should assume that Mr A has not reserved a benefit in the settled property nor has an interest in possession in the trust and is, therefore, subject to the POAT charge.)

The settlement comprises 'intangible' property of cash and shares with a value of £1,250,000 at the valuation date. In the tax year 2017/18 the trustees receive income of £60,000 which is chargeable to income tax on Mr A under *ITTOIA 2005, s 624*. A further £350,000 capital gains are realised, which are deemed to be Mr A's gains by virtue of *TCGA 1992, s 86*. In these circumstances, £27,000 income tax is payable on the £60,000 and £98,000 in CGT on the £350,000. The tax allowance (T) against the potential *Sch 15* charge is, therefore, £125,000. The chargeable amount (N) under *Sch 15* is 4.0% of £1,250,000 = £50,000. Since the tax allowance is greater than the chargeable amount, a charge under *Sch 15* will not arise.

Avoidance of double charge to income tax

9.66 There may be situations where:

- a chattel or land is caught by the rules applying to chattels or land; and

- there is also a charge in respect of intangible property which derives its value from the chattel or land.

In such situations, only one charge arises on the chattel or land and this will be the one which gives the largest chargeable amount. If this amount does not exceed the £5,000 *de minimis* limit no tax will be payable – the lower amount is disregarded completely.

Where the occupation, possession or use of any land or chattel is taxed as a benefit in kind in *Income Tax (Earnings and Pensions) Act 2003 (ITEPA 2003), Pt 3,* that Act takes precedence. However, if the chargeable amount under the pre-owned assets legislation exceeds the benefit in kind, the excess is charged under the pre-owned assets legislation (*FA 2004, Sch 15, para 18*).

The IHT election

9.67 The provisions of the pre-owned assets legislation are optional. The reason for this is that the provisions are simply a device to prevent the avoidance of IHT by exploiting gaps in the gifts with reservation legislation. The legislation has, therefore, provided taxpayers with the opportunity to opt back into the IHT rules. Such an option has to be made by the taxpayer in the form of an election. Owing to a defect in subsidiary legislation, HMRC have indicated that late elections will be accepted (Budget 2007, BN28), but it is unclear as to what extent. *FA 2007, s 66,* substituting *FA 2004, Sch 15, para 23(3),* states:

> 'The election must be made on or before:
>
> (a)   the relevant filing date, or
>
> (b)   such later date as an officer of Revenue and Customs may, in a particular case, allow.'

This provision applies from 21 March 2007.

This may provide a let-out for those who have faced hefty income tax charges.

Focus

Consideration should be given to making an election if the ultimate IHT charge is low. This might be the case if the estate will be quite small and, therefore, the nil rate band will not be used entirely or will only be slightly exceeded.

Chapter 10

Non-residents

SIGNPOSTS

- Residence status is an important factor in determining liability to UK income tax (see **10.1**).

- A statutory residence test applies from 6 April 2013. From the same date, the concept of 'ordinary residence' was effectively abolished for tax purposes, but overseas workday relief is retained and has been placed on a statutory footing (see **10.2**).

- A UK-domiciled individual coming to the UK will normally be treated as resident here from the date of his arrival, in which case he is liable to UK income tax on his worldwide income (see **10.8**).

- An individual who has left or is about to leave the UK should notify HMRC accordingly (see **10.14**).

- There are special rules that apply to non-UK resident sportsmen and entertainers (see **10.42**).

- An individual who is resident in the UK will be liable to UK tax on all their worldwide income (unless they claim to use the remittance basis because they are not UK domiciled (see **10.44**).

- The remittance basis may be available to UK-resident individuals who are not domiciled in the UK (see **10.57**).

- Tax relief may be available for tax suffered on foreign income under one of the numerous double taxation agreements (DTAs) held between the UK and other countries (see **10.70**).

- *Finance Act 2016* introduced additional obligations to deduct income tax at source from royalties paid to certain non-resident persons, subject to certain conditions (see **10.75**).

RESIDENCE STATUS

Residence of individuals

10.1   Historically, the meaning of 'residence' for tax purposes has been the same as its everyday English meaning. In The Oxford English Dictionary, the word 'reside' is defined as:

> 'To dwell permanently or for a considerable time, to have one's settled or usual abode, to live in or at a particular place.'

The tax tribunal would ultimately decide whether a taxpayer was resident or not in the UK in any tax year. Since this was a matter of fact rather than law, the courts would not interfere in such decisions unless no tribunal acting reasonably could have come to that decision on the evidence available. HMRC Claims Branch deal with the application of the residency rules.

Following a lengthy period of consultation, legislation was contained in the *Finance Act 2013* which introduced the statutory residence test (SRT) (*FA 2013, s 219* and *Sch 46*). The provisions apply from 6 April 2013. Guidance on the SRT can be found in the HMRC *Guidance note for Statutory Residence Test (SRT) (RDR3)* (www.gov.uk/government/uploads/system/uploads/attachment_data/file/458559/RDR3_govuk_hyperlink__updated_078500.pdf).

In addition to the statutory residence test, there are provisions to enable tax years to be split into resident and non-resident periods (previously, this treatment relied on extra-statutory concessions) and anti-avoidance provisions to prevent individuals from taking advantage of the new test to avoid tax. The test has three key elements: an automatic residence test, an automatic overseas test and a sufficient ties test. If the individual does not meet the automatic residence test or sufficient ties test for the relevant year, they are treated as not resident in the UK. A systematic approach to the tests is therefore required in order to determine an individual's residency status.

Statutory residence test

10.2   Automatic overseas tests

An individual who meets any of the automatic overseas tests for a tax year, is automatically treated as non-resident for that year. These tests should therefore be considered first:

First automatic overseas test

The individual was resident in the UK for one or more of the three tax years preceding the tax year and spends fewer than 16 days in the UK in the tax year. If an individual dies in the tax year, this test does not apply.

Second automatic overseas test

The individual was resident in the UK for none of the three tax years preceding the tax year and spends fewer than 46 days in the UK in the tax year.

Third automatic overseas test

The individual works full-time overseas over the tax year, without any significant breaks during the tax year from overseas work, and:

- spends fewer than 91 days in the UK in the tax year (see **10.10**),

- the number of days in the tax year on which the individual works for more than three hours in the UK is less than 31 days.

The third automatic overseas test does not apply if:

- the individual has a relevant job on board a vehicle, aircraft or ship at any time in the relevant tax year, and

- at least six of the trips that the individual makes in that year as part of that job are cross-border trips that:

    – begin in the UK;

    – end in the UK; or

    – begin and end in the UK.

Automatic UK tests

Subject to not meeting any of the automatic overseas tests, an individual will be resident in the UK for a tax year if they meet:

- any of the automatic UK tests set out below; or

- the sufficient ties test.

First automatic UK test

The individual spends 183 days or more in the UK in the tax year.

Second automatic UK test

The second automatic UK test is relevant if the individual has or had a home in the UK during all or part of the tax year.

The individual will meet this test if there is at least one period of 91 consecutive days, at least 30 days of which fall in the tax year, when:

- they have a home in the UK in which they spend a sufficient amount of time, and either they:

    – have no overseas home; or

    – have an overseas home or homes in each of which they spend no more than a permitted amount of time.

10.2 *Non-residents*

Where an individual has more than one home in the UK, each home needs to be considered separately.

Third automatic UK test

The individual works full-time in the UK for any period of 365 days, with no significant break from UK work and:

- all or part of that 365-day period falls within the tax year;

- more than 75% of the total number of days in the 365-day period, when they do more than three hours of work, are days when they do more than three hours of work in the UK;

- at least one day in the tax year is a day on which they do more than three hours of work in the UK.

An individual who meets these criteria will be resident under the third automatic UK test.

If a period of 365 days is identified where the individual has worked full-time in the UK, but does not then meet the 75% test relating to that 365-day period, they must consider whether there is another 365-day period when they do meet the 75% test. If there is no such period, they will not meet the third automatic UK test.

Sufficient ties test

An individual who does not meet any of the automatic overseas tests or any of the automatic UK tests should use the sufficient ties test to determine their UK residence status for a tax year. They will need to consider their connections to the UK, called ties, and determine whether the ties, taken together with the number of days spent in the UK, are sufficient for them to be considered UK resident for tax purposes for a particular tax year.

If the individual was not UK resident for any of the three tax years before the tax year under consideration, they will need to consider if they have any of these UK ties:

- a family tie;

- an accommodation tie;

- a work tie; and

- a 90-day tie.

An individual who was resident in the UK for one or more of the three tax years before the tax year under consideration will also need to consider whether they have a country tie.

Example 10.1—Residence (I)

In 2017/18, Jim earns a bonus of £5,000, although he does not receive it until 2018/19. He is resident in the UK in 2017/18 but, following a move abroad, he is non-UK resident in 2018/19. The bonus is chargeable to UK tax on the 'arising basis' in 2017/18.

Example 10.2—Residence (II)

Etienne lives in France but comes to work in the UK and is resident here in 2018/19. He is not chargeable on a bonus received in 2018/19 but earned in 2017/18 when he was not resident here.

The charge to income tax remains fundamentally the same, with the same available deductions.

Split tax year concession

10.3   Under the SRT (see **10.2**), an individual is either UK resident or non-UK resident for a full tax year and at all times in that tax year. However, if during a year that individual either starts to live or work abroad or comes from abroad to live or work in the UK, the tax year will be split into two parts if their circumstances meet specific criteria:

- a UK part for which they are charged to UK tax as a UK resident;

- an overseas part for which, for most purposes, they are charged to UK tax as a non-UK resident.

The taxpayer must be UK resident for a tax year under the SRT to meet the criteria for split year treatment for that year. They will not meet the split year criteria for a tax year for which they are non-UK resident under the SRT.

Split year treatment in the context of the SRT applies only to an individual in his or her individual capacity. It does not apply to individuals acting as personal representatives. It applies in a limited way to individuals acting as trustee of a settlement in determining the trustees' residence status:

- if the individual becomes or ceases to be a trustee of the settlement during the tax year,

- provided that the period they are a trustee falls within the overseas part of the tax year for that individual.

Split year treatment will not affect whether the individual is regarded as UK resident for the purposes of any double taxation arrangement.

10.4   The split tax year concession (see **10.3**) only applies to the self-employed if they are going abroad for at least three years. They will remain liable to UK tax to the extent that any part of the business is carried on in the UK. If the overseas country has a significantly more favourable tax regime, it may be worthwhile incorporating an offshore company with non-resident directors so that the exposure to UK tax is limited to the profits of the UK branch.

Where the partnership carries on business partly in the UK and partly abroad, the non-resident partner's taxable share in the UK is limited to his share of the profits of the trade carried on in the UK.

In *Shepherd v R & C Commrs* [2005] SpC 484, the taxpayer was an airline pilot who, prior to his retirement, claimed to have set up a home in Cyprus. He rented a fully furnished apartment, and then went on to purchase a property there. From the time he first rented the apartment, he ensured that his visits to the UK were less than the 91-day limit. In the year that concerned the appeal (1999/2000), his visits totalled only 80 days. He claimed that he had separated from his wife but they continued to share the matrimonial home throughout the period involved. In addition, he had described himself on his tax return as married and not separated and, when making a will in Cyprus, he left the property to his 'dearest wife'. He also remained on the electoral register and had mail sent to him there. He claimed that, when staying over in the UK between flights to and from Cyprus, he normally stayed with his parents; however, the Special Commissioner found that he stayed mainly at the matrimonial home. The Commissioner held that he was resident in the UK for 1999/2000 because he had gone abroad only for occasional residence. His continued, albeit on a much reduced scale, occupation of the matrimonial home indicated that he had not severed his connection with the UK sufficiently to show that his residence in Cyprus was anything other than occasional. His appeal in the High Court ([2007] BTC 426) was subsequently dismissed.

10.5   In *Grace v R & C Commrs* [2008] SpC 663, the taxpayer was an airline pilot who had formerly lived in the UK but, in 1997, he set up home in South Africa (the country of his birth) and claimed to be non-UK resident. His former wife and children continued to live in the UK but he only saw them on rare occasions. He maintained a house in the UK but only stayed there to rest before or after his flights.

The Special Commissioner held that, although Mr Grace was resident in the UK before October 1997, in that year there was a distinct break and, since then, his settled mode of life was in South Africa and not in the UK. This decision was found applying the principle established in *IR Commrs v Combe* (1932) 17 TC 405 that, if a person resident in the UK left for another country, and if there was a 'distinct break', then even if he returned for lengthy visits, he need not be resident if he had a settled mode of life elsewhere. The Special Commissioner then considered whether the taxpayer was ordinarily resident in the UK. *ICTA 1988, s 334* (now *ITA 2007, s 829*) did not apply, as the taxpayer's presence abroad from October 1997 was not for the purpose only of occasional residence abroad but for the purposes of continuous and settled residence in his house in South Africa and he only returned to the UK for the purpose of his work.

The High Court subsequently overturned the Special Commissioner's decision and held that there had been several errors in arriving at that decision. The judge said that 'temporary' (in former *ICTA 1988, s 336(2)*, now *ITA 2007, s 832*) was not descriptive of the taxpayer's presence but of the taxpayer's purpose. In turn, this meant that it was for the Special Commissioner to decide whether the reason for the taxpayer's presence in the UK was casual or transitory. The recurrent nature of his regular presence in the UK (*Shepherd v R & C Commrs* considered) led to the conclusion that his purpose for being in the UK was neither casual nor transitory. It was also found that the Special Commissioner was wrong in law to discount the reason for the taxpayer's regular presence in the UK in his own house as being attributable 'only' to his work. He said the Commissioner had overlooked the fact that someone may be here for the exigencies of work and still have his presence treated as voluntary.

Furthermore, the Commissioner was wrong in concluding that there had been a 'distinct break' in the taxpayer's life when he set up home in South Africa. That conclusion, the judge said, was inconsistent with the undisputed facts that the taxpayer had retained the house in the UK which remained furnished, continued the same employment, and continued to be present regularly in the UK for the purposes of that employment. All that happened after he set up home in South Africa was that he acquired another home there.

On appeal against the decision of the High Court, the Court of Appeal referred the case to the First-tier Tribunal (*Grace v R & C Commrs* [2009] BTC 704).

Ordinary residence

10.6   The concept of 'ordinary residence' was abolished from 6 April 2013 (*FA 2013, s 219* and *Sch 46*).

Formerly, individuals who were not ordinarily resident in the UK were taxed on the remittance basis on income from foreign employment duties where the income was paid by the UK employer provided the individual intended to leave the UK within three years of arrival. This is known as 'overseas work day relief'.

To prevent those who were entitled to overseas workday relief from being placed at a disadvantage, this relief continues in a statutory form from 6 April 2013 onwards. It only applies to individuals who are not domiciled in the UK, and it is available for the tax year in which an individual first becomes resident in the UK for tax purposes and the following two tax years. There is no requirement about the length of time that an individual intends to remain in the UK, but they have to have been non-resident for the three tax years before coming to work in the UK. There is transitional relief for those who currently benefit from the relief. In all other cases where a tax liability is determined by reference to ordinary residence, it will be determined solely by reference to residence status.

Transitional elections

10.7   An individual may elect (for these purposes only) to determine his residence status for one or more of years prior to 2013/14 (a 'pre-commencement year') by reference to the SRT rather than in accordance with the prior law. The election does not change an individual's actual tax residence status for the pre-commencement year or years nor does it affect his tax liability in that or those year or years.

UK domiciled individuals

10.8   A UK-domiciled individual coming to the UK will normally be treated as resident here from the date of his arrival, in which case he is liable to UK income tax on his worldwide income (*ITEPA 2003, Pt 2, Ch 4*) (see **10.44** for commentary on domicile). The following table (which has been adapted from the HMRC RDR1 booklet) shows the liability to tax on employment income according to the individual's residence status, and the place where the duties of the job are performed:

UK domiciled status	UK residence status	Arising basis (AB) or remittance basis (RB) claimed	Employment duties performed wholly or partly in the UK		Employment duties performed wholly outside the UK
			Duties performed in UK	Duties performed outside UK	
Domiciled within UK	1 Resident and ordinarily resident	AB	Liable[1]	Liable[1]	Liable[1]
	2 Resident and not ordinarily resident	2(a) AB	Liable	Liable	Liable
		2(b) RB	Liable	Liable on remittance	Liable on remittance
	3 Not resident	AB[2]	Liable	Not liable	Not liable

Notes:

1   Liable to pay UK tax unless subject to Seafarers' Earnings Deduction (SED) (see **10.30**).

2   For individuals not resident in the UK, the arising basis is limited to liability to UK tax on income arising in the UK.

Focus

Finance (No 2) Act 2017 contained a package of reforms to the 'non-dom' regime, which apply from April 2017 (*F(No 2)A 2017, ss 29 and 30*).From that date, those who have been resident in the UK for more than 15 out of the past 20 tax years will be treated as deemed UK domiciled for all tax purposes. This means that they will no longer be able to use the remittance basis (see **10.57**) and they will be deemed domiciled for inheritance tax purposes. In addition, those who had a domicile in the UK at the date of their birth will revert to having a UK domicile for tax purposes whenever they are resident in the UK, even if under general law they have acquired a domicile in another country.

The legislation also contains measures designed to help those who become deemed-domiciled after having been resident for 15 of the past 20 years to transition to the new regime.

Dual residence

10.9   It is possible to be resident in more than one country and, in some cases, there will be actual or potential double taxation of the same income. The UK has double taxation treaties with most countries and in most cases relief will be available; either the treaty will give one country the right to tax a particular type of income (eg rent from property located in that country), or it will provide for credit relief (ie one jurisdiction will permit the set-off of tax paid in the other country).

Focus

For a list of countries with which the UK has a double taxation agreement (DTA) in force, see the HMRC Digest of Double Taxation Treaties (www.gov.uk/government/publications/double-taxation-treaties-territory-residents-with-uk-income).

91-day test

10.10   The case of *Robert Gaines-Cooper v HMRC* [2006] SpC 568 attracted some attention from tax practitioners and their clients because there had been some suggestion that the decision changed the basis on which HMRC calculate the '91-day test' (see **10.2**). HMRC Brief 01/07, however, confirmed that this is incorrect.

HMRC believe that their guidance is clear that the '91-day test' applies only to individuals who have either left the UK and live elsewhere or who visit the UK on a regular basis. Where an individual has lived in the UK, the question of whether he has left the UK has to be decided first. Individuals who have left the

UK will continue to be regarded as UK resident if their visits to the UK average 91 days or more a tax year, taken over a maximum of up to four tax years.

HMRC's normal practice is to disregard days of arrival and departure in calculating days under the '91-day test'.

In considering the issues of residence, ordinary residence and domicile in the *Gaines-Cooper* case, the Commissioners needed to build up a full picture of Mr Gaines-Cooper's life. A very important element of the picture was the pattern of his presence in the UK compared to the pattern of his presence overseas. The Commissioners decided that, in looking at these patterns, it would be misleading wholly to disregard days of arrival and departure. They used Mr Gaines-Cooper's patterns of presence in the UK as part of the evidence of his lifestyle and habits during the years in question. Based on this, and a wide range of other evidence, the Commissioners found that he had been continuously resident in the UK. From HMRC's perspective, therefore, the '91-day test' was not relevant to the *Gaines-Cooper* case, since Mr Gaines-Cooper did not leave the UK.

In Brief 01/07, HMRC confirmed that there has been no change to their practice in relation to residence and the '91-day test'. Accordingly, they will continue to:

- follow the published guidance on residence issues, and apply this guidance fairly and consistently;

- treat an individual who has not left the UK as remaining resident here;

- consider all the relevant evidence, including the pattern of presence in the UK and elsewhere, in deciding whether or not an individual has left the UK; and

- apply the '91-day test' (where HMRC are satisfied that an individual has actually left the UK) as outlined in booklet HMRC6, normally disregarding days of arrival and departure in calculating days under this 'test'.

Following on from the Commissioners' decision, in *R (on the application of Davies & Anor) v R & C Commrs; R (on the application of Gaines-Cooper) v R & C Commrs* [2010] EWCA Civ 83, the Court of Appeal, dismissing applications for judicial review, clarified the interpretation of HMRC's 1999 edition of booklet IR20 in relation to leaving the UK to work full-time abroad and leaving the UK permanently and definitely, and held that HMRC had not been shown to have made any unannounced alteration in their interpretation of the guidance. The case continued its journey to the Supreme Court (*R (on the application of Davies & Anor) v R & C Commrs; R (on the application of Gaines-Cooper) v R & C Commrs* [2011] UKSC 47) and, on 19 October 2011, the court, by a majority, held that the guidance in IR20 did not dispense with the requirement of a 'distinct break' in order to obtain non-resident status, and that there was insufficient evidence of any settled practice on the part of HMRC giving rise to a legitimate expectation that the taxpayers would be treated as non-resident.

Returning to the UK

10.11   Generally, individuals returning to the UK from overseas postings will be resident in the UK from the date of return (*ITEPA 2003, Pt 2, Ch 5*).

Basis of assessment

10.12   Except in relation to certain foreign emoluments (see *ITEPA 2003, s 15*), any person who is resident in the UK, and UK domiciled, is liable to income tax on the whole of his earnings wherever earned and irrespective of whether they are remitted to the UK. The taxpayer may be entitled to a special deduction where his duties are carried out wholly or partly outside the UK (see below) and, in many cases, double taxation relief will apply (see **10.70**).

The place of performance of duties is of major importance in determining how payments are treated for income tax purposes. Where duties are ordinarily performed in the UK, emoluments during any absence from employment are related to UK duties unless, but for that absence, they would have been emoluments for duties performed outside the UK. Thus, an airline pilot's rest days were not attributable to duties performed outside the UK. In order to bring himself within the exception, the taxpayer would have to show that had he worked on those days his actual duties would have been performed outside the UK and it did not matter that most of his time was spent on duties abroad.

The relative levels of the emoluments received here and abroad may not reflect the relative duties performed here and abroad. The split may be made simply to suit the employee's convenience and there may be scope for tax planning in this area. He may, therefore, be remitting to the UK emoluments received abroad but attributable to the UK duties. Each case must be studied on its facts.

Focus

HMRC will accept that the total emoluments may be apportioned between UK and overseas duties on the basis of working days, unless there are special circumstances.

An employee who is not resident in the UK is only liable to tax on earnings from duties performed in the UK, under *ITEPA 2003, s 27*.

PERSONAL RELIEFS FOR NON-RESIDENTS

Personal allowances

10.13   Non-UK residents are generally not entitled to personal allowances and reliefs, unless the individual is (*ITA 2007, s 56*):

● a national of an EEA state;

- a person who is or has been a Crown servant;

- a person whose late spouse or late civil partner was employed as a Crown servant;

- a missionary;

- a person in the service of a British protectorate;

- a resident of the Isle of Man or Channel Islands; or

- a person who has been resident in the UK but is now resident abroad for the sake of his health or the health of a member of his family who resides with him.

In these cases, the non-resident is entitled to the personal reliefs to which residents are entitled.

To ensure compliance with certain aspects of the *Human Rights Act 1998*, legislation is contained in *FA 2009* to withdraw the entitlement for non-resident individuals who currently qualify for UK personal tax allowances and reliefs *solely* by virtue of being a Commonwealth citizen. Whilst the vast majority of individuals affected will still benefit through other means such as double taxation treaties, citizens of Bahamas, Cameroon, Cook Islands, Dominica, Maldives, Mozambique, Nauru, Niue, St Lucia, St Vincent & the Grenadines, Samoa, Tanzania, Tonga and Vanuatu may be affected (*FA 2009, s 5* and *Sch 1*).

EMPLOYMENT MATTERS

Introduction

10.14   Emoluments from an employment, including benefits in kind, are calculated under the normal tax rules. Apart from the travelling expense rules, expenses are deductible only according to the normal test of being wholly, exclusively and necessarily incurred in the performance of the duty of the employment.

Many international employers operate tax equalisation schemes, also known as tax protected pay or net pay. It is an arrangement that ensures that an employee has the same take home pay wherever employed. Payments under these schemes are taxable. 'Golden handshakes' are also taxable but, in addition to the general £30,000 allowance, substantial foreign service may give a full or further partial exemption (see **10.18**).

Stock options or share acquisition schemes may give rise to taxable income. Gains on the grant of an option escape tax if the individual is not resident and (until 5 April 2013) not ordinarily resident and his emoluments are foreign emoluments for duties wholly performed outside the UK. Gains on the exercise of an option will not necessarily escape tax if the individual is then non-resident. Gains arising in relation to share acquisition schemes are chargeable in the normal way, unless the employee is non-resident at the time the gain arises.

Form P85 is for completion by employees when they subsequently leave the UK. It is a voluntary, rather than statutory, form. Since self-assessment, the form is still required to be completed but, in addition, any individual who receives a tax return form is required to complete the 'Non-residence' supplementary pages. It should be noted that, since the introduction of self-assessment, HMRC have ceased to give residency rulings. This form may be relevant for those leaving the UK, and 'who may not be coming back or are going to work abroad full-time for at least a complete tax year'.

Focus

HMRC offer an online form service to claim tax relief or any tax refund due where a taxpayer has left, or is about to leave the UK. The service can be accessed at www.gov.uk/government/publications/income-tax-leaving-the-uk-getting-your-tax-right-p85.

Liability to tax

10.15 The tax treatment of employment income of individuals domiciled outside the UK depends on:

- the residence status of the employee;

- whether the duties are performed wholly abroad or wholly or partly in the UK;

- whether remuneration is classed as foreign emoluments.

Foreign emoluments are amounts paid by a non-resident employer (which includes a branch of a non-resident company or partnership) to a non-domiciled employee. An employer resident in the Republic of Ireland, or in the UK and abroad, cannot pay foreign emoluments.

Where there is a difference in treatment between UK earnings and overseas earnings, two separate contracts, one for UK and the other for foreign duties, are desirable. The contracts must be with separate employers, as it is not possible to have two contracts of employment with the same employer. The use of two contracts allows the employer to specify that the foreign duties attract a higher rate of remuneration, although they will be treated as one employment for tax purposes.

Incidental duties

10.16 Duties performed in the UK which are merely incidental to duties performed abroad are treated as if they were performed abroad (*ITEPA 2003, s 39*).

For the purpose of the 100% deduction for seafarers (see **10.30**), incidental duties performed abroad are treated as performed in the UK where the duties of the employment are in substance performed in the UK.

Whether duties performed in the UK are 'incidental duties' is a question of fact. It is the nature of the duties which is the most significant factor, but the time spent on such duties is also a factor to be taken into account (*ITEPA 2003, ss 341(6), (7), 376(4), (5)*).

HMRC guidance advises on whether certain items are regarded as incidental or not incidental to duties performed abroad:

Not incidental	**Incidental**
(1) Directors' meetings A company director, usually working abroad, attends directors' meetings in the UK.	(1) Overseas representative An overseas representative of a UK employer comes to the UK to report to the employer or receive fresh instructions.
(2) Three months or more Duties performed for an aggregate period of three months or more.	(2) Training An overseas employee visiting the UK for a training period not exceeding three months in a year and where no productive work is done by him in that time.

See also the HMRC paper entitled *Dual contracts: record keeping, enquiries, completion of Self Assessment Returns and interpretation of 'merely incidental' duties,* which can be found at www.gov.uk/government/publications/dual-contracts.

More than one job

10.17 Special provisions apply where the employee has two or more employments. These provisions are largely designed to prevent the 'loading' of earnings onto the overseas employment in order to avoid tax (*ITEPA 2003, ss 23(3), 24, 329(1), 331(2)*).

Where the duties of an employment and any associated employment (see below) are wholly performed abroad, the deductions referred to above will apply to all the earnings of the employment.

The 100% deduction for seafarers and the deduction relating to 'foreign emoluments' apply to only a proportion of the earnings from the employment abroad where the duties of the employment or any associated employment are not performed wholly outside the UK.

That proportion is one which is shown by the employee to be reasonable having regard to the nature of the duties and the time devoted to them within the UK and abroad and other relevant circumstances.

An employment is an 'associated employment' of another employment for these purposes if they are with the same person or with persons associated with each other. A company is associated with another if one of them has control of the other or both are under the control of the same person or persons. An individual or partnership is associated with another person (whether or not a company) if one of them has control of the other or both are under the control of the same person or persons.

Foreign service relief

10.18   Broadly, until 5 April 2018, under the foreign service relief rules, employees who received termination payments while working in the UK, but who had worked for their employer outside the UK for more than 75% of the last 20 years, did not have to pay any income tax on these payments. In addition, if an employee had worked abroad but did not meet the qualifying criteria for a 100% deduction, they may have been able to receive a smaller relief that was proportionate to their time worked outside the UK for that employer.

The foreign service, in general, must comprise one of the following (*ITEPA 2003, s 413(1)*):

• three-quarters of the whole period of service;

• the last ten years where the period of service exceeded ten years; or

• where the period of service exceeded 20 years, one-half of that period, including any ten of the last 20 years.

The government believes that the foreign service relief rules are outdated, unnecessary or no longer justifiable. Subsequently, new provisions have been enacted by Finance Act 2018 to ensure that employees who are UK resident in the tax year their employment is terminated will not be eligible for foreign service relief on their termination payments. Reforming foreign service relief in this way is designed to help achieve the government's aims of a fairer tax system.

The changes mean that those who have worked abroad but are resident in the UK in the year their employment is terminated will be taxed in the same way as others who haven't worked abroad. They will continue to benefit from the existing £30,000 income tax exemption and an unlimited employee National Insurance contributions (NICs) exemption for payments associated with the termination of employment.

The change will apply to those who have their employment terminated on or after 6 April 2018. However, the relief will cease even for payments and benefits actually received from 13 September 2017 (*FA 2018, s 10*).

The existing Statutory Residency Test (see **10.2**) will be used to determine whether employees are UK resident in the tax year they receive their termination award.

The relief is retained in cases where the employee is non-UK resident in the tax year in which the employment is terminated and the change is not extended to seafarers for whom the position on the relief essentially remains unchanged.

Travel expenses

10.19 Travelling expenses incurred by an employee necessarily in the performance of his duties are allowable in calculating chargeable income. *ITEPA 2003, s 370* allows a deduction for the employee's travel costs and expenses in certain cases where the employee's duties are performed abroad.

Expenses incurred in connection with certain overseas duties – either travel to take up a foreign employment with duties wholly overseas (and returning to the UK at the end of that employment), board and lodging while there or in travelling between an employment whose duties are at least partly overseas and any other employment – are eligible for relief if the employee is resident in the UK and the earnings are not foreign emoluments (*ITEPA 2003, ss 15* and *22*).

Expenses are apportioned where travel is partly for another purpose.

Where an employer provides travel facilities or reimburses an employee the cost of travel, the employee is entitled to a deduction for the cost of the travel facilities or sum reimbursed. This rule applies to:

- travel between any place in the UK and the place of performance of any of those duties outside the UK (and any return journey) by the spouse/civil partner or any child of the employee;

- travel from any place in the UK to the place of performance of any of those duties (and any return journey) by an employee whose duties are performed partly outside the UK and can only be performed outside the UK; and

- travel from the place of performance of any duties of an office or employment outside the UK to any place in the UK (and any return journey) by an employee absent from the UK performing the duties of an office or employment which can only be performed outside the UK.

Similar provisions apply to the travel expenses of non-UK domiciled employees.

ITEPA 2003, s 304A provides an exemption from income tax in relation to the subsistence allowances paid by a body of the EU located in the UK to experts who are seconded by their employers to work for the EU body. Relevant EU bodies include:

- the European Medicines Agency;

- the European Police College;

- the European Banking Authority; and

- any other body established by an EU instrument which is designated as a relevant EU body for the purposes of *s 304A*.

This measure has effect in relation to subsistence allowances paid in respect of periods beginning on or after 1 January 2011.

Before the travel expenses of the spouse or any child of the employee can attract the beneficial treatment, the following further conditions need to be met (*ITEPA 2003, s 371*).

Example 10.3—Overseas travel expenses

Marco works in France, but has to travel to the UK for a business meeting in London (the place of the business meeting is a temporary workplace), arranged for Monday morning at 9.00am. The cost of the journey would have been deductible for tax purposes had he met it himself.

Marco flies to the UK on Sunday evening; he disembarks his plane at 6:00am on Monday at Heathrow and after clearing immigration and customs leaves the terminal at 7.30am. Marco travels directly to his business meeting, arriving there at 8.45am. The meeting lasts two hours, after which he returns to the airport for a flight home the same day.

The time spent travelling from overseas, up to the point of disembarking at Heathrow, counts as work done overseas. Time spent travelling from disembarking at Heathrow to the place of his business meeting counts as work done in the UK, as does the duration of the meeting and the return journey to Heathrow. As Marco worked for more than three hours in the UK on this day, it is also a UK work day.

Travel costs and expenses of non-domiciled employees

10.20 Non-UK domiciled employees can claim a deduction for expenses from an employment for duties performed in the UK (*ITEPA 2003, s 373*). The deduction is given for the amount included in respect of (a) the provision of travel facilities for a journey made by the employee, or (b) the reimbursement of expenses incurred by the employee on such a journey. Two conditions must both be met.

The first condition is that the journey ends on, or during the period of five years beginning with, a date that is a 'qualifying arrival date' in relation to the employee.

The second condition is that the journey is made:

- from the country outside the UK in which the employee normally lives to a place in the UK in order to perform duties of the employment; or

- to that country from a place in the UK in order to return to that country after performing such duties.

If the journey has a dual purpose, the deduction is given for so much of the amount included in earnings as is properly attributable to the work purpose.

> **Example 10.4—Non-domiciled travel expenses (I)**
>
> Marcus, who is domiciled in Italy, divorces his wife. She has custody of their two children and takes them to live in her native New York. A journey made by the children to visit their father in the UK would not qualify under this provision if it was direct from New York (not the taxpayer's usual place of abode). Equally, a return journey could not qualify, as to do so it must follow a qualifying journey.

> **Example 10.5—Non-domiciled travel expenses (II)**
>
> Franco is domiciled in Italy and comes to the UK in June 2012 to work as a freelance IT consultant. He makes a home here, although he regularly returns to Italy for about six months a year. In January 2016, he gets a job in Italy in a UK company. He remains in Italy during his tenure of that employment. He returns to the UK in July 2018 to take up another post with the same company. Throughout this period, he maintains a house in the UK available for his use. He has a wife and family in Italy.
>
> Franco satisfies the conditions because:
>
> (1) he is non-resident in the two tax years before that in which he returns to the UK (being physically absent for the duration); and
>
> (2) he does not return to the UK at any time between July 2016 and July 2018.
>
> If he returns to the UK for any purpose in this latter period (eg for holiday or interview), he fails condition (2).

Employee's spouse's, civil partner's or child's travel

10.21 A deduction may be claimed for the travelling expenses in respect of (a) the provision of travel facilities for a journey made by the spouse, civil partner (*SI 2005/3229, reg 148(3)*) or child of the non-UK domiciled employee, or (b) the reimbursement of expenses incurred by the employee on such a journey. The following conditions must be met (*ITEPA 2003, s 374*):

Condition 1 – journey

The journey must:

- be made between the country outside the UK in which the employee normally lives and a place in the UK; and

- end on, or during the period of five years beginning with, a date that is a 'qualifying arrival date' in relation to the employee.

Condition 2 – employee's presence in the UK

The employee must be in the UK for a continuous period of at least 60 days (see **10.24**) for the purpose of performing the duties of one or more employments from which the employee receives earnings for duties performed in the UK.

Condition 3 – spouse, civil partner or child

The spouse, civil partner or child must be:

- accompanying the employee at the beginning of the 60-day period;

- visiting the employee during that period; or

- returning to the country outside the UK in which the employee normally lives, after so accompanying or visiting the employee.

'Child' includes a stepchild and an illegitimate child, but does not include any child who is aged 18 or over at the beginning of the outward journey (*ITEPA 2003, s 374(9)*).

The journey by a member of the employee's immediate family must be between the country outside the UK in which the employee normally lives and the place of performance of his duties in the UK.

Example 10.6—Travel expenses

Ed is posted to the Hong Kong office of his employer. He has been absent from the UK for a continuous period of more than 90 days. Ed and his wife, Sarah, plan to visit Thailand when his wife visits him. Sarah flies from London to Hong Kong and the two of them fly on to Thailand. Ed's employer pays for Sarah's return trip to Hong Kong.

The cost of the return journey between London and Hong Kong is deductible from Ed's employment earnings. However, where Ed has to arrange for his wife to fly directly to Thailand, where he would meet her, the employer again bearing the cost, the cost of the return trip between London and Thailand would not be deductible, since Thailand is not the place of the performance of Ed's duties. The entire cost would, therefore, have been disallowed.

Only two return journeys may be claimed by the same individual in a single tax year (*ITEPA 2003, s 374(8)*).

If the journey has a dual purpose, the deduction is given for so much of the amount included in earnings as is properly attributable to the work purpose.

Qualifying arrival date

10.22   A 'qualifying arrival date' is defined as the date on which a person arrives in the UK to perform duties of an employment from which he or she receives earnings for duties performed in the UK and which meets either of two conditions (*ITEPA 2003, s 375*):

(1)   the person has not been in the UK for any purpose during the period of two years ending with the day before the date.

(2)   the person was not resident in the UK in either of the two tax years preceding the tax year in which the date falls. If this condition is met and there are two or more dates in the tax year on which the person arrives in the UK to perform duties of an employment from which the person receives earnings for duties performed in the UK, the qualifying arrival date is the earliest of them.

Focus

For further information on arrival in the UK, see www.gov.uk/personal-tax/coming-to-uk.

Travel within a foreign country

10.23   Although travel may commence or end at any place in the UK, the travel to or from the country outside the UK in which the employee normally lives can, on a strict reading, only qualify if it is to or from the point of arrival or, as the case may be, departure in that country.

Example 10.7—Travel within a foreign country

Jack is domiciled in France and has lived for many years in Paris. He travels to take up a post with the London branch of a French manufacturing business. Rather than take a direct flight to London, he travels via Amsterdam, stopping over for one night between flights. His point of departure is Amsterdam. The flight from Paris to Amsterdam is not from the country outside the UK in which Jack normally lives, rather it is within it.

However, HMRC have confirmed that they will normally interpret the phrase 'usual place of abode' pragmatically, so that bona fide cases will qualify for relief.

Meaning of 'a continuous period of at least 60 days'

10.24 HMRC accept that, for the purposes of *ITEPA 2003, s 374(4)* only, employees satisfy the 60-day rule where:

- they spend at least two-thirds of their working days in the UK over a period of 60 days or more; and

- they are present in the UK for the purpose of performing the duties of their employment both at the start and at the end of this period.

Foreign expenses

10.25 Expenses incurred in providing board and lodging to enable an employee to perform the duties of his overseas employment are deductible if either the board and lodging outside the UK is provided directly by the employer, or the employee incurs the expense and is reimbursed by the employer, and the following conditions are met (*ITEPA 2003, s 376*):

- the duties of the employment are performed wholly outside the UK;

- the employee is resident in the UK; and

- in a case where the employer is a 'foreign employer', the employee is domiciled in the UK (apart from this, the employee's domicile is irrelevant).

Where the board and lodging is provided partly for the performance of the duties and partly for another purpose, only the expenses attributable to the former are allowable as a deduction.

Focus

The terms 'accommodation' and 'subsistence' are not defined in the legislation. However, HMRC's Employment Income Manual (at EIM34030) provides guidance on overseas accommodation, subsistence costs and expenses.

Example 10.8—Foreign expenses

Christopher is sent to Australia by his employer on business which takes one week to conclude. Whilst in Australia, he decides to take a further fortnight's holiday. The hotel expenses of the three weeks are paid for by the employer.

In these circumstances, only the hotel expenses relating to the first week are allowable as a deduction.

Double tax treaties

10.26 Many double taxation treaties provide that a resident of a foreign country who can claim the protection of the treaty will not be liable to UK tax on emoluments for duties performed in the UK if:

- the individual is present in the UK for periods not exceeding in total 183 days in any tax year;

- the emoluments are paid by an employer who is not resident in the UK; and

- the cost of the emoluments is not borne by a permanent establishment or fixed base that the employer has in the UK.

Treaties often exclude public entertainers and sports people from the protection of such a provision, and their earnings are often paid under deduction of tax (see **10.70**).

PAYE MATTERS

UK presence

10.27 If an employer has a trading presence in the UK, he will be required to deduct income tax and Class 1 NICs under PAYE from employees, regardless of whether he and/or the employee are non-resident. The remuneration will be charged to UK income tax.

Intermediaries

10.28 Primary legislation governs the PAYE liability of non-resident employers, and of those to whom employees are seconded in cases where the employer does not operate PAYE (*ITEPA 2003, ss 689* and *691*).

The legislation was amended with effect from 6 April 2014 to ensure that the correct amount of PAYE and NICs is paid when UK and UK continental shelf workers are employed by offshore companies or engaged by or through offshore employment intermediaries. Revised record-keeping and return requirements now apply to intermediaries placing workers with end clients but not deducting PAYE and NICs at source (*FA 2014, s 20*).

Focus

The legislation relating to employment agencies was strengthened with effect from 6 April 2014 by removing the obligation for personal service. Instead, the legislation focuses on whether the worker is subject to, or to the right of, supervision, direction or control as to the manner in which the duties are carried out (*FA 2014, s 16*). The concept of an agency contract

---

has also been removed from the legislation. These changes have been introduced to prevent the avoidance of PAYE and NICs by UK agencies engaging UK workers through non-UK agencies.

Dual contracts

10.29   Legislation in *FA 2014* is designed to ensure that non-domiciled individuals are taxed on overseas employment income on the 'arising basis'. This measure was introduced to prevent contrived arrangements by a small number of high-earning, UK resident, non-domiciled individuals who create what are typically artificial divisions between the duties of a UK employment and an employment overseas in order to obtain a tax advantage.

Broadly, the legislation:

- takes certain 'overseas' employment income out of the definition of 'chargeable overseas earnings';

- takes certain employment-related securities income out of the definition of 'foreign securities income'; and

- takes certain overseas employment income that is provided through a third party out of the calculation of third party employment income to which the remittance basis applies.

These changes apply to income associated with an overseas employment where:

- an individual has both UK and overseas employment(s), either with the same employer or where the UK employer is associated with an overseas employer;

- a UK and an overseas employment are related to each other; and

- the foreign tax rate that applies to the income associated with an overseas employment, calculated in accordance with the amount of foreign tax credit relief available against that income, is less than 65% of the UK's additional rate of tax (currently 45%).

Where income associated with an overseas employment meets all of the above criteria in a tax year, the income that this measure identifies will be taxed in the UK on the arising basis. Foreign tax credit relief available against any UK tax charge will be available in the usual way. Income from each overseas employment will be considered independently. The income and foreign tax credit relief available for all overseas employments are not, therefore, aggregated for the purposes of the 65% test.

This measure will not apply to overseas income that falls within the three-year period for overseas workday relief (set out at *ITEPA 2003, s 26*). If income associated with an overseas employment falls outside the parameters of this targeted measure, the existing rules will continue to apply.

This change has effect for general earnings and employment-related securities income from an overseas employment, and overseas employment income provided through third parties, arising on and after 6 April 2014. Income that arises on or after this date, but which is related to employment duties performed in a year prior to 2014/15, will not be subject to this legislation (*FA 2014, s 15* and *Sch 3*).

Foreign earnings deduction for seafarers

10.30   The 100% deduction in determining the foreign earnings which are brought into charge to income tax was withdrawn for all office holders, and for all employees except seafarers, with effect from 17 March 1998 (*ITEPA 2003, s 378*).

The definition of seafarers has been clarified to exclude explicitly those employed on offshore installations for oil or gas exploration or extraction. *FA 2004* included a measure to redefine 'offshore installation' to ensure that, from 6 April 2004, foreign earnings deduction remains available only to the parts of the shipping sector for whom it was intended.

Focus

Employees of the Royal Fleet Auxiliary have been able to claim seafarers' earnings deduction on a concessionary basis. *Finance Act 2018, s 7* has given the concession statutory authority with effect from 15 March 2018.

The deduction is calculated by reference to emoluments for the qualifying period after allowing such deductions as pension contributions, expenses and capital allowances.

To qualify for the 100% deduction, the duties of the employment must be:

- performed wholly or partly outside the UK; and

- performed in the course of a qualifying period consisting of at least 365 days, falling wholly or partly in any tax year.

For this purpose, seamen are generally treated as performing their duties abroad where the voyage, or any part of it, begins or ends outside the UK; this applies notwithstanding the provision which treats such duties as performed in the UK for most purposes. The days which a seafarer can spend in the UK as part of a qualifying period of absence are 183 days or one-half of the total days.

Note that the Department for Business, Energy & Industrial Strategy guidance entitled 'Guide to the application of the Equality Act and National Minimum

Wage for seafarers' specifies that all seafarers working in UK waters must be paid at least minimum wage rates (see www.gov.uk/government/publications/seafarers-employment-rights-and-minimum-wage).

10.31 Where duties of the employment are performed partly outside the UK, the earnings subject to the deduction are determined on a reasonable basis.

Where a period of leave immediately follows a qualifying period, the earnings attributable to that leave generally qualify for the 100% deduction (such period not being part of a qualifying period: see below).

A 'qualifying period' is a period of consecutive days which consists of days of absence from the UK. The qualifying period need not coincide with a complete tax year in order to take advantage of the deduction.

The date of departure from the UK counts as a day of absence (the test being whether an individual is present in the UK at midnight on a particular day); the date of arrival does not. Days spent abroad on holiday can be included towards the 365-day period.

For seafarers who have previously been resident in the UK and who return to the UK following a period of absence abroad during which they have not been resident in the UK, such absences are not taken into account when calculating the qualifying period (*FA 2004, s 136*; *ITEPA 2003, s 378*).

In *Pete Matthews and Keith Sidwick v HMRC* [2012] UKUT 229 (TCC) the Upper Tribunal upheld the First-tier Tribunal decision that two cruise ship entertainers were self-employed and therefore not entitled to the SED in *ITEPA 2003, s 378*. A significant number of cases may turn on this decision as, at the time the decision was released, a further 12 appeals on the same issue were stayed behind this case.

Focus

In *Cameron v R & C Commrs* [2012] EWHC 1174 (Admin), the High Court allowed the taxpayers' application for judicial review of HMRC's refusal of their claims for seafarers' earnings deduction (SED) or foreign earnings deduction (FED) where the taxpayers had a legitimate expectation that HMRC would allow their claims in accordance with their published guidance.

Employee of overseas employer

10.32 Where:

- an employee works for a person (the 'relevant person') other than his employer; but

- is still paid by his employer or an intermediary of his employer (see above) or of the relevant person;

- the *Income Tax (Pay As You Earn) Regulations 2003 (SI 2003/2682)* ('the *PAYE Regulations*') do not apply to the payer or, if he makes the payment as an intermediary of the employer or of the relevant person, the employer; and

- PAYE is not deducted or accounted for in accordance with the regulations by the payer or, if he makes the payment as an intermediary of the employer or of the relevant person, the employer,

the relevant person is required to account for PAYE on payments to the employee, grossed up if the payments are net of any income tax.

Where, under the 'notional payments' provisions (*ITEPA 2003, s 710*), an employer would be treated for the purposes of the *PAYE Regulations* as paying an amount to an employee, he is also treated for *ITEPA 2003, s 689* purposes as making a payment of that amount. Where this happens, the amount of assessable income which the employee is treated as receiving is regarded as a gross amount.

In determining whether a payment is made by an intermediary of the person for whom the employee works, the same approach is taken as in *ITEPA 2003, s 687(4)*.

From 1 April 2012, *Regulation (EC) 883/2004* was extended to cover Switzerland, which means that HMRC now treat Switzerland as being another EU Member State for social security purposes. The rules apply to anyone living or working in Switzerland. Depending on the circumstances of employment, employees may continue to pay UK NICs, or start paying Swiss contributions instead. Swiss employers employing UK employees working in the UK may also have to pay UK contributions. The rules also apply to self-employed people moving between the UK and Switzerland.

Mobile UK workforce

10.33 Where employees of a UK employer ('the contractor') work for another person, but continue to be paid by or on behalf of the contractor, and it is likely that PAYE will not be accounted for even though all parties are based in the UK, HMRC may give a direction that the person to whom the employees are seconded must deduct PAYE tax from any payments made by that person to the contractor in respect of the work done by the employees.

A direction must specify both the contractor and the person to whom the employees are seconded, must be given by notice to that person, and may be withdrawn at any time by notice to that person. HMRC must take 'such steps as are reasonably necessary' to ensure that the contractor is given a copy of any such notice as relates to him.

Payments to non-resident employees

10.34   Where an employee is not resident in the UK, and works partly in the UK and partly overseas, only some of his income from employment will be taxable under the charge on employment income provisions (*ITEPA 2003, s 690*). In such cases, the employer, or a person designated by the employer, may apply for a direction that a particular proportion of any payment made to the employee in a tax year should be treated as liable to PAYE. If, however, there is no direction in force, the entirety of any payment made to the employee in the tax year will be liable to PAYE.

An application for a direction must give 'such information as is available and is relevant to the application' (*ITEPA 2003, s 690(4)*). The application itself must be given by notice to the employer or the person designated by the employer, and must specify the employee and the tax year. The direction may be withdrawn by notice to the employer or designated person from a specified date, which must be no less than 30 days from the giving of the notice (*ITEPA 2003, s 690(6)*).

Whether or not a direction is in force, the validity of any assessment of the employee's income, and any right to repayment of overpaid tax or obligation to pay tax underpaid, remain unaffected.

Relevant payments

10.35   PAYE is to be applied on the making of a 'relevant payment' (*SI 2003/2682, reg 21(1)*). With certain exceptions (see below), the term 'relevant payment' is defined to mean a payment 'of, or on account of, net PAYE income'. 'Net PAYE income' is then defined as PAYE income, less allowable pension contributions and allowable donations to charity (as further defined in each case). To complete the circle, 'PAYE income' is defined in accordance with *ITEPA 2003, s 683* (ie encompassing employment income, pension income and social security income).

The following are excluded from the definition of 'relevant payment':

- PAYE social security income, but subject to the exceptions in *Pt 8* of the *PAYE Regulations*;
- UK social security pensions;
- excluded relocation expenses;
- excluded business expenses;
- excluded pecuniary liabilities; and
- excluded notional payments.

An employer who provides an employee with assessable income in the form of 'readily convertible assets' is treated as making a payment to the employee of an amount liable to PAYE. The PAYE net is similarly extended to remuneration by way of non-cash vouchers, credit tokens and cash vouchers. Payments of assessable income deemed to have been made under these provisions are called 'notional payments', and there are particular rules for accounting for tax on such payments.

Apart from statute, there is no obligation on an employer to operate PAYE in respect of a payment only part of which is assessable under the charge on employment income provisions.

An exception to this rule is provided by *ITEPA 2003, s 690*, which subjects to PAYE certain relevant payments to employees not resident in the UK, who work partly overseas and partly in the UK.

ITEPA 2003, s 304A (inserted by FA 2011, s 38) provides an exemption from income tax in relation to the subsistence allowances paid by a body of the EU located in the UK to experts who are seconded by their employers to work for the EU body. This exemption applies in relation to allowances paid in respect of periods beginning on or after 1 January 2011.

Short-term business visitors

10.36 HMRC allow a relaxation to the operation of PAYE concerning 'short-term business visitors' ('STBVs'). This usually applies to employees from overseas subsidiaries who come to work for a UK company. The UK company can apply to relax their obligation to operate PAYE on the relevant earnings of such an individual, by way of 'short-term business visitor arrangements' ('STBVAs', also known as 'EP Appendix 4'). These arrangements also relieve the individual of the need to file a self-assessment tax return. At the 2018 Autumn Budget, the government confirmed it would extend the PAYE special arrangement limit for UK workdays in the tax year, from 30 days or less to 60 days or less. This change will apply from April 2020.

TRADING

Charge on foreign income from trade, profession or vocation

10.37 Income of a UK resident derived from a trade, profession or vocation which is carried on wholly abroad is liable to tax only if it was remitted to the UK where the trader is:

- not domiciled in the UK; or

- a Commonwealth (including a British) citizen or a citizen of the Republic of Ireland and is not 'ordinarily resident' in the UK.

In all other cases, the income of a resident is liable to tax whether or not the income is remitted. Income arising in the Republic of Ireland is treated as if it arose in the UK but is nevertheless entitled to the same deductions (and subject to the same limitation of reliefs) as apply to trades etc carried on abroad.

The income of a non-resident derived from a trade carried on wholly abroad is not liable to tax. However, a non-resident trading in the UK through a branch or agency is liable to tax on consequent profits.

Partnerships

10.38   A trade carried on in partnership is treated as resident in the place that the business is controlled and managed, ignoring the residence status of the individual partners concerned.

Where a non-resident partnership trades both in the UK and overseas, a UK resident partner will be taxable on both the UK profits and the overseas profits. A non-resident partner will not be liable to UK income tax and the overseas profits (*ITTOIA 2005, s 849*).

Where a partnership has an overseas trade, and a UK resident partner who is not domiciled in the UK, he will only be liable to UK tax on profits from the overseas trade on a remittance basis. The usual rules apply to profits from the UK trade.

If a partner's residence status changes during a tax year, and that partnership's business is partly carried on in the UK and partly abroad, he will be treated as ceasing to be a partner at the time of the change, and then immediately becoming a partner again after the date of change. This means that separate tax calculations may be made for a tax year.

Trading in the UK

10.39   A 'non-UK resident' trading in the UK is only liable to UK tax where he is trading through a branch or agency.

Whether a person is trading in the UK through a branch or agency is a question of fact, but the distinction has to be made between trading with the UK and trading in the UK: soliciting orders in the UK will not by itself constitute trading in the UK. An important factor is whether the contract for sale or supply of services was made abroad, but the contract may not be conclusive.

UK resident trading wholly abroad

10.40   An individual who is resident in the UK and carries on a trade, profession or vocation wholly abroad, either alone or in partnership, is liable to tax on all his income from such a trade. The income is assessed on a current-year basis. Losses etc can only be set off against the income of that or another overseas source, foreign emoluments, other overseas income and certain pensions.

However, non-UK domiciled individuals will be liable to UK tax only on a remittance basis, where appropriate (*ITTOIA 2005, s 7*).

Expenses connected with foreign trades

10.41   Special rules apply to travel expenses and board and lodging expenses incurred by an individual taxpayer whose trade, profession or vocation is carried on wholly outside the UK, and who has failed to satisfy HMRC that he is not domiciled here.

Where the rules apply, the travel and board and lodging expenses are to be treated as deductible provided that the taxpayer's absence from the UK is wholly and exclusively for the purpose of performing the function of the foreign trade.

In certain circumstances, travel expenses of the taxpayer's spouse or civil partner and any children are deductible.

Travel between foreign trades is also deductible, subject to conditions (*ITTOIA 2005, ss 92–94*).

Non-resident entertainers and sportsmen

10.42   There is a system of withholding basic rate income tax from payments made to visiting, non-resident entertainers and sports personalities. Except where the activity in point is performed in the course of an office or employment, it is treated as if it were a trade, profession or vocation exercised in the UK and the income from it plus payments connected with it are chargeable to income tax on a current-year basis; it is stated that regulations dealing with the system generally can provide specifically for losses and reliefs (*ITA 2007, Pt 15, Ch 18 (ss 965–970)*).

Where a payment is made in respect of an appearance by a non-resident entertainer or sportsman in the UK, the payer must deduct tax at the basic rate. This rule does not apply if:

- the payment is below £1,000;

- the recipient has agreed a lower or nil rate of withholding tax with HMRC.

Tax is calculated on a current-year basis.

Non-residents trading through a branch or agency

10.43   Where non-residents carry on a trade in the UK through a permanent establishment, for the purposes of self-assessment, HMRC will, broadly, treat that permanent establishment as the non-resident's 'UK representative', and look to it for the performance of various tax obligations. Certain persons are excluded from being a UK representative.

The amount of income tax chargeable for any tax year on the total income of any person who is not resident in the UK is limited to the sum of (*ITA 2007, s 811*):

- tax deducted, or treated as deducted, at source (including tax credits) from income received under deduction of tax; and

- tax on the non-resident's total income computed without regard to (*ITA 2007, s 813*):

  - savings and investment income;

  - gains from disposals of certificates of deposit;

  - various social security benefits;

  - income arising from transactions carried out on the non-resident's behalf by brokers and investment managers who are not treated as the non-resident's UK representative (SP 1/01);

  - income designated for this purpose by the Treasury in regulations;

  - personal allowances;

  - relief under any double tax treaty.

The limitation on charge does not apply to the income of non-resident trustees if any of the trust's beneficiaries is an individual resident in the UK or a company resident in the UK (*ITA 2007, s 812*). 'Beneficiaries' are broadly defined to include both actual and potential beneficiaries who:

- are or ever might become entitled to receive income from the trust; or

- have income from the trust paid to them or applied for their benefit by legitimate exercise of the trustees' discretion,

and 'trust' income includes capital derived from accumulated income.

DOMICILE

Introduction

10.44 The charge to income tax and capital gains tax in the UK is largely founded on residence status. However, the domicile of an individual will also be of importance in determining his liability and the taxation of foreign emoluments under *ITEPA 2003*. This is particularly important following changes brought in by *FA 2008*, which apply from April 2008 (see **10.57**). Domicile is also important for the purposes of inheritance tax. The concept of domicile is one of general law and within the jurisdiction of the UK domicile is regarded as being the equivalent of a person's permanent home. Broadly, a person is domiciled in that country in which he makes his permanent home. An individual is not domiciled in the UK as such, but rather in one of the areas of jurisdiction that together constitute the UK, namely England and Wales, Scotland, and Northern Ireland.

There are three kinds of domicile:

- domicile of origin;
- domicile of choice; and
- domicile of dependency.

Domicile of origin

10.45 Every individual has a domicile which is acquired at birth and is known as a domicile of origin. In the case of a legitimate child this will be the domicile of his father, and in the instance of an illegitimate child that of his mother. There need be no connection between an individual's place of birth and his domicile of origin, eg a legitimate child born in England to a father of Scottish domicile would acquire a Scottish domicile of origin.

It is not possible to have more than one domicile. The domicile of origin subsists until it is displaced by a new domicile of either choice or dependency.

Domicile of origin is characterised by two factors, its permanence and the heavy burden of proof required to displace it. In *IR Commrs v Bullock* (1976) 51 TC 522, the taxpayer was born in Nova Scotia, Canada, in 1910 and his domicile of origin was there. He came to England in 1932 to join the Royal Air Force. He married an English wife and they visited Canada on a number of occasions. He hoped to persuade his wife that they should live there after his retirement. He retired in 1961. His wife did not wish to reside in Canada and the couple continued to live in England. In 1966, he executed a will appointing a Nova Scotia corporation as executor. The will contained a declaration that his domicile was in Nova Scotia, Canada, and that he intended to return to that country upon his wife's death. All his assets were in Canada. The Court of Appeal held that for the taxpayer to have acquired a domicile of choice in England he must have intended to make his home there until the end of his days unless and until something happens (which was not indefinite or vague). The possibility that the taxpayer would survive his wife was not unreal. He had not formed the intention necessary to acquire a domicile of choice in England and therefore his domicile of origin still subsisted.

In Bullock's case, 40 years of residence in England was insufficient to displace the taxpayer's domicile of origin. The domicile of origin can never be completely lost. Since a person cannot be without a domicile, English law automatically assumes a domicile of origin. Thus, if an individual abandons a domicile of choice without acquiring a new domicile of choice, his domicile will be one of origin ensuring that he is not without a domicile. In *Udny v Udny* (1869) LR 1 Sc & Div 441, Colonel Udny had a domicile of origin in Scotland. He acquired an English domicile of choice and resided in that country for some

32 years. He then left England and went to live in France where he resided for the following nine years. On these facts, the House of Lords held that upon his departure for France, Colonel Udny abandoned his English domicile of choice but did not acquire a French domicile of choice. In consequence, his Scottish domicile of origin revived.

Domicile of choice

10.46   A domicile of choice is that domicile which an individual of legal capacity, not being dependent for his domicile upon another person, may acquire by taking up residence in another country with the intention of permanently residing there. In order to establish a domicile of choice an individual must demonstrate both residence and intention.

In *Plummer v IR Commrs* [1987] BTC 543, the taxpayer's family moved to Guernsey, and it was her intention also to settle there. However, she remained in the UK to continue her education at school and, later, university. Her claim to have established a Guernsey domicile of choice failed, since Guernsey had not become her chief place of residence.

In *Executors of Moore deceased v IR Commrs* [2002] SpC 335, the taxpayer was a US citizen born in 1924, with a domicile of origin in the US. In 1942, he moved from Missouri to New York, where at some point he purchased an apartment which he sold in 1983. He then rented an apartment there. During the 1980s, the deceased and his partner spent time in England and the US. They purchased a holiday home in Ireland, which was sold in the early 1990s. In March 1991, the deceased was granted consent to enter the UK for the limited purposes of his employment as an artist. He purchased a flat in London. His leave to remain in the UK expired in March 1995, but he continued to live in London. There was no attempt to deport him. In October 1995, his partner died but the deceased continued to live in the UK. He renewed his US passport on which he travelled.

The deceased died in March 1997 in London, where his funeral took place. He had made US tax returns but no UK tax returns although, following his death, payment was made to the Revenue in respect of UK income tax and capital gains tax based upon his residency in the UK. He left two wills, one in US form dealing with his US assets and the other in English form disposing of the whole of his estate worldwide (apart from those assets in the US which were dealt with separately) to a wide range of beneficiaries and English charities. He also charged his UK estate with sole liability of all his just debts, funeral and testamentary expenses. The will was executed in London.

The Revenue issued a notice of determination that the deceased died domiciled in England and Wales. The US executors supported the notice but the UK executors appealed, contending that the deceased died domiciled outside England.

535

The Special Commissioner, in allowing the appeal, said that the issue was whether the deceased had acquired a domicile of choice in England. That required that he had a fixed and determined purpose to make England his permanent home. The intention did not have to be immutable, but an intention to make a home in a new country merely for a limited time or for some temporary or special purpose was insufficient. The true test was whether he intended to make his home in the new country until the end of his days unless and until something happened to make him change his mind. The burden of proof was on the Revenue to show on the balance of probabilities that the deceased acquired a domicile of choice in England (*IR Commrs v Bullock* (1976) 51 TC 522 applied).

On the evidence, it appeared that the deceased's living solely in London prior to his death was determined more by ill-health than by a desire to make England his permanent home. His nomadic existence just happened to end up in London, rather than being the result of his forming the intention to stay, as was illustrated by his short-term immigration status. He never really gave up his New York connections. There was no clear evidence that he really had the necessary intention to acquire a domicile in England and quite a lot of evidence that he kept up his connections with New York. Accordingly, he did not die domiciled in England and Wales.

10.47 In *Surveyor v IR Commrs* [2002] SpC 339, the taxpayer was born in England in 1958 and acquired from his father a domicile of origin in the UK. He went to work in Hong Kong in 1986 and, until 1991, he returned to the UK once or twice a year for holidays. He married a UK national who had been resident in Hong Kong since 1984. In 1991, the taxpayer became a partner in his firm and was given the option of returning to the UK. He refused on the basis that he saw Hong Kong as his home and had no intention of returning to the UK to live. By 1994, he had three children and he purchased an apartment in Hong Kong for use as his family home. It was sold in 1995, as it was too small to accommodate a family, but the taxpayer continued to live in rented accommodation in Hong Kong. After the early 1990s, the taxpayer rarely visited the UK, except on occasional business trips.

In 1997, when the handover of Hong Kong to China was imminent, the taxpayer and his wife applied for permanent resident status, as they desired to remain permanently in Hong Kong, even though it was not compulsory. In order to obtain that status, they had satisfied certain criteria, including seven years' continuous residence in Hong Kong and the possession of certain financial and academic or business qualifications. Thereafter, they were entitled to live and work in Hong Kong without needing a work permit and/or the sponsorship of an employer. The taxpayer could also travel in and out of Hong Kong using only his permanent resident's identity card and did not need a passport or visa. He would have been subject to restrictions if he had not acquired permanent resident status.

In 1999, the taxpayer built a holiday home in Thailand. From 2000 to 2002, he lived and worked in Singapore, because his employer relocated him there, although he returned to Hong Kong on a regular basis. In July 2002, the taxpayer left his job and returned to Hong Kong, where he purchased an apartment with the help of a Hong Kong-based mortgage.

In 1999 the taxpayer created a Jersey settlement which would have contained 'excluded property' for inheritance tax purposes if he was domiciled outside the UK at that time. The Revenue took the view that the taxpayer was domiciled in the UK but the taxpayer appealed to the Special Commissioners on the basis that he had established a domicile of choice in Hong Kong.

The Special Commissioner, in allowing the appeal, said that the intention to abandon a domicile had to be unequivocal and that the standard of proof was the balance of probabilities; however, so serious a matter as the acquisition of a domicile of choice was not to be lightly inferred from slight indications or casual words. There had to be 'convincing evidence' of a settled intention to reside in another place, otherwise the person remained domiciled in England. The test was whether the taxpayer intended to make his home in a new country until the end of his days unless and until something happened to make him change his mind.

Applying those principles to the present case, the evidence supported the conclusion that, at the date of the creation of the settlement in August 1999, the taxpayer had the intention to reside permanently in Hong Kong. At that time, his residence in Hong Kong was not for a limited period or for a particular purpose but was general and indefinite in its future contemplation. His intention was directed towards one country and that was Hong Kong. His family, social business and financial ties were all there.

The Revenue had argued that, when the taxpayer completed form DOM1 in 1999, he had stated that his intention for the future was to remain permanently in the Far East and that he was building a family residence in Thailand to meet those requirements. The Far East was not a territory and did not have a distinctive legal system, both of which were a requirement for domicile. However, the form also said that the taxpayer considered himself as domiciled in Hong Kong and the statements about the Thailand house had to be considered in that context. On the evidence, the existence of the house in Thailand did not alter the intention of the taxpayer to make Hong Kong his permanent home. It did not point to the conclusion that, in August 1999, it was the taxpayer's intention to reside permanently in more than one country; nor that he intended to settle in one of several countries. Moreover, the temporary move to Singapore did not affect the taxpayer's intention in August 1999 to reside permanently in Hong Kong.

Domicile and residence

10.48　Residence is a matter of fact. Alone, without the necessary intention, it will be insufficient to establish domicile. However, intention may be inferred from the fact of residence since an individual's residence in a particular country is generally regarded as being prima facie evidence that he is also domiciled in that country. Thus, whilst no particular length of residence is required to establish a domicile of choice, the greater the period of residence the more strongly an intention to permanently reside is to be inferred. In *IR Commrs v Duchess of Portland* [1982] BTC 65, Nourse J opined that:

> 'residence in a country for the purposes of the law of domicile is physical presence in that country as an inhabitant of it. If the necessary intention is also there, an existing domicile of choice can sometimes be abandoned and another domicile acquired or revived by a residence of short duration in a second country.'

However, in *IR Commrs v Bullock* (1976) 51 TC 522, a period of 40 years' residence in England was insufficient to displace the taxpayer's domicile of origin. In *Ramsay v Liverpool Royal Infirmary* [1930] AC 588, a man born in Scotland in 1845, and thus with a Scottish domicile of origin, left that country in 1892 and henceforth resided in the city of Liverpool, in England. Whilst this individual often stated that he was proud to be a Glasgow man, he expressed a determination never to return to Glasgow. He resided in Liverpool for the final 36 years of his life leaving England on only two occasions during that period, once to visit the USA and once to visit the Isle of Man. He arranged for his own burial in Liverpool. On these facts, a unanimous House of Lords held that he had died domiciled in Scotland.

In *Anderson (Executor of Muriel S Anderson) v IR Commrs* [1997] SpC 147, the deceased had lived in Scotland all his life until, in 1974, at the age of 64, he retired and sold his home in Scotland. He moved to a property which he acquired in Cornwall, where he died eight years later, and his ashes were scattered in Scotland. A Special Commissioner concluded that his domicile remained in Scotland.

These cases illustrate that, whilst residence is an essential element in establishing a domicile of choice, it is the intention of the individual that is the determining factor.

Intention

10.49   The intention which is required for the acquisition of a domicile of choice in a particular country is the intention to reside permanently or for an unlimited time in that country.

In *Re Furse (deceased); Furse v IR Commrs* [1980] 3 All ER 838, the testator had a domicile of origin in Rhode Island, USA. In 1923, at the age of 40, the testator and his family came to England, and the following year they purchased a farm in Sussex where the testator resided until his death in 1963. During his periods of residence in England the testator indicated that he would not return to the USA until such time as he was rendered incapable of leading an active life on his farm in England. Fox J held that in view of the fact that the testator's intention was to go on living his accustomed life on the farm in England and only to leave when he was no longer able to lead an active physical life there, it was clear that he had no intention, save on a vague and indefinite contingency, of leaving England. It followed that at the time of his death the testator had acquired a domicile of choice in England.

Although the merest possibility of a future contingency is probably insufficient to deny the acquisition of a domicile of choice, there is no doubt that a contingency which is both realistic and unambiguous (eg the end of a job) will have that effect. In practice, it will be rare to find a person who has consciously formed the requisite intention to acquire a domicile of choice; consequently, such an intention will normally have to be inferred from the individual's conduct. The courts will look for any instance which is evidence of a person's residence or of his intention to reside permanently in a country. As Scarman J observed in *In the Estate of Fuld (No 3)* [1968] P 675:

> 'Domicile cases require for their decision a detailed analysis and assessment of facts arising within that most subjective of all fields of legal inquiry – a man's mind.'

In the case of *Re Clore (dec'd)* [1982] Ch 456, the testator had received professional advice to acquire a foreign domicile. He followed the advice received and started to make arrangements to sever his more important connections with the UK. He retired as company chairman, instructed the sale of his two residences, bought an apartment in Monaco to which he removed some furniture, and made a Monaco will. Despite these actions, it was held on the evidence that he had not formed a settled intention to reside permanently in Monaco, and thus had not lost his English domicile.

It is impossible to formulate a rule specifying the weight to be given to particular evidence. All that can be gathered from the case law in this respect is that more reliance is placed upon conduct than upon declarations of intention, especially if they are oral.

Abandonment of domicile of choice

10.50   A domicile of choice is less retentive, and therefore more easily abandoned, than a domicile of origin (*Qureshi v Qureshi* [1972] Fam 173 at 191). There is some dispute as to the required intention necessary to abandon a domicile of choice. In seeking to abandon a domicile of choice in a particular country an individual must clearly cease to reside there. The uncertainty concerns whether such cessation of residence must be accompanied by:

- a positive intention not to return; or

- mere absence of any intention to return.

It must also be remembered that where a domicile of choice is abandoned, the domicile of origin will stand in its place unless and until it is replaced by a new domicile of choice.

Married women

10.51   Formerly the domicile of a married woman was dependent upon her husband's domicile. If he acquired a new domicile of choice then she acquired it too. She retained this domicile not only as long as her husband was alive and she was legally married to him, but also during widowhood or following divorce unless and until it was changed by the acquisition of another domicile.

This former rule was abolished by *Domicile and Matrimonial Proceedings Act 1973, s 1* (operative from 1 January 1974), and a married woman can now acquire a separate domicile from her husband.

Where a woman married prior to 1974, and thus acquired her husband's domicile upon marriage, she is treated as retaining that domicile, as a domicile of choice, or domicile of origin if it be so, until it is changed by the acquisition of a new domicile of choice or revival of the domicile of origin on or after 1 January 1974 (*Domicile and Matrimonial Proceedings Act 1973, s 1(2)*).

It would appear that a woman, living in England with her husband, who was married before 1 January 1974 will only be able to change her (now) domicile of choice by choosing to leave her husband for permanent residence abroad.

American wives of UK-domiciled taxpayers

10.52   A unique situation is afforded to US wives of British tax residents where the marriage took place before 1 January 1974. Under *art 4(4)* of the *US–UK Double Taxation Convention of 31 December 1975 (SI 1980/568)*, a pre-1974 marriage is regarded as having taken place on 1 January 1974, and thus the new law applies to the determination of the wife's domicile. The consequence is that a pre-1974 American wife has the best of both worlds. For income tax and capital gains tax purposes only, her domicile will be determined independently of her British husband's domicile, and she can claim to be domiciled in one of the states of the USA. If her claim is successful, her overseas income and capital gains will be assessed on the remittance basis. For capital transfer tax and inheritance tax purposes, a pre-1974 American wife will generally have her husband's UK domicile, and consequently enjoy the exemption for transfers between spouses. She will, in any case, have a deemed UK domicile for inheritance tax purposes after 17 out of 20 years of residence.

UK tax position of overseas voters

10.53   UK taxpayers resident abroad are required, if they wish to exercise their right to vote in the UK, to complete a declaration on their registration forms which states: 'I do not intend to reside permanently outside the United Kingdom'. In a written answer in the House of Lords on 17 October 1986 (Hansard, vol 480, col 1018) the Secretary of State for Employment considered the effect of signing such a declaration on the signatory's domicile and UK tax position. He said that making such a declaration would not affect the UK tax position of voters who were temporarily non-resident and maintained their links with the UK. However, where an individual with a UK domicile goes abroad and it becomes necessary to determine whether he retains his UK domicile or acquires a foreign domicile, any expression of his intentions (such as the declaration) would be only one of a number of factors to be taken into account, and the question of where he was domiciled would ultimately be resolved by looking at the extent to which he had in fact severed his ties with the UK so as to make his permanent home abroad.

In order to determine, for inheritance tax, capital gains tax and income tax purposes, whether a person is domiciled in the UK on or after 6 April 1996, the following factors are to be ignored (*FA 1996, s 200(1), (2)*):

- where a person does anything with a view to, or in connection with, being registered as an overseas elector; or

- where a person, when registered as an overseas elector, votes in any election in which he is entitled to vote by virtue of being registered.

A person is registered as an overseas elector if he is registered in any register mentioned in *Representation of the People Act 1983, s 12(1)* on account of an entitlement to vote conferred on him by *Representation of the People Act 1985, s 1*, or is registered under *Representation of the People Act 1985, s 3 (FA 1996, s 200(3))*.

Where a person's domicile is to be established for tax purposes, he may require that the above-mentioned factors should be taken into account (*FA 1996, s 200(4)*).

Domicile of dependency

10.54   The domicile of a dependent person is determined by the domicile of the person on whom he or she is dependent. Should the domicile of the latter change, the domicile of the dependent person will change accordingly. A dependent person cannot alone change his domicile. There are two categories of dependent persons: children and mentally incapacitated persons.

Children

10.55   At birth, a child acquires a domicile of origin. This will normally be the domicile of the father, unless the child is either illegitimate or born after the father's death, in which case it will be the domicile of the mother. Between the time of his birth and attaining the age of 16, an unmarried child is incapable of acquiring a domicile of choice by his own act. He may, of course, acquire a new domicile of dependency if that person upon whom he is dependent does so (but note the decision in *Re Beaumont* [1893] 3 Ch 490 where the court took the child's welfare into account upon the remarriage of her mother). Once a child reaches 16 years of age, he becomes capable of acquiring a domicile of choice in his own right (*Domicile and Matrimonial Proceedings Act 1973, s 3*). However, until he acquires an independent domicile, he will retain his domicile of dependency as a (now) domicile of choice (note the decision in *IR Commrs v Duchess of Portland* [1982] BTC 65: see **10.48**).

Domicile and Matrimonial Proceedings Act 1973, s 3 states that a married person under the age of 16 is capable of acquiring an independent domicile. Whilst English domiciled children are incapable of contracting marriage below this age, the provision will be important in relation to a child below that age whose foreign marriage is recognised here.

In Scotland, a minor with legal capacity, ie a girl of 12 years or over or a boy of 14 years or over, is capable of acquiring an independent domicile.

Mentally incapacitated persons

10.56   A mentally incapacitated person will be unable to acquire an independent domicile by his own act if he is incapable of forming the requisite intention. A mentally incapacitated child will, during infancy, continue to take his father's domicile as a domicile of dependency. Upon attaining majority such a person will probably continue to depend upon the domicile of his father. An adult who becomes mentally disordered probably retains the domicile he possessed prior to the disorder.

REMITTANCES

The remittance basis

10.57   The remittance basis of taxation has been in existence for some 200 years and has operated largely in its present form for about 90 years. However, significant changes were introduced in *FA 2008*, which mainly affect UK residents who are normally liable to UK tax on the whole of their worldwide income and gains arising in a tax year – the arising basis. The remittance basis is available to UK-resident individuals who are not domiciled in the UK, subject to certain conditions being satisfied. It provides for foreign-sourced income (and, in the case of non-domiciled individuals only, foreign sourced gains) to be charged to tax by reference to the extent to which they are remitted to, or received in, the UK. Under the remittance basis, tax is charged on the amount received in the UK on a current-year basis.

Where the remittance basis applies, it allows the taxpayer to defer tax on foreign income or gains that have arisen until amounts in respect of those income or gains are received in the UK (if they ever are). It does, however, have to be shown that what is received in the UK is 'in respect' of that income or gain.

Broadly, the legislation covers three categories of tax charge, namely relevant foreign income, employment income and capital gains. Historically, the remittance basis has applied automatically for both employment income and capital gains. With effect from 6 April 2008, the claims mechanism applies to all three categories of charge. It is therefore up to taxpayers who are UK resident but not domiciled to decide whether they wish to be taxed on the remittance basis for each tax year. Self-assessment returns allow those who are entitled to the remittance basis to make a claim if they so wish. Those eligible can choose from one tax year to the next whether they wish to be taxed on this basis.

Focus

HMRC will assume that taxpayers with unremitted foreign income and gains of less than £2,000 have used the remittance basis unless they are notified that the taxpayer wishes to be taxed under the arising basis. In addition, a claim to use the remittance basis will not be required where an individual has total UK income or gains of no more than £100 which has been taxed in the UK, provided they make no remittances to the UK in that tax year (*ITA 2007, ss 809D* and *809E*).

The obligation to file a self-assessment return on individuals with small amounts of income from overseas employment was removed with effect from 6 April 2008 where the overseas income is less than £10,000, and overseas bank interest is less than £100 in any tax year, all of which is subject to a foreign tax (*ITA 2007, Pt 14, Ch 1A (ss 828A–828D)*).

10.58   The changes to the remittance basis rules from April 2008 do not apply to those non-UK domiciled individuals whose unremitted income and/or gains for a tax year are less than £2,000 (see **10.65**). They will automatically be taxed on the remittance basis for that year, without the need for a claim (*ITA 2007, s 809C*). In addition, individuals entitled to claim the remittance basis who have no UK income or gains, and who do not remit any foreign income or gains, will not have to claim the remittance basis in years they are not liable to the remittance basis charge (RBC). This avoids them having to complete a self-assessment return only so they can claim the remittance basis and then have no tax to pay.

10.59   Emoluments are treated as received in the UK if they are paid, used or enjoyed in the UK, or transmitted or brought to the UK; amounts treated as remitted which are not directly received are sometimes known as 'constructive remittances'.

Income received in a tax year after the source of the income has ceased to exist is not taxable on the remittance basis so long as the remittance is not in the same tax year.

Income considered as remitted to the UK need not necessarily be paid to the taxpayer, but income which is properly alienated abroad to another person is not regarded as remitted to the UK by the original owner if the new owner sends that money to the UK.

It is sometimes difficult to distinguish between income and capital, but, in general, the proceeds of investments purchased abroad with income that would be taxable if remitted are liable to tax as income if those proceeds are themselves remitted.

The fact that sums remitted are derived from a bank overdraft is not in itself sufficient to establish that the remittance is out of capital.

However, investments purchased out of income before taking up residence in the UK may be realised and the money remitted without liability.

10.60   A non-domiciled individual who is aged 18 or over at any time in the tax year and satisfies certain qualifying conditions regarding residence may use the remittance basis for taxation of overseas income if they pay an annual tax charge. If the individual elects not to pay the charge, he will be charged to UK tax as though he were resident and domiciled in the UK for that tax year. In addition, someone who is UK resident, but not domiciled, who claims the remittance basis for taxing overseas income, is only able to claim personal allowances, married couple's allowance and blind person's allowance against their taxable income if their unremitted foreign income is less than £2,000 a year (see **10.65**) (*FA 2008, s 25* and *Sch 7*).

Overseas workday relief

10.61   From April 2013, overseas workday relief (OWR), which was previously dealt with by HMRC statement of practice 1/09, has been placed on a statutory footing, is now available to all non-domiciled individuals arriving in the UK who have not been resident in any of the previous three tax years (*ITEPA 2003, s 26A*). It is available for the tax year in which they become UK resident and the following two tax years. This measure broadly replicates the treatment which previously existed under the Statement of Practice referred to above for certain employees who are resident but not ordinarily resident in the UK. The legislation also includes some additional relaxation in the rules over and above the current treatment. See the HMRC guidance note entitled Overseas Workday Relief (RD4) (www.gov.uk/government/publications/rdr4-overseas-workday-relief-owr/overseas-workday-relief-rdr4) for further details.

Focus

The concept of 'ordinary residence' was generally abolished from 6 April 2013 (*FA 2013, s 219* and *Sch 46*). However, to prevent those who were entitled to overseas workday relief from being placed at a disadvantage, this relief will continue in a statutory form (see SP 1/09). It only applies to individuals who are not domiciled in the UK and is available for the tax year in which an individual first becomes resident in the UK for tax purposes and the following two tax years. There is no requirement about the length of time an individual intends to remain in the UK, but they will have to have been non-resident for the three tax years before coming to work in the UK. There is transitional relief for those who currently benefit from the relief. In all other cases where a tax liability is determined by reference to ordinary residence, it will be determined solely by reference to residence status.

Unremittable overseas income

10.62 Persons (including companies) who are liable to tax on their overseas income wherever it arises may be unable to remit the income to the UK. This income may be treated as income arising abroad and not chargeable to UK income tax where (*ITTOIA 2005, s 841*; *CTA 2009, s 1274*):

- a person is prevented from transferring to the UK, either by the laws of that territory or any executive action of its government or by the impossibility of obtaining foreign currency in that territory;

- the person has used reasonable endeavour to transfer; and

- that person has not realised in some other currency which he is not prevented from transferring to the UK.

Claims to this relief must be made not later than the first anniversary of the 31 January after the end of the tax year in which the income arises (*ITTOIA 2005, s 842*). The relief will be given only as long as the three conditions above continue to be satisfied, ie the tax liability is only postponed, not removed.

Remittance basis and personal allowances

10.63 Those who make a claim under *ITA 2007, s 809B* to be taxed on the remittance basis will lose their entitlement to various personal tax allowances (*ITA 2007, Pt 14, Ch A1*). *Section 809G* lists these as, for income tax purposes, personal allowance and blind person's allowance, tax reductions for married couples and civil partners, and payments for life insurance; and for capital gains tax (CGT), the annual exempt amount.

However, this does not apply to individuals who are eligible to use the remittance basis without a claim in a tax year because they meet the conditions set out in *s 809C* (because their unremitted income and gains for a tax year are less than £2,000). They retain their entitlement to all those various allowances and reliefs.

Annual charge

10.64   *Finance Act 2012, s 47* and *Sch 12* made various amendments to the remittance basis rules. The following paragraphs apply for the tax year 2012/13 and subsequent years.

The remittance basis may be claimed for a tax year if the individual:

- is aged 18 or over in that year; and

- meets the 12-year residence test or the 7-year residence test for that year.

An individual meets the 12-year residence test for a tax year if he or she has been UK resident in at least 12 of the 14 tax years immediately preceding that year (*ITA 2007, s 809C(1A)*).

An individual meets the 7-year residence test for a tax year if he or she does not meet the 12-year residence test for that year, but has been UK resident in at least seven of the nine tax years immediately preceding that year (*ITA 2007, s 809C(1B)*).

Where the remittance basis is claimed, the individual will be required to pay the remittance basis charge (RBC). The charges are as follows (*ITA 2007, s 809H*):

- for an individual who meets the 12-year residence test for that year, £60,000 from 6 April 2015 (previously £50,000) (*FA 2015, s 24*);

- for an individual who meets the 7-year residence test for that year, £30,000.

From 6 April 2015, a charge of £90,000 applies for people who have been resident in the UK for more than 17 of the past 20 years (*FA 2015, s 24*).

Focus

Finance (No 2) Act 2017 contains a package of reforms to the non-dom regime, which include a measure so that, from April 2017, those who have been resident in the UK for more than 15 out of the past 20 tax years will be treated as deemed UK domiciled for all tax purposes. This means that from that date, they may no longer use the remittance basis (see **10.57**). They will also be deemed domiciled for inheritance tax purposes from that date. In addition, those who had a domicile in the UK at the date of their birth will revert to having a UK domicile for tax purposes whenever they are resident in the UK, even if under general law they have acquired a domicile in another country. The legislation contains provisions to help those who become deemed-domiciled after having been resident for 15 of the past 20 years to transition to the new regime.

The Remittance Basis Charge (RBC), paid by non-UK domiciled individuals who have been resident in the UK for more than 12 of the past 14 years, and who wish to retain access to the remittance basis of taxation, was increased from £50,000 to £60,000 with effect from 6 April 2015. Also from that date, a new charge of £90,000 has been introduced for people who have been resident in the UK for more than 17 of the past 20 years (*FA 2015, s 24*). The current £30,000 charge will remain the same for those resident in the UK for seven of the past nine years (see above).

This charge is in addition to the tax liability for the year in question on any income and gains remitted to the UK, and any UK income or gains taxed on the arising basis. The RBC will be paid on nominated income and gains not remitted to the UK in the year. (These income and gains are called 'nominated' income and gains because the taxpayer is free to nominate the income and gains not remitted to the UK in the year on which the RBC is payable. For example, this could be £75,000 of unremitted foreign deposit interest on which UK tax was due at 40%, so leading to an income tax charge of £30,000.) If, in subsequent years, that 'nominated' income or gains upon which the RBC has been paid is, in fact, remitted to the UK, then that income or gains will not be taxed again.

However, there are ordering rules to ensure that if 'nominated' income or gains is, in fact, remitted when other untaxed income and gains remain unremitted, then that unremitted income and gains is treated as being remitted before the 'nominated' income and gains (*ITA 2007, ss 809H* and *809I*).

The nominated income rules were amended from April 2012 to allow individuals to remit up to £10 of overseas income or capital gains which they have nominated for the purposes of the annual remittance basis charge, without being taxed on that remittance and without becoming subject to the identification rules. This applies both for the purposes of the £30,000 and for the increased £60,000 charge (*ITA 2007, s 809I*).

The record keeping necessary for *ss 809H* and *809I* can be avoided if individuals ensure that 'nominated' income or gains upon which the RBC is paid are not remitted to the UK, or only remitted after the remittance of all other unremitted income and gains since the first year of residence from April 2008. If an individual is confident they will never need to remit that 'nominated' income or gains, paying the RBC will not involve any extra complexity or record keeping.

Focus

From April 2012, the charge to UK tax on overseas income or capital gains remitted to the UK for the purpose of making a commercial business investment in an unlisted company or a company listed on an exchange regulated market has been removed (*ITA 2007, s 809VA*). There are specific anti-avoidance provisions to ensure the investment is made on proper commercial terms.

£2,000 'de **minimis' rule**

10.65 The *FA 2008* changes referred to at **10.58** will not apply, for a particular tax year, to those whose unremitted foreign income and gains for that year are less than £2,000. The remittance basis will apply automatically to their overseas income and gains without a claim, and they will not lose personal allowances or be required to pay the RBC (see **10.64**). In the Explanatory Notes to *Finance Bill 2008*, HMRC gave the following two examples where the *de minimis* rule would be met for the year 2008/09:

Example 1:

Unremitted income and gains in 2008/09 = £1,500

Unremitted income and gains from previous years = £0

Example 2:

Unremitted income and gains in 2008/09 = £1,500

Unremitted income and gains from previous years = £4,000

Although the total of unremitted income and gains in Example 2 is £5,500, it is only the amount proper to the year of assessment which is considered for the *de minimis* rule.

Anti-avoidance measures

10.66 *FA 2008* introduced measures to close various loopholes and address certain flaws and anomalies in the way the rules previously operated. HMRC perceived that those eligible for the remittance basis could often arrange their affairs so that they received or enjoyed foreign income or gains in the UK without any liability to UK tax, even though they had in substance remitted the foreign income or gains to the UK. The general aim of the measures was to ensure that income or gains to which the remittance basis applies were only excluded from charge to UK tax where they were genuinely kept offshore and not brought to the UK. Where they are in effect remitted to the UK in such a manner that the individual has the use or enjoyment of them in the UK, the individual will be liable to tax on them if he has effectively remitted them to the UK.

'Ceased sources'

10.67 Under a long-standing interpretation of the legislation and case law in respect of relevant foreign income, HMRC have accepted that no tax liability can apply if the source of the income benefiting from the remittance basis no longer exists in the year of remittance – the 'source doctrine'. This means that if an individual arranges for a bank account to be closed at the end of one tax year and remits the interest in the next year, there was likely to be no liability. *FA 2008, Sch 7* overturned the 'source doctrine', so that a charge can be imposed where relevant foreign income that has benefited from the remittance basis is remitted, whether or not the source exists in the year of remittance. (That is already the case with employment income and capital gains, where the legislation is cast in terms preventing this outcome.)

'Cash only'

10.68   Prior to *FA 2008*, on the basis of case law, the general view was that relevant foreign income could only be taxed if it was brought into the UK as cash. So, if a remittance basis taxpayer turned relevant foreign income into an asset outside the UK and then imported that asset, it was unlikely that any charge would arise on the income (unless and until the asset was sold in the UK and there were cash proceeds). *FA 2008, Sch 7* contains legislation to ensure that money, property and services derived from relevant foreign income brought into the UK will be treated as a remittance and taxed as such.

Any asset purchased out of untaxed relevant foreign income which an individual or another relevant person owned on 11 March 2008 will be exempt from a charge under the remittance basis, for so long as that person owns it, even if the asset is outside the UK at that date and later imported.

Any asset purchased out of untaxed relevant foreign income and in the UK on 5 April 2008 will also be exempt from a charge under the remittance basis, for so long as the present owner owns it, even if the asset is later exported and then re-imported.

For the future, the following exemptions will be available to assets brought to the UK, purchased out of untaxed relevant foreign income:

- the 'personal use rule', applying to clothes, shoes, jewellery and watches, for the use of the individual or members or their immediate family;

- the 'repair rule' for assets brought to the UK for repair and restoration;

- the 'temporary importation rule' where assets are in the UK for less than a total period of 275 days; and

- assets costing less than £1,000.

There is also a 'public access rule', allowing exemption for works of art, collectors' items and antiques brought into the UK for public display.

If an asset is sold in the UK while any of these exemptions is in force, the exemption will cease at that point and the tax charge that arises under existing law will apply at that point.

If property meets the personal use rule, the repair rule or the public access rule then the time during which it meets any of those rules is taken into account in deciding whether it meets the temporary importation rule. So, for example, if an asset comes to the UK for repair, and that repair takes 75 days, then after the repair is complete it can be kept in the UK for a further 200 days under the temporary importation rule. Property to which the temporary importation rule applies remains exempt if, before the end of the 275-day period, it is then put on public display and meets the terms of the public access rule.

FA 2009 extended the scope of the exemptions that allow individuals using the remittance basis to bring property, which has been purchased out of overseas investments and savings, into the UK, to include property purchased out of foreign employment income and foreign chargeable gains, as well as relevant foreign income. The extension to the existing rules applies from 1 April 2008 (*FA 2009, Sch 27*).

Offshore mortgages

10.69   Previously, individuals paying tax on the remittance basis who borrowed money from a non-UK institution could repay the interest on that loan out of untaxed foreign income without giving rise to a tax charge on the remittance basis, even if the loan was advanced into the UK. Without special rules the effect of other changes to the legislation made by *FA 2008, Sch 7* would be that repayments on such loans advanced to the UK would be treated as a remittance on or after 6 April 2008. *Schedule 7, para 86* therefore provides 'grandfathering' provisions for certain loans made before 12 March 2008. Subject to conditions, interest payments out of untaxed relevant foreign income will not be treated as a remittance on or after 6 April 2008.

The loan must be made to the individual outside the UK before 12 March 2008. It must be for the sole purpose of enabling the individual to purchase a residential property in the UK. Before 6 April 2008 the money has to be received in the UK and used to acquire the property, and repayment of the debt has to be secured on that property.

These rules apply to interest payments for the remaining period of the loan, or until 5 April 2028 if sooner. If the terms of the loan are varied or any further advances made after 12 March 2008, the repayments will be treated as remittances from that point.

DOUBLE TAXATION RELIEF

Introduction

10.70   The UK has entered into numerous double tax agreements with other countries to mitigate the effect of double taxation of income and capital gains but far fewer in relation to gifts and inheritances.

Agreements or Treaties are made with one country in each case, but members of the Organisation for Economic Co-operation and Development have subscribed to a model form and many treaties follow that form. Where a treaty applies, it explains when UK domestic tax law applies and where the overseas tax law applies. The treaty does not override UK tax law in that the treaty cannot impose a liability. It can say which authority has the taxing rights if they exist and there would, otherwise, be double taxation. Double taxation arises because different countries employ different criteria to found their tax jurisdiction. For example, a US citizen who is taxable in the UK as a resident or because of a UK source of income will remain liable to US tax on worldwide income and gains by virtue of US citizenship.

Focus

A UK resident may claim double tax relief even where no treaty is in force. This relief is called unilateral relief. Relief will be given by a credit equal to the lower of the UK tax or foreign tax on the overseas income or capital gains. If there is no UK tax on the income, such as where profits are covered by current year losses, the foreign tax can be deducted in calculating the income or gains for UK tax.

A treaty will normally go further than allowing credit by assigning exclusive taxing jurisdiction to one country or other by limiting withholding taxes (eg on dividends, interest and royalties). Treaties can apply to dual residents but usually require an individual to be treated as a resident of only one country, determined by criteria in order of priority (eg permanent home, centre of vital interests, and nationality). They usually permit a country to tax business profits only if derived from a local permanent establishment. The permanent establishment is usually a fixed place of business defined in some detail. However, a permanent establishment might be a temporary site office or mobile home or caravan. The terms of the specific treaty must be checked. It is possible for a person to be taxed in one country on one type of income or profit but in another country for another type of income.

Credit is also available for overseas tax similar to inheritance tax charged on the gift of an asset, in lifetime or on death. Few treaties have been negotiated and many do not adequately cover lifetime gifts, because they were negotiated when the former estate duty was in force. In addition to deductions and credit they also lay down useful criteria for determining and so resolving conflicts over the domicile of an individual and the location of assets.

Forms of double tax relief

10.71   Double tax relief may be given in several different forms. These can usefully be categorised as follows:

Treaty exemption – Income which has been taxed in one territory is specifically exempt by treaty from tax in another territory. This method does not generally prevent the second territory taking the amount of exempt income into account when computing the tax to be charged on the remaining taxable income.

Credit relief – Relief may be provided either by treaty or unilaterally. Income which has been taxed in one territory (usually the territory of source) is not exempt from tax in the second territory, but the tax paid in the first territory in respect of that income is deductible from the tax payable in the second territory in respect of that income.

Deduction – Income which has been taxed in one territory is reduced by the amount of that tax in determining the amount of income which is taxed in the second territory (*TIOPA 2010, Pt 2*).

Model treaty provisions

10.72   Two chief methods of relieving double taxation are adopted in 'tax treaties'. First, taxing rights over certain classes of income are reserved entirely to the country of residence of the person deriving the income. Secondly, all other income may be taxed (in some cases, only to a limited extent) by the country of origin of that income; if the country of residence of the recipient also taxes that income, it must grant a credit against its tax for the tax levied by the country of origin.

Many tax treaties are based on the 1977 or 1992 Model Convention published by the Organisation for Economic Co-operation and Development. They usually provide that a national from one territory should not be treated more harshly than a national from the other territory (a 'non-discrimination clause'); though the EC Treaty requires similar treatment within the EC, the matter in point must fall within the provision for the reliefs effected by arrangements agreed with foreign governments.

Some of the usual exemption provisions of treaties are noted below, but it is emphasised that each treaty must be looked at individually for its specific provisions.

Business profits

10.73   The profits of any business carried on by a resident of country A is taxable only in country A, unless the business is carried on in country B through a permanent establishment (a fixed place of business, eg a branch, office, factory or mine) in country B. Where this is the case, the profits of the business are taxable in country B, but only to the extent that those profits are attributable to the permanent establishment.

Shipping, inland waterways and air transport

10.74   Profits from the operation of ships, aircraft or inland waterways transport are taxable only in the country in which the place of effective management of the relevant enterprise is situated.

Interest, dividends, royalties, non-government pensions

10.75 Interest, dividends, patent and copyright royalties, and non-government pensions are often taxable only in the country of residence or are taxed at a reduced rate in the other country.

Finance Act 2016 introduced additional obligations to deduct income tax at source from royalties paid to certain non-resident persons where:

- arrangements have been entered into which exploit the UK's double taxation agreements (DTAs) in order to ensure that little or no tax is paid on royalties either in the UK or anywhere in the world;

- the category of royalty is not currently one of those in respect of which there is an obligation to deduct tax under UK law; or

- royalties which do not otherwise have a source in the UK are connected with the business that a non-UK resident person carries on in the UK through a permanent establishment in the UK.

The measure has effect for payments made under tax avoidance arrangements from 17 March 2016. The change to the definition of royalties to which deduction of tax applies and the change to the source rules in respect of royalties paid under obligations which are connected with a permanent establishment in the UK has effect for payments made on or after the date of 28 June 2016 (*FA 2016, ss 40* and *41*).

Professional services

10.76 The income of a person in respect of professional services is generally only taxable in the country in which he is resident, unless he has a fixed base regularly available to him in the other country for the purpose of providing his services. However, actors, musicians and athletes are generally liable to tax in both countries.

Salaries and wages

10.77 Most salaries and wages are generally taxable only in the country of residence unless the employment is exercised in the other country, in which case income derived from such employment is also taxable in the other country. However, usually the treaty will contain a provision that the salary etc is only taxable in the country of residence if:

- the taxpayer is present in the other country for an aggregate period not exceeding 183 days in the relevant tax year;

- the salary etc is paid by, or on behalf of, an employer who is not resident in the other country; and

- the payments are not borne by a permanent establishment which the employer has in the other country.

However, actors, musicians and athletes are generally liable to tax in the country in which they perform.

Government salaries and pensions

10.78 Government pensions, salaries etc are generally taxable only in the country responsible for paying the pensions, salaries etc. However, the income is only taxable in the other country if the services are rendered in that country and the taxpayer is resident in, or is a citizen of, that country.

Teachers and researchers

10.79 Under some DTAs, teachers or professors who come to the UK to teach in schools, colleges, universities or other educational establishments for a period of two years or less can be treated as exempt from UK tax on their earnings from the teaching post. Temporary absences from the UK during this period normally count as part of the two years.

Some DTAs also cover individuals who engage in research. In such cases, the rules are normally the same as for teachers.

Where an individual covered by the exemption stays for more than two years, the exemption does not apply and they will be liable to UK tax on the whole of their earnings from the date of arrival in the UK. Some agreements only allow exemptions to be given if the earnings are liable to tax in the individual's home country.

In addition, where exemption has been granted for a visit (or visits) of up to two years, some DTAs do not allow further exemption for visits made at a later date.

Students and apprentices

10.80 Most DTAs allow overseas students or apprentices visiting the UK solely for full-time education or training exemption from UK income tax on payments from sources outside the UK for maintenance, education or training. A number of DTAs also provide that students or apprentices visiting the UK will be exempt from UK tax on certain earnings from employment here. Individual agreements impose various restrictions on this relief, including, for example, monetary limits and conditions as to the type of employment.

Entertainers, sportsmen and sportswomen

10.81 Under most DTAs, if an individual who is not resident in the UK comes to the UK as an entertainer, sportsman or sportswoman, any payments received will be liable to UK tax (*OECD Model, art 17*). This includes actors and musicians performing on stage or screen and those participating in all kinds of sports.

Personal allowances and reliefs

10.82   Many double tax agreements provide that individuals who are resident in country A are entitled to the same personal allowances, reliefs, and deductions for the purposes of tax in country B as subjects of country B who are not resident in that country.

Often, the double taxation agreement will exclude entitlement to the personal allowances etc where the income consists solely of dividends, interest or royalties.

To ensure compliance with certain aspects of the *Human Rights Act 1998*, entitlement for a non-resident individual who formerly qualified for UK personal tax allowances and reliefs solely by virtue of being a Commonwealth citizen was withdrawn with effect from 6 April 2010 (*FA 2009, Sch 1*). Whilst the vast majority of individuals affected will still benefit through other means such as double taxation treaties, citizens of Bahamas, Cameroon, Cook Islands, Dominica, Maldives, Mozambique, Nauru, Niue, St Lucia, St Vincent & the Grenadines, Samoa, Tanzania, Tonga, and Vanuatu may be affected.

Calculation of double tax credit relief available

10.83   In many cases, double tax agreements provide that where there is no deduction or exemption from UK tax, credit is to be given for any foreign tax which is paid and which corresponds to income tax whilst similar credit is given by 'unilateral relief'; this reduces the amount of UK tax chargeable except in certain cases where a non-resident company is connected with a state or province of a foreign territory which operates a 'unitary tax' regime. In general, a claim for relief by way of credit for foreign tax must be made within the period ending four years following the end of the tax year within which the income falls to be charged to tax (*TMA 1970, s 43*).

Taxpayers who have claimed relief for foreign tax must notify HMRC if there is an adjustment to the amount of foreign tax and the relief claimed has become excessive as a consequence. For trades, professions and vocations, there are special rules relating to the years of commencement and cessation.

An overseas dividend manufacturer may have his right to double tax relief restricted, in particular, in respect of tax credits on overseas dividends received when the tax credits have been offset against tax due on manufactured overseas dividends paid, or when the overseas dividends have been effectively paid on to a non-resident.

Where no credit is allowable, the foreign tax may be deducted. A person may elect that any treaty provision giving credit is ignored.

Guidance on residence

10.84   The gov.uk website has much useful guidance on residence, domicile and other aspects relating to international taxation. Readers may find the following links useful:

Tax on foreign income	https://www.gov.uk/tax-foreign-income/residence
RDR1: Residence, domicile and the remittance basis	https://www.gov.uk/government/publications/residence-domicile-and-remittance-basis-rules-uk-tax-liability
Income tax when arriving in the UK	https://www.gov.uk/tax-come-to-uk
Income tax when leaving the UK	https://www.gov.uk/tax-right-retire-abroad-return-to-uk
Tax on UK income if you live abroad	https://www.gov.uk/tax-uk-income-live-abroad
Double taxation treaties: non UK resident with UK income	https://www.gov.uk/government/publications/double-taxation-treaties-territory-residents-with-uk-income

Chapter 11

Income tax – UK and overseas tax planning considerations

SIGNPOSTS

- Individuals may wish to review their tax affairs before the end of each tax year to help minimise their annual liability to income tax (see **11.2**).

- Certain tax planning aspects may be considered by foreign nationals working in the UK and British citizens going abroad (see **11.7**).

- The extraction of profits from small 'family' companies is examined at **11.11**.

- Certain factors may be considered in making the decision as to whether to incorporate a business (see **11.19**).

UK TAX PLANNING CONSIDERATIONS

11.1   Proper tax and financial planning can lower and defer a liability to income tax, freeing up cash for investment, business or personal purposes. However, whilst the tax implications of any planned investments should play an important part in investment strategy, no transaction should be undertaken purely for tax reasons. The wider financial aspects must also be carefully considered, especially where its value represents a large part of the family fortunes or where it provides a livelihood for one or more members of the family.

The most basic form of year-end planning often involves pushing tax bills into the future by deferring income into the next year and accelerating deductions into the current year.

Individuals

11.2   The following points may be considered by taxpayers before the end of each tax year to help minimise their annual liability to income tax:

- Ensure that personal allowances and basic rate bands are fully utilised. Using personal allowances and basic rate bands may seem an obvious point, but is surprisingly frequently missed. Unused allowances are not available to be carried forward, so it is important to ensure that they are utilised each year. Simple planning can be applied, such as changing ownership of assets or creating an employment. However, care is needed to escape the anti-avoidance legislation.

- A spouse or civil partner who is not liable to income tax (or is not liable above the basic rate for a tax year) is entitled to transfer a set amount of their unused personal allowance to their spouse or civil partner, provided that the recipient of the transfer is not liable to income tax above the basic rate. For 2019/20 the maximum amount that can be transferred is £1,250 (rising from £1,190 for 2018/19). This can potentially mean a reduction in tax liability of £250 for 2019/20 (£238 for 2018/19).

Focus

For 2019/20, the maximum amount that can be transferred from one partner to the other is £1,250, which means that the spouse or civil partner receiving the transferred allowance will be entitled to a reduced income tax liability of up to £250 for 2019/20 (£1,250 × 20%).

The allowance was introduced on 6 April 2015. For 2015/16 it was worth £212. For 2016/17, the allowance was raised to £1,100, making it worth £220, for 2017/18 it was £1,150 making it worth £230, and for 2018/19 it was £1,190, making it worth £238. Backdated claims are possible, which means that a claim for all four years from 2015/16 to 2018/19 inclusive can be worth up to £900.

It is also possible to claim Marriage Allowance even where one partner has died since April 2015, providing all the eligibility criteria is satisfied (see **1.20**).

Claims can be made online via the gov.uk website at https://www.gov.uk/apply-marriage-allowance, or by calling the HMRC helpline on 0300 200 3300.

The Marriage Allowance should not be confused with Married Couple's Allowances (MCA), which may be claimed where one partner was born before 6 April 1935. For 2019/20, MCA can reduce the claimant's tax bill by between £345 and £891.50 a year. Further information on MCA can be found on the gov.uk website at www.gov.uk/married-couples-allowance.

- Ensure that tax is being paid at the lowest rate on investment income. If a spouse, or civil partner, pays tax at a different rate, consider transferring income-producing assets to give the income to the person paying at the lower rate.

- Tax-efficient investments are covered in detail in **Chapter 4**. However, as a general point, a review of bank and building society accounts should be made before the tax year end. Many people still have large sums of cash in ordinary accounts paying very little interest when they could be earning over 5% gross interest from specialist accounts. Make sure that ISA allowances have been fully utilised for all the family, where applicable.

- For 2019/20 (remaining unchanged from 2018/19), the ISA maximum subscription limit is £20,000 and there is no restriction on the amount that may be invested in a cash ISA. The overall investment limits on ISAs mean that a couple could save a substantial amount in tax-efficient savings accounts (see **4.25** for further commentary on ISAs).

- From April 2017, most adults aged under 40 can open a Lifetime ISA. Up to £4,000 can be saved each year and savers will receive a 25% bonus from the government on this money. Broadly, money invested in this type of account can be saved until the investor is 60 and used as retirement income, or it can be withdrawn to help buy a first home.

- Junior ISAs are available to UK resident children (under-18s). Junior ISAs are tax-relieved and have many features in common with existing ISA products. The maximum annual subscription for 2019/20 is £4,368 (£4,260 in 2018/19). Investments may be made in any combination of qualifying cash or stocks and shares investments. Withdrawals are not permitted until the named child has reached the age of 18, except in cases of terminal illness. Since April 2015 it has been possible to transfer Child Trust Funds (CTFs) to Junior ISAs.

- Help-to-buy ISAs are now available, enabling most first-time buyers to save up to £200 a month towards their new home and benefit from cash government incentives (see **4.26**).

- Innovative Finance ISAs were launched in 6 April 2016. This type of ISA can hold peer-to-peer (P2P) loans, which often pay significantly higher returns than cash accounts (see **4.29**).

- Regular sums can be invested in National Savings (some products offer a tax-free return, which is particularly attractive to 40% and 45% taxpayers), banks and building societies (see **4.31**). Those willing to accept the possibility of greater risk perhaps equalling greater reward might consider the stock market, stock market-linked investments or buy-to-let property.

- Ensure that adequate pension contributions have been made. Paying pension contributions can currently give tax relief at the individual's highest income tax rate.

- Consider paying into pensions for family members. The introduction of stakeholder pensions allow contributions to be made for all UK residents, even children, as there is no requirement to have any earnings. Consider making payments of up to £3,600 for family members, as the fund will grow in a tax-free environment. The net cost is only £2,880.

- Take advantage of tax exemptions. Everyone has a yearly capital gains exemption. In 2019/20, the exemption is £12,000, and gains up to this figure can be made without tax. Taxpayers should therefore consider realising gains from investments up to this figure. Gifts between spouses and civil partners are tax free, so it is possible to double the yearly exemptions available by giving shares or other investments to a spouse or civil partner. See *Capital Gains Tax* (Bloomsbury Professional) for commentary on utilising the capital gains tax annual exemption.

- Realise losses where possible. With regards to shares standing at a loss, consideration should be given to selling them so that the loss can be set against any gains made over and above the capital gains annual exemption. If the taxpayer wishes to retain the investment, it could be bought back by the spouse or partner, within an ISA. It will not be tax effective for the taxpayer to buy back the investment, unless he or she waits for 30 days before doing so. In addition, care must be taken not to fall foul of anti-avoidance legislation which prevents loss relief being claimed where certain arrangements exist, the main purpose, or one of the main purposes, of which is to secure a tax advantage (*TCGA 1992, s 16A*).

- Capital gains tax may be deferred through the use of an Enterprise Investment Scheme investment (see **4.39**).

- Making charitable donations via the Gift Aid scheme is an effective way to reduce taxable income. If donations have been made, it is important that the taxpayer has ticked for Gift Aid so that the charity can benefit from the basic rate tax relief. Higher rate taxpayers should make the necessary claim on their tax return for further relief. If future donations are planned, the taxpayer may wish to bring these forward to before 5 April to ensure the tax relief is obtained at an earlier date.

- Employees should check that their PAYE tax code number for the following tax year is correct and ensure that any inaccuracies are amended.

Minimising the additional rate of tax

11.3   The introduction of the additional 50% income tax rate, and the clawback of the personal allowance where income exceeds £100,000, meant that between 2010/11 and 2012/13 there was an effective 60% marginal rate of tax on income between £100,000 and approximately £112,000. Furthermore, there was also the prospect of a marginal 2% National Insurance charge on employment and business income, leading to a maximum rate of 62% in some cases. The reduction in the additional rate to 45% from 6 April 2013 helped relieve some marginal rate worries, but individuals could still be facing tax rates of up to 57%.

Many businesses will already be suffering the 50% tax rate on their profits, particularly if they have an accounting date early in the tax year. These businesses need to consider their future business structure carefully, and possibly use companies to run all of the business or be a partner.

Opportunities for careful planning of income and reliefs exist at the margins. For example, making a Gift Aid payment could drop taxable income below the £150,000 threshold and permit higher rate tax relief on pension contributions.

Businesses

11.4   The following points may be considered by businesses before the end of each tax year to help minimise their annual liability to income tax:

- The annual investment allowance (AIA) for capital allowances purposes is a 100% allowance for qualifying expenditure on machinery and plant. The AIA limit has been temporarily raised to £1m for expenditure incurred between 1 January 2019 and 31 December 2020. From 1 January 2021 it will revert to its former level of £200,000. Businesses considering significant expenditure on qualifying plant and machinery within the next, say, five years, may wish to consider doing so sooner rather than later to qualify for the increased AIAs and subsequently receive relief on the expenditure at an earlier date (see **7.57**).

- In essence, the AIA gives full tax relief for annual expenditure incurred by a business on plant and machinery up to the relevant annual investment limit (*CAA 2001, s 51A*). Expenditure must be incurred by a 'qualifying person', defined to mean an individual, a partnership consisting only of individuals, or a company (*CAA 2001, s 38A*) (see **7.57**). This means that businesses will receive immediate relief for their qualifying expenditure. The timing of expenditure will be important to ensure that relief is received sooner rather than later, where appropriate.

- If it is usual practice for the company to pay bonuses to directors or dividends to shareholders, careful consideration should be given as to whether payment should be made before or after the end of the tax year. This will affect the payment date for any tax and may affect the rate at which it is payable. Remember that any bonuses must be paid within nine months of the company's year-end to ensure tax relief for the company in that period.

- Where there are beneficial loans made to office-holders and employees, these should be reviewed prior to the end of the tax year and accounting year to minimise income tax, national insurance and corporation tax.

- Where remuneration can be justified, it may be beneficial to make payments to a spouse or other family members to reduce the overall tax and national insurance liability. The statutory threshold for the cash equivalent of beneficial loans to be treated as earnings of the employment is currently £10,000. As long as the total outstanding balances on all such loans do not exceed the threshold at any time in a tax year, there will be no tax charge.

- Review timing of disposal and acquisition of business assets to minimise tax or obtain tax deferral.

- Deferment of Class 2 and 4 National Insurance contributions should be obtained if Class 1 contributions will be paid on employment income.

- Employers may consider making tax-free gifts to staff, including:

    - *Long service awards.* Broadly, there will be no tax charge so long as the employee has been employed for at least 20 years and the article given has a value not exceeding £50 for each year of service.

    - *Suggestion scheme awards.* Such awards must be made under a properly constituted suggestion scheme, based on a set percentage of the expected financial benefit to the business. The maximum award allowed is £5,000. There is also a concession for 'encouragement awards' of £25 or less to reflect meritorious effort on the part of the employee concerned.

    - *Staff functions.* Staff annual functions (eg a dinner dance or Christmas party) are tax free where the total cost per person attending is not more than £150 per year (including VAT).

    - *Promotional gifts.* Such items are normally purchased for advertising purposes and must display a 'conspicuous advertisement'. Staff may receive promotional gifts tax free provided that the overall cost of the articles involved does not exceed £50 per person per year. Gifts of food, drink, tobacco or vouchers are specifically excluded.

    - *Medical treatment.* A tax exemption may apply for amounts up to £500 paid by employers for medical treatment for employees. The exemption applies to medical treatments recommended by employer-arranged occupational health services in addition to those recommended by the new Health and Work Service.

- If it is expected that profits from a business will be below the small profits threshold (£6,365 in 2019/20), exception from payment of Class 2 contributions can be applied for.

- A statutory exemption applies from 6 April 2016, which exempts from income tax and NICs low-value benefits-in-kind which meet certain qualifying conditions, including a £50 limit per individual benefit.

Qualifying 'trivial' benefits-in-kind provided to directors or other office holders of close companies, or to members of their families or households, is subject to an annual cap of £300 (see **6.46**).

National Insurance contributions

11.5   The following points may be considered by employers wishing to mitigate NICs:

- Increases in the amount that the employer contracts to contribute to company pension schemes.

- Share incentive plans (shares bought out of pre-tax and pre-NIC income).

- Small companies may consider disincorporation and instead operate as a sole trader or partnership.

- Reduction in salary and increase in bonus to reduce employee (not director) contributions.

- Payment of dividends instead of bonuses to owner-directors.

- Provision of childcare.

- If it is expected that profits from a business will be below the small profits threshold (£6,365 in 2019/20), exception from payment of Class 2 contributions can be applied for.

Focus

From 6 April 2015, employers are not required to pay secondary Class 1 National Insurance contributions on earnings paid up to the upper earnings limit to any employee under the age of 21.

Trusts

11.6   Trusts currently pay 45% income tax on most of their income unless they are 'life interest' trusts. Even higher rates may apply if trusts receive dividend income that is fully distributed. Trustees need to consider their position, particularly with regard to future investment policy, and time the distribution of funds to beneficiaries carefully. In some cases, trustees might consider the winding up of trusts (or converting to life interest trusts) to use the lower rate tax bands of beneficiaries. Trusts still have their uses to protect family wealth and avoid capital taxation.

Discretionary trustees, who face the punitive 45% rate on virtually all their income, should seriously consider giving one or more beneficiaries an entitlement to receive the trust income (known as an 'interest in possession'), in which event the 45% will not apply at the trust level. Any such appointment

563

may be revocable at any time, so that the trust can revert to discretionary nature if the trustees so decide at some future time.

The main rate of capital gains tax payable by trustees and personal representatives was reduced from 28% to 20% from 2016/17 (although it remains at 28% for gains on residential property not eligible for private residence relief). See *Capital Gains Tax* (Bloomsbury Professional) for further commentary on this.

OVERSEAS TAX PLANNING CONSIDERATIONS

11.7 This section takes a brief look at planning issues for foreign nationals working in the UK and for British citizens going abroad.

For foreign nationals coming to the UK, it is assumed that the individuals are not domiciled in the UK and, in the case of employees, it is further assumed that they are employed by non-resident employers so that their earnings qualify as chargeable overseas earnings (*ITEPA 2003, s 23(2)*).

Large numbers of British citizens now go to live abroad for various periods of time and for various reasons. Since tax is territorial, there will inevitably be tax considerations, and it is always best to plan well in advance of departure.

Residence

11.8 The key to most tax planning issues for income tax purposes will centre on residence status, so it is imperative to get this right from the outset of any transaction. It is possible to be resident in more than one country at any one time.

Once there has been a finding that a taxpayer is resident in the UK, then he is treated as resident for the whole of that tax year. HMRC, however, by concession will allow a tax year to be split so that a taxpayer will be treated as resident in the UK for only part of that tax year in certain circumstances (see **10.3**).

Working in the UK

11.9 Emoluments of foreign nationals working in the UK are calculated under the normal charging provisions of *ITEPA 2003* – this includes charges arising on benefits in kind. Apart from the travelling expense rules, expenses are deductible only according to the normal test of being wholly, exclusively and necessarily incurred in the performance of the duty of the employment. Pension contributions to an approved scheme are deductible, but the pension will be taxed when received, and, being UK source income, will remain permanently liable to UK income tax. Pensions paid on behalf of a foreign employer are not liable to UK tax.

It used to be possible for a UK-resident individual to obtain a deduction of 100% against earnings from abroad if they related to a period of absence of 365 days, even if those days did not include one complete income tax year. The deduction has been abolished for all qualifying periods beginning after 17 March 1998 except for qualifying seafarers (see **10.30**). An individual who is abroad for one complete tax year will, of course, not be resident. There were detailed rules for calculating days of absence, which could include weekends and rest days and travelling time. Careful planning is required to attract the 100% Seafarers' Earnings Deduction (SED).

Many international employers operate tax equalisation schemes, also known as tax protected pay or net pay. It is an arrangement that ensures that an employee has the same 'take home' pay wherever employed. Payments under these schemes are taxable. 'Golden handshakes' are also taxable but, in addition to the general £30,000 allowance, substantial foreign service may give a full or further partial exemption.

Where there is a difference in treatment between UK earnings and overseas earnings, two separate contracts, one for UK and the other for foreign duties, are desirable. The contracts must be with separate employers, as it is not possible to have two contracts of employment with the same employer. The use of two contracts allows the employer to specify that the foreign duties attract a higher rate of remuneration.

The following points may be considered by a foreign national taking up employment in the UK:

- Relief under a double tax treaty or exemption from UK tax may be obtained if the visitor is considered non-UK resident in any year and meets certain other treaty conditions.

- A claim for allowances on arrival in the UK may avoid the withholding of excessive PAYE deductions.

Working overseas

11.10   To achieve the most favourable tax treatment, it is essential to obtain detailed local advice on the tax system of the host country, and careful consideration of the double taxation agreement, where such an agreement exists. Many countries have more burdensome tax regimes than the UK. Historically, the traditional approach of UK tax advisers has been to try and minimise liability to UK taxes. However, while the UK's income tax rates remain some of the lowest in Europe, advisers may wish to consider whether it might be better to maximise that proportion of their clients' income over which the UK has sole taxing rights.

For planning purposes, the following points may be worth consideration:

- Advance planning is essential – the tax considerations of any proposed transaction should be considered well in advance of departure from the UK.

- HMRC booklet RDR1 is a useful reference guide (www.gov.uk/government/uploads/system/uploads/attachment_data/file/528018/RDR1-residence-domicile-remittance.pdf).

- A detailed knowledge of the local tax system of the host country is desirable.

- Consider timing and duration of visits to the UK, to avoid being classed as resident in a tax year if at all possible.

- The UK currently has comparatively low income tax rates. In attempting to mitigate a liability to UK income tax, check that that same income is not liable to a higher rate in the host country.

- Aim to minimise pre-return income when returning to the UK.

- Consider interaction of income tax and capital gains tax – conflicts may arise.

Focus

From April 2014, the capital gains tax private residence relief final period exemption was reduced from 36 months to 18 months (*FA 2014, s 58*). This is an anti-avoidance measure aimed at reducing the incentive for those with more than one home to 'exploit' the rules. Previously, where a property was used as an individual's only or main residence at any time during his or her ownership, the gain relating to the final 36 months of ownership would be free of tax when selling that home.

SMALL FAMILY COMPANIES

Extracting profits

11.11   Given the rates of income tax and corporation tax currently in force, it is often considered to be advantageous for a family company director/shareholder to draw little or no salary or dividends, but to retain all profits within the company to be taxed only at the lower (small companies or normal) corporation tax rate. Of course, unless the director/shareholder has other sources of income, taking an income in one form or another from the company will be necessary to meet living expenses and other financial commitments.

The decision as to whether to extract profits from the family company or retain them generally depends on what route will produce the most tax-effective overall benefit to the family. The most efficient tax planning strategy will normally be to pay out the company's income annually, by way of remuneration or dividends, rather than retaining it within the company, where it may become subject to the higher combined charges of corporation tax and capital gains tax.

The main rate of corporation tax for the 2019 financial year is 19%. *F(No 2) A 2015, s 7* sets the main rate of corporation tax for the financial year 2020 at 17% (*FA 2016, s 46*).

Remuneration versus dividends

11.12 The two main methods of extracting profits from a company are as remuneration and by way of dividend. Extraction of funds by way of a loan is not possible because of the company law restrictions and tax disadvantages (*CTA 2010, Pt 10, Ch 3* (loans to participators, etc)).

The tax effects of the two methods may be broadly contrasted as follows:

- Remuneration is deducted in arriving at the taxable profits of the company (provided the amount is justifiable (see *Copeman v William Flood & Sons Ltd* (1940) 24 TC 53), although HMRC rarely challenge the size of the directors' remuneration paid by trading companies where the directors are full-time working directors). The recipient is taxed on the remuneration through the PAYE system at the date of payment including a charge to NIC.

- Dividends are not deducted in arriving at the taxable profits.

Note that the extraction of profits by way of salary will give rise to a liability to NIC, whereas a dividend does not.

11.13 A number of other factors must be taken into account:

- A reduction in salary may result in a decreased entitlement to certain earnings-related social security benefits. It is important to note that a full NIC contribution record must be maintained to ensure maximum social security benefits.

- The lack of a salary charge in the accounts may increase the value for CGT and IHT purposes of holdings valued on the basis of earnings. In addition, a higher dividend payment will increase the value of a holding calculated on a dividend yield basis, although it is unlikely to affect the valuation of a major interest.

- Dividends are payable rateably to shareholders in proportion to their holdings in the company, which may not necessarily correspond to the relative efforts of the directors in earning the profits. Dividend waivers may assist in these circumstances, but care must be taken.

- Dividends can only be paid out of distributable profits whereas, at least in theory, remuneration can be paid out regardless of the level of profits.

- In the longer term, there is a risk that, at some future date, the relative advantages might be reversed at a time when the flexibility to switch between the two methods is restricted.

- The national minimum wage legislation should be considered, as this applies equally to directors under contracts of employment as it does to employees.

- Overall, it will normally be best to extract profits using a mixture of salary, benefits and dividends, which can be varied according to individual circumstances.

Distribution policy

11.14 In deciding how profits are to be extracted, the following aspects should be considered:

- The 10% tax credit attaching to dividends was abolished from 6 April 2016. From that date, the rates applicable to dividend income are the 7.5% ordinary rate up to the basic rate limit, the 32.5% dividend upper rate, and the dividend additional rate of 38.1% on dividends above the higher rate limit. Whilst the changes to the taxation of dividend income from April 2016 mean that most taxpayers will thereby pay less tax, people with a share portfolio valued at £140,000 a year or more will pay more. This is part of a strategy to reduce the incentive to incorporate businesses and take remuneration in the form of dividends.

- Individual needs of shareholders may differ – some may require income, others may be more interested in capital appreciation. These conflicting interests may be met by the issue of separate classes of shares with differing distribution rights.

- For the financial year 2019, the main rate of corporation tax remains at 19%, which means that the rate of tax payable on retained profits is potentially lower than current income tax rates.

Family members

11.15 For income tax purposes, it is generally desirable to spread income around a family to fully utilise annual personal allowances and to take full advantage of nil and lower rate tax thresholds.

The term 'family' includes all individuals who depend on a particular individual (eg the owner of the family company) for their financial well-being. This may include not only the spouse, civil partner and children but also aged relatives, retired domestic employees, etc. Care must be taken in this area not to fall foul of the 'settlements' legislation and other anti-avoidance measures in force at the time.

Distributions (usually dividends) from jointly owned shares in close companies are not automatically split 50/50 between husband and wife, but are taxed according to the actual proportions of ownership and entitlement to the income (*ITA 2007, s 836(3)*).

Possible methods of spreading income around the family include employing a spouse and/or children, waiving salary (to increase profits available as dividends) or dividends (to increase the amounts available to other shareholders), and transferring income-producing assets.

Some distributions of income to family members will not be beneficial for tax purposes, and to this effect, the following points should be borne in mind:

- a salary paid to spouse, civil partner, children or other dependants is a tax deductible expense of the company only if it can be justified in relation to the duties performed (see *Nicholson v HMRC* (TC06293) below);

- a salary paid to spouse, civil partner, children or other dependants will attract a liability to NIC if it is above the lower earnings limit; and

- the investment income of an infant child (ie an unmarried child below the age of 18) is taxed on his parents, where it arises from a gift by them.

Paying family members

11.16 In the recent case of *Nicholson v HMRC* (TC06293), the first-tier tax tribunal examined a deduction made in sole trader's accounts for his university student son. In this case, Mr Nicholson claimed that his son had been employed in promoting the business through internet and leaflet distribution and computer work. His wages had been calculated at a rate of £10 per hour for 15 hours per week, but unfortunately there was no evidence to support wages being paid on this basis. HMRC rejected the claim because of a lack of contemporaneous records preventing a successful reconciliation from the business bank statements.

Mr Nicholson claimed that payments to his son had been paid partly through the 'provision of goods'. He managed to identify £1,850 in cash by reference to his son's bank statements. He also substantiated a monthly direct debit of £18.51 in respect of his son's home insurance costs. However, the bulk of the claim was based on Mr Nicholson buying food and drink to help support his son at university.

The tribunal made reference to an earlier judgment in *Dollar & Dollar v Lyon (HM Inspector of Taxes)* [1981] CH D54 TC 459, which also involved payments to family members, and concluded that Mr Nicholson's payments were made out of 'natural parental love and affection'. There was a duality of purpose as the 'wages' had a major underlying 'private and personal' motive, and thus not for the purposes of the trade. The tribunal subsequently dismissed the appeal on the grounds that Mr Nicholson was doing nothing more than supporting his son at university.

In particular, this case highlights the importance of keeping proper records regarding the basis in which payments are to be made to children. The tribunal commented that the likelihood of a successful claim would have been increased had there been payment on a time-recorded basis, or a methodology in calculating the amount payable plus an accurate record of the hours worked. A direct link between the business account and the recipient's account would clearly be advisable.

Whilst there was no suggestion here that employing relatives is an issue in itself, the importance of paying a commercial rate for the work undertaken should be noted. The concept of 'equal pay for equal value' should help prevent a suggestion of dual purpose and thus, in turn, also help refute allegations of excessive payments to family members as a means of extracting monies from the business.

It is also important to remember that wherever payments are made to family members, certain other legal issues such as the national minimum wage should also be borne in mind.

Income shifting

11.17 On 25 July 2007, the House of Lords gave its judgment in the landmark case of *Jones v Garnett* [2007] UKHL 35 (also known as '*Arctic Systems Ltd*'). HMRC had previously lost this case in the Court of Appeal and, as a result, had appealed to the House of Lords. The case concerned dividends payments made by a company to Mrs Jones through which Mr Jones provided IT consultancy services. If the decision had gone against Mr and Mrs Jones, many married couples would have faced a very large tax and NIC cost, going back over the last six years.

In their judgment, their Lordships ruled that Mr and Mrs Jones were creating an arrangement in the nature of a settlement when they subscribed for one share each, and set up their company, Arctic Systems Ltd. However, the exemption for gifts between spouses also applied, and dividends paid to Mrs Jones were therefore not income arising under a settlement. The resulting decision meant that Mrs Jones (rather than Mr Jones) was assessable on the dividends she received from the family company, even though most of the profit was as a result of Mr Jones's efforts for the company.

Following the decision given in *Arctic Systems Ltd*, the government swiftly announced that it would effectively reverse the ruling by changing the law. A consultation was published in December 2007 with the intention of bringing in new legislation from 6 April 2008. The revised legislation focuses on 'income shifting arrangements that make use of companies or partnerships to gain a tax advantage'. While it was aimed at preventing the transfer of dividend income or partnership profits from a person who paid tax at 40% to an individual paying a lower rate of tax, the changes were widely drafted and caught situations in which a range of connected parties had invested capital in a business (eg businesses involving spouses, siblings and parents and children). The resulting outcry from the professional bodies and businesses subsequently prompted the government to announce its intention to delay indefinitely the introduction of the new legislation.

Disposal of shares

11.18 If a loss is made on the disposal of shares in the family company, the shareholder may in certain circumstances be able to obtain tax relief for it against income rather than against capital gains on other assets. This is only possible if the shares were acquired by subscription, not by purchasing them from an existing shareholder. For shares acquired on or after 6 April 1998, the company must be carrying on qualifying activities under the EIS provisions. The disposal must be the result of an arm's-length bargain, liquidation or of the shares becoming of negligible value.

For shares issued on or after 7 March 2001, the requirement that the company has to be unquoted both at the date of issue and at the date of disposal is replaced by one that it must be unquoted at the date of issue and that there must be no arrangements then in place for it to cease to be unquoted or for it to become a wholly owned subsidiary of a new holding company which is to cease to be unquoted.

If the director/shareholder lends money to the family company for the purposes of its trade and the debt becomes irrecoverable, it may be possible to claim a CGT loss. If relief under *TCGA 1992 s 253* is not possible, a loss can only be claimed if the loan qualifies as a debt on a security under *TCGA 1992, s 251*. Unfortunately, there is no statutory definition of 'debt on a security': *s 251* refers the reader back to *TCGA 1992, s 132(3)(b)* which states that:

> '"security" includes any loan stock or similar security whether of the Government of the United Kingdom or of any other government, or of any public or local authority of the United Kingdom or elsewhere, or of any company, and whether secured or unsecured.'

This merely provides guidance as to the type of instrument that is considered to be a 'security' and it leaves undefined the meaning of 'loan stock or similar security'.

Following the various *dicta* in *WT Ramsay Ltd v IR Commrs* [1982] AC 300, HMRC, in their Capital Gains Manual (CGTM53420–53436), have given their view of the characteristics which they consider need to be satisfied before a debt can qualify as a 'debt on a security'.

INCORPORATION

When and how to incorporate

11.19 When and how to incorporate a business will ultimately be a matter of personal choice. However, the following factors may be considered in making this decision.

Personal risk

11.20 As a business grows, so do the risks associated with it. Many individuals become reluctant to bear personal liability for increasingly large trade creditors and other business commitments. Running their business through the medium of a company creates a barrier between creditors and their private assets.

External investment

11.21 Particularly if the owners are managing a strongly growing business, a company presents greater opportunities to attract external capital and motivate employees through tax-efficient shares schemes. Where the owners consider that their business will be floated on a stock exchange in the future, share option schemes need to be established well before the flotation, to allow the maximum growth in value.

Pension provision

11.22 A company provides much more flexible opportunities to provide pension provision, both for the owner-managers and employees. If the company is making significant profits a company pension scheme can prove to be an effective tax shelter as well as provision for a retirement income.

Tax-efficient incorporation of a business

11.23 The difficulty faced by the owner wishing to transfer an unincorporated business to a company is that, without tax reliefs, capital gains tax is likely to be payable on the transfer of any chargeable assets. Since the business owner and the new company are connected persons for capital gains tax purposes, any transfer of the business to the company is treated as being at market value, whatever the actual purchase consideration. Two alternative incorporation routes seek to mitigate the consequences. The first, *TCGA 1992, s 162*, is a form of rollover relief provided specifically for this purpose, but it has some drawbacks that can make it unattractive. The alternative is to use the provisions of *TCGA 1992, s 165* and make a gift of the business to the new company.

Rollover relief on transfer to a company

11.24 No claim is required, as this relief is automatic. However, there are circumstances in which it is disadvantageous to use it.

The relief is a form of rollover relief; that is to say the gains on the business' chargeable assets, that would otherwise be subject to tax, are deducted from the cost of acquisition of the shares in the new company.

There are three aspects to the conditions that must be met for the relief to apply. These are:

- a person who is not a company transfers to a company a business as a going concern;

- the transfer is of the whole assets of the business, or the whole of those assets other than cash; and

- the business is so transferred wholly or partly in exchange for shares issued by the company to the person transferring the business.

The transferor has to be a person who is not a company. This can include an individual, two (or more) individuals in partnership, trustees or personal representatives. Sometimes, partnerships include companies as partners. In these circumstances, no relief is given to the corporate partner, but relief is not precluded for individual partners.

The business must be transferred wholly or partly in exchange for shares issued by the company to the individuals transferring the business.

Relief

11.25   There are three stages in calculating the relief, as follows:

(1)   calculate the gain or loss on each asset being transferred to the company;

(2)   set off any losses against the total gains to produce a figure for aggregate gains; and

(3)   split the aggregate gains between the amount attributable to consideration issued by the company in shares (including, by concession, assumption of trade liabilities) and the amount attributable to 'other consideration' (normally cash or debts).

Any gains attributable to non-share consideration are taxable immediately. Provided that the aggregate gains do not exceed the cost of the shares, the gains attributable to the share consideration are relieved in full (but otherwise will be restricted to the cost of the shares, with any excess being taxable immediately).

Incorporation using relief for gifts of business assets

11.26   As far as its application to business incorporation is concerned, the general scheme of *TCGA 1992, s 165* is uncomplicated. The first and overriding condition is that the relief applies to disposals 'otherwise than by way of bargains at arm's length'. Consequently, it applies both to outright gifts and sales which occur at a value less than market value. There are then three other types of condition, which are:

(1)   the transfer must be made by an individual;

(2)   the transfer must be made to a person who is resident in the UK; and

(3)   the assets transferred must be used in a trade, profession or vocation carried on by the transferor.

In the first condition, the term 'individual' includes partners (other than corporate partners). In some circumstances, it also applies to trustees.

Except where there are restrictions because an asset has not always been used for trade purposes, if no payment is received for the disposal, the full amount of the gain may be held over that otherwise would have been chargeable. So, there is no chargeable gain at the time of the disposal, but the amount of the held-over gain is deducted from the transferee company's base cost. The held-over gain is therefore brought into the capital gains computation automatically on any subsequent disposal of the assets by the company.

Transfer to a company relief or gift of business assets relief?

11.27   The choice of methods will depend entirely on the circumstances of the case. The gifts of business assets route is currently used more widely and this is due principally to the perceived defect in *s 162* that all assets (other than cash) have to be transferred to the company. This can involve considerable amounts of stamp duty being payable. The increase in the top rate of stamp duty to 5% for assets worth more than £1,000,000 increases this cost; ie 5% applies to instruments executed after 6 April 2011.

Using the *s 162* route, a significant problem may arise where the business is of a type that requires large premises that appreciate in value. Insofar as it is commercially possible, it is good tax planning to keep such assets outside a company, to avoid the owner being exposed to a potential double capital gains charge (once when the company sells the premises) and again, indirectly, when the owner sells his or her shares in the company. Using the gifts of business assets rules selectively enables the business owner to keep such assets outside the company.

Pre-incorporation losses

11.28   Where a claim has been made to carry forward losses from self-employment against future profits, but the business has been transferred to a company before all the losses have been used, relief for those losses may be given against income received from the company (*ITA 2007, s 86*).

The conditions for relief are that:

- the business must have been transferred to the company wholly or mainly in return for shares in the company (at least 80% of which are retained); and

- the trader continues to be the beneficial owner of the shares and the company must continue trading at least to 5 April following the date of transfer.

Losses may be set against any income derived by the individual from the company, whether by way of dividends, salary, rent or interest. The individual may make the set-off in the order that provides maximum benefit. (This is a change introduced with the enactment of *ITA 2007 – Explanatory Notes, Annex 1, Change 11.*)

Claims must be made through the tax return for the year in which the income is received, in the same way as for post-cessation expenses above.

DISINCORPORATION

11.29   It was announced in the Autumn Budget 2017 that disincorporation relief would not be extended beyond 31 March 2018. The following section therefore applies for relevant periods to that date.

Disincorporation relief, which was introduced from 1 April 2013, is designed to remove certain tax barriers that previously existed when companies transferred from incorporated status to sole trader or partnership status.

The relief is particularly relevant to small companies, but there are some potential problems to be aware of.

Broadly, disincorporation relief:

- allows a company to transfer its goodwill and land to its shareholders without a corporation tax charge arising on the transfer;

- requires the transfer of the company's business, as a going concern, to its shareholders;

- does not apply to stock or work in progress; and

- only applies to companies with qualifying assets with a total value of up to £100,000 ('qualifying assets' are goodwill and land and buildings used in the business).

The relief does not extend to any income tax charges that might arise on the shareholders where the company's assets are distributed to them.

The assets transferred to the shareholders will be treated as dividends *in specie*. As long as this does not push the shareholders into the higher rate, there will be no further income liability for the shareholders. Higher and additional rate taxpayers will face an income tax charge.

The underlying rationale for the relief was that it should mirror the reliefs available where an unincorporated business incorporates, so that a business would not face a tax charge solely for changing its legal form. The key problems, however, are the monetary limit on assets and the lack of relief for shareholder gains.

The asset cap potentially has the bizarre effect that a company that has created its goodwill from nothing could obtain relief on gains of up to £100,000, whereas another might have made gains of only £10,000 but be ineligible for the relief because its qualifying assets were worth £105,000.

Transfers of assets between a company and its shareholders are normally transfers between connected persons or related parties. Usually, transfers between connected persons or related parties are treated as taking place at market value for tax purposes, the result being that the transfer is taxed on the market value of the asset regardless of the amount paid by either party. This could result in the company having to pay a corporation tax charge in cases where the market value of the asset is more than its original cost or its tax written down value.

A claim to disincorporation relief allows qualifying assets to be transferred below market value so that no corporation tax charge arises to the company. The shareholders accept the reduced transfer value for all future capital gains computations.

Shareholders may still be liable to income tax or capital gains tax on the transfer of assets to them by the company. Shareholders may also be liable to capital gains tax if they dispose of the assets at a future date.

As claims are made jointly by the company and shareholders, a claim cannot be made if the company has already been closed down (struck off or wound up).

Focus

The £100,000 asset cap referred to above has raised particular concerns within the tax profession. A company may be at risk if it transfers its business to its shareholders and subsequently finds out that HMRC's idea of 'value' means that the £100,000 limit has been breached. This could very easily happen in relation to goodwill. Many small firms will not have given thought to the real value of their goodwill and, even with proper advice, it will be impossible for shareholders to know in advance what valuation will be acceptable to HMRC. If the limit is breached, no relief is due and the company may receive an unexpected corporation tax bill.

Index

[All references are to paragraph number]

A

Absolute interest in residue
taxation of estates, and 9.42–9.43

Accrued income scheme
savings and investment income, and 4.11

Accumulation and maintenance settlements
generally 9.23
non-resident trustees 9.29

Acquisition costs
relocation expenses and benefits, and 6.51

Active service, death on
pensions, and 5.39

Acts of Parliament
sources of law, and 1.5

Additional rate of tax
distributions, and 11.14
dividends, and 4.5
generally 1.49
gilts, and 4.24
minimisation 11.3
threshold 1.50

Adjusted net income
personal allowance, and 1.19

Adoption pay
taxable benefits, and 5.43

Age 18 to 25 trusts
generally 9.23
non-resident trustees 9.29

Age-related allowances
generally 1.23–1.24
rates 1.17

Agency workers
statutory sick pay, and 5.44

Air departure tax (ADT)
Scotland, in 3.4

Air transport
double taxation relief, and 10.74

Allocation of income to tax bands
deductions 1.61

Allocation of income to tax bands –
contd
double tax relief 1.62
example 1.60
generally 1.58
higher marginal rates, at
generally 1.59
savings income 1.60
introduction 1.47
order 1.52
partnerships, and
examples 7.101–7.103
generally 7.98
mixed membership, with 7.99
sideways losses 7.100
reliefs 1.61
savings income 1.60

Allowances
See also **Capital allowances**
age allowances 1.23–1.24
amounts 1.17
annual investment allowance 7.57
blind person's allowance 1.25
calculation of income tax, and 1.47
capital expenditure
cash basis, and 8.9
generally 8.8
first year allowances 7.52
introduction 1.16
marriage allowance 1.20
married couple's allowance 1.22
personal allowance
'adjusted net income' 1.19
generally 1.18
personal savings allowance 1.21
plant and machinery, and
annual investment allowance 7.57
first year allowances 7.52
writing down allowances 7.55–7.56
property income, and
capital expenditure 8.8–8.9

577

Motor vehicles – *contd*
  capital allowances, and – *contd*
    rules from 2009/10 7.64
    very low CO$_2$ emissions 7.65
  benefit scale rates, and
    from 6 April 2012 6.57
    taxable percentages 2012/13 to
      2017/18 6.58
    vans 6.60
  fuel rates, and 6.59

N

National insurance contributions (NICs)
  alignment of income tax, and, 6.43
  amounts 6.42
  Class 1
    contracting out 6.34
    employment allowance 6.35
    generally 6.33
  Class 1A
    generally 6.36
    miscellaneous 6.36
  Class 1B 6.37
  Class 2
    failure to notify liability to pay 2.53
    generally 6.38
    self-employment, and 7.86
  Class 3
    decision to pay 5.61–5.62
    eligibility 5.58
    employment income, and 6.39
    overview 5.57
    payment 5.60
    time limits 5.59
  Class 4
    generally 6.38
    self-employment, and 7.87
  contracting out 6.34
  employment allowance 6.35
  generally 6.32
  maximum amounts 6.40
  rates 6.42
  self-employment, and
    Class 2 7.86
    Class 4 7.87
    exemptions 7.89
    introduction 7.85
    maximum amount 7.88
    rates 7.89
  tax deductions 6.41

National insurance contributions (NICs)
  – *contd*
  year-end tax planning, and 11.5
National living wage
  generally 6.23
National minimum wage
  generally 6.22
  tips and service charges, and 6.71
National Savings
  exempt income, and 1.10
  generally 4.30
  introduction 4.2
  tax planning, and 11.2
Negligence
  enquiries into returns, and 2.69
Negotiations
  enquiries into returns, and 2.66
91-day test
  residence, and 10.10
Non-cash benefits
  pensions, and 5.17
Non-contributory benefits
  taxable benefits, and 5.55
Non-natural persons (NNPs)
  property income, and 8.52
Non-resident landlords scheme
  administration 8.46
  application for payment with no tax
    deducted 8.38–8.39
  armed forces personnel 8.45
  calculation of tax 8.49
  conditions for approval 8.39
  Crown servants 8.45
  deductible expenses 8.47–8.48
  letting agents
    generally 8.41
    obligations 8.42
  obligations under
    letting agents 8.42
    tenants 8.44
  overview 8.37
  penalties 8.51
  record keeping 8.51
  tenant-finders 8.50
  tenants
    generally 8.43
    obligations 8.44
  'usual place of abode' 8.40
Non-resident trustees
  liability to tax 9.29–9.30

Index

Self-employment – *contd*
  trading expenses – *contd*
    'wholly and exclusively' 7.28
    trading indicators 7.5
    voluntary simplified cash basis 7.24
    'wholly and exclusively' 7.28
Serial tax avoidance regime (STAR)
  generally 2.115
Service charges
  generally 6.70
  miscellaneous 6.70
  national minimum wage, and 6.71
Settled property
  trusts, and 9.1
Settlement
  PAYE, and 2.106
Settlements
  See also **Trusts**
  generally 9.1
Settlor
  trusts, and 9.4–9.5
Severe disablement allowance
  non-taxable benefits, and 5.41
Share farming
  See also **Farming**
  generally 7.112
Share Incentive Plans
  generally 6.108–6.110
Share loss relief
  calculation of income tax, and 1.55
Share options
  non-residents, and, 10.14
Share schemes
  Company Share Option Plan 6.113–6.114
  employee shareholder status 6.115
  Enterprise Management Incentive 6.107
  introduction 6.104
  non-residents, and, 10.14
  reportable events 6.105–6.106
  Save As You Earn Share Option 6.111–6.112
  Share Incentive Plans 6.108–6.110
Shares
  savings and investment income, and 4.32
Shari'a-compliant accounts
  generally 4.12
Shipping
  double taxation relief, and 10.74

Short-life assets
  capital allowances, and 7.67
Short-term business visitors
  foreign earnings deduction, and 10.36
Sick pay
  taxable benefits, and
    agency workers 5.44
    generally 5.43
Sideways losses
  partnerships, and 7.100
Simplification of tax
  self-employment, and
    cash basis 7.24
    expenses 7.26
    income 7.25
    introduction 7.23
    receipts 7.25
    simplified expenses 7.26
Single premium bonds
  chargeable event 4.59
  generally 4.58
  top-slicing relief 4.60
60-day rule
  non-residents, and 10.24
Small Company Enterprise Centre (SCEC)
  Enterprise Investment Scheme, and 4.49
Small family companies
  disposal of shares 11.18
  distribution policy 11.14
  extracting profits 11.11
  family members 11.15
  income shifting 11.17
  paying family members, 11.16
  remuneration/dividend issue 11.12–11.13
Smartphones
  non-taxable benefits, and 6.83
Social Fund payments
  non-taxable benefits, and 5.41
Social investment tax relief (SITR)
  generally 4.63
Social security benefits
  adoption pay 5.43
  contributory benefits 5.56
  disability benefits 5.43
  employment and support allowance 5.45–5.47
  exempt income, and 1.10
  incapacity benefit 5.45